Sentencing and Criminal Justice

Providing unrivalled coverage of one of the most high-profile stages in the criminal justice process, this book examines the key issues in sentencing policy and practice. It provides an up-to-date account of the legislation on sentencing together with the ever-increasing amount of Court of Appeal case law. The aim of the book is to examine English sentencing law in its context, drawing not only upon legislation and the decisions of the courts but also upon the findings of research and on theoretical justifications for punishment.

The analysis is given depth and perspective by examining the interaction between the law and the wider criminal justice system, including the prison and probation services. The book also discusses the influence of statements from politicians, the mass media and public opinion. It engages with the theory of sentencing and the reasons for depriving offenders of their liberty. It looks at the statistical evidence on the effectiveness of sentences, and pays particular attention to difficult questions about aggravating and mitigating factors in sentencing, the proper approach to dealing with persistent offenders, the relevance of race, gender and unemployment, and the growth of 'preventive' orders (such as anti-social behaviour orders) which are not sentences as such but which impose restrictions and obligations.

This new edition has been extensively revised so as to integrate the new laws introduced by the Criminal Justice Act 2003, which has brought sweeping reforms to English sentencing.

Andrew Ashworth is Vinerian Professor of English Law at the University of Oxford. His previous titles include *Principles of Criminal Law* (4th edn, 2003), *The Criminal Process* (3rd edn, 2005, with Mike Redmayne) and *Proportionate Sentencing* (2005, with Andrew von Hirsch).

The Law in Context Series

Editors: William Twining (University College London)
and Christopher McCrudden (Lincoln College, Oxford)

Since 1970 the Law in Context series has been in the forefront of the movement to broaden the study of law. It has been a vehicle for the publication of innovative scholarly books that treat law and legal phenomena critically in their social, political and economic contexts from a variety of perspectives. The series particularly aims to publish scholarly legal writing that brings fresh perspectives to bear on new and existing areas of law taught in universities. A contextual approach involves treating legal subjects broadly, using materials from other social sciences, and from any other discipline that helps to explain the operation in practice of the subject under discussion. It is hoped that this orientation is at once more stimulating and more realistic than the bare exposition of legal rules. The series includes original books that have a different emphasis from traditional legal textbooks, while maintaining the same high standards of scholarship. They are written primarily for undergraduate and graduate students of law and of other disciplines, but most also appeal to a wider readership. In the past, most books in the series have focused on English law, but recent publications include books on European law, globalisation, transnational legal processes, and comparative law.

Books in the Series
Anderson, Schum & Twining: *Analysis of Evidence*
Ashworth: *Sentencing and Criminal Justice*
Barton & Douglas: *Law and Parenthood*
Bell: *French Legal Cultures*
Bercusson: *European Labour Law*
Birkinshaw: *European Public Law*
Birkinshaw: *Freedom of Information: The Law, the Practice and the Ideal*
Cane: *Atiyah's Accidents, Compensation and the Law*
Clarke & Kohler: *Property Law*
Collins: *The Law of Contract*
Davies: *Perspectives on Labour Law*
De Sousa Santos: *Toward a New Legal Common Sense*
Diduck: *Law's Families*
Elworthy & Holder: *Environmental Protection: Text and Materials*
Fortin: *Children's Rights and the Developing Law*
Glover-Thomas: *Reconstructing Mental Health Law and Policy*
Gobert & Punch: *Rethinking Corporate Crime*
Harlow & Rawlings: *Law and Administration: Text and Materials*
Harris: *An Introduction to Law*
Harris: *Remedies in Contract and Tort*
Harvey: *Seeking Asylum in the UK: Problems and Prospects*
Hervey & McHale: *Health Law and the European Union*
Lacey & Wells: *Reconstructing Criminal Law*
Lewis: *Choice and the Legal Order: Rising above Politics*
Likosky: *Transnational Legal Processes*
Maughan & Webb: *Lawyering Skills and the Legal Process*
Moffat: *Trusts Law: Text and Materials*
Norrie: *Crime, Reason and History*
O'Dair: *Legal Ethics*

Sentencing and Criminal Justice

Fourth edition

Andrew Ashworth
Vinerian Professor of English Law,
University of Oxford

1 004 600 406

CAMBRIDGE UNIVERSITY PRESS
Cambridge, New York, Melbourne, Madrid, Cape Town, Singapore, São Paulo

Cambridge University Press
The Edinburgh Building, Cambridge CB2 2RU, UK

Published in the United States of America by Cambridge University Press, New York

www.cambridge.org
Information on this title: www.cambridge.org/9780521674058

First published by Weidenfeld & Nicolson 1992
Second edition published by the Butterworths Division of Reed Elsevier 1995
Third edition published by the Butterworths Division of Reed Elsevier 2002
This edition first published by Cambridge University Press 2005

Printed in the United Kingdom at the University Press, Cambridge

A catalogue record for this book is available from the British Library

ISBN-13 978-0-521-67405-8 paperback
ISBN-10 0-521-67405-0 paperback

Contents

Preface

In the five years since the third edition, the brisk pace of change in sentencing set in the 1990s has continued with vigour. Most significant is the Criminal Justice Act 2003. Over half of its 339 sections and 30 of its 38 schedules relate to sentencing. Not all of those provisions are yet in force – at the time of writing, it appears that the new sentence of custody plus and the raising of the magistrates' courts' sentencing limit from 6 to 12 months will not be brought in until autumn 2006. Several chapters have needed extensive rewriting in order to reflect the provisions of the 2003 Act. Attention has also been paid to other significant changes in sentencing – the continued rise in the prison population to over 75,000; the continued increase in reliance on the National Probation Service for risk management and rehabilitation in the community; the extension of social control through the anti-social behaviour order and the many other preventive orders and the concomitant blurring of boundaries, rights and responsibilities that this entails; the development of the guideline movement in sentencing, and the unexpected return of the Court of Appeal to the practice of laying down guidelines or 'guidance'; and many other changes.

I ceased to gather material for this edition at the end of March 2005, but room has been found for a few subsequent developments. I am grateful for the term's sabbatical leave granted by the University of Oxford to enable me to push forward with this project, and also to the Law Faculty at the University of Tasmania for its warm welcome and generous support during my visit in January–February 2005. I received helpful suggestions about the book from a number of colleagues, and my special thanks go to Elaine Player for commenting on a draft of Chapter 9 and to Julian Roberts for commenting on a draft of Chapter 6. And, above all, I owe a great debt to Von, whose support for me throughout this project was unwavering even though I had to spend much more time than anticipated at my desk.

Andrew Ashworth
All Souls College, Oxford
May 2005

Table of statutes

Table of cases

CHAPTER 1

An introduction to English sentencing

1.1 Courts and crimes

Although some common law crimes remain, most of the offences in English criminal law were created by statute and have a statutory maximum penalty. For the purposes of trial, offences were divided into three categories by the Criminal Law Act 1977 – offences triable only on indictment, offences triable only summarily, and offences triable either way. The most serious offences (e.g. murder, rape) are triable only on indictment, at the Crown Court. A large mass of less serious offences is triable only summarily, in magistrates' courts. The middle category of offences triable either way comprises most burglaries, thefts and deceptions. The first question in these cases concerns the defendant's intended plea: if the defendant indicates a plea of guilty, the magistrates must assume jurisdiction and proceed to sentence, unless they decide that their sentencing powers are insufficient. If the intended plea is not guilty, the defendant will be tried at a magistrates' court unless either the magistrates direct or the defendant elects that the case be tried at the Crown Court.

The Crown Court sits with a judge and jury. There are three levels of Crown Court centre: first-tier centres, where both civil and criminal cases are tried and where High Court judges and circuit judges preside; second-tier centres, where High Court judges or circuit judges preside but only deal with criminal cases; and third-tier centres, where circuit judges or recorders deal with criminal cases, being mostly offences triable either way. The types of criminal offence are divided into four classes, according to their gravity, and some can only be tried by a High Court judge, whereas others can be tried by circuit judges or recorders. In total, there are over 1,000 Crown Court sentencers. Circuit judges are full-time judges, although they may divide their time between civil and criminal work. Recorders and assistant recorders are part-time judges, whose main occupations are barristers, solicitors or (in a few instances) academics; most full-time judges start their judicial careers in this way. Appeals against sentence from the Crown Court go to the Court of Appeal and, if there is no point of law involved, the appeal requires the court's leave if it is to be heard. Applications for leave are dealt with by individual High Court judges.

Magistrates' courts deal with the least serious criminal offences. There are around 30,000 lay magistrates in England and Wales, divided into local benches, and a court normally consists of three magistrates. There are also full-time and part-time District Judges (Magistrates' Courts) (DJMC), formerly known as stipendiary magistrates, whose numbers have grown in recent years to over 200. A DJMC must be a barrister or solicitor of at least ten years' standing, and he or she sits alone – usually dealing with the longer or more complicated summary cases. The powers of magistrates' courts are limited to imposing a maximum of six months' imprisonment in respect of one offence (or a total of 12 months for two or more offences); these maxima are to be raised, when s. 154 of the Criminal Justice Act 2003 is brought into force, to 12 months for a single offence and 65 weeks for two or more offences. The maximum fine or compensation order that may be imposed by a magistrates' court is usually £5,000. Magistrates may, having heard the evidence in a case, commit it to the Crown Court for sentence, if they form the view that the offence was so serious that greater punishment should be inflicted than they have power to impose. As mentioned above, a defendant who indicates an intention to plead guilty to an either-way offence should be sentenced by the magistrates unless they decide that their powers are insufficient, in which case they should commit to the Crown Court for sentence. A person who has been sentenced in a magistrates' court may appeal against sentence to the Crown Court. The appeal takes the form of a complete rehearing of the case, before a circuit judge or recorder and two lay magistrates, and the Crown Court has the power to pass any sentence which the magistrates' court could have imposed, even if that sentence is more severe than the one they did in fact impose.[1]

Summary offences are little discussed in this book, although there are frequent references to sentencing in magistrates' courts (which also deal with many 'triable-either-way' offences). Most of the statistics quoted in part 3 of this chapter refer to 'indictable offences', which include those triable on indictment and those 'triable-either-way', whether tried in a magistrates' court or at the Crown Court.

1.2 The available sentences

Recent years have seen several major statutes bringing change to the sentencing structure, and three of them are particularly important for present purposes. The first is the Criminal Justice Act 1991, which was the first major attempt for over 40 years to establish a coherent sentencing structure. After a series of further statutes in the 1990s, Parliament consolidated sentencing law in the Powers of Criminal Courts (Sentencing) (PCCS) Act 2000. This consolidation was a wonderful idea, since it promised the great convenience of bringing the various powers together in one place. Sadly, the statute had already been overtaken by new provisions by the time it came into force, and after three years large parts of it were replaced by the now principal statute, the Criminal Justice Act 2003.

1 See Sprack (2004) for fuller details of these matters.

This part of the chapter gives a preliminary sketch of the courts' sentencing powers, referring also to the different sentences available in relation to young adult offenders (aged 18–21) and to juveniles. Most of these sentencing powers are discussed in detail in later chapters, and in part 4 of this chapter we examine the reasons why only a small proportion of the crimes committed in any one year result in an offender being sentenced in court.

1.2.1 Sentences for adult offenders

A court's duty in all cases involving injury, death, loss or damage is to consider making a *compensation order* in favour of the victim or, in a case of death, the victim's family. This forms part of a policy of increasing recognition of the needs, wishes and rights of the victims of crime. A court has a duty to give reasons for not making an order in a case where it has the power to do so. The provisions governing compensation orders are to be found in ss. 130–134 of the PCCS Act 2000. One important restriction is that the court should take account of the means of the offender when deciding whether to make an order and, if so deciding, for what amount. The consequence is that some victims whose offenders are impecunious will receive nothing from this source, and that victims in cases where an order is made may receive compensation for only part of their loss.[2] In 2002, over half of offenders convicted at magistrates' courts of indictable offences of criminal damage were ordered to pay compensation; as for those convicted of offences of violence, 33 per cent in the magistrates' courts and 17 per cent in the Crown Court were subjected to compensation orders. A compensation order will usually be made as well as another order, but it may be made as the sole order against an offender.

The most lenient course which an English court can take after conviction is to order an *absolute discharge*. The power is governed by s. 12 and Schedule 1 of the PCCS Act 2000. A conviction followed by an absolute discharge does not count as such for most future purposes. Formally, the court must be satisfied that it is 'inexpedient to inflict punishment'. In practice, the power is used in fewer than 1 per cent of cases, and is generally reserved for instances where there is very little moral guilt in the offence.

The power to grant a *conditional discharge* is also to be found in ss. 12–15 and Schedule 1 of the PCCS Act 2000, and once again the conviction does not count as such for most future purposes. The condition is that the offender must commit no offence within a period, of not more than three years, specified by the court. If the offender is convicted of an offence committed during that period, then he or she is liable to be sentenced for the original offence as well. Thus, the conditional discharge carries a threat of future punishment, as does also the power to 'bind

---

2 Victims of crimes of violence also have the possibility of applying to the Criminal Injuries Compensation Scheme: see below, ch. 10.4.

over' an offender to keep the peace and to be of good behaviour – in effect, a kind of suspended fine which some courts tend to use more frequently than others.[3] Conditional discharges continue to be used in substantial numbers of cases: of adult indictable offenders dealt with in 2002, some 14 per cent of males and 24 per cent of females received a discharge from the court, and almost all of these would be conditional discharges.

The *fine* remains the most used penal measure in English courts, largely because of its widespread use for summary offences. Its proportionate use for indictable offences has declined, to some 26 per cent of adult male indictable offences in 2002. Maximum fines are usually unlimited for indictable offences tried in the Crown Court, but in magistrates' courts the maximum fines have been banded in five levels. The leading principle (in s. 164 of the Criminal Justice Act 2003) is that the fine should reflect the seriousness of the offence and the offender's ability to pay; and a court should give priority to a compensation order over a fine where the offender has limited financial resources and appears unable to pay both. The use of imprisonment for non-payment of fines has declined in the last decade, as alternatives such as community service have been introduced, but some offenders are still committed to prison for non-payment, even though the original offence was not thought to merit custody.

The *community sentence* has been changed in major ways by the Criminal Justice Act 2003. In place of the plethora of different sentences hitherto available (e.g. community punishment, curfew orders, drug treatment and testing orders, and so forth), the Act introduces a new generic community sentence – the idea being that this will bring to courts both flexibility and (if they follow the guidelines) consistency. Section 148 of the 2003 Act states that a court must not pass a community sentence unless satisfied that the seriousness of the offence(s) is sufficient to warrant such a sentence. Having reached this decision, the court must then select the requirement(s) which (i) are most suitable for the offender and (ii) impose restrictions on the offender which are commensurate with the seriousness of the offence. The list of requirements largely corresponds to the separate orders available previously, and is as follows (for offenders aged 18 or over).

(a) an unpaid work requirement
(b) an activity requirement
(c) a programme requirement
(d) a prohibited activity requirement
(e) a curfew requirement
(f) an exclusion requirement
(g) a residence requirement
(h) a mental health treatment requirement

3 This power, deriving from the common law and the Justice of the Peace Act 1391, was reviewed by the Law Commission in 1994 and by the Home Office in 2003: see ch. 10.3 below.

(i) a drug rehabilitation requirement
(j) an alcohol treatment requirement
(k) a supervision requirement
(l) an attendance centre requirement (only for those aged 16–25)

Further discussion of the new order in Chapter 10 below will examine the prospects for greater consistency in the application of community sentences and for greater effectiveness in reducing reoffending.

Next in ascending order of severity is *imprisonment*. Before imposing a custodial sentence, the court must be satisfied, according to s. 152(2), that the offence was 'so serious that neither a fine nor a community sentence can be justified', a formula that requires the court to dismiss all lesser alternatives before resorting to custody. If it decides on custody, s. 153(2) states that the sentence should be for the shortest term 'commensurate with the seriousness of the offence'. In determining the length of any custodial sentence, courts are bound to apply any relevant guidelines, and to take due account of aggravating and mitigating factors (see Chapter 5), and of previous convictions (see Chapter 6).

When the court has decided that a sentence of imprisonment is justified and has decided on its length, it may still have the choice between a suspended sentence, intermittent custody and immediate prison. This applies where the court is minded to impose a sentence of less than one year. If it decides that there are grounds for suspending, it may suspend any sentence of between 28 and 51 weeks for a period of up to two years (s. 189 of the 2003 Act), during which time it may order the offender to comply with one or more requirements taken from the list available for community sentences (above). Non-compliance may result in return to court and the activation of the whole or part of the prison sentence. Alternatively, the court may take the view that intermittent custody is more appropriate, the period of between 28 and 51 weeks being converted into between 14 and 90 custodial days plus release on licence in the intermediate periods – see s. 183 of the 2003 Act. If the court believes that neither a suspended sentence nor intermittent custody is appropriate in the circumstances, and that a custodial term of under 12 months is proper, it will be able to impose a term of 'custody plus' in accordance with ss. 181–182 of the 2003 Act, when this is brought into force (probably autumn 2006). Until then, ordinary sentences of imprisonment remain available. The new form of sentence is designed to ensure that the use of imprisonment in this range includes a short period in prison followed by supervised release. There must first be a custodial period, of between 2 and 13 weeks as specified by the court; then there must be a period under supervision of at least 26 weeks, for which the court may impose one or more requirements from a list of eight of those available for community sentences. It remains to be seen what effects this new framework for custodial sentences under 12 months will have – on sentencing practice, on reducing reoffending, and on the prison population.

Standing in contrast to the general injunction to courts to impose the shortest proportionate custodial term (in s. 153(2)) are a small number of other provisions, usually justified on public protection grounds. Section 287 introduces a minimum sentence of five years' imprisonment for various offences of possessing firearms. This joins the minimum sentence of seven years for the third offence of trafficking class A drugs (s. 110 of the PCCS Act 2000) and three years for the third domestic burglary (s. 111 of the PCCS Act 2000). The 2003 Act also provides for severer forms of custodial sentence for dangerous offenders who are thought to present a significant risk of serious harm to members of the public. These sentences include life imprisonment, indefinite custody for public protection or (for those convicted of violent or sexual offences with maximum sentences between 2 and 10 years) extended sentences (see Chapter 6).

Both the use of custodial sentences and their average length have increased significantly in recent years: by 2002, some 30 per cent of male indictable offenders aged 21 or over and some 17 per cent of females received immediate imprisonment, compared with 18 per cent and 6 per cent respectively in 1992. The actual meaning of custodial sentences depends on the operation of the system of early release under the Criminal Justice Act 2003. In broad terms, all prisoners are released after serving half their sentence, but are then on licence and subject to recall at any time until the expiry of the full sentence. For some offenders serving four years or longer this means release at an earlier point than before; but for all prisoners serving 12 months or longer the impact of the sentence endures longer, since the licence conditions remain in force until the end of the nominal sentence (and not until the three-quarters point, as before). For those serving extended sentences the system is slightly different, in that they are not entitled to release after serving half their sentence; release thereafter is at the discretion of the Parole Board.[4]

It will be evident that the sentences available under the 2003 Act are, broadly, graduated in terms of severity. The least onerous are absolute and conditional discharges; on the next level are fines (which may occasionally rise almost to the level of custody); slightly higher and partly overlapping with fines is the community sentence, only to be imposed if the offence is 'serious enough'; and at the highest level come custodial sentences, usually requiring the court to be satisfied that neither a fine nor a community sentence could be justified and that imprisonment was therefore required.

There is a whole list of ancillary and/or preventive orders which may be made by the courts in appropriate cases. These range from orders for deportation, restitution orders, and disqualification from driving, to the more recent flush of preventive orders – notably, anti-social behaviour orders (ASBOs), exclusion from premises, exclusion from football grounds, and so on. In some circumstances the court is bound, or almost bound, to make an order – such as disqualification from working with children. In other cases, such as drug trafficking, a court is bound to follow the

---

4 For further details see ch. 9.5 below.

statutory procedure towards making an order for the confiscation of the offender's assets under the Proceeds of Crime Act 2002. Many of these ancillary orders are discussed in Chapter 11.

1.2.2 Sentences for young offenders

Sentencing powers regarding offenders aged under 21 fall broadly into two groups – first, offenders aged 18, 19 or 20, who are termed 'young adults' and dealt with in adult courts; and then offenders aged 10–17 inclusive, who are dealt with chiefly in the youth court.

The structure of sentencing for young adults is largely the same as that for adults, although young adults sent to custody have usually been placed in different establishments from adult prisoners. Otherwise, sentencing powers are fairly similar to those for adults, except that the *attendance centre order* is available only for those aged up to 25, as noted above. Attendance centres operate on Saturday afternoons and require offenders to participate in demanding (and usually physical) activities. The maximum order is 36 hours.

For young defendants under 18 both the procedure and the sentencing powers differ considerably. Their cases are dealt with in youth courts, except when there is a charge of a particularly grave crime. Very young children charged with murder, manslaughter and some other serious offences are tried in the Crown Court. However, where the defendants are as young as 11 or 12, special efforts must be made to ensure that the defendants can follow and participate in the trial: a Practice Direction on the appropriate procedures for such cases was issued in 2000,[5] but a recent decision of the European Court of Human Rights indicates that further changes of procedure will need to be made.[6]

However, cases of that kind are few. In practice, as we shall see in part 1.4 below, most offenders of this age are dealt with by a reprimand or final warning under the Crime and Disorder Act 1998, described more fully in Chapter 12. Section 37 of the 1998 Act declares that 'the principal aim of the youth justice system [is] to prevent offending by children and young persons', but this benevolent aim must be read in the light of the custody rate for young offenders – in 2002, 13 per cent for boys and 7 per cent for girls. For those who are prosecuted in court for the first time and plead guilty, the court is under a statutory duty to make a referral order under s. 16 of the PCCS Act 2000. The consequence of the referral order, described more fully in Chapter 12, part 12.1.2, is the drawing up of a 'youth offender contract' requiring certain commitments. In other cases the youth court has the same range of powers as do the ordinary courts when dealing with young adults, with two noticeable exceptions. The first is that when a youth court is dealing with a child under 16, it must require the attendance of the child's parents unless this would be

5 *Practice Direction: Young Defendants in the Crown Court* [2000] 2 All ER 284, applying the decision in *V and T* v. *United Kingdom* (2000) 30 EHRR 121.
6 *SC* v. *United Kingdom* [2004] Crim LR 130.

unreasonable, and it must bind over the parents to exercise control over the child unless it give reasons for not doing so. The second difference concerns custodial sentences, which have been relatively rare for young offenders. Details of the law are given in Chapter 12, but essentially a 'detention and training order' may only be made in certain standard lengths, as consolidated in ss. 100–107 of the PCCS Act 2000 (i.e. 4, 6, 8, 10, 12, 18 or 24 months, and not intermediate lengths).

1.3 The general statistical background

Some 5.9 million 'notifiable offences' (excluding minor crimes) were recorded by the police in 2003, showing a slight rise from 2002 to set against the overall decline in the volume of crime as measured by the British Crime Survey – down to 11.7 million crimes against households and individuals in 2003, compared with 12.3 million in 2002. Table 1 shows how the volume of crime as measured by the British Crime Survey was considerably higher in 1991 than it is in the early years of the twenty-first century, whereas the number of crimes recorded by the police has continued to grow steadily since 1991, although the major acceleration in the recorded crime rate came in the preceding decades. These differences between recorded crimes and the crime rate estimated by the British Crime Survey are discussed in section 1.4 below.

Table 1 also shows that the detection rate – proportion of recorded offences 'cleared up' by the police – declined substantially in the 1970s and 1980s, and in recent years has been hovering around 23 per cent, approximately half the rate of 1961. This does not imply that in all these cases a conviction was obtained or a formal caution administered, for the 'detected' category also includes offences traced to children under 10, cases where the victim is unable to give evidence, and offences 'taken into consideration' on other charges. The detection rate has always varied from offence to offence, however. Over three-quarters of offences of violence and sexual offences are usually cleared up, largely because the victim can usually identify the offender, who was often known to him or her anyway. In contrast, the proportion of burglaries and robberies cleared up remains at less than one-quarter.

Table 1 shows that, of the 1.4 million non-minor offences cleared up in 2003, some 486,000 resulted in either a finding of guilt for an indictable offence or a police caution for an indictable offence. The figure includes some 151,000 formal cautions, of which the majority were reprimands or warnings administered to offenders under 18. Some 335,000 persons were found guilty of indictable offences by the courts in 2003, and it may seem strange that so many fewer people were convicted in 2003 than in 1981, when the figure was 465,000 (see Table 1). One reason why this statistic appears strange is the wide disparity in the numbers of crimes recorded in the two years – 2.8 million in 1981, compared with 5.9 million in 2003. The explanation is to be found in a combination of factors – the decline in the detection rate from

Table 1. *Summary of criminal justice statistics, 1951, 1961, 1971, 1981, 1991, and 2001–2003*

England and Wales

	1951	1961	1971	1981	1991	2001[7]	2002[7]	2003[7]	2002–2003 (% change)
	(000)								
Crime measured by British Crime Survey	(1)	(1)	(1)	11,046	15,125	13,037	12,308	11,716	−5
Notifiable offences									
– offences recorded by the police[2]	525	807	1,666[3]	2,794	5,075	5,525	5,899	5,935	+1
– offences detected	247	361	775[3]	1,056	1,479	1,291	1,389	1,394	–
– detection rate (percentage)	47	45	45[3]	38	29	23	24	23	
Number of offenders cautioned[4]	(6)	70	109	154	279	230	225	242	+7
of which Indictable offences[5]	(6)	25	77	104	180	144	143	151	+5
Defendants proceeded against at magistrates' courts	736	1,161	1,796	2,294	1,985	1,838	1,925	2,001	+4
of which Indictable offences[5]	122	159	374	523	510	501	517	509	−2
Defendants found guilty at magistrates' courts	705	1,121	1,648	2,042	1,438	1,293	1,362	1,432	+5
of which Indictable offences[5]	115	151	282	402	269	270	281	278	−1
Defendants sentenced at the Crown Court after summary convictions	3	4	14	14	7	16	17	16	−1
Defendants tried at the Crown Court	20	34	48	79	100	77	76	80	+4
Defendants found guilty at the Crown Court	18	31	40	63	81	56	60	60	–
Total offenders founds guilty at both courts	723	1,152	1,688	2,105	1,519	1,350	1,421	1,491	+5
of which Indictable offences[5]	133	182	342	465	347	324	338	335	−1
Total offenders found guilty or cautioned[4]	723[6]	1,222	1,797	2,259	1,796	1,580	1,647	1,733	+5
of which Indictable offences[5]	133[6]	207	419	568	527	468	481	486	+1

[1] The British Crime Survey did not commence until 1982, where interviews were based on the previous year's experience of crime.

[2] Excluding other criminal damage of value £20 and under. Includes estimates for criminal damage over £20 for Merseyside and Metropolitan Police. Figures were affected by the new counting rules from 1998 onwards and by the NCRS from 2001/02 onwards.

[3] Adjusted to take account to the Criminal Damage Act 1971.

[4] Cautions, written warnings and all fixed penalties for summary motoring offences are not covered in this volume but are published in the Home Office Statistical Bulletin 'Motoring offences and breath tests'.

[5] Indictable offences include those triable either way.

[6] Cautions figures were not collected until 1954.

[7] Both British Crime Survey data and notifiable offences data are for the financial years, ie 2001/02, 2002/03 and 2003/04.

Source: Criminal Statistics 2003, Table 1.1.

Table 2. *Flows through the criminal justice system, 2003*

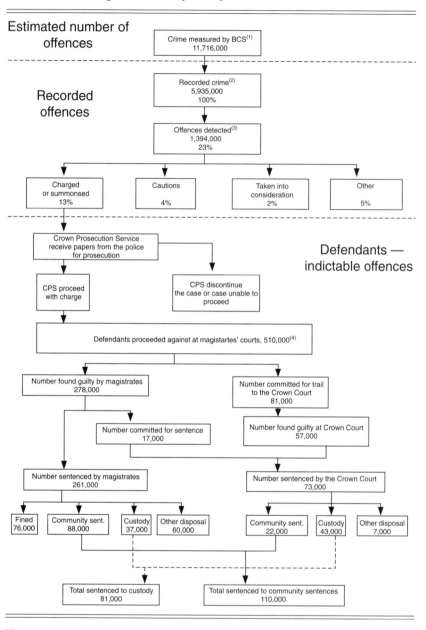

[1] Covers crimes against households and individuals, reported in the 2003/04 British Crime Survey interviews, that were not necessarily reported to the police. This set of offences is not strictly comparable to recorded crime.

[2] Covers all indictable, including triable either way, offences plus a few closely associated summary offences.

[3] In the financial year 2003/04.

[4] Adjusted for shortfalls of data.

Source: Criminal Statistics 2003 Table 1.1.

38 per cent in 1981 to 23 per cent in 2003, the increase in the use of police cautions (up from 104,000 to 151,000), and perhaps the increased discontinuance rate of prosecutions. Table 2 shows the progress of recorded offences through the criminal justice system, and will be discussed in part 1.4 below.

How do the courts use their sentencing powers? For this it is necessary to revert to the 2002 statistics,[7] and the details for the last decade are best presented in separate tables for adult offenders, for young adults (aged 18 and under 21), and for juveniles (aged under 18). Table 4 shows that for adults the use of immediate prison sentences rose from 18 per cent of all male indictable offenders in 1992 to 30 per cent in 2002; for women the rise was even steeper, from 6 per cent in 1992 to 17 per cent in 2002. The decade also saw increases in the proportionate use of community sentences, at the expense of fines. For young adult offenders, Table 5 shows a significant rise in the use of custody, from 15 per cent in 1992 to 26 per cent by 2002; the proportion of community sentences remains stable, whereas fines and discharged have declined slightly. Table 6 gives the figures for offenders aged 10–17 inclusive. Community sentences have increased significantly throughout, largely at the expense of discharges and attendance centres. While the rate of custody has increased relatively slightly for boys, it has shown an enormous increase for girls, from 2 per cent to 7 per cent over the decade.

What has been the effect of these sentencing patterns on the custodial population? Table 7 shows the average daily population of prisons and young offender institutions for the years 1992 to 2002. Starting from some 46,000 in 1992 (from which it fell back further in 1993), there has in the following years been a steep and unprecedented rise to an annual average of over 70,000 prisoners in 2002, and to over 75,000 in April 2004 and again in April 2005 – increases whose causes are discussed in some detail in Chapter 9 below. Moreover, the steep rise in the mid- and late 1990s is attributable almost entirely to the numbers of adult sentenced prisoners; while in previous decades the growth of the remand population was an important element in the rise in the prison population, remand prisoners contributed hardly at all to the recent increase. The same can be said of the numbers of young male offenders in custody, which appear to have stabilized in the last five years. However, the sharp rise in the female prison population (both young offenders and adults) has made a significant overall contribution, even though female offenders still account for only about 6 per cent of the prison population.

This brief discussion of changes in the prison population shows how sentencing and the prisons are merely parts of a wider process of criminal justice, in which factors such as remand decisions by magistrates, diversion decisions by the police, prosecution decisions by the Crown Prosecution Service, and so forth, have a significant role. We now turn to consider the various pre-trial stages in decision-making.

---

7 Unfortunately the Criminal Statistics series discontinued its sentencing tables in 2003, although they had appeared annually until 2002.

Table 3. Trends in BCS incidents of crime 1981 and 1991 to interviews held in 2003/04, with percentage change and statistical significance of change between 1995, 1997, 1999, 2001/02, 2002/03 and 2003/04 interviews

	1981	1991	1995	1997	1999	2001/02 interviews	2002/03 interviews	2003/04 interviews	% change 1995 to 2003/04	% change 1997 to 2003/04	% change 1999 to 2003/04	% change 2001/02 to 2003/04	% change 2003/03 to 2003/04
			(000)										
Property crime													
Vandalism	2,713	2,759	3,366	2,866	2,861	2,600	2,530	2,465	−27	−14	−14	−5	−3
Vehicle vandalism	1,558	1,685	1,826	1,609	1,594	1,509	1,515	1,437	−21	−11	−19	−6	1
Other vandalism	1,155	1,073	1,540	1,256	1,267	1,091	1,016	1,028	−33	−18	−19	−6	1
Burglary	749	1,380	1,770	1,621	1,290	967	972	943	−47	−42	−27	−3	−3
Attempts	276	511	772	768	523	416	411	410	−47	−47	−22	−1	<−1
Attempts and no loss	376	668	979	970	739	572	565	526	−46	−46	−29	−8	−7
With entry	474	869	998	852	767	552	560	533	−47	−37	−30	−3	−5
With loss	373	712	791	651	551	395	406	417	−47	−36	−24	6	3
All vehicle thefts	1,751	3,845	4,350	3,511	3,009	2,491	2,361	2,121	−51	−40	−30	−15	−10
Thefts from vehicle	1,286	2,424	2,544	2,200	1,849	1,494	1,422	1,337	−47	−39	−28	−11	−6
Theft of vehicles	285	522	510	378	336	315	278	241	−53	−36	−28	−23	−13
Attempts of and from	179	899	1,297	933	825	682	661	543	−58	−42	−34	−20	−18
Bicycle theft	216	569	673	541	400	367	358	370	−45	−32	−8	1	3
Other household theft	1,518	1,857	2,267	2,024	1,880	1,443	1,358	1,283	−43	−37	−32	−11	−5
Theft from the person	434	438	680	621	636	603	689	622	−9	<1	−2	3	−10
Snatch theft from person	86	79	80	83	58	74	88	116	46	40	101	57	32
Stealth theft from person	348	359	601	538	578	529	601	506	−16	−6	−12	−4	−16
Other thefts of personal property	1,586	1,739	2,069	1,935	1,554	1,405	1,342	1,321	−36	−32	−15	−6	−2

Violence

Common assault (includes some with minor injuries)	1,403	1,751	2,924	2,455	2,322	1,722	1,699	1,654	−43	−33	−29	−4	−3
Wounding	508	624	914	804	650	648	708	655	−28	−18	1	1	−8
Robbery	164	182	339	334	406	356	302	283	−17	−15	−30	−20	−6
All BCS violence	2,160	2,635	4,256	3,675	3,436	2,799	2,798	2,708	−36	−26	−21	−3	−3
Domestic violence	292	534	989	814	774	626	505	446	−55	−45	−42	−29	−12
Acquaintance	774	1,043	1,816	1,642	1,226	861	948	905	−50	−45	−26	5	−5
Stranger	844	797	1,004	784	953	882	955	958	−5	22	1	9	<1
Mugging (robbery and snatch theft)	250	259	419	417	464	430	390	399	−5	−4	−14	−7	2
All household crime	6,947	10,410	12,426	10,562	9,441	7,868	7,578	7,181	−42	−32	−24	−9	−5
All personal crime	4,094	4,733	6,926	6,148	5,569	4,733	4,741	4,535	−35	−26	−19	−4	−4
Old comparable crime	6,535	9,796	12,093	10,297	9,253	8,031	7,920	7,459	−38	−28	−19	−9	−5
Comparable crime	n/a	n/a	n/a	n/a	11,575	9,753	9,619	9,113	n/a	n/a	−21	−7	−5
All BCS crime	11,041	15,142	19,353	16,711	15,009	12,601	12,319	11,716	−39	−30	−22	−7	−5
Unweighted base	10,905	10,059	16,337	14,937	19,398	32,787	36,450	37,891					

Source: Dodd et al. (2004), Table 2.1.

Table 4. *Persons aged 21 and over sentenced for indictable offences by sex and type of sentence or order, 1992–2002*

England and Wales

Sex and year	Total number of persons sentenced	Absolute or conditional discharge	Fine	Community rehabilitation order(1)	Community punishment and order(1)	Community punishment and rehabilitation order(1)	Curfew order	Drug treatment and testing order	Imprisonment Fully suspended	Partly suspended	Unsuspended	Otherwise dealt with	Total immediate custody	Total community sentences
					Number sentenced for indictable offences (000)									
Males														
1992(2)	190.1	32.5	70.3	16.2	17.1	0.5	*	*	15.1	0.5	32.8	5.0	33.3	33.8
1993(2)	183.1	33.0	69.3	17.5	20.7	3.5	*	*	2.3	*	32.1	4.7	32.1	41.7
1994	187.0	30.1	67.3	20.3	21.1	4.6	*	*	1.9	*	37.0	4.6	37.0	46.0
1995	178.4	26.0	60.7	19.1	19.2	5.1	0.0	*	1.9	*	42.0	4.3	42.0	43.3
1996	175.6	24.6	57.1	19.1	17.4	5.7	0.1	*	2.1	*	44.9	4.6	44.9	42.3
1997	186.6	26.0	59.1	20.4	17.6	6.4	0.2	*	2.2	*	49.4	5.4	49.4	44.5
1998	197.7	27.0	62.5	21.8	18.0	6.9	0.3	(3)	2.1	*	53.2	5.8	53.2	47.0
1999	195.1	26.1	60.0	21.8	17.6	6.6	0.4	(2)	1.9	*	54.5	6.3	54.5	46.3
2000	184.7	24.8	52.1	21.0	17.0	6.0	0.7	0.2	1.8	*	55.1	5.9	55.1	45.0
2001	183.5	25.4	49.5	22.4	16.0	4.1	0.8	2.9	1.6	*	54.9	5.9	54.9	46.1
2002	197.0	27.0	52.1	23.9	16.6	4.4	1.3	3.6	1.4	*	59.7	6.9	59.7	49.8
Females														
1992(2)	28.5	10.2	7.7	4.6	1.5	0.1	*	*	1.9	0.1	1.8	0.6	1.8	6.2
1993(2)	27.6	9.4	8.6	4.6	1.8	0.4	*	*	0.4	*	1.9	0.6	1.9	6.7
1994	28.5	9.2	8.0	5.5	1.9	0.6	*	*	0.4	*	2.3	0.5	2.3	8.1
1995	26.8	8.0	7.0	5.3	1.9	0.7	–	*	0.5	*	2.8	0.5	2.8	7.9
1996	27.2	7.7	6.8	5.7	1.8	0.9	0.0	*	0.6	*	3.2	0.6	3.2	8.4
1997	30.3	8.3	7.3	6.3	2.0	1.0	0.0	*	0.7	*	4.0	0.7	4.0	9.3
1998	33.7	9.0	7.8	7.1	2.3	1.1	0.0	(3)	0.7	*	4.7	0.9	4.7	10.6
1999	34.8	8.6	7.8	7.4	2.6	1.2	0.1	(2)	0.7	*	5.4	1.0	5.4	11.2
2000	33.6	8.1	7.3	7.3	2.7	1.0	0.1	0.0	0.6	*	5.5	1.0	5.5	11.1
2001	33.5	8.2	6.8	7.1	2.6	0.7	0.1	0.5	0.5	*	5.7	1.1	5.7	11.1
2002	36.4	8.8	7.3	7.7	2.7	0.8	0.2	0.7	0.5	*	6.4	1.2	6.4	12.2

Percentage sentenced for indictable offences

Males

1992[2]	100	17	37	9		0	*	*	8	0	17	3	18	18
1993[2]	100	18	38	10		2	*	*	1	*	18	3	18	23
1994	100	16	36	11		2	*	*	1	*	20	2	20	25
1995	100	15	34	11		3	0	*	1	*	24	2	24	24
1996	100	14	33	10		3	0	*	1	*	26	3	26	24
1997	100	14	32	9		3	0	*	1	*	26	3	26	24
1998	100	14	32	9		4	0	(3)	1	*	27	3	27	24
1999	100	13	31	9		3	0	(2)	1	*	28	3	28	24
2000	100	13	28	9		3	0	0	1	*	30	3	30	24
2001	100	14	27	9		2	0	2	1	*	30	3	30	25
2002	100	14	26	8		2	1	2	1	*	30	3	30	25

Females

1992[2]	100	36	27	16	5	0	*	*	7	0	6	2	6	22
1993[2]	100	34	31	17	6	1	*	*	2	*	7	2	7	24
1994	100	32	28	19	7	2	*	*	2	*	8	2	8	28
1995	100	30	26	20	7	3	-	*	2	*	10	2	10	30
1996	100	28	25	21	7	3	0	*	2	*	12	2	12	31
1997	100	27	24	21	7	3	0	*	2	*	13	2	13	31
1998	100	27	23	21	7	3	0	(3)	2	*	14	3	14	31
1999	100	25	22	21	8	3	0	(2)	2	*	16	3	16	32
2000	100	24	22	21	8	3	0	0	2	*	16	3	16	33
2001	100	25	20	21	8	2	0	2	2	*	17	3	17	33
2002	100	24	20	21	7	2	1	2	1	*	17	3	17	33

[1] New names for these community sentences came into force in April 2001. They are community rehabilitation order (previously probation order), community punishment order (previously community service order) and community punishment and rehabilitation order (previously combination order).

[2] Improvement during 1992 in the data collection methods used by the Metropolitan Police have led to an increase in the number recorded as sentenced of about 2 per cent in 1993 for indictable offences (see paragraph 5, appendix 2).

[3] Numbers of drug treatment and testing orders given in pilot area in 1998 and 1999 are included in 'Otherwise dealt with'.

Source: Criminal Statistics 2002, Table 4.1.

Table 5. *Persons aged 18 to 20 sentenced for indictable offences by sex and type of sentence or order, 1992–2002*

England and Wales

Sex and year	Total number of persons sentenced	Absolute or conditional discharge	Fine	Community rehabilitation order[1]	Community punishment and order[1]	Attendance centre order	Community punishment and rehabilitation order[1]	Curfew order	Drug treatment and testing order	Young offender institution	Otherwise dealt with	Total immediate custody	Total community sentences
					Number sentenced for indictable offences (000)								
Males													
1992[2]	58.8	9.9	20.6	7.5	9.0	1.2	0.2	*	*	9.0	1.3	9.0	17.9
1993[2]	53.1	9.0	18.0	6.2	7.4	0.8	1.6	*	*	9.0	1.2	9.0	15.9
1994	50.1	8.1	15.5	6.3	6.9	0.7	2.0	*	*	9.6	1.1	9.6	15.9
1995	47.3	7.1	14.1	5.7	6.3	0.5	2.2	–	*	10.4	0.9	10.4	14.7
1996	46.2	6.6	13.3	5.3	5.8	0.5	2.4	0.0	*	11.2	1.0	11.2	14.0
1997	48.1	6.9	14.0	5.4	5.8	0.5	2.7	0.0	*	11.8	1.1	11.8	14.4
1998	51.6	7.0	15.5	5.6	6.3	0.5	2.9	0.1	(3)	12.5	1.1	12.5	15.4
1999	52.3	7.2	15.2	5.8	6.4	0.5	2.9	0.2	(3)	12.8	1.3	12.8	15.7
2000	49.8	6.5	13.8	5.5	6.3	0.4	2.6	0.3	0.0	13.1	1.3	13.1	15.1
2001	47.7	6.5	12.7	5.6	6.1	0.3	1.8	0.4	0.4	12.5	1.4	12.5	14.7
2002	46.2	6.3	12.3	5.2	6.0	0.3	2.0	0.4	0.4	12.0	1.3	12.0	14.3
Females													
1992[2]	7.3	2.9	2.1	1.4	0.5	0.0	0.0	*	*	0.3	0.1	0.3	1.9
1993[2]	6.3	2.3	2.0	1.0	0.4	0.0	0.1	*	*	0.3	0.1	0.3	1.6
1994	6.2	2.3	1.7	1.2	0.4	0.0	0.1	*	*	0.3	0.1	0.3	1.8
1995	5.7	1.9	1.5	1.2	0.4	0.0	0.2	–	*	0.4	0.1	0.4	1.8
1996	5.6	1.8	1.3	1.3	0.4	0.0	0.2	0.0	*	0.5	0.1	0.5	1.9
1997	6.2	1.9	1.4	1.4	0.5	0.0	0.3	0.0	*	0.6	0.1	0.6	2.2
1998	7.1	2.0	1.7	1.6	0.5	0.0	0.3	0.0	(3)	0.8	0.2	0.8	2.5
1999	7.6	2.1	1.8	1.7	0.6	0.0	0.3	0.0	(3)	0.9	0.2	0.9	2.7
2000	7.5	2.0	1.6	1.7	0.6	0.0	0.3	0.0	0.0	1.0	0.2	1.0	2.8
2001	6.9	1.8	1.4	1.6	0.6	0.0	0.2	0.0	0.1	0.9	0.2	0.9	2.6
2002	6.8	1.8	1.3	1.6	0.6	0.0	0.2	0.1	0.1	0.9	0.2	0.9	2.6

Percentage sentenced for indictable offences

Males

	Total											
1992[2]	100	17	35	13	15	2	0	*	*	15	2	30
1993[2]	100	17	34	12	14	1	3	*	*	17	2	30
1994	100	16	31	13	14	1	4	*	*	19	2	32
1995	100	15	30	12	13	1	5	*	–	22	2	31
1996	100	14	29	11	13	1	5	*	0	24	2	30
1997	100	14	29	11	12	1	6	*	0	25	2	30
1998	100	14	30	11	12	1	6	(3)	0	24	2	30
1999	100	14	29	11	12	1	6	(3)	0	24	2	30
2000	100	13	28	11	13	1	5	0	1	26	3	30
2001	100	14	27	12	13	1	4	1	1	26	3	31
2002	100	14	27	11	13	1	4	1	1	26	3	31

Females

	Total											
1992[2]	100	40	29	19	7	0	0	*	*	3	2	26
1993[2]	100	37	31	17	7	0	2	*	*	5	2	25
1994	100	36	27	20	7	0	2	*	*	5	2	29
1995	100	34	26	20	7	0	3	*	–	7	2	31
1996	100	32	23	22	8	0	4	*	0	9	2	34
1997	100	31	22	23	8	0	4	*	0	9	2	36
1998	100	28	23	23	8	0	5	(3)	0	11	2	36
1999	100	27	23	23	8	0	4	(3)	0	11	2	36
2000	100	26	22	23	9	0	4	0	1	13	2	37
2001	100	26	20	23	9	0	3	1	1	14	3	38
2002	100	26	19	23	9	0	3	2	2	14	3	38

[1] New names for these community sentences came into force in April 2001. They are community rehabilitation order (previously probation order), community punishment order (previously community service order) and community punishment and rehabilitation order (previously combination order).

[2] Improvement during 1992 in the data collection methods used by the Metropolitan Police have led to an increase in the number recorded as sentenced of about 2 per cent in 1993 for indictable offences (see paragraph 5, Appendix 2).

[3] Numbers of drug treatment and testing orders given in pilot area in 1998 and 1999 are included in 'Otherwise dealt with'.

Source: Criminal Statistics 2002, Table 4.10.

Table 6. *Persons aged 10 to 17 sentenced for indictable offences by sex and type of sentences or order 1992–2002*

England and Wales

Sex and Year	Total number of persons sentenced	Absolute or conditional discharge	Fine	Community rehabilitation order[1]	Supervision order[1]	Community punishment order[1]	Attendance centre order	Community punishment and rehabilitation order	Curfew order
				Number sentenced for indictable offences (000)					
Males									
1992[4]	33.7	1.8	5.7	2.1	4.0	3.0	3.9	0.1	*
1993[4]	31.6	10.3	3.4	1.2	5.3	2.4	4.3	0.6	*
1994	35.5	11.4	4.0	1.3	6.5	2.4	4.6	0.7	*
1995	37.2	11.6	4.1	1.4	7.1	2.5	4.6	0.7	0.0
1996	39.1	11.7	4.2	1.6	7.4	2.6	4.5	1.0	0.0
1997	40.7	12.0	4.5	1.7	7.5	2.8	4.5	1.2	0.0
1998	43.1	12.5	5.1	1.9	8.0	2.9	4.6	1.3	0.1
1999	43.9	12.0	5.3	1.9	7.8	3.0	4.8	1.3	0.2
2000	42.6	9.4	5.4	1.4	6.7	3.1	3.7	1.3	0.2
2001	43.4	6.7	5.2	1.4	6.4	2.6	2.9	1.2	0.8
2002	42.5	4.5	3.9	1.3	6.0	1.9	1.9	1.0	1.4
Females									
1992[4]	4.2	2.3	0.6	0.3	0.5	0.1	0.1	0.0	*
1993[4]	3.8	2.0	0.4	0.2	0.7	0.1	0.2	0.0	*
1994	4.8	2.5	0.4	0.2	0.9	0.1	0.3	0.0	*
1995	5.0	2.5	0.5	0.2	1.0	0.1	0.4	0.0	0.0
1996	5.2	2.5	0.5	0.3	1.1	0.2	0.4	0.0	0.0
1997	5.6	2.5	0.5	0.3	1.2	0.2	0.4	0.1	0.0
1998	6.4	2.9	0.6	0.4	1.5	0.2	0.4	0.1	0.0
1999	6.6	2.8	0.7	0.4	1.4	0.2	0.4	0.1	0.0
2000	6.7	2.1	0.7	0.3	1.3	0.3	0.4	0.1	0.0
2001	6.9	1.5	0.6	0.3	1.3	0.2	0.3	0.1	0.1
2002	6.7	0.9	0.4	0.2	1.1	0.1	0.2	0.1	0.1
				Percentage sentenced for indictable offences					
Males									
1992[4]	100	32	17	6	12	9	12	0	*
1993[4]	100	32	11	4	17	8	14	2	*
1994	100	32	11	4	18	7	13	2	*
1995	100	31	11	4	19	7	12	2	0
1996	100	30	11	4	19	7	12	2	0
1997	100	29	11	4	18	7	11	3	0
1998	100	29	12	4	19	7	11	3	0
1999	100	27	12	4	18	7	11	3	0
2000	100	22	13	3	16	7	9	3	1
2001	100	16	12	3	15	6	7	3	2
2002	100	11	9	3	14	5	4	2	3
Females									
1992[4]	100	54	15	8	12	3	3	0	*
1993[4]	100	52	11	5	19	3	5	1	*
1994	100	53	9	4	20	3	6	1	*
1995	100	50	10	4	20	3	7	1	0
1996	100	48	9	5	21	4	7	1	0
1997	100	45	9	6	22	4	7	2	0
1998	100	44	9	6	23	3	6	2	0
1999	100	42	10	6	22	3	6	2	0
2000	100	31	10	5	20	4	5	2	0
2001	100	22	9	5	18	3	4	2	1
2002	100	13	6	4	16	2	2	1	2

[1] New names for these community sentences came into force in April 2001. They are community rehabilitation order (previously probation order), community punishment order (previously community service order) and community punishment and rehabilitation order (previously combination order).

[2] Referral orders were introduced by the Youth Justice and Criminal Evidence Act 1999 and consolidated by Criminal Courts (Sentencing) Act 2000; they were implemented nationally on 1 April 2002.

Source: Criminal Statistics 2002, Table 4.10.

Reparation order	Action plan order	Drug treatment and testing order	Referral order[2]	S90–92 PCCS Act 2000[3]	Secure training order	Detention and training order	Young offender institution	Otherwise dealt with	Total immediate custody	Total community sentences
				Number sentenced for indictable offences (000)						
*	*	*	*	0.1	*	*	3.3	0.7	3.4	13.1
*	*	*	*	0.3	*	*	3.3	0.6	3.6	13.8
*	*	*	*	0.4	*	*	3.6	0.6	4.0	15.5
*	*	*	*	0.4	*	*	4.2	0.6	4.6	16.3
*	*	*	*	0.6	*	*	4.8	0.7	5.4	17.2
*	*	*	*	0.7	*	*	5.1	0.7	5.8	17.7
(5)	(5)	(5)	*	0.6	0.1	*	5.1	0.8	5.8	18.9
(5)	(5)	(5)	*	0.6	0.2	*	5.1	1.6	5.9	19.1
1.9	2.4	0.0	(5)	0.6	0.1	3.9	1.2	1.3	5.7	20.8
3.6	4.6	0.1	(5)	0.5	*	5.4	*	1.9	5.8	23.6
2.2	3.0	0.1	8.5	0.7	*	5.1	*	1.1	5.7	27.2
*	*	*	*	0.0	*	*	0.1	0.1	1.1	1.1
*	*	*	*	0.0	*	*	0.1	0.1	0.1	1.2
*	*	*	*	0.0	*	*	0.1	0.1	0.1	1.6
*	*	*	*	0.0	*	*	0.1	0.0	0.2	1.7
*	*	*	*	0.0	*	*	0.2	0.1	0.3	2.0
*	*	*	*	0.0	*	*	0.2	0.1	0.3	2.3
(5)	(5)	(5)	*	0.0	0.0	*	0.3	0.1	0.3	2.6
(5)	(5)	(5)	*	0.0	0.0	*	0.3	0.2	0.4	2.6
0.4	0.5	0.0	(5)	0.0	0.0	0.3	0.1	0.2	0.4	3.2
0.7	1.0	0.0	(5)	0.0	*	0.4	*	0.4	0.4	4.0
0.4	0.6	0.0	1.9	0.1	*	0.4	*	0.2	0.5	4.7
				Percentage sentenced for indictable offences						
*	*	*	*	0	*	*	10	2	10	39
*	*	*	*	1	*	*	10	2	11	44
*	*	*	*	1	*	*	10	2	11	44
*	*	*	*	1	*	*	11	2	12	44
*	*	*	*	2	*	*	12	2	14	44
*	*	*	*	2	*	*	13	2	14	43
(5)	(5)	(5)	*	1	0	*	12	2	13	44
(5)	(5)	(5)	*	1	0	*	12	4	13	43
4	6	0	(5)	1	0	9	3	3	13	49
8	11	0	(5)	1	*	12	*	4	13	54
5	7	0	20	2	*	12	*	3	13	64
*	*	*	*	0	*	*	2	3	2	27
*	*	*	*	0	*	*	2	1	3	32
*	*	*	*	0	*	*	3	1	3	34
*	*	*	*	0	*	*	3	1	3	35
*	*	*	*	1	*	*	3	1	4	38
*	*	*	*	1	*	*	4	2	5	40
(5)	(5)	(5)	*	0	0	*	4	2	5	40
(5)	(5)	(5)	*	0	0	*	5	3	5	39
5	7	0	(5)	0	0	5	1	3	6	49
11	14	0	(5)	0	*	5	*	5	6	58
6	9	0	29	1	*	6	*	3	7	71

[3] Section 53 of the Children and Young Persons Act 1933 was repealed on 25 August 2000 and its provisions were transferred to sections 90 to 92 of the Powers of Criminal Courts (Sentencing) Act 2000.

[4] Improvements during 1992 in the data collection methods used by the Metropolitan Police have led to an increase in the number recorded as sentenced of about 2 per cent in 1993 for indictable offences (see paragraph 5, Appendix 2).

[5] Numbers of reparation, action plan and drug treatment and testing orders given in pilot areas in 1998 and 1999 are included under 'Otherwise dealt with' as are referral orders given in pilot areas in 2000 and 2001.

Table 7. *Average population in custody:*[1] *by type of custody and sex*

England and Wales

Type of custody	1992	1993	1994	1995	1996	1997	1998	1999	2000	2001	2002
	Number of persons[2]										
All male and female											
Population in custody of which:	**45,817**	**44,566**	**48,794**	**51,047**	**55,281**	**61,114**	**65,298**	**64,771**	**64,602**	**66,301**	**70,861**
Population in Prison Service establishments	44,719	44,552	48,621	50,962	55,281	61,114	65,298	64,771	64,602	66,301	70,778
Population in police cells	1,098	14	173	85	–	–	–	–	–	–	83
All males											
Population in custody of which:	**44,240**	**43,005**	**46,983**	**49,068**	**53,019**	**58,439**	**62,194**	**61,523**	**61,252**	**62,560**	**66,562**
Population in Prisons Service establishments	43,157	42,991	46,810	48,983	53,019	58,439	62,194	61,523	61,252	62,560	66,479
Population in police cells	1,083	14	173	85	–	–	–	–	–	–	82
Prisoners on remand	**9,707**	**10,279**	**11,867**	**10,884**	**11,075**	**11,532**	**11,863**	**11,772**	**10,574**	**10,462**	**11,847**
Untried	7,805	7,687	8,818	8,077	8,004	8,057	7,730	7,513	6,701	6,494	7,231
Convicted unsentenced	1,902	2,592	3,049	2,807	3,071	3,475	4,133	4,258	3,873	3,969	4,616
Prisoners under sentence	**34,230**	**32,183**	**34,505**	**37,593**	**41,346**	**46,360**	**49,796**	**49,217**	**50,057**	**51,126**	**53,922**
Young offenders	**5,336**	**4,994**	**5,164**	**5,619**	**6,489**	**7,556**	**8,172**	**8,012**	**8,070**	**8,175**	**8,320**
Detention in a young offender institution/Detention & training order	5,169	4,836	5,020	5,486	6,389	7,439	8,035	7,869	7,925	8,030	8,170
Life (including Section 90 and custody for life)	105	84	84	81	80	105	122	135	141	139	148
In default of payment of a fine	62	74	60	52	20	12	15	8	4	5	2
Adults	**28,894**	**27,189**	**29,340**	**31,974**	**34,856**	**38,805**	**41,624**	**41,205**	**41,987**	**42,951**	**45,601**
Life	2,812	2,917	2,999	3,112	3,289	3,488	3,688	3,939	4,261	4,530	4,845
Immediate imprisonment (excl. life)	25,830	23,874	25,977	28,528	31,417	35,194	37,825	37,183	37,670	38,384	40,724
In default of payment of a fine	252	398	364	334	150	123	112	83	56	38	32
Non-criminal prisoners	**303**	**543**	**611**	**591**	**599**	**547**	**534**	**534**	**619**	**972**	**793**
Held under the 1971 Immigration Act	224	405	464	464	494	464	455	463	557	916	726
Others	79	137	147	127	105	83	78	71	61	56	67

All females

Population in custody of which:	**1,577**	**1,561**	**1,811**	**1,979**	**2,262**	**2,675**	**3,105**	**3,247**	**3,350**	**3,740**	**4,299**
Population in Prison Service establishments	1,562	1,561	1,811	1,979	2,262	2,675	3,105	3,247	3,350	3,740	4,299
Population in police cells	15	–	–	–	–	–	–	–	–	–	1
Prisoners on remand	**383**	**395**	**490**	**491**	**538**	**599**	**704**	**748**	**700**	**775**	**945**
Untried	271	285	351	344	371	396	426	434	396	430	496
Convicted unsentenced	112	110	139	147	167	203	278	313	304	345	449
Prisoners under sentence	**1,190**	**1,135**	**1,292**	**1,464**	**1,697**	**2,052**	**2,380**	**2,474**	**2,627**	**2,925**	**3,301**
Young offenders	**133**	**137**	**155**	**187**	**233**	**278**	**333**	**332**	**369**	**390**	**459**
Detention in a young offender institution/Detention & training order	125	129	148	179	225	268	328	328	363	378	446
Life (including Section 90 and custody for life)	5	5	5	6	6	9	5	4	6	11	13
In default of payment of a fine	3	3	2	2	2	1	–	1	–	1	–
Adults	**1,057**	**998**	**1,137**	**1,277**	**1,464**	**1,774**	**2,047**	**2,142**	**2,258**	**2,535**	**2,842**
Life	95	102	104	108	117	125	135	139	145	150	152
Immediate imprisonment (excl. life)	950	878	1,013	1,154	1,339	1,644	1,908	2,000	2,109	2,384	2,687
In default of payment of a fine	12	18	20	15	8	5	4	3	3	1	3
Non-criminal prisoners	**5**	**31**	**29**	**24**	**28**	**25**	**20**	**24**	**22**	**40**	**54**
Held under the 1971 Immigration Act	3	25	23	19	22	21	19	22	19	39	51
Other	2	6	6	5	6	4	1	2	2	1	2

(1) Included police cells.

(2) The components do not always add to the totals because they have been rounded independently.

Source: Prison Statistics 2002, Table 1.13.

1.4 The criminal process[8]

Sentencing is one of several stages at which decisions are taken in a criminal process that begins with decisions such as reporting a crime or arresting a suspect, and goes through to decisions to release a prisoner on parole or to revoke a community order. Occasionally, in debates about prison overcrowding, it has been suggested that that problem is a direct result of the sentencing policies of the courts. In a formal sense it is true: the people in prison have been sent there by the courts. But it is important to consider the matter more deeply. There are at least two possibilities – that the courts have changed their approach and are sending more offenders to prison, or that the number and/or composition of people coming before the courts have changed and sentencers' policies have remained unchanged. The latter possibility is much favoured by many judges and magistrates as an analysis of recent trends, notably the steep rise in the prison population,[9] and so we should first look into the evidence for variations of this kind. Where might these variations come from? An obvious answer might be 'the crime rate'. As 'the crime rate' increases, so sentencers will have to deal with more and more offenders. If they do not alter their sentencing practice, it follows that more offenders will be sent to prison. But the answer is too simple and too sweeping. Apart from the need to scrutinize the idea of 'the crime rate', it is vital to examine the effect of the many other decisions to be taken between reporting a crime and bringing an accused person before a court. The numbers sentenced may reflect changes in police investigation priorities or changes in the policies of the Crown Prosecution Service, rather than any increase or decrease in 'the crime rate'.

How can the number of crimes committed each year be measured? The best that the official criminal statistics can offer is the annual total of crimes recorded by the police. It will be recalled that the second line of figures in Table 1 above, 'Offences recorded by the police', shows trends in recorded crime. The statistics in that table are more representative of the crime rate than the numbers of offences which are detected or which result in a conviction (i.e. all the figures lower down Table 1), but they still give only a small part of the picture. The police are informed about crimes mostly by victims, but not all victims report incidents to the police. Of those crime victims who responded to the British Crime Survey and who failed to report the crimes to the police in 2003/04, some 72 per cent fell within the category of 'trivial/no loss/police would not (could not) do anything', and a further 22 per cent responded 'private/dealt with ourselves'. Other, less frequent reasons were a fear of reprisal or dislike of the police.[10] Thus, although the figures for serious offences recorded by the police have been the most comprehensive set of statistics published regularly over the decades, they are not a reliable indicator of the number of crimes being committed, or of fluctuations in the crime rate.

---

8 For an extended treatment of the issues summarized in this section, see Ashworth and Redmayne (2005) and Sanders and Young (2000). For selected readings, see Padfield (2003), chs. 2–6.
9 Hough et al. (2003), p. 30.   10 Dodd et al. (2004), p. 43.

Criminologists have attempted to estimate the number of unreported offences (sometimes called the 'dark figure' of crime) by two main methods. One is the self-report study, in which people are asked to divulge in confidence how many offences they have committed during a specified period of crime. An obvious defect of this approach is that some people may be reticent whereas others might exaggerate their deeds out of bravado. The second and more widely used method is to ask people to state in confidence the number of crimes of which they have been a victim during a specified period. If one then takes the results of such a study, known as a victimization study or crime survey, and compares them with the number of officially recorded crimes over the same period, an estimate of the proportion of crimes unrecorded can be made. This is the basis on which the British Crime Survey (BCS) has proceeded since 1981.[11] However, crime surveys are at their best when dealing with crimes with identifiable victims: the BCS covers violence, sexual offences, burglary, robbery, theft and damage. It is much more difficult to survey crimes against businesses and public authorities, although that has now been done separately.[12] And it is particularly hard to survey offences of which people are unlikely to think of themselves as victims, such as drug offences and consensual sexual crimes.

The BCS has been conducted frequently since the early 1980s, and consists of questions put to a large sample of citizens about crimes to which they have fallen victim in the past year. Although its scope is restricted to certain crimes, for the reasons just given, it does enable a comparison with the figures for crimes recorded by the police for those offences. It also enables comparisons of trends over time. What can be seen, from comparing the first line with the second line of figures in Table 1 above, is that 'Crime as measured by the British Crime Survey' peaked in 1991 and has been falling slowly but steadily since then. On the other hand, although the figures for 'Notifiable offences recorded by the police' also rose sharply during the 1980s, they have continued to rise steadily but relatively slowly since then. In other words, during the last decade the police have been recording more crimes, but members of the public have been suffering fewer crimes. Householders questioned about the offences of which they have been victim have been reporting fewer crimes committed against them, but the impression created by the police figures is that the crime rate is continuing its upward march.

If we follow the details of the BCS into Table 3, we see that in most categories of offence the number of incidents reported by householders reached its peak in 1995. Since then there has been a downward trend, which for some categories has been enormous. The ninth column of Table 3 shows the percentage decline from 1995 to 2003/04: for vehicle thefts the decline is 51 per cent, for burglary it is 47 per cent, for common assault (i.e. the least serious forms of assault) it is 43 per cent, for thefts of personal property it is 36 per cent, and for vandalism it is 27 per cent. There has been

11 The latest report is that of Dodd et al. (2004).
12 The Commercial Victimization Survey in 1994, summarized in Home Office *Digest 4* (1999), p. 8.

an overall decline in personal crimes since 1995 of some 35 per cent, and personal crimes include all violence, robbery and thefts from the person. It is evident that for robbery and woundings the decline has been less than for most other offences; but there is still a decline that contrasts with the considerable rise in such categories of offence recorded by the police. The BCS figures are more reliable over time since they have been subject to fewer changes of recording practice. For example, violent crimes recorded by the police showed an increase of no less than 12 per cent in the year between 2002/03 and 2003/04, but it is likely that this was caused (at least partly) by changes in recording practices.[13] All these statistics are particularly important, insofar as they are used by politicians and the media to support arguments about penal policy. The BCS shows a consistent decline in the rate at which people are becoming victims of crime, and yet this finding tends to be downplayed in the face of a continuing rise in the number of offences recorded by the police – even if changes in recording practices have a considerable influence.

The importance of changes in reporting habits is apparent when one considers that around three-quarters of offences which come to the notice of the police are reported by members of the public rather than 'discovered' by the police themselves.[14] Moreover, these reporting habits do not merely relate to the offences against individuals with which the BCS is concerned. Many companies learn of offences of fraud or thieving committed by their employees, and deal with them by dismissing or disciplining the employee without reporting an offence. As for the offences which the police discover for themselves, the numbers will be affected by levels, styles and targets of policing. In general, the police are much more likely to 'discover' offences committed in public places than crimes committed in the home or in business or financial settings. Furthermore, fluctuations in the number of recorded offences of possession of drugs, possession of child pornography or possession of obscene articles for gain might largely reflect priorities in police deployment. Thus, discovery of many of these crimes may bear little relation to variations in the actual rate of offending.

It is already clear, then, that the number of offences recorded by the police each year is a considerable under-estimate; that the number includes proportionately more offences against individuals and public order offences than offences by and against companies; and that fluctuations from year to year may reflect changes in reporting or recording practices rather than changes in the true level of crime. The next stage in the process sees another major quantitative change. We have observed that only 23 per cent of offences recorded by the police in 2002 were detected (Table 1 above, line 4). An offence is treated as 'detected' not only if a person is convicted or cautioned but also if the offence is 'taken into consideration' by the court on conviction for another offence,[15] or if the offence is believed to have been committed by a child under the age of criminal responsibility, or in a number of other cases where the police believe they have sufficient evidence but for some reason cannot

---

13 Dodd et al. (2004), pp. 9, 13.   14 Bottomley and Coleman (1981), p. 44.
15 This practice is discussed in ch. 8.1 below.

prosecute. The detection or 'clear-up' rate has declined gradually from 38 per cent in 1981. Some of this decline may be traceable to the increased reporting of relatively minor incidents (e.g. some thefts) which are difficult to detect. The rate is certainly higher for the more serious offences. For many years some three-quarters of offences of violence against the person and sexual offences have been 'cleared up', although the high figure owes as much to the fact that many victims recognize and can identify their attackers as to the greater efforts put into police work on these crimes. Fewer than 20 per cent of recorded burglaries and robberies were cleared up in 2002.

It is apparent from the definition of 'detected' that not all these offences result in a prosecution. In fact, both the police and the Crown Prosecution Service are urged to consider two factors, evidential sufficiency and whether prosecution is in the public interest. The police take no further action in some cases which are recorded as crimes but where the available evidence is considered weak – notably, no further action is taken in around 30 per cent of rape cases, largely because the complainant withdraws the complaint.[16] During the 1980s and early 1990s the police were encouraged to make greater use of formal cautions as an alternative to prosecution. This policy was pursued most vigorously in relation to juveniles, and the proportionate use of cautions increased until the mid-1990s. In 1994 the then Home Secretary issued a circular to the police which stated that only in exceptional circumstances should a caution be used for an indictable-only offence or for someone who had already been cautioned. After that, as Table 8 demonstrates, the overall cautioning rate has steadied somewhat – although it still remains well above the level of the 1980s. Cautions for offenders under 18 were replaced by warnings and reprimands under the Crime and Disorder Act 1998 (discussed further in Chapter 12), and Table 8 shows that the decline in diversion of young offenders in the mid-1990s has now steadied.

A new form of diversion is introduced by the Criminal Justice Act 2003, the conditional caution. This may only be directed by a crown prosecutor, although the police retain their power to dispose of an offence by means of a 'simple caution'. Section 23 of the 2003 Act sets out five conditions to be met before a conditional caution is given, and they include sufficient evidence to bring a charge, an admission from the defendant, and the latter's signature to a document setting out the conditions to which consent is given. The conditions may include requirements to participate in some rehabilitative, reparative or restorative programme. Failure to observe the conditions may result in the bringing of a prosecution for the original offence.

Not all criminal cases are handled by the police. Perhaps one-quarter of all prosecutions of adults for non-motoring offences are initiated by government departments, HM Customs and Excise, the Inland Revenue, the Post Office, the various inspectorates concerned with industrial safety, local authorities and their various departments (including trading standards), and occasionally private individuals.

---

16 Harris and Grace (1999), ch 3.

Table 8. Offenders[1] cautioned as a percentage of offenders found guilty or cautioned by type of offence, sex and age group, 1993–2003

England and Wales

Percentages

Year	All offenders[1]	Males[1]						Females					
		All ages	Aged 10–11	Aged 12–14	Aged 15–17	Aged 18–20	Aged 21 and over	All Ages	Aged 10–11	Aged 12–14	Aged 15–17	Aged 18–20	Aged 21 and over
Indictable offences[2]													
1993	41	37	96	83	59	32	26	60	99	95	80	52	46
1994	41	37	95	81	56	34	25	59	100	94	77	50	44
1995	41	37	94	79	54	35	26	59	99	93	76	51	44
1996	40	36	94	77	51	35	26	56	99	91	72	50	44
1997	38	35	93	74	49	34	26	52	98	89	68	48	42
1998	37	33	91	72	48	34	24	51	97	88	67	46	39
1999	34	31	87	69	45	31	22	48	96	87	64	44	36
2000	32	29	86	68	43	29	20	47	95	86	63	39	32
2001	31	28	86	66	42	28	19	46	95	85	64	39	32
2002	30	27	83	63	41	29	19	44	94	84	62	41	35
2003	32	28	85	66	44	31	20	45	92	83	65	44	33
Summary offences[2]													
1993	18	22	97	85	63	30	16	10	95	89	74	28	7
1994	18	21	97	82	60	29	15	9	99	86	67	27	6
1995	18	20	94	78	56	28	13	11	95	80	65	25	7
1996	16	19	95	79	55	29	12	10	97	82	60	23	6
1997	18	19	94	77	50	28	12	14	94	78	52	28	10
1998	17	18	92	73	47	26	11	15	98	79	53	28	10
1999	18	18	88	70	46	26	11	17	92	75	56	32	11
2000	15	16	86	67	44	24	9	12	92	75	56	26	7
2001	16	17	88	67	44	23	10	13	86	75	55	25	8
2002	14	15	85	63	41	22	9	13	92	72	54	25	8
2003	16	16	86	65	44	24	10	14	82	72	56	25	8

[1] Other offenders, i.e. companies, public bodies, etc. are included with males aged 21 and over.

[2] Excluding all motoring offences.

Source: Criminal Statistics 2003, Table 2.3.

Indeed, it is not just that these bodies bring around a quarter of non-motoring prosecutions. Equally significant is their widespread practice of avoiding prosecution wherever possible. For example, both HM Customs and Excise and the Inland Revenue have extensive powers of compounding, for example, which enable them to exact compliance plus a financial penalty without bringing a case to court.[17] Research also demonstrates the emphasis of the Health and Safety Commission and other inspectorates on obtaining compliance with the required standards, and their general practice of using prosecution only as a last resort.[18] Since many of these offences are typically committed by people who have moderate or good financial resources, it follows that the figures for crimes recorded by the police and for persons prosecuted may tend to give greater prominence to crimes committed by members of the lower socio-economic groups.

Returning to the types of crime with which the police concern themselves, the next question is whether to charge the defendant and if so, what offence to select. When the Crown Prosecution Service was created by the Prosecution of Offences Act 1985, this power remained with the police, and the main function of the CPS was to conduct a review of the file at a later stage. However, new charging arrangements introduced by the Criminal Justice Act 2003 transfer the power to charge to the CPS for all but minor cases. Police and prosecutors will usually work alongside one another in taking these decisions (although the CPS technically has the last word), and the hope is that the new arrangements will make for speed, better-quality preparation and therefore fewer cases discontinued or dismissed by the courts. In taking decisions either on initial charge or on later review, crown prosecutors are regulated by the *Code for Crown Prosecutors*.[19] In essence, they must take two related decisions. First, is the evidence sufficient for a prosecution? The code states that cases should only be brought where there is a 'realistic prospect of conviction'. Second, would a prosecution be 'in the public interest'? The code sets out a number of general criteria for and against prosecuting – most of them similar to the aggravating and mitigating factors in sentencing reviewed in Chapter 5 below. The two decisions are closely connected, and in practice there is considerable emphasis on pursuing serious charges and diverting less serious cases. The CPS has the power to alter the charge later or to discontinue a prosecution if this is thought to be appropriate.

The *Code for Crown Prosecutors* is not the only source of guidance for CPS decision-making. As is evident from their website, there is much available guidance on the proper approach to particular types of offence, and approved 'charging standards' for some offences.[20] No study of the effectiveness of this guidance has been published, and so it remains to be discovered whether it has brought about reductions in questionable practices. For example, s. 144 of the Criminal Justice Act 2003 gives legislative authority for a discount for pleading guilty. It is sometimes suggested that this gives an incentive to prosecutors to over-charge some cases, in

---

17 Roording (1996).   18 Hawkins (2003).
19 The latest version of the code was published in 2004: see Ashworth and Redmayne (2005), ch. 7.
20 www.cps.gov.uk.

the hope of inducing a bargain whereby the defendant agrees to plead guilty to a lesser offence (which may be the offence that should have been charged originally). On the other hand some cases may be under-charged, in order to have the case disposed of in the magistrates' court, where any plea of not guilty is less likely to succeed than it is in the Crown Court. Although it is not known how often these practices occur, they demonstrate that factors other than the intrinsic seriousness of the case may determine the charge brought and the way in which the evidence (or, on a guilty plea, the prosecutor's statement of facts) is presented. Moreover, the prosecutor's choice of charge may have a considerable effect on the sentence. The decision to charge a summary offence restricts the court's sentencing power. The decision to charge an offence triable either way, together with representations to the magistrates in favour of Crown Court trial, invariably results in the case being committed to the Crown Court, where the sentence may be some seven times as severe as a magistrates' court's sentence.[21]

The Crown Prosecution Service also has a role to play in any subsequent negotiations about the defendant's plea. Most cases end with a plea of guilty rather than a trial. In 2002–03 some 74 per cent of Crown Court cases involved a guilty plea, and in magistrates' courts the figure is almost 94 per cent.[22] However, not all these defendants began by pleading guilty: indeed, of those defendants in Hedderman and Moxon's study who had elected to go for trial in the Crown Court, no fewer than 82 per cent subsequently changed their plea to guilty.[23] Of those who thus changed their plea to guilty, some 51 per cent said that they 'expected some charges would be dropped or reduced, resulting in a lighter sentence' and a further 22 per cent now took the view that there was 'no chance of a not guilty plea succeeding'.[24] Since, as we shall see in Chapter 5, a plea of guilty should usually result in a significant reduction in sentence, these practices have implications for the powers of the courts as well as for the rights of the individual defendant. The finding of Baldwin and McConville (1978) that many such defendants felt under pressure from their lawyers to change their plea to guilty was hotly disputed by the legal establishment in the 1970s, but since then there has been a succession of cases in which judges were revealed to have played some part in negotiations, which would then have been relayed to the defendant by counsel.[25] Home Office research projects have confirmed the extensive influence of lawyers:

> The two most frequent reasons given for a change in advice on plea on the day scheduled for trial were 'a bargain with the prosecution' and 'information about probable sentence'. The most frequent forms of concession were that, in consideration of one or more pleas of guilty, the prosecution should offer no evidence, or agree to the defendant's being bound over, on other charges.[26]

---

21 Hedderman and Moxon (1992).   22 Crown Prosecution Service (2003), pp. 30, 33.
23 Hedderman and Moxon (1992), p. 22.   24 Hedderman and Moxon (1992), p. 24.
25 A number of cases are discussed in Ashworth and Redmayne (2005), ch. 10.
26 Riley and Vennard (1988), p. 20; also Hedderman and Moxon (1992), pp. 22–4.

Thus, even a matter of hours or minutes before a case is due to be tried, it can undergo changes which 'reconstruct' it. When it is presented to the court for sentence, the case may have been negotiated in certain ways so that it is qualitatively different from that originally brought by the police. One main purpose of enacting s. 144 of the Criminal Justice Act 2003 (requiring courts to consider a discount for a guilty plea) and s. 49 of the Criminal Procedure and Investigations Act 1996 ('plea before venue') was to place more pressure on defendants to plead guilty, and to do so at the earliest possible stage.[27] Unfortunately, that pressure falls upon the innocent as well as the guilty.

The main implication of this contextual discussion of the criminal process is that the cases which judges and magistrates have for sentence are qualitatively and quantitatively different from the 'real' amount of crime in society. This casts grave doubt upon pronouncements about crime, crime prevention and trends in crime which are based on the features of cases going through the courts. The qualitative differences stem from the several stages of selection, starting with the under-reporting of crimes in the home and crimes by and against businesses, continuing with the differential responses to crime by the police and the so-called regulatory agencies, taking in the differential diversion rates for juveniles and young adults, and ending with the plea negotiations which make some offences appear less serious than they were. The overall conclusion is that the types of case which come up for sentence are an imperfect reflection of the nature of crime in society.

The quantitative differences between the crimes actually committed and those coming up for sentence in court are immense. Taking the Home Office's own figures, compiled with the benefit of British Crime Survey data, we may start with the cautious assumption that some 45 per cent of offences in any one year are reported. Of those, only about 55 per cent are actually recorded by the police as crimes, for various reasons. That reduces the number of cases still within the criminal justice system to 24 per cent (i.e. 55 per cent of the 45 per cent reported). The detection rate for recorded crimes is less than a quarter, so the 24 per cent declines to 5.5 per cent of all offences that are cleared up. Of those offences that are cleared up, just over half result in a conviction or formal caution. This brings the figure to some 3 per cent of offences and, since about one-third of those result in a caution, sentencers probably deal with just over 2 per cent of actual offences in any one year. (Around 0.3 per cent of offences result in a custodial sentence.) The final figures would be higher for offences of violence, but lower for many thefts. Since these are the Home Office's own figures in *Digest 4* (1999) of information on the criminal justice system, they can hardly be treated as exaggerated. What the figures demonstrate is that, if criminal justice policy-makers expect sentencing to perform a major preventive function, they are looking in the wrong direction. As Baldock put it, in the context of attempts to reduce the prison population,

---

27 The import of s. 144, and the guidelines attached to it, will be discussed in ch. 5.4.1 below.

Prisons stand at the end of an elaborate process of selection by the public, police, courts and judges. Consequently, relatively small changes at any point in the process can have an amplified impact on the prison system. It is a mistake to seek the causes and remedies for the growth of the prison population by looking only at the very late stages of these processes, sentences of imprisonment. This is the tail end of the story and, as most of the attempts to 'reform' or counteract sentencing policy have shown, it is a tail which cannot easily be made to wag the dog.[28]

The argument, therefore, is that sentencers deal only with a small and selected sample of offences and offenders; that the preventive and other general effects of sentencing in these cases should not be overestimated; that any assumption that crime rates stand in some hydraulic relationship to sentence levels, so that crime will go down if sentences go up and vice versa, seems wildly unrealistic; and, on the basis of the selection of offences they deal with, that judges and magistrates are likely to have a somewhat skewed view of the crime problem as a whole.

Alongside those important points must also be placed another. At the beginning of this part of the chapter the question was raised whether the sharp increase in the use of custody in the last decade was a product of increases in the number of cases coming before courts for sentence, or of a change in the sentencing practices of the courts. As Table 1 above confirms, there has been no significant increase in the number of cases coming up for sentence. That suggests that the explanation lies in the greater severity of sentencing practices. However, Hough, Jacobson and Millie's interviews of judges and magistrates yielded a trio of other explanations – that judges were responding to the more repressive climate of opinion in society, that the offenders coming before the courts had more previous convictions, and that the offences were more serious.[29] The first of these three explanations concedes the point that sentences have become more severe. The second and third were investigated by the researchers, who found that the available statistics do not confirm either that the offenders being sentenced have more previous convictions than formerly[30] or that their offences are more serious. However, as they conclude, sentencers clearly believe that these are major factors, and those perceptions may influence their behaviour.

Prominent at the various stages of the criminal process is discretion. The police exercise it, the regulatory agencies exercise it, the Crown Prosecution Service exercises it, and so forth. Now it may well be true that the many and varied elements which are relevant to these decisions tell in favour of discretionary rather than strictly rule-bound decision-making. This is often said to be true of sentencing to a certain extent, and may be no less true of prosecution decisions. However, discretion brings not only advantages, in the shape of flexibility to respond to different combinations of facts, but also disadvantages, in that it may allow the individual views of the decision-maker to influence (deliberately or otherwise) the approach

---

28 Baldock (1980), pp. 149–50.   29 Hough et al. (2003), pp. 26–30.

30 The authors find some evidence of an increased proportion of persistent offenders in the categories of theft and handling, which may be related to drug use (Hough et al. (2003), p. 29), but it is not of sufficient magnitude to explain the steep overall rise in the use of custody.

taken. Replacing discretion with rigid rules may eliminate its advantages as well as its disadvantages. A wiser course may therefore be to attempt to structure the discretion, in an attempt to ensure that it is exercised broadly in line with some coherent policies.[31] Steps have been taken in this direction, in the form of Home Office circulars to the police on cautioning and the *Code for Crown Prosecutors*. However, the principles contained in these documents are fairly general, and criminological research establishes that other influences – such as easing one's own job, maintaining good relations with others, and personal or local preferences – often enter into practical decision-making.[32] Drafting and promulgating guidelines is therefore not enough to ensure that discretion is exercised along the right lines. At least two further steps should be taken. One is to foster positive and constructive attitudes amongst the key decision-makers, so that they understand the reasons for policies and become committed to carrying them out. The other is to create structures of accountability, in terms of both internal monitoring and external scrutiny or audit.

It is important to recall, finally, that the mechanisms for dealing with suspected offenders and prosecutions continue to differ according to the type of offence. Put crudely, 'white-collar crime' and so-called regulatory offences are unlikely to come to the attention of the police. Since the agencies dealing with those offences tend to regard prosecution as a last resort, the court system is likely to contain far more offenders of some kinds than offenders of other kinds. We will return to this problem of social justice at various points in the book.

1.5 The formal sources of sentencing decisions

The principal sources of English sentencing law are legislation, definitive sentencing guidelines and judicial decisions. In a less formal and weaker sense, the work of certain academic lawyers may be regarded as a source. The leading writer is D. A. Thomas of Cambridge University, a tireless collator of and commentator on sentencing decisions and legislation. Commentaries by Thomas on Court of Appeal decisions are to be found in the *Criminal Law Review*, as are articles on major pieces of sentencing legislation. Occasionally, these commentaries have been cited with approval in the Court of Appeal, thus suggesting that they may be regarded as at least a secondary source of law. However, recent years have also seen an increase in the number of works by other writers, both academic and practitioner, which draw together and comment on sentencing decisions and laws relevant to the Crown Court or to magistrates' courts.[33] In Scotland the leading work is Sheriff-Principal Nicholson's *Law and Practice of Sentencing in Scotland*,[34] but the Scottish sentencing

---

31 See Galligan (1987) for a thoughtful discussion.
32 For further discussion see Ashworth and Redmayne (2005), ch. 3.
33 E.g. Wasik (2003), a discerning commentary on sentencing laws and decisions; Banks (2003), which collates decisions excerpts from judgments without commentary; Archbold (2005), which assembles and comments on general sentencing legislation but less on judicial principles or particular offences; and Blackstone (2005), which comments both on legislation and on precedents applicable to particular offences.
34 The latest edition is Nicholson (2001).

system differs from that in England and Wales and is not included in the discussion below.[35]

1.5.1 Legislation

Statutes passed by Parliament establish the framework of English sentencing law, as will have been evident from parts 1 and 2 of this chapter. Statutes lay down a maximum sentence for almost every offence. Legislation (such as the Criminal Justice Act 2003) lays down the terms of the orders which a criminal court may make after conviction, and imposes restrictions on the making of orders in certain circumstances. Legislation also limits the powers of magistrates' courts, and provides for the circumstances in which cases can be committed to the Crown Court for sentence. All these provisions have to be interpreted by the courts, and some of the cases which go on appeal raise a particular point of statutory interpretation (about the extent of the courts' powers) rather than any general issue of principle (as to how the courts should exercise their powers).

The role of legislation as a source of English sentencing law has therefore largely been one of providing powers and setting outer limits to their use. Within those outer boundaries, sentencing practice has been characterized by considerable discretion, subject (as we shall see) to the general superintendence of the Court of Appeal. However, in recent years the legislature has increasingly made forays into the area previously left to judicial discretion. The high water mark of this is to be found in s. 269 and Schedule 21 of the Criminal Justice Act 2003: not only is life imprisonment the mandatory sentence for murder, but Parliament has now specified various starting points to which judges 'must have regard' when setting the minimum term to be served in a particular case.[36] This legislative steer must be added to the prescribed minimum sentences introduced by the Crime (Sentences) Act 1997, re-enacted in the PCCS Act 2000 and now supplemented by the Criminal Justice Act 2003. There is a myriad of other examples of changes in sentencing law (large and small) being introduced with increasing frequency, as well as major statutes such as the Proceeds of Crime Act 2002 and two statutes on youth sentencing, the Crime and Disorder Act 1998 and the Youth Justice and Criminal Evidence Act 1999. Thomas has produced a devastating critique of the methodology of these changes, highlighting the omissions and confusion resulting from late amendments, defective drafting, legislation by incorporation, staggered commencement dates, and ill-conceived transitional provisions.[37] He also makes the point that the overall amount of sentencing legislation is immense, and that the practical difficulties for sentencers are increased by its dispersal across several statutes. We have already noted that the attempt to consolidate sentencing law in the Powers of Criminal Courts (Sentencing) Act 2000 met with limited success, since Parliament began to change the law even before that

---

35 For an introduction to Scottish sentencing see Hutton (1999a).
36 For further discussion, see ch. 4.4.1 below.
37 Thomas (1997): the criticisms are no less applicable to legislation since then.

Act came into force, and the Criminal Justice Act 2003 now replaces substantial parts of it.

There is much substance in the complaints that sentencing laws are often poorly drafted[38] and scattered across several different statutes. But those criticisms should not lead us to overlook two other arguments – that important policy objectives (e.g. the making of a compensation order in favour of the victim wherever possible) cannot be accomplished without legislation; and that fairer sentencing outcomes may not come about if maximum discretion is left to judges and magistrates, despite their claims to the contrary. Both of these arguments call for full consideration, before it is concluded that most new sentencing legislation is a bad thing, or that there should be a moratorium on sentencing legislation. It may well be possible to present good arguments of principle for encouraging Parliament to introduce new sentencing policies in some spheres. But the benefits of frequently re-enacting legislative principles such as the principle that offending on bail should be treated as an aggravating factor, or that defendants who plead guilty should receive a discount (and the earlier the plea, the greater the discount), may be questioned. These arguments are taken further below, in Chapter 2 when discussing judicial independence and in Chapter 13 when discussing the future shape of sentencing.

1.5.2 Definitive sentencing guidelines

Guideline judgments handed down by the Court of Appeal became a salient feature of the sentencing system in the 1980s:[39] many of them are still in force, and they will be discussed in part 1.5.3 below. However, it was relatively rare for the Lord Chief Justice to deliver guideline judgments, and by the late 1990s they covered only a small proportion of offences. By ss. 80–81 of the Crime and Disorder Act 1998 two major changes were introduced: first, a Sentencing Advisory Panel was created to draft guidelines, consult widely on them, and then advise the Court of Appeal about the form that they should take; and second, the power of the Court of Appeal to give guideline judgments was restricted to offences on which it had received advice from the Sentencing Advisory Panel, although it was not bound to accept the Panel's advice. This arrangement continued for some years, producing new guideline judgments on racially aggravated offences[40] and on child pornography,[41] a revised guideline judgment on rape[42] and several others.

The 2003 Act changed the structure in major ways. The Sentencing Advisory Panel remains (s. 171) and will continue to devise draft guidelines, to consult members of the public and its statutory consultees about them, and then to prepare

---

38 This is not necessarily a criticism of parliamentary counsel: much depends on the brief they receive, usually from the Home Office.
39 The first guideline judgment issued by a lord chief justice was that for drug offences in *Aramah* (1982) 4 Cr App R (S) 407.
40 *Kelly and Donnelly* [2001] 2 Cr App R (S) 341.
41 *Oliver, Hartrey and Baldwin* [2003] 2 Cr App R (S) 64.
42 *Milberry et al.* [2003] 2 Cr App R (S) 142.

its advice. However, that advice goes not to the Court of Appeal but to a new body, the Sentencing Guidelines Council, which has the power to issue guidelines (s. 170). There were some problems with the previous machinery – SAP only had the power to propose guidelines relating to a 'particular category of offence', whereas there is a need for guidelines on types of sentence and matters of general principle; and the Court of Appeal could only issue guidelines as part of the judgment on an appeal before it, so it had to wait for an appropriate case to come along – but these could easily have been cured by legislative amendments. In its White Paper *Justice for All* the government put forward two further reasons for creating the Council – the need for comprehensive guidelines, and the importance of giving Parliament a role in 'considering and scrutinizing' draft guidelines.[43] Neither reason actually necessitated the creation of a further body, since SAP and its procedure could easily have been adapted to allow for this, but it was surely right in principle to separate the function of creating guidelines from that of deciding individual appeals.[44]

The new procedure is that the Council may only issue guidelines after receiving an advice from SAP. SAP may propose guidelines of its own motion, or after receiving a notification from the Council that guidelines on a particular subject are required.[45] SAP itself must follow its procedure of preparing a consultation paper,[46] having regard to such matters as sentencing practice, the cost and effectiveness of various forms of sentence, and public confidence; and then reviewing the responses and producing an advice for the Council. The Council must then consider framing guidelines and, if it decides to do so, it must first publish them as draft guidelines (having considered the matters enumerated in s. 170(5), such as cost and effectiveness, consistency etc.) and then consult the Home Secretary and the House of Commons Home Affairs Committee about them.[47] Having made any amendment to the draft that it considers appropriate, the Council 'may issue the guidelines as definitive guidelines' (s. 170(9)). Courts are placed under a duty to 'have regard to any guidelines which are relevant' to a particular case (s. 172(1)), and to give reasons for passing a sentence outside the range indicated by any guidelines (s. 174(2)(a)).

The structure and operation of this statutory procedure for creating guidelines will be discussed again below.[48] For present purposes it is important to note that

43 Home Office (2002), 5.17. The proposal built on the examination of the issues and options in ch. 8 of the Halliday report (Halliday, 2001), which argued that 'a clear code of sentencing guidelines' must be the aim if consistency is to be achieved (para. 8.7).

44 Strangely Schedule 37 of the CJA removes the restriction on the Court of Appeal issuing its own guidelines that had been in introduced in 1998 when the SAP was created. See further below, text at nn. 68–74.

45 The Council may decide thus to notify SAP of its own motion or after receiving a proposal from the Home Secretary: ss. 170(2), 171(1).

46 The consultation period is normally three months, and consequently the whole process of formulating an advice takes SAP several months. However, s. 171(4) empowers the Council to notify SAP that, because of 'the urgency of the case', it may dispense with its normal consultations.

47 The terms of s. 170(8) allow for other consultations too, as either the Lord Chancellor or the Council itself thinks appropriate.

48 The constitutional and political implications are discussed in ch. 2.2; the implications for the development of English sentencing are discussed in ch. 13.

the Council has been operating since March 2004, and issued three sets of definitive guidelines in December 2004, with more to come. It first issued *Overarching Principles: Seriousness*, a guideline that sets out the principles on culpability and harm that the Council, SAP and courts are to apply, and also elaborates on the 2003 Act's thresholds for custodial sentences and for community sentences. There is then a substantial document, *New Sentences: Criminal Justice Act 2003*, setting out guidelines for the use of the whole range of new forms of sentence introduced by the 2003 Act. The third guideline is *Reduction in Sentence for a Guilty Plea*, which gives guidance on the application of the long-standing sentence discount for guilty pleaders, altering the approach in some respects. Each of these guidelines is discussed in its appropriate sentencing context later in this book. Each guideline was issued as a draft, following the statutory procedure, and then examined by the Home Affairs Committee and commented upon by the Home Secretary.[49] It is noteworthy that none of these guidelines could properly have been produced under the pre-2003 scheme, since SAP had no power to propose guidelines on general principles or on types of sentence.[50]

1.5.3 Judicial decisions

Since the creation of the Court of Criminal Appeal in 1907, it has been possible for an offender to appeal against sentence. The Court formerly had the power to increase sentence on an appeal by a defendant, but this was abolished in 1966. However, since 1988 it has been possible for the Attorney General to refer to the Court of Appeal a sentence imposed by the Crown Court which is thought to be unduly lenient, and this is now done in over 100 cases per year. In such cases the Court has the power to increase the sentence if it concludes that that is appropriate. Further appeals to the House of Lords were extremely rare in sentencing cases between 1970 and 2000, but the amount of sentencing legislation means that some cases are now reaching the House of Lords on points of sentencing law.[51] However, the Court of Appeal remains the final appellate court in most sentencing cases.

The development of a worthwhile jurisprudence would not be possible in the absence of regular reporting of appellate decisions. This began in the *Criminal Law Review* in 1954, with brief reports, and gathered pace in 1970 with the publication of the first edition of Thomas's *Principles of Sentencing*, bringing together both reported and unreported cases into a single structured narrative. This book was influential in creating an atmosphere in which the various principles of sentencing came to be regarded more seriously, and more as an interconnected group. A further step

---

49 See House of Commons (2004).
50 In practice the statutory limitations on SAP did not constrain its operation: it responded to the Court of Appeal's request for guidelines on the use of the extended sentence, which the Court rapidly adopted in *Nelson* [2002] 1 Cr App R (S) 565.
51 For three recent examples, see *Revzi, Benjafield* [2002] 2 Cr App R (S) 313 (confiscation orders); *Pope* [2003] 1 Cr App R (S) 299 (confiscation orders); and *R v. Home Secretary, ex p. Uttley* [2004] UKHL 38 (relevance of Art. 7 of the European Convention on Human Rights to changes in early release laws).

forward came in 1979, when the publication of *Criminal Appeal Reports (Sentencing)* began. This series is devoted entirely to sentencing decisions, and appears to have been one factor in the increased citation of previous decisions to the Court of Appeal by counsel and by the court in its judgments. The encyclopaedia *Current Sentencing Practice* builds on this series of reports by collating decisions and arranging them according to subject matter, providing judges and practitioners with a ready source of reference on most issues of sentencing law.

Judicially created principles of sentencing have therefore gone through a case-by-case development, in the tradition of the common law. The reporting of decisions has increased, and with it references to earlier decided cases. A body of decisions worthy of being called a jurisprudence has grown up. From its earliest days, the Court of Criminal Appeal (now the Court of Appeal (Criminal Division)) established certain procedural principles. One was that the statutory maximum sentence should be reserved for the worst possible case.[52] Another was that the court should only alter a sentence if it is 'wrong in principle',[53] adapted latterly to Attorney General's references, so that a sentence will only be increased if it is 'outside the proper limits of a judge's discretion in cases such as this'.[54]

The numbers of reported decisions have now increased markedly, but many of them deal with the exercise of discretion in an area with little firm guidance (unless guidelines exist). It is over a quarter of a century since Lord Widgery CJ, in the Court of Appeal, rebuked counsel for seeking to refer the Court to some previous decisions.[55] The most cursory glance through volume one of the *Criminal Appeal Reports (Sentencing)* in 1979, and then through the latest annual volumes, will quickly reveal the more frequent reference to previous decisions. However, it remains true that most of the Court of Appeal's sentencing decisions consist of brief *ex tempore* judgments delivered shortly after hearing argument from counsel. Many of these decisions afford little guidance to other courts. The Court may sit in two or three divisions, which compounds the difficulty of ensuring consistency in its pronouncements, as Lord Lane CJ once explained:

> Sitting as we do in several divisions, each with a heavy workload, there are inevitably going to be discrepancies between different divisions of the Court of Appeal (Criminal Division), and there are going to be judgments of that court which trouble judges at first instance (and, I may add, sometime trouble the court which delivered the judgment).[56]

One consequence of burgeoning legislation and reported decisions on sentencing is that both the Court of Appeal and trial courts place greater reliance on counsel to draw their attention to relevant decisions. The Court of Appeal has stated on many occasions that counsel should draw a judge's attention to legislative restrictions if an unlawful sentence or order is about to be imposed,[57] and the same applies to

52 *Harrison* (1909) 2 Cr App R 94.   53 *Gumbs* (1926) 19 Cr App R 74.
54 *Attorney General's Reference No. 7 of 1989 (Thornton)* (1990) 12 Cr App R (S) 1, at p. 6.
55 In *Rees* [1978] Crim LR 298.   56 1982 1 *Bulletin of the Judicial Studies Board*, Foreword.
57 E.g. *Komsta and Murphy* (1990) 12 Cr App R (S) 63, *Hartrey* [1993] Crim LR 230.

guidelines[58] – although there are occasional cases decided without proper reference to authoritative guidelines.[59] There are surely enough sources on sentencing law to prevent this from happening.

If guidelines or guidance from the Court of Appeal exist, the trial judge has a duty to follow what the Court has laid down. The Court of Appeal in *Johnson* (1994) emphasized the trial judge's duty to follow its guidance:

> A judge when sentencing must pay attention to the guidance given by this Court and sentences should be broadly in line with guideline cases, unless there are factors applicable to the particular case which require or enable the judge to depart from the normal level of sentence. In such special cases the judge should indicate clearly the factor or factors which in his judgment allow departure from the tariff set by this Court. What a judge must not do is to state that he is applying some personal tariff because he considers the accepted range of sentences to be too high or too low.[60]

Although in this passage Roch LJ refers to guideline cases, the context suggests that his remarks apply generally to 'guidance' such as settled principles of sentencing.[61] The Court of Appeal has recently reiterated the need for trial judges to follow guidelines, adding that failure 'to do so can only cause public concern and affect the confidence of the public in the system'.[62] This injunction is now strengthened by the provisions in s. 174(2)(a) of the 2003 Act, requiring courts to give reasons for passing a sentence outside the range indicated by applicable guidelines (a provision not restricted to 'definitive guidelines' issued by the Council). Beyond that, the precedent value of a Court of Appeal decision on sentencing varies considerably, and seven different types of decision may fruitfully be distinguished.

1. Decisions by a full Court. Very rarely the Lord Chief Justice will convene a full Court of Appeal of five judges in order to hear a particular case. This usually signals the need to decide between two conflicting precedents, and it therefore follows that the decision of a full Court is authoritative and binding. A recent example is provided by *Simpson* (2004),[63] where the Court had to decide between conflicting decisions on the limits of the jurisdiction to make a confiscation order. Another example is *Sullivan* (2005),[64] where Lord Woolf convened a court of five judges in order to give general guidance on the transitional and other provisions in Schedules 21 and 22 to the Criminal Justice Act 2003, on the (politically sensitive) question of minimum terms of imprisonment for persons convicted of murder.

---

58 See *Panayioutou* (1989) 11 Cr App R (S) 535, where the Court of Appeal held that judges are entitled to have their attention drawn to relevant sentencing guidelines.
59 A clear example is *O'Brien* [2003] 2 Cr App R (S) 390, where the Court of Appeal succeeded in deciding an appeal on racially aggravated offences without the guideline decision being cited, although another (superseded) decision was cited.
60 (1994) 15 Cr App R (S) 827, at p. 830.   61 An example would be *Panayioutou* (above n. 58).
62 *Attorney General's Reference Nos. 37, 38 and others of 2003* [2004] 1 Cr App R (S) 499, at p. 503 per Kay LJ.
63 [2004] 1 Cr App R (S) 158.   64 [2005] 1 Cr App R (S) 308.

2. Guideline judgments. Of particular importance as precedents are guideline judgments, already mentioned above. A guideline judgment is a single judgment which sets out general parameters for dealing with several variations of a certain type of offence, considering the main aggravating and mitigating factors, and suggesting an appropriate starting point or range of sentences. This kind of judgment was pioneered in the 1970s by Lawton LJ,[65] and then taken over by Lord Lane when he became Lord Chief Justice. He developed the formulation of guideline judgments so that they set out a fairly elaborate framework within which judges should determine length of sentence. Lord Lane delivered around a dozen guideline judgments when presiding in the Court of Appeal, and in the 1990s both Lord Taylor CJ and Lord Bingham CJ continued to augment the stock of guideline judgments. These judgments acquire authority from the fact that the Lord Chief Justice laid them down: they are intended to bind lower courts, and are treated as doing so. In strict terms it might be argued that the sentencing guidelines in all these cases are massive obiter dicta, since much of what is said is not essential to the decision in the particular case. However, the key element is that they are intended and accepted as binding, in a way that most Court of Appeal judgments on sentence are not.

How strictly should guideline judgments be construed? Lord Taylor stated in an extrajudicial speech in 1993 that 'guideline cases merely set the general tariff, but judges are free to tailor the sentence to the facts of the particular case'.[66] This underlines the importance of courts responding to the particular facts of each case. But courts must do so within the framework set by the guideline judgment. This point may be made more forcefully in relation to guideline judgments between 1999 and 2004, since all of them were based (either entirely or to a large degree) on the advice of SAP, and their structure tends to be more definite than was typical of earlier judgments. However, the position after 2004 may revert to that before 1999. It will be recalled that, on the creation of the Sentencing Advisory Panel, the Court of Appeal lost its power to give guideline judgments without first referring the matter to SAP.[67] However, that restriction was repealed without replacement by the 2003 Act, and so it is technically possible for the Court to revert to its previous practice of giving occasional guideline judgments. Lord Woolf CJ stated that this would be unlikely to happen save in exceptional circumstances,[68] but in fact it has already occurred on several occasions. It may be possible to draw a distinction between guidelines and mere guidance, and senior judges have occasionally attempted to do so.[69] But some of the very recent decisions look very much like guidelines. In *Wisniewski*

---

65 See e.g. *Willis* (1974) 60 Cr App R 146 on buggery, and *Taylor, Roberts and Simons* (1977) 64 Cr App R (S) 182 on unlawful sexual intercourse.

66 Taylor (1993), p. 130.   67 Crime and Disorder Act 1998, s. 80(3).

68 In a response to the Criminal Justice Bill 2003: see House of Lords Select Committee on the Constitution (2003), Appendix 3.

69 Most famously in the 'mobile phones' case of *Attorney General's References Nos. 4 and 7 of 2002; and Q* [2002] 2 Cr App R (S) 345, where Lord Woolf CJ stated that he was not laying down guidelines (which the Court of Appeal was then not entitled to do, unless the matter had first been referred to SAP), but was merely summarizing the effect of existing decisions on street robbery.

(2005)[70] and in *Corran et al.* (2005)[71] the Court of Appeal handed down guidance and guidelines on new offences under the Sexual Offences Act 2003 which have not yet been the subject of definitive guidelines, and in doing so the Court referred to previous guideline decisions and to a relevant SAP Consultation Paper on that Act. In other words, the Court saw itself as filling the gap until the Council has been able to issue definitive guidelines. In *Pace* (2005)[72] the Court set out aggravating and mitigating factors applicable when sentencing for breach of a restraining order. In *Afonso* (2005)[73] the Court adjusted the existing guidelines relating to the supply of class A drugs. And in *Page et al.* (2004)[74] the Court purported to lay down guidelines for sentencing for theft from shops. In fact SAP was in the course of preparing consultation papers on both matters, but the Court again regarded it as necessary to fill the gap before any definitive guidelines were promulgated.

Whatever the merits of this development – on the one hand, the machinery of SAP and the Council, with its consultation periods, moves rather slowly; on the other hand, the Court cannot conduct any of the broader enquiries required of SAP and the Council – guideline judgments of the Court of Appeal must have less authority than the definitive guidelines laid down by the Council. Even so, the pre-2004 guideline judgments of the Court stand as authoritative until overtaken by Council guidelines, and it seems likely that subsequent guideline judgments may acquire a similar authority. The Court is usually presided over by the Vice-President, Rose LJ, and the ensuing judgments are surely more authoritative than the normal run of decisions.

3. Statutory interpretation. As the volume of legislation on sentencing increases, the Court of Appeal is more frequently called upon to interpret provisions in legislation. The most prominent recent example is the Proceeds of Crime Act 2002, which establishes a somewhat complex scheme for the making of orders confiscating the assets of offenders. On several occasions the Court was required to give its interpretation of the previous law, and very soon there will be a burgeoning of decisions on the 2002 Act. There will also be sections of the Criminal Justice Act 2003 that require interpretation. And, of course, definitive guidelines issued by the Council under statutory authority may also need interpreting.

4. Settled lines of decisions. Although individual Court of Appeal decisions on length or type of sentence may not be regarded as authoritative, a settled line of decisions – particularly on a point of principle – may acquire considerable authority. Examples of such a *jurisprudence constante* will be found throughout the book, and include the principle that it is rarely appropriate to combine a compensation order with a custodial sentence,[75] the principle that courts should not give a financial penalty just because the offender is able to pay,[76] and the principles on adjusting the length of custodial sentences for offenders who are ill.[77]

---

70 [2005] Crim LR 403.   71 [2005] Crim LR 404.   72 [2005] 1 Cr App R (S) 370.
73 [2005] Crim LR 73. For further examples see *Kolawole* [2005] Crim LR 245, on passport offences; and *Graham and Whatley* [2005] Crim LR 247, on benefit fraud.
74 Unreported, 8 Dec. 2004.   75 See *Panayioutou* (above, n. 58), and ch. 10.4 below.
76 See ch. 10.5 below.   77 See ch. 5.5 below.

5. *Policy decisions.* Occasionally the Court of Appeal makes a pronouncement on general sentencing policy, usually on the use of imprisonment for particular categories of offender. Lord Lane CJ did so in *Begum Bibi* (1980),[78] urging judges to give shorter sentences for less serious types of offence, and a similar message was repeated more recently by Rose LJ in *Ollerenshaw* (1999)[79] and by Lord Woolf CJ in *Kefford* (2002),[80] where it was said to be particularly applicable to 'economic offences'. Similarly in *Mills* (2002)[81] Lord Woolf CJ counselled a more restrained use of custody for women offenders. There is no doubt that judgments of this kind are intended to change practice and therefore to bind judges and magistrates, but it is difficult to tell what effects actually flow from them.

6. *Attorney General's References.* Under s. 36 of the Criminal Justice Act 1988 the Attorney General has the power to refer a sentence to the Court of Appeal on the ground that it appears to be unduly lenient. The Court of Appeal may increase the sentence if it thinks this appropriate, but will only do so if it adjudges the sentence to be unduly lenient rather than just lenient. Over 100 references per year are now made, with robbery, s. 18 woundings, causing death by dangerous driving and rape having been the offences most frequently referred.[82] In terms of binding authority, these cases are usually argued more fully than many other sentence appeals. For many years there was a difficulty in using some of the Reference cases as precedents because the Court of Appeal failed to state what the proper sentence would have been initially. The sentence substituted by the Court of Appeal cannot be a true guide to this, since the Court usually gives some discount to reflect the element of 'double jeopardy' and delay to which offenders are subjected in these cases. In recent years, however, the Court has made a point of stating what the original sentence should have been, before reducing it to reflect the 'double jeopardy' element.

7. *Ordinary sentence appeals.* Many appeals against sentence are dealt with relatively briefly. The judgment may say little more than that the sentence was too long in the circumstances. Perhaps the least satisfactory judgments, from the point of view of providing guidance, are those in which the Court holds that a custodial sentence was too long, or that the judge failed to give sufficient weight to the mitigation, and then reduces the length of the sentence so as to enable the offender's immediate release. The Court thereby acknowledges that it is unnecessary for the offender to remain longer in custody. What it usually does not do, in such a case, is to specify what the original sentence should have been – leaving a doubt about whether the sentence should have been even shorter, or should have been non-custodial. Both those alternatives imply that the offender has been deprived of liberty for too long, but the Court is usually reluctant to say this.

The purpose of distinguishing these seven types of Court of Appeal judgment is to demonstrate how the precedent value of a decision depends on the context. In terms of providing guidance for sentencers, the range of judgments remains

---

78 (1980) 2 Cr App R (S) 177.   79 [1999] 1 Cr App R (S) 65.   80 [2002] 2 Cr App R (S) 495.
81 [2002] 2 Cr App R (S) 229.   82 For an examination of the system see Shute (1999).

unbalanced. Decisions on non-custodial sentences are now increasing in number, but remain unusual. There are many judgments on issues of general principle, such as consecutive or concurrent sentences, or the approach to dealing with elderly or ill offenders. Most of the judgments, however, concern long custodial sentences or other orders imposed in serious cases. Thus the Court's precedents are richer as the seriousness of cases rises, and relatively poorer for cases at the lower end of the criminal calendar, where the bulk of the cases tried in the Crown Court lies.

This particular problem is magnified in respect of magistrates' courts. There are few Court of Appeal precedents that are directly applicable and, as we shall see in Chapter 2, part 2.7.1, attempts have been made to remedy the deficiency by devising special guidelines. The Sentencing Guidelines Council is charged with promulgating guidelines for the Crown Court and the magistrates' courts, and for the allocation of cases between the two levels of court,[83] and so it is expected that the Council will 'take over' the Magistrates' Courts Sentencing Guidelines when the time comes to reissue them.[84] However, the definitive guidelines *New Sentences: Criminal Justice Act 2003* are directly applicable to magistrates' courts, as are those on *Reduction in Sentence for a Guilty Plea*, and so the amount of authoritative guidance for the magistrates' courts seems bound to increase.

1.6 Informal influences on sentencing practice

The formal sources of sentencing law may be said to provide a kind of outer framework for sentencing decisions, and also some internal rules, principles and standards, but it is plain that a considerable amount of flexibility is left in the hands of the court in many cases. In sentencing there are so many, often conflicting, points to be taken into account that there are strong arguments in favour of discretion. Different combinations of facts present themselves, and rules may prove too rigid and too crude to yield sensible decisions. Without discretion, unfairness results from treating alike cases which are unalike. However, it is important to assess this reasoning with care. Speaking extrajudicially, Lord Lane CJ declared that 'sentencing consists in trying to reconcile a number of totally irreconcilable facts'.[85] The reference to 'facts' omits the relevance of principles to the assessment of those facts, and might give the impression that sentencing is somehow a matter of reconciling diverse facts. In reality it involves applying rules and principles to facts, and perhaps considering novel fact combinations in terms of what the principles should be. As the amount of guidance increases – more legislation, the advent of definitive guidelines, the continued growth of Court of Appeal decisions – the coverage of applicable principles will also increase, but there will continue to be cases in which new fact combinations raise new issues.

---

83 Criminal Justice Act 2003, s. 170.
84 The latest version of those guidelines was agreed in 2003 and came into force in January 2004.
85 HL Deb, vol. 486, col. 1295.

That is the argument for discretion, which is conceded by what may be termed 'the guideline movement', since guidelines are not tramlines and leave room for courts to depart from the guideline if new factors present themselves. That departure may then be challenged on appeal, which means that the exercise of discretion is reviewable. But can one be sure that legislative rules, definitive guidelines and Court of Appeal guidance are actually followed in practice? There are good reasons for believing that practice is varied in this respect. It is often said that Crown Court sentences are kept in check by the appeal system, but appellate control is largely dependent on the system for giving leave to appeal. This depends on the views of individual judges in sifting through bundles of transcripts – a hit and miss 'system', for which there is little guidance and where some High Court judges give leave to appeal more frequently than others. Thus some judges may pursue their own policies with little disturbance from above. Indeed, many of the judges and magistrates in the study by Hough, Jacobson and Millie maintained that the effects of sentencing guidelines in the Crown Court and in magistrates' courts had been to 'level up' sentences, reducing the tendencies towards leniency of some sentencers while leaving the already severe sentencers unaffected.[86] We have seen that in *Johnson* a trial judge was strongly denounced for pursuing his own view rather than the Court of Appeal's,[87] but that judge's approach was somewhat unsubtle. Practitioners are well aware of the predilections of certain judges and, although it would be wrong to exaggerate, there is still a significant problem of inconsistency.

Are the prospects for legislation, definitive guidelines and Court of Appeal guidance any better in the magistrates' courts? Research in the 1980s suggested that magistrates believed that legislation has to be interpreted in the light of 'common sense', which tended to mean their own views and practices,[88] and that Court of Appeal principles were not consistently reflected in the sentencing practice of magistrates.[89] More will be said about the influence of local bench cultures in the coming paragraphs. For the present it is sufficient to note that there are reasons for supposing that official national guidance is not always followed at local level. Thus, taking both Crown Court and magistrates' court sentencing together, the authors of a substantial Home Office study concluded thus:

> The stark fact is that where the case is heard does have a significant influence on the likelihood of custody in borderline cases, and on the length of any custodial sentence. There are also big differences in the way non-custodial options are used, which in turn is affected by variations in policy and practice between probation areas.[90]

Findings such as these make it likely that the increasing guidance for sentencers will not entirely succeed in determining decisions in individual cases. The government's objective of comprehensive sentencing guidelines may be worth supporting,

---

86 Hough et al. (2003), p. 25.   87 Above n. 66 and accompanying text.
88 Parker, Sumner and Jarvis (1989).   89 Henham (1991).
90 Flood-Page and Mackie (1998), p. 128.

but it would be naïve to believe that they will transform sentencing practice and reduce individual variations to negligible proportions. It therefore remains important to look into other determinants of sentencing decisions. One source of influence, alluded to in the above quotation, may be found in the working practices of others in the criminal justice system: in part 4 above we saw the influence of decisions by police and prosecutors, and in Chapter 11 the influence of probation officers and counsel will be discussed. A further possible source of influence is the complex of attitudes and beliefs held by different sentencers. In areas where there is discretion, such attitudes are likely to shape the court's approach to sentencing. This will be explored further in the paragraphs which follow.

What factors might be assumed to enter or influence a sentencer's thought processes when taking a decision in a particular case? Four groups of factors may be identified:

  I. Views on the facts of the case.
 II. Views on the principles of sentencing:
    (i) views on the gravity of offences;
    (ii) views on the aims, effectiveness and relative severity of the available types of sentence;
    (iii) views on the general principles of sentencing;
    (iv) views on the relative weight of aggravating and mitigating factors.
III. Views on crime and punishment:
    (i) views on the aims of sentencing;
    (ii) views on the causes of crime;
    (iii) views on the function of courts in passing sentence.
IV. Demographic features of sentencers:
    (i) age
    (ii) social class
    (iii) occupation
    (iv) urban or rural background
    (v) race
    (vi) gender
    (vii) religion
    (viii) political allegiance

It will be observed that groups I, II and III are expressed so as to emphasize the sentencer's *views* about the various factors: it is these perceptions, which may or may not correspond with authoritative or objective statements, which are likely to influence behaviour.

What is the relevance of the fourth group of factors? The argument must be that each of us projects into our daily decisions certain aspects of our personality which are traceable to one or more of the demographic features listed. Many of those who sit in the courts may maintain that they become accustomed to preventing their own personal preferences from influencing their decisions. However, there is no evidence of how successful they are in this, and in any event some sources of bias may be unconscious – a tendency to view matters from a particular perspective or to select certain kinds of information, which the sentencer does not realize. There is still much debate about the existence of racial bias in English sentencing: the evidence is reviewed in Chapter 7.2, which shows an over-representation of ethnic minorities in prison and an under-representation of ethnic minorities among sentencers. The possibility of age discrimination has been less widely discussed. Most sentencers are at least one generation older, and often two generations older, than most offenders, and they may fail to understand the context or meaning of certain behaviour by young people. Over 30 years ago Roger Hood found that the age of magistrates was related to the size of fine imposed in his dangerous driving cases, with older magistrates being relatively severe in two of the cases involving younger drivers and relatively lenient in the three cases involving older drivers, as compared with the fines imposed by their younger colleagues:[91] might this still be true? In his Canadian study, Hogarth also found a relationship between specific beliefs and the age of the sentencer, with older magistrates tending to minimize sociological explanations of crime and generally to be more offence-oriented than offender-oriented in their approach to sentencing.[92]

By what process might the demographic features in group IV influence sentencing practices? What should be made of the repeated findings that about three-quarters of High Court judges, and a substantial proportion of circuit judges, have attended public school and then Oxford or Cambridge?[93] Is it possible that one identified characteristic (high social class, or at least privileged education) might be associated with particular views? Could it be (see III(ii)) that judges with this background might tend to give less weight to social conditions or the effects of the criminal justice system itself as possible causes of offending?[94] Or that judges with this background might tend to take a more lenient view of income tax offences or fiscal offences by 'respectable' people, than they take of offences related to social security benefits or even of pick-pocketing small amounts?[95] This fourth group of factors raises a number of hypotheses about the influence of demographic factors on sentencing which remain to be more fully tested in England. Hood's study found that magistrates' attributes exerted only a limited effect on their sentencing,[96] but there is a need for a broader, up-to-date study.

Turning to the factors in group III, it seems inherently likely that in a system which allows a fair amount of discretion, the views of sentencers on crime and punishment will exert some influence. Sometimes the views in group III may be the product of demographic features listed in group IV. Sometimes a more powerful source will be the bench which a magistrate joins. Thus Hood found that members of the same bench, determining a sentence at home without consulting colleagues, were

---

91 Hood (1972), p. 140.   92 Hogarth (1971), p. 211.
93 See e.g. Oxford Pilot Study (1984), p. 32.   94 Oxford Pilot Study (1984), p. 27.
95 Oxford Pilot Study (1984), p. 25.   96 Hood (1972), pp. 140–3.

still 'more likely to do something similar to their colleagues than we would expect by chance', and he found 'evidence that certain assumptions about penal policy are shared by magistrates on the same bench'.[97] Tarling's study of 30 magistrates' courts also found that bench tradition was a major factor in explaining sentencing patterns.[98] Darbyshire's study of justices' clerks in the early 1980s suggests that the tradition of some benches can be traced to the influence of their clerk, who takes a major role in magistrates' training;[99] although the system has now changed, local influences are still considerable.

The same analysis cannot be applied to judges and recorders who sit in the Crown Court, since they sit alone. The Oxford pilot study in the early 1980s suggested that judges might be more likely to be influenced by colleagues at medium-sized court centres, where five or six judges tend to take lunch together. Such informal contacts reduce the isolation of the individual judge, but at the very small court centres this rarely happens, and at the larger court centres there may be so many different judges and recorders passing through (for a week or fortnight at a time) that little sense of collegiality can develop.[100] It is true that judges attend Judicial Studies Board refresher courses every three years, in addition to training days on their circuit, but it is not known to what extent this reduces the isolation.

Factor III(iii) raises the question of the functions which sentencers perceive themselves as having. A particular issue here is the extent to which they take account of public opinion in sentencing. Many of the judges interviewed in the Oxford pilot study regarded themselves as holding a balance between the more vociferous elements in the popular press and critics of other kinds, and aligned themselves more with 'informed public opinion' and the standards of 'right thinking members of the community'. There seemed to be a general assumption that these opinions and standards coincided with their own,[101] thus reinforcing Hogarth's finding that 'sentencers tend to define the operative constraints in a way which maximises concordance with their personal attitudes'.[102] The opinions and standards might well be associated with demographic factors such as social class and age. One difficulty with the notion of 'informed public opinion' is the repeated finding that many members of the public are ill-informed about court sentencing practices. On the other hand, many sentencers in the survey by Hough, Jacobson and Millie recognized that much public and media opinion is uninformed;[103] yet many of them also conceded that general shifts in the climate of public opinion affected sentencing levels. There is evidence from the 1996 British Crime Survey to the effect that a majority of those surveyed made substantial overestimates of the proportion of recorded crime that involves violence, were unaware of the range of sentences available to the courts, and underestimated the use of imprisonment by the courts for offences such as rape, mugging and burglary.[104] Insofar as courts are tempted to increase sentences

97 Hood (1972), p. 145.   98 Tarling (1979).   99 Darbyshire (1984).
100 Oxford Pilot Study (1984), pp. 34–6.   101 Oxford Pilot Study (1984), pp. 30–4.
102 Hogarth (1971), pp. 209–10.   103 Hough et al. (2003), pp. 53–4.
104 Hough and Roberts (1998).

in response to public criticisms of leniency in sentencing, when it seems clear that those criticisms are based on misunderstanding, that would be to allow error to breed error.

Turning to the factors in group II, one might expect that sentencers' views on the principles of sentencing would be closely related to their opinions on the aims of punishment. There is some evidence from Lemon's study that magistrates' views on crime and punishment do not determine their sentencing practices,[105] but that study needs replicating in the contemporary environment. Under the Criminal Justice Act 2003 a sentencer is required to have regard to a whole range of possible sentencing purposes and, although proportionality is a primary factor in the definitive guidelines,[106] the diversity of possible purposes may encourage some sentencers to go their own ways. Insofar as proportionality is recognized as the main criterion, there is relevance in Hood's research exercise in which a group of magistrates were asked to rank a number of offences in order of gravity. The results showed some overall similarity, although there were differences of opinion on the ranking of assault and of possessing an offensive weapon.[107] One difficulty of exercises of this kind is that, if subjects are asked to 'imagine a typical case of each offence when making comparisons', they may regard different kinds of case as typical. Moreover, Hood's research also suggested that disparities in sentencing become wider as cases become more unusual. Indeed, on the basis of his study, he concluded that there is 'general support for an explanation of sentencing which sees differences in the way magistrates perceive and categorize offences as an important factor in producing disparate sentences'.[108]

Hood regarded this merely as one important factor. He did not suggest that there is a simple relationship between regarding an offence as relatively grave and imposing a more severe sentence than colleagues. Clearly, however, this was a major factor for many of the sentencers interviewed by Hough, Jacobson and Millie – they perceived that offending was becoming more serious, and that they had to respond to this.[109] Some of the other influential factors might be found in group II(ii), sentencers' views of the aims, effectiveness and relative severity of the available forms of sentence. For some years certain sentencers have voiced disquiet about the organization of some types of community sentence, and may therefore have tended to use them less frequently. A variety of judicial opinions was uncovered in the Oxford pilot study,[110] most of them stemming from personal or reported experience rather than from the results of research. There is no evidence on whether increased judicial training in recent years has reduced this diversity of approaches, and it remains to be seen how the new arrangements under the 2003 Act are received by sentencers. Certainly the research by Hough, Jacobson and Millie found many

---

105 Lemon (1974).
106 See Sentencing Guidelines Council, *Overarching Principles: Seriousness* (2004).
107 Hood (1972), p. 99; for further discussion, see ch. 4.2 below.   108 Hood (1972), p. 141.
109 Hough et al. (2003), p. 30.   110 Oxford Pilot Study (1984), pp. 28–30.

more positive attitudes towards pre-sentence reports, drug treatment and testing orders, and other community-based developments.[111]

Similar points could be raised in relation to views on the relative weight of aggravating and mitigating factors (group II(iv)). It is one thing to assess the weight of one factor alone, and quite another thing to reconcile combinations of aggravating and mitigating factors in a single case. In her US research, Shari Diamond found that 'when both aggravating and mitigating factors are present . . . there is evidence of greater disagreement among judges'.[112] In England, a simulated sentencing exercise with magistrates and justices' clerks led Claire Corbett to conclude that, at least in the reasons they give, different sentencers tend to place different values on the same factors.[113]

In group I the only factor is the sentencer's view of the facts of the case. The importance of this is widely accepted, both by sentencers and by researchers. Sentencers are given to stating that 'no two cases are alike', and 'each case must turn on it own facts'. Indeed, Lord Lane went so far as to assert that sentencing 'is an art and not a science'.[114] Such statements are often used as an argument against rules on sentencing, particularly when they emanate from the legislature, and in favour of discretion. Flexibility is needed, it is said, so that the court may reflect the particular combination of facts in each individual case. Similarly, there are those who argue that the legal analysis of sentencing decisions, in terms of offence-related and offender-related matters, and aggravating or mitigating factors, is never able to capture the uniqueness of the individual case. On this view, it is only by paying attention to the details of 'whole case stories' that it is possible to make sense of sentencing, not through the inevitably artificial categories and constructions of commentators.[115] Again, this argument is correct up to a point: cases do differ considerably in the combination of material facts. It justifies the view that rules cannot cater fairly for all eventualities, but it certainly does not justify the conclusion that rules and principles ought therefore to be kept to a minimum. Indeed, many of the judges who argue that each case depends on its own facts will also maintain that experience is of great value in the difficult task of sentencing. This contains the seeds of its own refutation, as Hood has pointed out:

> Magistrates and judges . . . place particular value upon their experience in sentencing. Now, if this experience is to be of value, then all cases cannot be unique, they must be comparable at least in some respects; and even if it is agreed that all cases are unique in some sense, this cannot be decisive in the practice of sentencing, for frequently decisions are reached with the aid of 'experience'. There are, then, certain observable factors which magistrates will take into account in their consideration of the appropriate sentence.[116]

---

111 Hough et al. (2003), pp. 46–9.
112 Diamond (1981), p. 407.   113 Corbett (1987); see also Hood (1972), p. 124.
114 The words of Lord Lane CJ when refusing to allow the continuation of a research project on judges' sentencing practices: Oxford Pilot Study (1984), p. 64.
115 E.g. Tata (1997).   116 Hood (1962), p. 16.

Thus the element of truth in the proposition that the facts of individual cases differ must not be allowed to obscure the importance of two other propositions – that facts do not determine cases, rather it is the approach of the court to those facts which is crucial; and that it is possible to identify certain factors which have a major influence on sentence, even if other subsidiary factors vary considerably from case to case.[117]

However, investigation of the concept of 'the facts of the case' remains an important research question. Facts do not come ready-labelled as important or unimportant. It may be true that the prosecution's statement of facts, or even the defence speech in mitigation, might urge a certain approach on the court. But it is often the judge or magistrates who, in assessing the facts of the case, construct their picture of the salient facts by applying their own views on issues in groups II and III. An important element in this process of construction seems to be the court's impression of the defendant's character, gained from observation in court. It was apparent from observations during the Oxford pilot study that judges might be influenced by the defendant's appearance and attitude to the court.[118] Carol Hedderman's small study suggested that demeanour in court (such as appearing cocky, not doing as instructed, appearing calm rather than nervous and contrite) both influences the way in which magistrates react to a defendant and affects sentence severity, being one possible reason why women (who often appear more distressed than men) receive more lenient sentences.[119] Further support for this view may be derived from interviews with magistrates as part of a Home Office project on the sentencing of women, revealing that magistrates may react differently to those perceived to be deferential and those perceived to be arrogant, and that more women fall into the former category.[120] Judge Cooke came close to conceding the influence of these instant character assessments when ruminating on the possibility of sentencing by computer:

> At the end of the day, the exercise of discretion in sentencing must remain in human hands. You cannot program a computer to register the 'feel' of a case, or the impact that a defendant makes upon the sentencer.[121]

If, then, it is accepted that 'the facts of a case' are not an objective entity but to some extent a construction of the court, certainly in respect of the weight assigned to different elements, the problem of achieving consistency and therefore equality before the law in sentencing practice is revealed as acute. This is not to suggest that authoritative guidance exerts no influence; rather, the suggestion is that its influence is limited, especially where it leaves discretion to the courts.

---

117 On this last point, see Moxon (1988), p. 64.
118 Oxford Pilot Study (1984), pp. 20–4.   119 Hedderman (1990).
120 Hedderman and Gelsthorpe (1997), pp. 30–4; this study also questions the accuracy of perceptions of deference and arrogance, especially when interpreting the behaviour of members of ethnic minorities.
121 Cooke (1987), p. 58.

The issue gives way to a debate about the limits to which rules, principles and guidelines can go, before they become so rigid or complex as to be productive of more injustice than their absence. The judiciary has tended to defend broad discretion by arguing that sentencing is an art and not a science, and that it is essentially an exercise of judgment rather than a question of applying rules or guidelines. This goes too far, and the senior judiciary has surely acknowledged its untenability in embracing the development of 'guideline judgments', first in the Court of Appeal and then through the Sentencing Guidelines Council. On the other hand, an equally extreme view is the argument that sentencing could be reduced to a stable set of rules which allowed little or no discretion: many would reject that as unfair in its consequences. The arguments take place on the middle ground – in England, as to how far the legislature ought to go, and how detailed the guidelines should be.

The argument is not simply one of ensuring that 'rule of law' values apply in sentencing, however. There are also extralegal factors influential at other stages. As described in part 4 above, sentencing is merely one part of a larger process, in which the decisions – and the beliefs and concerns – of other people involved in the administration of criminal justice may affect outcomes. Indeed, David Garland urges that the contextual point is taken even more widely:

> The major cultural themes which appear in penality – conceptions of justice, of crime, religious forms, attitudes towards age, race, class, gender, and so on – did not develop independently there, nor do they stand on their own as isolated beliefs. Like all cultural elements they are enmeshed in wide belief-systems and mentalities, deriving their sense and credibility from their ability to resonate with established ways of thinking and understanding.[122]

This alludes to the setting of the criminal justice system within wider social and political currents in society, a point of particular relevance when considering custodial sentences in Chapter 9 and the notion of 'punishment in the community' in Chapter 10. No less important are the constitutional aspects of the debate over sentencing policy, and it is to those that we now turn in Chapter 2.

---

122 Garland (1990), p. 211.

CHAPTER 2

Sentencing and the constitution

Major changes in the sentencing field in recent years have raised several questions of a constitutional nature. To what extent does sentencing policy belong to the judiciary? Are there any limits beyond which the legislature may not go when legislating on sentencing? Where do new bodies such as the Sentencing Advisory Panel and the Sentencing Guidelines Council fit into the constitutional framework? What are the limits beyond which the executive may not go in determining how a sentence may be carried out? These are all live issues, but firm guidance is not always available. Sometimes the principle of judicial independence has been brought into the debate, often without clarifying matters. These and other matters will be discussed in this chapter, taking account of their implications not only for the higher judiciary but also for the magistracy and for the Judicial Studies Board.

2.1 The separation of powers in sentencing

The doctrine of the separation of powers still has some relevance in British constitutional theory, but the place of sentencing has never been entirely resolved. In principle, the legislature has control over sentencing powers and policies – subject since the Human Rights Act 1998 to the limitations of the European Convention on Human Rights (the Convention). The judiciary deals with the application of sentencing law and principles to individual offenders. And the executive is responsible for carrying out the sentences imposed. But each of these propositions requires further discussion.

One clear starting point is that the legislature has superior authority to the courts: if Parliament passes legislation, the courts must apply it. Thus, when Sir Ivor Jennings identified three characteristics of the English courts, the first was 'their subordination to the legislature'.[1] This is surely correct, and yet it cannot be taken to suggest that the judiciary should not develop policy on matters left aside by legislation. Thus Sir James Fitzjames Stephen went too far when he stated that, if the judiciary were to take upon themselves the task of formulating principles of sentencing, 'they would be assuming a power which the constitution does not

---

1 Jennings (1959), pp. 241–2.

give them'.[2] The statement is only trivially true: it is unhelpful because the British constitution does not explicitly 'give' the power to any organ. The starting point is surely the doctrine that the courts are subordinate to the legislature, from which it follows that any policy-making function delegated or simply left to the courts can be taken back by Parliament. Are there, then, any limits to the competence of either the legislature or the courts, bearing in mind that Parliament has superiority when it does decide to legislate?

If one looks at the history, then one finds that wide judicial discretion has only been a characteristic feature of English sentencing for the last hundred years or so. In the first half of the nineteenth century, there were two factors that considerably restricted judicial discretion. There were maximum and minimum sentences for many offences, and several statutes provided a multiplicity of different offences with different graded maxima. For much of the nineteenth century, judges were left with less discretion than their twentieth-century counterparts,[3] and any claim that a wide sentencing discretion 'belongs' to the judiciary is without historical foundation. It gains its plausibility only from the legislature's abandonment of minimum sentences in the twentieth century, and from the trend at one time to replace the plethora of narrowly defined offences, each with its separate maximum sentence, with a small number of 'broad band' offences with fairly high statutory maxima.[4] That approach was adopted in the Theft Act 1968 and the Criminal Damage Act 1971, both of which replaced large numbers of separate offences dating from the nineteenth century with a few broadly defined crimes. These statutes broadened the discretion of judges in sentencing, but that approach has now been abandoned, and statutes such as the Sexual Offences Act 2003 return to the former approach of a multiplicity of offences with separate maximum sentences.

This is not to suggest, however, that judges in the later nineteenth century were tightly constrained in their sentencing. In fact, there was ample evidence of sentencing disparities, as Sir Leon Radzinowicz and Roger Hood have demonstrated.[5] There was concern in the Home Office, and even a proposal in 1889 for a royal commission with a view to bringing about uniformity through legislation. Opposing this successfully, the then Lord Chancellor, Lord Halsbury, asserted that sentencing is the province of the judiciary.[6] A few years later, in 1901, Lord Alverstone CJ and six Queen's Bench judges drew up a Memorandum of Normal Punishments, which sought to establish standard punishments for normal cases.[7] Thus, while it is often assumed that it was the creation of the Court of Criminal Appeal in 1907 which institutionalized judicial control over practical sentencing standards, the Alverstone Memorandum a few years earlier marked a significant step in this direction – albeit as a response to much public and official agitation in the closing years of

---

2 Stephen (1885).   3 Thomas (1978); and Radzinowicz and Hood (1986), chs. 22, 23.
4 Thomas (1974).   5 Radzinowicz and Hood (1986), pp. 741–7.
6 Radzinowicz and Hood (1986), p. 754.
7 Radzinowicz and Hood (1986), pp. 755–8, and Advisory Council on the Penal System (1978), Appendix E.

the nineteenth century. None the less, the gradual (and recently rapid) accretion of sentencing decisions from the Court of Appeal must surely have strengthened the belief that this is a judicial province and that there was little need for detailed legislative provisions on sentencing.

That belief, widely shared in the judiciary, is a belief that judicial discretion supervised by the Court of Appeal is more likely to produce fair sentencing than greater statutory restrictions. It is certainly open to debate. But it is not the same as the principle of judicial independence, nor does it provide a basis for any principle that the legislature may not properly do more than set maximum sentences and introduce new forms of sentence. Thus when there was a fierce debate about the introduction of minimum sentences into English law, prior to the Crime (Sentences) Act 1997, the 'judicial independence' argument was abandoned and the policy issues faced squarely. As Lord Bingham put it,

> There is room for rational argument whether it is desirable to restrict the judges' sentencing discretion in the way suggested or not. But even this is not a constitutional argument. As Parliament can prescribe a maximum penalty without infringing the constitutional independence of the judges, so it can prescribe a minimum. This is, in the widest sense, a political question – a question of what is beneficial for the polity – not a constitutional question.[8]

When there was a constitutional challenge to an Australian statute which required a court to impose a specified penalty on conviction for a particular offence, the High Court of Australia dismissed it in these terms:

> It is both unusual and in general, in my opinion, undesirable that the court should not have a discretion in the imposition of sentences, for circumstances alter cases and it is a traditional function of a court of justice to endeavour to make the punishment appropriate to the circumstances as well as to the nature of the crime. But whether or not such discretion shall be given to the court in relation to a statutory offence is for the decision of the Parliament. It cannot be denied that there are circumstances which may warrant the imposition on the court of a duty to impose specific punishment. If Parliament chooses to deny the court such a discretion, and to impose such a duty, as I have mentioned the court must obey the statute in this respect assuming its validity in other respects. It is not, in my opinion, a breach of the Constitution, not to confide any discretion to the court as to the penalty to be imposed.[9]

The same argument may be applied to s. 269 of the Criminal Justice Act 2003, in which Parliament curtailed the judges' discretion to determine the minimum term to be served by a person convicted of murder, imposing a restrictive structure on the judges' powers.[10]

However, it is a different matter if the legislature purports to pass a law that mandates a certain sentence for a particular individual. This question was tested in

---

8 Bingham (1996), p. 25; see also Taylor (1996), p. 8.
9 *Palling* v. *Corfield* (1970) 123 CLR 52, *per* Barwick CJ at p. 65.   10 See below, ch. 4.4.1.

Australia, where the Community Protection Act 1994 of New South Wales authorized and required the state's courts to impose a sentence of six months' preventive detention on a specific individual for the protection of the community. In *Kable*[11] the High Court of Australia held the legislation invalid, on the ground that it violated the separation of powers by requiring the courts to act as if at the behest of the executive, and that this would undermine public confidence in the administration of justice.

The separation of powers therefore seems to confirm that Parliament has considerable authority over sentencing policy, subject to the Human Rights Act and subject to the limitation that the legislature cannot prescribe a sentence for a particular offender. The judiciary retains the power to deal with individual offenders. Sentencing powers can be regulated and restricted by statute, even to the extent of requiring the imposition of mandatory or mandatory minimum sentences, so long as those requirements do not breach the Human Rights Act by violating offenders' Convention rights.[12] So far as the executive is concerned, it is certainly not acceptable for the Home Secretary to determine how long persons convicted of murder should spend in prison, either as a minimum term or (subsequently) for public protection. Those are sentencing decisions that require, according to Article 6(1) of the Convention, an 'independent and impartial tribunal'.[13]

This leads into a final constitutional point about the judiciary – the true meaning of the principle of judicial independence. Although it has often been referred to rather extravagantly in the context of legislative sentencing reforms, the true meaning of the principle is that when passing sentence in each case, a judge or magistrate should be in a position to administer the law without fear or favour, affection or ill-will.[14] No pressures upon the court to decide one way or the other should be countenanced. Discretion should not be exercised on personal or political grounds: it should be an exercise of judgment according to legal principle. Appointments to the bench should not be politically motivated. Freedom from bias, from partiality and from undue influence is integral to any definition of the rule of law.

This principle is regarded as particularly important in some east European countries where judges in the Soviet era were tightly restricted and as political appointees were expected to follow approved paths. However, it is worth remembering that in this country 'judicial appointments were influenced by party political considerations, as well as merits, until well into the twentieth century', and that 'it is to the post-war Lord Chancellorship of Lord Jowitt that we look for the establishment of the modern practice'.[15] In this sphere, as well as in respect of the role of the

---

11 (1996) 189 CLR 51. The 'sentence' was also retrospective in effect. For the context and further discussion, see Fox and Freiberg (1999), pp. 38–40.

12 The Court of Appeal implied a broad exception into the automatic sentence of life imprisonment created by the Crime (Sentences) Act 1997 in its decision in *Offen (No. 2)* [2001] 2 Cr App R (S) 44. For further discussion of human rights constraints, see ch. 4.6 below.

13 *R. v. Home Secretary, ex p. Anderson* [2003] 1 AC 837, discussed in ch. 4.4.1 below.

14 For an illuminating history, see Stevens (1993).

15 Munro (1992), p. 4. For a broader international discussion see Shetreet and Deschenes (1985).

legislature, modern notions of judicial independence and the judicial function have a shorter history than many believe.

2.2 The Sentencing Advisory Panel and the Sentencing Guidelines Council

The constitutional arrangements for guidance on sentencing have been altered twice in recent years, first by the appointment of a Sentencing Advisory Panel under ss. 80–81 of the Crime and Disorder Act 1998, and second by the creation of the Sentencing Guidelines Council under ss. 169–170 of the Criminal Justice Act 2003. The work of these two bodies was introduced in part 1.5.2 of Chapter 1, and we now turn to consider their constitutional position.

The Panel, chaired by Professor Martin Wasik, was constituted in July 1999 with 11 members, and three further members have been added. Four of the members are sentencers (judges or magistrates), three are academics, four others have recent or current experience of the criminal justice system, and the remaining three are laypeople with no connection with criminal justice. The Panel meets every three to four weeks, usually for one day and occasionally for two days. Its method of working is to formulate a consultation paper, having reviewed the applicable law and statistics and any relevant research, and then to seek responses from its statutory consultees and from members of the public. The normal consultation period is three months, after which it considers the responses and any further information before formulating its Advice. The whole process takes several months from start to finish, not least because the Panel will normally be running two, three or more separate subjects at the same time. In its first five years of operation the Panel produced draft guidelines on about a dozen offences, which were submitted as Advice to the Court of Appeal. The Court acted on all but one of these Advices, issuing guidelines in a subsequent decision.

The arrangements were reviewed by the Halliday report in 2001, and in Chapter 8 the report argued that steps must be taken towards the formulation of comprehensive sentencing guidelines and that a new machinery should be considered. Halliday set out three alternative approaches,[16] and the government decided in favour of the creation of a council 'responsible for setting guidelines for the full range of criminal offences'.[17] The Council's remit (and that of the Panel) also extends to the promulgation of 'allocation guidelines', replacing the Mode of Trial Guidelines as a means of dividing the workload in criminal cases between the magistrates' courts and the Crown Court. The Panel (SAP) was to continue in operation, so as to carry out the preliminary work and to conduct its wide consultations, but the Council was to take ultimate responsibility for the form of the guidelines. The government's purposes in creating the Council also included a desire to make provision for Parliament to have a voice in the creation of guidelines, and to divorce

16 Halliday (2001), paras. 8.11–8.22.   17 Home Office (2002), para. 5.15.

the function of creating guidelines from that of deciding individual appeals (and therefore to take the function of creating guidelines away from the Court of Appeal). It was assumed that for this purpose an entirely judicial body was needed, and so SAP (with its diverse membership) would not be appropriate and instead a Council composed entirely of judicial members would be introduced, fully recognizing 'the importance of an independent judiciary'.[18] Thus the Criminal Justice Bill presented to Parliament in 2002 provided for a council consisting of seven members – the Lord Chief Justice, two Lords Justice of Appeal, a High Court judge, a Circuit judge, a District Judge (Magistrates' Courts), and a lay magistrate.

Then, as the bill was progressing through Parliament, the Court of Appeal received an advice from SAP on the sentencing of domestic burglars.[19] Lord Woolf CJ in the Court of Appeal gave a guideline judgment which accepted most of the Panel's advice but significantly lowered the starting points for first-time and second-time offenders who committed medium-level burglaries, proposing community sentences for them.[20] Although Lord Woolf took care to explain these changes by reference to various government policy statements, the popular press and subsequently the Home Secretary denounced the judgment as inappropriately lenient. The ensuing furore attracted media attention for some time, and the Home Secretary seems to have decided that an entirely judicial body could not be trusted with this important social function. The government brought forward amendments to the bill which would add five non-judicial members to the Council – persons experienced in, respectively, policing, criminal prosecution, criminal defence, the promotion of the welfare of victims of crime and the administration of sentences. It was believed that the person with experience of the administration of sentences would be a civil servant from the Home Office, and objection was taken to this in the House of Lords. To expand the Council from an entirely judicial body to a body with wider membership was one thing; but to extend its membership so as to include a serving civil servant, a member of the executive who would be bound to put forward departmental views, was quite another thing. The House of Lords Select Committee on the Constitution took advice on the matter and, concluding that such an appointee might not appear independent, expressed its 'concern at the proposal that a serving civil servant should act as a member of the Sentencing Guidelines Council'.[21] This part of the amendment was therefore dropped, although a senior civil servant (the director of the National Offender Management Service, then Martin Narey) is allowed to attend and speak at Council meetings.[22]

The original assumption that the membership of the Council should be entirely judicial presumably either was based on recognition that the creation of sentencing guidelines is a judicial function or was a political gambit to ensure that the judiciary remained supportive of the new arrangements. The former reasoning cannot be

18 Home Office (2002), para. 5.15.
19 Sentencing Advisory Panel, *Advice to the Court of Appeal – 8: Domestic Burglary* (2002).
20 *McInerney and Keating* [2003] 2 Cr App R (S) 240; see further Davies and Tyrer (2003).
21 House of Lords (2003), para 6.   22 CJA 2003, s. 167(9).

sustained now, since we have a Council with a diverse membership (albeit with a judicial majority). So two reasons for creating the Council remain – the need to divorce the creation of guidelines from the function of determining appeals, and the importance of providing an opportunity for parliamentary input into the process of creating guidelines. However, neither reason tells in favour of creating an additional body, when SAP already existed. SAP does not have a judicial majority, although it does have four sentencers and, if chaired by the Lord Chief Justice or another senior judge, its membership would surely not be inappropriate for such a body. Moreover, it has three lay members; and there is no reason why it should not have been required to consult Parliament in the same way that the Council is now obliged to do. Since, however, Parliament has decided to create a new, additional body rather than to alter the membership of SAP so as to fit it for the role of promulgating guidelines, it is certainly beneficial that the Council should have a mixed membership. It has been argued in previous editions of this work[23] that it is desirable to have a body with diverse experience in broad matters of penal policy, not merely because many judges have a tendency to support existing arrangements rather than to favour change,[24] but also because other perspectives have a legitimate place in the deliberations.

Three further matters call for comment from a constitutional point of view. The first concerns the propriety of the legislature delegating the function of creating and promulgating sentencing guidelines to a new, and not entirely judicial, body. This question was tested before the Supreme Court of the United States in a constitutional challenge to the US federal sentencing guidelines, which were formulated by the US Sentencing Commission pursuant to the Sentencing Reform Act of 1984. In denying the constitutional challenge by a majority of eight to one, the Supreme Court in *Mistretta* v. *United States* (1989)[25] maintained that, although at one time 'Congress delegated almost unfettered discretion to the sentencing judge to determine what the sentence should be within the customarily wide range', it remains the position that 'the scope of judicial discretion with respect to a sentence is subject to congressional control'. There was therefore nothing unconstitutional in a legislature taking back the wide discretion it had left to the courts and then delegating it, within statutorily defined limits, to an independent Sentencing Commission. This reasoning surely applies equally to the British constitution, in support of the guideline-creating power conferred on the Council. More recently, the Supreme Court's decision in *Blakely* v. *Washington* (2004)[26] has raised questions about the constitutionality of US guideline systems. The precise point of the case was that it was a denial of the appellant's constitutional right to trial by jury if his sentence was subjected to an enhancement, above the normal sentence range indicated by the guidelines, as a result of a decision by a judge and not a jury. However, the

---

23 See the final chapter of the first (1992) and second (1995) editions, containing proposals that may
    have had some influence on policy-making on this subject.
24 This is the principal counter-argument of Tonry (2004), ch. 5.
25 (1989) 109 S. Ct 647.   26 (2004) 124 S. Ct. 2531.

implication may be that every guideline system that provides for courts to move above the guideline range of sentences must also provide for such aggravating factors to be determined by a jury. Critics therefore argue that the decision spells the death of guideline systems, because legislatures will not want an enormous increase in jury trials and are therefore likely to abandon guidelines in favour of a return to wide judicial discretion in sentencing matters. If the jury gives its verdict on guilt and the judge has a wide discretion, there will be no unconstitutionality. However, if a sentencing guideline indicates a narrow 'normal range' of sentences (say, 49–53 months, as in *Blakely*) and the judge, after hearing evidence, decides to go higher than that range (adding three years for 'deliberate cruelty'), then the offender has been deprived of the right to jury trial on a crucial issue. It is not yet clear to what extent the existing guideline systems will be able to withstand the effects of *Blakely*.

A second constitutional issue concerns the alleged 'democratic deficit' in the pre-2003 arrangements for creating guidelines, and the insistence on giving Parliament and the Home Secretary a role in 'considering and scrutinizing' draft guidelines.[27] As argued in part 1 above, there is no reason of constitutional principle why Parliament should not pass detailed legislation on sentencing matters, and from the same standpoint there is no strong constitutional argument against the involvement of parliamentarians in proposing amendments to guidelines. At a political level, however, there is obviously a danger that politicians will be looking to either vote-winning or progress within the party rather than trying to take a considered and rounded view of the subject. It remains to be seen whether these new powers are used sensibly or for party political reasons. For the present, some comfort can be taken from the checks and balances in the 2003 Act: the Council is obliged to consult the Home Secretary and the House of Commons Home Affairs Committee, but it is not obliged to accept their comments and it has the final decision on the form of the guidelines it issues.

This leads to the third matter. The Council issues 'definitive guidelines', but what kind of law are these? They are not primary legislation, delegated legislation, or part of the judgment of a court. They have authority by virtue of the duty of sentencers to have regard to definitive guidelines (s. 172), but it is not clear in what other way their statutory authority is manifest. It is unlikely that an action for judicial review of a court that refused to follow a definitive guideline would be entertained: no doubt the applicant would be directed to use the normal channels of appeal against sentence. So, just as judicial sentencing guidelines seemed to acquire binding force even though in substance they were *obiter dicta* in relation to the case in which they were set out, it also appears that definitive guidelines will acquire their authority partly through the legislative origin of the power to create them, and partly through enforcement by the Court of Appeal.

---

27 Home Office (2002), para 5.17. The proposal built on the examination of the issues and options in ch. 8 of Halliday (2001).

2.3 The judiciary, the executive and sentencing policy

The discussion thus far has mainly concerned the constitutional authority of Parliament and the courts in sentencing matters, as well as taking account of the position of SAP and the Council. Where does the executive fit into this? It has long been accepted that there is a royal prerogative power to commute sentences, the prerogative of mercy, which has come to be exercised by the Home Secretary (a member of the executive). At some times past it has been employed vigorously, as by Churchill during his short period as Home Secretary in 1910–11: so alarmed was he by disparities and by several instances of extraordinarily severe sentences that he used the prerogative to order the immediate release of several prisoners.[28] The exercise of the prerogative has come under scrutiny at various times when the abolition of capital punishment has been debated,[29] but in recent times it has been used mainly in compassionate cases and other instances not related to sentencing policy.[30]

Until recently the Home Secretary had a prominent role in determining how long prisoners sentenced to life imprisonment should spend in custody. However, as noted above,[31] recent judicial decisions have confirmed that it is inconsistent with the Convention for decisions on the length of imprisonment to be taken by a member of the executive rather than by an 'independent and impartial tribunal'. Similarly, life prisoners should be able to have access to a court in order to determine the need for their continued detention (Art. 5(4) of the Convention), and it has been held that a 'court' for these purposes may be the Parole Board sitting with a judge as chair.[32]

Those authorities set the boundaries of executive power over individual sentences, but the rules and conventions are rather more fluid when it comes to executive attempts to influence the judiciary and judicial attempts to influence the executive. One firm principle must be that the courts are not obliged to defer to the executive. The House of Commons Expenditure Committee stated the position (albeit in rather dramatic fashion) in 1978:

> The starting point of our discussion must be recognition of the constitutional position of the judiciary as independent of the executive arm of Government and the legislature. This means that it would not be appropriate for the Home Office to tell the judges what to do, even if the result of judicial activity were to threaten the breakdown of the prison system, which is very nearly what has happened.[33]

One step down from 'telling the courts what to do' is trying to persuade the courts to follow a certain course. One example of this was the Home Office's action in sending a copy of the interim report of the Advisory Council on the Penal System,

---

28 Radzinowicz and Hood (1986), pp. 770–5.   29 Radzinowicz and Hood (1986), pp. 676–81.
30 Smith (1983).   31 See n. 13 above and accompanying text.
32 The two principal Strasbourg decisions on this point are *Thynne, Wilson and Gunnell* v. *U.K.* (1989) 13 EHRR 666 (discretionary life imprisonment) and *Stafford* v. *U.K.* (2002) 35 EHRR 1121 (life imprisonment for murder).
33 House of Commons Expenditure Committee (1978), para. 37; cf. Woolf (1991), para. 10.154.

The Length of Prison Sentences, to every judge and every bench of magistrates in 1977. This report offered evidence that longer sentences had no greater crime-preventive effect than shorter ones, and ended by 'inviting' the courts to 'make their contribution towards' solving the problem of prison overcrowding (i.e. by passing fewer and shorter prison sentences).[34] This is moderate, exhortatory language; but one could see that frequent missives of this kind from the executive to the judiciary might be thought to overstep the mark, not least because there is another, judge-led body (the Judicial Studies Board) that has the task of keeping judges informed.

One unusual source of advice to the judiciary in recent years was a joint announcement by the Home Secretary and the Lord Chancellor in 2002.[35] The contents of the statement were unremarkable, in the sense that they broadly endorsed the policies being pursued by the Court of Appeal. Thus the statement affirmed the importance of 'protecting the public from violent, sexual and other serious offenders', welcomed Lord Woolf CJ's stance on 'violent robbery', but advocated a greater use of community sentences for 'lesser offences' in order to reduce reoffending. However, a question arises about the authority of these two government ministers to issue a statement of this kind on sentencing policy. The Home Secretary is clearly a member of the executive. The Lord Chancellor's traditional role has involved membership of all three branches of government – the executive, the judiciary and the legislature. However, Lord Chancellors have typically played no part in sentencing policy, except perhaps when delivering speeches in their role as presidents of the Magistrates' Association. It is doubtful whether this joint announcement had any authoritative standing, and there is no evidence that it actually exerted any influence on magistrates or judges (independently of Court of Appeal guidance). Whatever happens to the office of Lord Chancellor under the projected constitutional reforms, it is unlikely that this source of advice on sentencing policy will be adopted again, and it remains unclear why it was used in the first place.

The involvement of government ministers is also relevant when we turn to consider influence in the other direction, from the judiciary to the executive. Although there is no direct consultative mechanism, it has surely been a frequent feature of initiatives in recent years that the executive has consulted the senior judiciary about policy proposals (e.g. on the introduction of the Sentencing Guidelines Council). It seems probable that the consultations have involved the Lord Chancellor and the Attorney General rather than the Home Secretary, but little is known about this. So far as history is concerned, two examples of judicial influence over policy come to mind. In 1981 the Home Office's proposals for the reform of the parole system were opposed by a small group of senior judges who met and then communicated their misgivings to the government, which subsequently dropped the proposals.[36] And the proposal in a 1986 White Paper[37] that the Judicial Studies Board should be

---

34 Advisory Council on the Penal System (1977), para. 12.
35 Lord Chancellor's Department, press notice 194/02.
36 Revealed by Lawton LJ in a letter to *The Times*, 27 Nov. 1981.
37 Home Office (1986), noted at [1986] Crim LR 281–4.

statutorily required to collate and publish the texts of all sentencing guideline judgments was subsequently dropped, apparently after opposition from the judiciary. These instances of resistance appear not to have been preceded by any round-table discussion with ministers or civil servants, nor, it appears, by any systematic canvassing of judicial opinion. They seem to have been based on the views of an 'inner circle' of senior judges, probably communicated by a highly placed judge, such as the Lord Chief Justice.

One forum in which senior judges are able to express their views on parliamentary bills is the House of Lords, where the Lord Chief Justice and the 'Law Lords' are entitled to sit. Their views have been influential on a number of occasions during the passage of bills, notably during the debates leading up to the passage of the Crime (Sentences) Act 1997, where they succeeded in forcing significant last-minute amendments. Colin Munro has argued, with some force, that 'the mingling of functions involved here is one which many constitutions would not permit, and in principle it is better avoided'.[38] It seems likely that if the proposed constitutional reforms result in the creation of a Supreme Court, the link with the House of Lords will be cut and the entitlement of senior judges to sit there will cease. Democratic theory would certainly find no place for what happened during the closing days of the 1992–7 government, when both the government and the Labour opposition supported the provisions in the Crime (Sentences) Bill providing for the automatic life sentence and two mandatory minimum provisions, whereas an alliance of Law Lords, bishops and Liberal Democrat peers forced the government (on account of shortage of parliamentary time) to accept amendments which emasculated the mandatory minimum provisions by inserting a broad power for courts to avoid a minimum sentence if it would be 'unjust in all the circumstances' to impose it.

Recent years have also seen a greater willingness among senior judges to give public addresses and to make use of the media to put over the judicial point of view. Three successive Lord Chief Justices – Lord Taylor, Lord Bingham and Lord Woolf – have taken full advantage of media interest in sentencing. Perhaps the most notable example of this was the day on which the then Home Secretary, Michael Howard, announced his proposals for mandatory and minimum sentences. Within the hour, Lord Taylor had given a press conference to denounce the proposals, arguing (among other things) that mandatory sentences would not deter offenders because detection rates are so low. Both he and Lord Bingham accepted invitations to deliver public lectures at which the same views were presented with fuller argument.[39] They continued the attack in debates in the House of Lords, where Lord Taylor's comment was withering: 'Never in the history of our criminal law have such far-reaching proposals been put forward on the strength of such flimsy and dubious evidence.'[40]

---

38 Munro (1992).   39 Taylor (1996), Bingham (1996).
40 HL Deb., 23 May 1996; in the same debate Lord Williams of Mostyn, who became Attorney General in the subsequent Labour government which supported the 1997 Act, criticized the bill as 'a perversion of justice. It is an infinite shame that matters of this sort are dealt with on the basis of mottoes at party conferences. It demeans our society.'

The engagement of senior judges in public debate about sentencing policy is here to stay.

2.4 The Judicial Studies Board

It is said that the first judicial conference devoted to sentencing matters was convened by Lord Parker CJ in 1963. In 1975 the Home Secretary, the Lord Chancellor and the Lord Chief Justice set up a committee under the chairmanship of Mr Justice (later Lord) Bridge, '(i) to review the machinery for disseminating information about the penal system and matters related to the treatment of offenders; (ii) to review the scope and content of training, and the methods whereby it is provided; and to make recommendations'. The committee's 1976 working paper used the term 'judicial training' in its title, a term to which some judges reacted strongly. As the committee put it in its 1978 report,

> It is said that 'training' implies that there are 'trainers' who can train people to be judges, and so long as this concept is capable of influencing the thought of those concerned with the provision of judicial training this must, despite all protestations to the contrary, represent a threat to judicial independence.[41]

This was a clear demonstration of extreme sensitivity at this time about judicial independence in its broadest sense. The Bridge Committee bowed to it by entitling its final report *Judicial Studies and Information*, although it did state that the fears expressed by some judges were exaggerated.[42] The report led to the establishment of a Judicial Studies Board (JSB) in 1979.

> From the start the Board's main purpose was to try to reduce inconsistencies in sentencing in the Crown Court, but its seminars also covered topical problems in criminal law and procedure and the proper conduct of criminal trials, with background talks on particular subjects such as probation, and included visits to penal institutions.[43]

From its original focus on Crown Court sentencing, the Judicial Studies Board was enlarged in 1985 and given much wider responsibilities which include training for magistrates and training for judges in criminal, family and civil matters.[44] The Board now has a full-time Director of Studies, who is a judge on secondment. Sentencing in the magistrates' courts is the concern of the Magisterial Committee, discussed in part 2.5.5 below. Sentencing in the Crown Court is one of the matters covered by the Criminal Committee of the JSB, which is composed of judges, senior civil servants, members of the JSB secretariat, and a barrister and an academic member.

The Criminal Committee organizes two types of course which are run two or three times a year. Induction courses are for newly appointed judges and recorders,

---

41 Bridge (1978), para. 1.6.   42 Bridge (1978), para. 3.20.   43 Glidewell (1992), p. 166.
44 For the latest report, see Judicial Studies Board (2004), and www.jsboard.gov.uk.

some of whom will have experience of criminal practice but some of whom will not. The main medium of training in this four-day residential course is the tutor group, each with half a dozen new recruits and a judge tutor, working through practical exercises. There are a few lectures on aspects of law, procedure and sentencing, and on equal treatment, and the culmination of the week's course is a mock trial in which different roles are assigned and the course director (a judge) presides and offers comments and guidance. For experienced judges there is the four-day residential Criminal Continuation course, which each judge who sits in criminal cases is called to attend every three years. There are lectures designed to update judges on changes affecting the criminal law, evidence, procedure and sentencing. There are also syndicate groups, in which judges work through prepared exercises on procedure and on sentencing, followed by a plenary session. In addition, the Criminal Committee runs a number of special courses for judges who try particular kinds of case – serious fraud, murder and manslaughter, and the twice-yearly Serious Sexual Offences Seminar. In early 2005 the Criminal Committee embarked on the massive operation of training all Crown Court judges on the reforms brought in by the Courts Act 2003, the Criminal Justice Act 2003 and the Sexual Offences Act 2003.

Judges also receive training in the circuit criminal seminars. Each circuit arranges seminars for its judges each year, with some attention devoted to a common theme agreed between the JSB Criminal Committee and the presiding judges. This means that the total training programme is considerable, and the relentless flow of new statutory provisions in recent years makes that essential. Pulling against that, however, is the pressure of business in the Crown Court and the consequent difficulty of securing the release of judges from their duties in order to attend judicial seminars or to act as course directors, course tutors or syndicate leaders.

2.5 The position of the magistracy

The magistracy presides over the lowest level of judicial sentencing. Magistrates deal with the vast majority of criminal cases, but in the past there has been little authoritative guidance for them. Although the Court of Appeal announced in *Newsome and Browne* (1970)[45] that one of its functions is to lay down guidance for the magistrates' courts, most of its decisions fall at the other end of the spectrum of gravity. Since the Court does not hear appeals direct from magistrates' courts, it is fairly rare for the Court to pronounce on an issue of direct relevance to the magistracy. (Indeed, it could be argued that the Court has in any event too little experience of sentencing at magistrates' court level to provide much practical guidance.) The work of the Sentencing Advisory Panel has led to the creation of some sentencing guidelines with direct relevance to magistrates' courts (e.g. those on handling stolen

45 [1970] 2 QB 711.

goods and on offensive weapons), and the Sentencing Guidelines Council is now mandated to work towards comprehensive sentencing guidelines applicable to both levels of court.

There have long been criticisms of the composition of the magistracy, and of the relative failure of efforts to make the bench more representative. Two articles by Penny Darbyshire raise some important issues about these matters, and about the training of magistrates and the powers of justices' clerks, which have a clear bearing on sentencing practices.[46] However, magistrates' courts in many areas also have one or more District Judges (Magistrates' Courts) sitting, and this raises other issues. Research in the mid-1990s found that stipendiary magistrates (now DJMCs) used custody more than lay magistrates (which, some would say, reflects the more serious cases with which they deal), and that provincial stipendiaries used custody almost twice as frequently as metropolitan 'stipes'.[47] These matters call for more detailed research. The position of the magistracy, and the division of work between lay justices and DJMCs, was reconsidered in the Auld Review, but no structural changes were proposed.[48]

In terms of sentencing powers, however, there is soon to be a major change in the magistrates' courts. The Criminal Justice Act 2003 will double their sentencing powers for a single offence, from 6 to 12 months.[49] This will inevitably have an effect on the types of case they try and they sentence, and the Sentencing Guidelines Council will need to replace the current guidance on Mode of Trial with new 'allocation guidelines'. The Council is also required to issue sentencing guidance for all courts, and it is assumed that the next set of Magistrates' Courts Sentencing Guidelines will be the product of SAP and the Council. For the present, however, there are diverse kinds of guidance and influence on magistrates' sentencing, and brief mention may be made of five sources.

2.5.1 The Magistrates' Association

This is a voluntary association, to which the vast majority of some 30,000 magistrates belong. It represents the magistracy in national debates, commenting on policy proposals, responding to consultation papers from bodies such as SAP and occasionally campaigning for or against a particular change in the law. The association has local branches which hold regular meetings on issues of interest to the magistracy.

At national level it has shown its concern for consistency in sentencing by offering its own guidance to its members. In 1966 the Association first circulated its *Suggestions for Road Traffic Penalties*, proposing starting points for all the common road traffic offences for which justices are called upon to pass sentence. The document

---

46 Darbyshire (1997a, 1997b); see also Padfield (2003), ch. 6.
47 Flood-Page and Mackie (1998), pp. 67–70.   48 Auld (2001), ch. 4.
49 It seems likely that this provision will be brought into force at the same time as the new sentence of custody plus (see ch. 9.4.4 below), probably in autumn 2006.

was updated several times.[50] Some local benches adapted (i.e. altered) the national penalty scales. In the 1980s several local benches supplemented their own versions of the Association's *Suggestions* by adding 'starting points' or guideline penalties for a few other common crimes. The county of Cheshire developed a short booklet of guidelines, and in 1987 Lord Hailsham, as Lord Chancellor and president of the Magistrates' Association, commended the Cheshire guidelines and floated the idea of some national guidelines. The Association was already working on this, and in 1989 it issued its *Sentencing Guide for Criminal Offences (other than Road Traffic) and Compensation Table*. This provided starting points for some twenty frequent offences, prefacing them with some general principles.[51] The guidelines for road traffic cases have now been incorporated in the general guidelines, which were reshaped and revised in 1992, 1993, 1997 and 2000. However, from the outset there was a major difficulty with the guidelines: they had absolutely no legal authority, being the product of a voluntary association, and justices' clerks knew perfectly well that they were under no obligation to follow them. Nonetheless, the Association performed an important function, in the absence of adequate guidance from any authoritative source, by adopting this 'do-it-yourself' approach.

2.5.2 The Magistrates' Courts Sentencing Guidelines

The above guidelines are now referred to as the Magistrates' Courts Sentencing Guidelines, signifying that the group devising the guidelines has members who are justices' clerks and others who are District Judges (Magistrates' Courts), and also signifying that both justices' clerks and DJMCs are prepared to share ownership of the guidelines. This does not alter the fact that the guidelines have no legal force or authority: they remain voluntary, although strenuous efforts were made to ensure that the latest version of the guidelines, which came into force in January 2004, were accepted by benches, clerks and DJMCs in all parts of the country. The format of the guidelines remains unchanged from the 2000 and previous versions. After an introductory section setting out general principles, each of the selected offences has a page to itself, and that page lists the maximum penalty, a suggested guideline level, some particular factors that may make the offence more or less serious, personal mitigation and other statutory matters that should be considered, such as the reduction for a guilty plea and the making of a compensation order. The guideline levels indicate either fine, community sentence, custody, or consideration of whether the case should be committed to the Crown Court.[52] As stated above, the Sentencing Guidelines Council will take over the guidelines in the coming years. Whether it decides to continue with them in a form similar to the present guidelines,

---

50 The Association also commissioned research on its effect: Hood (1972), and the discussion in Ashworth (2003b).

51 For discussion of the controversy preceding the Association's decision to issue the guidelines in 1989, see Ashworth (2003b).

52 See further ch. 4.4.15 below on proportionality and the guidelines.

or to attempt to extend its general offence guidelines to cover magistrates' courts and to dispense with separate guidance, remains to be seen.

2.5.3 The appeal system

A defendant may appeal against sentence from a magistrates' court to the Crown Court. The case is reheard there, and the Crown Court may impose any sentence which the magistrates could have imposed, even if the new sentence is more severe than the one actually imposed by the magistrates. The latter provision tends to operate as a disincentive, and appeals against magistrates' sentences are therefore fairly rare. However, it may be unwise to look to appeals to the Crown Court as a source of guidance for magistrates, since the results of appeals are not always reported back to the relevant magistrates in a meaningful way, and the sentencing approaches of the judges who sit in the Crown Court may vary anyway.

2.5.4 Local liaison judges

For each area, a Crown Court judge is appointed to be the liaison judge for the magistracy. That judge will often be asked to speak at local magistrates' conferences, and may participate in their training sessions. Some influence might thereby be exerted. In the past, there has been evidence that some liaison judges have encouraged the creation of local sentencing guidelines, or local guidelines on mode of trial decisions.[53] There are now national guidelines on both these matters, but it remains natural for lay magistrates to look to 'their' full-time professional judge for guidance. However, in principle a liaison judge has no authority to bind magistrates on such matters. Insofar as liaison judges pass on to local magistrates the guidance laid down by Parliament and by the Court of Appeal, this should of course, be binding. But there is nothing in the statutory powers of liaison judges which entitles them to expect that any views of theirs, not based on that guidance, should bind local magistrates.

2.5.5 The Judicial Studies Board

When the Board was reconstituted in 1985, one of its new functions was to supervise the training of magistrates. It now has a Magisterial Committee, chaired by a senior circuit judge and including some magistrates.[54] It organizes training courses for District Judges (Magistrates' Courts), and the JSB took over full responsibility for lay magistrates' training in April 2005, having previously had the role of adviser to the Lord Chancellor on this subject. Changes will be expected in its organization and delivery. In its early days it produced 'structured decision-making' cards for the guidance of magistrates on various decisions, including sentencing.[55] It subsequently produced bench books for the adult court and the youth court, to provide practical guidance on powers and decision-making. As the legislation on

---

53 Riley and Vennard (1988), pp. 12–13.   54 See Judicial Studies Board (2004), pp. 23–7.
55 Judicial Studies Board (1988), ch. 13; see also Barker and Sturges (1986).

sentencing becomes ever more complex, the task of training magistrates become more demanding. The provisions of the Criminal Justice Act 2003 require an immense training programme, and the staged introduction of the Act's sentencing provisions has as many disadvantages as advantages.

2.6 Conclusions

As sentencing becomes more of a political issue, its constitutional dimensions assume greater importance. Probably the greatest constitutional limitation on sentencing stems from the Human Rights Act and the Convention rights: they are discussed in Chapter 4.6 below, but we have noted already that the Home Secretary's powers over life sentence prisoners have been removed on grounds of incompatibility with the Convention. Major changes such as the creation of the Sentencing Advisory Panel and the Sentencing Guidelines Council have introduced constitutional novelties, but there seems little doubt that what Parliament has 'delegated', it can take back. We noted that this view has the powerful support of the US Supreme Court in *Mistretta* v. *United States*,[56] which considered counter-arguments based both on delegation of power and on the separation of powers.

The legislature has shown its continuing willingness to exercise its powers, not just in enacting the far-ranging sentencing reforms in the Criminal Justice Act 2003, but more particularly by introducing statutory starting points for judges when calculating the minimum term to be served by someone convicted of murder. This may be seen as part of an ongoing struggle for the upper hand in sentencing policy. At the same time the judiciary has become more open, even more militant, in advancing its views about proposed reforms of sentencing law. This was demonstrated by the public battle between Lord Taylor as Lord Chief Justice and Michael Howard as Home Secretary over the provisions that went into the Crime (Sentences) Act 1997, and there were further public disagreements between Lord Woolf as Lord Chief Justice and David Blunkett as Home Secretary in relation to sentencing for burglary in particular. One change in these debates is that most of the constitutional overtones have been abandoned, and the battles are now joined on the substantive issues rather than by invoking a high-sounding but flawed notion of judicial independence.

---

56 (1989) 109 S. Ct 647, above, part 1; but cf. the uncertainty arising from the recent decision in *Blakely* v. *Washington*, also discussed in part 1.

CHAPTER 3

Sentencing aims, principles and p

3.1 The aims of the criminal justice system

The 'criminal justice system' is not a structure which has been planned as a system. Nor is it so organized that the several interlocking parts operate harmoniously. In England and Wales, as in many other jurisdictions, the administration of criminal justice has grown in a piecemeal way over the years, with separate phases of development leaving their mark. To refer to a 'system' is therefore merely a convenience and an aspiration. It should not be assumed that the various arrangements were planned or actually operate as a system, although it remains necessary to recognize the interdependence of the different parts and to incorporate this into any planning.

It is important to distinguish the aims of the criminal justice system from the aims of sentencing, which merely relate to one element. The system encompasses a whole series of stages and decisions, from the initial investigation of crime, through the various pre-trial processes, the provisions of the criminal law, the trial, the forms of punishment, and then post-sentence decisions concerned with, for example, supervision, release from custody and recall procedures. It would hardly be possible to formulate a single meaningful 'aim of the criminal justice system' which applied to every stage. It is true that one might gather together a cluster of aims: for example, the prevention of crime, the fair treatment of suspects and defendants, due respect for the victims of crime, the fair labelling of offences according to their relative gravity and so on. But to combine these into some overarching aim such as 'the maintenance of a peaceful society through fair and just laws and procedures' is surely to descend into vacuity, since it gives no hint of the conflicts that arise and the priorities that need to be determined. The Home Office's first Statement of Purpose reveals the conflicts but fails to indicate priorities:

> To work with individuals and communities to build a safe, just and tolerant society enhancing opportunities for all and in which rights and responsibilities go hand in hand, and the protection and security of the public are maintained and enhanced.[1]

1 www.homeoffice.gov.uk.

This generalized purpose does not recognize that different stages may have their distinct aims and purposes. It needs supplementing with more focused aims, but those enumerated by the Home Office do not carry the issue much further. These are

(i) to reduce crime and the fear of crime, tackle youth crime and violent, sexual and drug-related crime, anti-social behaviour and disorder, increasing safety in the home and public spaces;

(ii) to reduce organized and international crime, including trafficking in drugs, people and weapons, and to combat terrorism and other threats to national security, in co-operation with European Union (EU) partners and the wider international community;

(iii) to ensure the effective delivery of justice, avoiding unnecessary delay, through efficient investigation, detection, prosecution, trial and court procedures. To minimize the threat to and intimidation of witnesses and to engage with and support victims; and

(iv) to deliver effective custodial and community sentences to reduce reoffending and protect the public, through the prison and probation services, in partnership with the Youth Justice Board.

These aims are undoubtedly important, even if the attempt to highlight some forms of crime results in leaving out others. However, once again, there is no acknowledgment of the inevitable conflicts, no reference to human rights, and no reference to appropriate international documents (e.g. European Convention on Human Rights, United Nations Convention on the Rights of the Child).

Unrealistic aims should not be set for individual decisions in the criminal justice system. We saw earlier[2] that only a small proportion of crimes come before the courts for a sentencing decision – around 2 per cent on Home Office figures. Even granted that publicity may make it appear that the courts are dealing with a higher proportion than this, the potential of sentencing for altering the frequency and patterns of offending in society is severely handicapped by the fact that relatively few offences result in the passing of a sentence. However, it may be assumed that sentencing fulfils an indispensable public function within the criminal justice system: without the panoply of police, penal agents and courts, there would surely be more crime. There is at least some evidence that law and order would break down in the absence of police, for example.[3] But it does not follow from any of this that increases in sentence levels will bring about increases in general crime prevention, as we shall see in the discussion of deterrence theory in part 3.3.2 below.

The conscientious pursuit of crime prevention is, however, a worthy objective of a criminal justice system as a whole, and considerable developments have taken place. Since at least the early 1980s the Home Office has devoted considerable attention

---

2 In ch. 1.4 above.

3 Evidence for this might be derived from the spread of lawbreaking, mostly property offences, during the police strikes in Melbourne in 1918 and Liverpool in 1919, and during the immobilization of the Danish police force in 1944. It is argued by Mathiesen (1990), pp. 62–3, that these were such atypical situations that they leave the propositions in the text as unsupported assertions.

to different forms of crime prevention, in order to identify and to carry forward the most effective methods of crime prevention. Some of these begin with family planning and parenting, through pre-school facilities to the identification and monitoring of children 'at risk' of offending.[4] Then there is situational crime prevention, which the Home Office has long encouraged through a variety of initiatives, such as altering the designs of buildings or vehicles in order to reduce the opportunity for certain kinds of crime. This 'target-hardening' approach has been used to increase surveillance (e.g. the now widespread use of cameras in public places, on public transport and in shopping centres), to make houses more secure against burglars, and so forth.[5] A further possibility is social crime prevention, although in the present government's policy this is often termed 'community crime prevention' and includes 'zero tolerance' approaches to incivilities as well as improvements to housing, social and recreational facilities, education and employment.[6] Techniques of policing may also offer possibilities for crime prevention, although the prospects of success are often grossly overestimated by references to 'more police on the beat' as a solution to alleged increases in the crime rate. There is, however, evidence that in some circumstances certain techniques of policing can bring crime prevention benefits.[7]

There is much promise in some crime prevention strategies, insofar as they are shown to reduce crime and thereby reduce the load on the law enforcement agencies and the labelling of people as offenders. The history of 'auto-crime' shows the considerable impact of introducing steering locks in the 1960s in reducing thefts and takings of cars – a far more significant reduction than could have been achieved by all but the most draconian sentencing policy – and in the 1990s motor manufacturers co-operated in improving car security as part of a renewed effort against these types of crime. However, although some crime prevention strategies appear so promising that they should be pursued with much greater vigour than at present, there are at least three drawbacks which must be borne in mind. One is that the number of small local projects far outstrips the amount of careful and rigorous evaluation. Schemes are often difficult to evaluate, and not just because one has to investigate possible 'displacement' effects, in the shape of lawbreaking of other kinds or in other areas. The political attractions of crime prevention initiatives are sometimes allowed to run ahead of proper assessments of their effectiveness.[8] A second danger is that the schemes will be used to spread the net of social control, promoting so-called 'community' initiatives in a way which increases state control over individuals, families and neighbourhoods and therefore brings other disadvantages. Insufficient attention has been paid to ethical issues in crime prevention, raised by a number of techniques (such as CCTV). A third unwelcome consequence is that situational approaches might conduce to the mentality of a 'fortress' society, surrounded by locks, bars and unbreakable articles. This might heighten fear of crime, even if it reduces objective risk. Despite these drawbacks, it remains the best policy to try

---

4 Graham (1998).   5 Ekblom (1998), Pease (1998).   6 Hope (1998).
7 Jordan (1998).   8 For an overview and critical discussion, see Bottoms (1990).

to prevent crime before it occurs, so long as this can be achieved within a rights-based framework. However, when the government abandoned its much-trumpeted 10-year Crime Reduction Programme in 2002, after only three years, it was evident that the main source of disappointment stemmed from setting over-ambitious targets too quickly, without proper monitoring and evaluation.[9]

If prevention does not work, then the state must be prepared to respond to an offence that has been committed. The immediate danger is that sentencing will be expected to function efficiently as a crime prevention mechanism, when there are well-documented reasons why this may not happen. Two clear reasons why sentencing and crime rates may vary independently are (i) that crime rates are affected by demographic factors such as the age profile of the population and by changes in the availability of desirable and stealable goods (such as mobile phones); (ii) that fewer than half of all crimes are reported to the police, as we saw in Chapter 1.4 above.[10] When there is a formal response to an offence this does not always mean prosecution–conviction–sentence, since, as we saw in Chapter 1.4, there are various methods of diversion available. For those cases that are brought to court, however, sentencing is a process that has considerable social significance in its own right. Conviction involves the public labelling of people as offenders. The sentencing decision can often be seen as the core of the labelling or censuring process by giving a judgment of 'how bad' the offence was, and by translating that judgment into the particular penal currency of this country at this time. Sentencing has an expressive function and, as Durkheim argued, 'the best punishment is that which puts the blame . . . in the most expressive but least costly form possible'.[11]

This expressive or censuring function is carried out by means of imposing coercive measures on convicted offenders. The imposition of punishment requires justification. We should not be satisfied with the proposition that anyone who commits any offence forfeits all rights, and may be dealt with by the state in whatever manner the courts decree. That would be to suggest that any convicted person is at the disposal of the criminal justice system, and has no relevant rights. Instead, we should seek strong justifications for contemporary sentencing practices, not least because of the increasing use of imprisonment and the greater restrictiveness of non-custodial sentences in many countries. But before turning to consider the possible rationales for sentencing, it is first necessary to say something about the institution of state punishment.

3.2 Justifying state punishment

Whence does the state acquire its right to punish, and what sustains it? A proper answer to these questions would require a substantial foray into political philosophy.

9 Maguire (2004).   10 See further Bottoms (2004), pp. 60–1.
11 Quoted in Garland (1990), p. 46.

All that can be done here is to sketch some of the lines of justification.[12] It is often assumed that the right to punish is simply one aspect of the modern sovereign state, but any such assumption is disputed by those who proclaim that victims and their families, or victims and communities (through restorative justice), ought to be central to responses to crime.[13]

Justifications for assigning the central role to the state are often derived from social contract theories, the essence of which is that citizens give up their 'natural' right to use force against those who attack their interests and hand it over to the state, in return for the state's promise to protect them by maintaining law and order.[14] Citizens retain a limited right of self-defence, but apart from that the state takes charge of enforcing the law, maintaining courts and providing the institutions of punishment. Without some such idea of contract, the co-operation on which society rests could not be attained, it is argued. The state then has the responsibility of ensuring peaceable co-operation, and one aspect of that is to establish a category of wrongs that amount to crimes. It is the state's task to provide police, prosecutors and courts to respond to these wrongs. Individual victims may bring civil actions against the perpetrators, but it is in principle for the state to prosecute and (on conviction) to provide the institutions of sentencing. Another approach would be to justify the state's role in punishment by reference to the need to displace individual revenge and retaliation by maintaining a social practice that constitutes an independent and authoritative response to crime.[15] This does not constitute the state as a 'proxy retaliator': the state has the duty to act with justice and with humanity in discharging the function of punishment, and often there may be a 'displacement gap' between what the public or the media would like to see by way of punishment, and what the state's institutions can and should provide. Regulating that gap and its social consequences is one of the modern state's more difficult obligations.

The importance of punishment being in the hands of state institutions rather than victims or other individuals resides in rule-of-law values. Decisions on punishment should be taken by an independent and impartial tribunal, not by individuals with an emotional involvement in the events. The outcome should not be dependent on whether the victim is vengeful or forgiving, but should be dependent on the impartial application of settled principles, notably principles that recognize the offender as a citizen capable of choice and that regard proportionality of sentence to offence as a key value.[16] The state therefore has the role of providing the institutions for an authoritative response to wrongs, which constitute a public valuation of the offender's conduct.[17] Sometimes these notions are expressed in terms of the state and its courts being more 'objective' than victims and their families, but one must

12 For accessible discussions, see MacCormick and Garland (1998), Gardner (1998) and Duff (2001).
13 E.g. Christie (1977).
14 See MacCormick and Garland (1998) for discussion and variations on this theme.
15 Gardner (1998).   16 Ashworth (2002).
17 See further von Hirsch and Ashworth (2005), ch 2.

beware of the concept of objectivity here. Issues of crime and punishment have become intensely political in recent years and, even if sentences are objective in the sense that they are not chosen by victims or their representatives, they are not objective in the sense of being free from the political posturing or vote-catching policies that have tended to shape sentencing legislation (and therefore judicial sentencing) in recent decades.

Thus whether one takes the justification for state punishment to be an aspect of the idea of a social contract, or (more pragmatically) to be the carrying out of a displacement function that is essential to social co-operation, there are problems in translating the justification to any particular criminal justice system. There are many signs of what David Garland has termed 'the decline of the sovereign State',[18] and, even if some of his analysis is less compelling than it might appear,[19] it is surely true that the simple model in which the state provides for the security of its subjects is not sustainable in many countries. Responsibility is being devolved to private entrepreneurs and to local authorities, and crime is perceived as a major social problem still. At some times in some countries, the legitimacy of the state and its institutions suffers collapse, and those dire circumstances would force reconsideration of the basic principles.[20] Thus we might conclude with Antony Duff that, although there may be justifications for the state taking responsibility for criminal justice, they are contingent on the state fulfilling its side of the agreement,[21] and in many countries that is in doubt. This area of doubt makes it all the more important to scrutinize the justifications for sentencing policy in general, for the types of sentence that are used, and for the conditions that they impose on offenders.

3.3 The rationales of sentencing

3.3.1 The argument for declaring a primary rationale

When judges are discussing sentencing, one of the most frequent topics is discretion. Some of the constitutional dimensions were mentioned in Chapter 2, but another dimension is the constant tension between flexibility and the rule of law. There are many who would agree that sentencers ought to have sufficient discretion to take account of the peculiar facts of individual cases. So be it. But does that remove the argument for bringing the rule of law as far into sentencing decisions as possible? The rule of law, in this context, means that judicial decisions should be taken openly and by reference to standards declared in advance.[22] It is one thing to agree that judges should be left with discretion, so they may adjust the sentence to fit the particular combination of facts in an individual case. It is quite another to suggest that judges should be free to choose what rationale of sentencing to adopt in particular cases or types of case. Freedom to select from among the various

18 Garland (2000).   19 Zedner (2002).   20 For references, see Ashworth (2002b), pp. 580–1.
21 Duff (2001), p. 197.   22 Raz (1979), ch. 11.

rationales is a freedom to determine policy, not a freedom to respond to unusual combinations of facts. It is more of a licence to judges to pursue their own penal philosophies than an encouragement to respond sensitively to the facts of each case.

It is fairly well established that a major source of disparity in sentencing is the difference in penal philosophies among judges and magistrates.[23] Yet many judges and magistrates place great importance on the freedom to pursue whatever approach they think appropriate 'on the facts of the case'.[24] One notable decision of the Supreme Court of Victoria expresses what many judges may believe:

> The purposes of punishment are manifold and each element will assume a different significance not only in different crimes but in the individual commission of each crime . . . Ultimately every sentence imposed represents a sentencing judge's instinctive synthesis of all the various aspects involved in the punitive process.[25]

The inscrutable idea of an 'instinctive synthesis' comes close to another notion, which is that the various aims of sentencing should be 'balanced' in each case. Indeed, the Sentencing Reform Act of 1984 in the United States required the US Sentencing Commission to devise guidelines that reflected proportionality, deterrence, public protection and offenders' treatment needs – aims that were listed without recognition that they conflict, and that priorities must be established. If there is thought to be some value in each of these purposes, what should be done?

It is often assumed that there are only two alternative courses: either (i) to declare a single rationale, or (ii) to allow sentencers a fairly free choice among several rationales. Critics of the first approach argue that it is too rigid, especially when there is such a wide range of crimes and criminals. They may then assume that the second approach is the only 'realistic' one. They may argue that the second approach is more 'balanced' or is 'multi-faceted', thereby contrasting its practicality with the academic, even ascetic regime of a single rationale. But there is a third possibility, which is both practical and consistent with the rule of law: (iii) to declare a primary rationale, and to provide that in certain types of case one or another rationale might be given priority. This approach has been operating in Sweden since 1989, with desert or proportionality as the primary rationale and other aims having priority in certain types of case.[26] It was also the approach embodied in the Criminal Justice Act 1991, with desert as the primary rationale and incapacitation having priority in certain types of case. And it received the approval of the Council of Europe in its recommendation on 'Consistency in Sentencing':

---

23 See Hogarth (1971), cited in ch. 1.6 above, and the wider review of research by the Canadian Sentencing Commission (1987), para. 4.1.2.
24 See ch. 1.6 above on this concept.
25 *Williscroft* [1975] VR 292, at pp. 299–300; see also *Young* [1990] VR 951.
26 For the text of the law in English, see von Hirsch and Jareborg (1989); for discussion, see Jareborg (1995).

A.1 The legislator, or other competent authorities where constitutional principles and legal traditions so allow, should endeavour to declare the rationales for sentencing.

A.2 Where necessary, and in particular where different rationales may be in conflict, indications should be given of ways of establishing possible priorities in the application of such rationales for sentencing.

A.3 Where possible, and in particular for certain classes of offences or offenders, a primary rationale should be declared.[27]

However, the government appears not to regard itself as bound by this kind of clearly structured approach. The scheme of the 1991 Act has been abandoned, and in its place we have a law that seems to embody the worst of 'pick-and-mix' sentencing. Section 142 of the Criminal Justice Act 2003 provides:

Any court dealing with an offender in respect of his offence must have regard to the following purposes of sentencing –

(a) the punishment of offenders,
(b) the reduction of crime (including its reduction by deterrence),
(c) the reform and rehabilitation of offenders,
(d) the protection of the public, and
(e) the making of reparation by offenders to persons affected by their offences.

This invites inconsistency, by requiring judges to consider a variety of different purposes and then, presumably, to give priority to one. However, it seems possible that its effect will be blunted by another provision in the 2003 Act, which the Sentencing Guidelines Council has adopted as the touchstone for its guidelines. Thus, having set out the terms of s. 142, the Council goes on to state that 'the sentencer must start by considering the seriousness of the offence', and then quotes s. 143(1):

In considering the seriousness of any offence, the court must consider the offender's culpability in committing the offence and any harm which the offence caused, was intended to cause or might foreseeably have caused.

The remainder of the Council's guideline on *Overarching Principles* focuses on the proportionality principle in s. 143, without returning to s. 142, and makes it clear that s. 143 will underpin the guidelines it issues.[28] It remains to be seen how closely the guidelines are followed, and what happens to any judge or magistrate who purports to 'have regard to' one of the purposes in s. 142 rather than to the guidelines.[29]

The enactment of s. 142 makes it all the more important to examine six contemporary rationales of sentencing: deterrence, rehabilitation, incapacitation, desert,

---

27 Council of Europe (1993), p. 6.   28 SGC, *Overarching Principles – Seriousness* (2004).

29 It should be mentioned that s. 142 does not apply to the sentencing of offenders under 18. However, there are also conflicting rationales in respect of them – s. 37 of the Crime and Disorder Act 1998 states that the aim should be 'to prevent offending by children and young persons', whereas s. 44 of the Children and Young Persons Act 1933 enjoins courts to 'have regard to the welfare of the child or young person'. See further ch. 12.1 below.

social theories, and reparation or restoration. Each of these aims has a considerable philosophical background and penological context, which cannot be set out in full here. Readers are referred to a recent anthology of readings, with commentary and bibliography, for further study.[30]

3.3.2 Deterrence[31]

Deterrence is one of several rationales of punishment which may be described as 'consequentialist', in the sense that it looks to the preventive consequences of sentences. In fact, deterrence is merely one possible method of producing crime prevention through sentencing: it relies on threats and fear, whereas rehabilitation and incapacitation adopt different methods of trying to achieve a similar end, as we shall see below. It is important to draw the distinction between individual (or special) deterrence and general deterrence. The latter aims at deterring other people from committing this kind of offence, whereas individual deterrence is concerned with deterring this particular person from reoffending. A system which regards individual deterrence as the main goal would presumably escalate sentences for persistent offenders, on the reasoning that if non-custodial penalties fail to deter then custody must be tried, and if one year's custody fails to deter, two years must be tried, and so on. It is not the gravity of the crime but the propensity to reoffend which should be the main determinant of the sentence. Although this approach seems to underlie the latest provision on persistent offenders,[32] it is rarely adopted as the primary rationale of a sentencing system.

   More significant is general deterrence. Jeremy Bentham was its chief proponent, and he started from the position that all punishment is pain and should therefore be avoided. However, punishment might be justified if the benefits (in terms of general deterrence) would outweigh the pain inflicted on the offender punished, and if the same benefits could not be achieved by non-punitive methods. Sentences should therefore be calculated to be sufficient to deter others from committing this kind of offence, no more and no less. The assumption is that citizens are rational beings, who will adjust their conduct according to the disincentives provided by sentencing law. The same assumption leads to a belief in marginal deterrence – that increasing penalty levels by a certain amount will result in a decline in offending. Modern economic theorists such as Richard Posner adopt a similar approach, viewing punishments as a kind of pricing system.[33] Less sweeping is the rational choice perspective, adopted by criminologists such as Ronald Clarke as an explanation of certain types of offending and used to generate specific preventive strategies. The argument is that particular types of crime tend to result from a form of rational calculation (usually termed 'bounded rationality'), and that the responses to such crimes should take account of this and combat it.[34]

---

30 Von Hirsch and Ashworth (1998).   31 Von Hirsch and Ashworth (1998), ch. 2.
32 S. 143(2) of the 2003 Act, analyzed in ch. 6.3.2 below.
33 Posner (1985), excerpted in von Hirsch and Ashworth (1998), ch. 2; see also Pyle (1995).
34 Cornish and Clarke (1986).

Criticisms of deterrence theory may be divided into the empirical and the principled. The main empirical criticism is that the factual data on which a deterrent system must be founded do not exist. Reliable findings about the marginal general deterrent effects of various types and levels of penalty for various crimes are hard to find. For example, sophisticated techniques have been applied in attempts to assess the deterrent efficacy of the death penalty, without yielding clear and reliable results.[35] A necessary element in research is a proper definition of deterrence, to establish that fear of the legal penalty was the particular factor that led to avoidance of the proscribed conduct. Deterrence must operate (if at all) through the potential offenders' minds, so it is essential that they know about the severity of the probable sentence, take this into account when deciding whether to offend, believe that there is a non-negligible risk of being caught, believe that the penalty will be applied to them if caught and sentenced, and refrain from offending for these reasons.[36] These subjective beliefs are vital components in the operation of deterrent policies, and all must therefore be investigated if research is to be reliable. Few studies satisfy these criteria, and they provide no basis for sentencing policies that involve increasing severity in order to reduce offending levels. This was the major finding of the Cambridge study, commissioned by the Home Office, although it did find that there was better evidence of the deterrent effect of a (believed) high risk of detection than of (believed) penalties.[37] The Halliday report reviewed the evidence and also concluded that the limited evidence 'provides no basis for making a causal connection between variations in sentence severity and differences in deterrent effects'.[38] A subsequent international review by Doob and Webster recognized the intuitive attraction of the deterrent hypothesis but still found that the evidence indicated 'that sentence severity has no effect on the level of crime in society'.[39]

There is a little research which suggests that certain forms of offence which tend to be committed by people who plan and think ahead may be susceptible to deterrent sentencing strategies: Richard Harding, for example, found that robbers tended to desist from arming themselves with guns if there was a significant extra penalty for carrying a firearm.[40] This may be taken to bear out the proposition that general deterrence is more likely to be effective for planned or 'professional' than for impulsive crimes, although Harding argues that deterrent sentences need to be combined with publicity and appropriate 'social learning' opportunities if they are to have significant preventive effects. A counterpoint is provided by David Riley's study of drink drivers, in which he shows that the problems of a general deterrent strategy lie in drivers' optimism about the risk of being caught, ignorance of the penalty, and ignorance of the amount of alcohol consumption needed to commit an offence.[41] Further studies have examined the potential deterrent effect of increased enforcement by the police, but it seems that a general crime prevention

---

35 Hood (2002), ch. 7.   36 See Bottoms (2004), p. 65.
37 Von Hirsch et al. (1999), chs. 3 and 7.   38 Halliday (2001), p. 129.
39 Doob and Webster (2003), p. 143.   40 Harding (1990).   41 Riley (1985).

strategy with publicity and attempts to change people's attitudes is likely to be more effective than either sentencing or enforcement changes alone.[42] Another area in which the potential for legal deterrence appears not to be great is burglary: interviews with burglars suggest that most of them are not rational calculators but rather short-term hedonists or eternal optimists.[43] Particularly interesting is the finding of Ros Burnett and Shadd Maruna that, although the majority of their convicted prisoners wanted to desist from crime after their release, only a minority succeeded in doing so and it tended to be a philosophy of hope that distinguished them. The notion of austere prison conditions as a deterrent was simply not enough.[44] This dearth of supporting evidence leaves some authors undaunted, since they argue that 'commonsense reasoning about general prevention' can be used instead.[45] There is a point here: general deterrence can indeed work, given the necessary favourable circumstances.[46] But the available research surely demonstrates the danger of generalizing from intuitions, or one's personal experience, to the probable reactions of others.[47] Reliable and precise evidence is required, and it is not available.

Principled criticisms of deterrence theory would apply whether or not there is satisfactory evidence of general deterrent effects. One such criticism is that the theory could justify the punishment of an innocent person if that were certain to deter several others: a simple utilitarian calculus would allow this to happen, without any respect for the rights of the innocent person. Another, more realistic criticism is that the theory can justify the imposition of a disproportionately harsh sentence on one offender in order to deter several others from committing a similar offence. This is the so-called 'exemplary sentence'. English judges have passed such sentences from time to time,[48] and some would argue that such decisions have been the product of political or 'media' pressure to respond to public anxiety about a certain type of crime. One incident which has become part of judicial lore is the passing of exemplary sentences on certain offenders after the Notting Hill race riots in 1958. It is argued that such sentences may be justified by the consequences, which in this case were reductions in racial troubles in Notting Hill (although there were similar troubles in other cities in the following months). But who can assert that it was the exemplary sentences which caused the reduction in the number of offences which otherwise would have taken place? Might it not be the case that the police had arrested and charged the ringleaders, and without them there would be no continuation? Or that increased police patrols dramatically increased the perceived risk of being caught? The Notting Hill case serves only to emphasize the formidable difficulties of gathering evidence on the effectiveness of exemplary sentences as short-term deterrents. There must be no other plausible explanations for the changes in people's behaviour: otherwise, one cannot be confident of interpreting a sequence of social events correctly.

42 Riley (1991).   43 Bennett and Wright (1984), chs. 5 and 6.
44 Burnett and Maruna (2004).   45 E.g. the classic book by Andenaes (1974).
46 Nagin (1998).   47 Mathiesen (1990), pp. 67–8, argues strongly on this point.
48 See the discussion in part 5 of this chapter.

These points emerge from the sequel to the Birmingham mugging case of *Storey* (1973).[49] A youth was ordered to be detained for 20 years for his part in the violent robbery of a drunken man. The sentence was widely publicized, both in Birmingham and in the national newspapers, as an exemplary sentence. Researchers were able to plot the rate of reported robberies in Birmingham and in two other cities during the months before and after the sentence was passed. The robbery rates seemed quite unaffected by the sentence in *Storey*: indeed, the rate of reported robberies in Birmingham had begun to rise before the trial and continued to increase before reaching a peak several weeks later. This calls into question the normal assumptions one would make about human behaviour, unless it is argued that the effect of *Storey* took several weeks to exert itself by reaching the ears of all potential robbers in Birmingham. The difficulty is that we do not understand the reasons, and this shows the problems of firm assertions about general deterrent effects.

The argument has returned to the empirical objection. The real test of the principled objection is this: even if one believes the Notting Hill anecdote, would this justify the extra-long sentences on the first people to be sentenced for the crime? Should, for example, an extra two years of one person's liberty be sacrificed in the hope of deterring several others? The objection to this is often expressed in the Kantian maxim, 'a person should always be treated as an end in himself [or herself], and never only as a means'. Respect for the moral worth and autonomy of the individual means that citizens should not be regarded merely as numbers, to be aggregated in some calculation of overall social benefit. It may be true that the fundamental justification for the whole institution of punishment is in terms of overall social benefit, in the same way as this is the justification for taxes. There are also plenty of other examples of compulsion 'for the greater good', such as quarantine, compulsory purchase of property and so on. These measures do not, however, have the censuring dimension which sentences have. Exemplary sentences, by heaping an undeserved portion of punishment on one offender in the hope of deterring others, are objectionable in that they penalize an individual in order to achieve a social goal – and do so without any real criterion of how much extra may be imposed. A deterrent theory which incorporates no restrictions to prevent this shows scant respect for individuals' choices and invests great power in the state and the judiciary.

There are several offences for which 'deterrent' rationales and sentence levels are a long-standing feature – robbery and drug trafficking being prime examples. The argument here is that it is necessary, in order to achieve a high level of general prevention for such offences, to impose penalties which are more severe than the proportionate sentence would be. The Court of Appeal frequently upholds sentences imposed on this ground; yet the empirical basis for expecting such policies to succeed is almost entirely lacking – we do not know whether all courts impose such sentences, whether this is known to offenders and potential offenders, whether this knowledge affects their reasoning processes, or is outweighed by other reasons

49 (1973) 57 Cr App R 240.

(chance of avoiding detection, prospects of gaining substantial money). Moreover, the judiciary seems confused on the issue. When Lord Taylor, as Lord Chief Justice, was arguing against the introduction of mandatory sentences into English law, he exposed the naivety of the government's belief that such penalties would have a significant deterrent effect, referring to the evidence against this and the evidence that the risk of detection was more powerful.[50] Yet he and his successors as Lord Chief Justice have presided in the Court of Appeal when many sentences based on just such general deterrent reasoning have been upheld.[51] Governments are also inconsistent on the point: only a few years earlier, a White Paper stated that 'it is unrealistic to construct sentencing arrangements on the assumption that most offenders will weigh up the possibilities in advance and base their conduct on rational calculation. Often they do not.'[52]

A number of mixed theories of punishment have been advanced in an attempt to preserve some elements of deterrence theory while avoiding the principled objections. The most notable is that of H. L. A. Hart,[53] who argued that the general justifying aim of punishment must be found in the prevention and control of crime, but that in deciding whom to punish and how much to punish the governing principle should be desert. That is, only the guilty should be punished, and then only in proportion to the seriousness of their offences. This does away with deterrence as a rationale for particular sentences, but, on the other hand, it finds no place for desert in the basic justification for punishment. There is a strong argument that in order to justify punishment there must be insistence on individual desert as well as overall social benefit.[54]

Sentences are not the only form of general deterrent flowing from the criminal justice system. In some cases it is the process that is the punishment – being prosecuted, appearing in court, receiving publicity in the local newspaper – rather than the sentence itself. In some cases the shame and embarrassment in relation to family and friends are said to have a more powerful effect than the sentence itself.[55] On the other hand, the deterrent effects of sentencing and of the process may be diluted considerably by enforcement policy, or at least by beliefs about the risk of detection. As we noted earlier, the evidence suggests that it is beliefs about the probability of detection rather than about the quantum of punishment which are more likely to influence human behaviour.[56] However, there is little detailed knowledge of the beliefs and thought processes of offenders and potential offenders, and the Cambridge study indicates a need for more focused research on these matters.[57] At a time when the detection rate for all crimes has fallen to around 23 per cent, and when burglary and robbery have detection rates of barely one-fifth, there are grounds for believing that any deterrent effect which sentence levels have upon the reasoning of potential offenders may be diluted considerably by the fairly low risk of detection. At

---

50 Taylor (1996), p. 10.   51 See n. 170 below.   52 Home Office (1990), para. 2.8.
53 Hart (1968).   54 Lacey (1988), pp. 46–56; von Hirsch (1993), ch. 2.
55 See the survey of young people by Willcock and Stokes (1963).
56 See the review by von Hirsch et al. (1999), ch. 6.   57 Von Hirsch et al. (1999), ch. 6.

any event, there is much less research in support of marginal deterrence by increasing the severity of penalties: few such effects have been reliably identified, and there are awkward questions such as how great an increase in severity is required, how that can be communicated to the target audience, whether the severity of penalties has already reached saturation point.[58] Thus, all the indications are that it is naïve to assume the kind of hydraulic relationship between court sentences and criminal behaviour that some find intuitively appealing.

3.3.3 Incapacitation[59]

A second possible rationale for sentencing is to incapacitate offenders, that is, to deal with them in such a way as to make them incapable of offending for substantial periods of time. In its popular form of 'public protection', this may be advanced as a general sentencing purpose.[60] However, it is usually confined to particular groups, such as 'dangerous' offenders, career criminals or other persistent offenders. Capital punishment and the severing of limbs could be included as incapacitative punishments, but there are formidable humanitarian arguments against such irreversible measures. The debate has usually concerned lengthy periods of imprisonment and of disqualification (e.g. from driving, from working with children, from being a company director). Some community measures, such as curfews, may raise similar problems.

What has been claimed for incapacitative sentencing strategies? This question receives detailed discussion below in the context of persistent and 'dangerous' offenders,[61] but two such strategies can be mentioned here. One is the imposition of long, incapacitative custodial sentences on offenders deemed to be 'dangerous'. It is claimed that one can identify certain offenders as 'dangerous', that is, as likely to commit serious offences if released into the community in the near future, and the risks to victims are so great that it is justifiable to detain such offenders for longer periods. The chief objection to this is over-prediction: studies suggest that incapacitative sentencing draws into its net more 'non-dangerous' than 'dangerous' offenders, with a 'false positive' rate that has often reached two out of every three. This means that any portion of punishment added to the proportionate sentence may be not only undeserved but also unnecessary to prevent that individual from committing a further serious offence.

The empirical basis of the second incapacitative strategy is likewise open to question. It was claimed by Greenwood in the United States that one can identify certain high-risk robbers and incarcerate them for substantial periods, achieving a reduction in the number of robberies and lowering sentence levels for other robbers.[62] The crime preventive benefits of this are obvious, but the strategy has been shown to have major flaws. A subsequent report in the United States for the National Academy of

58 Von Hirsch et al. (1999), ch. 10.
59 For fuller discussion and selected readings, see von Hirsch and Ashworth (1998), ch. 3.
60 As in s. 142(1)(d) of the Criminal Justice Act 2003.
61 See ch. 6.7 and 6.8 below.   62 Greenwood (1982).

Sciences demonstrated that Greenwood exaggerated the incapacitative effects and based his calculations on imprisoned robbers rather than robbers generally, and that a reworked version of his prediction method produced disappointing results.[63] The Halliday report reviewed the research on incapacitation, and concluded that 'the available evidence does not support the case for changing the [sentencing] framework . . . for the sole purpose of increasing an incapacitation effect'.[64] Despite these unpropitious findings, selective or none-too-selective incapacitative policies continue to have a political appeal: they underlie many 'three strikes and you're out' policies in the United States, and also the minimum sentences for third-time burglars and drug dealers introduced by the Crime (Sentences) Act 1997, the minimum sentence for possession of a firearm introduced by the Criminal Justice Act 2003, and the new 'dangerousness' sentences in that Act. Thus even governments supposedly committed to evidence-led policies find it irresistible to introduce incapacitative sentencing strategies in the face of poor penological prospects.[65]

Apart from the empirical objections, there is also a principled objection to incapacitative sentencing, which parallels the objection to general deterrent sentencing: individuals are being punished, over and above what they deserve, in the hope of protecting future victims from harm. In both cases it is essentially a moral objection to sacrificing one offender's liberty in the hope of increasing the future safety of others. The force of such an objection is particularly strong where the successful prediction rate is low, and yet its high moral content is often submerged by seductive references to increased public protection and public safety. The more difficult question is whether the objection should be given absolute force if a fairly high prediction rate could be achieved. There are some cases where the prison authorities, doctors and others feel sure that a certain prisoner presents a serious danger to others, in terms of violent or sexual assault. Should the Kantian objection be upheld even if there was an agreed high risk of serious offences? The Floud Committee thought that a just redistribution of risk should result in the prolonged detention of the high-risk offender rather than an increased danger to victims.[66] Some critics of their approach, who would wish to uphold an individual's right not to be punished more than is proportionate to the offence(s) committed, concede that in cases of 'vivid danger' it might be justifiable to lengthen detention for incapacitative purposes.[67] However, the better justification for doing so lies in the realistic prospect of a significant increase in public protection from doing so, rather than by comparing the offender's right with the rights of potential victims.[68] The point is an important one, because the emphasis of liberal theories on individual rights does not necessarily lead to absolute rights which ignore the social context and the possibility of conflicting rights. Thus, even the staunchest advocate of individual rights might concede that there are exceptional circumstances in which it is the

---

63 Blumstein et al. (1986); see also Zimring and Hawkins (1995).
64 Halliday (2001), para. 1.68.   65 See the thorough review by Zimring and Hawkins (1995).
66 Floud and Young (1981), supported by Walker (1982).
67 Notably Bottoms and Brownsword (1982).   68 See von Hirsch and Ashworth (2005), ch. 5.

right of the convicted offender which should yield. All this would depend on an acceptably high rate of successful prediction and, even then, since the isolation from the rest of society would be purely on preventive grounds, it is strongly arguable that the detention should not be in a prison but in some form of civil facility.[69]

3.3.4 Rehabilitation [70]

Like deterrence and incapacitation, the rehabilitative rationale for sentencing (sometimes termed 'resocialization') seeks to justify compulsory measures as a means of achieving the prevention of crime, the distinctive method involving the rehabilitation of the offender. This usually requires a range of sentences and facilities designed to offer various programmes of treatment. Sometimes the focus is on the modification of attitudes and of behavioural problems. Sometimes the aim is to provide education or skills, in the belief that these might enable offenders to find occupations other than crime. Thus the crucial questions for the sentencer concern the perceived needs of the offender, not the gravity of the offence committed. The rehabilitative approach is closely linked with those forms of positivist criminology which locate the causes of criminality in individual pathology or individual maladjustment, whether psychiatric, psychological or social. Whereas deterrence theory regards offenders as rational and calculating, rehabilitative theory is aimed at those who are regarded as being in need of help and support. One key element in determining those needs is a report from an expert – for example, a pre-sentence report prepared by a probation officer or, occasionally, a psychiatric report. Such a report will usually advise on the form of programme that matches the perceived needs of the offender, and the court may then make the appropriate order. In their heyday, the operation of these 'treatment models' often led to sentences that were indeterminate, on the basis that a person should only be released from obligations when, in the opinion of the experts, a cure had been effected.

This approach to sentencing reached its zenith in the 1960s, particularly in certain US jurisdictions. The 1970s are often said to have brought the decline of the rehabilitative ideal, but its adherents remain and the 1990s saw a revival of rehabilitation. Why did faith in the rehabilitative ideal decline in the 1970s? Two major concerns can be identified. One was the criticism that few of these treatment programmes seemed to be better at preventing reoffending than ordinary, non-treatment sentences. There had been many studies of the effectiveness of particular programmes, usually judging them on reconviction rates in subsequent years, and the conclusions of a widely publicized survey of the research by Martinson and others were represented as 'nothing works'.[71] In fact, Martinson disavowed such a totally negative conclusion,[72] and an English survey by Stephen Brody was more circumspect in pointing out that only a limited number of programmes had been tried and

---

69 Wood (1988).
70 For fuller discussion and selected readings, see von Hirsch and Ashworth (1998), ch. 1.
71 Martinson et al. (1974).   72 Martinson (1979).

evaluated.[73] Moreover, it was increasingly recognized that it would be more sensible to look for 'interaction effects' than for overall reductions in reconviction – in other words, there might be small groups of offenders for whom a certain kind of treatment has markedly better or markedly worse results, but such effects might not be apparent by looking simply at reconviction rates for all offenders.[74]

The second objection to rehabilitative policies is that they considerably increase the powers of so-called experts and recognize no right in individuals to be regarded as worthy of equal respect and concern. Indeterminate or even semi-determinate sentences place the release of offenders in the hands of prison or probation authorities, usually without firm criteria, clear accountability or avenues for challenge and reasoned decision-making. There is no question of recognizing an individual's right not to be subjected to compulsory state intervention which is disproportionate to the seriousness of the crime committed. Even if the crime is relatively minor, an offender who is assessed as needing help might be subject to state control for a considerable period. The motivation may be benevolent and 'in the person's best interests'. In effect the individual offender may be regarded more as a manipulable object than as a person with rights.[75]

The rehabilitative rationale has staged a revival in recent years. The response to the second, 'respect for personhood' objection is varied: some recognize that one route to successful rehabilitative programmes is for offenders to develop respect for the moral authority of those (notably probation officers) who are supervising their treatment,[76] whereas others (particularly, it must be said, in government circles) lay greater emphasis on notions of public safety and public interest that demand compliance by the offender within a chiefly punitive framework.[77] The response to the first, 'lack of evidence' objection has been to suggest that the 'meta-analysis' of large numbers of small rehabilitative schemes demonstrates that positive results can be obtained in favourable circumstances with selected offenders.[78] Enthusiasm for various kinds of cognitive-behavioural programme is high in some quarters, but the warning of a 1998 Home Office survey is still relevant: 'there have been . . . very few well-designed and carefully evaluated studies in this country of the effectiveness of programmes designed to rehabilitate and reduce the risk of reoffending'.[79] Even accepting that there are good reasons to devise and to evaluate new programmes, properly resourced and based on sound principles, this leaves several questions unanswered. Do we have rehabilitative programmes which could work for large numbers of offenders? Do we have programmes which could work for lesser, but still significant groups of offenders, whose suitability could be identified in advance?

73 Brody (1976).
74 Early English research into intensive probation (Folkard 1976) did not yield impressive results from this point of view.
75 See Allen (1981), excerpted in von Hirsch and Ashworth (1998), ch. 1.
76 For discussion see Rex (1998).
77 E.g. the language pervading the National Standards, discussed in ch. 10 below.
78 McGuire (1995), Hedderman and Sugg (1997) and Sherman et al. (1997).
79 Vennard and Hedderman (1998), p. 115.

Should these programmes be available to courts, even in cases where the duration of the programme exceeds the proportionate sentence? Even if all these questions are answered in the negative, there may be sound humanitarian reasons for continuing to experiment with rehabilitative programmes for offenders. However, respect for individual rights suggests that the duration of programmes should remain within the bounds set by proportionality,[80] and excessive claims of or targets for 'success in reducing reoffending' should be avoided. The latest (and mixed) results of programmes in custody are discussed in Chapter 9 below, and those of community programmes in Chapter 10 below.

3.3.5 Desert [81]

Desert theory is a modern form of retributive philosophy and, like retributivism, it has various shades and hues. Its leading proponent is undoubtedly Andrew von Hirsch, the author of the US report *Doing Justice* in 1976 and the writer of several subsequent articles and books.[82] He argues that punishment has two interlocking justifications. One element lies in the intuitive connection between desert and punishment: thus, desert is 'an integral part of everyday judgments of praise and blame',[83] and state punishment institutionalizes this censuring function. Thus, sentences communicate official censure or blame, the communication being chiefly to the offender but also to the victim and society at large. However, censure alone is not enough: the fallibility of human nature makes it necessary to attach a prudential reason to the normative one. Thus, the second justifying element lies in the underlying need for general deterrence: without police, courts and a penal system, 'it seems likely that victimising conduct would become so prevalent as to make life nasty and brutish, indeed'.[84] This preventive element of the rationale is regarded as a (contingent) foundation for the sentencing system, but it does not justify severe penalties: on the contrary, if the punishment were severe, it would 'drown out' the moral quality of the censure.[85]

The essence of desert or proportionality theory is thus that the sentence addresses the offender as a moral agent, as having the capacity to evaluate and to respond to an official evaluation of their conduct. This evaluation is communicated by imposing a proportionate sentence, and not any greater sentence that punishes the offender in order to achieve a preventive goal (by deterrence or incapacitation). In this way, proportionality theory respects rule of law values, and places limitations on state power over offenders. It is evident from this that the concept of proportionality is the touchstone, and two senses of the term must be distinguished with care. Ordinal proportionality concerns the relative seriousness of offences among themselves. Cardinal proportionality relates the ordinal ranking to a scale of punishments, and requires that the penalty should not be out of proportion to the gravity of

---

80 Rex (1998).   81 For fuller discussion and readings, see von Hirsch and Ashworth (1998).
82 See especially von Hirsch (1993) and von Hirsch and Ashworth (2005).
83 Von Hirsch (1986), p. 52.   84 Von Hirsch (1986), p. 48.
85 See further Narayan (1993); and von Hirsch (1993), ch. 2. Cf. the approach of Duff (2001), below.

the crime involved. Different countries have different anchoring points for their penalty scales, often evolved over the years without much conscious reflection and regarded as naturally appropriate. It is sometimes alleged that the rhetoric of desert is likely to lead to greater severity of penalties, but in the jurisdictions that embraced proportionality theory most fully – Finland, Sweden and Minnesota – that was certainly not the outcome. In some other jurisdictions, such as California, substantial increases in penalty levels did follow, but that was chiefly caused by the intrusion of incapacitative sentencing.[86] Leading writers on desert have insisted on restraint in the use of custody,[87] but in practice the implementation of policies depends on general political trends and judicial disposition in the jurisdiction concerned.

Nevertheless, it must be conceded that to draw the theoretical distinction between cardinal and ordinal proportionality is not to provide much concrete guidance on the severity level that is 'proportionate' to a particular kind of offence. It does suffice to rule out extreme punishments such as ten years' imprisonment for shoplifting; but the argument as to whether a person committing a particular house burglary deserves three years' imprisonment, three months or a community sentence has to be conducted on broader penological and social grounds. At this point desert theory needs to be supplemented with some other principles, such as the decremental strategy advocated by von Hirsch[88] or the principle of parsimony advocated by Norval Morris and by Michael Tonry.[89]

The parameters of ordinal proportionality are also contentious. Most countries have a fairly traditional ordering of offences, but this has usually not come to terms with modern offences concerned with, for example, safety risks or environmental crimes. Changes in the relative rankings of certain offences have taken place – for example, in England in recent decades offences such as child abuse and causing death by dangerous driving have been moved up-tariff – but without any overall theory of what makes offences more or less serious. In justifying a reduction in sentence levels for social security fraud, Lord Lane CJ stated that such offences are 'non-violent, non-sexual and non-frightening'.[90] Criteria of this kind need to be refined considerably if there is to be a framework which can cope not only with 'new' forms of criminality such as breaches of safety regulations and incitement to racial hatred, but also with the long-standing contrast between property crimes and offences against the person. The project of further refinement has been started by von Hirsch and Jareborg,[91] and an attempt to carry it forward is made in Chapter 4.3 below.

A different strain of desert theory is that developed by Antony Duff.[92] He regards the proportionality principle as central, but the essence of his theory is that sentences are communicative. The punishment forces the offender's attention to the

---

86 For further discussion, see von Hirsch and Ashworth (2005), ch. 6.
87 Notably von Hirsch, e.g. in (1993), ch. 3.   88 Von Hirsch (1993), chs. 3 and 5.
89 For a stimulating analysis, see Tonry (1994).   90 *Stewart* (1987) 9 Cr App R (S) 135, at p. 138.
91 Von Hirsch and Jareborg (1991); see further von Hirsch and Ashworth (2005), Appendix 3.
92 See particularly Duff (2001).

disapproval it conveys. The aim of the punishment is to bring the offender to repent of the wrongdoing, and to provide a means for the offender to 'work through' and express penitence. Punishment therefore has a significant psychological element, and the offender's response to the sentence may be seen as a kind of apology to the community wronged by the offence.[93]

Critics have attacked desert theory at various points. It is said to be unsatisfactory to rest such a coercive response, even partly, on the mere intuition that punishment is an appropriate or natural response to offending.[94] Furthermore, exactly what is deserving of blame and punishment – culpable acts or dispositions?[95] It is also said to be unfair to rest desert partly on individual culpability when strong social disadvantages may be at the root of much offending.[96] One answer to this is to recognize grounds for mitigation of sentence for any offender who has suffered significant social deprivation, while maintaining that the unequal distribution of wealth and opportunity in society ought to be tackled by means other than sentencing. Where social injustices are widespread, this 'does not diminish . . . the harmfulness of common victimising crimes', although it strengthens the case for reducing overall punishment levels.[97] Critics have also argued that the key concepts of ordinal and cardinal proportionality are too vague and open to divergent interpretations, but this should be regarded as a challenge rather than a barrier. The reasons for wishing to place principled limits on the state's power to punish are widely accepted. Thus it is significant that the Council of Europe's recommendation on *Consistency in Sentencing* (see part 3.2.1 of this chapter) states:

> A4. Whatever rationales for sentencing are declared, disproportionality between the seriousness of the offence and the sentence should be avoided.[98]

Similarly, critics such as Morris and Tonry[99] and Nicola Lacey[100] accept that disproportionate sentences cannot be justified, and therefore commit themselves to some form of desert reasoning. Support for a 'disproportionality' limit underlines the importance of desert theorists working towards criteria for ranking offences for the purpose of ordinal proportionality,[101] and towards a principled approach to the awkward question of the relevance of previous convictions to sentence, rationalizing the concessions to first offenders in terms of human frailty and evaluating the relevance of various types of previous record (see Chapter 6.2). Desert theorists have also tackled the problems of introducing proportionality into non-custodial sentencing (see Chapter 10.2). Many of the proposals require further refinement, but the strengths of proportionality theory are to be found in its apparent concordance

---

93 See Duff (2001) for the rich and detailed development of this theory. For criticisms, see von Hirsch and Ashworth (2005), ch. 7.
94 Cf. Lacey (1988), pp. 21–6, with Moore (1988).
95 For this and other points, see Walker (1991).
96 Mathiesen (1990), p. 121; and more broadly Lacey (1988), pp. 18–22.
97 von Hirsch (1993), pp. 107–8.   98 Council of Europe (1993), p. 6.
99 As restated in Tonry (1994).   100 See part 3.3.6 below.   101 See ch. 4.3 below.

with some widely held moral views, in its respect for the rights of the individual offender, and in its placing of limits on the powers of the state. Thomas Mathiesen has attacked desert theory for the implicit claims of precision and objectivity embodied in terms such as 'commensurate', 'ordinal and cardinal proportionality', 'culpability' and 'offence seriousness'.[102] A different interpretation would be that it is a belief in the importance of these terms to the justification of punishment, and the concomitant rule of law concerns, that continue to motivate desert theorists towards further enquiries on these topics.

3.3.6 Social theories of sentencing

Several contemporary writers are dissatisfied with the tendency of the four 'traditional' theories of punishment, especially desert theory, to deal with sentencing in isolation from its wider social and political setting. Various theories are being developed which attempt to make the approach to sentencing more responsive to social conditions and community expectations. Three examples of this tendency may be described briefly.[103]

In her work Barbara Hudson insists that priority should be given to crime prevention and to reducing the use of custody by the penal system. Changes in social policy relating to employment, education, housing and leisure facilities are far more important to justice than narrow debates about proportionality of sentence. And when it comes to sentencing, there should be greater concern with 'the problems of whole human beings' rather than with particular pieces of behaviour: the state should not 'privilege events over people' and should place more emphasis on the provision of rehabilitative opportunities. However, such developments at the sentencing stage should take place within a framework set by proportionality theory.[104]

Nicola Lacey likewise argues that the first step must be the state's recognition of its duty to foster a sense of community by providing proper facilities and fair opportunities for all citizens. Once this has been achieved in a community, punishment is justified as reinforcing the values that it has been decided to protect through criminal law. The proportionality principle would remain important in sentencing, but so would the conflicting value of promoting the welfare of the community. Lacey disagrees both with desert theorists and with preventionists in their insistence on assigning general priority to a single value: for her, while the core of each value must be preserved, compromises have to be negotiated separately and sensitively, with due attention to the avoidance of gender and racial bias. However, Lacey recognizes that community determinations of these issues raise further questions of limits and of enforcement, and that vigilance must be maintained in order to ensure that the arrangements remain inclusive and do not produce new forms of social exclusion.[105]

102 Mathiesen (1990), ch. 5 and *passim*.
103 See also the writings of Norrie and of Garland, excerpted and discussed in von Hirsch and Ashworth (1998), ch. 8.
104 E.g. Hudson (1995).   105 Lacey (1998), and excerpt 8.3 in von Hirsch and Ashworth (1998).

John Braithwaite and Phillip Pettit develop what they term a republican theory of criminal justice. Its central value is dominion, defined in terms of each citizen's ability to make life choices, within a social and political framework which each citizen has participated in shaping, and then to be protected in those choices. In its responses to offending, the criminal justice system should adopt a system of minimum intervention, but may pursue policies of prevention through sentencing where appropriate. Proportionality of sentence is not a primary concern. Indeed, republican theory would decouple censure from sentencing. Censure might be achieved more effectively by shaming and other forms of social reaction, and a particular sentence might be lower if the prospects for shaming seemed good. Otherwise, while the authors gesture vaguely towards upper limits of proportionality, they seem to accept that substantial sentences based on predictive and preventive rationales might be acceptable.[106]

These thumbnail sketches of complex theories should serve at least to demonstrate the continuing vitality of debate about the proper aims of sentencing. They have led, in their turn, to criticism, response and rebuttal.[107] However, as with all the theories outlined in this chapter, it is necessary to go to the original texts in order to acquire an appreciation of the precise steps by which both theories and critiques are constructed. What is characteristic of these social theories is that, to various extents, they assign greater importance to reducing overall levels of penalty and to removing wider social inequalities than to the relative fairness of individual sentences.

3.3.7 Restoration and reparation[108]

One of the major developments in criminal justice in the final quarter of the last century was the increasing recognition of the rights and needs of the victims of crime. This was clearly signalled by the United Nations in its *Declaration on the Basic Principles of Justice for Victims and Abuse of Power* in 1985, and in the government's *Victim's Charter* in 1990. It has also been manifest in at least two different ways in sentencing theory. One is the increased attention to victims' rights in the criminal justice system, including the granting of the right to make a victim personal statement to the court about the offence.[109] The second development will be the focus here – the growing number of restorative theories of criminal justice. The fundamental proposition is that justice to victims should become a central goal of the criminal justice system and of sentencing. This means that all the 'stakeholders' in the offence (the offender and the victim, their families, and the community) should become involved in discussions about the appropriate response to the offence. The

---

106 Braithwaite and Pettit (1990).
107 E.g. in extracts 7.2 and 7.3 of von Hirsch and Ashworth (1998).
108 For fuller discussion, see Johnstone (2002); for readings, see Johnstone (2003).
109 *Practice Direction: Victim Personal Statements* [2002] 1 Cr App R 69. Some jurisdictions go further and permit victims to make submissions on sentence: see further Ashworth (1993), Erez (1999), and ch. 11.8 below.

aim would be to bring about an apology, to ensure that the offender compensates the victim and the wider community for the effects of the crime, and to take steps to ensure that the offence is not repeated. Thus, as Lucia Zedner puts it,

> criminal justice should be less preoccupied with censuring code-breakers and focus instead on the process of restoring individual damage and repairing ruptured social bonds. In place of meeting pain with the infliction of further pain, a truly reparative system would seek the holistic restoration of the community. It would necessarily also challenge the claim of the state to respond to crime and would instead invite (or perhaps demand) the involvement of the community in the process of restoration.[110]

A considerable number of schemes of restorative justice are in place in different parts of the world. The first major initiative was that introduced in New Zealand by the Children, Young Persons and their Families Act 1989: young offenders are dealt with in 'family group conferences', in which a group including the victim and the offender and their families, together with a community representative as facilitator, formulate a plan for responding to the offence.[111] The best-known scheme in Australia is RISE in Canberra, in which persons charged with four types of offence (violence, property, shop theft, drunk-driving) were randomly allocated to court or to restorative justice. Interpretation of the results is problematic,[112] but it is claimed that victims who went to restorative justice conferences were much more satisfied with the procedure, and it appears that only violent offenders were less likely to reoffend following restorative justice, and not those who committed one of the other three types of offence. From her study of the South Australia project for young offenders, Kathleen Daly reports considerable victim satisfaction with the processes of restorative justice, although only a minority of conferences were in her view very well run. She also suggests that reoffending is likely to be determined by the usual factors (such as the number of previous convictions, and the offender's family and community ties), but that if an offender who participates in restorative justice is truly remorseful and accepting of the outcome, this may reduce reoffending.[113] Restorative justice has not been embraced so fully in this country, but a scheme of restorative cautioning started by Thames Valley police has now spread to other areas,[114] partly under the auspices of the Crime and Disorder Act 1998 for young offenders, which also includes 'restorative' conferencing as part of the response to a referral order for young offenders appearing in court for the first time.[115]

Restorative justice has considerable attractions as a constructive and socially inclusive way of responding to criminal behaviour. But there remain various problems of principle which trouble critics.[116] One is to determine the objectives of restorative justice: many statements suggest that it can lead to the healing of

110 Zedner (1994), p. 233.   111 See A. Morris (2002).   112 E.g. Kurki (2001).
113 Daly (2002).   114 See Hoyle and Young (2003).
115 On whether these interventions are rightly labelled 'restorative', see Morris and Gelsthorpe (2000) and Ball (2004).
116 For an enumeration of, and reply to, criticisms, see Morris (2002).

victims, restore the community and reduce reoffending, but there is no evidence that it can do all these things satisfactorily, and it seems likely that a focus on one may not enhance others. Moreover, the concept of restoring the community remains shrouded in mystery, as indeed does the identification of the relevant 'community'. If restorative justice is to be used for non-minor offences, then it is problematic to allow the victim and/or the victim's family to play a part in determining the response. In principle, such determinations should be made by an independent and impartial tribunal, and it is unconvincing to argue that offenders 'consent' to restorative processes in view of the pressures upon them.[117] If restorative justice is to be used, then at least there should be limits to the powers of conferences so as to ensure that proportionality constraints are not breached.[118] Advocates of restorative justice often complain that all these safeguards are unnecessary and that restorative justice is a positive experience which does not involve severity. However, the experience with rehabilitation in the 1960s warns of the dangers that the claims of enthusiasts might run ahead of the evidence and that the amount of control and coercion exerted over offenders might go beyond what is deserved for the offence.

3.3.8 Defining punishment

This discussion of restorative justice raises the question of the definition of punishment. Advocates of restorative justice are wont to say that they are not in the business of punishment and to contrast their approach with the punishment-oriented rationales considered above. On the classic definition of punishment offered by Hart, an agreement resulting from a restorative justice conference that imposes obligations on the offender certainly amounts to the infliction of pain or other unpleasant consequences by a court in consequence of an offence – at least insofar as the agreement goes beyond mere apology, reparation or compensation. Moreover, as Daly argues, the censure and reparative obligations flowing from a restorative justice conference may often be experienced by the offender as a punishment for the offence.[119] Advocates of restorative justice may counter this by arguing that a restorative justice agreement, involving restoration of the victim and of the wider community, is intended to be constructive rather than punitive. This points up the need to decide whether the definition of punishment should be dependent on what the person authorizing or inflicting it intends, on what the person receiving it perceives, or on some other model.

Hart's definition purports to take an objective view, dependent not on the purpose of what is done or the offender's perception of it, but rather on whether it fulfils certain criteria. A somewhat similar approach was adopted by the European Court of Human Rights when it had to decide whether an order depriving an offender of the alleged profits of crime amounted to a 'penalty' within the meaning of the

---

117 See further Ashworth (2002b).
118 On this and other matters, see von Hirsch and Ashworth (2005), ch. 9.
119 Daly (2002), p. 60.

Convention. The then legislation on drug trafficking required a judge, had been convicted of such an offence, to postpone sentencing in orde whether the offender had benefited from drug trafficking by receiving or other reward for it. Once the court was satisfied that there had b was empowered to assume that all the offender's assets, and everyth.... ʋwιιcu ιι the previous six years, were or represented the proceeds of drug trafficking, unless the offender showed otherwise. There were lengthy periods of imprisonment in the event of non-payment. Similar powers have now been re-enacted in the Proceeds of Crime Act 2002. In Strasbourg the question came up in the context of Article 7 of the Convention, which prohibits retrospective penalties.[120] It was conceded that the powers were retrospective. The question was whether deprivation of the profits of crime was a 'penalty'. In this context it is of no avail to state that it is a form of elementary justice that a person should not be allowed to profit from his or her wrong. The Court held that the confiscation order does amount to a 'penalty', since its purpose and the associated procedures were very much those of a punishment. It noted that the measure had punitive as well as preventive and reparative aims; that the order was calculated by reference to 'proceeds' rather than profits, and therefore had a reach beyond the mere restoration of the *status quo ante*; that the amount of the order could take account of the offender's culpability; and that the order was enforceable by a term of imprisonment in default.

The particular consequence of the Strasbourg ruling is that, where a confiscation order is made under the Proceeds of Crime Act 2002, this must be taken into account in deciding 'the overall penalty'.[121] Unlike the various preventive orders discussed in Chapter 12 below, it does amount to a penalty, since it is concerned to remove past profits rather than to bring about the prevention of future harm.

3.4 Some principles and policies

Justifying sentences and the sentencing system is not merely a matter of considering overall or ultimate aims. A number of discrete principles and policies may also impinge on either general sentencing policy or individual sentencing decisions. It would be extravagant to claim that there is a settled core of these principles and policies, which can be drawn together and put forward as a coherent group. The reality is that they form a fluctuating body at different stages in penal history, and are invoked selectively as the tides of penal politics ebb and flow. The penal system may be regarded as one of the institutions of society (along with the family, religion, the armed forces etc.), and in this context sentencing is an institution for the expression of social values as well as an instrumental means to a clinical penological end. An awareness of this wider context

120 *Welch* v. *United Kingdom* (1995) 20 EHRR 247.
121 A point already decided in England in *Joyce* (1989) 11 Cr App R (S) 253. See further discussion in ch. 11 below.

makes it easier to argue that the pursuit of values such as justice, humanity, tolerance, decency, humanity and civility should be part of any penal institution's self-consciousness – an intrinsic and constitutive aspect of its role – rather than a diversion from its 'real' goals or an inhibition on its capacity to be 'effective'.[122]

What might these values be, and how might they be expressed? Some attempt is made below to describe briefly six principles and policies which have some contemporary relevance – the first by virtue of legal authority, the others on moral, social and political grounds. Clearly, they may conflict among themselves; each one has an element of indeterminacy; and some of them raise as many questions as they solve. None the less, they are worth exploring.

3.4.1 The principle of respect for fundamental rights

The Human Rights Act 1998 requires all public authorities (including courts, prosecutors, prisons, offender management services) to act in conformity with the European Convention on Human Rights. While the Convention has rather less application to sentencing than to other stages of the criminal process, its provisions will have a distinct impact on some sentencing matters. These are discussed more fully in the appropriate parts of the book, but it is convenient to mention six points of impact here.

First, Article 3 of the Convention forbids torture and 'inhuman or degrading treatment or punishment': this rules out corporal punishment[123] and also, in conjunction with Protocol 6, capital punishment. If one considers the historical changes in the acceptability of punishment, there has been a movement away from corporal penalties – those which affect the body, in the sense of the direct infliction of pain – towards punishments which affect the mind. Such measures as amputation, torture and even corporal punishment are now regarded in this country as 'barbaric', as is capital punishment by many. Yet why is it that these forms of punishment are ruled out? If they might be effective as deterrents (of which evidence would be needed), why should a consequentialist or preventive theorist exclude them? If some of them might appear to be apt or proportionate responses to some types of crime, why should the desert theorist disavow them? One answer to this is human rights, and the meaning of Article 3 of the Convention. Although there is no objective or timeless benchmark of what is inhuman or degrading, the European Court of Human Rights takes the view that it depends partly on the age and condition of the persons subjected to the punishment, and partly on European trends and consensus. Thus there is considerable degradation in having to share a small cell with two other prisoners, with or without integral sanitation, for many hours at a stretch and with little opportunity, for example, for exercise. After many years, modern sensibilities are now turning against this and are accepting that it shows insufficient respect for

---

122 Garland (1990), pp. 291–2.
123 *Tyrer* v. *United Kingdom* (1978) 2 EHRR 1 (use of birch as punishment violates Art. 3).

human dignity.[124] Whether it will be held that wearing an electronic tag amounts to 'degrading punishment' remains to be tested.

Second, Articles 3 and 5 of the Convention may be invoked together or singly to rule out a disproportionate sentence. The Strasbourg Court has stated that life imprisonment for a small-value robbery might be so disproportionate as to amount to inhuman and degrading punishment, although it might be possible to justify it as a preventive sentence in certain circumstances.[125] Similarly, when holding in *Offen (No. 2)*[126] that the automatic sentence of life imprisonment for a second 'serious offence' should be made subject to a broader exception, Lord Woolf CJ drew upon Convention rights as part of his reasoning, noting that conviction of a 'serious offence' could result from a mere push that causes a fatal head injury:

> The offence is manslaughter. The offender may have committed another serious offence when a young man. A life sentence in such circumstances may well be arbitrary and disproportionate and contravene Article 5. It could also be a punishment which contravenes Article 3.

Third, Article 5 has also had a considerable impact on the procedures relating to life imprisonment. The Strasbourg Court, applying Article 5(4), has insisted that there must be provision for regular judicial review of the need for continued detention, applying this first to discretionary life sentences[127] and eventually to life imprisonment for murder.[128] The effect of this is to transfer to the Parole Board, chaired by a judge, the task of deciding how long a life prisoner needs to be detained in order to protect the public.

Fourth, Article 6 declares the right to a fair trial, and this includes the sentencing decision. Article 6 and its safeguards will therefore apply wherever proceedings result in the imposition of a 'penalty' on a person.[129] One result of this is to hold that the Home Secretary cannot set the minimum term for an offender convicted of murder, since he is not an 'independent and impartial tribunal' as required by Article 6.[130] It has also been held that court proceedings must be specially adapted where the defendant is a child, so as to facilitate meaningful participation.[131]

Fifth, Article 7 declares that no person may be subjected to a greater penalty than the one applicable at the time of the offence. We have already noted that English law's classification is not determinative, since the Strasbourg Court held that a

124 See the reports of the European Committee on the Prevention of Torture and Inhuman and Degrading Treatment, mentioned in ch. 9.1.3 below. See also *Napier* v. *Scottish Executive* [2004] UKHRR 881.
125 *Weeks* v. *United Kingdom* (1987) 10 EHRR 293.   126 [2001] 1 Cr App R 372.
127 *Thynne, Wilson and Gunnell* v. *United Kingdom* (1989) 13 EHRR 666.
128 *Stafford* v. *United Kingdom* (2002) 35 EHRR 1121, departing from its previous decision in *Wynne* v. *United Kingdom* (1994) 19 EHRR 333.
129 For the meaning of 'penalty', see *Welch* v. *United Kingdom*, n. 120 above.
130 As held by the House of Lords in *R.* v. *Home Secretary, ex p. Anderson* [2003] 1 AC 837, reviewing the previous Strasbourg decisions.
131 *V and T* v. *United Kingdom* (2000) 30 EHRR 121; *SC* v. *United Kingdom* [2005] Crim. LR 130.

confiscation order is a 'penalty',[132] although it seems that most of the preventive orders are not regarded as penalties.[133] Of more general significance is the principle that changes to sentencing law may not operate retrospectively.[134] This is particularly relevant in view of the frequent changes in sentencing powers introduced by legislation in recent years.

Sixth, Article 8.1 declares each person's right to respect for his private and family life, his home and his correspondence, and Article 8.2 sets out the circumstances in which interference with that right may be justified. Even where it is held that interference is justified, any sentence resulting from conviction must remain proportionate to the rationale for the interference and must reflect the fact that a right is being compromised. Thus, in the sado-masochism case of *Laskey* v. *United Kingdom*,[135] the European Court showed its willingness to scrutinize the severity of the sentence on this ground (the sentence imposed at trial had already been reduced by the Court of Appeal, and no further adjustment was thought necessary). The same proportionality principle applies to sentences for offences which involve a (justifiable) interference with a right under Article 9 (freedom of religion), Article 10 (freedom of expression) and Article 11 (freedom of assembly).[136]

The impact of the Convention on prisoners' rights has been more extensive, with a steady stream of decisions in Strasbourg and in the English courts.[137] However, it seems unlikely that the Charter of Fundamental Rights of the European Union will be allowed to exert a great effect on sentencing or penal policy. While it contains a number of provisions on criminal justice – particularly Article 49(3), that 'the severity of penalties must not be disproportionate to the criminal offence' – the government is concerned to ensure that its application is limited to EU directives and legislation based upon them.[138]

3.4.2 The principle of restraint in the use of custody

In recognition that imprisonment is a severe deprivation for most of those incarcerated, there has been widespread formal acceptance that it should be used with restraint. Draft Resolution VIII of the Eighth United Nations Congress on the Prevention of Crime and the Treatment of Offenders recommended that 'imprisonment should be used as a sanction of last resort',[139] and the Council of Europe had also adopted a similar policy some years earlier when advocating the wider use of non-custodial sanctions.[140] But these formal statements disappeared from view in the closing decade of the twentieth century, with burgeoning prison populations in many countries, notably in the United States and latterly in England and Wales. It is

---

132 Above, n. 120.
133 See e.g. *Ibbotson* v. *United Kingdom* (1999) 27 EHRR CD 332, holding that sex offender registration is not a penalty.
134 Cf. *Ghafoor* [2003] 1 Cr App R (S) 428 on the application of the principle in juvenile sentencing.
135 (1997) 24 EHRR 39.
136 For further analysis of these and related matters, see ch. 16 of Emmerson and Ashworth (2005).
137 See Livingstone, Owen and Macdonald (2003).
138 Cf. van Zyl Smit and Ashworth (2004) with Goldsmith (2004).
139 United Nations (1990), para. 5(e).   140 Council of Europe (1976), Res. 10.

fair to say that the principle of restraint was never wholly embraced in this country, since the Criminal Justice Act 1991 adopted a 'twin-track' approach, maintaining severe sentences for serious and 'dangerous' offenders while advocating reductions in the use of custody for the less serious offenders. But the then government did at least commit itself to the general proposition that prisons are 'an expensive way of making bad people worse',[141] and the principle of restraint was also advocated strongly by the Woolf Inquiry into the prison disturbances of 1990.[142] However, the tide then turned, and in 1993 the then Home Secretary, Michael Howard, declared that 'prison works' and sentencers were urged to make greater use of custody. In contrast Lord Woolf made several public statements critical of the government's approach, stating during a 1994 debate in the House of Lords that

> As a result of a change in climate, the importance of avoiding custody when it is appropriate to do so has been forgotten. A factor which has undoubtedly contributed to this change of climate is that the Government, who give a lead in these matters, have abandoned preaching the need for restraint in the use of prisons. The message which is being received loud and clear by all those involved . . . is that it is necessary to get tough with crime . . . It needs to be reiterated repeatedly that if prison is used when it is not necessary, then it is frustrating, not furthering, the objectives of the criminal justice system.[143]

However, the judiciary and magistracy found themselves unable to resist the political and media pressure for higher sentences, as Lord Bingham CJ subsequently admitted,[144] and the change of government in 1997 brought no change in the punitive rhetoric from ministers.

Yet this 'populist punitiveness',[145] while staunchly maintained in government publicity, is not unmitigated. Detailed policies and pronouncements yield evidence of other concerns. The Criminal Justice Act 2003 has some reductivist aspects – tighter language on the threshold for custody, tighter language on the length of custody[146] – and the guidelines laid down by the Sentencing Guidelines Council emphasize the decision processes through which the courts must go before they decide to impose a custodial sentence.[147] This is not to suggest that the present government is committed to restraint in the use of custody but dare not say so. Rather, the position appears to be that the preferred policy is again one of bifurcation, so that the government can support long sentences for serious offenders and for public protection, while at the same time promoting more constructive approaches to non-serious offenders.[148]

141 Home Office (1990), para. 2.7.   142 Woolf (1991), discussed in ch. 9.1 below.
143 HL Deb., 2 Feb. 1994. See also the interviews with senior judges in the *Observer*, 17 Oct. 1993, p. 3.
144 'Since 1993 the use of custody has increased very sharply, in response (it would seem likely) to certain highly publicized crimes, legislation, ministerial speeches and intense media pressure.' *Brewster* [1998] 1 Cr App R (S) 181, at p. 184.
145 The term coined by Tony Bottoms (1995).   146 See ch. 1.5 above.
147 Sentencing Guidelines Council, *Overarching Principles: Seriousness* (2004), Part E.
148 Cf. ch. 13 below on the three tracks of sentencing policy.

3.4.3 Managerialism and the policy of controlling public expenditure

Governments always have an eye to public expenditure, and this may be one reason why this government is so enthusiastic about the 'what works' approach – testing specific and targeted methods of dealing with offenders, especially in the community, so as to reduce reoffending.[149] It is notable, for example, that the Sentencing Guidelines Council is required to have regard, when framing sentencing guidelines, to 'the cost of different sentences and their relative effectiveness in preventing reoffending'.[150] However, this criterion has yet to be applied to the high rate of imprisonment in the UK jurisdictions. There is no evidence that the Treasury has questioned the economic benefits of a high custody rate: if they had done so successfully, this would reinforce the criminological arguments that prisons may be counter-productive and that 'more severe' does not mean 'more effective'. When the present government did commission inquiries into the effectiveness of imprisonment and other penal measures,[151] it showed little interest in the consistent findings that the present high custodial population is wasteful on so many grounds. The political mantra of not appearing to be 'soft on crime' trumps even economics in this sphere.

3.4.4 The principle of equality before the law

This is the principle that sentencing decisions should treat offenders equally, irrespective of their wealth, race, colour, sex, abilities, or employment or family status. English law now makes it a statutory aggravating factor if an offence is motivated or accompanied by hostility based on race, religion, sexual orientation or disability.[152] More long-standing are the precedents stating that offenders with wealth should not be allowed to 'buy themselves out of prison' by paying large fines or compensation.[153] This principle of equality hardly needs justification, for it is surely unjust that people should be penalized at the sentencing stage for any of these reasons. Yet in practice there are difficulties. As we shall see in Chapter 7, there is evidence of discrimination according to wealth, some evidence of race and sex discrimination in certain respects, and clear evidence of discrimination on grounds of employment status. The last is a peculiarly difficult issue: courts often try to pass a sentence which ensures that a person who has a job is able to keep it, although the implication is that unemployed offenders are discriminated against, since that source of sentence reduction is not open to them. This leads into the question, already discussed in parts 3.3.5 and 3.3.6 of this chapter, of whether it is right to speak of 'just' or 'fair' sentences in a society riven with inequality and injustice.

---

149 For discussion, see above, and more generally ch. 10 below.
150 Criminal Justice Act 2003, s. 170(5)(c).
151 See Moxon (1998), and also von Hirsch et al. (1999) for the Cambridge study of deterrence, carried out for the Home Office.
152 Criminal Justice Act 2003, ss. 145–146.
153 See *Markwick* (1953) 37 Cr App R 125 and other decisions discussed in ch. 7.5 below.

3.4.5 The principle of equal impact

This principle argues that sentences should be so calculated as to impose an equal impact on the offenders subjected to them. Or, to phrase the principle negatively, the system should strive to avoid grossly unequal impacts on offenders with differing resources and sensitivities, because that would be unjust. The most obvious application of the principle is to fines, which ought to be adjusted to reflect the different means of different offenders.[154] Another application may be to imprisonment for offenders who have some special mental or medical condition which may make custody significantly more painful,[155] although there may be an alternative justification based on compassion rather than equality of impact of sanctions.[156] Many of the questions raised by the principle of equal impact are discussed further in Chapter 7 below, where the problems of integrating it into a system of proportionate sentencing are examined.

3.4.6 The principle of parsimony

On the basis that all punishment is pain and ought therefore to be avoided or minimised where possible, Bentham argued for a principle of frugality in punishment:[157] in all cases the lowest sufficient punishment should be chosen. Norval Morris developed a similar principle of parsimony,[158] and this is urged in current debate by Michael Tonry.[159] What is not always clear is the level at which proponents are urging the principle. It could be regarded as a principle applicable to policy-makers – a broader version of the principle of restraint in the use of custody, perhaps phrased in terms of minimum intervention. This would recognize the punitive effects of the criminal process and publicity on many offenders, and would argue for the greater prominence of formal cautions and other diversionary measures for less serious forms of crime. It would also support the approach of reserving community penalties for cases that are too serious for a fine or conditional discharge, an approach implicit in the Criminal Justice Act 2003. A more thoroughgoing 'decremental strategy' would involve a progressive reduction in penalty levels over time.[160]

Alternatively, or even additionally, the principle of parsimony could be regarded as a principle for the sentencer in individual cases. The question is how far this should be taken, if the court has two cases before it – both offences of stealing, one by a person of lowly status (e.g. from a 'criminal' family or neighbourhood), the other by a citizen whose background leads the court to believe it unlikely that he will ever offend again. If the court gives a lesser punishment to the second one, it may be following the principle of parsimony, but would this be fair? It would certainly breach the principle of equality before the law (above). The same would apply if the court gave a lesser punishment to an employed offender than to an unemployed

---

154 See ch. 7.5 below for discussion.   155 See Ashworth and Player (1998).
156 Cf. von Hirsch and Ashworth (2005), Appendix C.   157 Bentham (1789), ch. xv, para. 11.
158 Morris (1974).   159 See e.g. Tonry (1994).
160 See Braithwaite and Pettit (1990), and von Hirsch (1993), ch. 5.

offender, on the basis that it would be unfortunate if the former were to lose a job, bringing hardship to the family and so on. It is argued in Chapter 7 below that, while the principle of parsimony ought to be pursued at the general or legislative level, the principle of equality before the law should prevail in individual sentencing decisions. But Morris and Tonry decry this as producing 'equality of misery', and advocate the principle of parsimony in individual sentencing decisions too.[161]

3.5 Sentencing rationales and English criminal justice

Whatever the philosophical and empirical objections to some rationales for punishment, there remains some support for each rationale, at least as applied to certain categories of case. This sometimes leads to the suggestion that some form of 'hybrid' approach should be devised, finding room for more than one rationale. If this is to be done, then (as the Council of Europe recommended)[162] consistency will only be possible if a primary rationale is declared, and the limited circumstances under which that rationale can be displaced are made clear. This approach is evident in the Swedish sentencing statute, which adopts desert as the primary rationale but makes provision for other rationales in defined spheres (such as general deterrence in the sentencing of drunk drivers).[163] The English Criminal Justice Act 1991 was intended to embody a similar approach, with desert as the primary rationale of sentencing, subject to incapacitation in a limited class of cases. However, a major difficulty was that the 1991 Act was not drafted in such a way as to make its scheme clear. Nowhere was desert or proportionality proclaimed as the primary rationale, and this both led to considerable misunderstanding and left room for spoiling tactics by those charged with interpreting and applying the Act.

The judiciary was never in favour of the 1991 Act and, after some of its provisions had been altered by the Criminal Justice Act 1993, the main parts of the legislation were rarely referred to in the Court of Appeal in the late 1990s. Instead, the preoccupation lay in opposing the then government's support for mandatory minimum sentences. When those sentences were introduced by the Crime (Sentences) Act 1997, albeit in a slightly attenuated form, the scheme of the 1991 Act was no longer part of judicial consciousness about sentencing – if indeed it ever was. But it still remained the law, and the government sought to pave the way for its removal by setting up the Review of the Sentencing Framework, England and Wales, chaired by a former senior civil servant at the Home Office, John Halliday. His brief from the Home Office suggested that the 1991 Act had become an impediment to proper sentencing – although it appeared to be exerting little practical effect at all – and urged him towards a sentencing approach that would place a greater priority on reducing reoffending and on punishing those who fail to respond to measures taken to reduce reoffending. In the event, Halliday reviewed the evidence on deterrence

---

161 Morris and Tonry (1990), discussed in ch. 7.7 below.
162 Council of Europe (1993), quoted in the text at n. 23 above.
163 Von Hirsch and Jareborg (1989).

and on incapacitation and concluded that there was too little evidence to say that either strategy had sufficient prospect of leading to crime reduction. He therefore advocated a modified form of proportionality rationale – that sentences should be proportionate to the seriousness of the offence and the seriousness of the criminal record.[164] This enabled him to address the government's concern about persistent offenders, while insisting that proportionality should remain the primary rationale.

The government broadly accepted Halliday's recommendation on persistent offenders (discussed further in Chapter 6.3.1 below), but still seemed confused about the proper place of proportionality. In its White Paper *Justice for All* it proclaimed that it would 'set out in legislation the purposes of sentencing' and require sentencers to consider them and to achieve 'the right balance' between them.[165] Halliday had not recommended this, and indeed had pointed out the shortcomings of the evidence on which policies of deterrence and public protection were based. Thus it is not just that the five purposes of sentencing conflict, but also that at least two of them (deterrence and incapacitation) were said by Halliday to have insufficient evidential foundations. Given this confusion, one wonders what instructions were given to parliamentary counsel at the time of drafting what was to become the Criminal Justice Act 2003. The result is ambiguous. On the one hand is the vacuous and incoherent s. 142, setting out five (conflicting) purposes of sentencing to which the court must have regard, as discussed in part 3.1 above. On the other hand, we find s. 143(1) on the meaning of the proportionality principle, which has now been adopted as the central principle for sentencing in the Sentencing Guidelines Council's first guidelines;[166] and we also find three key provisions of the 2003 Act that use proportionality as their touchstone – s. 148(1) stating that a community sentence should not be imposed unless the offence is serious enough to warrant such a sentence, s. 152(2) stating that a custodial sentence should not be imposed unless the offence is too serious for a community sentence or fine, and s. 153(2) stating that the custodial sentence should be 'for the shortest term . . . commensurate with the seriousness of the offence'.

This ambiguity makes it difficult to predict how, if at all, the 2003 Act will affect the approach to sentencing. The three words, 'if at all', are interposed because much depends on whether counsel base their arguments on the precise words of ss. 143(1), 147(1), 152(2) and 153(2), and how the Court of Appeal responds to such arguments. Unfortunately, the history of similar statutory provisions in the 1991 Act does not give grounds for optimism. Within two months of that Act's implementation, the Court of Appeal, led by the then Lord Chief Justice, handed down its judgment in *Cunningham* (1993).[167] The offender had been sentenced to four years' imprisonment for robbery, and in sentencing him the judge had said that 'others who might be tempted to follow your example must realize that a long deterrent sentence will follow'. Counsel submitted that deterrence was

---

164 Halliday (2001), para. 2.8.   165 Home Office (2002), paras. 5.8–5.9.
166 SGC, *Overarching Principles: Seriousness* (2004), discussed in part 3.1 above.
167 (1993) 14 Cr App R (S) 444.

no longer a legitimate consideration in sentencing under the 1991 Act. The 1990 White Paper came close to declaring this: it did not actually do so, but it is clear that disproportionate sentences based on general deterrence would rarely, if ever, be justified.[168] If that was read in conjunction with the wording of the relevant provision – the sentence 'shall be for such term . . . as is commensurate with the seriousness of the offence' – one would have thought that the answer was clear. Lord Taylor CJ thought otherwise. The judges, long accustomed to citing deterrence as a reason for sentences, were unwilling to give this up in the face of a mere statute. Lord Taylor therefore interpreted s. 2(2)(a) of the 1991 Act as follows:

> The purposes of a custodial sentence must primarily be to punish and to deter. Accordingly, the phrase 'commensurate with the seriousness of the offence' must mean commensurate with the punishment and deterrence which the seriousness of the offence requires.[169]

This flagrant misreading of the statute opened the way for the judges to continue largely with 'business as usual', the different sentence lengths for crimes reflecting not the relative seriousness of those offences, but rather an ad hoc mixture of deterrent and proportionality considerations. The only exception recognized by Lord Taylor was that the provision did prohibit a judge from lengthening a sentence in order to make an example of a particular offender. The upshot was that deterrence remained a relevant factor in setting general sentence levels, but it did not justify a judge in going above those levels in particular cases in the hope of enhancing the general deterrent effect.

Even a cursory glance at recent appellate judgments shows how frequently deterrence has continued to be cited as the rationale for a particular sentence.[170] Is Lord Taylor's construction of the phrase 'commensurate with the seriousness of the offence' in the 1991 Act to be carried over to the same phrase in s. 153(2) of the 2003 Act? Or will an abrupt change of direction be apparent in the months after the implementation of this part of the 2003 Act? The Sentencing Guidelines Council has expressed its preference for proportionality as the primary rationale for sentencing, but how will its guideline fare against the ingrained habits of the judiciary at all levels? This cannot be dismissed as a minor matter, given the frequency with which judges and the Court of Appeal support sentences by reference to general deterrence.[171] Moreover, it is not a point on which senior judges have been consistent. It will be recalled that Lord Taylor, who gave the pro-deterrence

---

168 Home Office (1990), para. 2.8; quotation in the text at n. 42 above.
169 (1993) 14 Cr App R (S) 444 at p. 447.
170 For four recent examples, from many, see Lord Woolf's judgment in the 'mobile phones' case of *Attorney General's References Nos. 4 and 7 of 2002, and Q* [2002] 2 Cr App R (S) 345; *Jarrett* [2003] 1 Cr App R (S) at p. 159; *Attorney General's Reference* [2003] 2 Cr App R (S) 55, at [8]; and *Omari* [2004] 2 Cr App R (S) 514.
171 It could be argued, however, that references to deterrence are simply the expression of aspirations, and do not imply that the court has passed a sentence above that which would be proportionate to the offence. That would have to be tested by research.

judgment in *Cunningham*, was a vociferous opponent of the then Home Secretary's assumption that the minimum sentences in the 1997 Act would act as deterrents. Lord Taylor argued that fear of detection is far more important than fear of the punishment in most cases, and that the evidence was that the government's strategy 'will not work'.[172] Is there any reason to suppose that the evidence would be more promising in respect of the deterrent sentences imposed by the judiciary?

Since the argument here is that the judiciary has long been attached to the idea of deterrent sentencing, it is apposite to raise questions about a related judicial favourite – the prevalence of the offence. Lord Taylor also discussed the idea of prevalence in his judgment in *Cunningham*, but here his approach was more circumspect. He did not support prevalence as a reason for increasing a sentence, except in situations where the prevalence of a type of offence creates fear in the community.[173] Over the years there has been evidence of courts regarding the prevalence of an offence as a general reason for increasing sentence levels for it, but that is open to at least two major objections – there is often no firm evidence of prevalence, and if prevalence really were a key factor in sentencing, this would have the absurd consequence that theft from shops (and even illegal parking) would be projected sharply up the tariff.[174] The Sentencing Guidelines Council has sought to lay down guidance on the use of the concept of prevalence to increase a sentence. In general, it states that sentences should not be increased on account of beliefs about the prevalence of a particular type of offence. But in 'exceptional local circumstances', and where there is 'supporting evidence from an external source' about the offence's prevalence, a court may impose a higher sentence than is proportionate to the seriousness of the offence. However, this would be 'exceptional', and 'sentencers must sentence within the sentencing guidelines once the prevalence has been addressed'.[175] This is a strong and restrictive guideline. Its effectiveness will depend on the success of the guidelines in overcoming a judicial culture that includes long-standing attachment to the importance of prevalence.

---

172 Taylor (1996), quoted more fully in ch. 2.1 above.
173 (1993) 14 Cr App R (S) 444, at p. 448.
174 A fine judgment by Lloyd LJ in the Court of Appeal in *Masagh* (1990) 12 Cr App R (S) 568 spelt out these objections very clearly, but sadly it appears not to have lessened judicial references to the concept.
175 SGC, *Overarching Principles: Seriousness* (2004), paras. 1.38–1.39.

CHAPTER 4

Elements of proportionality

This chapter explores the practical application of the proportionality principle in English sentencing. After examining the relevant provisions of the Criminal Justice Act 2003, we begin an exploration of the concept of proportionality in practice and in theory. Part 2 considers people's opinions about the relative seriousness of different offences, and part 3 discusses a possible theoretical framework for determining questions of offence-seriousness. Part 4 relates this framework to a selection of English offences, taking account of Court of Appeal decisions and of past sentencing practice. In part 5 we consider the variations in culpability, and part 6 draws in some perspectives on proportionality from European Community law and from European human rights law. Part 7 presents some provisional conclusions on the elements of proportionality.

4.1 The proportionality principle

In 1990 the Home Office left no doubt that the intention behind the reforms which became the Criminal Justice Act 1991 was to introduce 'a new legislative framework for sentencing, based on the seriousness of the offence or just deserts'.[1] Arguing that both rehabilitation and deterrence have drawbacks as purposes of sentencing, the White Paper asserted that

> If the punishment is just, and in proportion to the seriousness of the offence, then the victim, the victim's family and friends, and the public will be satisfied that the law has been upheld and there will be no desire for further retaliation or private revenge.[2]

As noted in Chapter 3.5 above, the 1991 Act failed to convey this message clearly, and led to some confusion. In the Criminal Justice Act 2003 the sources of confusion are much more plain to see, because, as noted in the previous chapter, s. 142 sets out five conflicting purposes of sentencing to which courts 'must have regard'.

However, other provisions of the 2003 Act appear to insist on proportionality of sentence to the seriousness of the offence. Thus s. 143(1) states that 'in considering the seriousness of any offence, the court must consider the offender's culpability in

---

1 Home Office (1990), para. 2.3.   2 Home Office (1990), para. 2.4.

committing the offence and any harm which the offence caused, was intended to cause or might forseeably have caused'. That leads on to the question of when, under the 2003 Act, seriousness is a relevant matter. The answer is that it is relevant to three vital threshold decisions. First, s. 148(1) states that a community sentence must not be passed unless the offence 'was serious enough to warrant such a sentence'. Second, s. 152(2) states that a court must not pass a custodial sentence unless the offence 'was so serious that neither a fine alone nor a community sentence can be justified for the offence'. This formulation requires a court to relate its assessment of the seriousness of the offence to the possible penalty of a fine or community sentence. And third, s. 153(2) states that, when a court does impose custody, the sentence 'must be for the shortest term that in the opinion of the court is commensurate with the seriousness of the offence'.

In part 5 of the previous chapter, we discussed the probable interpretation and impact of all these provisions. The general principles set out by the Sentencing Guidelines Council confirm that the proportionality principle is expected to play a major role in sentencing under the 2003 Act.[3] The question for the remainder of this chapter is how it should be decided which offences are more serious and which are less serious than others. How can a scale of ordinal proportionality be constructed? Some US systems have approached this by constructing sentencing 'grids', which classify offences into various groups and then assign guideline sentences to them, leaving the courts with more or less discretion.[4] In Finland, Article 6 of the Penal Code provides simply that 'punishment shall be measured so that it is in just proportion to the damage and danger caused by the offence and to the guilt of the offender manifested in the offence'.[5] Chapter 29 of the Swedish Criminal Code, introduced in 1989, provides that sentences should be based on the penal value of the offence: 'The penal value is determined with special regard to the harm, offence or risk which the conduct involved, what the accused realized or should have realized about it, and the intentions and motives of the accused.'[6]

Apart from s. 143(1), mentioned above, the 2003 Act in England and Wales contains no elaboration of the term 'seriousness of the offence'. One possible problem is the structure of the criminal law. Some English offences are relatively narrow in the conduct they specify (e.g. murder and rape, although it is possible to distinguish degrees of each offence). Many other offences cover broad areas of conduct without legal differentiation: robbery can involve anything from a push to snatch a purse to an armed hold-up of a bank, and the offence of theft has no subdivisions at all according to the value of the property or the circumstances of the offender. It follows from this that consideration of offence-seriousness sometimes becomes difficult to separate from a consideration of aggravating and mitigating factors. However, we shall devote Chapter 5 to the latter issue, and focus as far as possible on offence-seriousness itself here. The first task is to discover whether there are any

3 SGC, *Overarching Principles: Seriousness* (2004).   4 See Tonry (1996), chs. 2 and 3.
5 Lappi-Seppala (2001).   6 Jareborg (1995).

shared opinions on the relative seriousness of offence. The next task is to examine the problem from the point of view of a theory which can be put into practice.

4.2 Opinions about offence-seriousness

Opinion surveys have been conducted several times in different countries in attempts to ascertain public views on the relative seriousness of offences. It is not proposed to discuss all of them here, even though some have achieved considerable sophistication.[7] The origin of modern surveys is the scale devised by Sellin and Wolfgang in 1964, which has been claimed to produce similar rankings when applied to subjects with different occupations and social standing and to subjects in different countries.[8] We might focus on the results of the application of an improved version of their methodology to 500 citizens of London by Sparks, Genn and Dodd in the 1970s.[9] The results are presented in Table 9. The authors remarked that in general the ranking was 'agreeably rational' and that there was, as most other researchers have found, 'a broad concordance between the mean scores given by our sample' and the legal maxima.[10]

The generality of this kind of survey raises difficulties if the results are used as a touchstone of relative gravity. These surveys are usually based on very brief descriptions of different types of offence, and no steps are taken to examine the network of assumptions and beliefs which underlie the way in which subjects approach the task of ranking. For example, the authors lamented that the sale of marijuana to a 15-year-old received a higher average score than rape, remarking that this might have 'resulted from a general ignorance among our sample as to the nature of marijuana'.[11] One might add that it may also have suggested a general ignorance about the physical and psychological impact of rape at that time. Is it not possible that other answers were based on other ill-founded, popular assumptions? Could it not be said that the relatively low ranking of burglaries neglected the profound psychological effects which many burglaries have upon their victims?

This particular survey also ignored the difference between premeditated or planned offences and sudden or impulsive offences. There is a strong argument for saying that these differences in culpability exert a powerful effect both on sentencing practice and on people's judgments of crimes. Surveys which leave out this dimension are not only omitting a crucial element in the judgments but are also leaving that factor roaming 'loose', so it might enter into the assessments of different subjects in different ways. A survey by Leslie Sebba attempted to take account of the culpability dimension. He found not only that people's views of seriousness do differ according to the mental element specified, but also that when no mental element is specified they tend to regard the offence as intentional unless it is a 'regulatory'

7 For a recent summary see Roberts and Stalans (1997), ch. 4.
8 Cf. Roberts and Stalans (1997) with the Introduction to Sellin and Wolfgang (1978).
9 Sparks, Genn and Dodd (1977).   10 Sparks, Genn and Dodd (1977), p. 185.
11 Sparks, Genn and Dodd (1977), p. 185.

Table 9. *Citizens' assessments of relative seriousness of crimes*

Offence ranked by seriousness	Mean score	Standard deviation	Rank of mean score
Attack with blunt weapon causing death	10.67	0.90	1
Attack with knife causing death	10.64	1.01	2
Rape and beating, serious injuries	10.12	1.15	3
Attack with knife, serious injuries	9.52	1.51	4
Rape, no other injuries inflicted	8.98	2.03	6
Assault on police officer – serious injury	8.84	2.01	8
Attack, blunt weapon – minor injury	8.02	2.06	10
Assault on police officer – minor injury	7.79	2.32	12
Attack with fists – minor injury	6.71	2.37	18
Robbery of £25 + serious injury	8.96	1.81	7
Robbery of £25 + minor injuries	8.00	2.09	11
Robbery of £25 with no injuries	7.34	2.21	15
Burglary + assault, nothing stolen	7.53	2.17	13
Burglary + theft of £10 cash	5.42	2.60	27
Burglary + theft of £10 in property	5.35	2.49	29
Burglary – nothing taken	5.03	2.45	30
Obtaining £1,000 by fraud	7.37	2.72	14
Obtaining £100 by forged cheques	6.60	2.66	19
Embezzlement of £100	6.57	2.65	20
Theft of £100 property from car	6.49	2.47	21
Theft of £100 materials from work	6.25	2.53	22
Theft of £10 from wallet	6.10	2.61	23
Theft of £10 by employee from shop till	5.40	2.65	28
Theft of £10 property from car	4.95	2.36	31
Theft of £10 materials from work	4.91	2.55	32
Theft of goods worth £10 from shop	4.83	2.47	33
Reckless driving causing injury	8.58	2.02	9
Reckless driving £100 property damage	6.83	2.46	17
Sale of marijuana to person aged 15	9.13	2.41	5
Sale of marijuana to adult	7.08	3.45	16
Causing £50 damage to private property	6.04	2.53	24
Causing £50 damage to public property	5.47	2.51	26
Buying property known to be stolen	5.73	2.95	25

Source: Sparks, Genn and Dodd (1977), p. 184.

offence, where they tend to assume negligence only.[12] However, Sebba's survey was confined to the traditional legal categories of intention, recklessness and so on, and did not go further into possible differences between planned and impulsive crimes.[13]

To what extent do people from different backgrounds have different opinions? Analysis by Ken Pease of material from the 1984 *British Crime Survey*, which produced results fairly similar to those of Sparks, Genn and Dodd, showed that there were no significant differences according to the social class of the person questioned, and that victims tended not to rate offences as more serious than non-victims. Pease found that older people and women tended to regard all crimes as somewhat more serious than younger people and men.[14] Other international studies suggest that people with less formal education and living in smaller communities tend to regard all crimes as more serious.[15] All of this suggests that further research is needed to improve our knowledge of these factors.

Even then, the attitudes that are being measured may often be based on false beliefs, for it is well established that many members of the public have imperfect knowledge about the prevalence of crime, its effects on victims, and the level of sentences typically imposed by the courts.[16] Yet there must be explanations for the changes that have apparently taken place in the seriousness ranking of certain offences in recent years. Some offences have come to be regarded in a much more serious light. One is rape: greater publicity about the effects of rape, with research findings documenting this, have resulted in the police and the courts treating the offence as more serious.[17] Another such crime is causing death by dangerous driving: at one time this was treated as a 'mere' motoring offence, but increasing realization of the loss and devastation resulting and of the avoidability of such offences has led to public concern (to which the courts have responded by increasing levels of sentence).[18] On the other hand, some offences have come to be regarded as less serious. Social security frauds might fall into this category – in the early 1980s they were often regarded as particularly serious offences warranting custodial sentences, but attention was drawn to the low sums of money sometimes involved and to the comparatively lenient (indeed, usually non-criminal) treatment of tax frauds, and in 1986 the Court of Appeal called for a reduction in sentence levels for social security frauds without aggravating features, on the ground that they are non-violent, non-sexual and non-frightening.[19]

4.3 Developing parameters of ordinal proportionality

These examples of changes in the perceived seriousness of certain offences contain signposts to the difficulties ahead. The seriousness of rape may stem from the

---

12 Sebba (1980); see also Roberts and Stalans (1997), pp. 61–2.
13 See below, part 4.5.   14 Pease (1988).   15 Roberts and Stalans (1997), pp. 67–8.
16 Hough and Roberts (1998), ch. 2.   17 See part 4.4.7 below.   18 See part 4.4.4 below.
19 *Stewart* (1987) 9 Cr App R (S) 135; cf. the research by Cook (1989).

psychological as much as from the physical impact of the offence, and a scale of proportionality must take account of that. The same may be said of burglary, ostensibly an offence against property but which may have severe emotional effects. Causing death by dangerous driving is a homicide offence and therefore quite high on any scale. It is an offence of lesser culpability than murder or some forms of manslaughter, but how much should its seriousness be discounted from those crimes? There must be some way of comparing such offences with deliberate woundings and other non-fatal harms. Insider trading has no individual victim: it is a violation of the principles of the financial markets which may bring great profit to the offender without significant loss to any one individual (although perhaps loss of confidence in the market generally). Should the scale take account of profit gained, as an alternative to loss caused? Could the two be incorporated into a single scale? The same applies to social security frauds: it is more a question of gaining unfair financial advantage than causing specific losses.

The foremost modern attempt to establish some parameters for ordinal proportionality is that of Andrew von Hirsch and Nils Jareborg (1991).[20] Their approach, which deals only with crimes against individual victims, is to determine the effect of the typical case of particular crimes on the living standard of victims. The first question to be asked is what interests are violated or threatened by the standard case of the crime, and they identify four generic interests:

(i) physical integrity: health, safety and the avoidance of physical pain;
(ii) material support and amenity: includes nutrition, shelter and other basic amenities;
(iii) freedom from humiliation or degrading treatment; and
(iv) privacy and autonomy.

Additions could be made to this list, but their concern is to focus on paradigm cases of crimes with individual victims. They take the standard case in order to enhance the simplicity of the basic framework and in the knowledge that any non-standard features of the particular case can be taken into account when determining the offender's culpability and its effect on seriousness (did he know that the victim was elderly?), and when quantifying any compensation payable to the victim.

Once the nature of the interest(s) violated has been settled, the second step is to assess the effect of violating those interests on the living standards of the typical victim. These effects are banded into four levels:

(i) subsistence: survival with maintenance of elementary human functions – no satisfactions presupposed at this level;
(ii) minimal well-being: maintenance of a minimal level of comfort and dignity;
(iii) adequate well-being: maintenance of an 'adequate' level of comfort and dignity; and
(iv) significant enhancement: significant enhancement in quality of life above the merely adequate level.

20 For a recently revised version see von Hirsch. and Ashworth (2005), Appendix A.

The differences between the four levels are couched in fairly general terms, such as 'adequate' and 'significant', but this is inevitable if the search is for general principles. The scale is to be applied to the offence and the harm which it penalizes, and one of its advantages should be to cut through the conventions which result in 'traditional' crimes such as wounding being regarded as naturally more serious than 'modern' crimes such as dangerous driving or the maintenance of unsafe working conditions. The scale does not itself yield an index of ordinal proportionality, but deals with one crucial step in that direction.

Thus the violation of a protected interest is one key component of offence-seriousness, often expressed as harm or harmfulness but also including the concept of a wrong, since it is not merely the physical or psychological consequences but also the nature of the wrong done to a victim that is relevant in assessing seriousness.[21] A further step is to integrate into the calculation a judgment of culpability, which in some instances may have a considerable effect on the ultimate ranking of an offence. For example, manslaughter is usually thought to be a serious offence, and the harm involved is death, which ranks as a level (i) interest. But if the culpability involved is no more than the culpability for an ordinary assault (which is sufficient in English law), one might expect that form of manslaughter to appear much lower down the scale than most other homicides. In terms of culpability, therefore, one question is the degree of purpose and awareness which the offender had – usually interpreted in English law as intention, knowledge, recklessness or mere negligence – and another question is the magnitude of the harm or wrong to which that mental element related. If the offender intended an assault but caused a death, one should not treat it as an intentional causing of death.

A further component, in addition to culpability, is the remoteness of the offence from the occurrence of the harm. The law contains several offences which do not require the actual infliction of the harm concerned, such as offences of attempt (e.g. attempted robbery, attempted rape), offences of endangerment and risk-creation (e.g. dangerous driving, drunk driving, unsafe working conditions), and protective or preparatory offences (e.g. possession of an offensive weapon or of equipment for counterfeiting). A scale of offence-seriousness should discount the level of particular offences according to their remoteness from the resulting harm, but the extent of that discounting is likely to be a matter of controversy. There are some who attribute great significance to the occurrence of the harm, and who would correspondingly make a considerable reduction in the level of seriousness if the crime consisted merely of an abortive attempt, or an unrealized risk, or possession without offensive use. On the other hand, there are those who would judge the offender primarily on what he or she believed would or might happen, and would make only a small distinction according to whether the harm actually resulted or not.[22]

21 For an elaboration of this distinction in the context of rape, see Gardner and Shute (2000).
22 For discussion and further references see Ashworth (2003a), pp. 158–61.

The discussion so far has identified four main stages in the process of assessing offence-seriousness, following the von Hirsch-Jareborg principles. At the first stage it is a question of determining the interests violated. At the second stage there is a preliminary quantification of the effect of a typical case on a victim's living standards. At the third stage account is taken of the culpability of the offender. And at the fourth stage there may be a reduction in the level of seriousness to reflect the remoteness of the actual harm. The authors themselves demonstrate the application of their principles to a range of crimes, and show how effect might be given to the four stages by devising a harm scale. Once the second stage has been reached, there is a need to transfer those quantifications of effect on living standards on to some kind of harm scale. The authors recognize that this could be a more or less elaborate scale. It might, for example, be a 100-point numerical scale, but they reject this as evincing a 'misleading sense of precision'[23] and prefer a scale with five broad bands, each of them containing room for further differentiations of degree. Thus, the causing of a serious injury might be valued at level (ii) in terms of its effect on a typical victim's living standard, since it leaves the victim only with a minimal level of comfort and dignity; this might correspond to level (ii) on the harm scale, but it might then be reduced because the offender was merely reckless, or because the offence was merely an attempt.

Let us take stock of the argument so far. The previous paragraph has represented the von Hirsch-Jareborg principles in terms of four stages in gauging the seriousness of harms. One criticism might be that the parameters are vague and indefinitely expressed, with the result that they will allow room for inconsistencies in outcome between different people using the same scale. This should be conceded, but is it truly a criticism? Does it not presuppose that it is possible to devise a scale which has great numerical precision, and yet which is sufficiently sensitive to the different combinations of facts? Surely the best that can be hoped for is a uniform approach which establishes a common methodology for determining these awkward questions. Another criticism might be that the principles are far too complex to be of practical use. This should not be conceded, for much of the authors' enterprise has been to formalize the intellectual processes which sometimes take place, albeit impressionistically and even inconsistently, in the minds of those who have to decide these questions. In the English system, these are primarily questions for legislators when setting the maximum penalty for a new offence. When judges have to pass sentence for a new or unusual crime, they may also tend to follow some such course of reasoning. The alternative method is to reason by analogy, but the analogies are not always available and in any event presuppose a framework of this general type.

A more searching question is whether the authors' self-imposed restriction to crimes with individual victims does not impair the utility of their scheme. It is understandable that they should wish to construct some principles on firm ground before moving to the more intractable areas, but in the context of a pressing need

---

23 Von Hirsch. and Jareborg (1991), p. 28.

to develop parameters of proportionality for English sentencing some additions and adaptations must be made. For example, the crime of theft covers a wide range of different situations, some involving individual victims and some not. Of those which do involve individual victims, some contain elements which have a wider significance. An example might be a theft in breach of trust, in which a solicitor misappropriates a client's funds. It is not just the effect on the typical victim's standard of living which determines the seriousness of the offence, but also the breach of trust by a solicitor on whom citizens tend to rely. This may be seen as a 'public' element in a crime with an individual victim. Nor can this be convincingly put aside as an aggravating feature rather than an integral feature of the crime, for it is questionable whether there is any such clear dividing line. Different legal systems incorporate different elements into the definitions of their crimes.

Moreover, many thefts are takings from companies. It would not seem fruitful to explore the 'living standards' of companies, because the effect of one particular theft on a corporate economy may not be large. The controversial question is whether the negligible effect on the victim makes the crime less serious, or whether it would not be better to focus on the gain to the offender. There is, perhaps, an argument for saying that, in general, it is slightly less serious to steal from a company than from an individual, because the offence is likely to have less of an impact on the victim, possibly because the company may be said to have facilitated the offence through its method of trading. (Clearly there are exceptions, in the shape of individual millionaires and of small businesses with few reserves, but we are concerned with the typical case.) Is there any reason why a person who steals £10,000 from the company which employs him should be judged by the effect of that theft on the typical company, without any comparison of the seriousness of appropriating £10,000 from a non-corporate source? Surely it is at least relevant that the offender is £10,000 richer, whereas the person who steals smaller amounts from individual victims has gained far less. This chain of reasoning suggests that, at the second stage of the von Hirsch-Jareborg principles, it would be proper to introduce the notion of 'benefit to the living standard of the typical offender' as an alternative to the impact on the living standard of the typical victim. The receipt of £10,000 would significantly enhance the living standards of most people, and this suggests that an offence involving such a gain should be placed high in the fourth category – perhaps at level (iv) or (iii) of the seriousness scale, before culpability and mitigation are taken into account.

This modification might also have some utility for thefts of public property. There is no sense in exploring the living standard of the state: it is far more appropriate to consider the gain to the offender, in terms of the benefit to the typical person of receiving that amount. However, whereas most offences against companies are economic crimes which can be expressed in terms of gain to the offender, some offences against the state have no economic element at all. Perjury is regarded as an offence against the administration of justice (although it can have consequences for the liberty of an individual victim in some cases). Is there any way of integrating offences such as perjury into the four generic interests described by von Hirsch and Jareborg? They do not claim that their list is complete, and it is confined to crimes with individual victims. It is difficult to imagine how one could add a single generic interest to take care of all offences against the state, since they range from espionage down to failures to complete returns for statistical and other purposes. Treason and espionage might threaten the very foundations of the state, and might therefore be placed close to murder at the top of any scale, but it is less easy to see how perjury could be accommodated other than by introducing a generic interest to cater explicitly for offences against the administration of justice. That merely postpones the problem to the next stage – how can it be incorporated into a living standard scale? Neither loss nor gain applies in most such cases.

How might a modified version of the von Hirsch-Jareborg scheme be presented? It could be characterized as a decision sequence along the following lines, and applicable to any conduct prohibited by the criminal law:

(i) four or more harm dimensions: physical integrity; material support and amenity; freedom from humiliation; privacy/autonomy; integrity of the administration of justice;
(ii) living standard impact or benefit in the typical case: subsistence; minimal well-being; adequate well-being; enhanced well-being;
(iii) map on to a seriousness scale of, for example, five levels;
(iv) culpability: planned, impulsive, knowing, reckless, negligent and so on; adjust level on seriousness scale accordingly;
(v) remoteness: completed, attempted, risked, preliminary or preventive offence; degree of involvement or participation in the offence; adjust level on seriousness scale accordingly;
(vi) aggravation and mitigation: assess the various factors, and adjust the level on seriousness scale accordingly; and
(vii) transfer from seriousness scale to commensurate sentence.

Little has been said about the final step in this sequence, and yet we have seen that several threshold decisions under the 2003 Act require this. The discussion thus far has concentrated on issues of relative seriousness as between offences (ordinal proportionality). How can the sentence be commensurate with the relative seriousness of the offence?

It is tempting to answer that it cannot.[24] The seriousness of offences forms one scale, and the severity of punishments another. There is no natural or inevitable relationship between them: the relationship can only be conventional and symbolic.[25] If there is a shared desire to alter the conventions, a change can be brought about: Dutch judges and prosecutors lowered their sentencing levels in the early 1950s,[26]

---

24 Walker (1991), ch. 12.
25 Lacey (1988), pp. 20–1; cf. her later acceptance that 'proportionality to socially acknowledged gravity could serve a useful function in underlining community values', even if other functions would also be important (p. 194).
26 Downes (1988).

and English juvenile courts did so in the 1980s,[27] whereas English courts in the 1990s raised their sentencing levels.[28] Despite this conventional or symbolic element, it can be argued that certain punishments would be excessive for certain crimes. If, for example, three years' imprisonment were the norm for theft from a shop, one could argue that this is not commensurate. The foundations for the argument would have to be located in loose notions of equivalence which are unspecific in their central zones but which contain outer limits. It is not a *lex talionis*, which assumes a 'natural' equivalence between crime and punishment, but a looser formula which excludes punishments which impose far greater hardships on the offender than does the crime on victims and society in general. Thus, one might argue that because a particular shop theft causes only minor loss to the shop and only a minor gain to the offender, it cannot possibly justify the loss of a person's liberty for as long as three years. Into that argument must go some propositions about the use of custody, such as the policy of restraint (stated in Chapter 3.3.2 above). By this means it might be possible to argue that there is such a thing as utter disproportionality, even if there is no such thing as absolute proportionality.

Within those outer limits, however, conventional modes of thought have tended to play a major part, together with the influence of the media and of politicians. Lord Bingham CJ acknowledged this strong political element:

> From 1987 to 1992 the use of custody generally declined, probably in response to legislation, ministerial speeches and the White Paper on 'Crime, Justice and Protecting the Public'. Since 1993 the use of custody has increased very sharply, in response (it would seem likely) to certain highly publicized crimes, legislation, ministerial speeches and intense media pressure.[29]

Detailed analysis of the issues of lengths of custody or degrees of restriction on liberty in the community will be left over to Chapters 9 and 10, where the specific policies bearing on them will be discussed. But there remain difficult questions about the numerical representation of differentials between offences and about the calibration of the punishment scale.

Catherine Fitzmaurice and Ken Pease (1986) have raised various questions about this neglected aspect of sentencing. If it is decided that one offence is twice as serious as another, does it follow that it should attract double the penalty? Hypothetical exercises conducted with three judges suggested that there may be differences in the way in which incremental seriousness is reflected, with some judges having a steep and others a shallow slope.[30] There is no absolute reason why twice the seriousness should lead to double the sentence, especially when the experienced severity of a sentence might itself increase more steeply as months and years are added on. Thus, criminological knowledge about the typical impact of sentences might be relevant to devising both a sentence severity scale and a ratio of commensurability.

---

27 See ch. 12.7 below.   28 As seen in ch. 1.3 above.
29 *Brewster* [1998] 1 Cr App R (S) 181, at p. 184.   30 Fitzmaurice and Pease (1986), p. 87.

On the other hand, one might promote a scale which shows a degree of tolerance of minor crimes and a marked abhorrence of very serious crimes: the reasoning here would be that a typical rape is not twice as serious as the typical house burglary, but four times as serious. This would produce a ratio of commensurability which might be represented by a stepped upward curve: many minor crimes would receive minor penalties; in the middle range of crimes the increases in sentence severity are normal; but, for the most serious crimes, sentence severity increases steeply. This approximates to the twin-track or bifurcated policy, often associated with treating serious and violent crime severely while lowering the scale of response to most property crime. Whether this is truly an aspect of proportionality or rather a pragmatic compromise to appease the media by scapegoating certain offenders is a matter for debate.

This leads us to the calibration of the scale of punishment severity. How should the differentials between offences of varying seriousness be marked? It is well known that in nineteenth-century England the tendency had been to pass custodial sentences of the lengths previously used as periods of transportation. Parliament tended to create maximum penalties by using the 'seven times table' – indeed, many offences still have maxima of 7 or 14 years – and the courts followed.[31] No less a figure than the 'supreme commander of the Victorian prison system', Sir Edmund du Cane, a man 'identified with stern discipline, rigidity . . . and faith in the deterrent force of penal discipline',[32] questioned whether these old conventions were not resulting in the infliction of unnecessary suffering. A further challenge came from the scientist Sir Francis Galton in 1895, in an article which showed how shorter sentences tended to cluster round three, six, nine and twelve months, and how longer sentences tended to be rounded into years, with even larger gaps in the upper echelons. Galton argued that 'runs of figures like these testify to some powerful cause of disturbance which interferes with the orderly distribution of punishment in conformity with penal deserts'.[33] Those remarks are no less apposite today. The courts have 'preferred numbers', and there is no reason of principle why a completely different mode of calibration could not be chosen. When a court wishes to make a 'just noticeable difference' from a six-month sentence, the tendency is to give nine months – not seven or eight. When it wishes to signal a 'just noticeable difference' from a sentence of eight years' imprisonment, it may go to ten years instead of nine. These are preferred numbers, and their use 'probably protects sentencers from thinking about what a sentence means in practice'.[34]

Could a wholly different set of conventions be selected? It has been argued for a long time that one approach would be to express all terms of custody under one year in weeks, and those above one year in months. Sentencers could be urged to use decimal rather than duodecimal scales. And, more especially, courts could

---

31 See Thomas (1978) and Advisory Council on the Penal System (1978), paras. 36–66 and Appendix K.
32 The quotations are taken from Radzinowicz and Hood (1986), p. 747.
33 See Fitzmaurice and Pease (1986), pp. 103–4.   34 Fitzmaurice and Pease (1986), p. 113.

be urged to make fuller use of intermediate points. One way of achieving this is to demonstrate the difference between adding one month and three months to a six-month sentence: that difference would (with conditional release) amount to some 30 days and nights longer incarcerated. Could not the relativity which the court wishes to mark be achieved by a further 15 or 20 days and nights? A step in this direction has been taken by the 2003 Act: s. 181 states that the term of a prison sentence of less than 12 months 'must be expressed in weeks', and the whole of its configuration is calculated by reference to weeks.[35] Does this amount to belated statutory recognition that numbers have consequences, and conventions can produce extra pain, as du Cane and Galton showed a hundred years ago? Perhaps this can be heralded as a step towards restraint in the use of custody, a principle that behoves us to re-examine conventional elements in sentencing rather than to assume that the espousal of proportionality cloaks them with respectability.

4.4 Offence-seriousness in practice

This examination of some of the problems of establishing a scale of ordinal proportionality and relating it to sentence severity has left us with few clear prescriptions, but it has raised many questions about current practices. The only committee of inquiry into English sentence levels in recent years, the Advisory Council on the Penal System (1978), concentrated on levels of imprisonment without much discussion of relativities between offences. Judicial decision-making is an unlikely context for a general discussion of the overall sentencing structure, but in *Turner* (1975)[36] Lawton LJ did deliver some general remarks on this subject. The problem with which the Court of Appeal had to grapple was the proper level of sentences for serious armed robberies. Lawton LJ decided that this could only be approached by considering the normal sentence for murder, and then relating sentences for other serious crimes to it. So he began with the rough calculation that a case of murder without mitigating circumstances would probably result in the offender serving 15 years in prison. This represented a determinate prison sentence of $22\frac{1}{2}$ years, less the one-third remission which was deducted at that time. Since 'it is not in the public interest that even for grave crimes, sentences should be passed which do not correlate sensibly and fairly' with the sentence for murder, it followed that the sentences for other crimes of high seriousness should be ranged beneath 22 years. Lawton LJ went on to describe a group of 'wholly abnormal' crimes, including 'bomb outrages, acts of political terrorism and possibly in future acts of political kidnapping', which should be placed on the next rung of the ladder, beneath the notional sentence for murder. No figure was set, but other decisions suggest that the range from 20 to 22 years was thought appropriate.[37] Beneath this group there

---

35 For detailed discussion see ch. 9.4.4 below.   36 (1975) 61 Cr App R 67, at pp. 89–91.
37 E.g. *Termine* (1977) 64 Cr App R 299, where a sentence of 21 years was upheld for a siege with guns in which hostages were taken and political demands made.

are crimes which are 'very grave and all too frequent', such as armed robberies of banks. For these the starting point was held to be 15 years, going up to 18 years for two such robberies.

More will be said about robbery sentences below. The merit of Sir Frederick Lawton's judgment is that it stands as a rare judicial attempt to reflect on the logic of the sentencing structure. Even though there have been major changes to the sentencing structure since 1975 – notably, remission on prison sentences has been abolished, and the effective period of detention of many murderers has lengthened – there has been no fundamental rethinking of the *Turner* approach. On a few occasions sentences longer than 22 years have been upheld for non-homicide offences, but it is possible to reconcile them with the *Turner* logic. For example, in *Al-Banna* (1984)[38] sentences of 30 and 35 years were upheld on men who had attempted to assassinate the Israeli ambassador to the United Kingdom, wounding him severely in the process. The appeal was argued on the basis that, had the attempt succeeded, the men would only have been subject to recommendations to serve a minimum of 20 years for murder. The Court of Appeal dismissed this argument, saying that minimum recommendations of 30 to 35 years would have been appropriate for a political assassination. In terms of the *Turner* logic, this case is treated as equivalent to an aggravated murder, and no discount is apparently given for the fact that it was a mere attempt rather than the completed crime. An even longer sentence was upheld in *Hindawi* (1988).[39] The offender had placed a bomb in a bag carried by his pregnant girlfriend, who was about to embark on an aircraft carrying some 370 people. The bomb was timed to explode when the aircraft was in mid-flight, but was discovered at the airport. For the offence of attempting to place on an aircraft an explosive device likely to destroy or damage the aircraft, Hindawi was sentenced to 45 years. Stating that 'it is no thanks to this applicant that his plot did not succeed in destroying 360 or 370 lives', the Court of Appeal upheld the sentence as 'not a day too long'. Once again, the case appears to be treated as an attempted murder of hundreds of people: there is no apparent discount for the fact that the offence was merely an attempt, and the numbers involved aggravate the offence considerably. More difficult to reconcile is *K.* (2003),[40] where the Court of Appeal upheld a sentence of 26 years for conspiracy to import heroin in a case where 44 kg of the drug had been found in the offender's possession. The Court accepted that 30 years was an appropriate starting point for the ringleader of such a conspiracy. It will be argued in part 4.4.5 below that such sentences are out of proportion to those for murder, rape and other very serious crimes.

The remainder of this part of the chapter is devoted to an examination of the sentence levels for selected crimes. This is a fit subject for a whole book, and therefore all that can be achieved here is to assess the broad relativities between certain crimes. Almost all the selected offences are regularly punished by imprisonment

38 (1984) 6 Cr App R (S) 426.   39 (1988) 10 Cr App R (S) 104.
40 [2003] 1 Cr App R (S) 22.

in England, and much more will be said in Chapter 9 about the use of custody. While it is important to remember that the numbers do represent years and months of deprivation of liberty, the focus of concern here is on the relativities and their justifications – on ordinal rather than cardinal proportionality.

4.4.1 Murder

The judgment in *Turner* was undoubtedly right to assign a central place to the sentence for murder when working out the sentencing structure. Since the Murder (Abolition of Death Penalty) Act 1969, the only sentence that a court may pass for murder is life imprisonment. The sentence for murder is divided into two portions: the first is now known as the minimum term (formerly, the tariff period), and is intended to reflect the relative gravity of the particular offence. It is a term that is served in full, and the early release provisions applicable to all determinate custodial sentences do not apply here. Once the minimum term expires, release is determined by considerations of public protection, and a murderer who is thought still to present a danger may be detained for many years longer.[41] Until recently the determination of both portions of the mandatory life sentence was a matter for the Home Secretary. He set the minimum term, having received the recommendation of the trial judge and the Lord Chief Justice on the matter. And he set the release date, having received the recommendation of the Parole Board.[42] In 1994 the European Court of Human Rights confirmed that this practice was compatible with Articles 5 and 6 of the Convention,[43] largely on the ground that murder is a special offence to which special considerations should apply, but the Court then began to move away from this approach. In 1999, in the well-known decision in *V and T v. United Kingdom*,[44] it held that the setting of the tariff period for a juvenile convicted of murder amounted to the fixing of a sentence and should therefore be carried out by an 'independent and impartial tribunal'. For the Home Secretary to do this was a breach of Article 6(1). The Court attempted to distinguish young offenders from adults, but it was only a matter of time before this fragile distinction collapsed. This occurred in *Stafford v. United Kingdom* (2002),[45] which removed the Home Secretary's right to determine release from the second part of the mandatory life sentence. It was not long before the English courts held, in *R. (on application of Anderson) v. Secretary of State for the Home Department* (2002),[46] that it was incompatible with Article 6 for the Home Secretary to set the minimum period in murder cases because he is not an 'independent and impartial tribunal'.

David Blunkett, the then Home Secretary, reacted angrily to this decision, inevitable though it was, and vowed to neutralize its effect through legislation.

---

41 See Cullen and Newell (1999).   42 See Padfield (2003), ch. 10.
43 *Wynne v. U.K.* (1994) 19 EHRR 333.   44 (1999) 30 EHRR 121.
45 (2002) 35 EHRR 1121.
46 [2003] 1 AC 837; see also *Lychniak and Pyrah* [2002] UKHL 47, and previous decisions such as *R. v. Secretary of State for the Home Department, ex p. Doody* [1994] 1 AC 531 and *R v. Secretary of State for the Home Department, ex p. Hindley* [2001] 1 AC 410.

Section 269 of the Criminal Justice Act 2003 essentially requires a court, when setting the minimum term to be served by a person convicted of murder, to have regard to the principles set out in Schedule 21 to the Act. The structure of that Schedule is to indicate three starting points:

- a whole life minimum term for exceptionally serious cases, such as premeditated killings of two or more people, sexual or sadistic child murders, or political murders;
- 30 years for particularly serious cases such as murders of police or prison officers, murders involving firearms, sexual or sadistic killings, or murders aggravated by racial or sexual orientation;
- 15 years for other murders not falling within either of the higher categories.

However, the language in Schedule 21 is not constraining. Although criteria are enumerated for the whole life and 30-year starting points, they are expressed as factors that would 'normally' indicate such a sentence. There is then provision for the court to take account of any further relevant factors, and an explicit statement that 'detailed consideration of aggravating and mitigating factors may result in a minimum term of any length (whatever the starting point)'. The Lord Chief Justice amended the previous guidance to reflect the 2003 provisions when he issued a Practice Direction in May 2004.[47] When he discussed the effect of the Schedule in *Sullivan* (2005),[48] he emphasized that s. 269(3) states that the judge must specify the minimum term that 'the court considers appropriate', and indeed went on to say that so long as the judge bore in mind the principles set out in Schedule 21, 'he is not bound to follow them' – although an explanation for departing from them should be given. Lord Woolf also emphasized that to compare the minimum term with a determinate sentence one should double it: in other words, a minimum term of 15 years is the equivalent of a determinate sentence of about 30 years.[49] He also drew attention to the inclusion in Schedule 21 of the discount for pleading guilty, although subsequent guidelines from the Sentencing Guidelines Council state that the discount in murder cases should be roughly half that for determinate sentences, in order to achieve a similar effect in practice.[50] Much of the judgment in *Sullivan* deals with the difficult technicalities in the transitional provisions, contained largely in Schedule 22 and relevant to those already serving sentences for murder.[51]

The justifications for having a mandatory penalty for murder remain controversial. The offence has variable degrees of seriousness, and can sometimes be less serious than a manslaughter. The mandatory sentence applies without any finding

47 *Practice Direction (Mandatory Life Sentences)*, May 2004.
48 [2005] 1 Cr App R (S) 308.
49 This is because a determinate sentence of 30 years means 15 years in prison (followed by 15 years on supervised licence: see ch. 9.5 below), whereas a minimum term for murder is not subject to the general provisions on early release and is served in full.
50 SGC, *Reduction in Sentence for a Guilty Plea* (2004), paras 6.1–6.5; see below, ch. 5.4.1.
51 See further Taylor, Wasik and Leng (2004), pp. 215–16. Any retrospectivity difficulties have been alleviated by the decision of the House of Lords in R. v. *Secretary of State for the Home Department, ex p. Uttley* [2004] UKHL 38.

of dangerousness,[52] and yet the two stages of the life sentence apply to all murderers. Previously the retentionist argument was that only the Home Secretary can protect the public from danger, an argument of doubtful force aside from political populism. Now that the Home Secretary's role has gone, sentences for murder should surely be put on the same footing as sentences for all other serious crimes. If the murderer fulfils the criteria for life imprisonment, on account of a finding of dangerousness, that will be the proper course.[53] In the absence of such a finding, the courts should impose determinate sentences.[54]

4.4.2 Attempted murder

We saw earlier, from the decisions in *Al-Banna* and *Hindawi*, that very high sentences can be passed in cases which are either charged as attempted murder or amount to that in fact. The culpability required for attempted murder is an intent to kill, which (paradoxically) is a higher degree of culpability than required for murder, where an intention to cause grievous bodily harm will suffice. Both those decisions adhere strongly to the view that the sentence should be based on the result intended by the offender, rather than the actual outcome of his efforts. This accords with the principle endorsed by the Sentencing Guidelines Council for cases where the harm is much less than intended: 'the culpability of the offender . . . should be the initial factor in determining the seriousness of an offence'.[55] However, it is more than possible that this point of principle was overshadowed in the judges' minds by the terrorist element in *Al-Banna* and *Hindawi*. If one looks at other decisions on attempted murder, one finds that cases which have no political or professional element and which occur in a 'domestic' setting have tended to receive sentences of around 10 to 12 years after a guilty plea – with *Gibson* (1997)[56] receiving ten years for trying to hold his wife hostage and then stabbing her twice with a filleting knife, *Rahman* (1998)[57] receiving 11 years for attacking his wife with a knife, slashing her throat and almost causing her death, and *Bedford* (1992)[58] receiving ten years for throwing petrol over his wife, igniting it and shutting her inside a room, where she received 40 per cent burns to her body.

There seems to be a significant gap between these sentence lengths and those prescribed by the 2003 Act as starting points for murder sentences. Murders involving political motivation have a starting point of a whole life tariff, while the 'domestic' cases (not involving child victims) would seem to fall within the residual category of murders with a starting point of 15 years. Much will depend on other mitigating and aggravating factors, of course, but we must recall that the minimum terms

---

52 Cf. the reasoning in *Offen (no. 2)* [2001] 2 Cr App R (S) 44 in respect of the automatic life sentence.
53 See the discussion of this sentence below, ch. 6.8.
54 For suggestions about how this might be done, see Wasik (2000), pp. 174–83. For analysis and international comparisons, see van Zyl Smit (2002).
55 SGC, *Overarching Principles: Seriousness* (2004), para. 1.19.
56 [1997] 2 Cr App R (S) 292.   57 [1998] 1 Cr App R (S) 391.
58 (1993) 14 Cr App R (S) 336.

for murder are calculating on 'real time', and must therefore be doubled in order to make a true comparison with ordinary sentences. This opens up an enormous gap between murder and attempted murder, particularly in the so-called domestic cases. There is a strong argument to the effect that some murder cases are over-sentenced, but it is equally possible to argue that attempted murders in domestic settings do not show sufficient respect for the value of life. Attempted murders are all intentional offences, and on the von Hirsch-Jareborg scale they rank as highly culpable attacks on physical integrity, creating a threat to the victim's very subsistence. Their seriousness ranking might be reduced slightly because the offence is incomplete, being a mere attempt, but in principle the decisions in *Al-Banna* and *Hindawi* were right to minimize any reduction. The pressing question is whether the differentials between attempted murders with political motivation and those in a 'domestic' setting should be so great.[59]

4.4.3 Manslaughter

This is a single offence with several different legal bases. For present purposes, three types of manslaughter should be distinguished – manslaughter by reason of diminished responsibility, manslaughter upon provocation and constructive manslaughter. All forms of manslaughter involve the culpable causing of death, and on the von Hirsch-Jareborg scale would be classified as attacks on physical integrity which affect (nay, obliterate) subsistence. The offence is complete, not attempted, and so it is the question of culpability which becomes crucial. Since the harm is the most serious of all, to what extent should lesser culpability reduce the seriousness of the offence?

In manslaughter by reason of diminished responsibility, the case is essentially one of murder reduced to manslaughter because an abnormality of mind 'substantially impaired' the offender's responsibility. The leading case of *Chambers* (1983)[60] sets out three principal sentencing options, once the judge has reviewed the psychiatric report(s) on the offender. Where the psychiatric evidence points to a condition that requires treatment and falls within the relevant Mental Health Act provisions, the court should make a hospital order, usually without limit of time.[61] If there is no recommendation in favour of a hospital order, and the offender is considered dangerous, the conditions for a life sentence or imprisonment for public protection may be met.[62] In other cases the court may impose a determinate sentence of imprisonment – which may be as long as ten years, but is more typically in the three- to five-year range. This is a clear compromise between punishment and treatment: the reasoning is that the length of sentence should reflect the portion of responsibility which is left after the mental abnormality has been deducted.[63]

---

59 Stuart-Smith LJ expressed doubts about this in *Bedford*, ibid., at p. 338, but these appear not to have been taken up elsewhere.
60 (1983) 5 Cr App R (S) 190.
61 See ch. 12.3 below. For a recent decision, see *Walton* [2004] 1 Cr App R (S) 234.
62 See ch. 6.8 below.   63 For an example, see *Cutlan* [1998] 1 Cr App R (S) 1.

In cases of manslaughter upon provocation, there are two leading decisions that have given general consideration to the issues. The first was *A-G's Reference No. 33 of 1996 (Latham)*,[64] where the Court of Appeal was urged to raise the tariff for provocation cases involving a weapon with which the offender had forearmed himself. The Court accepted that there appeared to be a tariff of four to seven years for provocation cases involving a knife, and they held that this was too low. The Court approved *Pittendrigh* (1996),[65] where a sentence of 12 years was held to be appropriate on conviction of an offence committed with a shotgun which the offender was carrying, and it went on to hold that a range of 10–12 years would be appropriate where the offender had forearmed himself with a knife.

The second leading case is *Attorney General's Reference Nos. 74, 95 and 118 of 2002 (Suratan and others)*,[66] where counsel for the Attorney General set out to argue that the normal range of sentences in cases of provocation arising from infidelity by one partner was between five and seven years, and that this was inappropriately low for two principal reasons – that possessiveness and jealousy are no longer acceptable reasons for loss of self-control, and that sentences of such length are too low compared with sentence levels for kindred offences. The Court did not 'seriously disagree with' the proposition that the normal range for cases of jealousy or unfaithfulness was five to seven years. It also accepted the point that sentences for attempted murder in a domestic context tend to be around 10 years, as we saw in part 4.4.2 above. However, the Court held that in cases where provocation is established,[67] a judge must assume that the offender lost self-control as a result of provocation that was enough to provoke a reasonable person, to the extent of reducing murder to manslaughter. This differentiates the cases from the attempted murders used as a comparison (although in those cases there is no defence of provocation available to be put to the jury), and so the judge must keep faith with the verdict of manslaughter. Thus the Court endorsed the sentence range of five–seven years as a starting point in this type of case.

Subsequently the Sentencing Advisory Panel has considered the issues and has proposed guidelines to the Sentencing Guidelines Council.[68] The Panel recognizes that these cases involve the taking of life, but also recognizes the strong element of provocation in some types of case. It argues that infidelity of itself should not amount to a high level of provocation, but that long-term taunting may do so, and that actual or anticipated violence will generally be regarded as stronger provocation than infidelity or offensive words unless the latter amounts to psychological bullying. It devotes considerable attention to the significance of a lapse of time and the use

64 [1997] 2 Cr App R (S) 10.   65 [1996] 1 Cr App R (S) 65.
66 [2003] 2 Cr App R (S) 273.
67 Since the change in the substantive law made by the House of Lords in *Morgan Smith* [2001] 1 AC 146, also discussed by the Court in this case, the Crown Prosecution Service will ordinarily not accept a plea of guilty to manslaughter on grounds of provocation, and will insist on a jury verdict after a trial for murder. Cf. now *Holley* [2005] UKPC 23.
68 SAP, *Manslaughter by Reason of Provocation* (2004).

of a weapon, arguing that there may be cases where such factors do not necessarily indicate greater culpability. The Panel concludes by proposing three sentencing ranges as starting points – 10–12 years where the provocation is low, four–nine years where the provocation is substantial, and two–three years where the provocation is high, contemplating that there may be exceptional cases where a non-custodial sentence is appropriate (perhaps involving long-term physical abuse with the threat of more to come). In *Howell* (1998),[69] where a woman killed her partner after receiving repeated physical abuse, the Court of Appeal held that three-and-a-half years was an appropriate sentence where the killing was with a shotgun; and a sentence of three years was upheld in *Grainger* (1997),[70] where a carving knife was the weapon. The Court of Appeal has rarely considered cases where a non-custodial sentence has been passed, but in *Gardner* (1992),[71] where a woman had killed her bullying partner (at a time when she was suffering from depression), the Court replaced custody with a probation order.

Sentences at this relatively low level raise deep problems of principle, as the Panel recognized. Since these are offences involving death caused intentionally (or at least with the intent of causing serious injury), how could one justify sentences as low as three years' imprisonment, or even lesser sentences? The harm is of the highest order on any scale, so the focus must be on the culpability. The argument must be that the factors set out by the Court in the *Suratan* reference and accepted by the Panel – the loss of self-control, and the element of partial justification for that loss of control – justify placing such cases so low on the scale of offence-seriousness. In some such cases, perhaps such as *Gardner* and *Grainger* above, it is almost argued that death or serious injury was deserved by the deceased's conduct, or at least that that was a strong factor when allied to the extreme emotional torment of the offender that resulted. Others, however, would argue that if the conditions of self-defence are not made out, the sentence should always be high enough to mark the taking of a life.

The third type of manslaughter, where death results from an unlawful act or from gross negligence, brings another awkward conflict to the surface. The offence varies widely in its seriousness, some of the cases being close to the borderline with murder and being sentenced accordingly.[72] Difficult problems of principle occur at the lower end of the scale, where liability for constructive manslaughter derives from an assault or other relatively minor crime which results in death. In the leading case of *Coleman* (1991),[73] Lord Lane CJ gave guidance for sentencing in cases where death results from a fall caused by a single punch. He distinguished such cases carefully from more serious ones in which the actual blow caused the injury, or where a weapon was used, or where a victim on the ground was kicked about the

---

69 [1998] 1 Cr App R (S) 229.   70 [1997] 1 Cr App R (S) 369.
71 (1992) 14 Cr App R (S) 364; it may have been relevant that she had already spent nine months in prison.
72 E.g. *Hussain* [2004] 2 Cr App R (S) 497, where a sentence of 18 years was upheld for manslaughter by participating in the petrol bombing of a house, resulting in the death of eight people.
73 (1991) 13 Cr App R (S) 508, followed in *Edwards* [2001] 2 Cr App R (S) 540.

head. He held that 12 months' imprisonment should be the starting point in cases where it was the fall that caused the death after a single blow: the sentence should be higher if the offender had a record of violence or if more than one blow was struck, and lower if the blow was unpremeditated and only of moderate force. Thus in *Grad* (2004)[74] the Court of Appeal reduced from 18 to 9 months a sentence for manslaughter by a single punch to the head, which resulted in a haemorrhage and immediate death due to an unusual combination of medical factors.

The conflict here is between sentencing based on the intrinsic gravity of the conduct itself, taking account of the offender's fault, and sentencing based to some extent on the unexpected and unfortunate result. Research findings suggest that public perceptions of conduct are heavily dependent on the harm actually resulting.[75] However, since the resulting harm is nothing more than a twist of fate, the fault-based approach is surely fairer. To argue that the offender should be punished for causing the death is unconvincing, and may confuse the justice of a compensation claim with the justice of punishment. Many people inflict minor assaults without causing anything more than minor injuries, and there is really nothing other than misfortune to distinguish those thousands of cases from the few which happen to cause death. If there is to be a slightly higher penalty where death occurred, this can only be explained as an attempt to placate public opinion or the victim's family. The proper approach, endorsed by the Sentencing Guidelines Council, is that the sentence should be governed not by the vagaries of chance but by what the offender believed he was doing or risking, or at least what was reasonably foreseeable at the time of the conduct.[76]

4.4.4 Causing death by bad driving

Two offences may be discussed here – causing death by dangerous driving, and causing death by careless driving while under the influence of alcohol. The former was the subject of an early guideline judgment, *Boswell* (1984),[77] in which Lord Lane CJ emphasized the seriousness of these offences and called upon judges to impose longer sentences. In 1993 Parliament raised the maximum sentences for both offences from five to ten years' imprisonment, and the 2003 Act further raised the maxima to 14 years.[78] The latest sentencing guidelines, stemming from the advice of the Sentencing Advisory Panel,[79] were handed down in the judgment in *Cooksley* (2003),[80] before the further increase in maximum penalty. The Court

---

74 [2004] 2 Cr App R (S) 218; cf. *Cheetham and Baker* [2004] 2 Cr App R (S) 278, where the Court reached a slightly different conclusion.

75 Cf. Mitchell (1998) with Robinson and Darley (1995).

76 For discussion and references, see Ashworth (2003a), pp. 158–61; see also SGC, *Overarching Principles: Seriousness* (2004), para. 1.18: 'where unusually serious harm results and was unintended and beyond the control of the offender, culpability will be significantly influenced by the extent to which the harm could have been foreseen'.

77 (1984) 6 Cr App R (S) 257.

78 Criminal Justice Act 2003, s. 285; the maximum for aggravated vehicle-taking causing death is also raised to 14 years by this section.

79 SAP, *Causing Death by Dangerous Driving* (2003).   80 [2004] 1 Cr App R (S) 1.

accepted the various aggravating and mitigating factors set out by the Panel, and endorsed four levels of starting points. For the highest culpability involving the presence of three or more aggravating factors, the Court indicated a starting point of six years, with sentences up to the then maximum of 10 years. In *Noble* (2003),[81] the Court upheld a sentence of 10 years on an offender who caused six deaths by driving at excessive speed while two-and-a-half times over the drink-driving limit and who then claimed that someone else had been driving. At the next level comes a four- or five-year starting point, for offences with one or two aggravating factors and no substantial mitigation. Below that come cases involving a momentary error of judgment or bad driving over a short distance, where the starting point is two to three years. Thus in *Braid* (2002),[82] where a young driver overtook a lorry on a bend and caused one death and a serious injury, with no aggravating factor present, the Court had reduced the sentence from two years to 18 months' detention. The Court in *Cooksley* thought that two years should have stood. At the lowest of the four levels come cases with strong mitigating and no aggravating factors, where the starting point should be 12–18 months. In *Attorney General's Reference No. 85 of 2003 (Eversham)*,[83] the offender failed to notice a driver turning right, braked suddenly, swerved on to the opposite carriageway and caused a collision in which the other driver (not wearing a seatbelt) was killed. The Court held that a suspended sentence was unduly lenient, because the facts of the case were not sufficiently exceptional to justify going below the custody threshold, and substituted a sentence of eight months.

Where the offence is one of causing death by careless driving while under the influence of alcohol, the chief determinants of sentence should be the degree of carelessness and the quantity of alcohol taken. In practice the average length of custodial sentence for this offence was 42 months in 1999 and 38 months in 2000, compared with 34 months and 37 months respectively for causing death by dangerous driving. Moreover, for causing death by dangerous driving there were around twenty cases each year (or some 10 per cent) in which a non-custodial sentence was given. There were no such sentences for causing death by careless driving while under the influence of alcohol, presumably because the taking of alcohol establishes a certain degree of culpability in all those cases.

Many of the more serious forms of dangerous driving involve several minutes of highly irregular driving, during which the offender either realizes the risk of serious injury or death resulting or is foolishly optimistic about his own ability to avoid the risk created. In terms of the von Hirsch-Jareborg scale, these offences violate the value of physical integrity, and deprive the victim of subsistence. In principle the culpability is much lower than for an intentional causing of death or injury, but that point cannot be carried too far. Cars are familiar everyday objects, with more socially beneficial uses than a gun, dagger or axe (in most contexts), but it is surely

---

81 [2003] 1 Cr App R (S) 312.
82 [2002] 2 Cr App R (S) 509.   83 [2004] 2 Cr App R (S) 371.

the reckless creation of an avoidable risk of death (or at least serious injury) that justifies the recent raising of this offence in the scale of relative seriousness. However, there remains the awkward theoretical question of the extent to which courts should mark the difference between bad driving that causes a risk of death, a single death, or more than one death. In some instances the driver should know that several lives are being put at risk, as where there are others in the car or where the vehicle is a coach or minibus. This should be an aggravating factor. But in other circumstances the causing of more than one death may be a matter of chance, as the Court of Appeal has recognized. But the Court's view is that, 'rather illogical' as it is, 'in the public's estimation it is a factor which people in general do take into account. People do regard killing three as more criminal than killing one. That is a fact of life which this court recognizes.'[84] The Court in *Cooksley* took the same view, adding that any increase 'must remain proportionate to the nature of an offence which does not involve any intent to injure'.[85]

4.4.5 Drug trafficking

Offences involving the importation or supply of prohibited drugs rank high in the current English scale of ordinal proportionality. They were the subject of the first of Lord Lane's guideline judgments, in *Aramah* (1982).[86] Since then, Parliament has increased the maximum penalty under the Misuse of Drugs Act 1971 from 14 years to life imprisonment, and the *Aramah* guidelines have been revised and progressively replaced by specific guidelines on different types of prohibited drugs (as described below). Sentences of imprisonment are not the only form of censure and deprivation for drug traffickers: the courts also have extensive duties to order confiscation of their assets, consolidated in the Proceeds of Crime Act 2002. The general approach in sentencing is to distinguish between importation, supply and mere possession, and to distinguish between drugs in classes A, B and C.

In recent years the Court of Appeal has been recasting the *Aramah* guidelines in terms of the weight of the drugs imported, rather than the more nebulous and contested notion of street value. Starting with class A drugs, the leading case is now *Aroyewumi* (1994),[87] where Lord Taylor CJ stated that sentences for the importation of 500 g of heroin or cocaine should be around ten years, and for 5 kg around 14 years. These figures related to drugs of 100 per cent purity: appropriate adjustments should be made for less pure substances, and where the offender was deceived by the supplier about purity.[88] Lord Taylor was satisfied that this change was not an increase, but merely a reformulation. Four years' imprisonment is regarded as the lowest sentence for the importation of any appreciable amount. Guidelines of

84 *Pettipher* (1989) 11 Cr App R (S) 321 at p. 323.
85 [2004] 1 Cr App R (S) 1 at p. 14.   86 (1982) 4 Cr App R (S) 407.
87 (1994) 16 Cr App R (S) 211; the case is sometimes given the name of a co-appellant, Aranguren.
88 For a deception case, where the sentence was based on average purity, see *Patel and Varshney* [1994] Crim LR 772.

a similar kind were laid down in *Warren and Beeley* (1996)[89] for Ecstasy, another class A drug. The court held that for the importation of 5,000 tablets the appropriate sentence would be around ten years, and for 50,000 tablets around 14 years. In *Main and Johnston* (1997)[90] the importation ran to over 1.2 million tablets, and the Court of Appeal upheld sentences of 24 years. In *Ellis and Avis* (2000)[91] there was a conspiracy to import some 115,000 tablets at 75 per cent purity: discounting for the purity level, the sentence was calculated on the basis of 88,000 tablets and, since the conspiracy was not brought to fruition, the court held that 16 years would be appropriate. On the same model, guidelines for LSD cases were laid down in *Hurley* (1998),[92] with ten years for a quantity of 25,000 squares or dosage units, and 14 years for 250,000. A similar formula was adopted in *Mashaollahi* (2001) in respect of opium.[93]

Turning to class B drugs, guidelines for cannabis cases were laid down in *Ronchetti* (1998),[94] using the same model. For importation of 500 kg the guideline sentence would be ten years; counsel invited the court to indicate a guideline for 100 kg, and a range of seven to eight years was suggested. Amphetamines, also class B drugs, were dealt with in a guideline judgment in *Wijs* (1998).[95] This is rather more detailed than some of the earlier judgments, and it indicates sentence ranges from up to two years' imprisonment for up to 500 g, through four to seven years for the range between 2.5 and 10 kg, and then 10 years and above for 15 kg or more. All the guidelines are chiefly aimed at importers and dealers, and following the *Aramah* approach they should be heavily discounted in cases of possession for personal use. Thus in *Elder and Pyle* (1993),[96] where it was accepted that the offenders were importing 1 kg of cannabis for their personal use, the Court of Appeal held that the offence was not so serious that only custody could be justified.

Where should drugs offences be placed on a scale of ordinal proportionality? A number of arguments have been advanced. In *Aramah* it was said that the huge profits of drug smuggling attract 'the worst type of criminal', since the profits may exceed those of robbing banks. Although there are no victims suffering loss in the usual sense, the gain to offenders may be substantial. But a major difference from robbery is the absence of violence or threat of violence as an element in the offences. Lord Lane also said that rivalry between gangs 'may be a fruitful source of violence and internecine strife'; but unless those offences are proved, it is wrong to allow such speculative and secondary consequences to raise valuations of the seriousness of drug offences. Lord Lane added another secondary consequence: that people addicted to the drugs imported by these offenders have to resort to crime in order to pay for the drugs. This leads to 'the most horrifying aspect': 'the degradation

89 [1996] 1 Cr App R (S) 233.   90 [1997] 2 Cr App R (S) 63.
91 [2000] 1 Cr App R (S) 38.   92 [1998] 1 Cr App R (S) 299.
93 [2001] 1 Cr App R (S) 330, broadly adopting the advice in SAP, *Importation and Possession of Opium* (2000).
94 [1998] 2 Cr App R (S) 100.   95 [1998] 2 Cr App R (S) 436.
96 (1993) 15 Cr App R (S) 514.

and suffering and not infrequent death which the drug brings to the addict. It is not difficult to understand why in some parts of the world traffickers in heroin in any substantial quantity are sentenced to death and executed.'[97] This hints at the argument that drug dealing is in effect a preliminary to homicide, since drug traffickers tempt addicts into a kind of physical and mental disintegration which may lead to death. In order to sustain this argument, it is necessary to rely on a large slice of paternalism, for those who use heroin must be supposed to have been rational citizens when they began, even if their addiction subsequently saps their free will. In other words, they cannot be said to be victims in the ordinary sense of unwilling participants. Even if their living standards have declined spectacularly, there may have been no force, fear or fraud. At most, then, the analogy is with aiding and abetting suicide, not murder.

The profits involved might be thought to increase the seriousness of the crime, but in order to rank it high on the von Hirsch-Jareborg scale one would have to regard it as threatening the value of physical integrity; as threatening subsistence, or at least minimal well-being; and as having high culpability (in terms of planning). However high the culpability, there would still be the problem that the offence is, at its strongest, a preliminary or protective crime which lies fairly remote from causing people's deaths. Only by adopting a strong form of paternalism and regarding offences of importation or supply as (indirect) victimizing crimes can this argument proceed. It is doubtful whether, even if persuasive, those considerations justify sentences double the length of those for rape or serious cases of causing death by dangerous driving. Indeed, some determinate sentences are well in excess of sentences for those offences or for armed robbery – notably, the 24 years imposed for large-scale importation of Ecstasy tablets in *Main and Johnston*[98] and the 26 years upheld for conspiracy to import heroin in *K*.[99] If sentences of that length can be justified at all, it must be general deterrence rather than proportionality that is dominant – in other words, these offences stand outside a tariff or hierarchy of sentences based on seriousness. The various international conventions on the control of narcotics and other drugs may lend pragmatic support to this. However, we saw in Chapter 3.3.2 above that the justifications for deterrent sentencing are themselves not well supported.

4.4.6 Serious woundings

We have already noted that attempted murders tend to result in sentences of ten years' imprisonment upwards, which may again be seen as reflecting a subjective principle of sentencing. Slight or extensive as the injuries may be in those cases, the intention with which they were inflicted is crucial.[100] On the same principle, there are serious woundings which receive higher sentences than manslaughter. The offence of wounding with intent to cause grievous bodily harm may involve

97 (1982) 4 Cr App R (S) 407 at pp. 408–9.   98 Above, n. 90.   99 Above, n. 40.
100 See SGC, *Overarching Principles: Seriousness* (2004), para. 1.19, and the discussion of attempted murder in part 4.4.2 above.

the same fault element as murder in English law, and in one case a sentence of 12 years was upheld for shooting a police officer twice, blinding him and inflicting other injuries.[101] The use of a firearm was a strong aggravating factor in that case, and in *Davies* (1986),[102] where a man pleaded guilty to attacking his wife with a hammer, causing the loss of an eye and other serious injuries, the Court of Appeal upheld a sentence of seven years for wounding with intent – a level similar to that for manslaughter upon provocation, again showing the power of provocation in reducing the length of manslaughter sentences in English law. While sentences on conviction for wounding with intent, without provocation, may be in the 7 to 10 years range if the offence involves an axe, knife or hammer, the normal range for 'glassing' or striking someone on the head with a bottle has been put at two-and-a-half to five years.[103] Many of these cases are impulsive, the glass or bottle being picked up and used spontaneously, but where there is some degree of deliberation, a starting point of four to six years may be appropriate.[104]

These offences do harm to physical integrity and to autonomy, in von Hirsch and Jareborg's terms. Their effect is mostly in terms of minimal well-being rather than subsistence, and mitigation and aggravation again assume a critical role. English courts seem to dwell largely on the degree of deliberation and the dangerousness of the weapon used, placing the offence within a wide range, from around 18 months up to 12 years. In many of the cases, the injury done to the victim is far in excess of the injury in robbery cases sentenced at the same level, a point to be borne in mind when robbery is discussed in paragraph 4.4.9 below.

4.4.7 Rape

Rape is one of the offences whose known profile has changed considerably in the last twenty years. In 1985 there were just under 2,000 reported rapes, with stranger rapes, rape by intimates ('relationship rapes') and acquaintance rapes in roughly equal proportions. In 1996 there were some 6,000 reported rapes: stranger rapes had not increased in number and thus now formed only 12 per cent of the total, whereas reported relationship rapes accounted for 43 per cent and rapes by acquaintances for 45 per cent.[105] Data from the British Crime Survey suggest that current partners are responsible for some 45 per cent of rapes, and strangers only for 8 per cent.[106]

There have been major changes in the substantive law. The Sexual Offences Act 2003 expanded the definition of rape to include oral as well as vaginal and anal penetration by a penis, and introduced a new range of other serious sexual offences (see 4.4.8 below). Just before that Act was passed the Court of Appeal, responding to an Advice from the Sentencing Advisory Panel, handed down revised guidelines

101 *Chesterman* (1984) 6 Cr App R (S) 151.   102 (1986) 8 Cr App R (S) 97.
103 *Attorney General's Reference No. 41 of 1994* (1995) 16 Cr App R (S) 792; the difficulty of sentencing s. 18 cases is manifested in the figures for references by the Attorney General, of which s. 18 cases made up 22 per cent between 1988 and 1998: Shute (1999), p. 608.
104 *Attorney General's Reference No. 14 of 2000* [2001] 1 Cr App R (S) 55.
105 Harris and Grace (1999), p. 6.   106 Myhill and Allen (2002), ch. 5.

for the sentencing of rape,[107] and those guidelines will shortly be revised by the Sentencing Guidelines Council to take account of the structure of the 2003 Act.[108]

How seriously should rape be ranked on the ladder of offences? Some two-thirds of rapes involve some violence or threat of violence, and many involve the infliction of other sexual indignities.[109] However, the fundamental interests violated by sexual attacks are autonomy and choice in sexual matters. It is not just that victims are wronged by the invasion of their right to respect for private life, of which sexual autonomy is a central feature.[110] The distinctly sexual element brings in other values and disvalues – self-expression, intimacy, shared relationships; shame, humiliation, exploitation and objectification – which are often crucial to understanding the effects of sexual victimization.[111] In terms of the von Hirsch-Jareborg scale, then, there will usually be humiliation and deprivation of privacy and autonomy to a significant degree, often compounded by a threat to physical integrity. The typical effect on the victim is therefore likely to be at the level of minimal well-being. It is not thought that most rapes are planned, in the way that armed robberies often are, but the culpability will usually be high because the offender will know perfectly well what is being done.[112]

The guidelines handed down by the Court of Appeal in *Millberry* (2003)[113] retain the general structure and levels of the previous guidelines in *Billam* (1986),[114] with some minor but significant changes. The structure involves three levels of starting points. The general starting point for a conviction of rape after a contested trial is five years. A higher starting point of eight years is indicated where one or more of seven aggravating factors is present – rape by two or more offenders, offender in a position of trust, an element of abduction, rape of a child or other vulnerable victim, rape aggravated by discrimination (such as race or homophobic rape), repeated penetration in the course of a single attack, and rape by an offender with a life-threatening sexually transmitted disease. Above this, there is a 15-year starting point for campaigns of rape, and rapists held to constitute a danger to the public will fall within the new dangerousness sentences.[115] From the appropriate starting point the court would move downwards to take account of any mitigating factors, and upwards to take account of any aggravating factors not otherwise built into the sentence. This means that a rape without aggravating factors to which the offender pleaded guilty could attract a sentence as low as four or even three-and-a-half years. However, the figures for 2000 showed that the average custodial term was seven years and four months for those convicted after a trial, and six years and seven months for those pleading guilty, figures that demonstrate the frequency of aggravating factors in rape cases.[116]

107 *Millberry* [2003] 2 Cr App R (S) 142, superseding *Billam* (1986) 82 Cr App R 347.
108 SAP, *Sexual Offences Act 2003* (2005).   109 Harris and Grace (1999), p. 19.
110 This is emphasized by the jurisprudence on Art. 8 of the Convention – e.g. *Sutherland and Morris v. United Kingdom* (1997) 24 EHRR CD22, para. 57.
111 For further discussion, cf. Lacey (1998) with Gardner and Shute (2000).
112 For similar analysis see SAP, *Sexual Offences Act 2003*.
113 [2003] 2 Cr App R (S) 142.   114 (1986) 82 Cr App R 347.
115 See below, ch. 6.8.   116 See SAP, *Rape* (2002), Annex A.

What was new about the Panel's Advice and the Court of Appeal's guidelines in *Millberry* was a change in the approach to relationship rape, where the parties had recently been or were still involved in a sexual relationship. The Panel commissioned empirical research into views of rape among a sample of members of the public, including some rape victims.[117] One of the clear outcomes of this research was the view that relationship rape was no less traumatic and therefore no less serious than stranger rape, because, although the latter was frightening, the breach of intimate trust involved in relationship rape could have equally deep effects on the victim. The Panel therefore recommended, and the Court of Appeal accepted, that the starting points should be the same whether it was a stranger rape or relationship rape. This was a departure from the previous case law,[118] and there is evidence that it is now being followed in the courts.[119] The *Millberry* guidelines also make it clear that the approach to sentence should the same whether the victim is a woman or a man, and whether the rape was vaginal or anal.

It remains open to argument whether the sentence levels for rape correlate sensibly with those for other serious crimes. Although the average sentence is around seven years, because of the frequency of aggravating features, some might argue that the basic starting point of five years is too low when compared with some sentences for persistent pickpockets and people who use fear created by an imitation weapon (such as a cucumber or banana) in order to rob someone of a few hundred pounds. It will be necessary to return to this subject after discussing sentences for robbery.

4.4.8 Other sexual offences

The Sexual Offences Act 2003 has introduced major reforms of the law, and the Sentencing Advisory Panel has responded by proposing guidelines in respect of all the new offences.[120] This has been a complex enterprise, not least because the 2003 Act contains large numbers of offences and some of them overlap to a considerable degree. However, the Sexual Offences Act has been brought into force for offences committed on or after 1 May 2004, and it has therefore been necessary for the courts to deal with some offences without the benefit of any guidelines – until the Sentencing Guidelines Council is able to complete its statutory procedures and issue definitive guidelines. The Court of Appeal has therefore stepped into the breach and has given guidance on the new offence of assault by penetration (contrary to s. 2 of the Sexual Offences Act 2003) in *Attorney General's Reference No. 104 of 2004 (Garvey)* (2005).[121] The Court quoted from the Panel's consultation paper on the Sexual Offences Act 2003, and took the view that digital penetration of the vagina should be sentenced more severely under s. 2 than under the previous offence of indecent assault. The Court held that the sentence for digital penetration

---

117 Clarke, Moran-Ellis and Sleney (2002).
118 E.g. *W* (1993) 14 Cr App R (S) 256, and *M* (1995) 16 Cr App R (S) 770.
119 See *Price* [2003] 2 Cr App R (S) 440, and *Attorney General's References Nos. 37, 38, 44, 53 et al.* [2004] 1 Cr App R (S) 499 at p. 511.
120 SAP, *Sexual Offences Act 2003* (2005).   121 [2005] Crim LR 150.

of a woman after entering her house as a trespasser and getting into her bed while she was sleeping should properly have been four years, rather than the 18 months imposed. Similarly, in *Wisniewski* (2005)[122] the Court gave guidance on sentencing for battery with intent to commit a sexual offence, and in *Corran et al.* (2005)[123] it gave more general guidance on various offences under the Sexual Offences Act 2003.

The new structure of sexual offences is intended to give added protection to the vulnerable, to be gender-neutral as far as possible, and to provide for sentences proportionate to the wrongdoing of the particular offence. Some maxima are increased (as in the case of digital penetration, which was previously classified as indecent assault with a maximum of 10 years, but now falls within the life-carrying offence of assault by penetration), and other maxima are reduced (e.g. incest between adults, which now has a maximum of two rather than seven years).

4.4.9 Robbery

The decision in *Turner* (1975)[124] remains the leading authority on serious armed robberies, whereas the more recent judgment in *Attorney General's References Nos. 4 and 7 of 2002; Q* (2002)[125] contains guidance on street robberies. Reported robberies have increased considerably in number in recent years, from some 36,000 in 1990 to some 66,000 in 1999 and 101,000 in 2003.[126] In 2002 the government introduced a Street Crime Initiative, involving a five-month focus of co-ordinated services (police, prosecutors, courts) on preventing, detecting and dealing swiftly with street robberies, and the figures for the year from the start of the initiative showed a reduction of some 17 per cent in reported street robberies.[127] These reductions are welcome, although there remain unanswered questions about whether they have been achieved at the cost of neglecting other offences. But the key question concerns the levels at which robberies ought to be sentenced.

The inquiry must begin with the definition of the offence.[128] The crime of robbery is made up of two elements, theft and the use or threat of force in order to steal. It is immediately apparent that the amount of force required to turn a theft into a robbery may vary tremendously, from tugging at an arm in order to effect the release of a bag through to the use of firearms or other weapons coupled with threats to kill. When violence is threatened or used in other circumstances, the law offers a graduated scale of crimes, from murder through attempted murder, grievous bodily harm, unlawful wounding and assault occasioning actually bodily harm down to assault. Each of those offences against the person has its own sentence range. But in the context of robbery there is no such division according to the seriousness of the violence done or threatened: robbery is robbery. In principle, the sentence ranges

---

122 [2005] Crim LR 403.   123 [2005] Crim LR 404.
124 Above, p. 114.   125 [2002] 2 Cr App R (S) 77.
126 The last figure relates to the 2003/04 year: Dodd et al. (2004), p. 9.
127 Home Office (2003).
128 The arguments that follow are elaborated more fully in Ashworth (2002a).

for robbery ought to reflect and to be closely related to the scales for the various offences against the person, but in practice there is little evidence of that, and the use of the single word 'robbery' to cover such a wide range of seriousness may not conduce to clarity in sentencing practice.

Sentencing practice for crimes of robbery can be divided into five gradations. At the top stand the so-called 'first division robberies' with extra aggravating factors such as kidnapping: decisions such as *Schultz* (1996)[129] show that some such crimes may be sentenced as high as 25 years, although 20 years is a more general starting point. Just below them come the professional armed robberies of banks or security vehicles with which the *Turner* judgment was concerned, for which the range is 15–18 years.[130] Below those offences come the less serious bank robberies, still involving a firearm but not bearing a professional hallmark: for example, in *Copeland and Hegarty* (1994)[131] the Court of Appeal reduced the sentence from 13 to 10 years on the grounds that it was not professionally carried out, there were elements of incompetence, and therefore the fear caused may have been less. At around the same 10–12 year starting point come violent robberies in the home, a group of cases in which the violence is often considerable but the money taken not great. An example is provided by *Attorney General's Reference No. 89 of 1999 (Farrow)* (2000),[132] where the offender forced his way into a house, threatened the elderly occupant with a knife, pulled a cable round his neck until he lost consciousness, and then stole some £120. The Court of Appeal stated that the proper sentence should have been 10 years' imprisonment. In this group of cases, the violence is rightly regarded as more important than the theft. The fourth group of cases consists of robberies of post offices, off-licences and small shops and the like, usually with an imitation firearm or other forms of threat, and usually not yielding large sums of money. A typical example would be *Clarke* (1994),[133] where the offender had entered a bank, pointed an imitation gun at a cashier and obtained some £2,000, and the Court of Appeal upheld a sentence of seven years on a guilty plea, which suggests that the range would perhaps go up to nine years after a trial.

There is a difficulty in determining whether offences in that fourth category are sentenced at the right level. Often they involve no injury (although there is fear), an imitation weapon is used and the sums taken are not high. Imitation weapons (and bananas, cucumbers and other items made to look like pistols) are not to be taken lightly, but they are clearly less dangerous to people and may not give rise to such

---

129 [1996] 1 Cr App R (S) 451.
130 In *Betson* [2004] 2 Cr App R (S) 270, an audacious and professional attempt to steal diamonds from the Millennium Dome, the Court reduced the sentences to 15 and 12 years on the basis that no direct use or threat of violence had been contemplated.
131 (1994) 15 Cr App R (S) 601; cf. *Parkinson* [2003] 2 Cr App R (S) 160, where the Court held that 14 years was appropriate for robbery of a building society with an imitation gun, where the offender had similar previous convictions.
132 [2000] 2 Cr App R (S) 382.
133 (1994) 15 Cr App R (S) 15; see also *Attorney General's Reference No. 7 of 1991 (Khan)* (1993) 14 Cr App R (S) 122.

lasting trauma. If attention is focused on the element of fear created in the victim, which is usually the most serious feature of these offences, questions may properly be raised about starting points of seven, eight or nine years when the general starting point for rape after a trial is five years. Similar questions of comparability arise in relation to the fifth group of cases, the street robberies. Here, the value of what is taken is not usually high (a mobile phone, a handbag), and so the focus should be on the violence or threat of violence. The judgment of Lord Woolf CJ in *Attorney General's References Nos. 4 and 7 of 2002, and Q*[134] created a difficulty here. Having begun by outlining the rapid rise in numbers of thefts and robberies in which mobile phones were taken, his Lordship stated:

> Faced with that background the courts have no alternative but to adopt a robust sentencing policy towards those who commit these offences. Those who do so must understand that they will be punished severely. Custodial sentences will be the only option available to the courts when these offences are committed, unless there are exceptional circumstances. That will apply irrespective of the age of the offender and irrespective of whether the offender has previous convictions. However, both those factors are very important when a judge comes to decide on the length of sentence.[135]

The sentence range indicated was between 18 months and 5 years. This crucial passage creates several problems. It focuses on mobile phones when they are really of small value, and instead it should focus on the use or threat of violence. It fails to recognize that many such offences take place between teenagers in circumstances that might not normally be regarded as a matter for prosecution or at least for serious sanction, and where courts have typically passed non-custodial sentences (in 2000 half of robbery offenders aged 10–17 received community sentences). Lord Woolf's reference to custody being almost inevitable 'irrespective of the age of the offender' seemed to indicate an enormous shift of policy, which the Youth Justice Board certainly thought unwise,[136] and which sits awkwardly with Lord Woolf's general advocacy of more constructive methods of reducing reoffending. And the passage fails to draw a proper distinction between serious incidents of street robbery involving knives, claw hammers and other weapons (as in the appeals heard in that case) and the many other cases where far less force is used or threatened.

The result of this decision seems to have been an escalation in sentences for offences falling within the fifth category. Thus in *Attorney General's References Nos. 150 and 151 of 2002* (2003)[137] two offenders aged 18 and 20 had robbed one schoolboy of his mobile phone and gold ring by means of unspecific threats, and then made threats and eventually kicked another schoolboy once and punched him twice, without him yielding his phone to his attackers. The Court of Appeal held that community sentences were unduly lenient for these offences, and stated that

---

134 [2002] 2 Cr App R (S) 345.   135 Ibid., at p. 348.
136 Youth Justice Board (2002), referring to the constructive efforts to reduce youth offending through community sentences.
137 [2003] 2 Cr App R (S) 658.

four years' detention would have been the proper sentence. This is very high for young offenders in a case in which no weapon had been carried, threatened or used. The element of theft is not major, and it is doubtful whether the Court would have imposed sentences anywhere near four years for assault occasioning actual bodily harm, which is the most serious offence of violence consistent with the facts.

The Sentencing Advisory Panel has proposed new guidelines on robbery that would attempt to draw courts towards focusing more clearly on the amount of violence threatened or used, and not to give undue weight to the label 'robbery'.[138] The Panel draws attention to the wide range of forms of robbery, and to the frequency of community sentences when dealing with young offenders. This would be more consistent with the kind of objective assessment of these cases indicated by the von Hirsch-Jareborg scale. Applying that approach, the element of theft would not be greatly significant in most of the cases, especially in the fifth category, and the principal task would be to assess the gravity of the attack on the victim's physical integrity, including psychological harm. It would therefore be preferable to think in terms of the level of the violence involved or threatened (grievous bodily harm, actual bodily harm or a mere assault) and to make the assessment of relative seriousness on that ground. Such a revised approach would probably indicate the reduction of many robbery sentences, and this would meet with opposition from those who would depict it as an 'invitation to rob'. Such language can be deployed in respect of any reassessment of the sentencing structure that leads to the lowering of some sentences; and it is only justifiable on its own terms if there is a clear relationship between sentence levels and robbery levels, whereas the figures from the Street Crime Initiative suggest that it is policing and prosecution practices that are more important than any marginal deterrence derived from variations in the sentence level.[139]

4.4.10 Burglary

For sentencing purposes this offence is usually subdivided into two distinct types, burglaries of dwellings and burglaries of commercial or industrial premises. The Criminal Justice Act 1991 confirmed this by reducing the maximum penalty for non-residential burglary to 10 years, below the 14 years for residential burglary. The distinction is that the commercial burglaries are often viewed as theft combined with damage, whereas the residential burglaries may additionally cause significant psychological harm to the householder, chiefly because of the invasion of the home and personal possessions and sometimes because of the loss of treasured mementos. The possible effects were documented by Maguire (1982), who found that over a quarter of victims of residential burglary suffer quite serious shock as a result of the offence, and that the lives of some two-thirds of victims are affected for a period of weeks following the offence. Courts have sometimes implied that burglary of an

---

138 SAP, *Robbery* (2004).
139 See further von Hirsch, Bottoms, Burney and Wikstrom (1999), discussed in ch. 3.3.2 above.

occupied house at night almost amounts to an offence of violence – presumably because there is thought to be considerable risk of violence, although in Maguire's study the burglar and householder came face to face in only 4 per cent of cases.[140]

Sentencing practice even in residential burglary cases has always been diverse. The law classifies as burglary an incident in which someone walks through an open kitchen door and steals a radio-cassette recorder, and in his guideline judgment in *Brewster* (1998),[141] Lord Bingham CJ made it clear that not all cases of domestic burglary are so serious that only a custodial sentence can be justified. A Home Office analysis of domestic burglars aged 18 and over who were sentenced in March 1996 found that, of those sentenced at the Crown Court, where this was the first domestic burglary some 68 per cent were sentenced to custody with an average sentence length of 15.9 months; where it was the second domestic burglary, 84 per cent went to prison with an average sentence of 14.8 months; and where it was the third or subsequent domestic burglary conviction, 86 per cent went to prison with an average sentence of 19.6 months.[142] Parliament thought that the element of 'progression' should be steeper, in order to deter and/or incapacitate repeat domestic burglars, and so s. 4 of the Crime (Sentence) Act 1997 introduced a minimum sentence for the third domestic burglary. In outline,[143] that section requires a court to pass a sentence of three years' imprisonment for the third domestic burglary unless it would be 'unjust in all the circumstances' to do so, but a burglary conviction only qualifies for this purpose if it relates to a crime committed after conviction of another qualifying burglary. This means that the provision did not begin to bite until about 2003, because to qualify a burglar had to have a sequence of conviction – sentence – conviction – sentence – conviction, each offence of conviction being committed after conviction for the previous one.

The Sentencing Advisory Panel took the view that this required the setting of new guidelines for this offence, and in its Advice it began from the proposition that the third domestic burglary should have a starting point of three years' imprisonment, and that the first and second burglary should therefore be ranged in steps up to that level. The Panel had commissioned research into public attitudes towards burglary, and from the results it derived the concept of a 'standard burglary' (involving theft of electrical goods and/or jewellery, damage to the house and some turmoil within it, no direct violence but trauma to the victim). It proposed a starting point of nine months for the first standard burglary (less for a lower level burglary) and 18 months for the second, arriving at the three-year minimum for the third, before taking account of aggravating and mitigating factors.[144] The Court of Appeal in *McInerney and Keating* (2003)[145] gave general support to the Panel's analysis of the issues but held that more emphasis needed to be given to constructive efforts to break the cycle of offending. Lord Woolf CJ noted that a custodial sentence of

---

140 Maguire (1982), pp. 129ff.   141 [1998] 1 Cr App R (S) 181.
142 Reported in Lord Bingham's judgment, ibid., p. 184.
143 The provision is discussed more fully in the context of persistent offenders in ch. 6.7 below.
144 SAP, *Domestic Burglary* (2002).   145 [2003] 2 Cr App R (S) 240.

nine months would mean some four-and-a-half months in prison, less any time on home detention curfew, and that such a brief period in custody might be less helpful than a well-planned and enforced community sentence. He quoted passages from a report by the Social Exclusion Unit lamenting the inability of prison to turn people away from reoffending.[146] This led him to propose a starting point of a community sentence for the first, and even for the second, domestic burglary. This is closer to Lord Woolf's general approach to imprisonment than his remarks on robbery,[147] but it resulted in a public furore about judicial leniency and condemnation by the Home Secretary.[148] However, the guidelines have not been abrogated and the force of Lord Woolf's reasoning remains unimpaired. The judgment also recognizes that the minimum sentence 'gives the sentencer a fairly substantial degree of discretion as to the categories of situations where the presumption can be rebutted',[149] and that after the third qualifying conviction 'the increase in sentencing levels should slow significantly . . . [in order] to retain a degree of proportionality between the level of sentence for burglary and other serious offences'.[150]

This is an important consideration, and its force will be considered particularly when discussing persistent offenders in Chapter 6.7 below. Even if much longer sentences are justifiable for so-called professional burglars[151] – and that point is arguable, since such sentences are at the same level as that of an aggravated rape – there are other persistent burglars who have been manifestly over-sentenced. Thus in *Woods* (1998)[152] an offender with 121 previous convictions and 23 previous prison sentences, who was 'essentially a vagrant', broke into a vicarage, put a few items in a bag and then fell asleep, to be awoken by the vicar. The trial judge found his way to a sentence of six years' imprisonment for this pathetic offence; the Court of Appeal recognized that that was too high, and yet only reduced it to four years. This is still far too high for this relatively minor case involving an offender whose crimes are not particularly menacing. If it was his previous convictions that lengthened the sentence, then this is a questionable interpretation of the nature of his criminal record – he is hardly a professional criminal. More generally, the decided cases on burglary and the minimum sentence raise questions about relativities with other offences such as rape and serious woundings.

4.4.11 Theft in breach of trust

One form of so-called 'white-collar crime' which may yield considerable financial gain for the offender is theft in breach of trust. English law has a single offence of theft: the present category is for sentencing purposes only, and extends to other offences such as false accounting. It includes solicitors, bank managers, building

146 Ibid., at paras. 38–39.   147 See part 4.4.9 of this chapter, above.
148 For suggestions that Lord Woolf's guidelines were significantly lower than practice, see Davies and Tyrer (2003), although that research takes no account of the effect of mitigating factors.
149 [2003] 2 Cr App R (S) 240 at para. 16.   150 Ibid., at para. 48.
151 *Brewster* (above, n. 141), 10 years upheld; *Jenkins* [2002] 1 Cr App R (S) 22, 8 years upheld.
152 [1998] 2 Cr App R (S) 237.

society cashiers, club treasurers and others who divert funds which are under their control. Post office employees who steal from the mail are sentenced on a similar basis.[153]

Why should such offences be regarded as particularly serious? The answer, at least in relation to public officials and members of the professions, is that they are selected for their positions so that ordinary people can rely upon them. As Cox put it in the nineteenth century, professional people 'trade upon their honesty. They sell their trustworthiness.'[154] The Court of Appeal has commented that 'if people cannot deal with solicitors in absolute reliance on their honesty, the business of the country would be seriously affected in all sorts of ways'.[155] The same reasoning presumably underlies the Inland Revenue's readiness to bring prosecutions against accountants found to have made false declarations for taxation purposes, which contrasts with their extreme reluctance to prosecute other taxpayers even where considerable sums have been underpaid.[156] What this seems to suggest is that the gravamen of theft in breach of trust stems not merely from the loss to the victim but also from the public significance of the breach of professional responsibility. It is not merely the effect on the victim's living standard, but the fact that the loss was inflicted by someone who is supposed to preserve and protect that living standard. The professional status of the offender has been betrayed, and that renders the crime more serious. There are other factors which affect the seriousness of these offences: on the one hand, they usually involve planning and often continue over a substantial period of time, and on the other hand they are usually committed by people of previous good character who suffer many consequential deprivations (loss of job prospects, loss of pension rights) as a result of conviction. The public element of breach of trust creates a difficulty for the von Hirsch-Jareborg framework, since there is no necessary impact on the living standard of the typical victim (who may be corporate, or simply one of many small depositors suffering small losses). If these cases are to be accommodated, some kind of public dimension must be added.

In his guideline judgment in *Barrick* (1985),[157] Lord Lane CJ concluded that sentencing levels for breach of trust by professional people had become too low – perhaps because the courts had been giving too great a mitigating effect to the secondary consequences of conviction. He stated that 'professional men should expect to be punished as severely as the others [he had referred to thefts from the mail by postal workers]; and in some cases more severely'. The guidelines, subsequently amended by the Court in *Clark* (1998),[158] propose that for sums up to £17,500, sentences of up to 21 months should be contemplated; for £17,500 to £100,000 the range should be two to three years; for £100,000 to £250,000, three to four years; for £250,000 to £1 million, between five and nine years; and for £1 million or more, terms of 10 years upwards should be considered. Although the maximum for theft

153 E.g. *Poulter* (1985) 7 Cr App R (S) 260.   154 Cox (1877), p. 55.
155 *Wooding* [1978] Crim LR 701.   156 Roording (1996).
157 (1985) 7 Cr App R (S) 142.   158 [1998] 2 Cr App R (S) 95.

is now seven years' imprisonment, those offences involving two or more people may be charged as conspiracy to defraud (which has a maximum of 10 years), and many of the others involve several charges, so that consecutive sentences will be appropriate.[159] In *Barrick* some nine factors relevant to seriousness were set out, including the proposition that the higher the offender's rank, the more serious the offence.

To what extent these guidelines are translated into practice remains an open question. The survey of sentencing in the mid-1990s by Flood-Page and Mackie found that, even in the Crown Court, just over half of the cases of theft in breach of trust did not receive a custodial sentence, sometimes because the money was repaid, sometimes because of personal mitigating factors.[160] It seems likely that some courts are still over-impressed with the mitigation in these cases, despite the warning in *Barrick* that the secondary consequences of conviction should not be taken into account, and the result may be that white-collar offenders benefit from a leniency which is not shown to others who steal items of much lower value, such as wallets and handbags.

4.4.12 Theft from the person

Another form of behaviour covered by English law's single offence of theft is theft from the person, often taking the form of pickpocketing. Many of the offenders have considerable criminal records, making it difficult to make direct comparisons with theft in breach of trust, save to say that a single offence in that category may often involve a greater sum than repeated offences of pickpocketing. When discussing burglary of a dwelling, it was argued that the psychological harm which often results increases the offence's seriousness. Does pickpocketing have any similar feature?

In its report on mode of trial in 1975, the James Committee took the view that pickpocketing should be regarded as a particularly serious form of theft:

> Theft from the person, particularly pickpocketing, seems to us to fall into a different category. It is generally regarded as a particularly offensive and frightening type of theft, in some ways akin to robbery and burglary in its invasion of a person's privacy; the amount stolen bears little or no relation to the 'criminality' of the offence because the pickpocket cannot know the amount until he completes the theft; and the offence tends to be committed by gangs, which often operate on a semi-professional basis.

This combination of factors is certainly sufficient to take pickpocketing above theft from a shop or stall, but the Committee's reasoning begs a number of questions. It may be true that a pickpocket rarely knows how much is likely to be gained from the offence, although that can be said of many burglars when they enter houses. It is not known how victims of pickpocketing are affected by the offence: we have

---

159 For an investment fraud for which a sentence of seven years was held appropriate, see *Attorney General's References Nos. 48, 49, 50 and 51 of 2002 (Paulssen and others)* [2003] 2 Cr App R (S) 192.

160 Flood-Page and Mackie (1998), p. 85.

no findings comparable with those on burglary, and there are intuitive reasons for believing that the consequences will usually be less traumatic, although they may still be significant.

The involvement of gangs and of 'semi-professional' offenders, referred to by the James Committee, continues to have a significant effect on sentences for this type of offence. For an isolated offence, by offenders whose record does not suggest frequent pickpocketing, a sentence as long as 12 months' imprisonment has been held proper – the offence was an attempt to steal a purse from a woman's handbag.[161] Sentences as long as five years were upheld in *Freeman* (1989)[162] and *Whitrid* (1989)[163] for men with previous convictions for pickpocketing, who worked in gangs and were described as professional criminals. However, five years is close to the maximum for theft (seven years); the reliance on deterrent reasoning is open to the doubts expressed in Chapter 3.2.2; and the reliance on that judicial favourite, 'prevalence', was criticized in part 1 of this chapter. In *Gwillim-Jones* (2002)[164] the Court of Appeal reviewed the authorities on theft and attempted theft of handbags and upheld a sentence of three years on a man with over 90 previous convictions. In *McGhee and Hughes* (2004)[165] the Court reduced from five to four years the sentences on two men who picked the pockets of elderly victims in a hotel.

Are these sentences at the appropriate level? In determining the commensurate sentence, courts ought to focus on three elements: the amount taken, the psychological effect on the victim once the loss is discovered, and perhaps any secondary fears among tourists and others preyed upon by pickpockets. The last point is rather remote and imponderable, and the psychological consequences for victims – the main distinguishing mark of this type of theft – are inadequately documented and easily exaggerated. The offence invades the privacy of the victim, but the typical diminution of living standard is unlikely to be great. The amounts taken pale into insignificance when compared with frauds and breaches of trust involving many thousands of pounds, often sentenced at a much lower level than the offences of bag theft or pickpocketing (as is evident from 4.4.11 above). The culpability may be high where the offenders are classified as 'professional', but the offence is surely in the lowest band of the von Hirsch-Jareborg scale. Pickpocketing should be ranked as considerably less serious than burglary, and there is insufficient justification for reliance on assertions about prevalence, deterrence and 'professionalism' rather than on the modest amounts proved to have been stolen.

4.4.13 Handling stolen goods

In 2001 the Sentencing Advisory Panel proposed sentencing guidelines on handling stolen goods as part of its programme of proposing guidelines for frequently committed offences. The guidelines were set in the context of a distinction between sexual, violent or frightening offences and other property offences, with handling

161 *Smith and Read* [1997] 1 Cr App R (S) 342.   162 (1989) 11 Cr App R (S) 398.
163 (1989) 11 Cr App R (S) 403.   164 [2002] 1 Cr App R (S) 19.
165 [2004] 1 Cr App R (S) 399.

falling into the latter category – unless the handler knew that the goods had been obtained through a violent offence, such as robbery. In *Webbe* (2002)[166] the Court of Appeal handed down guidelines based largely on the Panel's advice. Having set out lists of aggravating and mitigating factors, it divided handling offences into three levels for sentencing purposes. At the lowest level are cases where property valued at less than £1,000 has been acquired for resale, or property of slightly higher value for personal use, and where the offender is young or has no record of dishonesty: a fine or community sentence would be the usual starting point. The custody threshold would be reached in a second group of offences characterized by a more sophisticated approach or a record of dishonesty. In the higher range of 12 months to four years would fall offences committed in the course of a business, or where the offender is an organizer or distributor of the proceeds of crime, and where the value is up to £100,000. The *Webbe* guidelines have been applied in cases such as *Dixon* (2002)[167] to reduce from three years to 18 months a sentence for assisting in the retention of goods worth some £255,000 from a recent burglary, by storing the goods at his home; and *Gwyer* (2002)[168] to justify a sentence of four years for a man who was part of a professional operation to 'sell on' antiques obtained by burglary and was convicted on nine counts of handling.

In terms of the von Hirsch-Jareborg scale, offences of handling will mostly be at the lowest end of the spectrum. They do not usually affect the victim's physical integrity, freedom from humiliation or privacy and autonomy, and their effect on 'material support and amenity' will usually not be great. If they diminish the victim's 'living standard', that diminution will usually be at the level of enhancements of the quality of life. There may be exceptions to these propositions – a handler who knowingly feeds off a violent robbery, or who knowingly takes property that is central to a person's life – but they would be unusual cases. Those who regard handling as a particularly serious offence argue that it is handlers who support thieves, burglars and robbers, and that therefore their offences take on some of the gravity of those other crimes. If burglary is known to be the source of particular goods, the handler bears some responsibility for the misery or deeper psychological effects typically felt by a householder whose house is burgled. But even if that argument is accepted, it is surely the burglars who bear most of the responsibility for inflicting such psychological harm, and the handler's responsibility is more remote and more attenuated. However, this is a difficult question, which is crucial – as we shall now see – in the context of indecent photographs of children.

4.4.14 Child pornography

In 2001 the Court of Appeal asked the Sentencing Advisory Panel to draw up guidelines on offences involving child pornography,[169] and also in 2001 the maximum penalty for possessing an indecent photograph of a child was increased from six

---

166 [2002] 1 Cr App R (S) 82.   167 [2002] 2 Cr App R (S) 18.
168 [2002] 2 Cr App R (S) 246; see also *Chalcraft and Campbell* [2002] 2 Cr App R (S) 172, where *Webbe* was applied but where an element of entrapment was held to justify a reduction in sentence.
169 In *Wild (No. 1)* [2002] 1 Cr App R (S) 37.

months to five years, and the maximum for making, distributing or publishing such photographs was increased from 3 to 10 years.[170] The Panel's advice was substantially followed by the Court of Appeal in *Oliver* (2003),[171] where guidelines were laid down. The centrepiece is a five-level scale of images, according to the relative seriousness of the activity they portray. The guidelines also rest on the nature of the offender's involvement (from mere viewing to actual involvement in production or distribution), and on the number of images involved, which in some cases run to hundreds or thousands. Where the offender merely downloads (and does not distribute) images at level 1 or a small number of images at level 2, a community sentence would usually be appropriate. But the custody threshold is reached when a person downloads many images at level 2 or a small number at level 3, and from there upwards the levels of imprisonment depend on the number of images at levels 3, 4 or 5. From these starting points, of course, courts would take account of mitigating and aggravating factors in arriving at an appropriate sentence.[172] The guidelines in *Oliver* have been much cited in cases dealing with those who have downloaded child pornography from the Internet, but there remain important questions of principle relevant to assessing the relative seriousness of such offences.

On the von Hirsch-Jareborg scale, the actual making of indecent photographs of children may infringe two significant interests – freedom from humiliation or degrading treatment of the children, and their privacy and autonomy. In some cases, perhaps many, the photographed activities may have a lasting effect on their psychological adjustment.[173] However, to what extent should an offender who merely downloads images already available be sentenced on the basis of involvement in the exploitation of young children? The Panel's view, accepted by the Court, was that

> an offender convicted for possession of child pornography should be treated as being to some degree complicit in the original child sexual abuse which was involved in the production of the images. The level of sentence for possession should also reflect the continuing damage which is done to the victim or victims, through copying and further dissemination of the pornographic images.[174]

The argument in the first sentence is similar to that often applied to the offence of handling stolen goods, and its relationship to the original offence (burglary, robbery or theft) whereby the goods were obtained. The argument is either an expressive one – that the offender signifies his endorsement or support for the activities depicted by downloading the images – or a deterrent one – that if people did

---

170 By s. 41 Criminal Justice and Court Services Act 2000.
171 [2003] 2 Cr App R (S) 64, adopting SAP, *Offences involving Child Pornography* (2002).
172 E.g. *Tatam* [2005] 1 Cr App R (S) 256, downloading some half a million indecent images of children, including over 3,000 showing penetrative sexual activity involving children. The Court upheld the sentence of five years' imprisonment, with an extended sentence (see ch. 6.8 for the new form of extended sentence).
173 For such a case, involving the actual taking of photographs of very young children, see *Saunders* [2004] 2 Cr App R (S) 459 – firmly stated by the Court to be 'not an *Oliver* case' because of the direct involvement of the offender in the activities themselves.
174 SAP, *Offences involving Child Pornography*, para. 13.

not download the images there would be no incentive for them to be made. The deterrent point is arguable, since there are certainly some people who take such photographs for their own use only.[175] The expressive point is stronger, for how could a person who knowingly downloads such an image protest that he does not condone the activities depicted? His downloading may be remote from the original making of the image, but in the absence of any plea of mistake he must to some extent be endorsing what was done. This may explain why downloading such images of children cannot be de-coupled from the making of them, but it remains for discussion whether the sentence levels indicated by *Oliver* are too low, about right, or too high.[176]

4.4.15 The Magistrates' Courts guidelines

More will be written in Chapter 9, below, on the approach of the Court of Appeal to the lower reaches of the 'tariff' and on other relevant guidelines. Before 1999, when the Sentencing Advisory Panel started work, one problem was that the Court of Appeal had little opportunity to deal with the general run of non-serious crime that is the daily diet of the magistrates' courts and of many Crown Court sittings. Perhaps because the Court of Appeal's pronouncements on relatively non-serious crime were infrequent and unconvincing, the Magistrates' Association began to draw up its own guidelines. Now they are drawn up by a group including justices' clerks and district judges, and are known as the *Magistrates' Court Sentencing Guidelines*.[177] Each of the selected offences has a page devoted to it: the page begins by indicating a guideline level of sentence (i.e. either fine/discharge, community penalty or custody), then sets out some of the factors that will make each offence more or less serious, and then draws attention to personal mitigating factors. Leaving out the section on road traffic offences, some of the principal guideline levels in the latest (2004) version are as follows:

　　1. *Guideline – custody*. Affray; aggravated vehicle-taking; assault occasioning actual bodily harm; assault on a police officer; breach of an anti-social behaviour order; harassment, alarm or distress with intent; harassment causing fear of violence; possessing an offensive weapon or a bladed instrument; racially aggravated common assault;[178] racially aggravated threatening behaviour; racially aggravated harassment, alarm or distress with intent; racially aggravated harassment causing fear of violence; theft in breach of trust.

　　2. *Guideline – community penalty*. Animal cruelty; burglary not in a dwelling; common assault; cultivation of cannabis; disorderly behaviour with intent to cause harassment, alarm or distress; evasion of duty; going equipped to steal; harassment, alarm or distress; interference with a vehicle; handling stolen goods; obtaining by

---

175 E.g. *Saunders*, above n. 173.
176 SAP is revisiting its earlier Advice in the context of its proposals on sentencing under the Sexual Offences Act 2003.
177 For fuller discussion of their origins, see ch. 2.5 above.
178 In these three lists, 'racially aggravated' is shorthand for offences aggravated by race, religion, disability or sexual orientation. See below, ch. 7.2.

deception; possession of class A drug; racially aggravated criminal damage; racially aggravated harassment, alarm or distress; racially aggravated disorderly behaviour; school non-attendance; social security fraud; taking a vehicle without the owner's consent; theft; threatening behaviour.

3. *Guideline – fine or discharge.* Criminal damage; cultivation of cannabis; disorderly behaviour; drunk and disorderly; making off without payment; non-payment of television licence; obstructing a police officer; possessing a class B or C drug.

These are merely guidelines or 'starting points', and of course the sentence in each case should reflect not merely any factors which make the particular offence more or less serious, but also mitigating factors personal to the offender. Several of the distinctions reflect points already discussed above (e.g. the difference between domestic burglary and other burglaries), and other distinctions based on aggravating factors (e.g. that between common assault and assault on a police officer) are discussed in Chapter 5. The guidelines have undoubtedly become more severe since they were first drafted in 1989, and one feature of the 2004 guidelines was the removal of several offences for which the guideline was previously custody into a higher category that requires the court to consider whether its sentencing powers are sufficient to deal with the case – for example, aggravated assault, actual bodily harm or unlawful wounding or grievous bodily harm, the possession of indecent photographs of children, the production or supply of class A, B or C drugs, and violent disorder.

As mentioned in Chapter 2.5.2 above, these guidelines appear to be adopted by a majority of areas, and the co-option of justices' clerks and district judges was designed to persuade benches and courts in all areas to adopt them. The latest (2004) version will be the last to be produced in this way, since the Sentencing Guidelines Council now has responsibility for setting guidelines for all courts. Presumably the Sentencing Advisory Panel will soon start work on a revision of the guidelines, with a view to submitting them to the Council for eventual approval as definitive guidelines. That, for the first time, would cloak the guidelines with legal authority.

4.5 Individual culpability

So far, this chapter has concentrated on one of the elements of proportionality – offence-seriousness – and on one of the components of offence-seriousness – the harm done or risked by the offender's conduct. We now turn to the other principal dimension of offence-seriousness, the culpability of the individual offender.

> Harm refers to the injury done or risked by the criminal act. Culpability refers to the factors of intent, motive and circumstance that determine how much the offender should be held accountable for his act. Culpability, in turn, affects the assessment of harm. The consequences that should be considered in gauging the harmfulness of an act should be those that can fairly be attributed to the actor's choice.[179]

---

179 Von Hirsch (1986), pp. 64–5.

A number of the discussions in part 4.4 above turn on the degree of offender's culpability. It is now time to explore the relevant principles.

In English law most of the offences discussed in part 4.4 above require proof of an intention to cause the prohibited harm, or proof of recklessness in that regard. This is sometimes termed the subjective principle of criminal liability: for most of the serious offences, criminal liability depends on the offender's choice or awareness of what he was doing.[180] While courts may deliberate over whether or not the offender can be said to have intended a particular result, the question at the sentencing stage is rather different. The concept of intention in English law is wide enough to comprise a whole range of mental states, from planning, through deliberation, to a hastily conceived intent, a 'spur of the moment' decision and an impulsive response to a situation. Any of these mental attitudes satisfies the definition of intention in English law: so long as the offender realized for a split-second the nature of the act, it is likely to be held intentional. However, one might wish to argue that the premeditated offender is more culpable than the one who acts on the spur of the moment. As Bentham put it, the longer the offender continued under the influence of anti-social motives, the more convincing is the evidence that he has rejected social motives.[181] So there are degrees of culpability within the concept of intention, running from the careful plan down to the sudden impulse.

Exactly the same might be said of the legal concept of recklessness. It is usually defined in terms of awareness of risk, but the degree of culpability surely varies according to the magnitude of the risk and the amount of calculation involved. Although the term 'reckless' may be thought to suggest a carefree act executed with abandon, there is a scale of recklessness running along two dimensions: first, there is the anticipated degree of risk that the harm will materialize, from a high to a low risk; second, there is a similar scale to that within intention, running from a carefully calculated risk, through to a deliberate risk and a sudden risk, to impulsive risk taking. Once again, the decision on criminal liability does not supply the sentencer with the fine detail necessary for an estimate of culpability. It is possible that some of the more calculated forms of recklessness might be adjudged more serious than impulsive forms of intention. Tom Hadden has argued that courts should be required to determine issues such as premeditation or impulse at trial:[182] he accepted that this would add considerably to the length and complexity of proceedings, which some would regard as sufficient to condemn the proposal, but he makes the strong point that these decisions are no less important for the offender than the 'intention or recklessness' decision which the law now requires.

A further point is that the two key legal concepts of intention and recklessness do not exhaust the factors which do, and should, influence judgments of culpability. As a matter of law, there is a range of possible defences to criminal liability – insanity, duress, mistake of fact, and to some extent mistake of law and intoxication. English

---

180 For fuller discussion see Ashworth (2003a), ch. 5.
181 Bentham (1789), ch. XI, para. 42.   182 Hadden (1968), pp. 534–5.

law confines each of these defences narrowly,[183] and does so partly because effect can be given at the sentencing stage to variations in culpability. So it is important to consider whether a case contains an element of duress, mistake, entrapment by the police or provocation. As Martin Wasik has argued, there is a 'scale of excuse, running downwards from excusing conditions, through partial excuses to mitigating factors'.[184] Thus, provocation and entrapment do not constitute general defences in English law (though provocation may reduce murder to manslaughter), but courts are expected to take them into account when assessing culpability for the purpose of sentencing. The claims of particular excuses to be included as full defences or merely reflected in sentencing will not be discussed in detail here.[185] The important point is to recognize that culpability is a wider issue than cognition, as represented by the two legal terms of intention and recklessness, and that it extends to a wide range of volitional and situational factors.

Indeed, the boundaries should be pushed further still. It is not simply that consideration of a claim of duress or provocation may take the sentencer beyond the offender's awareness of what he was doing, to his control over his emotions and the pressures exerted by others. There are at least two further issues – the question whether individuals should generally be held responsible for their behaviour and their intentions, and the question whether culpability might be reduced by a disadvantaged social background or an unsatisfactory upbringing. As we shall see, the questions are interconnected.

The first of these issues is raised by determinists, who argue that all our behaviour is determined and therefore it is neither sensible nor fair to hold people responsible even when they appear to have intended to cause a particular harm. However, very few people hold this extreme form of determinism, and it has been convincingly argued that there is insufficient justification for regarding determinism as either true or false.[186] So there is no reason to abandon the common-sense view that in most matters we have some degree of choice whether to act or refrain from acting. This is a qualified statement, because even English law accepts that there are some occasions when behaviour can be regarded as so heavily determined by other factors as not to justify any blame. This is so where the defence of insanity or the defence of duress succeeds. These may be regarded as atypical cases which do not defeat the general proposition that most people have sufficient freedom of action for most of the time so that one can properly judge people in terms of culpability and responsibility.

There is a second challenge, and this comes not from philosophical arguments about freedom of the will but from criminological arguments about the causes of crime. In their speeches in mitigation of sentence, lawyers sometimes refer to the fact that the offender had a difficult family background or has been subject to several social disadvantages. Should this be accorded any effect in judging culpability?

---

183 Ashworth (2003a), ch. 6.   184 Wasik (1982), p. 524.
185 See Wasik (1982), Wasik (1983) and Ashworth (2003a), ch. 6.9.   186 Kenny (1978).

Table 10. *Association between social background and 'delinquency'*

Characteristic	Percentage of those with characteristic found 'delinquent'	Percentage of those without characteristic found 'delinquent'
Lowest income (poor)	33	17
Large family (five or more children)	32	17
Criminal parent	36	16
Known delinquent sibling	45	15
Bad parental behaviour	32	16
Parental separation before boy reached age 10	39	19
Teachers' ratings of boys 'most troublesome' at age 8	38	12

Source: Based on West (1973), p. 191.

There are research findings, based on a detailed follow-up of the careers of some 800 boys, which show that certain background factors tend to be associated strongly with subsequent criminality. West and Farrington's Cambridge study produced the findings shown in Table 10.

The figures in Table 10 show the percentage of boys with each characteristic who were later detected in lawbreaking. Although it might be tempting to argue that an individual with a known delinquent sibling has less chance of avoiding detection than one without a known delinquent sibling, not least because the police and others might tend to identify a 'problem family', the key question is whether the offending behaviour of such boys is less under their control. This is not a strong inference, since proportionately more of those with delinquent siblings were not detected in delinquency (55 per cent) than were (45 per cent). A different approach might be to take a cluster of characteristics: the Cambridge study found that over half of the boys with three or more of the five adversities (low family income, large family size, parental criminality, low intelligence and poor parental behaviour) became delinquent. Since these characteristics, taken together, suggest that the boys had from an early age been subject to influences which were not conducive to law-abidance, there is some basis for the argument as to whether they should be treated as less culpable than those who have had the benefit of more benign influences. As Roger Hood argues, one must question whether these five adversities do not themselves 'arise, to some considerable extent, from wider socio-economic and cultural circumstances'.[187] Economic, employment and education policy all have a profound effect on the way in which people live. This is a point which criminologists

187 Hood (1987), p. 532.

of various hues have been making for years – from the Marxists who emphasize the organization of the means of production, through Robert Merton's US version of anomie theory, to left-realists such as John Lea and Jock Young, who argue that the key issue is relative deprivation: 'people's perception of unjustified inequalities, and of being excluded from the glittering prizes of capitalist society – material wealth or individual status and prestige – and marginalization from legitimate channels of redressing the balance'.[188]

In a survey of human development and criminal careers, David Farrington has demonstrated the wide range of family situation, social and economic factors that are correlated with offending behaviour, and indeed with other behavioural traits such as daring, the pursuit of excitement, and sexual intercourse and drinking at an early age.[189] Some support for the social arguments comes from a Home Office study of trends in crime by Simon Field: by examining recorded crime rates and economic fluctuations, he suggested that 'the economic circumstances of individuals play a role in the causation of crime'. Thus

> in years when people are increasing their spending very little, or even reducing it, property crime tends to grow relatively quickly, whereas during years when people are rapidly increasing their expenditure, property crime tends to grow less rapidly or even fall. In England and Wales the relationship has held throughout the twentieth century, and has been particularly strong in the last 20 years.[190]

Findings such as these may tend to confirm the general causal relationship between economic policy and crime, and they may therefore strengthen the argument that an offender with an appropriately disadvantaged background might be regarded as less culpable.

Strong arguments have, however, been ranged against this. It can be contended that these are general issues of social policy which can be tackled only through 'broad and slow social processes', and the need is to deal with individual cases now. Wilson and Herrnstein accept that criminality derives to a considerable extent from attitudes which are socially conditioned, but nevertheless conclude that 'the very process by which we learn to avoid crime requires that the courts act as if crime were wholly the result of free choice'.[191] In other words, desirable as it may be to work for long-term alleviation of the social problems associated with crime, the proper short-term approach is to regard offenders as rational, choosing citizens and not to reduce sentences wholesale because of the imperfections of social policy. This analysis is unacceptable. True, the findings of criminological surveys must be shown to have implications for particular cases before any reduced culpability can be contemplated. But if there is evidence that a person's offending derives in some significant measure from upbringing or social background, that should be a ground

188 Lea and Young (1993), p. ix.   189 Farrington (1997).   190 Field (1990).
191 Wilson and Herrnstein (1985), pp. 528–9; cf. Hood (1987), pp. 533–4.

for reduced culpability. There remains the counter-argument that by no means all people with such backgrounds fall into crime (or are detected in crime); but there are strong social grounds for recognizing a diminished degree of responsibility among people with these characteristics, even though the extent of the reduction in responsibility will vary in individual cases.[192]

We have seen, therefore, that the assessment of culpability has various dimensions. At the level of legal liability it usually turns on intention, recklessness and a limited group of excusing defences. Where the offender's case has elements of an excusing condition but falls outside the narrow legal definition for a defence, this should be a good ground for reduced culpability. And there are wider factors of family background and social conditions which may, in appropriate cases, reduce the offender's culpability. These instances of reduced culpability might be regarded either as mitigating factors or as questions of culpability, and there seems to be no firm dividing line between them. Moreover, all the grounds for reduced culpability have within them differences of degree. Just as the legal concepts of intention and recklessness were shown to cover different degrees of culpability, so there are different degrees of such factors as provocation too. However, these details will not be pursued here.[193]

4.6 Proportionality, human rights and European law

It is important here to note briefly the various ways in which European laws require the proportionality of sentences to offences. In Chapter 3.4.1 above the effects of European human rights law were mentioned, and it was observed that proportionality constraints can be found in Articles 3 and 5 of the European Convention on Human Rights, and also in the various articles (such as Art. 8 on respect for private life) that allow limited interference with Convention rights. A further source of proportionality constraints in English law may be found in European Community law. It is well known that European Community law maintains a right of free movement, but equally it enables member states to penalize those who fail to carry the required documentation to take advantage of that right. The European Court of Justice has insisted that sentences for breach must remain in proportion to the relevant right: any penalty 'which is so disproportionate to the gravity of the infringement that it becomes an obstacle to the exercise of that freedom' is inconsistent with Community law.[194] This is a general doctrine of Community law, which is applicable in other similar circumstances.[195] It has been reinforced by the provision,

---

192 Cf. Hudson (1998) with Hutton (1999).
193 For discussion of provocation and intoxication in relation to sentencing, see Ashworth (1983), pp. 167–73.
194 *Casati* [1981] ECR 2595, para. 27; see also *Pieck* [1980] ECR 2171, and discussion by Guldenmund, Harding and Sherlock (1995), pp. 110–17.
195 On which, see Baker (1998), pp. 371–3.

in the Charter of Fundamental Rights that forms part of the new Constitution for Europe, that 'the severity of penalties must not be disproportionate to the criminal offence'.[196]

4.7 Proportionality and offence-seriousness

This chapter has considered ways of gauging the seriousness of the harm caused or threatened by various offences; the principal issues involved in assessing culpability; and the problem of 'discounting' seriousness to reflect remoteness from the harm. Issues of aggravation and mitigation have been left over to Chapter 5. The effect of previous convictions is reserved for Chapter 6. The problems raised by proportionality in cases where the offender has to be sentenced for two or more offences will be examined in Chapter 8: these are difficult problems, since most discussions assume that it is two individual offences which are to be compared. Lastly, there is also the difficulty of achieving some kind of proportionality between the seriousness of the offence and the severity of the sentence, aired in part 4.3 above and discussed in Chapters 9 and 10. The present chapter is therefore little more than an exploration of one key concept in proportionality, the seriousness of the offence.

In practice, all the elements of proportionality constantly come into play. The justification for divorcing the treatment of offence-seriousness from that of the use of custodial sentences is to enable careful analysis. It has been noted that the Criminal Justice Act 2003 retains the concept of 'commensurability', despite the destructive interpretation by the Court of Appeal of the equivalent provision in the 1991 Act.[197] However, the 2003 Act also requires courts, in s. 142, to have regard to five separate and conflicting purposes of sentencing. Although the Sentencing Guidelines Council has insisted that the priority is to ensure that sentences are proportionate, s. 142 sows the seeds of confusion.

It is evident from part 4.4 of this chapter that there is already some confusion in the setting of sentence levels, and that considerations of proportionality are not always uppermost. The conflicting rationales emerge clearly if the sentencing approaches to rape and attempted murder are compared with those to robbery and drug dealing. In part 4.4 of this chapter a modified version of the approach proposed by von Hirsch and Jareborg was applied to these and other offences. It can be strongly argued that the starting points for armed robberies and drug importation fail to stand in a proportionate relationship to those for rape (five or eight years) and the normal range for attempted murder between friends (10 to 12 years). Where rape and attempted murder strike at very basic elements in one's living standard, robbery and drug smuggling may often be more remote or diluted. Thus the courts have tended to justify their sentencing approaches to robbery and

---

196 Art. II.49(3), discussed by van Zyl Smit and Ashworth (2004).
197 In *Cunningham* (1993) 14 Cr App R (S) 444, discussed in ch. 3.5 above.

drug smuggling on general deterrent grounds. This raises the question whether in this respect English sentencing attributes more importance to property than to physical safety. Drug smuggling is immensely profitable and, although attempts have been made to justify its high position on grounds of (remote) threat of harm to others, it seems that profitability is a central concern – even when sentencing drug couriers.[198] It seems unlikely that armed robbery would be ranked so highly if the two constituent parts were treated separately: the threats or use of force involved would not themselves attract substantial sentences, and many building society robberies and street robberies yield fairly modest sums of money. If it is the deterrent rationale that gives these offences their high position on the tariff, then the evidence in its favour must be examined. Recent careful examinations of the general evidence demonstrate that there is no adequate empirical basis for believing that the marginal deterrent gains from increasing sentence levels above what is proportionate are likely to be significant.[199]

In some fields it appears that mitigating factors have such an enormous effect as to upset the natural ranking. Attention was drawn earlier to the sentence range for manslaughter upon provocation: it rarely attracts more than seven or eight years' imprisonment, which puts it parallel not only with many rapes but also, more tellingly, with many robberies of building societies and sub-post offices involving no actual force and little money. Generally, it may be a manifestation of the emphasis on profit and property: the result is to undervalue human life compared to property. The argument becomes even stronger when sentences in the three- to five-year range are approved for 'professional' pickpocketing. Even if it were established by evidence that pickpocketing has a psychological impact on victims comparable to that found in research into the impact of burglary – and at present there is no such evidence – it is surely excessive for the sentencing range for professional pickpocketing to be so close to that for rape.

Another point concerns the effect of unintended consequences upon sentence. We noted the courts' tendency to take these into account in sentencing for manslaughter and for causing death by bad driving. Much less significance is attributed to the unintended deaths resulting from the unlawful act in manslaughter than in causing death by bad driving, and this is logical. Much of the conduct constituting the unlawful act in manslaughter is of a fairly minor nature, with little to put the offender on notice of the risk of death. On the other hand, it is well known that driving dangerously or with excessive alcohol creates risks for the safety and lives of others, supporting the greater emphasis placed on resulting deaths in those cases.

---

198 See *Attuh-Benson* [2005] Crim LR 243, where counsel attacked the appropriateness of using deterrent sentences against mere couriers, but the Court of Appeal reasserted its policy.
199 See Halliday (2001), p. 129, Bottoms (2004), pp. 63–6, and ch. 3.3.2 above.

These and many other issues have already received some discussion in this chapter. One pervasive question is whether factors which mitigate or aggravate the seriousness of an offence are not sometimes allowed to exert a greater effect on sentence than the nature of the offence itself. Should a planned offence be so much more serious, even if the sum of money involved is small? Should the fact that the victim is elderly take the offence above the normal range? Should the element of provocation take the case so far beneath the normal range? We now turn, in Chapter 5, to examine mitigating and aggravating factors.

CHAPTER 5

Aggravation and mitigation

5.1 Some preliminary problems of principle

The concepts of aggravation and mitigation have tended to attract little close examination or theoretical discussion. Perhaps this is because the factors recognized as aggravating or mitigating are thought to be uncomplicated or uncontroversial, or (in the terminology of the English judiciary) 'well known' and 'well established'. However, it will be argued in this chapter that many of them raise contentious issues. These issues assume particular importance now for three particular reasons:

- several aggravating factors and one mitigating factor are statutory requirements under the Criminal Justice Act 2003, as we shall see;
- s. 166 of the 2003 Act reaffirms that the various statutory thresholds for imposing custodial sentences and community sentences should not be read as 'prevent[ing] a court from mitigating an offender's sentence by taking into account such matters as, in the opinion of the court, are relevant in mitigation of sentence'; and
- s. 174(2) of the 2003 Act requires the court in any case to 'mention any aggravating or mitigating factors which the court has regarded as being of particular importance'.

For these three reasons, the analysis of the justifications for particular aggravating and mitigating factors becomes a more pressing task than may hitherto have been supposed. Moreover, the sentencing research by Hough, Jacobson and Millie shows that it was chiefly the influence of personal mitigating factors that often made the difference between a community sentence and a custodial sentence in cases 'on the cusp'.[1]

The restatement in s. 166 of the power to mitigate sentence is broadly framed, and immediately it raises the question whether justifications for taking account of some personal mitigating factors may be found outside the fundamental rationale of sentencing – which, as argued in Chapters 3 and 4, is that the sentence should be proportionate to the seriousness of the offence. This would not necessarily be illogical: it was argued in Chapter 3.4 above that it is possible to defend a sentencing system which has a primary rationale and which then allows certain other rationales

---

1 Hough et al. (2003), pp. 39–43.

to have priority in respect of certain types of crime or types of offender. The key requirement is that the justifications be strong and specific. Similarly, the notion that all aggravating and mitigating factors ought necessarily to be linked to the primary rationale must be rejected as too astringent a view, particularly in the context of a branch of the law so closely entwined with social policy and so politically sensitive as sentencing. It would be odd and probably inconsistent if the central core of aggravating and mitigating factors were not linked to the primary rationale, but there is no reason why additional factors should not be recognized. Everything depends on careful examination of the justifications for these factors.

One reason why the main aggravating and mitigating factors should be related to the primary rationale is that their status as such might be purely adventitious. One legal system may have distinct offences of robbery and armed robbery, the latter defined so as to penalize robbery involving the use or threatened use of a gun. Another, such as England and Wales, might have a single offence of robbery, and might treat the use or threatened use of a gun as an aggravating factor. Similarly, some countries have separate offences of theft, graded according to the amount stolen or perhaps the position held by the person stealing, whereas English law treats such factors as aggravating factors in a single offence of theft. It may therefore be a matter of legislative tradition whether such factors are part of the definition of the crime or are left to sentencing, but it should make no difference to the arguments needed to justify the factor as aggravating. The definitions of offences should in general be coherent with the primary rationale of sentencing,[2] and the same should apply to factors which could readily be treated as elements in the definitions of offences.

A further preliminary question concerns the practical relationship between aggravating and mitigating factors. It is often right to suppose that the opposite of a mitigating factor will count as aggravating (e.g. impulsive reactions may justify mitigation and premeditation may be aggravating), and this applies particularly where the two factors can be represented as extreme points on a spectrum. However, there may be other circumstances in which the absence of a mitigating factor should not count as aggravating. There has been some debate in England about the implications of the sentencing 'discount' for pleading guilty: clearly, a person who pleads not guilty and is convicted cannot receive this discount, and so the sentence will be higher than for someone who pleaded guilty to a similar offence. But does that mean that pleading not guilty and putting the prosecution to proof is an aggravating factor? Pleading not guilty certainly has a potential cost that pleading guilty does not have; but in principle the person who is convicted after a not guilty plea should receive the normal sentence, not an aggravated sentence. In essence, therefore, there are three forms of response to factors in each case – aggravating, neutral and mitigating. These may simply represent points on a spectrum (e.g. between impulsivity and premeditation). But where the factor relates to the presence or absence of a single element (e.g. pleading guilty or not guilty), there is a question

2 For a sophisticated discussion of these issues, see Jareborg (1988).

as to how they should be characterized. The wrong approach is to assume that the opposite or negative of a mitigating factor is necessarily aggravating; it might be neutral, as demonstrated by the theory of the discount for a guilty plea. Similarly, it is widely accepted to be an aggravating factor if the offence is committed against an elderly or a very young victim, but it would be absurd to claim mitigation on the basis that the victim was aged between, say, 20 and 50. That is simply a neutral factor.

5.2 Aggravation as increased seriousness

5.2.1 Statutory aggravating factors

English law now requires courts to treat certain factors as aggravating. The Criminal Justice Act 2003 sets out four such factors. The first – previous convictions for relevant and recent offences – will be discussed fully in Chapter 6.3 below. The other three – offence committed on bail; racial or religious aggravation; aggravation related to disability or sexual orientation – will be discussed here.

1. Offence committed on bail. S. 143(3) of the Criminal Justice Act 2003 states that 'in considering the seriousness of any offence committed while the offender was on bail, the court must treat the fact that it was committed in those circumstances as an aggravating factor'. This restates a principle recognized for some years,[3] but what is its justification? The fact that the offence was committed during a period when the offender was on bail does not increase the harm caused by the offence, nor does it increase the culpability of the offender in relation to that crime. Presumably the argument is that it constitutes an act of defiance of the court, or a breach of the trust placed in the offender by releasing him on bail pending the hearing of his case, or at least demonstrates that he has failed to heed the element of official censure implicit in the commencement of proceedings against him.[4] Since it is also a principle that the sentence for an offence committed on bail should be consecutive to the sentence for the original offence,[5] the aggravating effect of this factor ought to be relatively small. The consecutive principle will increase the sentence anyway, and the argument that aggravating the sentence is likely to have an additional deterrent effect is as unsubstantiated as most claims about deterrence.[6]

2. Racial or religious aggravation. The Crime and Disorder Act 1998 introduced racially aggravated forms of wounding and assault (s. 29), criminal damage (s. 30), public order offences (s. 31) and harassment (s. 32). There is also a more general provision, now re-enacted as s. 145(2) of the Criminal Justice Act 2003, that 'if an offence was racially or religiously aggravated, the court must treat that fact as an aggravating factor, and must state in open court that the offence was so

---

3 It is substantially a re-enactment of s. 151 PCCS Act 2000 and s. 29(2) of the CJA 1991.
4 There is, of course, room for argument about whether the bringing of a prosecution can be said to imply censure at that stage (see Ashworth and Redmayne (2005), ch. 8); and the analysis may depend on whether D intends to plead guilty or to contest guilt.
5 See ch. 8.2.3 below.   6 See ch. 3.3.2 above.

aggravated'. The definition of 'racially aggravated' is given in s. 28 of the 1998 Act, and includes conduct that is either racially motivated or involves the offender demonstrating towards the victim 'hostility based on the victim's membership (or presumed membership) of a racial group'. A parallel definition now applies to 'religious aggravation'.[7]

When the specific racially aggravated offences were enacted in 1998, they created a sentencing problem, since, in order to conform to existing conventions, Parliament increased the sentences for the different offences by different proportions – for example, the maximum for common assault rose from six months to two years if racially aggravated (a fourfold increase), whereas the maximum for a s. 20 wounding or a s. 47 assault rose from five to seven years if racially aggravated (an increase of under a half). Moreover, it was clear from the statutory scheme that, if the offence of conviction is one that has a racially or religiously aggravated version, of which the offender has not been convicted, it would be wrong for the court to take account of any racial or religious element so as to aggravate the sentence. These were prominent factors in leading the Sentencing Advisory Panel to propose guidelines for racially aggravated offences in 2000.[8] The Panel, noting the legislative intent of identifying racial crimes so as to mark them out for specific condemnation, proposed a scheme of enhancements to deal with this type of case. The Court of Appeal considered the Panel's advice in *Kelly and Donnelly* (2001),[9] and accepted it in part. It accepted the proposal that courts should first state what the sentence would be without the racial (or religious) element, and then state the sentence including that element. As Rose LJ commented, 'this will lead to transparency in sentencing, which will be of benefit to the public and, indeed, to this Court if subsequently the sentence passed is the subject of challenge'.[10] The Panel had gone on to propose that the enhancement should normally be between 40 and 70 per cent of the sentence for the basic offence, but the Court of Appeal preferred to leave it to the judge to consider the appropriate overall sentence without any such guideline. One feature of the Panel's advice is always to identify factors that make an offence (or, in this instance, racial or religious aggravation) more or less serious. The Court of Appeal agreed with the Panel's proposed factors, which included among the aggravating factors a pattern of racist conduct, membership of a racist group, deliberate humiliation of the victim and repeated or prolonged expressions of racial hostility. Two factors that might make the behaviour less serious were identified as the relative brevity of the racist conduct, and cases where there was no evidence of racial motivation and any racial abuse was minor or incidental. The same considerations now apply to religious aggravation.

Increasing sentences for these reasons may be seen as generally justified on the ground of reaffirming and enhancing social values of toleration and respect for

---

7 Its origin may be found in s. 39 of the Anti-Terrorism, Crime and Security Act 2001.
8 SAP, *Racially Aggravated Offences: Advice to the Court of Appeal* (2000).
9 [2001] 2 Cr App R (S) 341.
10 Ibid., at p. 347. The Court thus reversed what it had held in the earlier decision in *Saunders* [2000] 2 Cr App R (S) 71.

the variety of racial and religious groups, and more specifically as marking the humiliating effect on victims that such conduct often has. Whether or not Parliament was right to enact a handful of specific racially and religiously aggravated offences, the general principle of aggravation of sentence on such grounds is surely correct, and one that coheres with the principle of proportionality in sentencing. The approach laid down in *Kelly and Donnelly* for racially and religiously aggravated offences should be applied more widely, so that, wherever a sentence is increased to take account of racial or religious aggravation, the court should both state this and identify the enhancement added for this reason.

3. *Aggravation related to disability or sexual orientation.* S. 146 of the 2003 Act introduces a new statutory aggravating factor, similar in its wording to that applicable to racially and religiously aggravated cases. Courts are required to treat as aggravated offences in which the offender was wholly or partly motivated by, or has demonstrated hostility based on, either the sexual orientation or presumed sexual orientation of the victim, or a disability or presumed disability of the victim. Thus where male homosexuals are singled out for assault, or where during the course of an attack an offender makes a homophobic remark, courts 'must treat' that fact as aggravating the offence and 'must state in open court that the offence was committed in such circumstances'.[11] Presumably courts should approach the task of sentencing such cases in a manner consistent with the guidelines in *Kelly and Donnelly* on racial aggravation. There is a difference in the statutory framework, since there are no specific offences that have a version with a higher maximum penalty for aggravation related to disability or sexual orientation, but the general principle – and the justifications for it – are surely the same.

5.2.2 General aggravating factors recognized in definitive guidelines

In its guideline *Overarching Principles: Seriousness*, the Sentencing Guidelines Council set out a number of general aggravating factors, or 'factors indicating higher culpability'. The list is not intended to be exhaustive, and it includes the statutory aggravating factors already mentioned, but it may be useful to draw attention to the other factors:

planning of an offence
intention to commit more serious harm than actually resulted from the offence
offenders operating in groups or gangs
commission of the offence for financial gain (where this is not inherent in the offence itself)
high level of profit from the offence
attempt to conceal or dispose of evidence
failure to respond to warnings or concerns expressed by others about the offender's behaviour
offence committed whilst on licence
offence motivated by hostility towards a minority group, or members of it

11 The words of s. 146(3) of the 2003 Act.

deliberate targeting of vulnerable victim(s)

commission of an offence while under the influence of alcohol or drugs

use of a weapon to frighten or injure the victim

deliberate and gratuitous violence or damage to property, over and above what is needed to carry out the offence

abuse of power

abuse of position of trust[12]

The Council's assumption is that these factors indicate greater culpability, and are therefore compatible with the principle of proportionality. We may consider whether this is right, examining at least some of the factors listed.[13]

Greater culpability is probably the answer where an offender commits a crime against a vulnerable victim: there is a widely shared view that it is worse to take advantage of a relatively helpless person, and so the offender is more culpable if aware that the victim is specially vulnerable (e.g. old, very young, disabled, etc.). Thus in *Attorney General's Reference Nos. 38 and 39 of 2004 (Randall and Donaghue)* (2005)[14] the Court of Appeal regarded the robbery as particularly heinous because the offenders had targeted the home of a man whom they knew to have learning disabilities. In *O'Brien* (2002),[15] D had tricked his way into the house of a woman of 81 by pretending to be an employee of a water company, and had then stolen £200, a watch and a mobile phone. He had a record of committing similar offences, and the judge sentenced him to nine years' imprisonment – very high on the scale for burglary, especially when the amount involved was so low.[16] The Court of Appeal reduced the sentence slightly to eight years on the ground that the original sentence did not adequately reflect the guilty plea, but the Court stated that the offender's

speciality is vulnerable elderly people. He tricks them into allowing him into their homes and he steals their property. He serves his prison sentences and then very soon thereafter resumes his similar criminal activities. This type of burglary casts a shadow on the lives of elderly people: they begin to dread the unexpected knock on the front door.

The Court agreed with the sentencing judge's comment that 'society rightly reserves its deepest censure for those who prey on vulnerable groups such as the elderly'. This same point is evident in several other appellate decisions.[17] Decisions on violence against young children also emphasize their helplessness as a prominent reason for aggravating the sentence in these cases.[18] Martin Wasik, examining the relevant justifications, has argued that there is not only greater culpability but there

---

12 SGC, *Overarching Principles: Seriousness*, para. 1.22.

13 Several similar factors are recognized in Swedish sentencing law: see von Hirsch and Jareborg (1989).

14 [2005] 1 Cr App R (S) 267.   15 [2002] 2 Cr App R (S) 560.   16 See ch. 4.4.10 above.

17 E.g. *Attorney General's Reference No. 108 of 2001 (Tullius)* [2002] 2 Cr App R (S) 294 (snatching bag from woman of 88, causing her to fall and suffer serious injury); *McDonnell* [2003] 2 Cr App R (S) 117 (distraction burglaries and robberies at homes of elderly people); *Marcus* [2004] 1 Cr App R (S) 258 (robbery and wounding of two elderly people in their home).

18 E.g. *Boswell* (1982) 4 Cr App R (S) 317.

may also be greater harm in these cases – and the quotation from *O'Brien* suggests that the harm may be to older people generally, not just to the victims in the particular case. However, it remains for discussion whether the aggravating effect of selecting an elderly victim should be as great as it appears to be in some cases, such as *O'Brien*, where it might be said that the aggravating factor seems more important to sentence than the underlying offence. Research in the 1980s suggested that having an elderly victim was the factor most strongly associated with the use of immediate custody, and with longer custodial sentences, in the Crown Court.[19]

Where an offence is committed by two or more people, the justification for aggravating the sentence probably lies in the greater harm which it is believed to involve – although the Council's guideline suggests that 'offenders operating in groups or gangs' increases the culpability element. That may be so where a group of people come together in order 'by weight of numbers to pursue a common and unlawful purpose'.[20] However, in other cases where two or more offenders confront a victim, a significant factor is that the victim is likely to be in greater fear and to feel a greater sense of helplessness. The element of additional fear in such circumstances has been emphasized in several public order cases such as *Rogers-Hinks* (1989),[21] involving violence among football supporters travelling on a North Sea ferry. The offenders themselves may not generally understand or consider this factor, but it is something of which they ought to be aware. Another argument leading to aggravation in these cases might be that group pressure to continue may make such offences less likely to be abandoned, and that group dynamics may lead to greater harm or damage being caused.[22] Some group offences may be described as 'organized crime', when teams or systems operate so as to maximize profit. Whether they are charged as conspiracy or not, the courts treat even the organized theft of moderate sums as particularly serious where there is evidence of organization or selection of vulnerable victims.[23] Sentencers should, however, draw a distinction between the ringleader and fringe participants,[24] as the guideline itself affirms.

Elements of planning or organization may also be present in crimes committed by individuals. A person who plans a crime is generally more culpable, because the offence is premeditated and the offender is therefore more fully confirmed in his anti-social motivation than someone who acts on impulse. (An exception to this is where the planning is directed at minimizing the harmful results of the offence.) Planned lawbreaking constitutes a great threat to society, since it betokens a considered attack on social values, with greater commitment and perhaps continuity than a spontaneous crime.[25]

19 Moxon (1988), p. 9; see also p. 31.
20 *Caird et al.* (1970) 54 Cr App R 499, per Sachs LJ at p. 507.   21 (1989) 11 Cr App R (S) 234.
22 E.g. Lord Lane CJ in *Pilgrim* (1983) 5 Cr App R (S) 140, 'mob violence feeds upon itself'.
23 Cf. *Freeman* (1989) 11 Cr App R (S) 398, discussed in ch. 4.4.12 above, with *Masagh* (1990) 12 Cr App R (S) 568.
24 As emphasized in decisions such as *Keys and Sween* (1986) 8 Cr App R (S) 444, and *Chapman* [1999] 2 Cr App R (S) 374.
25 For fuller discussion of this point, see ch. 4.5 above.

The guideline is also justified in regarding a failure to respond to warnings by others as an aggravating factor. This may evidence a callous indifference to the consequences of one's actions, a factor that has emerged in various different types of offence. Thus, where the offender has caused death by dangerous driving, it is an established aggravating factor that he ignored warnings or pleas from passengers to slow down.[26] Similarly, in relation to breaches of health and safety laws, 'inactivity in the face of previous incidents and previous complaints' was regarded as aggravating the seriousness of the offences.[27]

Where breach of trust or abuse of authority is an element in the crime, the force of aggravation comes more from the social context of the offence. The crime may be unplanned, committed by an individual and not involving any violence or threats. But trust is fundamental to many social relationships, as argued in Chapter 4.4.11 above, and one of the burdens of trust or authority is an undertaking of incorruptibility. As the Court of Appeal stated in a case involving a stockbroker, breaches of trust 'undermine public confidence, because the matters of financial dealing with which this man was involved cannot be carried out unless confidence is reposed in those who carry out these transactions on behalf of members of the public'.[28] The same applies to offences committed by police officers, as the Court of Appeal recently stated:

> It is critical that the public retain full confidence in our police force. A feature of the trust that must exist is that the public can expect that they will not be assaulted by officers even if they are being a nuisance. Any erosion of that basic but reasonable expectation will do profound harm to the good relationship that must exist between the public and the police service.[29]

The courts' reasoning has sometimes been based on deterrence: people in positions of trust or authority will inevitably have great temptation placed before them, and the law must match this with strong sentences for succumbing. But that is a doubtful argument in itself, since there will usually be other disastrous consequences of being caught offending in such a position (loss of job, loss of pension and other rights, inability to find comparable employment) which will render a strong sentence less necessary on deterrent reasoning. The fundamental importance of networks of trust and authority for the smooth operation of society is surely sufficient explanation of the additional harm. A recent survey suggests that breach of trust is now the factor most strongly associated with the imposition of custodial sentences in the Crown Court.[30]

---

26 As reaffirmed in the guideline decision of *Cooksley* [2004] 1 Cr App R (S) 1 at p. 12 ('disregard of warnings from fellow passengers').

27 *Firth Vickers Centrispinning Ltd* [1998] 1 Cr App R (S) 293.

28 *Per* Stephen Brown LJ in *Dawson* (1987) 9 Cr App R (S) 248. See also the quotation from Cox in ch. 4.4.11 above.

29 *Dunn* [2003] 2 Cr App R (S) 535 at p. 540. See also *Nazir* [2003] 2 Cr App R (S) 671, and, for an offence by a prison officer, *Mills* [2005] 1 Cr App R (S) 180.

30 Flood-Page and Mackie (1998), p. 11.

It may be worth considering at this point the claims of a connected factor that is not included in the Guideline list but which is often thought to be aggravating – that the offence was committed *against* a public official. Should an attack on a police officer be regarded as more grave than an attack on an ordinary citizen? One answer is that police officers are expected to place themselves in vulnerable positions sometimes, as part of their job, and that people who take advantage of this commit a worse offence. Probably this line of argument could be connected with that in the previous paragraph: society needs people to undertake policing and other positions of authority, and a person who knowingly attacks such an official is striking against a fundamental institution in a way that one who attacks a private citizen is not. Because of its great social significance, it should be regarded as more serious. Thus in *Attorney General's Reference No. 35 of 1995 (Hartley)* Lord Taylor CJ made it clear that the use of violence against a police officer 'who was merely acting in the exercise of his duty' was an aggravated offence;[31] the Court of Appeal also increased the sentence in *Attorney General's Reference No. 99 of 2003 (Vidler)* for similar reasons.[32]

From this brief consideration of general aggravating factors, it is evident that the courts have not always tended to justify them in terms of their effect in increasing the seriousness of the offence. Instead, courts have often adopted the terminology of deterrence, probably without reflecting on the different rationales of sentencing. It is true that in a carefully constructed theory of deterrence the concept of proportionality is important, since Bentham devoted a whole chapter to it and included such injunctions as 'venture more against a great offence than a small one'.[33] However, the suggestion here is that each of the above factors is rightly regarded as increasing the seriousness of offences, although the foundations of the 'breach of trust' factor may be thought rather nebulous.

5.2.3 Specific aggravating factors

The number of aggravating factors specific to individual offences is enormous, and no purpose would be served by enumerating them here. Examples may readily be found in the various guideline judgments: thus in *Cooksley* (2004)[34] the Court set out aggravating factors for the offence of causing death by dangerous driving, including a number of specific factors such as 'driving when knowingly deprived of adequate sleep or rest'; in *McInerney and Keating* (2003)[35] the Court followed the Sentencing Advisory Panel in listing high-level aggravating factors and medium-level aggravating factors in burglary, and among the latter was the fact that the victim was at home when the offence was committed; and in *Oliver and Hartrey* (2003)[36] the specific aggravating factors included the fact that indecent photographs of children had themselves been shown to children.

---

31 [1996] 1 Cr App R (S) 413 at p. 415.   32 [2005] 1 Cr App R (S) 150.
33 Bentham (1789), ch. XIV, rule 2.   34 [2004] 1 Cr App R (S) 1 at p. 12.
35 [2003] 2 Cr App R (S) 240 at p. 252.   36 [2003] 2 Cr App R (S) 64 at p. 73.

The identification of specific aggravating factors was also a feature of earlier guideline judgments laid down by the Court of Appeal. Thus, in *Stewart* (1987),[37] where Lord Lane CJ laid down guidelines for sentencing in cases of frauds relating to social security and other state benefits, the aggravating factors identified were (i) where the frauds were committed over a lengthy period; (ii) where the fraud began by deliberate deception rather than by omission; (iii) where the money was spent on unnecessary luxuries (rather than essential supplies); and, of course, (iv) where the fraud was a carefully organized operation. That last factor is general, and factors (i) and (ii) clearly relate to the particular type of offence. Factor (iii) seems to concern events after the commission of the offence(s), but in reality its significance is probably related to culpability and motivation: a person motivated to commit the offence out of greed should not receive the mitigation which the desperately poor person should. The latter may have a more or less weak version of the defence of necessity, but it is arguable that the absence of such a claim should be neutral rather than aggravating, unless avarice and covetousness are to qualify as general aggravating factors.

Nothing more will be said about aggravating factors at this stage. By and large, those which have been discussed can be related to the seriousness of the offence, in terms of either culpability or harmfulness, but the discussion of crimes involving abuse of authority shows that the concept of harmfulness may have wider social dimensions than appear at first sight. This and other theoretical issues will be pursued after the mitigating factors have been discussed.

5.3 Mitigation as diminished seriousness

The factors which have been recognized as mitigating sentences in England are a much more heterogeneous collection than the aggravating factors. There is only one statutory mitigating factor that courts are required to take into account, the plea of guilty, and that is independent of the seriousness of the offence (see part 5.4.1 below). Apart from that, there is merely the permissive s. 166(1) of the Criminal Justice Act 2003, stating that the statutory thresholds for imposing custody or a community sentence should not prevent a court from mitigating a sentence by taking account of 'any such matters as, in the opinion of the court, are relevant in mitigation of sentence'. In this chapter, personal mitigating factors will be left for discussion in part 5.4 below, and here the focus will be on mitigating factors that reduce the seriousness of an offence. The distinction between general mitigating factors and those relevant only to particular types of offence will be adopted again, and it will be observed that some reflect the reduced harmfulness of the offence, and many more reflect the diminished culpability of the offender.

---

37 (1987) 9 Cr App R (S) 135 at p. 139.

5.3.1 Specific mitigating factors

Just as most sentencing guidelines set out some offence-specific aggravating factors, so they also list some offence-specific mitigating factors (although usually fewer). Thus, in relation to social security frauds, the specific mitigating factors recognized by the Court of Appeal in *Stewart* [38] were the fact that the offence arose from an omission rather than an active deception, the fact that the money was spent on necessary living expenses, any voluntary repayments and any matters special to the offender, such as illness or family difficulties. The omission/commission distinction presumably relates to culpability, as does the 'necessity' element – obtaining money to pay for the necessities of life exhibits low culpability. Culpability also seems to be the object of the reference to family difficulties, but the reference to voluntary repayments raises the question of the proper significance to be attributed to events after the commission of the offence. This is discussed in parts 5.4.1 and 5.4.2 below.

Among the specific mitigating factors enumerated in the guideline judgment on causing death by dangerous driving was 'the fact that the offender has also been seriously injured as a result of the accident caused by dangerous driving'[39] – which is similar to a provision in the Swedish sentencing law, based on the curious notion of 'natural punishment'.[40] A final example is provided by the guideline on burglary, where only four rather obvious grounds for regarding offences as less serious can be mustered – a first offence; nothing or only property of very low value is stolen; the offender played only a minor part in the burglary; and there is no damage or disturbance to the property.[41] These are fairly standard factors relating to proportionality.

5.3.2 General mitigating factors related to seriousness

We have noted that the seriousness of an offence may be analysed in terms of the harmfulness or potential harmfulness of the conduct, and the culpability of the offender. In the former category fall such factors as the small amount of damage caused or property taken, or the minor role of the offender. But it is in the latter category that we find the core of mitigation – factors personal to the offender which are treated as reducing culpability. Thus, it is generally treated as mitigation where the offence was committed impulsively or suddenly: this lies at the opposite end of the spectrum from planning and premeditation, which are treated as aggravating, whereas an intentional but unplanned offence might perhaps be neutral. Where the offender is young, this may also be treated as a mitigating factor. The age of criminal responsibility is 10 in English law, and it is relatively unusual for anyone under 14 to be convicted of an offence. It is logical to suggest that offenders in their teens might be slightly less responsible than older offenders, being more impressionable, more

---

38 Ibid.   39 *Cooksley* [2004] 1 Cr App R (S) 1 at p. 13.
40 See below, part 5.4.5.   41 *McInerney and Keating* [2003] 2 Cr App R (S) 240 at p. 253.

easily led and less controlled in their behaviour.[42] In these cases, as in all others, we are concerned with general arguments and their foundations, and in practice much depends on the court's assessment of the facts in the particular case.

A further group of cases involving reduced culpability consists of those who fail to bring themselves within the narrow confines of criminal law defences such as insanity, duress, necessity or mistake of law. Indeed, many of those defences are restricted tightly in the expectation that courts will award substantial mitigation of sentence where the circumstances fall just outside the legal requirements for a defence.[43] One example would be where an offender is suffering from a psychiatric disorder falling short of providing an insanity defence: thus in *Attorney General's Reference No. 37 of 2004 (Dawson)* (2005)[44] the Court of Appeal held that a community rehabilitation order with a condition of psychiatric treatment was not unduly lenient for attempted robbery by an offender suffering from clinical depression. Another example would be where the offender had a right to defend himself from attack but used excessive force in doing so.[45] In this kind of case the harm done remains the same, but its context and social meaning are less serious than an offence with no colour of justification. On the boundary between partial justification and partial excuse lies provocation, a frequent mitigating factor that draws upon the degree of provocation received and the impulsivity of the offender's response.[46]

Turning to the entrapment of an offender by the police or an agent provocateur, the English courts have declared that it may be sufficiently fundamental to justify staying the prosecution for abuse of process,[47] but that lesser degrees of entrapment ought to be a matter of mitigation in appropriate cases. The Court of Appeal has reduced sentences where there has been a significant element of entrapment.[48] Turning to cases where the offender has been under exceptional stress or emotional pressure, this will generally be regarded as mitigation, on the basis of reduced culpability.[49] This is one of a number of factors regarded as insufficient to amount to a complete defence to liability but appropriate for mitigation, which may be substantial in an appropriate case. A further example might be the person who steals in order to provide comforts for a dying relative. Thus conditions which involve partial exculpation rather than total exculpation often provide prima facie grounds for mitigation.

---

42 For elaboration, see von Hirsch and Ashworth (2005), ch. 3.
43 See Wasik (1983) for a full discussion. An example of mistake of law is *Tierney* (1990) 12 Cr App R (S) 216.
44 [2005] 1 Cr App R (S) 295; see also *Attorney General's Reference No. 83 of 2001 (Fidler)* [2002] 1 Cr App R (S) 588, community rehabilitation order upheld for robber suffering from schizophrenia.
45 See the unreported case of *Evans* (1974), discussed by Thomas (1979) p. 372 and by Wasik (1983) p. 456.
46 See Ashworth (1975), Horder (1989), and on the theory von Hirsch and Jareborg (1988).
47 *Looseley* [2001] 1 WLR 2060.   48 E.g. *Chalcraft and Campbell* [2002] 2 Cr App R (S) 172.
49 As in some cases of violence against young children: e.g. post-natal depression in *Isaac* [1998] 1 Cr App R (S) 266.

5.4 Personal mitigation

Research shows that in practice the range of factors advanced in mitigation is enormously wide.[50] An obvious mitigating factor is the previous good character of the offender: proportionality theory argues in favour of dealing more leniently with an offence that can be interpreted as an isolated lapse, recognizing human frailty and yet showing respect for the offender as a rational individual, capable of responding to the censure inherent in the sentence imposed. But this justification quickly evaporates as the offender gathers previous convictions, as we shall see in the detailed discussion of this issue in Chapter 6.2 below. We now step away from concepts of proportionality and offence-seriousness, to consider what other forms of mitigation might properly be admitted. The factors gathered together as 'personal mitigation' in the paragraphs that follow range from a guilty plea to other factors contributing to the smooth running of the criminal justice system, general social contributions and the impact of the sentence on the offender. In respect of each, the questions are whether and to what extent courts should take account of these matters, many of which have no bearing on either the seriousness of the offence or the culpability of the offender.

5.4.1 Statutory reduction of sentence for a plea of guilty

It was well settled in the English common law of sentencing that a plea of guilty should normally attract a reduction of sentence, and that the scale of the reduction should be greater, the earlier the plea was intimated.[51] However, in 1994 the government decided, following the report of the Royal Commission on Criminal Justice,[52] that what is usually known as the 'guilty plea discount' should be put into statutory form. In 2004 the Sentencing Guidelines Council handed down a definitive guideline on the reduction in sentence for a guilty plea. Having explained the law and the guideline, we go on below to discuss the available statistics, and the deep issues of principle raised by the guilty plea discount.

1. The statutory provision. The provision that originated in s. 48 of the Criminal Justice and Public Order Act 1994 is now to be found in s. 144 of the Criminal Justice Act 2003:

(1) In determining what sentence to pass on an offender who has pleaded guilty to an offence in proceedings before that or another court, a court must take into account:

(a) the stage in the proceedings for the offence at which the offender indicated his intention to plead guilty, and

(b) the circumstances in which this indication was given.

(2) In the case of an offence the sentence for which falls to be imposed under subsection (2) of ss. 110 or 111 of the Sentencing Act,[53] nothing in that subsection prevents

---

50 See the study by Shapland (1981).
51 See, for example, *De Haan* [1968] 2 QB 108, and *Buffery* (1993) 14 Cr App R (S) 511.
52 Royal Commission on Criminal Justice (1993), ch. 7.
53 This is shorthand for the Powers of Criminal Courts (Sentencing) Act 2000.

the court, after taking account of any matter referred to in subsection (1) of this section, from imposing any sentence which is not less than 80 per cent of that specified in that subsection.

This must be read in conjunction with s. 174(2)(d), which provides that courts must,

> where as a result of taking into account any matter referred to in s. 144(1), the court imposes a punishment on the offender which is less severe than the punishment it would otherwise have imposed, state that fact.

What is clear from the terms of s. 144 is that the discount applies to all courts, both magistrates' courts and the Crown Court, and to all forms of sentence, not just custody. There is no reference to a different principle for murder cases, and therefore the calculation of the minimum term to be served by a person convicted of murder should take the discount into account, albeit in a somewhat diminished form.[54] Subsection (2) modifies the approach for the two prescribed sentences, the minimum of three years for the third domestic burglary and the minimum of seven years for the third offence of dealing class A drugs.[55] Here the discount is limited to 20 per cent, presumably to emphasize the stringency of the minimum sentences while furnishing some encouragement to plead guilty, and it remains important for courts to consider it.[56] However, the Act includes no corresponding reference to the minimum sentence of five years for possession of a firearm,[57] and so the Court of Appeal held that no discount could be given for pleading guilty to that offence.[58] The omission of this offence from s. 144(2) appears to have been an oversight, and an example of the problems of legislation so large and cumbersome as the 2003 Act. The Court of Appeal might have been bolder and allowed the discount out of equity.

Since its inception, however, the legislation on discounts for pleading guilty has not been clear. Subsection (1) is drafted in a remarkably allusive manner. Not only does it fail to say anything about the scale of discounts, but it fails even to spell out the principle that the discount should be larger, the earlier the guilty plea is intimated. In the result, the Court of Appeal dealt with a succession of appeals on the subject between 1994 and 2004, and this underlined the need to establish guidance on the proper approach to sentencing in guilty plea cases.

2. *The SGC's guideline.* The Council prefaces its guideline with a restatement of the purpose of the guilty plea discount in the following terms:

---

54 This was a controversial issue in the drawing up of the Council's guideline on the subject: see House of Commons (2004) for discussion of the issue and the public and government response to it.
55 Discussed in detail in ch. 6.7 below.
56 Cf. *Smith* [2003] 1 Cr App R (S) 630 (judge apparently failed to consider giving discount to burglar).
57 S. 51A(2) of the Firearms Act 1968, inserted by s. 287 CJA 2003.
58 *Jordan* [2005] CLW/05/08/1.

A reduction in sentence is appropriate because a guilty plea avoids the need for a trial (thus enabling other cases to be disposed of more expeditiously), shortens the gap between charge and sentence, saves considerable cost, and, in the case of an early plea, saves victims and witnesses from the concern about having to give evidence.[59]

The first three factors mentioned (speeding up the system, reducing time on remand, and cost) are all pragmatic reasons related to the smooth running of the system. The discount thus appears as an incentive to contribute to the speed of criminal justice. The fourth factor – saving anxiety and distress for victims and witnesses – promises significant relief for those who would otherwise have to give evidence. Although this reason is probably valid in most cases, it should be noted that some victims and witnesses insist that they would rather (if they had the choice) undergo the pains of giving evidence if it meant that the offender received a longer sentence (i.e. no discount).[60]

Two points are missing from the Council's list of justifications. The first is any mention of remorse in this connection. Traditionally judges have cited remorse as a major justification for the guilty plea discount.[61] One difficulty is how courts can discern genuine contrition from sheer realism in recognizing (often with legal advice) that pleading guilty leads to lower sentences. Remorse-based reasoning is surely implausible in cases where the guilty plea occurs at the last minute, or in the early stages of the trial,[62] and it must be dubious in other cases where the court only sees the defendant for sentence. Sentencers often refer to remorse as a factor that can tip them away from imposing a custodial sentence, but at least some of them acknowledge the difficulty of assessing whether it is genuine.[63] Should remorse be relevant? If the argument is that the offender's acceptance of his wrongdoing means that less punishment is needed to deter or to reform, that is questionable on two grounds – whether deterrent or rehabilitative considerations should be given such weight, and whether the assumption is in fact true. The Council's guideline does refer to remorse, but states that courts should address both that and other mitigating factors separately from the guilty plea. This preserves the doubtful inclusion of remorse as a general mitigating factor, but keeps it apart from the guilty plea discount.

Also missing from the Council's guideline is any reference to the dangers of the guilty plea discount in terms of inducing innocent people to plead guilty. The Panel expressed some concern about this, and took the view that a 40 per cent discount would be simply too much encouragement to plead guilty.[64] The Council, not commenting on these matters, presumably takes the view that it is simply giving

---

59 SGC, *Reduction in Sentence for a Guilty Plea* (2004), para. 2.1. The guideline was based on the Advice from SAP, *Reduction in Sentence for a Guilty Plea* (2004).
60 This was a finding of the research on rape commissioned by the Panel: see Clarke, Moran-Ellis and Sleny (2002).
61 E.g. *Fraser* (1982) 4 Cr App R (S) 254, *Archer* [1998] 2 Cr App R (S) 76.
62 As in the former leading case of *De Haan* [1968] 2 QB 108.   63 Hough et al. (2003), p. 41.
64 SAP, *Reduction in Sentence for a Guilty Plea*, para. 11 and paras. 21–24.

guidance on how to administer the law as it is. However, in the context of a study of the principles on which sentences are and should be based, this is a factor that must not be ignored. We return to it in part 5.4.1.4 below.

The guideline states that the level of sentence reduction should be on a sliding scale from a maximum of one-third where the guilty plea was entered or intimated at the first reasonable opportunity, reducing to one-quarter if the trial date has already been set, and to one-tenth if the plea is tendered at the 'door of the court' or after the trial has begun.[65] Annex 2 to the guideline gives illustrations of what may be regarded as the 'first reasonable opportunity' to intimate a plea, recognizing that it is unfair to expect a defendant to enter a guilty plea if the legal adviser has not been given sufficient information about the precise nature of the charge. The guideline insists that, even for those who change plea at the start of a trial, there must always be some incentive or reward.[66] In cases where an early guilty plea is entered but then the offender's version of the circumstances of the offence is rejected in a *Newton* hearing, some of the normal reduction in sentence may be lost.[67] Thus procedurally the guideline recommends the following approach:

- decide on the sentence for the offence(s), taking account of aggravating and mitigating factors;
- select the amount of reduction for the guilty plea by reference to the sliding scale;
- apply the reduction to the sentence decided on; and
- pronounce the sentence, stating what the sentence would have been if there had been no reduction as a result of the guilty plea.[68]

Although there are references throughout the guideline to 'the sliding scale', this does not apply well to cases in which the discount has the effect of reducing a custodial sentence to a community sentence. The guideline states plainly that 'the reduction principle may properly form the basis for imposing . . . an alternative to an immediate custodial sentence'.[69] This is a logical application of the discount, but (i) it is a crucial and momentous decision for the offender, capable of exerting considerable pressure to plead guilty; and (ii) such decisions cannot be based on the 'sliding scale' as such. Applying the logic of the guideline, only an early guilty plea could reduce a custodial sentence of, say, 13 weeks to a suspended sentence or community sentence; whereas a later plea might still be accorded the effect of reducing, say, a two-week sentence in the same way.

At common law there was scattered authority allowing the discount to be withheld in certain circumstances, but the Council has now reconsidered the proper approach. The guideline states roundly that 'there is no reason why credit should be withheld or reduced' on the ground that the offender was caught 'red-handed'.[70]

---

65   Essentially, this follows the lines of the proposal by Auld (2001), p. 441.
66   Cf. *Okee and West* [1998] 2 Cr App R (S) 199, stating that 'the 10 per cent [discount] given by the learned judge in these circumstances seems to this court to have been ample'.
67   Cf. *Hassall* [2000] 1 Cr App R (S) 67.
68   This adapts the diagram at para. 3.1 of the SGC guideline.   69   Ibid., para. 2.6.
70   Ibid., para. 5.2; cf. the common law to the contrary, exemplified in *Landy* (1995) 16 Cr App R (S) 908 and criticized in the 3rd edn of this work, p. 144.

If the purpose of giving credit is to encourage the guilty to enter their plea at the earliest opportunity, the discount should be given in these cases too. There was some doubt at common law whether the discount should be given to offenders sentenced as dangerous: the guideline now states that the discount should apply to the proportionate part of the sentence (i.e. the minimum term) 'but not the public protection element of the sentence'.[71] The guideline goes on to emphasize that courts may not withhold the discount because they believe the maximum sentence for the offence is too low,[72] but a magistrates' court or any court dealing with a young offender may give the maximum permissible sentence if satisfied that a longer sentence (at the Crown Court, or a sentence of long-term detention for a youth) would have been justified in the absence of a guilty plea.[73] It remains to be seen how closely the courts follow the new guideline. Earlier research by Henham suggested that that compliance with the statutory requirements (then s. 48 of the 1994 Act) was variable, from 39 per cent to 75 per cent of cases at different Crown Court centres, and that references to the stage at which the plea had been entered were also variable.[74]

3. *The statistics*. Figures from the *Criminal Statistics 2002* show that the overall differences in Crown Court custodial sentences between those who plead guilty and those who are convicted are considerable: thus, in 2002 some 76 per cent of adult males pleading not guilty who were convicted received custodial sentences, compared with 62 per cent of those pleading guilty, and the average lengths of custodial sentences were 44 months and 27 months respectively.[75] This is almost a 40 per cent reduction, an even wider differential than that disclosed by David Moxon (22 per cent)[76] or by Roger Hood (31 per cent),[77] although the study by Flood-Page and Mackie in the mid-1990s also showed an average reduction approaching 40 per cent.[78] However, it is important to note that the *Criminal Statistics* record net sentences which already reflect the impact of previous convictions or mitigating factors. When Hood controlled for (took account of) the usual variables in analysing his data, a difference of ten months was reduced to one of three months.[79]

The 2002 figures in Table 11 are intriguing in that they show that for some offences the average sentence on a plea of guilty was *higher* than on conviction after a trial. What might be the explanation for the higher sentences for those who plead guilty to causing death by dangerous driving, and the small difference for indecent assaults and for 'other woundings'? The commentary in the *Criminal Statistics* suggests that some of the guilty pleas might be late pleas, or the offences may be more serious, or the offenders may have more previous convictions than those who go to trial. Those are all possible factors, and Hood's findings (above) suggest that if all factors are taken into account the differences tend to diminish. The

---

71 SGC guideline, para. 5.1. Cf. *Lovett* [2003] 1 Cr App R (S) 319.
72 Ibid., para. 5.3. For an example, see *March* [2002] 2 Cr App R (S) 448.
73 Ibid., paras. 5.5 and 5.6; long-term detention of juveniles is discussed in ch. 12.1 below.
74 Henham (2001), esp. pp. 18–20.
75 *Criminal Statistics 2002*, Table 4C. The 2002 statistics are used in this chapter because the 2003 volume of statistics contains no corresponding table.
76 Moxon (1988), p. 32.   77 Hood (1992), p. 125.
78 Flood-Page and Mackie (1998), pp. 90–1.   79 Hood (1992), p. 125.

Table 11. *Males aged 21 and over sentenced for indicable offences at the Crown Court: plea rates and custodial sentencing for selected offences, 2002*

England and Wales

Offence[1]	Pleaded guilty (%)	Custody rate (%)		Average sentence length (months)	
		Guilty	Not guilty[2]	Guilty	Not guilty
Violence against the person					
Causing death by dangerous driving	75	87	(88)	42.1	33.1
Wounding or other act endangering life	58	90	94	46.9	57.7
Threat or conspiracy to murder	79	58	(71)	27.9	36.1
Other violence against the person	84	51	57	15.0	16.5
All violence against the person	79	55	72	21.6	34.9
Sexual offences					
Rape	39	96	99	80.4	90.6
Indecent assault on a female	63	65	83	28.2	28.5
Indecent assault on a male	69	72	84	33.2	32.1
All sexual offences	61	71	89	36.9	52.9
Burglary					
In a building other than a dwelling	95	74	69	18.8	28.5
In a dwelling	94	77	84	24.9	29.9
All burglary	94	77	82	24.3	34.0
Theft and handling stolen goods					
Other theft or unauthorised taking	91	55	(59)	12.8	22.2
Handling stolen goods	90	50	45	11.9	18.7
Theft from the person of another	91	61	58	12.7	16.7
Theft by an employee	89	42	(63)	14.1	17.3
Theft from shops	94	61	34	7.1	8.1
All theft and handling stolen goods	92	59	51	11.5	17.2
Fraud and forgery					
Other forgery	90	65	(73)	12.3	15.7
Other fraud	88	53	65	15.1	26.8
All fraud and forgery	88	53	65	14.2	23.7
Criminal damage					
Arson	88	62	(81)	33.3	48.0
All criminal damage	89	39	48	29.0	41.4
Drug offences					
Trafficking	84	77	92	35.0	58.9
Possession	95	28	(30)	10.7	11.7
All drug offences	86	70	89	36.1	65.8

[1] Only those offences where at least 100 pleaded guilty or not guilty are shown separately.
[2] Figures given in parentheses indicate that percentage is based on fewer than 50 cases.
Source: Criminal Statistics 2002, Table 4D.

commentary adds that 'it is likely that for some offences, such as indecent assault on a female, those pleading guilty may originally have been charged with more serious offences (rape in this example) and are, therefore, at the more serious end of the offences within the class shown'.[80] This is plausible, and could also account for the figures for indecent assault on a male (an offence that could be reduced from rape or buggery).[81] But a different explanation is required for the startling figures for causing death by dangerous driving, and it is probably that those who plead guilty are persuaded that there is really no point in contesting the case because the offence was such a bad one, whereas those who do contest it are those whose offence is at the lower end of the scale, just above the boundary between dangerous and careless driving.

Research may also help to cast light on two further issues. The first is whether courts differentiate, in the sentencing discount, between early and late guilty pleas. Evidence from the mid-1990s suggested that defendants who delayed their change of plea until the last minute sometimes received a discount not much less than that for early pleaders:

> Last minute guilty pleas attracted smaller discounts. Offenders who intimated that they would plead guilty from the outset were more likely to receive a shorter sentence than those who initially pleaded not guilty but changed their plea before trial; these, in turn, received a shorter sentence than those who were convicted after a trial . . . The average length of sentence where the offender had pleaded guilty from the start was 21.8 months compared to 24.6 months where they had initially pleaded not guilty but eventually pleaded guilty and 36.4 months where the offender pleaded not guilty and was convicted after a trial.[82]

This may suggest that the Council's guideline of no more than a 10 per cent reduction for late guilty-pleaders calls for a significant change of practice. Moreover, those who change their plea at the door of the court or at the start of the trial can hardly advance certain lines of mitigation (reformed lifestyle, reparation to victim, even remorse) that may tend to bolster the effect of an early plea. The impact of the new guideline must therefore be carefully monitored.

Another issue on which the statistics cast light is whether in practice a guilty plea affects the choice of penalty as well as affecting its quantum. Table 11 demonstrates significantly lower custody rates for those who plead guilty than for those who are convicted after a trial,[83] but in Flood-Page and Mackie's study it was only in relation to drug offences that there was a statistically significant relationship between plea

---

80 *Criminal Statistics 2002*, para. 4.27.
81 The offence of indecent assault was abolished by the Sexual Offences Act 2003, but the same argument may turn out to be true of its principal replacement, the offence of sexual assault.
82 Flood-Page and Mackie (1998), pp. 91–2.
83 The exception is the category of theft and handling, and this is perhaps because many of those who are caught red-handed (e.g. on CCTV or with the goods in their possession) do not contest their guilt and have previous convictions, whereas first offenders may contest a higher proportion of cases.

and the probability of receiving a custodial sentence.[84] We have noted that the Council's guideline recognizes that a guilty plea can reduce a custodial sentence to a community order (and indeed a community order to a fine). Once again, the impact of the guideline will need to be assessed.

4. *Is the discount justifiable?* What are the justifications for the guilty plea discount? It has been noted that in the Council's guideline, following the advice from the Panel, the rationale of the discount is stated in terms of public interest (reduction in public expenditure, speedier trials etc.) and in terms of minimizing the stress on victims and witnesses. The reference to the public interest in this context must be to a net calculation, in the sense that the benefits are thought to be worth foregoing any additional public protection that might accrue from passing longer sentences (and not giving any discount).

However, there are other principles that the criminal justice system ought to respect – notably, the presumption of innocence and the principle of non-discrimination – and they pull in the opposite direction. Thus Article 6.2 of the European Convention on Human Rights declares the presumption of innocence. Is it not therefore a person's right to have the case against her or him proved beyond reasonable doubt? Is it proper that a person who insists on that should, in the result, be treated more severely at the sentencing stage if convicted? It seems a weak response to maintain that pleading not guilty is not an aggravating factor, but simply a neutral factor, whereas pleading guilty is a form of mitigation – although the European Commission on Human Rights accepted this view when examining the issue over thirty years ago.[85] Surely an inevitable consequence of the discount for pleading guilty is that a plea of not guilty has its price for defendants. Nor is this simply a matter of the length of custodial sentences: we have seen that the decision between custody and a non-custodial sentence can be influenced too. This serves to underline the pressures on defendants who believe, perhaps as a result of what their lawyers have suggested, that a custodial sentence would follow conviction whereas a non-custodial sentence might follow a guilty plea. There is evidence that some innocent defendants succumb to this pressure and decide to 'cut their losses' by pleading guilty: research carried out for the Royal Commission on Criminal Justice suggested that up to 11 per cent of guilty pleaders claim innocence.[86] The Royal Commission report did not deny this, but held that this 'risk' must be 'weighed against the benefits to the system and to defendants of encouraging those who are in fact guilty to plead guilty'.[87] This is a dreadful example of the 'balancing' metaphor, assigning no special priority to avoiding the fundamental harm of convicting innocent individuals. The Home Office remains attracted by the possibility

---

84 Flood-Page and Mackie (1998), p. 90; this contrasts with the findings of Moxon (1988), p. 32, and Hood (1992), pp. 87, 191–2, both of whom found a clear effect.
85 *X v. United Kingdom* (1972) 3 DR 10 at p. 16; a Commission decision of such antiquity has no great authority, and the issue would need to be argued afresh.
86 Zander and Henderson (1993), pp. 138–42; McConville and Bridges (1993).
87 Royal Commission on Criminal Justice (1993), para. 7.44, criticized by Ashworth and Redmayne (2005), ch. 10, and by Darbyshire (2000).

of introducing a system whereby 'defendants could seek an advance indication of the sentence they would get if they pleaded guilty', but it does recognize the need for safeguards to ensure that innocent defendants are not thereby put under pressure.[88] Whether that risk can be reduced in practice remains to be seen, but no such system has yet come into force.

It may be argued that the guilty plea discount is not only contrary to the spirit of the presumption of innocence declared by Article 6.2 of the European Convention on Human Rights, but also contrary to Article 14, which declares that all the rights in the Convention 'shall be secured without discrimination on any ground such as sex, race, colour . . .'. In his study of race and sentencing, Hood found that defendants from an Afro-Caribbean background tend to plead not guilty more frequently than whites (and tend to be acquitted more frequently), but that those who are convicted receive longer sentences largely, but not exclusively, because they have forfeited their 'discount'.[89] This can be regarded as a form of indirect discrimination: a general principle (the sentence discount) has a disproportionate impact on members of ethnic minorities simply because they more frequently exercise a right (the right to be presumed innocent until convicted). Hood argued that this supplies another reason to reconsider the discount. The Royal Commission stated merely that the policy of offering sentence discounts 'should be kept under review'[90] – an utterance of startling pusillanimity. The Auld Review did take this issue seriously, but favoured the view that the source of the injustice probably lay elsewhere than in the sentence discount.[91]

5.4.2 Assisting the criminal justice system

We have seen that the foremost rationale for the guilty plea discount is the offender's contribution to the smooth and cost-effective running of the criminal justice system. The same rationale underlies two other forms of personal mitigation. First, appellate decisions hold that an offender's conduct in admitting his offence before it is even discovered by others should be regarded as mitigation. In *R (on application of DPP) v. Salisbury Justices* (2003)[92] the offender, having taken drink, burgled the flat of an elderly lady and stole her handbag. The next day he walked into a police station and frankly confessed to the crime, saying that he had been drunk and very much regretted what he had done. He returned the property taken. Although he had many previous convictions for burglary, he had stayed out of trouble for over two years, and the circumstances of his voluntary admission of guilt without any prompting from the police were a major factor in the court's decision to order him merely to pay compensation to the victim. The Divisional Court declined to grant judicial

---

88 Home Office (2002), paras. 4.41–4.44, following the recommendations in Auld (2001), pp. 434–4.

89 Hood (1992), p. 125, stating that two-thirds of the 'race effect' in sentencing stems from the forfeiture of the discount by pleading not guilty.

90 Royal Commission on Criminal Justice (1993), para. 7.58.

91 Auld (2001), pp. 440–1. See now the development in *Goodyear* [2005] 3 All ER 117.

92 [2003] 1 Cr App R (S) 560. For an earlier authority, see *Claydon* (1994) 15 Cr App R (S) 526. See also *O* [2004] 1 Cr App R (S) 130, which is on the boundary between an early guilty plea and an unprompted confession.

review of the justices' decision, accepting that 'the very special facts' of the offence and of his reaction to committing it were sufficient reasons for the sentence. It greatly assists both the police and the victim to have a report and a full confession without the need for much investigation, and this assistance should be marked.

A second form of post-offence conduct applies the same reasoning directly: a person who assists the prosecution by giving evidence to the police and/or evidence in court which enables the detection of other offenders ought to receive some credit. There is established authority for this where the assistance is given before the offender is sentenced,[93] whereas guidance laid down by the Court of Appeal in *A and B* (1999)[94] confirms that a defendant who pleads not guilty, is convicted at the trial and sentenced, and subsequently gives assistance to the authorities, cannot expect to have his sentence reduced on appeal. Lord Bingham justified this by stating that the Court of Appeal is there to review material that was before the sentencing court, not to conduct a sentencing exercise afresh. The result is that an offender with such claims should press them before the Parole Board or the Home Office. The only exception contemplated in *A and B* is where a defendant gives assistance at an early stage and pleads guilty, but the true worth of the assistance only becomes evident at a later stage. In such cases the sentence may properly be reduced on appeal to reflect the extra assistance.

5.4.3 Voluntary reparation

Another source of mitigation deriving from events after the commission of the offence is where the offender has paid compensation or made reparation to the victim before the case comes to trial. In the context of a growing emphasis on compensation for victims, it might be thought that such conduct by an offender is meritorious and deserves some reward for its contribution to the goals of the criminal justice system. Indeed, for over thirty years there has been a statutory provision which allows a court to defer sentence for up to six months in order to have regard to an offender's conduct after conviction, including the making of reparation to the victim, and the Criminal Justice Act 2003 seeks to give this new prominence.[95] Where the offender makes reparation without such prompting from the court, should this not be regarded as positive mitigation? Perhaps there is an analogy with cases of voluntarily giving oneself up to the authorities: an offender who voluntarily pays compensation may be taken to show genuine remorse and concern for the victim. However, as in guilty plea cases, this may or may not be so. In practice, both may be calculated responses to a system whose rules promise

---

93 *Lowe* (1977) 66 Cr App R 122, *Sivan* (1988) 10 Cr App R (S) 282. Such information is often passed to the judge in a 'brown envelope' by the prosecution: see further *X (No. 2)* [1999] 2 Cr App R (S) 294.
94 [1999] 1 Cr App R (S) 52.
95 Criminal Justice Act 2003, Schedule 23, replacing ss. 1–2 of the Powers of Criminal Courts (Sentencing) Act 2000. See SGC, *New Sentences: Criminal Justice Act 2003*, paras. 2.2.1 *et seq.*, and ch. 10.7 below.

mitigation for guilty pleas and voluntary compensation, and any good legal adviser would surely inform a defendant of the probable benefits which might accrue from taking either or both of these courses.

Even if the court is satisfied that there is genuine concern for the victim, there are reasons of equity against reducing the sentence on this ground, as was recognized in *Crosby and Hayes* (1974).[96] In that case two offenders had made efforts to pay compensation, but one had the financial capacity to do so and the other did not. The Court of Appeal held that to give them different sentences, for the sole reason that one had a source of finance which the other did not, was wrong in principle and 'not a firm foundation for the administration of justice'. The principle of equality before the law (see Chapter 7, below) therefore militates against this ground of mitigation. The point is obvious where there are two or more co-offenders in the same case, but it should apply no less to any case where an offender claims credit for paying compensation to a victim voluntarily. No doubt some courts, if persuaded of the offender's genuine sorrow about the offence, will reduce the sentence somewhat to reflect the voluntary reparation, but the compromise with principle is clear. It is, in blunt terms, middle-class mitigation.

5.4.4 Worthy social contributions

There are several decisions in which the Court of Appeal has upheld or advocated the practice of giving credit to an offender for 'good deeds' which are quite unrelated to the offence. For example, in *Reid* (1982)[97] the Court of Appeal reduced a custodial sentence for burglary in the light of the offender's conduct, whilst awaiting trial, of attempting to rescue three children from a blazing house. That conduct, observed the Court, might justify the conclusion that 'the appellant was a much better and more valuable member of society than his criminal activities' would lead one to suppose. There are other decisions of a similar kind, concerning actions such as saving a child from drowning[98] and attending to an injured police officer. Nor is it only spectacular incidents which may tell in the offender's favour. In *Ingham* (1980)[99] the Court of Appeal reduced a sentence because the offender had 'done quite a lot of voluntary work', which the Court took as evidence that he had shown 'social responsibility' and 'has got inclinations to serve others rather than to prey upon them'.

To grant mitigation on these grounds implies that passing sentence is a form of social accounting, and that courts should draw up a kind of balance sheet when sentencing. The offence(s) committed would be the major factor on the minus side; and any creditable social acts would be major factors on the plus side. One argument in favour of recognizing such social contributions is that good deeds, like remorse,

---

96 (1974) 60 Cr App R 234.   97 (1982) 4 Cr App R (S) 280.
98 *Keightley* [1972] Crim LR 272.
99 (1980) 2 Cr App R (S) 184; see also *Whitehead* [1996] 1 Cr App R (S) 111, at p. 114: 'she is of positively good character, having contributed much to her locality . . . and has worked with the scout cubs'.

suggest that the offender needs less punishment in order to reintegrate him or her into society. But even if it were justifiable to give preference to rehabilitative reasoning at this point, what is the evidence for asserting that those who do occasional good deeds are less likely to reoffend than those who cannot claim such 'social contributions'? In any event, is it a court's proper function to concern itself with these matters? The court is passing sentence for the particular crime(s) committed. It should not be interested in inquiring either into any bad social deeds the offender has been involved in, except previous offences, or into any good social deeds. The only way to support the practice of taking these factors into account is by means of some modified Durkheimian concept of sentencing as a form of moral/social reinforcement, whereby courts which failed to recognize major social contributions of the offender might be taken symbolically to down-grade those contributions, and that might in turn be regarded as weakening instead of strengthening the collective conscience of society.

5.4.5 The probable impact of the sentence on the offender

There is plenty of support in the Court of Appeal's precedents for mitigation based on such factors as the age or physical or mental condition of the offender, the effect of a sentence on others and the effect of a sentence on the offender's career. These have some similarity with paragraph 5 of Chapter 29 of the Swedish Criminal Code, which provides that:

> in determining the punishment, the court shall to a reasonable extent, apart from the penal value, consider:
>
> 1. whether the accused as a consequence of the crime has suffered serious bodily harm; . . .
> 5. whether the accused as a consequence of the crime has experienced or is likely to experience discharge from employment or other disability or extraordinary difficulty in the performance of his work or trade;
> 6. whether a punishment imposed according to the crime's penal value would affect the accused unreasonably severely, due to advanced age or bad health . . .

Let us examine the foundations for these supposed mitigating factors.

We saw earlier that injury to the offender is recognized as a mitigating factor in the offence of causing death by dangerous driving,[100] and there are other English decisions that accept this as a mitigating factor.[101] Why is this factor thought relevant? The reasoning may draw upon the kind of 'social accounting' criticized in the previous section, or the argument may be that the sentence will have a greater impact on the offender in view of her or his physical condition (see below). The Swedish approach seems to be that this should be regarded as a form of 'natural justice', in the sense that the offender has 'already been punished to some extent', by

---

100 The guideline decision in *Cooksley* [2004] 1 Cr App R (S) 1 at p. 13, cited in part 5.3.2 above.
101 E.g. *Barbery* (1975) 62 Cr App R 248, sentence reduced because the offender's hand was severed during the commission of the offence.

the injuries resulting from the offence. However, it is 'natural' punishment only in a (weak) metaphorical sense. Should courts attempt to regulate the total amount of pain to which an offender is subjected in consequence of an offence, or should they ignore these collateral matters? If they are to do the former, how far should they go – should an offender who is ostracized by the rest of his family after the offence receive a lesser punishment?

At this point the argument merges into the next issue to be considered: what about the effect of the crime on the offender's career? The English decisions on collateral consequences of this kind seem to fall into two categories. Where the crime is unrelated to the offender's employment, there is often a willingness to take account of such matters as the loss of a job and, with it, the loss of pension rights.[102] But where the crime arises out of the offender's employment and may be regarded as an abuse of a position of trust, it is usually stated that no allowance should be made for these collateral matters. Thus, in the guideline case of *Barrick* (1985)[103] on thefts in breach of trust, the Court of Appeal made it clear that loss of job and loss of employment prospects are not to be regarded as mitigating factors. For example,

> Despite the great punishment that offenders of this sort bring upon themselves, the court should nevertheless pass a sufficiently substantial term of imprisonment to mark publicly the gravity of the offence.

> It is practically certain . . . [that] he will never again in his life be able to secure similar employment, with all that that means in the shape of disgrace for himself and hardship for himself and also his family.

Whether judicial practice is consistent with these exhortations is open to doubt. Although Lord Lane CJ held that 'it will not usually be appropriate in cases of serious breach of trust to suspend any part of the sentence', the results of empirical research in the mid-1990s showed that only half of all thefts in breach of trust tried at the Crown Court resulted in immediate custody, and that the proportion of suspended sentences was much higher than for other offences (8 per cent compared with 3 per cent).[104] There seems little doubt that some offenders who commit relatively serious offences of this kind still receive greater mitigation of sentence than the guidelines and other principles would indicate.

Is there any merit in this source of mitigation? Once courts begin to take account of collateral consequences, is this not a step towards the idea of wider social accounting which was rejected in the previous section? One difference is that we are referring here to collateral consequences of the offence, not to social deeds unconnected with the crime. In many cases one can argue that these collateral consequences are a concomitant of the professional responsibility which the offender undertook. Moreover, there is a discrimination argument here too. If collateral consequences were accepted as a regular mitigating factor, this would operate in favour of members of

---

102 E.g. *Stanley* (1981) 3 Cr App R (S) 373, an army sergeant convicted of perjury; *Pearson* (1989) 11 Cr App R (S) 391, a young man hoping to join the army.
103 (1985) 7 Cr App R (S) 142, updated in *Clark* [1998] 2 Cr App R (S) 95; see ch. 4.4.11 above.
104 Flood-Page and Mackie (1998), pp. 85–6.

the professional classes and against 'common thieves' who would be either unemployed or working in jobs where a criminal record is no barrier. It would surely be wrong to support a principle which institutionalized discrimination between employed and unemployed offenders.[105]

A more secure basis for mitigation is found in those cases where the normal sentence might have an exceptional impact on the particular offender. This may be relevant when the offender is very young, very old, or suffering from a life-threatening illness, for in such cases a substantial custodial sentence might be especially hard to bear. Insofar as there is a principle that sentences ought to have a roughly equal impact on offenders, this suggests that where an offender is likely to suffer from the sentence to a significantly different degree than most other people, there is a case for reducing its length.[106] In relation to the very young, the influence of this rationale was evident in the European Court of Human Rights in *T and V v. UK* (2000),[107] emphasizing that whether a punishment is 'degrading' depends to some extent on 'the sex, age and state of health' of the person. In several cases the Court of Appeal has allowed some reduction in the length of sentences imposed on elderly offenders, even though recognizing that a sentence of eight years on a man of 79 means that he 'may not be able to live any part of his life in the community again'.[108] A sentence of normal length on a person of advanced years may take most of his remaining days, but it may be argued that such a sentence on a young man in the flower of youth may be no less catastrophic in a different sense. There may be room for the alternative argument that prison is harder for a man of, say, 80; but perhaps that is a separate issue, to be dealt with on the principles that follow.

In relation to acute and/or terminal medical conditions, the leading decision of *Bernard* (1997)[109] yields two general principles. First, a medical condition that might at some unspecified future date either affect life expectancy or the prison authorities' ability to treat the offender satisfactorily is not a reason for a court to interfere with the sentence that would otherwise be appropriate, but it might be a matter which can be brought to the attention of the Home Secretary. Prisoners who are HIV positive fall into this category. Second, a serious medical condition, even when it is difficult to treat in prison, does not entitle the offender to a reduced sentence, although a court might impose a lesser sentence as an act of mercy. The second principle is unsatisfactory, inasmuch as it appears to leave the matter entirely at the discretion of the court.[110] The principle ought to be that such conditions should be

---

105 On the other hand, it is important to ensure that any collateral orders made against white-collar offenders (e.g. disqualification from company directorship) are kept in proportion: see Wasik and von Hirsch (1997).

106 Cf. Ashworth and Player (1998) with von Hirsch and Ashworth (2005), Appendix C.

107 (2000) 30 EHRR 121, para. 70.

108 *John Francis C* (1993) 14 Cr App R (S) 562; cf. *Harold Nicholas S* [1998] 1 Cr App R (S) 261, where the trial judge had consulted actuarial tables in calculating the sentence on a man aged 82.

109 [1997] 1 Cr App R (S) 135, discussed by Ashworth and Player (1998).

110 In *Stevens* [2003] 1 Cr App R (S) 32 the Court suspended a prison sentence on account of the offender's 'serious heart condition . . . with a poor prognosis and the real probability of a custodial sentence causing many problems'.

taken into account; exactly how this should be done is a practical question for the court.

A more difficult group of cases is where the probable reaction of other prisoners makes it inevitable that an offender will serve much of the prison sentence in solitary confinement for his own protection, or where the offender has been attacked and victimized by other prisoners. The Court of Appeal has stated that 'a defendant's treatment by other inmates is not generally a factor to which this court can properly have regard', and that the defendant should rather proceed through official complaints procedures or by petitioning the Home Secretary for compassionate early release.[111]

Other cases sometimes mentioned in this context are those where another person or persons may suffer abnormally as a result of the sentence imposed on the offender. It is rare for any reduction of sentence to be accorded on the ground that the offender's family will suffer,[112] because this is regarded as a normal concomitant of imprisonment, but the approach is different where a family member is suffering from a life-threatening disease. There are cases in which the Court of Appeal has reduced sentences on that account 'out of mercy'.[113] Perhaps the most frequent example of this line of mitigation is that of a mother caring for young children. Although there are some decisions in which mothers have had prison sentences reduced or suspended so as to allow them to care for their young children,[114] there are others that take a harder line:

> This Court is always most reluctant to see a mother of young children sentenced to a term of imprisonment. Unhappily it is sometimes inevitable . . . No one can fail to be moved by the children's plight but sadly the picture painted is all too familiar in cases where a young mother becomes involved in serious criminal activity. The circumstances which have been described to us are in no way exceptional.[115]

Courts have sometimes been willing to avoid a custodial sentence where the offender is pregnant,[116] and the new sentence of intermittent custody was said to be for 'women offenders who have children' because it minimizes the potential disruption to a child's life and reduces their risk of growing up in care;[117] but such alternatives may be considered impossible where the crime is regarded as serious. The absence of a clear principle is often converted into the language of 'showing mercy', and this is common in cases where the ground for the concession is the effect of the offender's sentence on third parties, particularly those considered vulnerable. One case which provides an unusual example of that rationale is *Olliver*

---

111 *Nall-Cain (Lord Brocket)* [1998] 2 Cr App R (S) 145 at p. 150.

112 Cf. *Grant* (1990) 12 Cr App R (S) 441.

113 E.g. *Haleth* (1982) 4 Cr App R (S) 178, son suffering from kidney disease.

114 E.g. *Whitehead* [1996] 1 Cr App R (S) 1, *Bowden* [1998] 2 Cr App R (S) 7.

115 *Smith* [2002] 1 Cr App R (S) 258 at p. 261, upholding 12 months' imprisonment for conspiracy to evade customs duty of some £70,000. It is notable that a recent Home Office White Paper stated, under the heading 'What is not working', that 'prison can break up families . . . 125,000 children are affected by the imprisonment of a parent each year': Home Office (2002), p. 85.

116 E.g. *Beaumont* (1987) 9 Cr App R (S) 342.   117 Home Office (2002), para. 5.34.

and Olliver (1989),[118] where two brothers convicted of moderately serious offences of violence received suspended sentences and fines, rather than immediate imprisonment, largely on the basis that the livelihoods of some 23 employees in their carpentry business depended on their continued liberty. This, surely, is not a matter of mitigation of sentence properly so called; it is rather a case of mercy being shown to offenders so as to avoid harmful consequences to uninvolved third parties. For the offender, it is a windfall.

5.5 Mitigation and aggravation in practice

This exploration of the sources of mitigation and aggravation has not been exhaustive and has touched upon only some of the many problems they present in sentencing. What has emerged clearly, however, is the great power of aggravating and mitigating factors. Thus the research by Hough, Jacobson and Millie shows that mitigating factors play a crucial role in deciding whether a case that is 'on the cusp' of custody can be dealt with by a form of non-custodial sentence. Whereas the cases sent to custody turn on the seriousness of the offence or the offender's previous record, the key factors in bringing a 'cusp' case down to a community sentence were mitigating factors such as remorse, guilty plea, motivation to address personal problems, family responsibilities, or good employment record or prospects.[119] The sentencers seemed to engage in a kind of moral assessment of the offender and his or her prospects:

> This emphasis on the personal undoubtedly makes the sentencing process a highly subjective one, in which the individual sentencer (or group of sentencers, in the case of magistrates) has to assess the intentions and capabilities of the offender and his or her attitude towards the offence, and offending, such as the presence or absence of remorse and the determination to stop offending. These assessments feed judgements about responsibility and culpability. In other words, sentencers' decisions are framed within a set of explicitly ethical concepts.[120]

These moral assessments take place in a particular context, in which the defence advocate will attempt to construct the offender's character in a particular way, and in which the sentencer(s) may draw inferences from the offender's demeanour in court and other actions.[121]

We have noted that legislation and definitive guidelines now establish the legal effect of some aggravating and mitigating factors, and that may have an effect on the approach of sentencers to these moral assessments. But this formalization does not exhaust the debate about the justifications for and practical effect of mitigating and aggravating factors. Three further questions will be discussed here, all of them demonstrating the close links between practice and theory. First, if a

---

118 (1989) 11 Cr App R (S) 10.   119 Hough et al. (2003), pp. 36–7.
120 Hough et al. (2003), p. 41.   121 See further ch. 1.6 above.

mitigating factor is present, is the offender entitled to a reduction in sentence or is this discretionary? Second, are there some kinds of offence for which normal mitigating factors may have only a negligible effect? Third, how should courts deal with a mixture of aggravating and mitigating factors?

1. *Is mitigation an entitlement?* David Thomas, on the basis of a synthesis of early English decisions, argued that it is not.[122] The early cases suggested that judges might withhold mitigation when they wished to pursue some other penal objective such as deterrence, but the present sentencing framework seems unlikely to allow the same flexibility. It is true that there is only one statutory mitigating factor – the guilty plea discount – and that the terms of s. 166 of the 2003 Act are permissive (leaving the court free to 'take into account any such matters as, in the opinion of the court, are relevant in mitigation of sentence'). However, the trend in the guidelines on sentencing for particular offences is to try to assess the arguments for and against admitting certain aggravating and mitigating factors, and it may not be long before some general guidelines on the subject are developed. It is inadequate for courts simply to state that they are allowing a factor to mitigate 'out of mercy', as if that absolves them from principled justification. Applying principles to particular facts allows room for judgment and discretion, but this should be preceded by arguments about the justifications for allowing the factor to mitigate at all. Once a certain ground for mitigation is authoritatively accepted, then it should be an entitlement – unless in a particular case there is an exceptional countervailing reason.

2. *Does the effect of mitigation vary according to the seriousness of the offence?* The discussion of the guilty plea discount shows that the reduction of sentence is intended to be proportionately the same, no matter whether the sentence is lengthy imprisonment or a mere fine (although there are, as noted above, policy-driven exceptions for mandatory minimum sentences and for murder). However, that approach does not apply to all mitigating factors, the most obvious example being previous good character. A first offender can expect to be dealt with much more leniently than a repeat offender. However, an offender whose first offence is rape or armed robbery cannot expect a significant discount: here, the gravity of the offence is held to overpower the usual claim to mitigation, and the 'concession to human frailty' reasoning looks rather thin. Thus, in *Turner* (1975)[123] Lawton LJ stated that 'the fact that a man has not much of a criminal record, if any at all, is not a powerful factor to be taken into consideration when the court is dealing with cases of this gravity'. The reasoning behind this is to be discussed in detail in Chapter 6 below, but essentially it is that the basis of the mitigation for a first offence is human frailty, and where the first offence is such an egregious wrong, there seems to be no strong ground for regarding the offence as a mere lapse.

3. *Dealing with a mixture of aggravating and mitigating factors.* In practice it is rare for a single mitigating or aggravating factor to appear on its own. In many

---

122 Thomas (1979) p. 47; see also pp. 35–7, 194.   123 (1975) 61 Cr App R 67 at p. 91.

cases there are two or more mitigating factors and, not uncommonly, two or more aggravating factors as well. How should a court gauge the overall effect of such elements? Research suggests that this is a source of considerable disparity in sentencing,[124] and that even where guidelines have been laid down for an offence the absence of clear guidance on weighting produces manifest disparity.[125] The typical structure of English guidelines is to indicate various starting points, and then to say that certain aggravating and mitigating factors can take the sentence up or down from that point – without proposing a weighting for individual factors, let alone suggesting which ones are typically more significant. This would probably be regarded as too detailed a task, and too open to variation according to the facts of individual cases. A typical judicial response would be that each case is different and has to be treated on its own facts. That argument is both true and untrue: it is true at a purely descriptive level, but cannot be true of a judge's interpretation of those facts, since there are bound to be some assumptions about their relevance and weight.[126] Little judicial effort has been made to examine those assumptions. In the United States the federal guidelines assign some two or three points to several factors: the court starts with a 'base level' of points for the category of offence, and then adds and subtracts in order to reflect the presence and strength of various aggravating and mitigating factors. The total number of points is then converted into a range of guideline sentences. This system appears unduly mechanistic, but that criticism can only be sustained if the comparison with ordinary discretionary or impressionistic sentencing is carefully made. The difficulty is that far too little is known about the actual calculations of judges and magistrates in England. They have a tendency to retreat behind the 'no two cases are the same' argument, and to fail to recognize that there are issues of principle to be resolved.

5.6 Aggravation and mitigation in theory

Diverse reasons for recognizing particular aggravating and mitigating factors have been considered in this chapter. In principle, aggravating and mitigating factors should flow from the same source as the rationale(s) of sentencing. If, for example, rehabilitation or resocialization of offenders were the leading rationale, then matters such as remorse and contrition on the part of the offender might assume central importance. But where proportionality is the primary rationale, any mitigation based on remorse requires separate and strong justification. We have identified various aggravating factors that are coherent with proportionality theory, but questions have been raised about the weight to be attached to those factors. One would expect proportionality theory to insist that no aggravating or mitigating factor should be allowed to take a sentence outside the sentencing range appropriate to the nature of the crime committed, but any such principle has been placed under strain by several

---

124 For English research, see Corbett (1987); for the United States, see Zeisel and Diamond (1977).
125 Ranyard, Hebenton and Pease (1994), pp. 208, 216.   126 See the discussion in ch. 1.6 above.

English decisions. Thus we saw in part 5.2.2 above that, where the victim is elderly or disabled, the sentence may be far higher than the offence would normally attract – to the extent that the age and vulnerability of the victim overshadows the intrinsic seriousness of the crime. In some cases where an offence is planned or organized, such as pickpocketing, courts have also imposed sentences out of proportion to the amount stolen, because the offender appears 'professional'.[127] Is it right to accord such an overpowering effect to an aggravating factor?

Some of the factors discussed in this chapter are quite unrelated to proportionality, but are accepted in pursuit of other policies on, for example, the use of imprisonment or the treatment of victims. The task is to examine their justifications independently. It was contended in part 5.4.2 above that offenders who, by their post-offence conduct, make a contribution to the smooth running of the criminal justice system or to its goals, ought to receive some mitigation. This recognizes that sentencing forms part of the criminal justice system in a given social context. But it was argued in part 5.4.1 that the same ought not to apply to the guilty plea discount, because reducing sentences significantly on that account goes too far towards undermining important rights of defendants which should not be sacrificed. It was also submitted, in part 5.4.1 above, that courts should take account of any abnormal impact which the normal sentence would have on an individual offender. Bentham argued strongly for this principle of equal impact in the context of his deterrent theory of punishment,[128] and similar arguments justify its place in a theory which relies on proportionality of punishment. However, it is merely a principle and not an absolute rule, and the possibilities of its conflicting with other principles such as the principle of non-discrimination (equality before the law) will be explored more fully in Chapter 7.

Arguments were presented in part 5.4.5 above against the relevance of the collateral consequences of conviction as mitigating factors, and in part 5.4.4 above against any attempt at wider social accounting such as mitigation for saving a child from drowning. It is not merely that sentencers would not know where to stop if they purported to draw up a balance sheet of the offender's social contributions; it is that the arguments of policy or principle to support this approach seem insufficient, unless the modified Durkheimian view of the courts' function is adopted.

There is a growing argument for some attempt at a co-ordinated framework for aggravation and mitigation. The rise in statutory aggravating factors and the enactment of s. 174(2)(e) of the 2003 Act, requiring courts to 'mention any aggravating or mitigating factors which the court has regarded as being of particular importance', should lead to a fresh and searching examination of the justifications for the various factors. Just as guidelines can assist in establishing a common structure for the sentencing of particular offences, so guidance on general principles can and should conduce to consistency for the same reason.

127 See above, ch. 4.4.12, and below, ch. 6.4.
128 Cf. Bentham (1789), ch. XIV, para. 14, with von Hirsch and Ashworth (2005), Appendix C.

CHAPTER 6

Persistence, prevention and prediction

In the course of this chapter there will be detailed discussion of a group of sentencing issues which lead to considerable practical and theoretical difficulties. After a brief historical introduction, part 2 explores three possible approaches to sentencing persistent offenders, and part 3 considers the relevant provisions of the Criminal Justice Act 2003. Parts 4 and 5 examine two specific problems, those of 'professional' criminals and of petty persistent offenders. In Part 6 a new approach to prevention is examined – the use of anti-social behaviour orders. Part 7 of the chapter turns to the question of selective incapacitation as a strategy for preventing crime, referring to the minimum sentences in English law. In part 8 the 'dangerousness' provisions of the 2003 Act are examined, and some concluding thoughts are found in part 9. Throughout these topics there are linking themes concerned with the promotion of security and the assessment of risk of future criminal behaviour. The invocation of such rationales amounts to a departure from the proportionality principle, and close attention will be paid to the justifications for this.

6.1 Historical introduction

The history of English measures aimed specifically at persistent offenders seems to be widely acknowledged to be a history of failure. The judges have had sufficient discretion, for the last hundred years at least, to allow them to pass fairly long sentences on persistent serious criminals without invoking any special powers. But penal reformers and governments have invariably felt that no major set of reforms would be complete without making further special provision for persistent offenders. The Gladstone Committee in 1895 argued in favour of a special measure against persistent thieves and robbers, who would otherwise serve a succession of fairly short sentences and therefore return frequently to prey on the community. The Committee's proposals led, after much debate,[1] to the Prevention of Crime Act 1908. This empowered a court to impose, upon an offender with three previous felony convictions since the age of 16, a sentence of preventive detention of between five and ten years, in addition to the normal sentence for the crime (a

---

1 Radzinowicz and Hood (1986), pp. 265–78.

so-called 'double track' system). The practical focus of the Act was soon revised when Churchill became Home Secretary. He took the view that the Act, as it was being administered, concentrated unduly on mere repetition in lawbreaking, and he exposed the minor nature of some of the offences which had led to the imposition of preventive detention. He issued a new circular which declared that 'mere pilfering, unaccompanied by any serious aggravation, can never justify' preventive detention, and propounded the general test of whether the nature of the crime was 'such as to indicate that the offender is not merely a nuisance but a serious danger to society'.[2] The aim of preventive detention thus became that of 'protecting society from the worst class of professional criminal'. In fact, the courts often found their ordinary sentencing powers sufficient in such cases, and so the use of preventive detention declined.

A new form of preventive detention was introduced in the Criminal Justice Act 1948 for persistent offenders aged 30 or over, being a sentence of 5 to 14 years instead of (not in addition to) the normal sentence. The Dove-Wilson Committee in 1932 had proposed this as suitable chiefly for 'professional criminals who deliberately make a living by preying on the public',[3] but when the legislation was introduced in 1948 the government envisaged that it would also cover 'the relatively trivial [persistent] offender'.[4] Judges soon found themselves passing sentences of preventive detention on offenders whose records, while showing persistence, were not serious. In the late 1950s the judges increasingly set their faces against this, and in 1962 the Lord Chief Justice went so far as to issue a Practice Direction to restrict the use of preventive detention.[5] Following a gloomy report from the Advisory Council on the Treatment of Offenders (1963) and two other studies which demonstrated the minor nature of many of the offences committed by those subjected to preventive detention,[6] the sentence virtually fell into disuse.

The next measure to be introduced was the extended sentence: the Criminal Justice Act 1967 empowered a court to extend a sentence beyond the normal length or (in limited circumstances) beyond the statutory maximum where it apprehended the need, in view of the offender's record, to protect the public. The White Paper of 1965 had proposed the extended sentence for those offenders who constitute 'a real menace to society',[7] but a parliamentary amendment which would have required the court to have regard to the gravity of the current offence was not accepted by the government. Once again the courts soon found that those falling within the ambit of the sentence could hardly be described as real menaces, and at no stage did the extended sentence play a significant part in sentencing practice.

In some respects the Criminal Justice Act 1991 was a slight improvement, since s. 2(2)(b) permitted courts to pass a longer than proportionate sentence for a violent or sexual offence if it was of opinion 'that only such a sentence would be adequate

---

2 Radzinowicz and Hood (1986), p. 285.   3 Dove-Wilson (1932), para. 42.
4 Hammond and Chayen (1963), p. 11.   5 See [1962] 1 All ER 671.
6 Hammond and Chayen (1963), West (1963).   7 Home Office (1965).

to protect the public from serious harm from him'. The Act did attempt to define 'violent', 'sexual' and 'serious harm', but the provision was vague on crucial issues and unacceptably wide in its scope as interpreted by the courts.[8] The power to impose longer than proportionate sentences appears to have been used relatively rarely in recent years, perhaps (again) because courts tend to give long sentences for serious offences anyway. Thus a brief historical survey reveals two recurrent difficulties. First, legislation on persistent offenders has usually been framed in broad terms, often without clear and precise guidance about the types of offender to be included and excluded. Second, and more fundamentally, there has been little agreement about the group or groups of offenders who should be the target of special sentences. Terms such as 'professional criminals' and 'real menaces' have been used without much effort at precision, and when the law did eventually specify violent and sexual offenders, many of those included were at the lowest end of the scale.

6.2 Three approaches to punishing persistence

The differing views which have been expressed on the sentencing of persistent offenders do not always fall neatly into categories, but three paradigms are (i) flat-rate sentencing, (ii) the cumulative principle, and (iii) progressive loss of mitigation. The aim here is to offer a description of each approach, to consider its rationale, and to weigh the advantages and disadvantages.[9]

6.2.1 Flat-rate sentencing

According to this approach, the sentence should be governed by the crime and not at all by the offender's prior record. This view has been advanced by a small group of desert theorists, most notably George Fletcher[10] and Richard Singer.[11] Their argument, in brief, is that an offender's desert should be measured by reference to the crime committed, in terms of its harmfulness and the offender's culpability in relation to it. Any previous offences cannot have a bearing on this. Indeed, not only are they irrelevant to the calculation, but to take them into account would be to punish the offender twice over – if sentence has already been passed for the previous offences, it is unjust to increase the sentence for a subsequent crime on account of a previously punished offence. Fletcher suggests that desert theorists who do take account of previous offences are indulging in a covert preventionist strategy. Since the increased sentence cannot be justified on desert grounds, says Fletcher, such writers are really trying to achieve a modest amount of individual prevention or incapacitation in such cases.

There are few practical examples of flat-rate sentencing schemes. Illegal parking of cars is one: the penalty does not increase according to the number of previous offences, and one could commit the offence every day without ever receiving more

---

8 See the 3rd edn of this work, pp. 183–9.   9 For fuller discussion see Roberts (1997).
10 Fletcher (1978), pp. 460–6.   11 Singer (1979), ch. 5.

than the fixed penalty. Many other minor offences have fixed penalties or such low maximum fines that they may be viewed as flat-rate offences. If a case goes to court, that creates an opportunity for the penalty to be mitigated for a poor or first-time offender – an opportunity ruled out by flat-rate sentencing. Indeed, since there can be no concession for the impecunious or first offender, the practical question arises of the level at which flat-rate penalties might be set if they are to be defended as proportionate.

6.2.2 The cumulative principle

Since at least the mid-nineteenth century there has been support for the cumulative principle of sentencing persistent offenders. The basic idea is that, for each new offence, the sentence should be more severe than for the previous offence. In this way sentences should be cumulative, with a view to deterring the individual offender from repeating the crimes. Perhaps the best-known exponent of the cumulative principle was the Gloucestershire magistrate Barwick Lloyd Baker. In 1863 he proposed that for a first felony conviction the punishment should be one week or ten days' prison on bread and water; for the second conviction 12 months' imprisonment; for the third, seven years' penal servitude; and for a fourth, penal servitude for life or for some very long period which would allow surveillance on ticket-of-leave for the greater part of the criminal's life. He saw this as achieving protection through individual deterrence, and had no doubts about its fairness: 'if you tell a man clearly what will be the punishment of a crime before he commits it, there can be no injustice in inflicting it'.[12]

That harsh approach made no allowances for the fact that some offences were minor and some stemmed from human weakness or poverty rather than 'wickedness'. It met with considerable opposition, notably from Francis Hopwood, Recorder of Liverpool towards the end of the nineteenth century, who strenuously denounced heavy penalties for petty recidivists. The Lord Chief Justice of the time, Lord Coleridge, appeared to have had greater sympathy with Hopwood's approach, since he maintained that he would inflict punishment only 'for the particular offence for which the prisoner is being tried before me'. But even Lord Coleridge admitted that some of his colleagues had 'different guiding thoughts'.[13]

Although Baker's rationale was deterrence, incapacitation might also be invoked in support of the cumulative approach, especially in view of the contemporary emphasis on security and risk. If so, how might one identify the offenders against whom the principle should be applied? Or is it contended that society is justified in protecting itself against all persistent offenders? Baker had argued that cumulative sentencing of habitual misdemeanants would reduce the incidence of petty offences by some 60,000 a year.[14] There are Home Office statistics showing that offenders with five or more previous convictions are 87 per cent likely to be convicted of another

---

12 See Radzinowicz and Hood (1986), pp. 237–8 and references.
13 Radzinowicz and Hood (1979), pp. 1311–12.   14 Radzinowicz and Hood (1980), p. 1330.

offence within six years.[15] However, most of these offences are towards the lower end of the scale of criminality: the high rates of recidivism are for lesser crimes, and the cumulative principle therefore tends to heap punishment on minor and relatively non-threatening offenders. The second and related question is whether, even if there was evidence that cumulative sentencing would 'work', it would satisfy the requirements of fairness. Would it be acceptable if the sentencing system prescribed penalties of ascending severity for recidivists, especially if their offences were minor? Would it be any more acceptable if the extra detention was under non-punitive conditions, perhaps similar to quarantine? These fairness issues are taken up in part 7 of this chapter, where proposals for the selective incapacitation of certain types of offender are reviewed.

The more common rationale for cumulative sentencing is individual prevention. This was Baker's main argument: cumulative penalties would deter the offender or, if they did not, he would in effect 'with his eyes open deliberately sentence himself'.[16] Several questions are raised by this claim. Are all, or even most, persistent offenders the rationally motivated wicked offenders that it assumes? The historical evidence of measures against persistent offenders, reviewed briefly in part 1 of this chapter, suggests that many of them are not.[17] Among them are people who are socially disadvantaged, others who are in personal turmoil, and others who are mentally disturbed. Even if such offenders are regarded as a threat to the public, the cause of their offending indicates that more constructive measures should be taken, and the concept of fairness underlying the proportionality principle should place a limit to the power that may be taken over them. For dangerous offenders it may be argued that people who offend repeatedly forfeit any right to be regarded as full rights-bearing members of society, or that any rights which such people have ought to be set against the rights of their potential victims, so that the rights of a person who has been shown to reoffend repeatedly may justifiably be overridden in order to preserve the rights of others. These and other arguments are considered in part 8 of this chapter. But for the socially disadvantaged or mentally disturbed, this is not an appropriate standpoint.

Would the cumulative strategy be effective in preventing crime? This depends not only on such factors as knowledge of the penalties among offenders and the absence of countervailing considerations (e.g. low detection rate, absence of proper social provision for people in need), but also on the effectiveness of the penalty. English law has long had one form of cumulative sentencing – the penalty points system for road traffic offenders. When a court sentences an offender for certain traffic offences, it may (or must) impose a number of penalty points, and when an offender accumulates 12 points an immediate disqualification from driving follows. The justifications for having this system for motoring offences and not for other

---

15 Philpotts and Lancucki (1979), p. 16; see also Lloyd, Mair and Hough (1994).
16 Radzinowicz and Hood (1986), p. 238.
17 Radzinowicz and Hood (1986), chs. 8–12, on these debates in the nineteenth century.

crimes have yet to be debated widely; but when it comes to a preventive system based on sentences of imprisonment, the objection was pointed out as long ago as 1932 by the Dove-Wilson Committee:

> the inference is that present methods not only fail to check the criminal propensities of such people, but may actually cause progressive deterioration by habituating offenders to prison conditions which weaken rather than strengthen their characters.[18]

Thus the repeated use of prison sentences may be counter-productive, making these offenders less able to live law-abiding lives and more likely to reoffend on release. If the cumulative principle is based on individual deterrence, and if the point of deterrence is to protect the public, heavy reliance on imprisonment for this purpose may not only go against the principle of restraint (see Chapter 3.4.2) but also be to a significant extent self-defeating.

On the basis of a review of the available evidence some ten years ago on the typical characteristics of criminal careers, David Farrington argued that 'since a high proportion of offenders desist after the first or second offence, significant criminal justice interventions might be delayed until the third offence. Diversionary measures might be appropriate after the first or second offence.'[19] This drives a further wedge between cumulative sentencing and prevention. If prevention is to be the chief concern, it does not follow that cumulative sentencing is the most effective way of achieving this, particularly after two or three convictions, and particularly if incarceration is involved. Like many penal policies, it may have a superficial attractiveness to politicians and the media because it appears 'tough', but it relies on crude assumptions about the causes of offending and on a failure to grasp the criminogenic effects of the penal system itself.[20]

6.2.3 Progressive loss of mitigation

This approach to the sentencing of persistent offenders differs from flat-rate sentencing in making some allowance for previous record, and differs from the cumulative principle in placing limits on the influence of previous record and in deferring to an overall concept of proportionality. The principle of progressive loss of mitigation really consists of two parts: one is that a first offender should receive a reduction of sentence, and the other is that with second and subsequent offences an offender should progressively lose that mitigation. How soon all the mitigation is lost is a question for discussion later, but clearly the principle assumes a limit beyond which the sentence cannot go, no matter how many previous convictions the offender has. The gravity of the current offence(s) is taken to set a 'ceiling' for the sentence: a bad previous record should mean that the offender loses this source of mitigation, but the record should not be treated as an aggravating factor. As Thomas put it, a bad

18 Dove-Wilson (1932), para. 3.   19 Farrington (1997), pp. 564–5.
20 On the indices of risk of offending and how to respond to them, see Farrington (2002).

record 'will not justify the imposition of a term of imprisonment in excess of the permissible ceiling for the facts of the immediate offence'.[21]

What is the theory underlying progressive loss of mitigation? It is an approach characteristically adopted by desert theorists, who view proportionality to the seriousness of the offence as the chief determinant of sentence. We saw earlier that some desert theorists adopt flat-rate sentencing for recidivists. Why would a desert theorist wish to dilute an offence-based system of sentencing (harm plus culpability) by incorporating an element relating to the offender's past history? The argument, restated and refined by Andrew von Hirsch,[22] is based on the idea of a lapse. Ordinary people do have occasional aberrations. Human weakness is not so unusual. The sentencing system should recognize not only this, but also the capacity of people to respond to censure, and to ensure that their future conduct conforms to the law. This is embodied in the idea of giving someone a 'second chance'.[23] So the justification for the discount for first offenders rests partly on recognition of human fallibility, and partly on respect for people's ability to respond to the censure expressed in the sentence. The justification for the gradual losing of that mitigation on second and subsequent convictions is that the 'second chance' has been given and not taken: the offender has forfeited the tolerance, and its associated sentence discount, because the subsequent criminal choices show insufficient response to the public censure. In principle, therefore, the second offence deserves greater censure than the first (unless there is good reason to indicate otherwise), and the third offence may be censured fully. But the seriousness of the offence must remain the primary determinant of sentence, and therefore sentences imposed on repeat offenders should not cumulate so as to lead to custodial terms greater than the current offence could justify.

One possible counter-argument is that the notion of lapse appears to take no account of the possibility that a first offender might have planned an offence meticulously and might have been fully aware of the gravity of the wrongdoing. However, the 'second chance' theory turns on the ability to respond to censure and punishment, not on mere awareness of wrongdoing. A second counter-argument is that the justifications offered seem to assume that all offending is based on rational choice, and to ignore the findings of criminological research. Thus rational choice (of a kind) may be evinced by those who adopt a particular lifestyle, such as career burglars.[24] But some recidivism is largely a concomitant of going to particular places and associating with particular people, as with people who frequently become involved in violence associated with drinking in public houses.[25] Some may stem

---

21 Thomas (1979), p. 41.
22 Von Hirsch and Ashworth (1998), ch. 4.7; von Hirsch and Ashworth (2005).
23 Cf. Bagaric (2001), ch. 10.3.1, for the counter-argument that the moral notion of lapse is inappropriate for matters so serious as criminal convictions. However, it is questionable whether every criminal offence is sufficiently serious to remove the moral force of the argument from lapse. Bagaric also argues that the idea of a discount for first offenders is a subterfuge, and that in reality we are discussing the claim of previous convictions to operate as an aggravating factor. For contrary arguments, see ch. 5.1 above.
24 E.g. Maguire (1982), Bennett and Wright (1984).   25 Walmsley (1986), pp. 17–18.

from contacts made within penal institutions, where information is exchanged and alliances formed.[26] A large amount of recidivism may be associated with drug use.[27] And, more generally, some is part of a cycle of social deprivation and/or personal turmoil, which may or may not be deepened by the experience of imprisonment, as with the so-called petty persistent offenders.[28] Studies of desistance from crime, which focus on the circumstances in which offenders typically give up offending, have long indicated the relevance of stable relationships, a child, a job and other prosaic factors in a person's life.[29] In this context it is important to note two of the recommendations of the Council of Europe on sentencing:

D1 Previous convictions should not, at any stage in the criminal justice system, be used mechanically as a factor working against the defendant.

D2 Although it may be justifiable to take account of the offender's previous criminal record within the declared rationales for sentencing, the sentence should be kept in proportion to the seriousness of the current offence(s).[30]

Proposition D1 emphasizes the importance of considering the reasons for reoffending in each case. This does not present problems for desert theorists, for, as we saw in Chapter 4.5, they can accept grounds for mitigation based on diminished capacity, social deprivation and so forth. Proposition D2 recognizes that, even in those countries where prevention is the primary rationale of sentencing, there should be a proportionality constraint in the sentencing of persistent offenders. The great merit of the 'second chance' idea is that a clear principle of fairness is accorded a central place.[31] Thus, progressive loss of mitigation assumes that a second and a third offence deserve greater censure, but it accords with the Council of Europe in leaving room for other responses if other explanations for reoffending seem persuasive and in insisting on a firm proportionality constraint. This last point distinguishes it clearly from the cumulative approach, which may result in long sentences for persistent but non-serious offenders.

At common law the Court of Appeal frequently restated the theory of progressive loss of mitigation and the proportionality constraint on sentencing persistent offenders. The leading case was probably *Queen* (1981),[32] where the offender had countersigned and attempted to cash a cheque for £50 belonging to someone else. He was sentenced to 18 months' imprisonment. The Court of Appeal, accepting that he had probably been sentenced on his 'appalling' record of thefts and deceptions, reduced the sentence to allow his immediate release. Kenneth Jones J held that it is wrong in principle to sentence an offender on his record:

---

26 See ch. 9.2 below.
27 'Of social variables, drug misuse is most strongly linked with the likelihood of reconviction': Halliday (2001), Appendix 3, para. 11.
28 See this chapter, part 6.5.   29 E.g. West (1963), Burnett (1994), Maruna (2001).
30 Council of Europe (1993).
31 Cf. Bagaric (2001), ch. 10, for the contrary argument that only by adopting flat-rate sentencing can bias against the poor and disadvantaged be reduced significantly.
32 (1981) 3 Cr App R (S) 245.

> The proper way to look at the matter is to decide on a sentence which is appropriate for the offence for which the prisoner is before the court. Then in deciding whether that sentence should be imposed or whether the court can properly extend some leniency to the offender, the court must have regard to those matters which tell in his favour; and equally to those matters which tell against him, in particular his record of previous convictions.[33]

The gravity of the offence should set the ceiling, and even an appalling prior record should not take the sentence above it. However, while the rhetoric of the courts embraced the principle, the reality of sentencing recidivists was often different. Moreover, the courts often seemed unaware of the difference, and managed to say one thing and do another in the same case. In *Bailey* (1988)[34] the offender stood convicted of two offences – one was theft of several ladies' nightdresses, which he had seized from a shop and taken to his solicitor's office nearby; the other was burglary of a hospital, in the form of taking four packets of frozen cod fillets from a hospital freezer. The trial judge imposed two years' imprisonment for the theft, and 18 months consecutive for the burglary, totalling three-and-a-half years. The offender's record was described by the Court of Appeal as 'truly appalling': it stretched back over 25 years, though most were 'comparatively petty thefts'. The trial judge evidently imposed the sentence in order to incapacitate Bailey for a lengthy time (a version of the cumulative principle), but the Court of Appeal held that this was wrong in principle. Stocker LJ went on:

> It is of course manifest that a convicted criminal's past record forms part of the matrix upon which he falls to be sentenced. Clearly no court would be likely to impose a sentence of imprisonment for a first offender of the same length that might be appropriate for a person with a substantial criminal record. To that extent the past record is a relevant factor to be taken into account. On the other hand, as has often been said by this court . . . the sentence imposed must be related to the gravity of the offences in relation to which it is imposed . . . Whilst fully understanding the motive which impelled the learned judge to impose a total sentence of three and a half years, we feel bound to say that those sentences bore so little relationship to the gravity of the offences that even having regard to the appalling background of this appellant, they cannot possibly be justified.[35]

The court went on to reduce the sentences to 15 months for the theft, and three months consecutive for the burglary which yielded the frozen cod fillets.

The statement of principle in this case is fairly clear. Although it is often shortened to 'it is wrong to sentence on record', the court shows appreciation of the relevance of the prior record, within limits, to the sentence. But what are those limits? They were supposed to be set by reference to the gravity of the offence(s), and to constitute the ceiling beyond which the sentence should not go. But the scarcity of clear guidelines for sentencing meant that ceilings were often somewhat plastic. By what benchmark is 15 months' imprisonment a proper ceiling for a rather feeble theft of nightdresses,

---

33 Ibid., at p. 255.   34 (1988) 10 Cr App R (S) 231.   35 Ibid., at p. 233.

which resulted in the recovery of the stolen property fairly soon after the event? The Court of Appeal's decision in *Bailey* shows that the rhetoric of the courts has often been different from the reality of their sentencing practice, and that the principle of progressive loss of mitigation cannot operate without reasonably firm sentence ranges.

The principle of progressive mitigation was not applied at common law to all crimes, even in theory. A different approach, more akin to flat-rate sentencing, applied to grave crimes. In his pioneering judgment in *Turner* (1975),[36] on sentencing levels for armed robbery and for grave crimes in general, Lawton LJ stated that 'the fact that a man has not much of a criminal record, if any at all, is not a powerful factor to be taken into consideration when the court is dealing with cases of this gravity'. Similarly, the guideline judgment on rape states that 'the defendant's good character, although it should not be ignored, does not justify a substantial reduction of what would otherwise be the appropriate sentence'.[37] If this restriction is to be explained, it must be along the lines that little concession to human weakness should be made where there is egregious wrongdoing. The usual 'concession to human frailty' implies that the offence can be seen as an unfortunate lapse, whereas there is less room for compassion for those who succumb to the temptation to commit a grave crime. Presumably this approach implies a kind of sliding scale, with the general 'concession to human frailty' approach to first offenders gradually giving way to a harder line. Rape has a starting point of at least five years' imprisonment, and so perhaps it is at that level that the concession tapers off.

6.3 Previous convictions and the Criminal Justice Act 2003

Section 143(2) of the 2003 Act introduces a new provision on the sentencing of repeat offenders. As such, it takes its place in a panoply of measures introduced by the government to tackle persistent offending. The discussion here begins by analysing official policy in respect of persistent offenders; it then examines the new legislative provision in some detail; and finally it considers what impact the new law is likely to have on sentencing practice, on the prisons, and on public protection.

6.3.1 Policy on persistent offenders[38]

Sentencing policy for persistent offenders should be seen in the broader context of the criminal justice system. In recent years the government has required local Criminal Justice Boards to develop schemes for targeting persistent offenders in terms of investigation and detection, aiming at 'prolific offenders who are responsible for a disproportionate amount of crime'.[39] The Persistent Offender Scheme defined a 'core persistent offender' as someone aged 18 or over who has been convicted of six

---

36 (1975) 61 Cr App R 67 at p. 91, discussed in ch. 4.4.9 above.
37 *Millberry* [2003] 2 Cr App R (S) 142 at pp. 152–3, adopting SAP, *Advice to the Court of Appeal: Rape* (2002), para. 46.
38 For detailed discussion see Wasik (1987), Roberts (1997), and von Hirsch and Roberts (2004).
39 Home Office (2002), p. 1.

or more recordable offences in the last 12 months. A recent inspection report on the scheme found that the most common offence by far was theft from shops, at 36 per cent of all those falling within the definition. Only 5 per cent of qualifying offences were burglary in a dwelling.[40] This demonstrates an abject failure to understand the lessons of history in respect of policy on persistent offenders, as described in part 6.1 above, and it is hardly surprising that the first recommendation made in the Joint Inspection Report is that the definition be narrowed so as 'to identify a more limited number of priority offenders'.[41] The report therefore recognizes the confusion between mere repeat offending and the idea of targeting priority offenders, but it stops short of indicating exactly who the priority offenders should be. It goes on to suggest that these should be identified locally, but the lack of specificity suggests that policy on persistent offending is still wallowing in a vitiating uncertainty. The report states that the needs of the offenders currently included in the scheme are similar to those in the general offending population – notably, 'problems with thinking skills, drug misuse, employment training and education, accommodation, lifestyle, attitudes and finance'. [42] The role of alcohol and substance misuse should be given even greater emphasis:

> The 100,000 most persistent offenders share a common profile. Half are under 21 and nearly three-quarters started offending between 13 and 15. Nearly two-thirds are hard drug users. More than a third were in care as children. Half have no qualifications at all and nearly half have been excluded from school. Three-quarters have no work and little or no legal income.

This important quotation comes not from a criminological textbook but from a major Home Office framework document.[43] However, it has been ignored too frequently by the Home Office since it was written. The quotation also points up a third difficulty with the prolific offender policy – the reference to 100,000 persistent offenders who commit about 50 per cent of serious crimes in any one year. The Halliday report was pessimistic about the crime-preventive effects of targeting this group,[44] and the Carter report referred to evidence that each year some 40 per cent of persistent offenders will stop offending without further official intervention and that many of these are replaced by new persistent offenders. Carter concluded that 'historically, incapacitation is only associated with small falls in crime',[45] and thus shared Halliday's view that subjecting this group to longer sentences would not have the large crime-preventive effects sometimes assumed. Criminological research shows that many criminal careers are short-lived, and mostly among males aged 15–25, and that there is a variety of personal and social-structural explanations of why offenders desist after a few years.[46] The constant renewal of the stock of repeat

40 Joint Inspection Report (2004), para. 6.13.
41 Joint Inspection Report (2004), para. 7.8.
42 Joint Inspection Report (2004), para. 6.14.   43 Home Office (2001), Appendix B, para. B.7.
44 Halliday (2001), Appendix 6; cf. Appendix 3, on criminal careers.
45 Carter (2003), pp. 15–16.   46 See Bottoms, Shapland et al. (2004), p. 370 and *passim*.

offenders is a well-known explanation of why incapacitative sentencing policies are less effective than some expect.

What, then, should be the policy in dealing with persistent offenders, and why? The Halliday review concluded that the proper approach to sentencing persistent offenders was unclear and therefore probably inconsistent – a diagnosis that could hardly be disputed, given the gap between the rhetoric of the common law and the practice of the courts (set out in part 6.2.3 above) and given the extraordinary fact that the legislative provision on sentencing persistent offenders introduced by the Criminal Justice Act 1993 was never formally considered by the Court of Appeal during its 12 years in force. How, then, should the law be 'clarified'?

> Clarification needs to be based on a clear presumption that sentence severity should increase as a consequence of sufficiently recent and relevant previous convictions. The justification for this modified principle is twofold. A continuing course of criminal conduct in the face of repeated attempts by the State to correct it, calls for increasing denunciation and retribution, notwithstanding that earlier crimes have already been punished. In addition, persistent criminality justifies the more intensive efforts to reform and rehabilitate which become possible within a more intrusive and punitive sentence. As it happens, because previous convictions are a strong indicator of risks of reoffending, this presumption would also, coincidentally, take such risks into account. For all these reasons, the new presumption would serve to target resources on the offenders who commit a disproportionate amount of crime and are most likely to reoffend. The new presumption must be governed by the proportionality principle, to avoid excessively severe and therefore unjust punishments. To do this, clear guidelines demonstrating the 'gearing' between offence seriousness, seriousness of record, and bands of acceptable sentences, will be needed, building on the guidelines already established or under development.[47]

Four points may be made about this key passage. First, it puts forward two reasons for modifying the proportionality principle, and with it the principle of progressive loss of mitigation. To argue that repeated convictions necessarily amount to some kind of defiance of the state and thus supply a justification for increased severity is doubtful for a number of reasons. Notably, it is doubtful because it assumes that the motivation for and causes of reoffending can properly be seen as defiance of the state and its efforts: the quotation from the Home Office set out above[48] shows what kinds of offender are to be found in this group, and it is therefore wrong to assume that they are all rational calculators who are deliberately thumbing their noses at the state. And it is doubtful, in any event, whether it is justifiable to treat any defiance of the state as an aggravating factor: to treat 'insubordination' as a serious evil in itself, aside from any harm resulting from or risked by the conduct, is a form of authoritarianism inconsistent with proper democratic principles.[49] Halliday did not argue that his recidivist premium was justified by reference to deterrence or

---

47 Halliday (2001), para. 2.7.   48 See text at n. 43 above.
49 See von Hirsch and Roberts (2004), p. 649.

to incapacitation. His primary rationales appear to be denunciation and a version of proportionality that treats an offender as deserving more for each subsequent offence, both of which are connected with his flawed idea of defiance.

Second, when the above passage does recognize that some persistent offenders need rehabilitation, it insists that this should be carried out within 'a more intrusive and punitive sentence'. Granted that such a significant proportion of persistent offending is drug-related,[50] does this mean that drug treatment for persistent offenders should generally be carried out in custody? Is that the right policy, in terms of either the seriousness of the individual offences or the effectiveness of the treatment? Or is it a recognition that funding for Drug Treatment and Testing Orders has not always been adequate, with the result that custodial institutions tend to offer a better prospect?[51]

Third, Halliday linked his policy towards persistent offenders with findings on risk, as set out in Appendix 3 of his report. He cites abundant evidence that the best predictor of reconviction is the number of previous convictions, but fails to notice that absent from the data is any assessment of the relative seriousness of the individual offences. This is a fault line running through many discussions of risk and crime prevention. The passage refers to offenders who commit a disproportionate amount of crime. Is it 'crime' in general that policies should be designed to reduce or, in a system of limited resources, is it not wiser to target offences that are of particular concern – notably, the more serious ones? As we shall see, this ambiguity flows through many official statements on persistent offending.

Fourth, and despite the rhetoric earlier in the passage, Halliday insisted that there should be upper limits (or ceilings) in order to prevent 'excessive severity' when sentencing offenders with a long record. This appears to place his proposals midway between progressive loss of mitigation (whose ceilings would, on his view, afford insufficient room for escalation of sentences for repeat offenders) and an unbridled cumulative approach, which he rejected explicitly: 'a cumulative approach would lead to disproportionate outcomes. As a general principle, the increased severity in sentence must retain a defensible relationship with the offences under sentence.'[52] When he went on to give examples of the scale of enhancement for previous convictions that he envisaged, it was clear that they were well above existing levels. For example, in relation to domestic burglary and handling stolen goods he pointed out that 14 years was the statutory maximum and that few cases, even those of offenders with several previous convictions, were sentenced in the upper quartiles of those ranges.

As we shall see below, the Halliday approach has not been followed in all respects in the new legislation. When the Home Office set out its policy in the White Paper, it had relatively little to say on this subject:

---

50 'Of social variables, drug misuse is most strongly linked with the likelihood of reconviction': Halliday (2001), Appendix 3, para. 11.
51 Joint Inspection Report (2002), ch. 5 (on the street crime initiative).
52 Halliday (2001), para. 2.15.

Persistent offending should also justify a more severe view and more intensive efforts at preventing reoffending. Increased punishment will be the outcome for those offenders who have consistently failed to respond to previous sentences. We will ensure that such an outcome is explicit in the statutory framework for sentencing.[53]

However, an element of confusion appeared in its more general declarations. The most repressive policies were to be directed at 'serious, dangerous and seriously persistent offenders',[54] a phrase that contains a crucial ambiguity about whether the persistent offenders have committed serious offences, or are merely frequent repeaters of offences at any level of seriousness. Similar confusion runs through the Carter review. On the one hand it recognized the problem with the claim about the 100,000 persistent offenders,[55] it urged the greater use of curfews and non-custodial interventions, it pointed to the strong link between persistent offending and drug problems, and it recognized that the result of 'the strict management of drug offenders . . . is a risk of rapidly increasing the prison population'.[56] On the other hand it criticized the courts for giving 'greater emphasis to the seriousness of the offence rather than the number of previous convictions',[57] referred enthusiastically to the 'risk assessment of offenders' without any reference to the seriousness of the offences 'risked',[58] and capped it all by advocating 'a clear gradient of sentencing severity, which increases with the number of previous offences' without any reference to the seriousness of the offending.[59]

Official policy on persistent offenders therefore suffers from ambiguity and inconsistency. There is considerable emphasis on risk of reoffending, but often without distinguishing serious from less serious offences. The main feature of the response to persistent offending is one of escalating severity, and that assumes that increased punitiveness is justified, that defiance makes offences more serious, and that offenders are rational actors (whereas Home Office evidence shows that these are often the most disadvantaged people, and that drug addiction plays a major part). Little account has been taken of criminological findings on criminal careers and desistance, and on using the desistance research to reorientate the response to recidivism towards a more constructive handling of the relatively few crime-prone years of many of these offenders.[60]

6.3.2 The new law

Section 143(2) of the Criminal Justice Act 2003 provides:

In considering the seriousness of an offence ('the current offence') committed by an offender who has one or more previous convictions, the court must treat each previous conviction as an aggravating factor if (in the case of that conviction) the court considers that it can reasonably be so treated having regard, in particular, to –

---

53 Home Office (2002), para. 5.10.   54 Home Office (2002), para. 5.7.
55 Carter (2003), p. 16.   56 Carter (2003), p. 29.   57 Carter (2003), p. 18.
58 Carter (2003), pp. 27–8.   59 Carter (2003), p. 29.
60 See now Bottoms, Shapland et al. (2004).

(a) the nature of the offence to which the conviction relates and its relevance to the current offence, and

(b) the time that has elapsed since the conviction.

The drafting of this provision indicates that a court is bound to treat each previous conviction as a factor that aggravates the current offence, and must do so each time the offender is sentenced.[61] Thus, if a person who was sentenced in April 2005 for an offence, and had five previous offences that were taken to aggravate the sentence, were to come up for sentence again in May 2006, the court would be required to treat each of his (now) six previous convictions as aggravating the sentence.

It may be argued that the force of the mandatory words, 'must treat . . . as an aggravating factor', is considerably softened by the later clause, 'if the court considers that it can reasonably be so treated'. But a more straightforward reading would be that the court's decision on whether a previous conviction 'can' (should?) be treated as aggravating is to be determined by its assessment of its relevance and recency, as set out in (a) and (b), and not by any broader views about whether previous convictions should be allowed to increase sentence. The Explanatory Notes to the Act state baldly that recent and relevant convictions 'should be regarded as an aggravating factor which should increase the severity of the sentence'.

What should be the criterion of whether prior convictions are relevant to the current offence? The Halliday report noted that most persistent offenders have a mixed criminal record, and therefore argued that 'less weight should be given to whether previous and current offences are in the same category', so that 'the key point is whether the previous offences justify a more severe view'.[62] Insofar as this suggests that the seriousness of the previous offences is the crucial issue, it seems difficult to reconcile with reference in s. 143(2) to relevance, which may be taken to indicate a similarity of subject matter. In the past, the practice in sentencing for offences of violence has been for courts to pay more attention to previous convictions for offences of violence than to others; and the same might be said of sexual cases.[63] Where there is a record of offences of dishonesty or burglary, courts may decide to treat the person as a 'professional' (see part 6.4 below). However, both Appendix 3 of the Halliday report and David Farrington's review of criminal career research lead to the conclusion that the typical pattern is a small degree of specialization 'superimposed on a great deal of generality or versatility in offending', and that the majority of offences of violent offenders are non-violent.[64] This raises the question whether mere similarity of offence category, rather than targeting particular types of victim, should be relevant at all. It could also be argued that the notion of lapse, underlying the concession of first offenders, should not be

61 Convictions from other jurisdictions may also be taken into account (subsections (4) and (5)), but it is unclear whether a conviction followed by a discharge counts as a previous conviction in this context.

62 Halliday (2001), para. 2.17; later in the same paragraph, however, the report states that 'completely disparate . . . previous convictions should be given less weight'.

63 See Wasik (1987), pp. 108–9.   64 Farrington (1997), p. 380.

applied simply to the heterogeneous category of 'crime'. Human weakness in losing one's temper momentarily and punching another may be regarded as different from human frailty in succumbing to the temptation of economic crime. There is therefore some ground for arguing that a first offence of violence by someone with previous property convictions should be treated as 'out of character', and should be mitigated to some extent. But this argument cannot be pressed too far. It would be absurd to imply that everyone is entitled to one 'discounted' crime of violence, one 'discounted' fraud, one 'discounted' sexual offence and so on. Thus Halliday suggested that the seriousness of the offences is the primary determinant, in terms of 'whether there is a continuing course of criminal conduct'.[65] Section 143(2)(a) seems to have a different emphasis, and a narrower notion of relevance – defined according to types or categories of offending – may take root.

There is widespread agreement that a gap in offending should be taken to diminish the effect of previous convictions, and s. 143(2)(b) accordingly requires courts to have regard to the time that has elapsed since each previous conviction. An example of this from the common law is *Fox* (1980),[66] where the Court of Appeal reduced the sentence on a man aged 35 convicted of grievous bodily harm who had two previous convictions many years earlier: 'In our judgment, his previous record of violence when he was in his late teens and mid-twenties should have been left out of account in deciding what action to take.' Various justifications may be offered for this concession – for example the offender deserves credit for going straight, or the present offence is to some extent 'out of character' in terms of his recent behaviour, or the conviction-free gap makes it less likely that he will reoffend – but the most straightforward approach is to affirm the underlying principle of the Rehabilitation of Offenders Act 1974. Generally speaking, it is unnecessarily harsh if a person has to bear the burden of previous convictions indefinitely: after a number of years a person should be able to regain full rights as a citizen, and such a principle may even provide an incentive not to reoffend. Many US guideline systems provide for the 'decay' of previous convictions after 10 years, and this has been adopted, for example, in the proposed South African sentencing code.[67]

What is missing from s. 143(2) is any reference to an overall proportionality constraint, as recommended by the Council of Europe and adopted, for example, in Sweden.[68] The wording of s. 143(2) seems consistent with a cumulative approach that increases the severity of the sentence on each subsequent conviction, allowing sentences (e.g. for theft from shops) to ascend to two, two-and-a-half or three years'

---

65 Halliday (2001), para. 2.17.

66 (1980) 2 Cr App R (S) 188; see also *Bleasdale* (1984) 6 Cr App R (S) 177 (four years without trouble for a man of 22 'is an important feature in his favour').

67 South African Law Reform Commission (2000), s. 42: 'where a period of 10 years has passed from the date of completion of the last sentence and the date of commission of any subsequent offence . . . the last conviction and all convictions prior to that must be disregarded for the purposes of sentencing'.

68 Von Hirsch and Jareborg (1989): see ch. 29.4, 'the court shall . . . to a reasonable extent take the offender's previous criminality into account'.

imprisonment. We have seen that Halliday insisted on a proportionality constraint. Section 143(1) may be taken to indicate a general principle of proportionality in sentencing but, as we saw in Chapter 3.5 above, s. 142 requires courts to have regard to other purposes of sentencing such as deterrence and public protection – which may be thought to authorize long sentences for persistent offenders. However, in Parliament it was said that s. 143(2) was not intended to lead to disproportionate sentences,[69] and it therefore falls to the Sentencing Guidelines Council to ensure that this intention is carried through into the relevant guidelines.

Finally, we should return to the mandatory wording of s. 143(2). Does the injunction that 'the court must treat each previous conviction as an aggravating factor' mean that Parliament intended to rule out the use of community sentences for repeat offenders? At one level it does not: a first offence may warrant a fine, and the two or three subsequent offences may justify only community sentences. The question then is whether the offence – say, theft from shops – is so serious that a custodial sentence can be justified for a repeat offender. If the answer is yes,[70] then it may seem inconsistent with the principle of treating each previous conviction as aggravating if a court is to decide on a community sentence. For example, some such offenders commit frequent thefts of items such as toiletries, with a view to selling them in order to raise money to buy drugs.[71] The offender may come before the court with 30, 40 or more previous convictions. If the court wishes to tackle what it regards as the underlying cause of offending (drug-taking) by making a community order, would it be lawful to do so? Halliday himself wanted to see community sentences used more widely in such cases, but there was always a conflict with his proposed policy on persistent offending,[72] and the mandatory wording of s. 143(2) heightens the conflict. On one view a court would be acting unlawfully if it dealt with an offender, whose record disclosed many recent and relevant convictions, by means of a community sentence: each previous conviction would be an aggravating factor, and the starting point for theft would therefore be a significant custodial sentence. Only if there were a guideline that placed a low ceiling on sentences for repeated non-serious offending would there be a possibility of imposing a community sentence. And even then, would not the court have to demonstrate compliance with s. 143(2) by saying that the previous convictions do aggravate the sentence but that it still falls beneath the custody threshold?[73]

---

69 Baroness Scotland, HL Deb. 24 Feb. 2003.
70 See *Page et al.*, unreported, 8 Dec. 2004, where Rose LJ held that persistent shop theft on a minor scale might justify one month's imprisonment; a history of persistent similar offending on a significant scale 'would often merit no more than 12 to 18 months'; but where offences were attributable to drug addiction, a community sentence aimed at tackling that addiction would often be appropriate. See further ch. 10.6 below.
71 See the instructive discussion of such a case by Jones (2002).
72 Jones (2002), pp. 185–6, citing Halliday (2001), para. 6.6.
73 Cf. cases where drug treatment and testing orders were imposed for offences serious enough to attract up to three years' custody, e.g. *Kelly* [2003] 1 Cr App R (S) 472 and *Belli* [2004] 1 Cr App R (S) 490, and below, ch. 10.6.3.10.

6.3.3 The probable outcomes

Having considered the policy towards persistent offenders generally, and the specific terms of s. 143(2), we now turn to consider the probable effects of the new law. Three spheres of impact will be assessed – sentencing practice, the prison population, and public protection.

1. Sentencing practice. Halliday envisaged that the principal constraint on sentencers would be definitive guidelines from the Sentencing Guidelines Council, which he expected to identify different starting points according to the weight of the previous criminal record. The only current guidelines with this degree of detail are those for domestic burglary, handed down by the Court of Appeal in *McInerney and Keating* (2003)[74] before the 2003 Act was passed. These establish distinct starting points for first-time, second-time and third-time domestic burglars committing a 'standard' burglary, and are therefore along the lines suggested by Halliday. This approach was taken because of the minimum sentence for the third domestic burglary (see part 6.7 below), and the belief that previous record is more important in burglary (presumably because it has a relatively high proportion of specialists, unlike many other crimes). But how might a court, applying the 2003 Act, deal with a case such as *Woods* (1998)?[75] A vicar returned to his vicarage to find the offender dozing on the floor, having broken in and put various items from the house in a bag ready to take with him. The offender had 121 previous convictions for offences of burglary and theft, not of great seriousness, and had been released from prison only 21 days before the burglary. The trial judge sentenced him to six years' imprisonment, saying that there was no hope of rehabilitating or deterring the offender and that therefore an incapacitative sentence was needed in order to protect the public. The Court of Appeal acceded to the proposition that the offender was not a professional but an incompetent yet frequent opportunist, usually looking for food or money. The Court reduced the sentence from six to four years. This was still a wholly disproportionate sentence for a burglary that is fairly low down the scale. Under the 2003 Act a court would be bound to find that his previous convictions were both recent and relevant, but the sentencing guidelines (underpinned by the minimum sentence for the third domestic burglary) would indicate a starting point of at least three years. If a court were really to regard each of his 121 convictions as aggravating the current offence, then it might well impose a sentence even longer than the four years upheld in *Woods*. There is nothing in s. 143(2) to direct courts to keep sentences for minor offences low, and it will fall to the Sentencing Guidelines Council to reinforce what Baroness Scotland stated in the parliamentary debates.

One of the curious features of the pre-2003 law was that the Court of Appeal failed to analyse (and only rarely referred to)[76] the statutory provision on persistent offenders. That is unlikely to happen under the 2003 Act, and indeed the Court of Appeal may be called upon to interpret s. 143(2) before the Council has laid down

---

74 [2003] 2 Cr App R (S) 240, discussed above, ch. 4.4.11.   75 [1998] 2 Cr App R (S) 237.
76 A rare example was *Spencer and Carby* (1995) 16 Cr App R (S) 482 at pp. 485–6.

any definitive guideline on it. The provision will certainly allow courts to continue to impose lengthy sentences on 'professional criminals' (see part 6.4 below), and unless relatively tight guidelines for particular offences are created, it is possible that s. 143(2) will encourage a further upward drift in sentences for recidivists – unless the courts take the view, not uncommon in these situations, that the new provision actually encapsulates the principles on which they have been acting for some time.[77]

2. *The prison population.* Those remarks about the effect of the new provision on sentencing practice have obvious implications for the prison population. If the courts simply take the view that s. 143(2) confirms their present approach, there will be little change in the prison population. But if the courts take literally the injunction to treat each previous conviction as an aggravating factor, and if there are no firm ceilings in place, then there will be a growing 'recidivist premium' in sentencing which will translate into increases in the prison population. Halliday suggested that some 3,000–6,000 extra prison places would be required, but this estimate was based on several contingencies.[78] If there is an increase, then it will be predominantly in respect of property offenders – since they typically accumulate more previous convictions than other types of offender.[79] This brings the discussion back to the crucial ambiguity in the government's policy statements: it proclaims that the toughest sentences will be reserved for violent and sexual offenders, but then adds 'and seriously persistent offenders',[80] an unclear phrase that may include those who commit non-serious property offences with great frequency. As argued in part 6.3.2 above, the wording of s. 143(2) may be taken to preclude courts from making community orders that require, say, submission to drug testing and treatment, in cases of offenders with several convictions for property offences. If these constructive alternatives are ruled out, then more custodial sentences for recidivists will result.

3. *Public protection.* At a general level the new legislation on persistent offenders may be seen as part of the government's emphasis on security, public protection and the reduction of risk to members of the public.[81] But when risk is discussed, it is usually the risk of physical and sexual harm that is regarded as the main object of protection. As argued above, what may happen if s. 143(2) changes sentencing practice is that more property offenders will receive longer sentences. If that occurs, it will not promise greater protection from sexual or violent offences. Will it even provide greater protection from property offences? The official figures show that this is unlikely to occur. Halliday accepted that the prison population would have to increase by some 10,000 in order to reduce the incidence of crime by 1 per cent,[82] and he concluded that neither a gain in incapacitative effect nor a gain in deterrent

---

77 This view was certainly put to Halliday (2001): 'many sentencers say they already do so, but it has not been possible to establish the extent or effects of current practice' (para. 9.12).
78 Halliday (2001), para. 9.13 and Appendix 7.   79 Von Hirsch and Roberts (2004), p. 651.
80 Home Office (2002), para. 5.7 (cited above, nn. 53–54).
81 E.g. Hudson (2003), Zedner (2003), Ashworth (2004b).
82 Halliday (2001), Appendix 6, p. 130; cf. the different calculation in the Carter report (2003), p. 16, also making the point that the fall in the number of young people in the population was a factor in reducing the crime rate.

effect could be relied on as a justification for his proposals – although he hoped that some such effects might be felt.[83] It was probably for these reasons that he had to rest his proposals on the argument that persistent offenders deserve longer sentences for continuing to offend despite the state's attempts to turn them away from crime.

6.4 The problem of 'professional' criminals

In the past, as we saw in part 6.1 of this chapter, severe policies against persistent offenders have often been rationalized on the ground that they are aimed at 'professional criminals', even though they have often swept many minor offenders into the net. Courts still describe certain offenders as 'professional', raising questions about the justification for singling out this group, and questions of definition. It is fairly clear that the courts' aim is either deterrence or public protection. The argument seems to be that professional criminals set themselves deliberately against the rest of society and endeavour systematically to exploit opportunities for crime to reap the benefits. Thus, there is no question of human weakness in this group, no occasional succumbing to temptation: they are perceived to be rational calculators, and the response should be a tough one.

But how is this group to be defined? It is one thing to affirm the existence of professional criminals ruthlessly and systematically exploiting law-abiding citizens. It is another to ensure that this group of offenders is so defined as to include only those who meet the description and to exclude others. As we saw in part 6.1 above, early in the last century Churchill 'was appalled to find that repetition was the criterion for imposing preventive detention, irrespective of the gravity of the offences committed'. There were long lists of offenders sentenced to preventive detention 'for such trivialities as stealing a pair of boots, or two shillings, or four dishes, or handkerchiefs, or fowls or slates or whatever'.[84] Is there a contemporary equivalent of this? The courts have tended to use the adjective 'professional' in relation to persistent pickpockets and bag-snatchers when justifying long sentences. Thus in *Freeman* (1989)[85] the Court of Appeal upheld a sentence of five years on a persistent pickpocket who was described as a professional; in *O'Rourke* (1994)[86] the Court upheld a sentence of three years on a persistent handbag thief; in *Spencer and Carby* (1995)[87] similar sentences were upheld on offenders described as professional pickpockets; and in *Gwillim-Jones* (2002)[88] a sentence of three years was upheld on a professional handbag thief. Thus the adjective 'professional' appears to suggest that crime is the offender's principal source of income, or it is a regular source of income, or the offences are planned to maximize profit and minimize the risk of detection,

83 Halliday (2001), paras. 1.62–1.68. See also von Hirsch and Roberts (2004), pp. 649–50.
84 Radzinowicz and Hood (1986), p. 283.
85 (1989) 11 Cr App R (S) 398; see also *Whitrid* (1989) 11 Cr App R (S) 403, and the discussion in ch. 4.4.12 above.
86 (1994) 15 Cr App R (S) 650; see also *Glide* (1989) 11 Cr App R (S) 319.
87 (1995) 16 Cr App R (S) 482.   88 [2002] 1 Cr App R (S) 19.

or the offences are executed with great skill, or simply that the offender commits acquisitive offences frequently.[89] But are all offences committed in one of those sets of circumstances sufficiently serious to justify such long sentences? Many of the convictions are for theft of items of small value, or even for attempted theft, and in principle they are 'worth' no more than a community sentence. Moreover, custody is unlikely to change the lifestyle of these offenders, whereas targeted interventions under the umbrella of a community sentence may now have a chance of doing so.[90]

The concept of a professional criminal may trade on its association with organized crime, conjuring up images of entrepreneurs who meticulously plan their offences.[91] The two concepts must be kept separate when small-time thieves are being sentenced. There are some individuals whose criminality would seem to be clearly professional, in the sense that their skill, planning and calculation of lucrative gains would bring them within most definitions – one example being the career of A. E. Brewster, who has repeatedly committed high-value burglaries at luxurious houses and flats in central London, serving long sentences (ten years and nine years upheld in the two Court of Appeal cases) and then returning to the same occupation.[92] Evidence of involvement in organized crime, for example through major armed robberies or trafficking in illegal immigrants, may warrant the term 'professional'. But the application of that term to pickpockets and handbag thieves, as a reason for imposing sentences in the same range as some rapes and serious woundings, cannot be justified. The terms of s. 143(2) of the 2003 Act would seem to encourage rather than discourage long sentences for such offenders, as we saw in part 6.3 above, and that supplies a further reason for reconsidering the use of the adjective 'professional'.

6.5 Persistent petty offenders

Prison surveys have revealed that a significant number of those in custody are there mainly because of their social rootlessness and the repeated commission of minor offences, often of a 'nuisance' or public order kind. Some of these offences would seem to fall into the category of cases which it is not in the public interest to prosecute, as the Woolf Inquiry concluded,[93] and in some cases a prosecution is brought simply to shift a problem from one agency to another. As a Home Office study found, 'the homeless poor may be persistently taken to court, and hence persistently returned to prison, because of a persistent failure to provide for them in any other way'.[94]

---

89 Note also the varying definitions of 'professional' used by the judges in the study by Davies and Tyrer (2003).
90 See ch. 10.6 below.
91 See the extensive discussion of definitions of organized crime by Levi (2002).
92 *Brewster* (1980) 2 Cr App R (S) 191 and [1998] 1 Cr App R (S) 181; see also *Jenkins* [2002] 1 Cr App R (S) 22.
93 Woolf (1991), paras. 10.106, 10.164.   94 Fairhead (1981), p. 2.

However, there are two sections in the 2003 Act which raise the possibility of disproportionately severe sentences on this type of offender. First, although s. 152(2) of the Criminal Justice Act 2003 should only permit the imposition of a custodial sentence if the offence is so serious that neither a fine nor a community sentence is an adequate sentence, the extent to which this will be blunted in practice by the provision on persistent offenders in s. 143(2) remains to be seen. The Home Office has supported 'diverting from prison minor offenders for whom a very short stay in prison serves little purpose',[95] without noting the contrary tendency of s. 143(2). But if s. 152(2) is to be given its proper force, courts should find themselves following the spirit of Lawton LJ's judgment in *Clarke* (1975),[96] where he declared (albeit in a case involving an element of mental disorder) that courts should not be used as 'dustbins for the difficult' and varied a sentence of 18 months' imprisonment, for damaging a flowerpot, to a fine of £2. This amounted to a strong declaration that most of these people are offenders only incidentally or symptomatically, and should properly be the concern of the social services. The provision of support and care for them should not be the responsibility of the criminal justice system. It is a wider social problem concerning the provision of education, housing, training and (where necessary) community care. But s. 143(2) may be taken to point in another direction.

Second, s. 151 of the Act empowers a court to impose a community sentence on an offender who has been fined on at least three previous occasions, and where (despite the effect of s. 143(2)) the court would not regard the current offence as serious enough to warrant a community sentence.[97] The court must decide that it is in the interests of justice to make such an order and to take the offender up-tariff in this way. The SGC's guidelines emphasize that courts should only impose a community sentence in the lowest range of seriousness in these cases, and warn that:

> Where an offender is being sentenced for a non-imprisonable offence or offences, great care will be needed in assessing whether a community sentence is appropriate since failure to comply could result in a custodial sentence.[98]

However, the danger exists that petty offenders will be sent to prison if courts embark on this route. This effect of s. 151 must be carefully monitored.

6.6 The prevention of 'anti-social behaviour'

Another part of the present government's strategy against persistent offending is the anti-social behaviour order (ASBO). It was in the same year as the Human Rights Act became law, 1998, that the ASBO was introduced by s. 1 of the Crime and Disorder Act.[99] It is a civil order, made by magistrates sitting as a civil court on application by the police, local authority or landlord, that imposes restrictive

---

95 Home Office (2004), para. 23.   96 (1975) 61 Cr App R 320.
97 This substantially re-enacts s. 59 of the Powers of Criminal Courts (Sentencing) Act 2000.
98 SGC, *New Sentences: Criminal Justice Act 2003*, para. 1.1.10.
99 For discussion of the conflicting policies of the two statutes, see Ashworth (2004a).

conditions on a person for at least two years. The magistrates must be satisfied that the person has caused harassment, alarm or distress to others, and that the order is necessary to protect local people from further such acts. The order may prohibit the person from doing anything that might expose people to further anti-social acts (not necessarily of the same type as already proved). It is also an order that may be made by a criminal court after convicting a person of an offence. Breach of the order is a criminal offence with a maximum sentence of five years' imprisonment.

Why are ASBOs relevant here? The reason, in brief, is that they may be made in respect of behaviour that could be non-criminal or criminal, and when they are made in respect of criminal behaviour, this is in reality a response to persistent offending. The ASBO could have been described as the Trojan horse of government policy in respect of persistent offenders, were it not for the fact that there has been no secrecy and indeed that the government advocated ASBOs vigorously at a time when neither local authorities, nor the police, nor the courts showed much enthusiasm for them.[100] But the number of orders is now increasing: although only 3,826 were made between their introduction in 1999 and September 2004, some 20 per cent of them were made in the last six months of this period. A high proportion were made against young people – at least 45 per cent were imposed on persons under 18.[101] This increasing use brings the arguments of principle against them into sharp relief. Four arguments may be considered briefly.

First, there is no definition of anti-social behaviour.[102] Causing harassment, alarm or distress may encompass anything from youths gathering on a street corner and forcing passers-by to walk in the road, or begging in the street, up to serious crimes such as burglary and robbery. Originally the discussions were about nuisance neighbours, noise in the night, dumping rubbish in inconvenient places, and so forth. But the concept of anti-social behaviour is not limited to non-criminal conduct. As seen in the leading case,[103] allegations of burglary may lead to the exclusion of a person from whole districts of a city, including that person's home. And the ASBO may be used in respect of conduct that is criminal but non-imprisonable, such as begging or soliciting for prostitution.[104] Orders are now imposed on conviction, rather than on application in civil proceedings, in an increasing proportion of cases.[105]

Second, there is no limit on the number or breadth of the conditions that may be imposed, although in *C* v. *Sunderland Youth Court* (2004)[106] the Divisional

---

100 See the figures for the early years in Campbell (2002).
101 Home Office press release 042/2005 (the age of 5 per cent of defendants was not recorded); Campbell (2002, p. 8) found that 58 per cent of orders were made against persons under 18.
102 See Ramsay (2004).
103 *Clingham* v. *Kensington and Chelsea Royal LBC; R. (McCann)* v. *Crown Court at Manchester* [2003] 1 AC 787.
104 On the latter, see *Chief Constable of Lancashire* v. *Potter* [2003] EWHC 2272.
105 Home Office Press Release 042/2005 records that 59 per cent of orders were in civil proceedings and 41 per cent on conviction over the whole 1999–2004 period. As orders on conviction have only been possible since 2002, this suggests that they may now account for over half of ASBOs being made.
106 [2004] 1 Cr App R (S) 443 at p. 458.

Court stated that 'magistrates must give very careful consideration to what is an appropriate area for an order' and must specify it precisely. The imposition of 10 or even 15 conditions is not unusual,[107] and yet there is no provision for support during the currency of an ASBO. It follows that young people, or others leading rather chaotic lives, seem to be 'set up to fail'. Some 42 per cent of ASBOs are breached,[108] far higher than the proportion of conditional sentences and licence provisions that are breached.

Third, the penalties for breach may be out of all proportion to the original behaviour. The maximum is five years' imprisonment – well above that for many criminal offences, and of course a particularly severe measure for non-criminal behaviour or the commission of a criminal offence that is non-imprisonable. The latest report states that 'of those persons who breached their ASBO on one or more occasions, 55 per cent received immediate custody on the first or later occasion. 46 per cent of young people received immediate custody.'[109] Just as there is no proportionality constraint in the legislation of sentencing persistent offenders, so also there is no such constraint in respect of the penalty for breaching an ASBO. It seems that the government's view is that breach of an ASBO is treated as a form of defiance that justifies a severe response, whether it constitutes criminal behaviour or essentially non-criminal behaviour such as entering a shopping mall or street from which the ASBO excludes the defendant.[110] Moreover, it has been suggested that a person convicted of the offence of breaching an ASBO should be sentenced for the 'pattern of behaviour' including the conduct giving rise to the making of the order – an approach inconsistent with proper principles of sentencing.[111] Long sentences have certainly been upheld for breach of an ASBO: in *Braxton* (2005)[112] the Court of Appeal upheld a sentence of three-and-a-half years' imprisonment on a man who repeatedly breached an order by approaching people aggressively in the street and asking for money.

Fourth, an ASBO must be for at least two years, and may be for longer. Two years is a particularly long time for a youth, and also for many others who live relatively chaotic lives. A 10-year order on a youth of 18 has passed without adverse comment.[113] Combined with the absence of any supervision requirement for an ASBO, this seems to be another reason for the high breach rate.

In conclusion, the ASBO may be seen – particularly in the increasing proportion of cases where it is made on conviction of a criminal offence – as one of several possible responses to persistent offending. In its present form[114] it is a response with some especially severe components: wide-ranging prohibitions may be included,

107 Burney (2002), Campbell (2002).   108 Home Office Press Release 042/2005.   109 Ibid.
110 The Home Office reports that 'of those entering custody, 31 per cent were dealt with for breach of ASBO alone and only 17 per cent (30) juveniles were dealt with for a breach of ASBO alone' (ibid.).
111 See Ashworth (2004a), pp. 278–9.   112 [2005] 1 Cr App R (S) 167.
113 *Verdi* [2005] 1 Cr App R (S) 197.
114 In a different form, it might be seen as a less serious and more constructive response to persistent offending than that embodied in s. 143(2), permitting an offender to take liberty on conditions. However, even for that, the grounds for making the order should be established in criminal proceedings, the order should be shorter, and the penalty for breach should be less draconian.

without support for the (often young) defendant, breach of any condition constitutes a criminal offence and a custodial sentence often follows. Insofar as ASBOs are used for minor offences such as begging and soliciting for prostitution, they open up the possibility of far higher penalties than Parliament has provided, and are likely to sweep into prison many people in the category of 'petty persistent offenders' considered in part 6.5 above. Insofar as ASBOs are used for otherwise non-criminal conduct, the use of custody is even more disproportionate and indefensible. The Home Office seems committed to the 'broken windows' theory: 'if a window is broken or a wall is covered in graffiti it can contribute to an environment in which crime takes hold, particularly if intervention is not prompt and effective'.[115] Even if the premise is sound, it should be used as a basis for preventive measures within the community and not as a reason to impose disproportionate criminal penalties.

6.7 Minimum sentences and selective incapacitation

It was noted above that supporters of the cumulative principle for sentencing recidivists have regarded the principle as a significant measure of crime prevention, even though the evidence for this is unpromising. Moreover, the claim is weakened by its failure to distinguish serious from non-serious offenders. Thus, although the statistics indicate that a person with five or more previous convictions is 90 per cent likely to commit another offence within six years, and probably fairly soon,[116] they do not tell us what type of crime that will be. The historical evidence suggests that pursuit of the cumulative principle would result in severe sentences for minor offenders.[117] Serious offenders are likely to receive substantial sentences on proportionality grounds, which have the side-effect of incapacitating them for a few years at a time.

Some twenty years ago it was claimed that a policy of lengthening prison sentences for selected robbers and burglars would have significant benefits in preventing lucrative and feared offences.[118] However, a reassessment of the data by the US National Academy of Sciences concluded that they did not provide a secure basis for an effective policy of selective incapacitation.[119] Moreover, the data took insufficient account of the rate at which such offenders would desist from crime voluntarily.[120] Even if the predictive techniques could be refined, would such a policy be justified? Selective incapacitation would involve the imposition of disproportionately long sentences on a few offenders, identified not just by reference to their prior criminal record but also (in Greenwood's model) by reference to life-style factors such as drug

---

115 Home Office (2003), para. 1.8. This White Paper foreshadowed the Anti-Social Behaviour Act 2003, which contains a number of measures on matters such as parental responsibilities, powers to disperse groups and high hedges, but which does not touch the substance of ASBOs.
116 See e.g. Halliday (2001), Appendix 3.
117 See part 6.1 of this chapter.   118 Greenwood (1982).
119 Blumstein et al. (1986); see also in von Hirsch and Ashworth (1998) essays 3.6 (Wilson), 3.7 (von Hirsch) and 3.8 (Tonry).
120 On which see Burnett and Maruna (2004) and, generally, Maruna and Immarigeon (2004).

use and employment record. The latter criterion raises issues of equality before the law and unequal treatment of the disadvantaged, which are discussed further in Chapter 7. A deeper question of principle is whether an offender may justifiably be sentenced more severely than is proportionate to the current offence(s).

In the United States this question has been answered in the affirmative, for reasons that mix deterrence, incapacitation and retributive arguments. Over the last ten years several states have introduced cumulative sentencing laws under the popularized banner of 'three strikes and you're out', providing for lengthy or indefinite imprisonment on the third conviction. The Californian 'three strikes' law introduced in 1994 is probably the broadest in its effects, mandating a doubled sentence on the second serious felony and 25 years to life on the third felony conviction. There is no restriction on the types of offence involved, and, although the first two convictions must be for 'serious felonies', that category includes burglary. In 1994 the US Congress introduced a 'three strikes' law for the federal jurisdiction: it provides for life imprisonment on the third 'strike', but all three convictions must be for drug trafficking or for violent crime (broadly defined). A careful examination of the effects of the California law by Zimring et al. shows that the mandatory 'three-strikes' sentence was imposed in only about 10 per cent of eligible cases because of prosecutorial and other discretion, that there is little evidence of a significant crime-preventive effect (and the Governor in 1999 vetoed a bill which would have funded research into the effects of the law) and that even the political legend of 'three-strikes' laws as a new tough policy against crime is a falsehood, in that the previous laws were hardly less repressive.[121]

English interest in such expressive and repressive policies culminated in the Crime (Sentences) Act 1997, which introduced three minimum sentences. The most severe of these measures, the automatic life sentence, was abolished by the Criminal Justice Act 2003 to make way for a new, and no less repressive, sentencing framework for dangerous offenders (see part 6.8 below). Here we will examine the two others, conceived as minimum (or 'prescribed') sentences for third-time offenders. Section 3 of the 1997 Act (now consolidated as s. 110 of the Powers of Criminal Courts (Sentencing) Act 2000) requires a court to pass a sentence of at least seven years' imprisonment on a class A drug dealer who has two previous convictions for similar offences, unless it would be 'unjust to do so in all the circumstances'. This created the impression that Parliament was taking a firm stand against drug dealers, when in fact it would be normal for a third-time class A drug dealer to receive a higher sentence than seven years in any event,[122] unless there were strong mitigating factors. In *Hickson* (2002)[123] the trial judge had misinterpreted the section in two ways. First, he failed to notice that a discount of up to 20 per cent for a guilty plea is possible.[124] Second, he assumed that 'exceptional circumstances' had to be

---

121 Zimring, Hawkins and Kamin (2001).
122 As in *Willoughby* [2003] 2 Cr App R (S) 257.   123 [2002] 1 Cr App R (S) 298.
124 See now s. 144(2) of the 2003 Act, discussed in ch. 5.4.7 above. However, the 2003 Act also contains provisions to the effect that a released prisoner's licence endures until the end of the nominal

established if the court were to go below the minimum, whereas the less demanding phrase 'unjust ... in all the circumstances' applies. Although the Court of Appeal gave the full discount for pleading guilty, it upheld the minimum sentence of five years seven months, despite the fact that some 14 years had elapsed since the offender's last conviction (for possession of one-and-a-half ounces of heroin with intent to supply). In *Pearce* (2005)[125] the Court of Appeal confirmed the minimum sentence in a case where it was the offender's fourth offence of class A drug trafficking, even though the offence and the previous offences may have been committed under the intimidation of her partner.

Section 4 of the 1997 Act (now consolidated as s. 111 of the 2000 Act) requires a court to pass a sentence of at least three years' imprisonment on a domestic burglar aged at least 18 who has two previous convictions for domestic burglary, each of them after 1 December 1999, and each of them in respect of an offence committed after the previous conviction.[126] Again, the court does not have to impose the 'prescribed sentence' if it would be unjust in all the circumstances to do so; and, of course, it is free to go above the prescribed sentence, on the normal proportionality principles. As with the minimum sentence for drug trafficking, a discount of up to 20 per cent is available for a guilty plea.[127] Guidelines for domestic burglary were handed down in *McInerney and Keating* (2003),[128] where Lord Woolf CJ gave three examples of circumstances in which it may be unjust to impose the minimum sentence:

> The sentence could be unjust if two of the offences were committed many years earlier than the third offence; or if the offender made real efforts to reform or conquer his drug or alcohol addiction, but some personal tragedy triggers the third offence; or if the first two offences were committed when the offender was not yet 16.[129]

The flexibility of the phrase 'unjust . . . in all the circumstances' has not yet been tested, and it is not known how many minimum sentences have been passed. In some cases the court would have sentenced at or beyond the minimum anyway, but in others it would not. No research is available to show either the impact of this minimum sentence on the prison population or its impact on crime prevention. However, it must be admitted that this minimum sentence has less mandatory

---

sentence, and the Sentencing Guidelines Council has advised that sentence lengths should be reduced by some 15 per cent in order to take account of this greater onerousness (below, ch. 9.5). Perhaps the 'unjust in all the circumstances' exception might be used to give effect to this reduction.

125 [2005] 1 Cr App R (S) 364.

126 The trial judge misunderstood the required sequence in *Hoare* [2004] 2 Cr App R (S) 261, and consequently thought himself bound by the minimum sentence legislation when he was not.

127 See also n. 124 above.

128 [2003] 2 Cr App R (S) 240, discussed in ch. 2.2 and ch. 4.4.10 above.

129 Ibid., at p. 251. Note that the first example accords with the well-known principle of recency, whereby a gap in offending should tell in the offender's favour, but that principle was not applied in *Willoughby*, n. 122 above.

force than those of many other jurisdictions, since 'unjust in all the circumstances' is a potentially wide exception. It is to be noted that the minimum sentence not discussed here because it is not confined to persistent offenders – the minimum of five years for any firearms offence[130] – only has 'exceptional circumstances' as its escape clause, a rather narrow concept.

Why did the then government promote these provisions, and why did the present government implement them? The primary rationale was deterrent – 'severe deterrent sentences for those who deal in hard drugs are . . . essential'[131] – and we have seen how vigorously that was attacked by Lord Taylor CJ on the ground that the low detection rate would weaken any deterrent effect.[132] But there was also an incapacitative element to the government's case. There is little doubt that the idea behind these prescribed or minimum sentences was borrowed from the United States, but it was borrowed without due attention to the evidence on their operation. In a study of the evidence, Michael Tonry found a number of weaknesses in the strategy, and two of them may be mentioned here.[133] First, 'there is little basis for believing that mandatory penalties have any significant effects on rates of serious crime'. A noticeable deterrent effect is unlikely because of the high probability of avoiding detection, and the incapacitative effects are little greater than those of ordinary sentences. Second, insofar as minimum sentences have a potential for injustice, they may lead prosecutors and judges to find ways of circumventing them. The English 'escape clause' is fairly broad, as we have seen, but plea negotiations may take on a different structure as defence counsel seek to avoid the accumulation of 'qualifying' offences.

It is therefore clear that the evidence does not sound in favour of these minimum sentences. They should be seen as a form of political symbolism designed to bolster the political fortunes of the government, and they are unworthy of any government that purports to engage in evidence-led policy-making.[134] But minimum sentences are attractive to governments the world over. In the United States they have been attacked on the principled ground that they may lead to disproportionate and therefore 'cruel and unusual punishment' under the US Constitution. In *Lockyer* v. *Andrade* (2003)[135] the offender had been sentenced to twice life with a minimum of 50 years' imprisonment, consisting of two sentences of life imprisonment (each with a minimum term of 25 years), for two incidents of theft involving a total of 11 blank video tapes. The majority of judges in the Supreme Court held that this did not violate the 'gross disproportionality' test under the Constitution. The minority commented that 'if Andrade's sentence is not grossly disproportionate, the principle has no meaning'.[136]

---

130 CJA 2003, s. 287.   131 Home Office (1996), para. 11.2.   132 See ch. 2.1 above.
133 Tonry (1996), ch. 5. For a more recent assessment, see Doob and Webster (2003).
134 See the powerful argument of Tonry (2004), ch. 1.
135 (2003) 123 S. Ct 1166, discussed by van Zyl Smit and Ashworth (2004).
136 Ibid., at p. 1179, per Souter J.

6.8 'Dangerous offenders' and the 2003 Act

Chapter 5 of Part 12 of the Criminal Justice Act 2003 comprises ss. 224–236 and is headed 'Dangerous Offenders'. It introduces an entirely new regime for the sentencing of offenders classified as dangerous, and replaces the automatic life sentence,[137] longer than proportionate sentences for sexual and violent offenders,[138] extended sentences (although they are preserved in a slightly different form), and to a large extent the discretionary sentence of life imprisonment. Under the 2003 Act, offenders who fulfil the conditions for classification as 'dangerous' are likely to be subjected to one of three levels of sentence – imprisonment for life, imprisonment for public protection, or an extended sentence. The legislation provides a mandatory framework, using the word 'must' frequently, but it also embodies an attempt to comply with Article 5 of the Convention by requiring, as a precondition of imposing one of the new measures, a judgment by the court that this offender presents a significant risk of serious harm to members of the public. Whether the new provisions are compliant with the Convention and defensible on principle and on penological grounds are matters to be considered below. First, the requirements of the legislation in respect of life imprisonment, imprisonment for public protection and extended sentences must be examined.

1. Imprisonment for life. The most severe sentence that can be imposed on a dangerous offender under these provisions is life imprisonment or, in the case of an offender under 18, detention for life. It appears that the powers under the Act replace the common law criteria for imposing discretionary life imprisonment: that power was always reserved for cases in which an offender had committed a grave offence and appeared so unstable as to be likely to remain a serious danger to the public, and where the consequences of future offences would be specially injurious.[139] Under s. 225 of the 2003 Act, a court must impose a sentence of life imprisonment on an offender if five conditions are fulfilled:

- the offender stands convicted of an offence with a maximum of life imprisonment,
- it qualifies as a 'serious offence' within s. 224,
- it was committed on or after 4 April 2005 (the commencement date),
- the court considers that the seriousness of the offence(s) justifies the imposition of life imprisonment, and
- the court is of the opinion that there is a significant risk of serious harm from his committing further specified offences.

These requirements constitute a much more formalized and perhaps restrictive version of the common law power to impose life imprisonment, and they are mandatory. The last condition is elaborated in s. 229 and will be discussed in paragraph 4 below. That judgment is crucial to the imposition of the life sentence. However, so

---

137 On which see the 3rd edn of this work, pp. 193–6.   138 See ibid., pp. 183–9.
139 See *Hodgson* (1967) 52 Cr App R 113 and *Attorney General's Reference No. 32 of 1996* [1997] 1 Cr App R (S) 261, and the discussion in the 3rd edn of this work at pp. 189–93.

is the fourth condition – that the current offence, or that offence and others associated with it (broadly, of which the offender is convicted on the same occasion), is serious enough to justify imposing life. There was always a seriousness threshold at common law, but it was not entirely clear where it was located. There was some authority suggesting that the current offence(s) had to be worth at least a sentence of seven years' imprisonment,[140] although more recently the Court suggested that a prediction of future grave offences might be more important than the seriousness of the current offence.[141] The latter approach is not compatible with the wording of s. 225(2)(b) of the 2003 Act, which requires the court to be satisfied that the current offence is sufficiently serious for a life sentence. It is not known where the threshold will be placed, but it is thought that it would be difficult to argue that an offence worth less than seven years should be sufficient to qualify the offender for a life sentence. The threshold may be higher.

Turning to the other three conditions, clearly the offence must carry a life maximum. It may then seem strange to require that it should also be a 'serious offence', but that is what s. 225(1)(a) states. In fact a 'serious offence' is one of the 'specified offences' listed in Schedule 15 that carries either life imprisonment or at least 10 years, and so this condition adds nothing to the first condition. The fact that the new dangerous offender provisions apply only to offences committed on or after 4 April 2005 means that the common law relating to discretionary life imprisonment continues to apply to offences committed earlier and not yet sentenced.[142]

Where these conditions are satisfied, the court must sentence the offender to life imprisonment. In doing so it should specify a minimum term – by taking the determinate sentence that would be proportionate to the current offence(s), halving it to take account of normal release provisions, and then subtracting any period spent on remand.[143] Once the minimum term has expired, the offender's release is a matter for the Parole Board, adopting the criteria of risk set out in Part 2 of the Crime (Sentences) Act 1997.

2. Imprisonment for public protection. The Halliday report recommended the creation of a new sentence for dangerous sexual or violent offenders, one that would slot in beneath the life sentence and provide for discretionary release of these offenders during the second half of their determinate sentence.[144] The Home Office went further:

> We want to ensure that the public are adequately protected from those offenders whose offences do not currently attract a maximum penalty of life imprisonment but who are nevertheless assessed as dangerous. We believe that such offenders should remain in

---

140 *Gray* [1983] Crim LR 691.
141 *Chapman* [2000] 1 Cr App R (S) 377, *per* Lord Bingham CJ at p. 385.
142 S. 226 provides for sentences of detention for life for offenders under 18 in broadly similar circumstances. But see paragraph 4 below on the assessment of dangerousness.
143 *Marklew and Lambert* [1999] 1 Cr App R (S) 6; *Attoney-General's Reference No. 3 of 2004 (Akuffo)* [2005] 1 Cr App R (S) 230 at p. 240.
144 Halliday (2001), paras. 4.25–4.35.

custody until their risks are considered manageable in the community. For this reason we propose to develop an indeterminate sentence for sexual and violent offenders who have been assessed and considered dangerous. The offender would be required to serve a minimum term and would then remain in prison beyond this time, until the Parole Board was completely satisfied that the risk had sufficiently diminished for that person to be released and supervised in the community. The offender could remain on licence for the rest of their life.[145]

The indeterminate sentence thus foreshadowed has been enacted by the 2003 Act. A court must impose a sentence of imprisonment for public protection where an offender has been convicted of a 'serious offence' committed after the commencement date, and where the court is of the opinion that the offender fulfils the dangerousness requirement. As we have seen, a 'serious offence' may be one of the 'specified offences' that carries life imprisonment or a maximum of at least 10 years. Many of them will be sexual or violent offences with high maxima, and it is perfectly possible for a court to impose a sentence of imprisonment for public protection for an offence that carries a maximum of life – if the court does not consider that the current offence is so serious as to justify a life sentence.[146]

In its effect, a sentence of imprisonment for public protection falls little short of life imprisonment – but it applies to 'serious offences' for which life imprisonment is unavailable, and the court does not have to be satisfied that the offence reaches the threshold of seriousness appropriate for a life sentence. This removes the proportionality constraint, and opens the possibility of indeterminate sentences for burglary with intent or for causing death by dangerous driving, for example. A court is required to set a minimum term commensurate with the seriousness of the offence, as for a life sentence. After the expiry of that minimum term, the offender will remain in prison until the Parole Board is satisfied that it is no longer necessary for the protection of the public that he should be detained; the offender will then be released on a licence that will remain in force for the rest of his life, unless on application the Parole Board determines that it is no longer necessary for the protection of the public that the licence should remain in force.[147] The rights of the offender are therefore chiefly rights to regular review of the need for continued detention.

3. Extended sentences. Whereas life imprisonment and imprisonment for public protection may only be imposed where the offence of conviction is both a 'specified offence' and a 'serious offence' – meaning that the relevant statutory maximum is 10 years or more – the extended sentence applies to all 'specified offences' which are not 'serious offences' – meaning that the relevant statutory maximum is between two and 10 years. Among these, which are listed in Schedule 15, are offences such as

---

145 Home Office (2002), para. 5.41.
146 The corresponding provision for offenders under 18 in section 226(3) is different, permitting a court to impose detention for public protection only if it believes that an extended sentence (below) would not provide adequate protection for the public.
147 CJA 2003, Schedule 18.

assault occasioning actual bodily harm (maximum, five years), affray (maximum, three years), assault with intent to resist arrest (maximum, two years), various child sex offences for which the maximum is five years if the offender is aged under 18 (Sexual Offences Act 2003, ss. 9–12), and any aiding or abetting or attempt to commit a listed offence. As with the life sentence and imprisonment for public protection, the trigger condition is that the court considers that there is a significant risk of serious harm to others (see paragraph 4 below). If the court is satisfied that that condition is fulfilled, it 'must impose on the offender an extended term of imprisonment' (s. 227(2)), that being a sentence consisting of the custodial term appropriate to the current offence(s) plus an extension period during which the offender will be subject to a licence.

Extended sentences were available in a slightly different form under s. 85 of the Powers of Criminal Courts (Sentencing) Act 2000, consolidating previous legislation. Under that provision the court had a discretion whether or not to impose an extended sentence, and the Court of Appeal handed down guidelines on the exercise of that power in *Nelson* (2002).[148] Now the courts have no discretion, once they decide that the 'trigger condition' is fulfilled. However, that part of the *Nelson* judgment relating to the length of the extension period may still be relevant. Section 227(2)(b) of the 2003 Act states that the extension period should be 'of such length as the court considers necessary for the purpose of protecting members of the public from serious harm occasioned by the commission by him of further specified offences', although s. 227(4) limits the extension period to five years for specified violent offences and eight years for specified sexual offences. The *Nelson* judgment pointed out that there is nothing inconsistent in having an 'appropriate custodial term' of one or two years and then a considerably longer extension period, since the criteria are different. The former should be proportionate to the seriousness of the current offence(s), whereas the latter is determined by predictions of future behaviour. Even though the offender may actually serve some or most of the extension period in prison if the licence conditions are violated, 'it would be illogical to require strict proportionality between the duration of the extension period and the seriousness of the offence', although proportionality does 'have some relevance' to the overall sentence.[149] The effect of an extended sentence is that the offender is eligible for release after serving half the custodial term, but release is conditional on a direction from the Parole Board that it is 'satisfied that it is no longer necessary for the protection of the public that the prisoner should be confined'.[150] Thus an offender with a second conviction for assault occasioning actual bodily harm is likely to fall within this category. The extended sentence means that the offender may serve more than half of the nominal custodial term, as well as being released on licence and therefore subject to recall for the remainder of the extension

148 [2002] 1 Cr App R (S) 565, following SAP, *Advice to the Court of Appeal on Extended Sentences* (2001).
149 *Nelson*, at p. 571.   150 CJA 2003, s. 247(3).

period. It is evident that the key element in this sentence is the trigger condition of dangerousness, and to that we now turn.

4. *Dangerousness – the trigger condition.* The mandatory terms of the 2003 Act's dangerousness provisions, requiring courts (in given circumstances) to impose a life sentence or imprisonment for public protection or an extended sentence, are contingent on the fulfilment of a trigger condition. So long as the current offence falls within the required categories, a court must impose a dangerousness sentence if it:

> is of the opinion that there is significant risk to members of the public of serious harm occasioned by the commission by him of further specified offences.[151]

The relevant risk is that this offender will commit further specified offences (which may be either offences of violence or sexual offences, as set out in the lengthy lists in Schedule 15). The court must be satisfied that such further offences would cause 'serious harm', a term defined by s. 224 as meaning 'death or serious personal injury, whether physical or psychological'. This is similar to the definition in the 1991 Act,[152] but it is likely to have to do much more work because of the extensive list of 'specified offences' in the 2003 Act. In view of the severely constraining effects of the new dangerousness provisions, courts should construe 'serious personal injury' restrictively rather than broadly.

Moreover, the 2003 Act requires the court to be satisfied that there is a 'significant risk' of serious harm in the future. Parliament could have selected the adjective 'substantial' but it did not. It can therefore be argued that 'significant' means not insignificant, or more than minimal, and certainly sufficient to justify taking strong measures to guard against the materialization of the risk. Section 229 of the Act goes on to lay down the manner in which courts should approach the task of assessing dangerousness. For offenders over 18 who have previously been convicted of a relevant offence,[153] there is a presumption of dangerousness unless the court considers that 'it would be unreasonable to conclude that there is such a risk', having taken account of information about this offence, about previous offences and about the offender. This is a draconian provision that appears even to go beyond the automatic life sentence repealed by the 2003 Act, since it would sweep into the dangerousness category any adult convicted of a second offence of affray or assault occasioning actual bodily harm and require the court to impose an extended sentence – unless it found that the risk was not 'significant' or that 'serious harm' was not likely to eventuate. Moreover, there is no requirement that the previous offence be recent (as under s. 143(2), discussed in part 6.3 above), or that it should be relevant in the sense of similar (it could be an offence of affray, whereas the

---

151 CJA 2003, ss. 225(1)(b), 226(1)(b), 227(1)(b) and 228(1)(b)(i), applying to all three forms of sentence and to offenders aged 18 and under 18.
152 Criminal Justice Act s. 31(3), discussed in the 3rd edn, pp. 185–6.
153 This term includes all specified offences and their Scots and Northern Irish equivalents: see Schedules 15, 16 and 17.

current offence is sexual). Whether the presumption is compatible with Articles 5 and 6 of the Convention is also open to debate: in principle, the court ought to be able to assess freely the degree of risk to the public, rather than being constrained by a presumption.

Where the offender does not have a previous conviction for a relevant offence, or is under 18, there is no such presumption. Instead, the court is required to take account of the nature and circumstances of the current offence, of 'any pattern of behaviour of which the offence forms part', and 'any information about the offender which is before it'.[154] It is regrettable that there is no requirement to obtain a pre-sentence report or a psychiatric report to assist the court, although the court must have regard to such reports if they are available. Exactly what constitutes a 'pattern of behaviour' in this context remains to be determined, but it seems possible that a sentence of detention for public protection could be required to be imposed on an offender of 17 before the court for a third street robbery, unless the court concludes that the offences do not create a risk of serious harm. In all these instances, much turns on predictions as to the offender's behaviour in the years to come. How reliable are these predictions?

5. The empirical evidence. The difficulties of predicting whether a particular person will constitute a danger to others are well documented in the criminological literature. The Floud Committee's survey of the available studies two decades ago revealed that no method of prediction had managed to do better than predicting one false positive for every true positive, that is a 50 per cent success rate in predicting 'dangerousness'. Indeed, many of the prediction methods had only a one-third success rate.[155] Part of the problem is that really serious crimes are rare events, and therefore particularly hard to predict with accuracy. The Floud Report also confirmed that actuarial methods of prediction, based on selected objective characteristics of the offender, were generally more reliable than clinical predictions, based on the judgment of experienced diagnosticians – an important finding, since there is a natural tendency in the courts to respect the judgments of experienced psychiatrists, despite this evidence of fallibility. Around the same time there was a Home Office study by Brody and Tarling, which involved clinicians reviewing the records of over 700 prisoners and selecting those who might be termed 'dangerous' on certain criteria. Of those who were so classified, 48 had been released and their records were examined for the five years following release. It was found that nine of them committed 'dangerous' offences during that period. This means that, if all of them had been detained for an additional five years on the basis of the prediction of dangerousness, there would have been nine true positives and 39 false positives – a 'success rate' of around 20 per cent only. It is also noteworthy, since public protection is often said to be the aim here, that nine of the 700 non-dangerous offenders who had been released had also committed a 'dangerous' offence during the

---

154 CJA 2003, s. 229(2).   155 Floud and Young (1981), Appendix C.

five-year period.[156] In other words, the risk of being the victim of one of these serious offences was as great from the large number of 'non-dangerous' as from the small number of 'dangerous' offenders.

It is also true that, even if the current offence is one of violence, this does not suggest that any subsequent offending will be of the same kind.[157] More recently, Hood and Shute have pointed out the difficulty of using offences of conviction (or previous offences) as the main index of 'high risk'.[158] And Hood et al. have also shown that fewer that 10 per cent of serious sexual offenders released from prison commit another sex offence within six years, and that Parole Board members tend to overestimate considerably the risk presented by sex offenders. As they comment, 'attempts to predict reconviction when the "base rate" is low inevitably produce a high rate of "false positives"'.[159] Subsequent research on the risk assessment of offenders believed to be 'dangerous' gives few grounds for optimism:[160] there is little research into the effectiveness of predictions of serious harm by offenders who are not diagnosed as mentally disordered, and the predictions for those who are so diagnosed still do not have a high rate of success.[161]

6. Arguments of principle. Despite the poor prospects for accurate predictions at even a 50 per cent rate, the imposition of disproportionate sentences on offenders believed to be dangerous remains attractive to politicians and legislators, and to some extent to members of the judiciary. How, if at all, can such disproportionate deprivations of liberty be justified? The Floud Committee concluded that the question is really a matter of the just redistribution of risk, between a known offender and a potential victim of a predicted offence. It is a moral choice between competing claims: who should bear the risk? Generally, they argued, everyone is presumed to be free of harmful intentions. But once a person has manifested, by committing a serious crime, the capacity to entertain and to implement harmful intentions, that presumption no longer applies. It may therefore be justifiable to redistribute the risk of future harms by protecting the potential victims (who are unlikely to have harmful intentions) and by burdening the known offender (who has lost the benefit of the presumption). Although they proposed various procedural safeguards for defendants before a protective sentence could be imposed, the Committee concluded that the redistribution of risk should favour potential victims.[162]

The philosophy of the 2003 Act bears some similarity to the Floud approach, and there are four major objections to it. First, it might be argued that the right to be presumed free from harmful intentions should not be extinguished indefinitely if a person commits a grave offence. Article 6(2) of the Convention proclaims the presumption of innocence at each new trial, no matter how many previous convictions the defendant may have, and in determinations of dangerousness this should be given some weight rather than none at all.[163] Second, the notion of just

156 Brody and Tarling (1981), pp. 29–30.   157 See Farrington, above, nn. 19–20.
158 Hood and Shute (1996).   159 Hood, Shute, Feilzer and Wilcox (2002).
160 Brown (1998); Brown and Pratt (2000).   161 Monahan (2004).
162 Floud and Young (1981), chs. 3 and 4.   163 Wood (1988).

redistribution of risk ignores the moral claims of proportionality. For one thing, it is arguable that an offender has a right not to receive greater punishment than is proportionate to the crime – a right deriving from the Kantian proposition that no person should be used merely as a means to a social end. For another, rights are not simply to be weighed and traded off according to marginal preferences or 'balancing'. Moreover, the idea of a balance between the rights of the offender and the rights of the potential victim is flawed, since the offender's right is against the state, and it is being compared with the state's justification for overriding it. Bottoms and Brownsword, assuming that the rights do conflict, seek to restrain the state's power through a requirement that additional protective detention be permissible only where there is 'vivid danger' to the public.[164] An alternative approach would be to argue that the proportionality principle should be overridden only where harmful consequences of an extraordinary character would otherwise occur.[165] However, such circumstances would hardly ever arise in the present context, because we are discussing the justification for detaining an offender after the expiry of the proportionate sentence – which requires confident predictions some years ahead. This is just where predictions are most fallible. Third, this expanded use of life imprisonment (and imprisonment for public protection) makes discretionary release the crucial decision, and once again it turns on assessments of risk. Dirk van Zyl Smit has argued convincingly against the expanding use of life imprisonment,[166] and in England and Wales the new regime is no better than that which it replaces. Fourth, might the Floud arguments be sufficient to support a kind of civil detention, even if they cannot support additional punishment? Quarantine is an established form of civil detention for those carrying life-threatening diseases, and it is not generally viewed as punishment. Might it not be possible, if the problems of prediction and definition could be acceptably reduced, to retain proportionate sentencing and to introduce a form of civil confinement for the 'dangerous' after the expiry of their sentence?[167] The difficulty lies with the qualification: although civil detention may be slightly easier to justify than imprisonment, it is questionable whether the tools for sufficiently accurate prediction exist in the context of 'dangerousness'.

6.9 Conclusion

Both persistent offenders and those predicted to be dangerous present difficulties for the theory and practice of sentencing. As this chapter shows, the current trend (evident in s. 143(2) of the 2003 Act) is in the direction of a cumulative principle, and tends to neglect the work of criminologists and practitioners on desistance from crime. Unless clear guidance to the contrary is given, courts will (continue to) concentrate on the offender's record rather than the current offence, at least after two or three convictions. This is objectionable because the offence is then used as

---

164 Bottoms and Brownsword (1982).
165 See von Hirsch and Ashworth (2005), ch. 4, adapting Dworkin.
166 Van Zyl Smit (2002).   167 Cf. Wood (1988).

a mere peg on which to hang severe preventive measures, with little regard for the seriousness of the current offence. This is already the approach to offenders labelled as 'professional', whose sentences often range well beyond the facts of the offence(s) of conviction. The same objection can be levelled at anti-social behaviour orders, which have both a high breach rate and a high custody rate for breach, even when the behaviour in question is either non-criminal or non-imprisonable.

It has been noted that some kind of incapacitative or 'public protection' sentence is found politically attractive in many jurisdictions. The 2003 Act has introduced a regime of three 'dangerousness' measures of ascending severity – extended sentences, imprisonment for public protection and life imprisonment – supported by a legislative framework that obliges courts to impose such sentences in given circumstances. Not only are the procedural safeguards in the 2003 Act inadequate for such severe sentences, but dangerous offender provisions of this kind are (and are well known to be) based on theoretically and criminologically doubtful foundations. The government is using the political irresistibility of the claim of public protection to promote increasing repressive measures. There is no political constituency of support for persons labelled 'dangerous', but there remain strong arguments based on principle and on human rights for continuing to press home criticisms of these measures.

CHAPTER 7

Equality before the law

7.1 The principle and its challengers

The constitutions of many countries proclaim a principle of equality before the law or non-discrimination, or at least a general principle of equality. There is no British Constitution as such, but the Human Rights Act 1998 brings into UK law most articles of the European Convention on Human Rights. Article 14 declares that the enjoyment of all the rights declared in the Convention shall be secured 'without discrimination on any ground such as sex, race, colour, language, religion, political or other opinion, national or social origin, association with a national minority, property, birth or other status'. This is not a general principle of non-discrimination, since it applies only to discrimination in respect of rights declared in the Convention, but it is nevertheless important. Protocol 12 to the Convention includes substantive and broader protection against discrimination, but it does not bind a member state unless that state ratifies it.[1]

Apart from Article 14, English law contains no general principle of non-discrimination. This deficiency ought to be rectified: non-discrimination is a key aspect of the principle of equality before the law. Discrimination is wrong because it treats persons with certain attributes as worthy of less respect than others. Equality before the law declares that every person is entitled to equal respect from the law and its processes. There have been significant steps in recent years, notably the extension of the race relations legislation to the police and other criminal justice agencies by the Race Relations (Amendment) Act 2000.

It might be argued that a direct statement of the anti-discrimination principle would be superfluous where the proportionality principle has priority in sentencing. On that principle, sentences should be determined by reference to the seriousness of the offence; that involves consideration of the factors discussed in Chapters 4, 5 and 6, not others. This, however, brings us to the thematic questions in this chapter. Does English sentencing practice give grounds for believing that discriminatory factors are present in some cases? Even if discriminatory elements are not evident as primary reasons for sentence, do they exert an indirect influence through other

1 Wintemute (2004).

factors such as unemployment, previous record or previous remand in custody? And, if so, should the principle of non-discrimination always be accorded greater weight than other relevant principles?

The first and second questions are matters for empirical inquiry, and the evidence will be reviewed briefly below in relation to race, gender, employment status, social status and other factors. The focus here is on sentencing but, as argued in Chapter 1.4, sentencing is merely a single stage in a sequence of decisions in the criminal process, and practices at earlier stages might exert a considerable (though perhaps unrecognized) influence on sentencing. On some of the points the available evidence is inconclusive, and definitive studies are awaited.

The third question goes to the foundations of sentencing policy. It is sometimes presented as the issue of whether the sentencing system should simply try to avoid discrimination in its own decisions, or whether sentences should be calculated in an effort to counteract discriminatory forces which are known to operate more widely – leading in some instances to a kind of positive discrimination. This is an issue which we should keep in view, but there are more specific issues too. How should the principle of parsimony be related to the principle of equality before the law? Norval Morris and Michael Tonry put their answer strongly: 'To insist that criminal A go to jail or prison because resources are lacking to deal sensibly with criminal B is to pay excessive tribute to an illusory ideal of equality.'[2] They are content to see a white or employed person receive a non-custodial sentence in the same circumstances in which a black or unemployed person would be incarcerated. This furthers parsimony, in the sense that fewer people would be incarcerated by subordinating the principle of equality before the law in such instances. Morris and Tonry would rather have the system discriminatory than uniformly punitive. Others would argue that equality before the law is simply not negotiable: it is a principle which should not be compromised, and any concerns about over-punitiveness should be tackled through the overall system rather than by discriminating between individual offenders.

Another aspect of this argument is that available statistics tend to suggest that those who suffer from certain social disadvantages (e.g. unemployed, no fixed address, no close family ties) are more likely to be reconvicted than those who are socially well established. A preventive sentencing strategy might therefore lead to the imposition of more onerous sentences on the disadvantaged, and correspondingly less onerous sentences on the well established. This, however, would be to pursue prevention at a fairly superficial level. Prevention at a deeper level requires a social strategy which tackles housing, employment, community facilities and related matters. To pursue preventive strategies through sentencing is as short-sighted as it is unjust. It tends to scapegoat a vulnerable group rather than to seek a longer-lasting solution.

References will be made to these themes in various parts below, and the arguments of principle will be reviewed in a concluding discussion.

2 Morris and Tonry (1990), p. 33.

7.2 Race[3]

The clearest application of the principle of equality before the law is that no person should be sentenced more severely on account of race or colour. If sentencing is based strictly on the seriousness of the offence, discrimination on this ground should not occur. However, we have noted that although proportionality is the overriding principle of English sentencing according to the Sentencing Guidelines Council, s. 142 of the Criminal Justice Act 2003 requires courts to have regard to a miscellany of conflicting purposes. If this is interpreted as bestowing considerable discretion on the courts, then it will leave room for elements of discrimination to creep into sentencing, whether consciously or unconsciously. Is there any evidence to suggest that it might do so? Is there evidence that blacks or Asians are treated more severely than whites?[4] The most cited figures are that, while some 1 to 2 per cent of the general population is black, some 15 per cent of the male prison population and almost one-quarter of the female prison population are black.[5] Does this indicate discrimination in sentencing?

First, it must be recalled that the offenders who come up for sentence in the courts are a selected group, resulting from various patterns of reporting, investigating and filtering in the pre-trial stages. The importance of regarding the sentence of the court as merely one stage in a lengthy process, signalled in Chapter 1.4, must be emphasized here.[6] It can be shown, for example, that blacks have been more likely to be stopped on the streets than whites or Asians, by a factor of around five to one.[7] These findings have been refined by Tony Jefferson and Monica Walker, whose study of the address and place of arrest of 5,000 people arrested during a six-month period showed that blacks have a higher arrest rate in predominantly white areas and that whites have a higher arrest rate in predominantly black areas.[8] There is evidence that white juveniles have been far more likely than black juveniles to be cautioned rather than prosecuted.[9] The charges brought against black people show a relatively high rate of victimless, preparatory and public order offences,[10] and a high rate of charges of robbery.[11] The extent to which these differences reflect real offending patterns or the influence of racial stereotypes on reporting and investigation remains to be examined. However, they certainly have consequences in the criminal process, inasmuch as a higher proportion of blacks appear at the Crown Court rather than the magistrates' courts[12] – notably because robbery is triable only in the Crown Court

---

3 Bowling and Phillips (2002).
4 The term 'blacks' is used here to refer to people from an African-Caribbean background, the term 'Asians' includes both people from a background in the Indian sub-continent and those of south-east Asian origin. Neither term is ideal.
5 See ch. 9.6.3 below.   6 See further Fitzgerald (1993) and Bowling and Phillips (2002).
7 Home Office (1999), Table 3.2.   8 Jefferson and Walker (1992).
9 Landau and Nathan (1983), discussed by Fitzgerald (1993), pp. 17–18.
10 Hood (1992), pp. 144–5. This category included drug offences.
11 Home Office (1999), Table 5.5, showed that some 54 per cent of persons arrested in London for robbery were black.
12 Hood (1992), p. 51, and Fitzgerald (1993), p. 21.

and not because more blacks elect to be tried there – and, partly in consequence, a higher proportion of blacks are remanded in custody.[13]

These findings go to establish that it would be a mistake to point to the sentencing statistics for black and white offenders or, even worse, the numbers of black and white offenders in prison, and to argue that the racial imbalance demonstrates discrimination in sentencing. The courts could pursue an absolutely impartial sentencing policy in relation to the already skewed group of offenders coming before them, and the results would appear discriminatory. The need, therefore, is for research which takes proper account of all the major variables in sentencing (e.g. type of offence, previous convictions and so forth), which distinguishes at least between blacks, Asians and whites (rather than grouping blacks and Asians together),[14] which distinguishes between the Crown Court and magistrates' courts, and which has sufficiently large numbers of non-whites in its sample. The study carried out in the West Midlands by Roger Hood (1992) meets most of these desiderata, although it was confined to Crown Court cases.

Hood's sample comprised 2,884 males, of whom half were white and half non-white (the latter including roughly twice as many blacks as Asians), and 443 females. It was therefore one of the largest samples of Crown Court sentencing ever processed, and it produced a number of familiar findings apart from racial issues. Thus custody rates varied among the courts studied, and this sentencing inconsistency persisted even after account had been taken of the different offence-mix and offender-mix of the various courts. Hood's methodology included the calculation of expectancy scores for sentencing, based on the characteristics of offences and offenders apart from race, in an attempt to show whether race did exert an independent effect. One result of this exercise was to show that a higher proportion of blacks fell into the high-risk (of custody) category, whereas a higher proportion of Asians fell into the lowest risk category.[15]

Comparing expected custody rates with actual custody rates, Hood found a 'residual race difference' of the order of a 5 per cent greater probability of a black offender being sent to prison, which was greater at one court and lower at another.[16] The origins of this appeared to reside in the tendency of particular judges to deal relatively harshly with some blacks with low or medium expectancies of custody. The two characteristics of black offenders most highly correlated with severity were being aged 21 or over, and being unemployed.[17] If, therefore, we return to consider the fact that the proportion of black males in prison is around seven times as high as that in the general population, what causal inferences can be drawn from Hood's study? He estimated that the bulk of the difference, some 70 per cent, was accounted

13 Hood (1992), pp. 148–9.
14 The Prison Statistics now distinguish between 'South Asians' and 'Chinese and other'.
15 Hood (1992), pp. 68, 197; cf. Flood-Page and Mackie (1998), who, in a smaller study with less sophisticated analysis, found that custody rates for white, black and Asian offenders were broadly similar in both magistrates' courts and the Crown Court.
16 Hood (1992), p. 78.   17 Hood (1992), p. 86 and ch. 6 generally.

for by the number of blacks appearing at the Crown Court for sentence: this, in other words, reflects the influence of all the pre-trial decisions and filters discussed above. This should not be represented as a cumulative bias: the research suggests discrimination at several stages, but not at every stage.[18]

What of the remaining 30 per cent of the difference? Hood estimated that some 10 per cent was accounted for by the more serious nature of the offences of which black offenders were convicted. No research has yet determined the extent to which blacks are disproportionately involved in more serious types of crime, or the extent to which the figures merely reflect stereotyping, labelling and deviancy amplification by the public and law enforcement officers.[19] A further 13 per cent was attributable to the imposition of longer sentences on black offenders, which was traced almost entirely to the greater propensity of black defendants to plead not guilty and, therefore, the unavailability to them of the sentence discount for pleading guilty.[20] The remaining 7 per cent was accounted for by the greater use of custody than expected. If the same analysis is carried out for black offenders under 21, some 92 per cent of the difference was attributable to the numbers appearing for sentence and the seriousness of their cases. Hood states that these estimates 'must be regarded with a degree of caution',[21] and in respect of sentencing decisions he argues that 'in most respects Asian offenders did not fare worse than whites, nor did all Afro-Caribbeans'.[22] None the less, this remains Britain's most careful and wide-ranging examination of race and the sentencing of male offenders,[23] and it makes a powerful case for vigilance rather than complacency about the existence of racial discrimination in sentencing.

The problem of race in sentencing must be seen at three different levels, at least. First, there is the broadest level of social policy: unless there is an end to racial discrimination in society, it is likely to manifest itself in criminal justice no less than elsewhere. Although the Race Relations Act 1965 may be regarded as rather timid in retrospect, it was a first excursus into a hitherto unregulated field of social behaviour, at a time when strong views against immigration were often expressed. Since then the legislation has been strengthened, and the Race Relations Act 1976 both created the Commission for Racial Equality and set out to penalize both direct and indirect discrimination on grounds of race. As noted earlier, the Race Relations (Amendment) Act 2000 extended the legislation to cover the police and other criminal justice agencies, on the recommendation of the MacPherson Report. However, race issues are often woven into public concern about immigration and asylum seekers. In terms of social policy, they cannot and should not be isolated

---

18 Indeed, blacks have a higher acquittal rate: Fitzgerald (1993), p. 22.
19 See Cook and Hudson (1993), pp. 9–10.
20 Hood (1992), pp. 124–5; issues around the guilty plea discount are discussed in ch. 5.4.1 above.
21 Hood (1992), p. 130.   22 Hood (1992), p. 183.
23 Ch. 11 of Hood's book discusses the sentencing of women, but the numbers of blacks and Asians in the sample were relatively small.

from more general inequalities in matters of wealth, employment and housing. This point is taken further in part 7.7 below.

Second, there is the level of criminal justice administration. Racial awareness training of judges and magistrates has increased in recent years, through the work of the Equal Treatment Advisory Committee (known as ETAC). In respect of judicial training, for example, ETAC advises on the structure of the sentencing and procedure exercises that judges are asked to discuss during their seminars. Training of this kind may help to remove prejudices of which sentencers may be unaware – for example, one study found evidence that magistrates were influenced by demeanour in court and might misinterpret the body language of some defendants as 'arrogance', leading to an unsympathetic response.[24] A recent study by Hood, Shute and Seemungal found that there were no major differences in the proportions of white, blacks and Asians who felt unfairly treated in the criminal courts. They did find that one-fifth of black defendants in the Crown Court believed that they had suffered unfair treatment as a result of racial bias (as did one in eight Asian defendants), proportions that are lower than some might expect but which are still unacceptably high.[25]

Third, there is the level of criminal justice policy. Various initiatives, policies or targets may have impacts that amount to at least indirect indiscrimination. Thus, in the context of US criminal justice, Michael Tonry has argued that the 'war on drugs' has had racially discriminatory effects, and has resulted in the sacrifice of black youths (imprisoned at an extraordinarily high rate) in pursuit of a drug-control policy with no better prospects of success than certain less repressive and less discriminatory alternatives would have.[26] A similar analysis of sentencing for drug offences and robbery in this country would be likely to raise stark questions of the same kind. For example, the label 'robbery' probably has an inflationary effect on sentences that might disappear if the offence of robbery were abolished, leaving prosecutors and sentencers to focus on the theft and any offence against the person committed.[27]

7.3 Gender[28]

Just as racial discrimination in many fields is outlawed by the Race Relations Act, so sex discrimination in some fields is outlawed by the Sex Discrimination Act. And, as we saw in the previous paragraph, the provision in s. 95(1)(b) of the 1991 Act on the publication of information about discriminatory practices applies expressly to sex discrimination. Is there any evidence of discrimination against, or for, women in the sentencing system?

The general statistics suggest that women are favourably treated at the sentencing stage. Some 24 per cent of adult women received a discharge for indictable offences

---

24 Hedderman and Gelsthorpe (1997), pp. 33–4.   25 Hood, Shute and Seemungal (2003).
26 Tonry (1995), esp. ch. 3.   27 Ashworth (2002b).
28 In addition to the works cited below, there are chapter-length treatments by Edwards (1993), Hudson (1998) and Heidensohn (2002).

in 2002, compared with 14 per cent of adult men; 33 per cent of women received a community sentence, compared with 25 per cent of men; and 17 per cent of adult women received immediate custody, compared with 30 per cent of men. If there is any discrimination suggested by these figures, it is against men, not women.

However, the figures cannot be taken at face value. Much depends, in the first instance, on the types of offence typically committed by men and by women. Some 66 per cent of females found guilty or cautioned for indictable offences have committed theft, usually shop theft, compared with only 44 per cent of males. For burglary and drug offences, the positions are reversed.[29] A second variable is the court in which an offender is sentenced: a higher proportion of women are sentenced by magistrates' courts, and the research evidence shows that the Crown Court tends to pass significantly more severe sentences in comparable cases.[30] A third variable is criminal record: in Moxon's Crown Court survey some 46 per cent of the females were first offenders, compared with 22 per cent of the males. The average number of previous convictions was 5.3 for males and 2.1 for females.[31]

A small study by David Farrington and Allison Morris found that, taking account of variations in type of offence and previous record, the gender of the offender seemed to have little or no independent effect on sentence.[32] A subsequent study by Lizanne Dowds and Carol Hedderman found that, taking account of the usual variables, women shoplifters were less likely than men to receive a custodial sentence, whether as first offenders (1 per cent and 8 per cent respectively) or as repeat offenders (5 per cent and 15 per cent).[33] Women were more likely to receive a community sentence and to receive a discharge, but this seemed to be because sentencers were often reluctant to fine a woman in circumstances where they would fine a man.[34] Insofar as this is true, it may mean that some women received a more severe sentence (a community sentence) that some men, because they were thought unable to pay a fine.

However, it has long been suggested that the whole orientation of sentencing for women is different: the emphasis in pre-sentence reports, speeches in mitigation and sentencing seems to be on some pathological or abnormal explanation for the offending.[35] This might be a separate strand of explanation for the higher use of community sentences, particularly those involving supervision. Thus, Farrington and Morris found that divorced and separated women received relatively more severe sentences than married women, as did women regarded as 'deviant' (e.g. unmarried

---

29 Flood-Page and Mackie (1998), p. 134.
30 Hedderman and Hough (1994), drawing on Hedderman and Moxon (1992).
31 Moxon (1988), pp. 53–4.   32 Farrington and Morris (1983).
33 Dowds and Hedderman (1997), p. 11.
34 Magistrates interviewed by Gelsthorpe and Loucks (1997), ch. 4, were often reluctant to fine women because they had no independent means and/or because taking money from them might make their child-care responsibilities more difficult.
35 Gelsthorpe and Loucks (1997), ch. 3, recording the tendency of the magistrates they interviewed to regard women offenders as 'troubled' rather than 'troublesome'.

mothers with no employment) rather than as 'normal'.[36] The other side of this coin is that the traditional family unit is adopted as the centre of normality. Where women do have family responsibilities, these sometimes militate in their favour;[37] those with less conventional lifestyles tend to be viewed unsympathetically, as do those who fail to exhibit expected female responses in court (tearful, apologetic, respectful).[38] When dealing with most female offenders, however, it appears that magistrates give much greater weight to mitigating factors and, in particular, strive harder to avoid a custodial sentence than when sentencing a male.[39]

Are women treated more leniently? In overall terms the answer might appear to be affirmative; but, on the basis of their research projects, Dowds and Hedderman and Gelsthorpe and Loucks draw a different conclusion. They point out that

> men and women stood an equal chance of going to prison for a first violent offence. However, among repeat offenders, women were less likely to receive a custodial sentence.
>
> Women first offenders were significantly less likely than equivalent men to receive a prison sentence for a drug offence, but recidivists were equally likely to go to prison.[40]

This shows, the authors argue, that women do not consistently receive more lenient treatment than men. Rather, their sentencing patterns are more likely to reflect 'the fact that men and women who come to court differ across a wide range of factors which sentencers take into consideration when determining an appropriate sentence'.[41] This refers to the effect on women's sentencing of factors such as the primary responsibility for child care, no independent income and a more respectful or remorseful attitude in court. But one could certainly argue that the patterns found by these authors point to heavily stereotypical reasoning by some sentencers.[42] Indeed, as suggested above, there may be two sets of divergent social stereotypes at play here – a form of chivalry that regards women as behaving irrationally if they offend ('troubled', 'disturbed') and therefore as deserving sympathy, and a form of rejection which bears down harshly on women who depart from conventional social roles.[43]

It can be strongly argued that the focus should not just be on gender but also on other reasons why women and men may be treated unfairly by the criminal justice system. We have already met one example of this: black women. The figures quoted in part 2 above showed that a quarter of the female prison population are black, around 13 times as many as in the general population. Some of these will be on remand, but that in itself is a cause for concern. Some will be convicted or alleged drug couriers from other countries. The justifications for imprisoning

36 Farrington and Morris (1983).
37 On the mitigating effect of such factors, see ch. 5.4.5 above.
38 See the remarks of the magistrates quoted by Gelsthorpe and Loucks (1997), pp. 30–4.
39 Gelsthorpe and Loucks (1997), ch. 4.
40 Gelsthorpe and Loucks (1997), p. vii.   41 Gelsthorpe and Loucks (1997), p. 55.
42 See also the study of male and female child-killers by Wilczynski (1997), identifying different official responses to the two groups.
43 See Morris (1988).

women in these and other cases need re-examination: the proportionate use of custodial sentences for women has grown even more steeply for women than for men in recent years: for adult men the rise was from 18 per cent in 1992 to 30 per cent in 2002, whereas for women it was from 6 per cent to 17 per cent. The report of the Committee on Women's Imprisonment made a strong case for reversing this trend, and for wider use of diversion to respond to the needs of women offenders.[44] The government created a Women's Offending Reduction Programme in 2001, but it is not clear what effects it has had. The Probation Service has begun to develop what is known as the 'Real Women Programme', involving special forms of group work aimed specifically at women offenders, particularly those convicted of acquisitive crimes, but evaluation remains at an early stage.[45]

Is it right in principle that women should receive equal treatment to men? The answer, surely, is that the same principles should be applicable to both. This might still mean that women would generally receive lesser sentences, inasmuch as their crimes are less serious and their previous records better. It might also mean that women can more frequently have the benefit of certain mitigating factors connected with family responsibilities, even if the same principle is capable of operating in favour of men. But that raises the question of whether family responsibilities should be regarded as so central to mitigation. Mary Eaton has argued that 'by judging both female and male defendants in the context of their families, the court displays not impartiality, or equality of treatment, but its role in preserving differences based on sexual inequality'.[46] This questions the role that courts should and could perform when sentencing. Are they to attempt to equalize the treatment of the sexes through sentencing and, if so, how? One practical step would be to ensure that the full range of sentencing options is available for women, especially those with child-care responsibilities, and that they are tailored to women's needs rather than based on research relating to male offenders.[47] A further practical step would be to ensure that sentencers receive 'gender awareness' training, partly because many courts deal with women so rarely, and partly to encourage them 'to reflect on how cultural and gender-specific stereotypes inform their practices and perceptions in the courtroom in ways which could lead to unfair sentencing'.[48] The general question about sentencers' responsibilities in relation to wider social inequalities must be left until part 7.7 below.

7.4 Employment status

We have already seen, in Chapter 5.4.5 above, that a good work record may constitute a powerful factor in mitigation. Understandable as it is that courts should wish to avoid passing a sentence which will result in an offender losing a job, one result of

44 Prison Reform Trust (2000); see further ch. 9.6.2 below.
45 Home Office (2004).   46 Eaton (1986), p. 98.
47 This is the point of the Real Women Programme, above n. 45.
48 Gelsthorpe and Loucks (1997), p. 58.

this approach may be that unemployed offenders come off worse. This ground of mitigation is unavailable to them. The significance of the problem is clear from a survey in the mid-1990s, showing that some two-thirds of sentenced offenders in the magistrates' courts and in the Crown Court were unemployed.[49] Particularly interesting, in the light of the discussion in part 7.2 above, was the finding that in magistrates' courts 75 per cent of black offenders were unemployed, compared with 64 per cent of white offenders and 48 per cent of Asians; the figures for the Crown Court were somewhat similar, at 77 per cent, 65 per cent and 64 per cent respectively.[50] Is there evidence that sentencing practice discriminates against the unemployed?

Four surveys might be mentioned. The first, by Iain Crow and Frances Simon, studied six magistrates' courts with different patterns of custody use in three areas with different unemployment rates. Their broad finding was that the effect of employment status on sentencing was generally small. Like many other English researchers, they found that the type of offence and the offender's criminal record were the most powerful factors. However, there were some distinct patterns among the six courts. They all tended to use fines more for employed people, whereas unemployed people tended to receive more probation, discharges and other sentences (including custody). Even so, they found that unemployed offenders who were fined were more likely to default – largely because fines tend not to be reduced in road traffic cases to reflect the offender's means.[51]

Some of these findings received support from Moxon's study of sentencing in the Crown Court. Unemployed offenders were more likely to be placed on probation, and less likely to be fined, than employed offenders.[52] Being employed was associated with a lower probability of custody than being unemployed, and offenders who said that they had secured a job between crime and conviction also tended to have a lower chance of custody. Those who were unemployed also tended to receive longer custodial sentences, but it was suggested that this may simply mean that they had committed more serious offences and were therefore more likely to have been dismissed from their job, or remanded in custody and lost their job, and so forth.

Third, Flood-Page and Mackie's study of sentencing in the mid-1990s shows the effect of employment status on courts' use of the fine. In the magistrates' courts some 82 per cent of employed first offenders were fined, compared with 57 per cent of unemployed first offenders; for recidivists the contrast was between 53 per cent and 43 per cent.[53] In the Crown Court a higher proportion of those given custodial sentences were unemployed (64 per cent) than employed (47 per cent).[54] These findings tend to confirm those from a 1994 Home Office survey, which showed

49 Flood-Page and Mackie (1998), pp. 117–19.

50 The study of race and sentencing by Hood (1992) showed that being unemployed was a significant factor in producing greater sentence severity for black offenders aged 21 and over, although not for whites or Asians.

51 Crow and Simon (1989).   52 Moxon (1988), pp. 44, 47.

53 Flood-Page and Mackie (1998), p. 49.   54 Flood-Page and Mackie (1998), p. 79.

that the unemployed are much more likely to receive a custodial sentence and less likely to receive a fine.[55] Although none of these figures should be taken at face value without analysis of type of offence, previous convictions and other significant variables, they remain strongly suggestive.

Fourth, the research by Hough, Jacobson and Millie on sentencers' decision-making in cases on the cusp of custody shows that having a job or good employment prospects would often militate in favour of a community sentence. 'An existing job and home, family support, or family responsibilities, are likewise viewed as encouraging aspects of an offender's life', leading to the inference that they are less likely to breach a community sentence because they have 'more to lose'. This emphasis on having a job suggests, the authors comment, that 'offenders who are already socially and economically disadvantaged are likely to suffer further disadvantage in the sentencing process'.[56]

These four surveys yield at least some suggestive evidence of discrimination on grounds of employment status. One might wish to argue that the problem here is different from discrimination on grounds of race or sex. It is not so much a matter of discrimination against the unemployed: if there is a difference in treatment, it may result from the extending of leniency to those in employment. This, the argument goes, can be justified on quite separate grounds. As Lord Lane CJ reasoned, there is

> [a] desire if possible to keep people out of prison who can be dealt with otherwise, and that is much to be applauded, because as we know, prison places at the moment are extremely valuable, and if people can be dealt with properly by means of non-custodial sentences, and fines are possibly the best of all the non-custodial sentences, then that should be done.[57]

The reasoning can be strengthened by adding that it is not only the expense but also the effects of prison which justify restraint in its use. But is the general argument sound? The case in which Lord Lane spoke these words concerned two brothers who had committed fairly serious offences of violence. The trial judge imposed suspended sentences of imprisonment combined with large fines. One reason was that the brothers were in employment. Another (with which we are not concerned here)[58] was that the jobs of some 23 others depended on the continuation of the brothers' business. By thus discriminating in their favour because they were in employment, were the courts not in effect discriminating against the unemployed? Tony Bottoms pointed out that suspended sentences were sometimes used for persons of 'education and intelligence' and for 'white-collar' offenders when they would not be used for people without those characteristics, and he argued that this amounts to 'the suspension of terms of imprisonment for middle-class offenders'[59] – an observation that may become pertinent again, if the suspended sentence comes to

---

55 Home Office Special Data Collection Exercise (1994), paras. 15–20.
56 Hough et al. (2003), p. 42.   57 *Olliver and Olliver* (1989) 11 Cr App R (S) 10 at p. 13.
58 See ch. 5.4.5 above.   59 Bottoms (1981), p. 18.

be widely used under the 2003 Act.[60] Similarly, Hough, Jacobson and Millie identified a good employment record as a factor that sentencers might treat as tipping
a borderline case away from a custodial disposal.[61] Such decisions may be regarded
as preferring the principle of parsimony over the principle of equality before the
law. Lesser punishments are given to one group on grounds of parsimony, although
other offenders who are similarly placed in terms of offence and criminal record
receive no such concession. The only way to pursue equality here is to offer no
concession at all based on employment.

A further complicating factor is the principle of equal impact: thus Moxon found
that unemployed offenders who were placed on community service tended to be
given a greater number of hours, perhaps because it was thought that they had
more spare time.[62] The results of these decisions on community service orders are
discriminatory, even though the intent is not. This conflict of principles is discussed
in part 7.7 below. A more specific question is whether we are justified in placing
such emphasis on employment. Just as Eaton attacks the emphasis placed on the
conventional family by sentencers, so one might criticize the influential role that
the work ethic seems to play in sentencing. It is certainly true that there should be
no direct inference from the status of being employed, resulting in the ascription of
moral or social superiority to employed people over unemployed people. There is
no general link between, for example, unemployment and fault or unemployment
and lack of respect for family responsibilities. Unemployment rates tend to result
more from changes in government economic policy or world trading conditions
than from outbreaks of inadequacy among groups of employees.

Indeed, a related question is whether unemployment might not be considered to
be a possible mitigating factor, at least in cases of thefts of necessary items. There is
some remote authority for this in the guideline judgment on social security fraud in
Stewart, where Lord Lane CJ suggested that courts should look more favourably on
cases in which the proceeds were used for 'the provision of household necessities'
than those in which 'unnecessary luxury' was the objective.[63] Although some might
baulk at calling this a mitigating factor, it certainly takes the crime towards the lower
rather than the upper end of the range of seriousness. Need is a less anti-social and
selfish motive than greed, and the distinction is one of which unemployed offenders
might properly have the benefit.

7.5 Financial circumstances

The principle of equality before the law indicates that poor offenders should not, on
account of their poverty, be treated less favourably than wealthy offenders. In practice, the situation is no less likely to arise the other way round, as with employment

---

60 See ch. 9.4.2 below.   61 Hough et al. (2003), p. 42 and ch. 4 generally.
62 Moxon (1988), p. 46; cf. Oxford pilot study (1984), p. 29.
63 (1987) 9 Cr App R (S) 135 at p. 139.

status. It may be less that courts aim to penalize those without financial resources, and more that courts find themselves able to take a lenient course with an offender who has financial resources. In terms of sentencing principles, however, this route to leniency has long been declared to be wrong. In the well-known case of *Markwick* (1953),[64] a wealthy member of a golf club had been fined £500 for stealing two shillings and sixpence from a golf club changing room, in circumstances which had cast suspicion on others. He appealed against this sentence to the Court of Criminal Appeal, which responded with a rare exercise of its power (since removed) to increase the severity of sentences on defence appeals. Sentencing Markwick to two months' imprisonment, Lord Goddard CJ remarked that in such a case a high fine 'would give persons of means an opportunity of buying themselves out of being sent to prison . . . There should be no suggestion that there is one law for the rich and one for the poor.'

The same principle has been stated for like cases. Thus, in *Copley* (1979)[65] Lane LJ observed that 'it is not open to persons who participate in crime and plead guilty to try to buy their way out of prison, or to buy shorter sentences, by offering money in the way of compensation'. Some defence lawyers still advance pleas in mitigation based, explicitly or implicitly, on the offender's ability to pay a substantial fine or substantial compensation. Such attempts to persuade a court to act contrary to principle may succeed occasionally, but they may also misfire. Far from persuading a court to suspend a sentence and impose a financial penalty, the court might give both immediate prison and a financial penalty.[66]

There is also some judicial authority for the converse principle, that an offender should not be given a more severe penalty simply because the court regards him or her as incapable of paying a sufficient fine.[67] In practice, however, there have been distinctly different patterns of disposal according to whether or not the offender is unemployed, as the findings set out in part 7.4 above demonstrate. Unemployed offenders are less likely to be fined and more likely to receive other sentences, particularly discharges and community service orders. Lack of financial resources is likely to go with unemployment here, and so the findings might be interpreted as showing that some relatively poor offenders receive an absolute or conditional discharge rather than a fine (which may be more lenient), whereas others receive community service instead of a fine (which is more severe).

No research project has set out to examine the relationship between financial resources and sentencing as such, but there has always been a strong suggestion that defendants with means may receive better treatment. The spread of legal aid and of duty solicitor schemes may have reduced the imbalance, but it remains true that legal costs lead some defendants to defend themselves and that, despite any efforts made by the clerk on their behalf, they may be at a disadvantage compared

---

64 (1953) 37 Cr App R 125.   65 (1979) 1 Cr App R (S) 55.
66 Cf. *Olliver and Olliver* (1989) 11 Cr App R (S) 10, discussed in ch. 10.5.5 below, with *Fairbairn* (1980) 2 Cr App R (S) 284.
67 E.g. *Myers* [1980] Crim LR 191, *Ball* (1981) 3 Cr App R (S) 283.

with the legally aided defendant, not to mention the defendant with a retained solicitor or barrister. Moreover, it has been strongly argued that class differences exert considerable influence in the courtroom, whether or not the defendant is represented.[68] Perhaps the greatest influence, however, occurs before cases come to court. From the outset there is a greater probability that 'white-collar' offenders will be dealt with outside the formal criminal process. Offences committed by companies and their officers are likely to be processed by statutory agencies such as the Health and Safety Executive and the various industrial inspectorates, for whom prosecution is a last resort.[69] Those who commit income tax offences are unlikely to be prosecuted, whereas those who commit social security frauds remain more likely to be prosecuted, despite the changes in the mid-1980s.[70] The result is that shoplifting and other small thefts are likely to be prosecuted, whereas larger appropriations of property in less visible and more privileged settings will be dealt with in other ways. Thus, the criminal justice system is structured in ways that favour the wealthy over the poor. The egalitarian principles declared by the Court of Appeal in relation to sentencing would, even if faithfully and invariably applied, merely assist in moderating the overall discrimination.

Whether steps should be taken at the sentencing stage to try to counteract the inequalities in the system as a whole is discussed later. Moderating those inequalities is, however, a worthy goal. The principle of equality before the law points in this direction. So too does the principle of equal impact: where a court decides to impose a financial penalty, such as a fine or compensation order, it should ensure that it is adjusted to the means of the offender. In the present context the most important aspect is that the size of the fine be reduced for an offender of limited means, a principle long established in the law. The courts resisted the corollary that fines should be increased for the wealthy, but since 1991 there have been legislative provisions embracing the principle of equal impact and stating that the fine should reflect the means of the offender, whether the effect is to increase or reduce its amount.[71] Recent years have seen a revival of official interest in the kind of 'day fine' system used in other European countries, discussed in Chapter 10.5 below, and if there is to be a reversal of the decline in fining and adherence to the principle of equality of impact, some such system must be adopted again.

At a theoretical level, does the principle of equal impact conflict with the proportionality principle? Could it be said that a fine of £7,000 for a theft in breach of trust involving property valued at £700 is disproportionate?[72] The answer is to be found in a separation between the gravity of the offence and the means of the offender. Proportionality should govern the process of estimating the gravity of the offence, taking account of aggravating and mitigating factors. Only when the relative seriousness of the offence has been assessed should the court turn to the offender's

---

68 McBarnet (1981).   69 See Hawkins (2003), and ch. 1.4 above.
70 Cook (1989).   71 Fully discussed in ch. 10.5 below.
72 As argued unsuccessfully in *Fairbairn* (1980) 2 Cr App R (S) 315.

financial resources and strive to achieve equal impact. To say, 'a fine of £7,000 is disproportionate for an offence involving £700', is to make the wrong comparison. The £7,000 ought to be compared with the relative seriousness of the offence and the offender's means; it should not be related directly to the amount involved in the offence, since that is only one of the factors relevant to its seriousness (breach of trust being another). Under the kind of day fine system used widely in other European countries and some US jurisdictions,[73] the point is made much clearer by announcing the fines, not in terms of the actual sum ordered to be paid, but in terms of the number of 'days' or 'units' (which represent the seriousness of the offence). There is thus no inconsistency between the proportionality principle and the principle of equal impact.

The latter principle is, however, compromised to some extent for reasons of administrative efficiency. Two forms of compromise can be mentioned. One is the standardized nature of some of the calculations which form part of any system of unit fines or day fines. They sacrifice maximum accuracy in individual cases in order to achieve a relatively rapid processing of large numbers of cases in the lower courts. Such systems can therefore claim greater equality of impact, not perfect equality. So long as the compromise is relatively generous to those least able to pay, it may be acceptable. The second form of compromise is inherent in the fixed penalty system: a large number of motoring offences and an increasing number of other offences have a fixed financial penalty, which does not vary according to the means of the offender. It is true that any offender has the alternative of going to court rather than accepting the fixed penalty, but there are obvious uncertainties and other disincentives attendant on this course. Some magistrates maintain that anyone who can afford to run a car can afford a penalty of this size, but that is too simplistic an approach, and there is a case for re-examining the impact of fixed penalties on the economically disadvantaged.

7.6 Social status

The principle of equality before the law requires that offenders should not be sentenced more favourably because of their social status or 'respectability'. In practice, social status is likely to be bound up closely with other factors already discussed, such as employment and financial circumstances. But there are a few cases in which the Court of Criminal Appeal considered the proper approach to sentencing someone who, until the offence, held a high social position. Both in *Cargill* (1913)[74] and in *Fell* (1963)[75] it was held that the proper approach is to pass sentence according to the seriousness of the offence. Where the offence involves a breach of trust, the gravity of that breach will generally be greater if the offender's position was higher. However, courts should not go further and increase the sentence because the offender has set a bad example to other citizens; even if this is so, it was held

---

73 Greene (1998).   74 [1913] 2 KB 671.   75 [1963] Crim LR 207.

to be counterbalanced by the probability that such offenders will suffer relatively greater deprivations and losses than others.

The fact that there is appellate authority for the application of the principle of equality before the law in sentencing does not exclude the possibility that other factors may operate at earlier stages. As with race and financial resources, it remains probable that social status is sometimes influential at the stage of deciding whether or not to prosecute, or even whether or not to report, certain cases. 'Young people' in one part of a city might receive an informal warning for 'rowdiness' or 'high spirits', whereas 'youths' in another area might be prosecuted or formally cautioned for similar behaviour interpreted as 'disorder'.

7.7 Equality, parsimony and risk

Inequality in sentencing is sometimes linked with inconsistency, a frequent battle-cry of those who attack English sentencing practice. It is a fundamental principle that like cases should be treated alike, and different cases differently. The practical significance of this principle depends, however, on authoritative agreement on which resemblances and which differences are to count as relevant or irrelevant. This is where the principle of equality before the law has its application, in arguing that certain differences should be excluded and rendered irrelevant to sentencing decisions. On a proportionality rationale, equality before the law at the sentencing stage is assured *if* the proportionality principle applies throughout sentencing, and *if* there are no significant amounts of unaccountable discretion in practical sentencing. Neither of these conditions seems to be satisfied by English sentencing. There is a major exception to the proportionality principle in the 2003 Act, in the dangerousness provisions (see Chapter 6.8 above). Moreover, the development of mitigating factors has largely been left to the courts themselves – so that, as we have seen in this chapter, parts 7.3 and 7.4, domestic responsibilities for women and employment for men act as mitigating factors, especially in relation to custodial sentences.[76] There is good reason to pay renewed attention to the practical application in sentencing decisions of the principle of equality before the law.

What this chapter has shown, however, is the complexity of doing so. Equality before the law is not the only principle or policy which may be relevant here, and so there are conflicts to be resolved. One obvious conflict is that between equality before the law and efficiency in the administration of justice: to what extent, and under what circumstances, might it be acceptable to forego maximum equality of impact in fines in order to expedite the processing of cases in magistrates' courts? Are the supposed effectiveness and administrative efficiency of on-the-spot fines sufficient reasons to outweigh the principle of equal impact? Another conflict is that between equality before the law and the principle of parsimony, or restraint in the use of imprisonment. There are strong arguments for imposing lesser punishments

76 See Hudson (1998), p. 231.

when they seem likely to be no less effective than the greater punishment; but should that be done if it results in giving preference to an employed over an unemployed offender, or a white over a black offender? Is this not discrimination? Should it be absolutely forbidden, or does parsimony have stronger claims?

Before these questions are debated, it is worth discussing further the concept of discrimination. It has been observed above that the effect of taking account of a positive factor in mitigation of sentence – e.g. that the offender has a steady job, or that the offender has paid compensation to the victim – may be to discriminate against others who are less fortunate. In exactly similar cases, the unemployed or poor offender would receive a more severe sentence. Now it can certainly be said that this does not amount to using unemployment or poverty as an aggravating factor: as argued in Chapter 5.1 above, there are not two but three notional effects which factors may have upon sentence – aggravating, neutral and mitigating. In theory, therefore, unemployment and poverty would be neutral factors whereas the 'steady job' and payment of compensation would mitigate. Yet the effect of taking account of these mitigating factors is to discriminate on grounds which should not form the basis of differences in sentencing, that is employment status and financial resources. The motivation behind the mitigation of sentence may be laudable, but the effect is discriminatory. If these grounds of mitigation are to be justified, then, it must be by reference to values which are regarded as superior to equality before the law. Can such a justification be found?

As we saw in part 7.1 of this chapter, Norval Morris and Michael Tonry argue that the principle of parsimony ought to be accorded greater weight than the principle of equality before the law. In their view, proportionality merely sets loose outer limits to the severity and leniency of punishments for particular crimes. They argue that the concept of cardinal proportionality is so uncertain in its application that this undermines the whole basis of desert theory. There are no criteria for determining the anchoring points of the scale, they say, and therefore there can be no compelling reason why judgments of ordinal proportionality should be accorded absolute priority. Reasonable people may differ about the appropriate levels of punishment for different types of crime, and the avoidance of manifest disproportion is all that can be achieved. It is therefore preferable to allow the principle of parsimony to lead to lower sentences in suitable cases, so long as the sentences are not disproportionately low:

> A developed punishment theory requires recognition that precise equivalency of punishment between equally undeserving criminals in the distribution of punishments is in practice unattainable and in theory undesirable. We argue that all that can be achieved is a rough equivalence of punishment that will allow room for the principled distribution of punishments on utilitarian grounds, unfettered by the miserable aim of making suffering equally painful.[77]

77 Morris and Tonry (1990), p. 31.

The utilitarian aim to which Morris and Tonry refer is the principle of parsimony. They apply it particularly to certain prison sentences:

> Imprisonment is expensive and unnecessary for some convicted felons who present no serious threat to the community and whose imprisonment is not necessary for deterrent purposes, and yet whose crime and criminal record could properly attract a prison sentence. Are we to allow an excessive regard for equality of suffering to preclude rational allocation of scarce prison space and staff?[78]

Morris and Tonry make it clear that one result of their approach would be that a white, middle-class offender is likely to receive a more lenient sentence than a black offender living on state benefits, if there are community treatment facilities in the first locality which are unavailable in the second.[79] They characterize the principle of equality before the law as a principle of equality of suffering, since it refuses to allow more lenient sentences for certain offenders if the result would be to discriminate on improper grounds against others. They oppose equality of suffering because their utilitarian concern is the reduction of suffering in as many cases as possible. They deny that this will infringe the principle of equality before the law *in the long run*, because they argue that one result of their scheme will be to produce more community sanctions for offenders of all races and social classes.[80] If intermediate punishments were seen to work for white, middle-class offenders, they might then be expanded so as to be available for all. Inequality of treatment in the short run should be tolerated in order to bring greater equality in the longer term.

Considering their approach on its own terms, is it more likely that the overall amount of suffering generated by their approach (discrimination in the short term, in order to show that community sanctions perform acceptably) would be less than the suffering generated by an approach which insisted on equality before the law, but yet which involved efforts to introduce more community sanctions which the courts would use? Much depends on the political system, on the attitudes of sentencers, on government funding and so on. The difficulty in the United States, as Morris and Tonry describe it, is to gain acceptance for community sanctions for offenders now sent to prison. Many states have no fines, and relatively few other sanctions. The position in this country is different: there is a wide range of available alternatives, and the problem is to ensure that they are used in a more extensive and more principled way. The problem here is as much one of discrimination as of a general unwillingness to use fines, and to use community sentences for offenders now sent to prison.[81] It is hard to be confident that Morris and Tonry's approach would reduce overall suffering in England and Wales, whatever the probabilities elsewhere.

On theoretical grounds, however, their analysis cannot be accepted. To caricature equality before the law as equality of suffering is surely a rather blinkered approach.

---

78 Morris and Tonry (1990), p. 90.   79 Morris and Tonry (1990), p. 33.
80 Morris and Tonry (1990), p. 33.
81 See the findings of Hood (1992), p. 141, on the disinclination of probation officers and courts to contemplate community sentences for black offenders.

Equality before the law is a fundamental value which cannot simply be cast aside: it stands for propositions about respect for human dignity, and impartiality in the administration of criminal justice. This is not to say that it should be regarded as absolute and inviolable. But the principle should be recognized as fundamental in most modern societies, not simply to be traded for gains in efficiency and so forth. If there are situations in which it has to be weighed against other principles such as parsimony, the two principles should be considered not only in their intrinsic strength but also in their wider social effects. Discrimination in the criminal justice system may alienate sections of the community and contribute to racial tensions or class divisions, as well as undermining respect for the administration of criminal justice. Moreover, Morris and Tonry's approach is not the only possible one. They seem to assume that the principle of parsimony entails the reduction of individual sentences wherever possible; another interpretation is that it requires a general lowering of punishment levels and expansion of community sanctions,[82] and not discriminatory distinctions among individual offenders. On the same reasoning, there should be no special pleading for women offenders: 'feminist criminologists and legal theorists are not asking for special-case leniency, but . . . are challenging the present assumption that the male penal norm is generalisable'.[83] Reducing levels of penalty for males would be a splendid application of the principle of parsimony.

Commitment to the principle of equality before the law may appear empty when there is so much inequality evident in society. Social unfairness may be largely the product of the social structure, and its roots are likely to be found in institutional arrangements rather than in the actions of a few individuals.[84] There is also the argument that remedying social inequality in such fields as housing, employment and education is likely to be a more potent means of crime reduction than specific measures taken through the criminal justice system. It is trite to say that the criminal justice system can have little effect on crime unless the social system is altered in certain ways. It is also trite to say that the sentencing system, dealing with only a small proportion of offences each year, can be expected to have far less influence on patterns of lawbreaking than certain strategies of crime prevention, whether situational or social. Equally, as we have seen, the sentencing system can only deal with those offenders who are prosecuted to conviction.

In the absence of a fairly adjusted social system and criminal justice system, notions of proportionality and desert in the allocation of punishment are placed under strain. Desert theorists can respond to that strain by advocating a decremental strategy so as to achieve greater parsimony, but, as Andrew von Hirsch has argued,

> The sentencing of convicted persons cannot wait until underlying social ills are remedied, nor can it be abandoned until they are addressed . . . Addressing fundamental social ills (desirable and, indeed, essential as this is) cannot constitute a substitute for trying to make sentencing policy more coherent and fair.[85]

82 See ch. 3.4 above.   83 Hudson (1998), p. 248.   84 Cook and Hudson (1993), pp. 9–10.
85 Von Hirsch (1993), p. 98; see also von Hirsch and Ashworth (2005), ch. 6.

Thus both proportionality, as giving effect to the principle of equality before the law, and parsimony must be regarded as goals. However, there must be greater recognition of the skewed nature of the sample of offenders who appear before the courts: too many statements by magistrates and judges contain the assumption that the offenders who are prosecuted represent a fair cross-section of all offenders, and that increases or decreases in offenders for sentence always represent real fluctuations in patterns of offending. This recognition, no less than improved policies of recruitment and training among criminal justice agencies, must form part of future sentencing developments.

Finally, it is important to signal the dangers to the principle of equality before the law that flow from the increasing emphasis on risk assessment. We have seen in Chapter 6 how significant the idea of prediction is in sentencing law, and we shall see in Chapter 12 how prominent a place is coming to be given to risk assessment in the social response to offending by young people and by the mentally disordered. The greater the focus on risk, the greater the focus on what might be termed 'non-legal' variables – that is not just previous convictions, but upbringing, family size, income and housing.[86] Reliance on these factors is highly likely to lead to direct and indirect discrimination. The direct discrimination would be against the poor and unemployed. The indirect discrimination would be against those who fall disproportionately within the categories of high risk, such as certain ethnic minorities and single mothers. The threat to equality before the law in the 'risk society' is therefore a real one, and righteous pronouncements on 'community safety' must be scrutinized closely from this point of view.

86 See further Farrington (2002).

CHAPTER 8

Multiple offenders

This chapter, like Chapter 6, deals with some of the problems posed by the sentencing of persistent offenders. Its focus, however, is on offenders who come before the courts in a different context. In Chapter 6 the main concern was with the sentencing of recidivists – those who offend repeatedly, despite the fact that they have experienced criminal sanctions. The main concern here is with offenders who commit a number of offences before they are detected and convicted, so that the court has to sentence them on one occasion for several offences. Not all the offenders whom the courts have to sentence for several crimes could be described as 'persistent offenders', for in some cases the offender has been involved in a single incident which gives rise to a number of charges and convictions. But many 'multiple offenders', whom the courts have to sentence for more than one offence, are people who have been committing offences over a period of weeks, months or even years before they appear in court, and they then face a number of charges. The criminal record of such multiple offenders may vary: some of them will be recidivists too, having experienced a number of criminal sanctions in the past, whilst others will fall into that seemingly incongruous category of 'persistent first offenders' – those who, when they are convicted for the first time, are convicted of several offences which show that they are accustomed to lawbreaking, if not to the criminal process.

The focus of this chapter, then, will be on multiple offenders, some of whom are being sentenced for a number of offences arising from a single incident, but most of whom will be being sentenced for offences committed at different times during the period before their court appearance. Wherever proportionality between the seriousness of the case and the severity of the sentence is a leading principle, multiple offenders give rise to difficulties both theoretical and practical. It is one thing to compare a residential burglary with a rape; it is quite another thing to draw comparisons of gravity between two, four or six residential burglaries and a single rape. Before tackling these problems, however, the various procedural methods of dealing with multiple offenders must be briefly explained.

8.1 Charging the multiple offender

What approach should the police and prosecutors take when it emerges that a suspected offender may have committed more than one offence? A full answer to this question would import a mass of technical detail; for present purposes, a sketch of the four main avenues open to the prosecution should provide a sufficient basis for the remainder of the discussion.

8.1.1 Charge all offences

The straightforward approach is to charge all the offences of which the prosecution have sufficient evidence. This has the disadvantage that the indictment could be so long as to make it very difficult for the court to deal fairly and accurately with the various charges against the defendant. If there is a plea of not guilty, the task of a jury dealing with a lengthy indictment may be formidable and beyond what is reasonable to expect of them. For this reason, it has long been accepted that the prosecution may, and indeed ought to, bring no charge in respect of relatively trivial incidents where the defendant already faces a number of more serious charges.[1] To some extent it remains in the prosecution's interest to bring a number of charges against a defendant, since they may then agree not to proceed with some of the charges in exchange for the defendant's agreement to plead guilty to the others. Where a defendant does plead guilty to some charges and it appears to the prosecution that he is likely to receive a broadly appropriate sentence for those offences, it will usually be right for the prosecution to drop any further charges to which he pleads not guilty. This requires, and will usually receive, the trial judge's consent.[2]

8.1.2 Charge specimen offences

Where the prosecution have evidence of a course of offending over a considerable period, usually but not necessarily against the same victim (e.g. sexual offences against children, thefts from an employer), they may decide to charge only a few incidents as 'specimen counts'. The chosen 'specimen counts' should relate to the most serious of the alleged offences, and the purpose is to avoid complicating a single trial with too many charges and to avoid the need for several trials, while giving the judge a sufficient basis for a proportionate sentence. This is obviously easier for the prosecution, since it spares them the burden of adducing evidence in relation to each one of a long series of offences. But if the defendant is unwilling to admit to the offences not charged, can the court sentence as if they were proved, simply because the prosecution described its charges as specimens (of a longer course of offending)? In the leading decision of *Canavan and Kidd* (1998),[3] Lord Bingham CJ declared that

---

1 E.g. Lawton LJ in *Ambrose* (1973) 57 Cr App R 538.
2 *Broad* (1979) 68 Cr App R 281.   3 [1998] 1 Cr App R (S) 243.

A defendant is not to be convicted of any offence with which he is charged unless and until his guilt is proved. Such guilt may be proved by his own admission or (on indictment) by the verdict of a jury. He may be sentenced only for an offence proved against him (by admission or verdict) or which he has admitted and asked the court to take into consideration when passing sentence. If, as we think, these are basic principles underlying the administration of the criminal law, it is not easy to see how a defendant can lawfully be punished for offences for which he has not been indicted and which he has denied or declined to admit.

He added that 'prosecuting authorities will wish, in the light of this decision . . . to include more counts in some indictments', and expressed the view that this would not be unduly burdensome. Although the principle thus enunciated is an important principle of fairness, it was not always followed at trials.[4] However, Parliament has now introduced a new procedure for cases in which the prosecution wish to prefer specimen charges. Under s. 17 of the Domestic Violence, Crime and Victims Act 2004, the prosecution may apply to a Crown Court judge to have some of the counts in an indictment tried by judge alone, while others are tried by jury. This means that the prosecution may charge a considerable number of offences, and then satisfy the judge that some of them may fairly be regarded as samples of the others. If the judge decides that trial by jury of every count would be impracticable, that the counts to be tried by jury are a sample, and that it is in the interests of justice to proceed in this way, the judge may make an order for trial of the other counts by judge alone. The jury trial then proceeds, and if the defendant is convicted 'on a count which can be regarded as a sample of other counts to be tried in those proceedings', the judge may then try the defendant on the other counts, giving a reasoned judgment (s. 19). In most cases the defendant will probably change the plea to guilty of these other offences, but the new procedure gives the prosecution an opportunity to circumvent the problem of principle presented by *Canavan and Kidd.*

8.1.3 Prefer a general charge

Another approach, when there is evidence of a course of offending over a long period, is to frame a general charge. If two or more people have been involved, a charge of conspiracy may have procedural advantages for the prosecution and open the way to higher sentences. Similar advantages may flow from a 'general deficiency' count in cases of repeated defalcation.

8.1.4 Offences taken into consideration

The prosecution may invite a defendant to ask the court to take other offences into consideration when sentencing him for the crimes charged. The House of Lords has laid down that a defendant should be informed explicitly of each offence and asked to consent to the court taking each one into consideration when sentencing.[5] The

---

4 One of the many decisions finding a breach was *Pardue* [2004] 1 Cr App R (S) 105.
5 *DPP* v. *Anderson* [1978] AC 964.

offences thus taken into consideration do not rank as convictions, but the court is likely to increase the sentence in order to take account of them, and the procedure is a relatively informal and expeditious way of disposing of a long series of offences which are not especially serious in nature.

8.2 Concurrent or consecutive?

At the outset, the limitations of any theoretical discussion of the sentencing of multiple offenders must be openly avowed. Because of the wide variety of combinations of offences in particular cases, and the equally wide variations in the time-span of the offending with which the court has to deal, it would unwise to adopt too dogmatic an approach. Indeed, David Thomas, after identifying two general principles, recognized the existence of decisions 'which do not lend themselves to any generalization'.[6] On the other hand, this wide variation in the circumstances in which courts may be confronted with the problem of sentencing a multiple offender should not be allowed to stifle the search for some general principles.

Just as the straightforward approach to prosecuting is to bring a charge in respect of each offence of which there is prima facie evidence, so the straightforward approach to sentencing is to impose a sentence for each offence of which there is a conviction. The offender who is convicted of one crime receives one sentence; the offender who is convicted of three crimes receives three sentences, each one additional to the others. The logic of this approach, however, is far from perfect. It begins to appear less straightforward when it is realized that, in certain instances, the law may provide (and the prosecution charge) a number of offences where in theory one would suffice, and in other instances the law may provide (and the prosecution charge) one offence where it would be natural to think of two or three. For example, the offence of aggravated burglary contrary to s. 10 of the Theft Act 1968 is apt to cover a case where a person commits burglary and has with him a firearm, an offensive weapon or an explosive; therefore it is not necessary to charge such a person on one count with burglary and on a separate count with the offence of possessing a firearm, offensive weapon or explosive substance. The law provides a single offence, aggravated burglary, and the sentencer will naturally take account of both elements of the crime (the burglary and the possession offence) in his calculations. On the other hand, crimes such as manslaughter and robbery do not specify the use of a weapon; whilst prosecutors will usually add a charge under the Firearms Act 1968 if the accused was carrying a firearm, it would be unusual to add a charge of possessing an offensive weapon to a charge of manslaughter or robbery (since the maximum penalty for offensive weapons is four years' imprisonment).

From the point of view of calculating the total sentence, it should be immaterial whether a firearms charge is added in such a case or not. The sentencer has all the facts, the maximum sentence for manslaughter or robbery is sufficiently high to

6 Thomas (1979), p. 55.

allow full account to be taken of any such aggravating factor, and it is highly unlikely that these features of the case would be overlooked. But there would be a choice as to how the sentence is expressed. If only manslaughter or robbery were charged, obviously there would be a single sentence. If there were an additional conviction under the Firearms Act, in theory the sentencer has a choice: if the decision is that, say, nine years is the appropriate total sentence, this total be expressed in terms of two consecutive sentences (e.g. six years for robbery, three years for the firearm) or in terms of two concurrent sentences (e.g. nine years for robbery, with three years concurrent for the firearm). The straightforward approach cannot deal with this kind of problem, since it overlooks the vagaries of prosecutorial discretion and of the shape of English criminal law. In some fields of activity the law provides several separate offences, in other fields a single encompassing crime. Merely to add a sentence for each conviction ignores these quirks of history and convention.

This is not necessarily to suggest that prosecutors are abusing the criminal process if, for example, they add a firearms charge to a principal charge of robbery or manslaughter when it is perfectly clear that the maximum sentence for the principal crime can accommodate any sentence the court might wish to pass. There are at least four independent reasons for adding a charge relating to firearms (or explosives). It ensures (i) that the user or carrier of firearms is clearly and separately labelled, in court, in public and in his criminal record, as an offender willing to resort to such means: if consistency can be attained among prosecutors and sentencers, then the form of a criminal record will become a reliable indicator of whether or not the offender is concerned with firearms, and this may assist in subsequent sentencing (and parole) decisions; (ii) that the defendant has a distinct opportunity to challenge this aspect of the prosecution case; and (iii) that if for some reason he is acquitted on the principal charge, he may nevertheless be convicted on this ground; and (iv) in any event the firearms offence might also relate to times and places other than those of the principal offence. The second point might be met by more rigorous fact-finding procedures before sentence, and the fourth by regarding this as a 'fringe' activity which does not justify cluttering the indictment where there are much more serious charges. But the first point may be considered important: the special heinousness of firearms offences should be marked, even if the principal charge is very serious in itself. If this is accepted, then the offender will be convicted of two crimes as a result of a single incident. This bare fact – whether he is convicted of two separate crimes, or the whole incident is brought under the umbrella of one crime – should have no influence on the total sentence, despite the procedural questions about the most appropriate approach.

8.2.1 The idea of concurrence[7]

Where a court has to pass sentence for two or more offences, the sentences might in theory be made concurrent or consecutive. Taking the question at the level of

---

7 For a learned analysis of this notion in continental law, see Jareborg (1998).

principle, what does the notion of concurrence imply? Its most obvious reference is temporal: offences committed concurrently ought to receive concurrent sentences. Of course, concurrence in time is not a precise concept: if one offence follows immediately upon another, or even rapidly upon another, one might be tempted to refer to them as occurring at the same time and to treat them as parts of the same incident. On the other hand, the longer an incident continues, the more serious it usually is; therefore, irrespective of the procedural issue of whether a continuing series of offences is thought to call for concurrent or consecutive sentences, it is surely right that such a series of offences should be regarded *ceteris paribus* as a more serious manifestation of criminality than a single such offence and as justifying a greater total sentence.

Even where there is exact temporal concurrence, however, there might be other reasons for arguing that concurrent sentences would be inappropriate. Consider a case of burglary in which the offender enters the house, begins to steal items and to pack them into a bag, is surprised by the occupier and strikes the occupier in order to make good his escape. It would generally be said that the offence of violence was committed at the same time as the burglary (although in strict legal terms the offence of burglary might have been complete at the time he entered the house);[8] in principle an offence of burglary accompanied by violence ought to be regarded as more serious than burglary without violence; the crime of burglary is not sufficiently broad to encompass all cases of violence;[9] therefore, it could be both logically and morally appropriate to pass consecutive and not concurrent sentences. Although the offences were concurrent in point of time, they violated different kinds of legal prohibition (i.e. offences against property, offences against the person). The offender ought to be labelled both as a property offender and as a violent offender, and his criminality should be viewed more seriously than if he had committed the property offence alone. However, there are still conceptual problems (do violent offences and sexual offences violate the same or different interest?),[10] and these should be noted as an early indication of the problems to be encountered throughout this chapter.

8.2.2 The general principle

English courts broadly follow the approach outlined above, so that where two or more offences are separately charged and they form part of a 'single transaction', the court should generally impose concurrent sentences. It is very difficult to construct a workable definition of a 'single transaction', especially since it seems to be little more than a pragmatic device for limiting overall sentences rather than a reflection of a sharp category distinction. However, there are some clear cases, of which

---

8 This would be true if the burglary were charged under s. 9(1)(a) rather than s. 9(1)(b) of the Theft Act 1968.
9 Burglary contrary to s. 9(1)(b) includes the infliction of grievous bodily harm, but no lesser form of violence. Aggravated burglary (s. 10) involves the carrying, not the use, of a weapon.
10 Wells (1992), ch. 2.

King (2000)[11] is an example. The offender pleaded guilty to dangerous driving and to driving while unfit through drugs, having crashed his lorry into a parked car when under the influence of diazepam. The Court of Appeal held that, as the dangerous driving arose out of the taking of drugs, 'it was not correct to impose consecutive sentences'. The sentences were made concurrent. On the other hand, the court has recognized that concurrence in time is insufficient to justify concurrent sentences where the offences are of different types, upholding consecutive sentences where (for example) a person who has driven with an excess alcohol level then attempts to bribe a police officer to refrain from administering the breath test.[12] The same approach has been taken in cases of burglary accompanied by violence.[13] Interpreted in terms of proximity in time and proximity in type of offence, then, the 'single transaction' principle embodies the general approach.[14] On the same general principle, offences committed on separate occasions against different victims should result in consecutive sentences.[15]

8.2.3 Four possible exceptions

At least four possible exceptions to the general principle appear to be established. The first is where an offender is convicted of both an offence against the person and a firearms offence. It has been thought right that the carrying of a firearm be marked not only by the separate conviction but also by a separate sentence. A long-standing authority is *Faulkner* (1972):[16] the offender was seen on the roof of a warehouse and chased by the police, and was subsequently convicted of various offences including conspiracy to steal, assault and offences contrary to the Firearms Act. He was sentenced to three years' imprisonment for the firearms and three years consecutive for the other offences. On appeal it was argued that the offences formed part of a single transaction and ought to attract concurrent sentences. The Court, dismissing the appeal, held that if an offender carried a firearm with intent when pursuing a criminal enterprise, a consecutive sentence should be imposed in order to discourage such conduct. This is deterrent reasoning, but a similar result can be reached by referring to the need to mark the special seriousness of firearms offences. In *French* (1982)[17] the Court of Appeal endorsed this as the correct approach. Although it recognized that it is simpler to charge only the principal offence, be it robbery or conspiracy to steal, for example, and then to reflect the carrying of a firearm in the sentence for that, it stated that prosecutors ought to charge the firearms offence separately. This gives the defendant the opportunity to dispute an issue on which he will subsequently be sentenced. The judge should then impose a

---

11 [2000] 1 Cr App R (S) 105.   12 See Thomas (1979), p. 55.   13 Thomas (1979), p. 55.
14 In the Australian state of Victoria, s. 16 of the Sentencing Act 1991 lays down a general presumption that sentences should be concurrent, which is said to embody the common law: see Fox and Freiberg (1999), pp. 706–29.
15 See e.g. *Attorney General's Reference No. 89 of 1998* [2000] 1 Cr App R (S) 49.
16 (1972) 56 Cr App R 594.   17 (1982) 4 Cr App R (S) 57.

consecutive sentence, but should ensure that the 'totality of sentences is correct in all the circumstances of the case', so that the offender 'is not sentenced twice over for carrying a gun'.[18] The same principle of consecutive sentencing has been stated for cases where there is also a conviction for carrying an offensive weapon or bladed instrument,[19] but it is not clear how commonly it is applied.

The second exception concerns assaults on the police or upon others attempting to arrest the offender, and may not be a true exception. This is because, where a police officer is assaulted whilst trying to effect the arrest of someone who is in the course of committing another offence, the other offence may well be of a different type and committed against a different victim, each of which would take the case outside the concurrent principle in any event. None the less, where a case involves an unwarranted attack on lawful authority this supplies an independent reason for imposing consecutive sentences. As the Court of Appeal remarked in *Kastercum* (1972),[20] consecutive sentences are generally preferable to emphasize the gravity of assaulting the police as a means of escape.

The third exception may also not be regarded as a true exception, for the same reasons. It is that, where an offender attempts to pervert the course of justice in respect of an offence already committed, the sentence for attempting to pervert the course of justice ought to be consecutive. This was held in *Attorney General's Reference (No. 1 of 1990)*.[21] Again, it can be argued that there is a clear temporal difference between the original offence and the subsequent attempt to pervert the course of justice – in this case, while the defendant was awaiting trial – and so concurrent sentences would hardly be appropriate.

The fourth exception is along similar lines. Section 143(3) of the Criminal Justice Act 2003 provides that the fact that an offence was committed while on bail on another charge should be treated as an aggravating factor. There is a long-standing principle that this should also result in a consecutive sentence. However, it seems wrong that both principles should apply together and cumulatively: either one principle or the other should apply, but surely both should not result in enhancements of the total sentence.

8.2.4 The scope of the general principle

It has been emphasized that neither the general principle nor the four possible exceptions operate precisely, but the brief discussion shows that the choice of approach may have significant consequences for the offender and raise questions of policy.

---

18 To the same effect, *Kent* [2004] 2 Cr App R (S) 367: judge correct to pass consecutive sentence for firearms offence when sentencing for manslaughter, but total sentence reduced from 15 to 12 years.
19 *Attorney General's Reference No. 46 of 1997* [1998] 2 Cr App R (S) 338, and see the guideline decision in *Celaire and Poulton* [2003] 1 Cr App R (S) 610.
20 (1972) 56 Cr App R 298, followed in *Wellington* (1988) 10 Cr App R (S) 384.
21 (1990) 12 Cr App R (S).

Although it has been suggested that repetition of the same offence against one victim may be treated as a single transaction,[22] perhaps because it could be said that, in general, the repetition of an offence against an 'established' victim evinces less wickedness than the selection of a new victim, this is not always true and on some facts the repeated victimization of one individual may show no less wickedness.[23] Thus, if all other factors are held constant – a given number of offences committed over a given period; the nature and circumstances of violence, or the amounts involved in theft or fraud, or the degree of sexual violation – it is hard to see why the mere fact that the offences were committed against the same victim or, as the case may be, against different victims should make a substantial difference to the seriousness of the case. It is equally hard to see why the probably slight difference in overall gravity should be reflected in a decision to impose concurrent rather than consecutive sentences.

8.3 Effect of the statutory principle

The practical importance of principles for sentencing multiple offenders emerged clearly from Moxon's Crown Court survey. Some 62 per cent of all cases involved more than one offence, and 20 per cent involved other offences taken into consideration. Moreover, the number of offences for which the offender was convicted was correlated strongly to the probability of a custodial sentence: 36 per cent of those convicted on one count only received an immediate custodial sentence, rising to 48 per cent on two counts, 60 per cent on three counts and 68 per cent on four or more counts.[24]

Between 1988 and 1993 there was a succession of legislative changes relevant to sentencing for multiple offences,[25] but the law has now been settled for a decade and is incorporated into the key provisions of the Criminal Justice Act 2003. It was noted above that three key provisions in the 2003 Act apply the proportionality principle: s. 148(1) states that a community sentence should not be imposed unless the offence is serious enough to warrant such a sentence, s. 152(2) states that a custodial sentence should not be imposed unless the offence is too serious for a community sentence or a fine, and s. 153(2) states that a custodial sentence should be 'for the shortest term . . . commensurate with the seriousness of the offence'. On all three occasions, the legislation does not merely refer to the seriousness of the offence but adds 'or the combination of the offence and one or more other offences associated with it'. This means that, when considering one of the seriousness thresholds, the court may aggregate the offences for which it is passing sentence.

---

22 Thomas (1979), p. 54.
23 E.g. three successive burglaries of one elderly woman by the offender in *Rogers* [1998] 1 Cr App R (S) 402.
24 Moxon (1988), p. 9.   25 See the 3rd edn of this work at pp. 224–5.

It will be seen that, in this context, the key phrase is 'other offences associated with it'. Section 161 of the PCCS Act 2000 states that an offence is associated with another if:

(a) the offender is convicted of it in proceedings in which he is convicted of the other offence, or (although convicted of it in earlier proceedings) is sentenced for it at the same time as he is sentenced for that offence; or

(b) the offender admits the commission of it in proceedings in which he is sentenced for the other offence and requests the court to take it into consideration in sentencing him for that offence.

Paragraph (b) is a straightforward reference to offences taken into consideration, discussed in part 8.1.4 above. It is important to note that it does not extend to cases where the convictions are on specimen counts and the court wishes to impose a sentence or compensation order in respect of other offences in the alleged course of conduct. The wording of paragraph (a) also calls for careful interpretation. In w*Crawford* (1993)[26] the Court of Appeal held that when a person is sentenced for an offence committed within the operational period of a suspended sentence, the original offence for which the suspended sentence was imposed cannot be treated as an 'associated offence'. The offender is not convicted of it in the present proceedings, and neither does the court sentence him for it in the present proceedings – it merely activates a sentence already imposed. The position differs, however, where a court deals with an offender for breach of a conditional discharge and uses its power to impose a new sentence for the offence for which the conditional discharge was originally imposed. This does amount to sentencing the offender for that offence, and so it becomes an 'associated offence' within paragraph (a). This applies equally in cases where a new sentence is passed following the revocation of a community sentence.[27]

8.4 Consecutive sentences and the totality principle

Where it is appropriate to impose consecutive sentences rather than concurrent sentences, for one of the reasons suggested in part 8.2 above, the basic approach is for the court to calculate separate sentences for each of the offences and then to add them together. This could, however, lead to a high overall sentence – placing thefts alongside rape, or burglaries alongside robbery, in terms of length of custody. The courts have therefore evolved a principle which Thomas has called 'the totality principle', which requires a court to consider the overall sentence in relation to the totality of the offending and in relation to sentence levels for other crimes. Section 166 of the 2003 Act preserves the principle by stating that nothing in the Act should prevent a court, 'in the case of an offender who is convicted of one or more other offences, from mitigating his sentence by applying any rule of law as to

---

26 (1993) 14 Cr App R (S) 782.   27 See further ch. 10.6.6 below.

the totality of sentences'. Whether the principle has matured into a rule of law is a nice question, but the import of the provision is clear. What is the substance of the totality principle at common law?

8.4.1 Totality and proportionality

Early authority may be found in an unreported judgment in 1972:

> When cases of multiplicity of offences come before the court, the court must not content itself by doing the arithmetic and passing the sentence which the arithmetic produces. It must look at the totality of the criminal behaviour and ask itself what is the appropriate sentence for all the offences.[28]

The application of such a principle would clearly produce what is in effect a discount for bulk offending. If the sentencer is expected to impose a sentence which is lower than the total which has been reached by a correct assessment of the gravity of each individual offence, then it follows that the offender will receive a lower total sentence than he would have received if he had been before the court on a number of separate occasions for the same number of offences. This is strikingly demonstrated in cases where an offender asks the court to take numerous other offences into consideration, although in those cases some might justify the discount as an incentive for the offender to own up and thereby to enable the crimes to be 'cleared up'. In most cases where a multiple offender is sentenced, however, the offender is being given a discount because his total sentence appears excessive, and that is because he managed to commit so many offences before being caught.

Implicit in the principle is a rather different sense of proportionality than that commonly used. The point is not whether one type of offence is *ceteris paribus* more heinous than another; it is a question of how a series of offences, sometimes all of the same kind and sometimes of different kinds, can be brought into a conceptual scheme which relates principally to single offences. The problem is illustrated by the Court of Appeal's remarks in *Holderness*, a case described by Thomas in the following terms:

> The appellant received sentences totalling four years' imprisonment for a variety of charges, primarily motoring offences. The court stated that the sentencer had failed to 'take the step . . . of standing back and looking at the overall effect of the sentences', and that if he had done so, 'he would have at once appreciated that he was imposing the kind of sentence which is imposed for really serious crime'. The sentence was reduced to twenty-seven months.[29]

The total sentence of four years passed by the trial judge was not impugned as an aggregate of the sentences appropriate for each individual crime. What the sentencer had failed to do was to consider that total sentence in relation to other crimes which would attract such long terms of imprisonment – perhaps a single

---

28 *Barton* (1972), cited by Thomas (1979), pp. 56–7.   29 Thomas (1979), p. 58.

serious wounding or a rape. It was argued in Chapter 4 that some progress can be made towards criteria of proportionality between different types of offence. We can give reasons why a single middle-range rape is *ceteris paribus* more serious than a single middle-range burglary or a single offence of driving while disqualified. But what reasons can be given for saying that a middle-range rape is not more serious than four burglaries or nine cases of taking cars? Assuming there is agreement on what constitutes a middle-range burglary,[30] it still seems implausible merely to 'do the arithmetic' and to rest content with that. 'Doing the arithmetic' might mean that a rape is given five years, that four burglaries at 12 months each amount to four years, and that nine offences of theft from shops at four months each amount to three years. There is a feeling that any calculation which results in such a close approximation of sentences between a rape (five years) and a moderate number of burglaries or of thefts from shops goes against common sense. This feeling may lead to assertions such as 'no number of offences of taking cars can be regarded as morally so heinous as a middle-range rape' or 'no number of non-violent middle-range burglaries can be regarded as the moral equivalent of a single unprovoked serious wounding'. Yet assertions of this kind, even if acceptable, merely lay down outer limits rather than providing the hapless sentencer with guidance on the proper approach to such comparisons.

If we turn aside from the moral issue and inquire into popular judgments of the seriousness of a multiplicity of offences, the position is no clearer. Since Sellin and Wolfgang constructed their index of 'offence-seriousness' nearly thirty years ago, there have been many criticisms of their methods and assumptions, and the issue of multiple offences provides a stern testing-ground.[31] An experiment by Ken Pease and collaborators[32] suggested not merely that the popular conception of the relative severity of two rapes is not simply double that of one rape, but that two rapes might be regarded as more than twice as serious as one. This might differ according to the lapse of time between the two crimes, and whether they were committed against the same victim or separate victims. It clearly suggests that popular judgments of these matters are not straightforward.

How should a court approach the calculation when large numbers of offences have been proved or admitted? If the leading principle is to retain some overall proportionality with the seriousness of the type of offence involved, it follows that each extra offence must have a diminishing incremental effect on the overall sentence. Thus, the results of German research on the subject by Hans-Jorg Albrecht are presented by Nils Jareborg as follows:

> The average 'cost' for one burglary was 7.9 months, for three burglaries 15.6 months (97 per cent added for two more crimes), for five burglaries 22.9 months (47 per cent), for seven burglaries 24.6 months (7 per cent), and for 9 burglaries 26 months (6 per cent

---

30 In the guideline decision of *McInerney and Keating* [2003] 2 Cr App R (S) 240, above ch. 4.4.10, the Court (following SAP) described a 'standard burglary' and used this as a marker.
31 Sellin and Wolfgang (1978), Introduction, discussed in ch. 4.2 above.   32 Pease et al. (1974).

added for two more crimes). A rough norm resulting from the data indicates that the total sentence is found halfway between the punishment for the most serious crime and the sum of punishments for all the crimes. It was also apparent that the upper limit of the scale of penalties used in practice (not the statutory maximum) had a steering effect. This is strikingly similar to English Court of Appeal practice.[33]

No such study has been done in this country, and English courts are unlikely to set out the detailed calculations. But the German approach seems to fit with a rational reconstruction of cases such as *Bosanquet* (1991),[34] where the offender pleaded guilty to eight residential burglaries and three attempted burglaries, with another 59 residential burglaries taken into consideration. The Court of Appeal upheld the total sentence of four years without going into the details of the calculation. It is evident that the overriding principle was to keep the total sentence approximately within the appropriate range for burglary, and out of the ranges reserved for more serious types of offence, although incidentally this must mean that many of his burglaries had a negligible effect on the overall sentence.[35]

8.4.2 The totality principle in operation

In his discussion of the totality principle, Thomas identified two sub-principles which the Court of Appeal appears to use as a guide in this difficult area. The first is that

> the aggregate sentence should not be longer than the upper limit of the normal bracket of sentences for the category of cases in which the most serious offence committed by the offender would be placed. This formulation would allow an aggregate sentence longer than the sentence which would be passed for the most serious offence if it stood alone, but would ensure that the sentence bore some recognizable relationship to the gravity of that offence.[36]

There have been exceptional cases in which even consecutive maximum sentences have been upheld, most notoriously *Blake*,[37] but the above proposition is advanced as the general principle. It was accepted as such by the Advisory Council on the Penal System in 1978, and they went on to propose three 'ground rules' for sentencing multiple offenders. The first was that

> Sentences passed on the same occasion for a number of offences should not in total exceed the maximum that could have been imposed for the most serious of the offences, unless the criterion for exceeding the maximum is satisfied.[38]

---

33 Jareborg (1998), p. 135.   34 (1991) 12 Cr App R (S) 646.
35 Higher sentences have been given, even for individual burglaries, and the overall sentence in this
   case would probably be longer today: see ch. 4.4.10 above.
36 Thomas (1979), p. 9.
37 [1962] 2 QB 377 (three consecutive maxima of 14 years upheld for espionage).
38 ACPS (1978), para. 219.

Such an approach is undoubtedly simpler for sentencers, and it conforms to the principle of restraint in the use of custody. It is broadly similar to the approach of many continental European countries, in which courts are expected to calculate a total sentence by reference to the most serious of the offences. Thus, in German law,

> the total sentence is constructed by enhancing the severest punishment, and if different types of punishment are involved by enhancing the severest type of punishment. The construction is based on a comprehensive judgment of the offender's person and the individual offences.[39]

Whereas English courts sometimes agonize over whether to impose concurrent or consecutive sentences, the continental approach is to focus on the overall sentence – although with keen attention to doctrinal issues of concurrence when deciding what that total sentence should be.

The second sub-principle identified by Thomas was that the total sentence should not be such as to impose a crushing burden on an offender whose prospects are not hopeless – in effect, a last throwback to rehabilitation. According to Thomas, this sub-principle operated so as to allow the sentencer to give some effect to mitigating factors in reducing the total sentence, even though they have already been taken into account once. The origins of the sub-principle lie in rehabilitative notions, perhaps supported by the principle of restraint in the use of custody. It has been discussed little in recent appellate decisions, but in Austin Lovegrove's recent study it seemed to be concern for the crushing effect of the sentence on the offender rather than concern about the proportionality principle that led judges to consider the totality of the sentence.[40]

8.4.3 Totality and non-custodial sentencing

Although most of the authorities on the totality principle concern custodial sentencing, that is largely because most of the Court of Appeal's judgments in general deal with custody. Courts ought surely to have regard to the same principle when dealing with a multiplicity of less serious offences which result in either community orders or fines. The totality principle is preserved by the 2003 Act for all forms of sentence. Authority for its application to fines may be found in *Chelmsford Crown Court, ex p. Birchall* (1989).[41] Between 12 July and 19 July one year, the offender was driving his lorry between a quarry and some roadworks fulfilling a contract. Investigators found that on ten of these journeys the lorry had been overweight. Sentencing him for ten offences, a magistrates' court simply added together the fines for each of the offences, producing a total fine of £7,600. The Crown Court dismissed his appeal against sentence. The Court of Appeal held that the sentence was 'truly astonishing', in that the lower courts had simply 'applied a rigid formula to each offence' and had then added up the resulting fines to produce a total. The

39 Jareborg (1998), p. 133, summarizing s. 52 of the German Penal Code.
40 Lovegrove (2004).   41 (1989) 11 Cr App R (S) 510.

main point in the decision to reduce the fine to £1,300 was that proper account had not been taken of the offender's means, but the Court of Appeal also deprecated the failure to have regard to the totality principle.

8.4.4 Totality as a limiting principle?

The discussion thus far has followed the conventional approach, presenting the totality principle as a limiting or restraining principle bolstered by a conception of overall proportionality. However, there is some evidence that, in practice, judges do not always proceed by first calculating the appropriate sentence for each offence, then adding them together, and then reducing the total so as to arrive at a fair total. Thus, Marianne Wells, in her detailed study of sentencing for multiple offences in Western Australia, argues that many cases show a 'top-down' approach which starts with the totality principle rather than ending with it.

> The totality principle becomes the primary determinant of whether the total sentence is appropriate; considerations of whether the individual sentences are correctly calculated and rightly made cumulative [i.e. consecutive] are subsumed in the general question of whether the total sentence is appropriate.[42]

This leads her to suggest that on some occasions the principle drives the sentence rather than limiting it. Austin Lovegrove, in his detailed study, also concluded that the totality principle is determining as well as limiting in its effects.[43]

English sentencing practice seems to be variable in this respect. In *Clugston* (1992),[44] where the offender had obtained over £5,000 by some hundred deceptions yielding £50 each, the Court approved an aggregate sentence of three years' imprisonment without any mention of the appropriate sentence for each offence taken separately. On the other hand, in *Attorney General's Reference (No. 31 of 1993)*[45] the offender had been given seven separate sentences for various offences of attempted robbery, possession of firearms and possession of an offensive weapon, committed on three separate occasions. The total sentence of four years was found to be unduly lenient and the Court of Appeal, bearing in mind the double jeopardy factor, increased the sentence to seven years. In doing so, the Court stated that it had regard 'for the overall totality of the sentence', and the machinery it chose was to make the sentence on the first indictment concurrent – although, on a strict approach, it should have been consecutive. This approach appears to be quite common: the overall sentence is what is important, and the consecutive/concurrent issue is sometimes regarded as a matter of detail, or even irrelevance.[46] Thus, in some cases the principle does appear to have a limiting effect, whereas there are others, perhaps many, in which it is the starting point rather than a final constraint.

---

42 Wells (1992), p. 43.
43 Lovegrove (1997). See also Lovegrove (2004) for detailed analysis of the reasoning of judges in Victoria when sentencing multiple offenders.
44 (1992) 13 Cr App R (S) 165.   45 (1995) 16 Cr App R (S) 90.
46 For another example, see *Ebanks* [1998] 2 Cr App R (S) 339.

8.5 Multiple offenders and proportionality

The theoretical difficulties encountered in this chapter derive from the fact that both proportionality theory and much popular thinking are tied to relativities between single offences. All the detailed discussion of proportionality in Chapter 4 was concerned with individual offences. How can multiple offending be integrated into such a scheme?

The answer suggested here is that a kind of overall proportionality should be preserved. This means that, no matter how many offences of a particular kind an offender is found to have committed, the sentence should remain in the range appropriate to that type of offence. This is to some extent a pragmatic solution. It is, of course, extremely vague in its import – almost inevitably so, in view of the theoretical problems of comparing one offence with several others in a single scale of seriousness. It comes close to another pragmatic approach – that the court should normally keep within the range of sentences appropriate for the most serious offence of the group for which sentence is being passed. This was recommended in 1978 by the Advisory Council on the Penal System[47] and is similar to the approach taken in several other European countries. The choice appears to lie between two possible applications of the proportionality doctrine. As Wells argues,

> it is one thing to say that, even though all the sentences are appropriate and proportionate to the individual offences and rightly made cumulative, the total is excessive by reference to a more serious offence; it is quite another to say that, in the same circumstances, the total is excessive in relation to the total conduct involved. If the sentence is reduced because it exceeds the normal range of sentences for a more serious offence, it does not necessarily follow that the reduced sentence is proportionate to the total conduct.[48]

The present English approach adopts the former, more restrictive approach. Tony Bottoms, in a careful examination of the issues, argues that the totality principle can be justified as a rational exercise of mercy.[49] Another approach would be to conclude that, since there are arguments on both sides, it is fitting that the principle of restraint in the use of custody should decide between them.

47 See n. 38 above and accompanying text.   48 Wells (1992), p. 38.
49 Bottoms (1998), pp. 63–70.

CHAPTER 9

Custodial sentencing

The aim of this chapter is to examine the law and practice relating to custodial sentences. Imprisonment involves deprivation of liberty and is the most onerous and intrusive sentence available in this and other European countries. Deprivation of liberty and incarceration in a punitive institution require special justification. To begin that process, it is necessary to understand the practical meaning of custodial sentences. This depends on the various provisions for calculating the proportion of the nominal sentence that the offender will spend in custody, on the conditions in which prisoners are held, and on the terms on which they are later released. The chapter begins with an outline of the state of English prisons. It then considers principles and policies for the use of custodial sentences, assessing the extent to which the principle of restraint, the policy of bifurcation or a blurred approach best characterizes English sentencing. There is then an analysis of the statutory threshold for imposing custody, and also the prevailing approach to long custodial sentences, noting significant changes introduced by the 2003 Act. The chapter concludes with a brief discussion of various groups of prisoners who raise particular issues of principle.

The use of incarceration and deprivation of liberty as a punishment raises fundamental questions of social and penal policy, as well as engaging several individual rights declared by the European Convention on Human Rights. In the context of criminal justice policy, we should note that the size of the prison population is determined, to a considerable extent, by sentencing law and practice; and that both the law and sentencing practice seem to be more strongly influenced by penal policy, political strategy and media pressure than by variations in crime rates.

9.1 The state of the prisons

What have been the conditions in English prisons in recent years, and what are they likely to be in the foreseeable future? The brief survey here looks at trends in the prison population, at the prison estate and at recent problems in the prisons.

9.1.1 The prison population

There have been significant changes in the prison population during the last two decades. In 1980 it stood at a little over 42,000; by 1988 it had reached almost 50,000, but it then fell again, to a low of 40,606 in December 1992; from 1993 it rose steeply, reaching 66,000 at the end of 1999, thereafter continuing to rise more slowly to some 75,000 in April 2004 and again in April 2005. It must be borne in mind that prisons do not only hold sentenced offenders, and that the figures for the prison population include prisoners held on remand. However, the steep rise in the prison population since 1993 is almost entirely attributable to an increase in the numbers of sentenced prisoners held. In round figures, some 11,000 of the average number of 43,000 prisoners held in 1993 were on remand, whereas in 2002 the figure was 12,790 out of almost 70,000. Thus, an increasingly high proportion of the prison population – some five-sixths – consists of sentenced offenders, sent to prison by the courts.

9.1.2 The prison estate

When an offender is sentenced to custody in England and Wales, there are two administrative but critical decisions to be taken by the Prison Service. The first decision is to place the offender in one of the security classifications, from A (high risk) to D (suitable for open conditions). The security classification of each prisoner is a 'continuing responsibility' of the Prison Service,[1] and so it should be reconsidered from time to time. It is important not only because it determines the restrictiveness of the regime to which the prisoner will be subject, but also because it governs the second decision – the allocation of the prisoner to a particular establishment. There is a list of factors that should be taken into account in this allocation decision,[2] but there is inevitably a significant amount of discretion, often exercised purely on grounds of administrative convenience (i.e. available space).

According to their security classification, female offenders are sent to open or closed women's prisons or, if under 21, to a young offender institution. Male young offenders go to young offender institutions, whereas adult male prisoners may be sent to open or closed prisons, according to their security classification. Prisoners sentenced to 18 months or less may serve the whole sentence in a local prison, if they are not considered suitable for open conditions. Prisoners serving longer sentences are likely to be sent to a 'training prison'. Regimes differ considerably between local and training prisons, with fewer activities and more time locked in cells at the former. This is partly because local prisons usually hold remand prisoners, whose stay in prison may be relatively short and may involve frequent trips to and from court, and partly because local prisons tend to be overcrowded, with a consequent difficulty of

---

1   R. v. *Home Secretary, ex p. Duggan* [1994] 3 All ER 271.
2   Livingstone, Owen and Macdonald (2003), p. 147; see their ch. 4 generally on classification and allocation of prisoners.

providing adequate supervision, work etc. for all inmates. These observations are taken further in part 9.1.3 below.

Since the early 1990s there has been a substantial expansion in the prison estate. By building new prisons, extending existing institutions and contracting with private operators, governments have increased the 'certified normal accommodation' of prison service establishments from over 40,000 to over 60,000. But the rise in the number of prisoners has continued to outstrip the supply of places, and therefore the building programme has not solved some of the endemic problems of English prisons.

9.1.3 The problems of the prison system[3]

If sentences of imprisonment are to be justified, the justifications must extend not simply to depriving an offender of liberty but also to incarcerating the offender in the particular conditions that obtain in the relevant prison system. If England and Wales had a prison system that complied fully with all international standards and with the targets set for the Prison Service itself, custodial sentences would still require strong justification, as indeed the legal framework indicates. But when, as will be demonstrated, those receiving custodial sentences find themselves in the hands of a prison system that consistently falls short of both international standards and its own targets, the burden of justifying a custodial sentence is a heavy one, and the length of any sentence calls for close scrutiny.

Under prevailing public service arrangements, several 'Key Performance Indicators' are set for the Prison Service each year. It is always open to argument whether the targets are the most relevant ones, and whether each one is fair. In 2003–04 the Prison Service reported that it met its targets on reducing the number of escapes, ensuring that over 8,000 prisoners completed offending behaviour programmes, reducing the number of days lost to staff sickness, increasing the proportion of minority ethnic staff, increasing the number of prisoners achieving basic skills awards, ensuring that more prisoners have resettlement arrangements, and ensuring the timely arrival of prisoner escorts.[4] However, it also reported that it failed to meet its targets on the rate of positive drug tests, increasing the average number of hours that prisoners spend in purposeful activity, reducing overcrowding, reducing suicides, increasing the numbers completing sex offender treatment programmes, and reducing the number of serious assaults on staff. Recent reports of Her Majesty's Chief Inspector of Prisons present a similar picture of improved performance in some respects and persisting problems in other areas.

Many of the endemic problems stem from the single fact of overcrowding. As the Chief Inspector put it in her 2003–04 report, 'the levelling off of the prison population is, in reality, the difference between a manageable crisis and an unmanageable one'.[5] Some establishments have been operating at well over their certified normal

---

3 For fuller discussion, see Cavadino and Dignan (2002), chs. 6, 7 and 8, and Morgan (2002).
4 Prison Service (2004), pp. 10–11.   5 HMCI Prisons (2004), p. 7.

accommodation for several years, with a consequent strain on officers, prisoners and the regime itself. Even the figure of 'certified normal accommodation' for prison establishments as a whole cannot be relied upon, since at any one time there may be empty accommodation in some regions or in some types of establishment (e.g. open prisons) while other establishments are over-full. In 2003–04 the Chief Inspector found Leeds prison holding 1250 prisoners, some 60 per cent above its certified normal accommodation, and one wing in Cardiff prison had a certified normal accommodation of 96 but was holding 184 prisoners.[6] Thus the overcrowding of cells constructed for one person remains a feature of local prisons up and down the country, with the result that many of their inmates – some on short sentences, many on remand – have to submit to unsatisfactory conditions.

> In the worst of our overcrowded local prisons, prisoners may spend 23 hours a day in a shared cell with an unscreened toilet. The best locals are working hard to sustain standards of humanity and respect; but even they are failing to deliver the activity and resettlement opportunities that prisoners need if society is to be protected from reoffending.[7]

The European Committee for the Prevention of Torture, Inhuman and Degrading Treatment (CPT) visited four prisons in England and Wales in 2001: it observed that 'much remains to be done to achieve the objective of holding all prisoners in "a safe, decent and healthy environment"',[8] and specifically criticized the conditions under which some inmates were held two to a cell measuring 8.5 metres square or less, sometimes without properly partitioned lavatories.[9]

The reasons for the persistent overcrowding seem to involve a complex mixture of geographical demands, an excess of accommodation in open institutions, the need to close wings of some prisons in order to refurbish them, and, of course, the fact that the prison building programme has not kept pace with the number of people sent into custody. The effects of overcrowding are felt in a variety of ways, and the implications are well documented. Thus in his examination of the causes of the disturbance at Strangeways Prison, Manchester, in 1990, Lord Woolf found that

> A large proportion of the inmates were sympathetic to the instigators of the disturbance and antagonistic towards the Prison Service because of the conditions in which they were housed at the time at Strangeways . . . As the inmates repeatedly told the Inquiry, if they were treated like animals they would behave like animals. The prison was overcrowded, and the inmates provided with insufficient activities and association.[10]

The effect of overcrowding on inmate activity is obvious and troubling. In her 2003–04 report the Chief Inspector commented that 'no local prison that we inspected was able to offer enough proper work and training for its population'. The

6 HMCI Prisons (2004), p. 44.   7 HMCI Prisons (2003), p. 3.   8 CPT (2001), p. 19.
9 CPT (2001), p. 23; see also p. 45.   10 Woolf (1991), para. 3.432.

reasons included lack of funding, and lack of space and infrastructure. 'Two-thirds of prisoners at Brixton, and a third at Lincoln, had no work at all; and many of the remainder were under-occupied in routine domestic tasks.'[11] The CPT commented adversely on the poor provision of constructive activities for prisoners in its 2001 report,[12] and the Chief Inspector's observations show that this issue has still not been tackled adequately. Moreover, it is not solely a problem in local prisons: the Chief Inspector found that the provision of work and education in training prisons was far better than in local prisons, but added that 'often provision could not match demand, and too many prisoners were unemployed, or employed in mundane tasks that brought no qualifications'.[13] The Prison Service target was 'to ensure that prisoners spend on average at least 24 hours per week engaged in purposeful activity', and the out-turn was 23.2 hours.[14] A careful reading of the Chief Inspector's reports demonstrates what a low target this is – taking in both local and training prisons – and how contestable the definition of 'purposeful activity' may be.

The Prison Service reported that it exceeded its target of ensuring the completion by prisoners of offending behaviour programmes in 2003–04, and fell a little short of its target for sex offender treatment programmes. There has been much emphasis on these courses in recent years as a major step towards reducing re-offending among released prisoners. However, the Prison Service admits that 'delivery [of these programmes] on a large scale presents many challenges', and it refers to the 'disappointing evaluation' of two such programmes. The Prison Service is now said to be assessing 'what works with whom in order to optimise the impact of programmes'.[15] Thus whether a numerical target, with similar courses for virtually all prisoners, is the right approach needs to be reconsidered.

In its 2001 report the CPT commented adversely on the amount of exercise time made available to inmates in the prisons it visited: it pointed out that the relevant Prison Rule is worded flexibly, whereas 'the basic requirement of at least one hour of outdoor exercise per day is a fundamental safeguard for prisoners', and recommended that the rule should be amended.[16] It was this kind of shortcoming, allied to the overcrowding and poor sanitation arrangements, that led the CPT to classify the conditions in English prisons as 'inhuman and degrading' on its first visit in 1992.[17] We have seen that the Chief Inspector has recently commented adversely on the fact that some inmates of local prisons still spend 23 hours per day in their cells.[18] Section 6 of the Human Rights Act 1998 now requires all public authorities, including the Prison Service, to ensure that their activities comply with the European Convention on Human Rights. Of particular importance is Article 3,

---

11 HMCI Prisons (2004), p. 44.   12 CPT (2001), p. 45.
13 HMCI Prisons (2004), p. 46 (giving details of training prisons with insufficient activity). On p. 8 it is said that only 5 of the 18 training prisons inspected were providing sufficient work and education. Cf. HMCI Prisons (1997), p. 11, for similar comments some years earlier.
14 Prison Service (2004), p. 10.   15 Prison Service (2004), pp. 31–2.
16 CPT (2001), pp. 25, 45.   17 CPT (1992).
18 See n. 7 above, and accompanying text.

which prohibits torture and inhuman or degrading treatment or punishment. Article 3 itself does not set out the standards to be attained, but the European Minimum Standards do so, and the Strasbourg Court (and therefore, one surmises, the courts of this country) would be expected to refer to those standards when considering issues of inhuman or degrading treatment. The only attempt by an individual prisoner to go to Strasbourg to establish a violation of Article 3 through British prison conditions was declared inadmissible by the European Commission in 1993:[19] this was not a strong case on the basis of overcrowding, since the applicant was in solitary confinement at the time of his application and therefore not suffering the effects of overcrowding. However, the Scots courts have found a violation of Article 3 amounting to degrading treatment where a prisoner was held in a small cell with another prisoner for 20 hours a day, with slopping out, one hour's walking exercise per day and little other recreation.[20] English prisons do not have slopping out, but they do have toilets in cells and sometimes keep prisoners locked in for more than 20 hours per day.

9.2 The use of imprisonment

Before examining the law relating to custodial sentencing, it is instructive to consider the evidence on the use of imprisonment by the courts of England and Wales. How does the overall imprisonment rate relate to that of other similar countries? What kinds of offender are imprisoned, and for how long, in English prisons?

9.2.1 International comparisons

The traditional way of comparing the relative severity of different sentencing systems has been to refer to the Council of Europe's table of prisoners per 100,000 of population in various European countries, which has consistently shown the United Kingdom at or around the top in recent years. Chris Nuttall and Ken Pease have argued strongly that this table is useless as a basis for sensible comparisons:

> National differences thus calculated are impossible to interpret. They could be attributed, *inter alia*, to country differences in age profile, crime rates, clearance rates, conviction rates, judicial severity, parole differences, or any combination of these or other factors.[21]

These are important points. At present there is no method of international comparison that avoids even most of the weaknesses of the Council of Europe data. Certainly the International Bar Association's survey was no better: it did obtain indications from 'representative legal practitioners' in many countries of the

---

19 *Delazarus* v. *United Kingdom*, App No 17525/1990.
20 *Napier* v. *Scottish Ministers* [2004] UKHRR 881; the implications of the decision are discussed by Lawson and Mukherjee (2004).
21 Nuttall and Pease (1994), p. 316.

sentence range appropriate to certain test cases, but there is no reason to suppose that the sentencers in all or any of the participating countries were typical, or had recourse to objective statistics in order to confirm their indicated sentences.[22] The only way of resolving the question would be to determine whether, for certain given offences, an English court would be more likely to imprison, or likely to imprison for longer, than courts in other countries with somewhat similar demographic features. It is unlikely that this question could be resolved by resort to official statistics, since they are not sufficiently refined to draw the necessary distinctions among the types of offender coming before the courts. A proper inquiry would have to take account of differences in legal definition, the circumstances of offences, the previous record of the offender and other aggravating and mitigating factors.

It is nonetheless evident that international comparisons consistently suggest that some countries, particularly those in Scandinavia, succeed in using custody distinctly more sparingly. This raises the question whether English sentencing levels might be lowered without adverse consequences for the crime rate or, put another way, for the risk of victimization. This might be established if it were shown that two countries with similar demographic features had different rates of punitiveness in sentencing, measured by the relative uses of imprisonment for crimes of a similar nature (i.e. a similar 'crime-mix'). Such calculations are difficult to undertake if all proper precautions are taken, but a few pointers can be derived from the latest international comparisons published by the Home Office. Taking figures for 2002–03, it records that England and Wales had the second highest imprisonment rate among European Union countries, at 141 per 100,000, followed by Spain (138) and Portugal (137). Countries with which the UK is often compared economically and socially were using imprisonment at somewhat lower rates (e.g. France 93, Germany 98).[23] The general trend in almost all countries has been upwards. This is, however, a crude measure that is open to the strictures of Nuttall and Pease, cited above. The 33 per cent increase in the English prison population between 1992 and 1997 was similar to that in South Africa, Russia and the United States (three of the more punitive jurisdictions in the world), but below the 50 per cent rises in the Netherlands, Portugal and the Czech Republic. The proportion of the English prison population serving sentences below 12 months in 1997 was 15 per cent, well below that in France (29 per cent), Sweden (36 per cent), the Netherlands (37 per cent) and Norway (59 per cent), although in Portugal the proportion was only 5 per cent.

Can it be argued that more and longer prison sentences are effective in deterring criminals from offending and reoffending? One attempt to link imprisonment rates to crime rates is that of David Farrington and Patrick Langan.[24] Their argument, briefly put, is that a comparison of incarceration rates in the United States and in England and Wales between 1981 and 1986–7 shows two things. First, it shows that

---

22 Discussed by Pease (1994), pp. 121–3.   23 Walmsley (2003).
24 Farrington and Langan (1992).

the risk of conviction and imprisonment for property crimes in England declined significantly during this period, although the same risk did not decrease for crimes of violence, and the risk increased for both types of crime in the United States. Second, it shows that recorded property crimes increased significantly in England and Wales during that period, and recorded violent crimes increased only modestly, whereas in the United States recorded crime in both categories fell markedly. The analysis is constructed with care, as one would expect, but the conclusions are necessarily tentative and partial. The authors appear to wish to raise the possibility, merely, that the two trends may be connected: that crime rates are responsive to the risk of custody, so that a high-custody policy may be crime-preventive. In order to substantiate this, however, a much fuller and deeper analysis would be needed. The authors recognize that, even allowing for the fact that the comparison was confined to two countries at only two points of time, they have not investigated the machinery by which any supposed deterrent or incapacitative effect might operate. If the claim is that 'prison works' through deterring potential offenders, it would have to be found, for example, that potential property offenders in England in the early 1980s were aware of the declining risk of conviction and imprisonment and that this affected their decision-making. In fact, what the Farrington and Langan studies show is that there is a significant link between the certainty of punishment and offending rates, but not between the severity of punishment and offending rates.[25] If the claim is that 'prison works' through incapacitating a considerable number of offenders, it is important to examine that claim in the context of the fact that only some 3 per cent of offenders in any one year go to court, and an even smaller percentage go to prison. In the absence of a clear causal link, it is best to keep faith with the reports from the US National Academy of Sciences which argue that any incapacitative effects are likely to be marginal.

What about the incapacitative effect of holding more offenders in English prisons? The figures are inevitably dominated by high-volume offences such as theft rather than the offences from which people most want protection.[26] Some would argue that the cause-and-effect claim could be made quite simply by looking at the decline in recorded crime: have we not witnessed a plain demonstration of the hydraulic effect, with more people in prison resulting in less crime in society? Between 1997 and 2002 the sentenced prison population increased from 48,412 to 71,498;[27] between 1997 and 2002 the British Crime Survey showed a 25 per cent fall in crimes committed, although that decrease has slowed in recent years.[28] Does this not show that the high imprisonment policy has worked? No: as suggested above, the

25 See the searching discussion of the Farrington-Langan studies by von Hirsch et al. (1999), pp. 25–8.
26 The Halliday report (2001, p. 130) stated that around 10,000 more prisoners would be needed to reduce the incidence of crime by 1 per cent. The Carter review (2003, p. 16) concluded that the increase in the prison population since 1997 might have reduced crime by 5 per cent, adding: 'the fall in the number of young people over the same period is estimated to have reduced crime by a similar amount'.
27 Prison Service (2003). In early 2005 the prison population exceeded 75,000.
28 Home Office Statistical Bulletin 07/03, p. 26 and Table 3.01.

Table 12. *Sentenced prison population*

Offence	Males			Females		
	1982	1992	2002	1982	1992	2002
Rape	561	1,582	2,918	1	2	5
Burglary	10,855	5,349	8,922	82	51	230
Robbery	2,504	4,174	7,197	50	56	310
Theft etc.	7,913	3,710	4,282	402	243	462
Drugs	905	2,899	8,724	90	259	1,331
Sentenced total	35,011	34,389	53,967	989	1,175	3,339

Source: Based on Prison Statistics 2002, Table 1.6.

simple inference cannot be drawn.[29] There is probably a small incapacitation effect, but the crime rate began to decline before the steep rise in imprisonment, there has also been a decline in the number of young people in society (the most crime-prone age group), and international comparisons show declines in crime rates in recent years in countries where the use of imprisonment has not escalated.[30]

9.2.2 The courts and custodial sentencing

Trends in custodial sentencing have an impact on the prison population in two ways – in terms of the number of custodial sentences handed down by the courts, and in terms of the length of those sentences. In addition, as elaborated in part 9.5 below, the provisions for early release of prisoners affect the numbers in prison.

The composition of the sentenced prison population has changed markedly in the last two decades. As the figures in Table 12 demonstrate, in 1982 and in 1992 the total numbers were the same but there had been significant shifts away from persons sentenced for burglary or for theft towards people imprisoned for serious sexual offences and drugs offences. For males, the 2002 figures show that the numbers serving prison sentences for burglary and for theft remain below the 1982 levels, but that there have been significant increases in every other group. In 2002 there were almost six times as many rapists and nine times as many drug offenders in prison as 20 years earlier. Between 1992 and 2002 there was a more than 50 per cent rise in the male sentenced prison population, with drug offenders, burglars and robbers showing particularly high rates of increase. The female sentenced prison population almost trebled between 1992 and 2002, with the same three groups of offenders (drugs, burglars and robbers) leading the way.

The steep increases between 1992 and 2002 reflect both a proportionately higher use of imprisonment by the Crown Court and by magistrates' courts, and a tendency to give longer sentences, particularly in the Crown Court. Thus the percentage

---

29 See nn. 21–23 above.   30 Tonry (2004), ch. 3.

Table 13. *Prison population by length of sentence*

Sentence length	Males		Females	
	1992	2002	1992	2002
Up to 6 months	3,465	5,139	156	425
6+ to 12 months	3,544	3,763	145	327
1+ to 3 years	11,567	14,656	368	1,007
3+ to 5 years	5,822	13,040	186	765
5+ to 10 years	5,710	9,773	202	539
10+ years	1,377	2,614	22	111
Life	2,904	4,982	96	165
Total	34,389	53,967	1,175	3,339

Source: Based on Prison Statistics 2002, Table 1.6.

of adults aged 21 and over sent to prison by magistrates' courts increased from 5 per cent in 1992 to 18 per cent in 2002, perhaps reflecting the more serious nature of the cases sentenced,[31] and for the Crown Court the rise was from 47 to 66 per cent. For the same group, average sentences remain about the same in magistrates' courts (2.5 months in 2002), but average sentences in the Crown Court are now one-third longer, having increased from 21.1 months in 1992 to 27.8 months in 2002.[32]

The changing profile of the prison population can be seen from Table 13, which shows a particularly sharp rise in medium- and long-term prisoners, both males and females. The numbers of female prisoners in each category have doubled and sometimes trebled. For males there was also a significant (50 per cent) increase in those serving sentences of up to six months. However, if we focus on the sentencing practices of the courts by considering receptions into prison (rather than the average population), the figures show that by far the largest increase between 1991 and 2001 was in offenders sentenced to less than 12 months (increased by a factor of one-and-a-half).[33] One suggestion is that significant numbers of 'those who previously might have been given a community penalty are now serving short prison sentences', which might explain why there has been such an increase in prisoners serving up to six months, why the average length of magistrates' sentences has not increased, and why the average increase in Crown Court sentence length is less than might have been expected.[34] Table 13 also shows that the numbers serving over six months and up to three years have increased modestly; but it is the number of prisoners sentenced to three years or longer who have swelled the prison population – more

31 Although the proportionate use of custody by magistrates' courts for driving while disqualified, a summary offence, rose from 18 per cent in 1991 to 47 per cent in 2001, which suggests a change of policy rather than a change in clientele: Hough et al. (2003), p. 13.
32 *Criminal Statistics 2002*, ch. 4.   33 See Hough et al. (2003), p. 14.
34 Hough et al. (2003), p. 13.

than double the prisoners serving sentences between 3 and 10 years than a decade ago, and almost the same degree of increase in those serving 10 years or over.

The particular problems of women prisoners are discussed in part 9.6.2 below, where some demographic features of the prison population are examined in greater detail.

9.3 Principles for the use of custodial sentences

The above discussion of the problems of the prison system draws attention to the conditions in which English prisoners may serve their sentences. The fact that these conditions sometimes (or often) fall short of international standards makes it necessary to seek even stronger justifications for imposing a prison sentence,[35] and add weight to the principle of restraint in the use of custody. As we saw in Chapter 3.3.2, there is now widespread international assent to the principle of restraint in the use of imprisonment. Resolution VIII of the Eighth United Nations Congress on the Prevention of Crime and the Treatment of Offenders (1990) states in paragraph 5(e) that 'imprisonment should be used as a sanction of last resort'. The Council of Europe has likewise declared a policy of encouraging the use of non-custodial sentences and reserving custodial sentences for the most serious types of offence.[36] However, the international survey by Dirk van Zyl Smit and Frieder Dünkel demonstrates the continuing centrality of imprisonment to the sentencing policy of most nations:

> The sentence of imprisonment remains the backbone of the system of penal sanctions – in spite of repeated proclamations at international congresses and in resolutions of the United Nations and the Council of Europe and other regional bodies that imprisonment should be seen solely as an *ultima ratio*. Alternatives to imprisonment continue in most countries to derive their credibility from the residual function of imprisonment, which, in as far as the death penalty has been abolished, is the most serious reaction to conduct that is seen as particularly dangerous to society or that repeatedly contravenes the law. This is strikingly demonstrated by the threat of imprisonment being used as the primary sanction for infringement of conditions of probation or the failure to pay a fine.[37]

Increases in the use of imprisonment are often policy choices rather than responses to objectively demonstrable rises in crime rates, and they may be policy choices of other agencies (such as the police and prosecutors) and not just the courts.[38] In England and Wales the official policies are somewhat diverse (some would say, confused). During the second part of the 1990s Michael Howard, as Home Secretary, pronounced that 'prison works', and his successors, Jack Straw and David Blunkett, continued an expansionist prison policy.[39] However, as will be argued below, there are also recent statements and policies that favour

---

35 See Kleinig (1998) on related issues.   36 Council of Europe (1992).
37 Van Zyl Smit and Dünkel (2001), p. 796.
38 For such an explanation of recent rises in imprisonment in Germany, see Suhling (2003).
39 For the politics of 'prison works', see Windlesham (1996), ch. 4; see further Morgan (2002), and Cavadino and Dignan (2002), ch. 6.

bifurcation – pursuing restraint in the use of custody in some less serious cases, but more substantial use of custody in more serious cases; and consequently there are many, in the courts and elsewhere, who complain of 'mixed messages' from the government. The establishment of the Youth Justice Board in 1999 has exerted some unifying effect on policy and practice in respect of young offenders. Whether the setting up of the National Offender Management Service (NOMS), to provide an integrated system encompassing prisons and community sanctions, brings greater clarity and constancy of purpose – as well as real improvements in practice, particularly in the prisons – remains to be tested.

9.3.1 Justifying restraint in the use of custody

The true principle of restraint in the use of custody is one which argues for the use of non-custodial sentences instead of custodial ones, and which argues for shorter custodial sentences instead of longer ones. The UN declaration (above), which refers to imprisonment as a sanction of last resort, is an inferior formulation because it implies that custody may justifiably be used for someone who persistently commits minor offences, and for whom other measures have been tried. Brief consideration is given here to three justifications for the principle of restraint – doubts about the reformative potential of custody, doubts about its individual deterrent effect, and humanitarian concerns.

(i) Doubts about the rehabilitative potential of penal institutions. In the 1930s Alexander Paterson, one of the most influential of Prison Commissioners, declared that 'it is impossible to train men for freedom in a condition of captivity'. By 1977 the mood of scepticism, encouraged by the works of criminologists,[40] had found its way into the official publication *Prisons and the Prisoner*:

> Experience in recent years has led increasingly to scepticism about the compatibility of rehabilitation in this traditional, paternalistic form with the practicalities of day-to-day life in custody. The coercion which is inherent in a custodial sentence and the very nature of 'total institutions' tend to direct the whole of the inmates' individual and group energies towards adjustment to the austerely unnatural conditions; towards alienation from authority; and thus towards rejection of any rehabilitative goals towards which the staff may be working.[41]

Important as it was to attempt to devise constructive regimes and to give prison staff a sense of purpose, the air of resignation in official publications continued and perhaps reached its zenith in 1990 when a White Paper argued that prison 'can be an expensive way of making bad people worse'.[42] Whether and to what extent the experience of imprisonment makes offenders worse may be difficult to establish; but such factors as loss of employment, loss of housing, loss of contact with family, increased financial problems and possible deterioration in physical and mental

40 For the then research, see Hood and Sparks (1970), ch. 8.
41 Home Office (1977), para. 17.   42 Home Office (1990), para. 2.7.

health must all be taken into account.[43] For many years the reconviction figures for released prisoners have been poor. It may be true that most of those who enter custody have previous convictions, many of them having several. But a comparative survey of reconviction rates following various types of sentence, which took account of age, type of offence and previous record, found that custodial sentences performed slightly worse than expected for all offenders other than the few first offenders. In general terms, the proportion reconvicted within two years of release was 54 per cent for prison, 49 per cent for community service, 42 per cent for 'straight' probation and 63 per cent for probation with additional requirements.[44]

A few years ago a decision was taken to try to reverse this position, and to take advantage of the findings of the 'What Works' movement to devise programmes for prisoners that would reduce reoffending. The Prison Service had a target of 8,444 prisoners completing offending behaviour programmes in 2003–04, and some 9,169 prisoners actually completed such programmes. As noted earlier, the Prison Service recognizes that the evaluations of these programmes have not yet produced evidence of reductions in reoffending.[45] The target of NOMS for 2004–05 is the lower figure of '7,000 offender behaviour programmes completed by prisoners, including 5,490 living skill programmes and 1,100 sex offender programmes in public prisons, and 330 living skills programmes and 80 sex offender treatment programmes in contracted prisons'.[46] On the basis of a review of English and US research studies, it has been claimed that

> evaluation surveys confirm a realistic approach that, on the one hand, does not deny the serious problems of offender rehabilitation, especially under the conditions of closed institutions, but, on the other hand, recognizes the opportunities for effective intervention that can be provided by prison authorities.[47]

However, as the Prison Service is finding, to expect good results from implementing such programmes in the conditions obtaining in the English prison system may be unrealistic. A review by Colin Roberts of three evaluations of offending behaviour programmes in prisons shows that the promising results of the first phase, in the mid-1990s, have not been maintained in later years, and that there were mixed results in one-year and two-year reconviction studies. Roberts suggests that, if there has been a downturn in effectivensss, this may be explained by the enthusiasm of the staff and the volunteers in the early programmes compared with the much-expanded programmes now delivered.[48] More prosaically, the Prison Service also offers various detoxification and drug intervention programmes to prisoners, but the Chief Inspector has commented on their 'patchy' provision and on the counter-effects of the availability of drugs in many institutions.[49] In the prison conditions that

43 Social Exclusion Unit (2002).   44 Lloyd, Mair and Hough (1994).
45 Prison Service (2004), pp. 31–2.   46 NOMS (2004).
47 Van Zyl Smit and Dünkel (2001), p. 823.
48 Roberts, C. (2004), pp. 136–42; see also Wilkinson (2005).
49 HMCI Prisons (2004), p. 8.

currently obtain in England and Wales, therefore, doubts about the rehabilitative potential of penal institutions are well grounded.

(ii) Doubts about the preventive effect of custody. When Mr Howard was Home Secretary, from 1993 to 1997, he proclaimed that 'prison works'. This could hardly stand as a reference to deterrence or to rehabilitation, since the reconviction figures within two years give no cause for encouragement in that respect – nor do the figures for desistance from crime in the 10 years following release.[50] It may be true to say that 'prison works' in that it succeeds in incapacitating almost all prisoners (except the very few who escape) for the duration of their sentences. But this hardly seems a persuasive basis for penal policy, since (i) it is a short-sighted kind of effectiveness when so many of the prisoners then reoffend on release; (ii) it is also short-sighted if there is little possibility of innovative schemes for prisoners, especially in the context of considerable overcrowding in local prisons; and (iii) the impact of keeping these offenders in prison is slight in terms of additional security for the ordinary citizen since, as we saw in Chapter 1.4, fewer than 3 per cent of offences result in conviction, and many of those are not sentenced to imprisonment. It follows that the threat to a citizen's safety and security is not likely to be diminished significantly by imprisoning 70,000 rather than 40,000 people. When in the United States the National Academy of Sciences investigated the incapacitative effect of imprisonment on the crime rate, they found it to be marginal. The Halliday report reached the same conclusion.[51] There is also little evidence of any general deterrent effect from greater use of custody.[52] It is therefore clear that the preventive effects of custody are frequently overestimated.

(iii) Human rights and humanitarian concerns. It is simply not acceptable for state institutions to operate in violation of human rights. There is already plenty of evidence, in reports from the CPT, that English penal establishments fall below international standards in several respects. It will take individual cases to determine whether breaches are taking place, and a Scots decision finding a violation was noted above.[53] The former Chief Inspector of Prisons took the UN *Basic Principles for the Treatment of Prisoners* (1990) as a benchmark for assessing the acceptability of English prison conditions,[54] and the government ought to take much more seriously the task of ensuring that proper minimum standards are achieved (and surpassed) in the prisons. To the extent that they are not, this may be a reason for closing certain institutions. It is certainly a strong argument for reducing the number of people sent to prison and the length of their sentences.

Greater weight is sometimes placed on a related argument, that imprisonment should be used less because the prisons are overcrowded. There is some logic in this: a given number of months incarcerated in overcrowded conditions may be as

---

50 See Burnett and Maruna (2004), tracing the careers of some 130 offenders released in 1992, on whose reactions to prison Mr Howard had originally placed reliance.
51 Halliday (2001), Appendix 3.
52 Von Hirsch, Bottoms, Burney and Wikstrom (1999); Halliday (2001).
53 Above n. 20 and accompanying text.   54 HMCI Prisons (1997).

punitive as a longer period in less unpleasant conditions.[55] But it shares with the human rights argument a temporary dimension. Overcrowding could be removed by a massive programme of prison building. This, however, would be the opposite of restraint in the use of custody. If, for example, the government were to commit itself to provide 100,000 prison places in conditions that fulfil international standards and human rights, the present arguments would be met but the principle of restraint in the use of custody would be undermined rather than advanced. In practice, the human rights and overcrowding arguments ought to have considerable purchase in England and Wales at present because there is no immediate prospect of significant improvement. But their limitations should not be overlooked.

A more durable line of reasoning stems from the inevitable pains of imprisonment. Custody entails a deprivation of freedom of movement, which is one of the most basic rights, and often involves considerable 'hard treatment'.[56] Loss of liberty takes away the freedom to associate with one's family and friends, and separates one from home and private life as well as from open society. Prison is therefore a severe restriction on ordinary human liberties, far above those imposed by most non-custodial sentences. And that restriction of liberties impinges not just on the offender but also on the offender's family and dependants. These considerations suggest that custody should not be used without some special reasons, and should be reserved for the most serious cases of lawbreaking. In particular, they suggest that custody should not simply be seen as the top rung of a ladder which starts with discharges and runs upwards through fines and community penalties. The imposition of a custodial sentence restricts liberty to a far greater degree than any other sentence, and for that reason should require special justification.

9.3.2 Bifurcation or mixed messages?

Home Office policy in recent years seems consistent with the idea of bifurcated responses to offending, commending long sentences for serious offenders and a reduction in sentence severity for minor offenders:

> Custody has an important role to play in punishing offenders and protecting the public. But it is an expensive resource which should be focused on dangerous, serious and seriously persistent offenders and those who have consistently breached community sentences... For those who are not serious, dangerous or seriously persistent offenders, we need to provide a genuine third option to sentencers in addition to custody and community punishment. For this reason we will introduce new and reformed sentences that combine community and custodial sentences.[57]

The then Home Secretary also put his name to a joint press release with the Lord Chancellor calling for the greater use of community sentences for non-violent

---

55 See the reasoning in *Upton* (1980) 71 Cr App R 102, *Mills* [2002] 2 Cr App R (S) 229 at p. 233 ('in a borderline case . . . it is very important that those who have responsibilities for sentencing take into account the overcrowding in women's prisons'), and *Kefford* [2002] 2 Cr App R (S) 495 at p. 497 ('the courts must accept the realities of the situation', i.e. overcrowding).
56 Kleinig (1998).   57 Home Office (2002), paras. 5.6–5.7.

offences,[58] and in his response to the Carter review referred to 'diverting from prison minor offenders for whom a very short stay in prison serves little purpose'.[59] However, these parts of the government's message are rarely given prominence in public speeches, where the focus is usually on long prison sentences in the name of public protection. This creates the risk that the policy of bifurcation will give greater weight to one of the 'twin tracks' than the other. Moreover, the boundary between the two is also likely to be put under even more pressure by the graduated severity of sentences that will be imposed on persistent offenders, in the absence of any proportionality constraint.[60]

Bifurcation quickly translates into blurring if there is an element of looseness in fixing the boundary between the two tracks, and this is evident in other events of recent years. It is perhaps not surprising that several of the sentencers interviewed by Hough, Jacobson and Millie complained about 'mixed messages' from both politicians and the senior judiciary.[61] In 2002 Lord Woolf called for stronger deterrent sentences against street robbers,[62] and then for less use of custody for economic crimes, especially when committed by women.[63] However, even if there was a clear distinction between violent offences (robbery) and non-violent offences ('economic crimes'), that was thought to have been put in doubt when Lord Woolf departed from SAP's proposed sentencing levels on domestic burglary by calling for the greater use of community sentences for certain first- and second-time burglars.[64] That judgment drew strong criticism from Mr Blunkett as Home Secretary, from sections of the media and from some sentencers.[65] Less publicity was accorded to the fact that the foundation stone for Lord Woolf's argument that public protection would be improved rather than reduced by giving fewer custodial sentences to first- and second-time burglars was a report from the government's own Social Exclusion Unit that spelt out the shortcomings of imprisonment as a form of public protection, criticizing it as expensive and counter-productive.[66] What this public disagreement shows is that the positioning of the two tracks of bifurcation policy is open to debate, and that often politicians may be more interested in making political capital out of an issue than of spelling out the reasons for their policy. If imprisonment policy really is one of bifurcation, then Home Secretaries should be willing openly to support the principle of restraint in the use of custody for cases falling within the lower of the two tracks. Interestingly, a research project by Bottoms and Wilson into public attitudes was able to include a question directly about Lord

---

58 Lord Chancellor's Department (2002).
59 Home Office (2004), para. 23; paras. 18–19 refer, without approval, to the rising severity of sentencing in the previous decade.
60 See above, ch. 6.3.   61 Hough et al. (2003), p. 53.
62 Attorney General's Reference Nos. 4 and 7 of 2002; and Q [2002] 2 Cr App R (S) 345.
63 In Mills and in Kefford, above, n. 55. Cf the detailed deconstruction of the Mills judgment in part 6(b) below.
64 McInerney and Keating [2003] 2 Cr App R (S) 240.
65 Charted in Davies and Tyrer (2003).
66 McInerney and Keating [2003] 2 Cr App R (S) 240, at pp. 256–8, quoting from Social Exclusion Unit (2002).

Woolf's burglary guidelines, and some 70 per cent of the responses supported his approach.[67] The research was conducted in Sheffield, the city often referred to by the then Home Secretary, Mr Blunkett, as his barometer on crime. Once again, careful research demonstrates differences between the true opinions of the public, and those voiced by politicians and the media.

9.4 The custody threshold and short custodial sentences

In part 9.3.2 above we considered the evidence for the proposition that the government's prison policy is one of bifurcation, preserving a strong response to serious offences and 'dangerous' offenders but seeking a reduction in the use of custody for less serious offences. We have noted that the White Paper of 2002 stated that 'for those who are not serious, dangerous or seriously persistent offenders, we need to provide a genuine third option to sentencers in addition to custody and community punishment'.[68] Part of the strategy is to introduce a new 'customized community sentence', discussed further in Chapter 10 below. Another part of the strategy is to introduce three new forms of short custodial sentence, for those offenders for whom 'short prison sentences will continue to be appropriate'. A fundamental problem with the pre-2003 Act regime of short sentences was that there was no element of supervision: prisoners serving less than 12 months were released after serving half the nominal term, but without proper support. The new strategy is to emphasize 'our overall aim of reducing reoffending' by ensuring that offenders on short sentences 'have proper support, supervision and follow-through of education programmes, drug treatment and anger management schemes in the community'.[69] This is to be achieved by creating three new forms of sentence – the suspended sentence, intermittent custody, and custody plus. These are examined below, after the primary legislative provision has been considered.

9.4.1 The custody threshold

Section 152(2) of the Criminal Justice Act 2003 provides:

> The court must not pass a custodial sentence unless it is of the opinion that the offence, or the combination of the offence and one or more offences associated with it, was so serious that neither a fine alone nor a community sentence can be justified for the offence.

This is very similar to the wording of s. 1(2)(a) of the 1991 Act,[70] save that 'must' has been substituted for 'shall', and that the closing phrase was formerly 'so serious that only such a sentence [i.e. custody] can be justified', whereas now a court ought to consider whether a fine or a community sentence could be justified. Only if the

---

67 Bottoms and Wilson (2004), pp. 394–5.
68 Home Office (2002), para. 5.7.   69 Home Office (2002), paras. 5.22–5.23.
70 Broadly speaking, an offence is 'associated with' the current offence if it is one for which the court is passing sentence on the same occasion: *Baverstock* (1993) 14 Cr App R (S) 471, *Godfrey* (1993) 14 Cr App R (S) 804.

court concludes that the case is too serious for either of those measures is a custodial sentence lawful.

How will the courts deal with this provision? Under the 1991 Act the Court of Appeal initially adopted the test of whether 'right-thinking members of the public, knowing all the facts, [would] feel that justice had not been done by the passing of any sentence other than a custodial one'.[71] This was strenuously attacked as vague and inappropriate,[72] and in dealing with a number of appeals against short custodial sentences in *Howells* (1999), Lord Bingham CJ recognized the force of these and other criticisms:

> it cannot be said that the 'right-thinking members of the public' test is very helpful, since the sentencing court has no means of ascertaining the views of right-thinking members of the public and inevitably attributes to such right-thinking members its own views ...
> In the end, the sentencing court is bound to give effect to its own subjective judgment of what justice requires on the peculiar facts of the case before it.[73]

However, Lord Bingham went on to argue that there is no bright line indicating the custody threshold, and in offering guidance to courts he merely listed familiar aggravating and mitigating circumstances that courts should take into account – premeditation, provocation, previous convictions, guilty plea and so forth. It was noted above that there are several judicial pronouncements on the need to reserve custody for serious cases and, where it is thought inevitable, to make sentences as short as possible, particularly for women and for those convicted of 'economic' offences.[74] The joint statement from the Home Secretary and Lord Chancellor in 2002 affirmed the importance of prison sentences for 'serious and violent crime' but then also referred to 'the need to keep prison as a last resort in other cases'. Short custodial sentences were criticized on the ground that they

> provide little opportunity to tackle reoffending and indeed can often make things worse – disrupting family and work life while putting offenders who have committed relatively minor crimes in the company of more serious offenders . . . For those who do not need to be in custody, the National Probation Service, with its central focus on reducing reoffending, means that rigorously enforced community based sentences offer a real and tough alternative.[75]

The Sentencing Guidelines Council has sought to reinforce the purpose of s. 152(2) by emphasizing two principles:

- the clear intention of the threshold test is to reserve prison as a punishment for the most serious offences;
- passing the custody threshold does *not* mean that a custodial sentence should be deemed inevitable, and custody can still be avoided in the light of personal

---

71 The test was originally laid down by Lawton LJ in *Bradbourn* (1985) 7 Cr App R (S) 180, and applied to the 1991 Act in *Cox* (1993) 14 Cr App R (S) 479.
72 Ashworth and von Hirsch (1997).   73 [1999] 1 Cr App R (S) 335 at p. 337.
74 See e.g. *Mills* and *Kefford* (both above, n. 55), per Lord Woolf CJ.
75 Lord Chancellor's Department (2002).

mitigation or where there is a suitable intervention in the community which provides sufficient restriction (by way of punishment) while addressing the rehabilitation of the offender to prevent future crime. For example, a prolific offender who
currently could expect a short custodial sentence . . . might more appropriately
receive a suitable community sentence.[76]

The import of the new legislation on the custody threshold is therefore fairly clear.
Custody should be used more sparingly, especially for 'economic' offences and for
women. The figures for receptions into prison under sentence show, however, that
the largest category remains 'theft and handling' (almost 16,000 in 2002), followed
by 'motoring offences' (12,000 in 2002, including drink-driving).[77] Moreover, even
in cases that do cross the threshold into custody, mitigating factors may have the
result in bringing the sentence back 'below the line'. This was the message of the
leading case under the 1991 Act, *Cox* (1993),[78] where the offender's relative youth
and the fact that he had only one previous conviction combined to bring the sentence
for an offence that passed the custody threshold down to a community penalty. It is
also clear from the guideline on reduction of sentence for guilty plea that a timely
plea of guilty may, in appropriate cases, be accorded the effect of reducing a custodial
sentence to a non-custodial one.[79]

There remains an abiding difficulty, however, in identifying where the threshold
should fall. In *Verdi* (2005)[80] the Court of Appeal held that a deterrent sentence of
18 months was appropriate for a youth of 18 who pleaded guilty to nine offences of
spraying graffiti on London Underground trains, offences described as 'an unpleasant nuisance' which each year cost the train operators some £10 million for cleaning.
In *Stephens* (2002)[81] a man admitted 'chipping' mobile telephones as a means of
defrauding the service providers of money for calls made. The Court of Appeal
reduced the sentence from 18 to 12 months on an early guilty plea, but the question
is whether an 'economic' offence of this kind justifies such a sentence. In *Seymour*
(2002)[82] the offender was convicted of obtaining £3,000 by deception from a householder by pretending that roofing work had been carried out when it had not. The
Court of Appeal upheld the sentence of 15 months for this 'economic' offence. Are
cases like this so far above the custody threshold?

The sentencing research by Hough, Jacobson and Millie took the custody threshold as its particular focus. They found no consistent differences in the types of offence
that fell either side of the custody threshold, but they did find particular factors that
'tipped the decision one way or the other'.[83] For decisions resulting in custody, it
was the intrinsic seriousness of the offence or the offender's record of convictions

---

76 SGC, *Overarching Principles: Seriousness* (2004), para. 1.32.
77 Prison Statistics 2002, Table 4.5.   78 (1993) 14 Cr App R (S) 479.
79 SGC, *Reduction in Sentence for a Guilty Plea* (2004), para. 2.6, discussed in ch. 5.4.1 above.
80 [2005] 1 Cr App R (S) 197.   81 [2002] 2 Cr App R (S) 291.
82 [2002] 2 Cr App R (S) 442.
83 Hough et al. (2003), pp. 36–8. This finding is significant when interpreting the study by Davies
   and Tyrer (2003), which suggests more punitive attitudes but leaves mitigating factors largely out
   of account.

or breaches that appeared to dominate. For cases resulting in a non-custodial disposal, a whole range of mitigating factors seemed capable of swaying the decision – remorse, guilty plea, motivation to address underlying personal problems, family responsibilities, good employment record or prospects and a previous good record. Often the assessment of these mitigating factors came down to a moral judgment of the offender, making the sentencing process 'highly subjective'.[84]

In the face of findings such as these, there is a considerable challenge for sentencing guidelines. Efforts have been made in some recent guidelines to give some indications about the positioning of the custody threshold,[85] but a recent judgment from the Court of Appeal – not based on proposals from the Sentencing Advisory Panel or the Council – demonstrates the problem. In *Page* (2004)[86] the Court gave little consideration to the interplay of the various aggravating and mitigating factors, and contemplated a short custodial sentence for a persistent minor offender. The Court stated that shoplifting was a classic offence for which custody should be the last resort, but it has often been pointed out that this is not a propitious formula.[87] Using custody as a 'last resort' may mean using it because the offender has previously experienced other forms of sentence, whereas custody ought to be reserved for serious offences. The Council was wise to avoid the 'last resort' principle in its guideline on s. 152(2). More than one-quarter of women sentenced to custody in 2002 were sentenced for theft from a shop, which surely suggests that the processes of reasoning in these cases (as revealed by the Hough, Jacobson and Millie research) require attention. More immediately, a downturn in the use of custody ought to result if the SGC's guideline on s. 152(2) is closely followed. Certainly the new statutory provision requires courts to consider whether a fine or a community sentence is sufficient to deal with the case. But it is more likely that attention will focus, not on the small changes of wording embodied in s. 152(2), but on the introduction of the three new measures to be considered below.

9.4.2 The suspended sentence

The first of the three new custodial sentences of 51 weeks or less is the suspended sentence. It may look odd to discuss this first, since its effect is that the offender does not go into custody, but the shape of the new legislation makes this the logical starting point. As we shall see, the principal custodial sentence of 51 weeks or less is 'custody plus'; but that should not be imposed if a sentence of intermittent custody can be justified; and that should not be imposed if a suspended sentence can be justified. Moreover, none of the three sentences should be imposed unless s. 152(2) is satisfied. So the discussion here started with an analysis of s. 152(2),

---

84 Hough et al. (2003), p. 41; cf. the discussion in ch. 5.5 above.
85 E.g. *Oliver* [2003] 2 Cr App R (S) 64 at p. 72, on indecent photographs of children; *Webbe* [2002] 1 Cr App R (S) 82, on handling stolen goods.
86 8 Dec. 2004, with Rose LJ presiding.
87 In previous editions of this work; see also Hough et al. (2003), p. 36.

requiring courts to consider whether a fine alone or a community sentence will suffice to deal with the case. Assuming that that threshold has been passed, and that there are insufficient mitigating factors to bring the case below the threshold, the court must then turn its attention to the appropriateness of a suspended sentence.

According to s. 189 of the 2003 Act, the term of imprisonment to be suspended must be between 28 and 51 weeks, and it seems to follow that the court must be satisfied that the offence(s) it is dealing with warrant(s) a custodial term of that length. When a court imposes a suspended sentence it may order the offender to comply, during the 'supervision period', with one or more of the requirements listed in s. 190 – essentially a list of 12 possible requirements, each of which can also form part of a community sentence.[88] The operational period (i.e. of the suspension) should be between six months and two years, and the supervision period (within which the requirements take effect) must not be longer than the operational period. The offender is liable to be ordered to serve the term of imprisonment if either there is non-compliance with a requirement during the supervision period, or the offender commits an offence during the operational period. There are new provisions for the periodic review of a suspended sentence, when the court may assess the offender's progress (ss. 191–192). An offender who breaches a community requirement should normally be given a warning on the first occasion, and then brought to court on the second. There are detailed provisions for dealing with breaches of suspended sentences in Schedule 12 of the 2003 Act. Essentially, paragraph 8(2) provides that the court must order the custodial term to take effect, either in whole or in part, unless it concludes that it would be unjust to do so, in which case there are powers to amend the order in various ways.

The Sentencing Guidelines Council has issued a guideline that encompasses the suspended sentence. It is important to recall that the suspended sentence has been part of English sentencing law since 1967, in some shape or form, and that its history is not one of unmitigated success. One long-standing complaint is that it has been regarded as a let-off, with no serious consequences for many offenders, and this factor has certainly been tackled by the new legislation. It will be expected that a court will add community requirements to the sentence, and so it will be a demanding sentence in its own right, even apart from the suspension of the prison sentence. On the other hand, the Council is concerned that the requirements should not be too onerous:

> Because of the clear deterrent threat involved in a suspended sentence, requirements imposed as part of that sentence should generally be less onerous than those imposed as part of a community sentence. A court wishing to impose onerous or intensive requirements on an offender should reconsider its decision to suspend sentence and consider whether a community sentence might be more appropriate.[89]

---

88 For this reason the details are discussed in ch. 10.6 below.
89 SGC, *New Sentences: Criminal Justice Act 2003* (2004), para. 2.2.14.

Another criticism of the suspended sentence has been its use in cases where an immediate custodial sentence would not be justified. As Bottoms showed, ever since its introduction there has been a conflict between the official aim of the suspended sentence, avoiding prison, and the way in which many sentencers regard it – the sword of Damocles.[90] In other words, there has always been a body of opinion among sentencers to the effect that the suspended sentence is merely another non-custodial sentence with a sharper threat to it, and not in any real sense a custodial sentence. Against this background, it is hardly surprising that in the early days suspended sentences were imposed in large numbers, some of them were breached, and in the event the hoped-for reduction in the prison population failed to occur. The Council's guideline seeks to tackle this 'malfunction' of the suspended sentence by reiterating the sequence of decisions implicit in the statutory framework:

(a) Has the custody threshold been passed?
(b) If so, is it unavoidable that a custodial sentence be imposed?
(c) If so, can that sentence be suspended (sentencers should be clear that they would have imposed a custodial sentence if the power to suspend had not been available)?[91]

Whether this reiteration will be sufficient to prevent a return to the pre-1991 practice, whereby suspended sentences were often imposed on people who would not otherwise have been sentenced to imprisonment, remains to be seen. One problem with it is that the logic may be thought imperfect. In taking step (b) above, and deciding that a case which passes the custody threshold can be brought below the threshold, the court must take account of all mitigating and aggravating factors – once. Then in deciding (c), whether there are factors justifying the suspension of a sentence that cannot be brought below the custody threshold, the court must consider the same aggravating and mitigating factors – again. If a plea of guilty, or having only one previous conviction, or having a young dependent child, is thought insufficient to bring a case below the custody threshold, can it then be held sufficient to justify suspending? If there is to be a positive answer to this question, it must consist of two elements – one, that in theory it is possible to think of a given set of mitigating factors being not quite strong enough to justify bringing a custodial sentence down to a community sentence but having sufficient strength to justify suspending the custodial sentence; and the other, an admission that the line is necessarily a fine one.

It is evident from this discussion that there are several ways in which the new suspended sentence could malfunction – it could be imposed where prison itself would not be; it could be made longer than an immediate sentence would have been; the requirements added to it may be unduly onerous; and (perhaps consequently) more cases may be breached and result in actual imprisonment. On the other hand, if courts follow the Council's guidelines carefully and make use of their powers to

90 Bottoms (1981).
91 SGC, *New Sentences: Criminal Justice Act 2003* (2004), para. 2.2.11.

review the progress of offenders on suspended sentences, there is the possibility of taking out of prison a fair number of offenders who might otherwise have been sent there, and of doing so without damage to public safety. That happened in Canada when the conditional sentence was introduced, albeit with some different features.[92]

9.4.3 Intermittent custody

The government was keen to introduce intermittent custody as a sentence 'suitable for those currently receiving short sentences who are not dangerous and who do not have to be held in secure accommodation to protect the public'.[93] This immediately raises an important question, since being dangerous is not and has never been a criterion for an immediate prison sentence – nor has public protection. The principal criterion at present is the seriousness of the offence(s), as s. 152(2) makes clear. If dangerousness or the need for public protection were instated as the threshold test for prison, the number of custodial sentences would surely show a significant decline.

Keeping to the law as it is, s. 183 of the 2003 Act empowers a court to order that any term of imprisonment between 28 and 51 weeks should take effect as an intermittent custody order, so long as there are facilities in the particular court area.[94] The court must specify the number of custodial days, which may be between 14 and 90, the remainder of the term being served on licence. The licence may include requirements of one or more of four kinds – unpaid work, activity requirement, programme requirement, or prohibited activity requirement. The offender must consent to the making of an intermittent custody order.

In what circumstances should intermittent custody be imposed? It is clear that the custody threshold must be passed, and the court must be satisfied that a suspended sentence cannot be justified. Thus steps (a), (b) and (c) for the imposition of suspended sentences must be taken, and a further step (d) considered: if the sentence cannot be suspended, can it be served intermittently?[95] In its guideline the Council accepts that 'public safety should always be the paramount consideration', so that this sentence should not 'be used for sex offenders or those convicted of serious offences of either violence or burglary'.[96] It goes on to suggest that it may be suitable for those who are 'full-time carers; employed; or in education'. This echoes the White Paper, which added that intermittent custody 'could be especially effective for some women offenders who have children, which could result in fewer children growing up in care or starting life in jail'.[97] There are some who would argue that giving priority to offenders who are in employment or in education may be discriminatory, a charge often brought against the suspended sentence in times past, and that any measure that discriminates in this way should be opposed. This points to the paradox in trying to keep people in jobs or to keep families together, when

92 Roberts, J. (2003), (2004).   93 Home Office (2002), para. 5.34.
94 Intermittent custody was introduced on a pilot basis in 2004 and is not yet available to all courts.
95 SGC, *New Sentences: Criminal Justice Act 2003*, para. 2.3.11.
96 Ibid., para. 2.3.9.   97 Home Office (2002), para. 5.34. Cf. above, ch. 5.

it is a question of allocating scarce penal resources such as intermittent custody. The Council takes this point in its guideline, and states that 'courts should strive to ensure that the intermittent custody provisions are applied in a way that limits discrimination and they should, in principle, be considered for all offenders'. But this aspect of intermittent custody ought to be carefully monitored.

In practice, intermittent custody is vulnerable to many of the possible malfunctions described earlier in relation to suspended sentences. Will courts use it where otherwise a suspended sentence or even a community sentence might have been imposed? The guideline is designed to avoid this, through its rigorous (a) to (d) decision sequence, but the history of suspended sentence provisions is not encouraging. Some will doubtless raise the same question – how mitigating factors that fail to save an offender from custody and are thought insufficient to justify suspension of the sentence may nevertheless be held sufficient to justify intermittent custody. The reply is almost the same, except insofar as intermittent custody proves to be targeted on the particular groups mentioned above. Will courts lengthen the term when imposing intermittent custody? The Council argues that courts should actually *shorten* the term when ordering the sentence to be served intermittently, because it will be more disruptive of life to have to leave one's family to travel to the custodial establishment each weekend. It therefore declares that 'once a court has decided that an offender should be sent to prison and has determined the length of the sentence, it should reduce the overall length of the sentence because it is to be served intermittently'.[98] What effect this will have remains to be seen. Will courts impose onerous licence requirements on those who receive the favourable sentence of intermittent custody? The Council warns against this, arguing that offenders will participate in full programmes during the weekends and that any conditions imposed during the week should be negative (such as curfew or prohibited activity) rather than positive requirements.[99]

The pilot projects of intermittent custody have been in operation for some time, and careful evaluation is awaited. But no less important than completion rates, breach rates and so forth is the question of the types of offender for which intermittent custody is imposed, compared with the types who receive community sentences, suspended sentences and immediate custody. We have seen that the distinctions that have to be drawn between a community sentence, a suspended sentence, intermittent custody and immediate custody may be very fine ones; it seems likely that they will turn on the disposition of the court rather than on objective factors connected with offence or offender, but that remains to be established.

9.4.4 Custody plus

It was observed in part 9.4.1 that the government thought that the previous arrangements for custodial sentences under 12 months were difficult to defend. The Halliday report had denounced them on three main grounds – that the offender served half

---

98 SGC, *New Sentences: Criminal Justice Act 2003*, para. 2.3.13.   99 Ibid., para. 2.3.12.

the sentence and was then released without support, so that the second half of the sentence was 'meaningless and ineffective'; that the custodial part was usually too short for any constructive programmes inside prison; and that reconviction rates for short-term prisoners were unacceptably high.[100] The Halliday report went on to show that the courts' usage of sentences under 12 months had risen by two-thirds between 1989 (27,000) and 1999 (45,000), with sentences under three months increasing by no less than 167 per cent in that period. On examining which types of offender were receiving sentences under 12 months, Halliday found

> large numbers of persistent offenders, with multiple problems and high risks of re-offending, whose offences (and record) are serious enough to justify a custodial sentence, but not so serious that longer prison sentences would be justified. A more effective recipe for failure could hardly be conceived.[101]

Halliday's response to the various problems of short custodial terms was to propose a new sentence of 'custody plus', made up of a custodial portion and a period of supervision (with conditions) in the community, with the clear objective of engaging the offender in programmes aimed at reducing reoffending. The custodial portion would be limited to three months and therefore shorter than some current sentences, but Halliday advocated this as a strengthening rather than a weakening of the requirements imposed on this group of offenders.[102] The government accepted Halliday's diagnosis of the problem and his remedy,[103] and so s. 181 of the 2003 Act replaces all terms of imprisonment for less than 12 months with the new sentence of custody plus.

The overall term of the sentence must be between 28 and 51 weeks;[104] the custodial portion must be between 2 weeks and 13 weeks; but in calculating the overall sentence, the court should ensure that the licence period is at least 26 weeks in length. This means, for example, that it would be unlawful for a court to impose the minimum sentence of 28 weeks and direct four weeks in custody and the remainder on licence. If the court wishes a custodial period of four weeks, it will have to add at least 26 weeks on licence, to make 30 weeks in total. The court is also empowered, by s. 181(3)(b), to require the licence to be granted on conditions that correspond (broadly) with the requirements that may be imposed on an offender made subject to a community order (see Chapter 10.6 below). Alternatively, it may leave the licence conditions to be determined by NOMS at the time of release.

Custody plus is a bold and positive step towards reducing reoffending, but if it is to be even a modest success it must avoid some obvious pitfalls. The first is that its chief aim is to reduce reoffending, and to do so among a group of offenders that includes many difficult cases (persistent minor offenders, often socially dislocated or

---

100 Halliday (2001), paras. 1.16–1.19 and 3.1–3.8, with Appendix 6.
101 Halliday (2001), para. 3.1.   102 Halliday (2001), para. 3.19.
103 Home Office (2002a), paras. 5.22 – 5.26.
104 The sentencing powers of magistrates will be increased to 12 months for one offence when s. 154 of the 2003 Act is brought into force, probably in autumn 2006.

otherwise disadvantaged). The question is whether there are effective interventions for this group – a question of evaluation to which we return in Chapter 10 below – and indeed whether the criminal justice system has the capacity to change behaviour if social, educational and employment policy changes are not also in place. It must be said that the available evidence is not yet persuasive. A second obvious pitfall is that the new sentence may be more widely used by the courts. It seems clear that this is not what the government intends, since custody plus is now to be underpinned by the suspended sentence and by intermittent custody and it is hoped that they will 'divert' some offenders who might otherwise have received a short immediate custodial sentence. But if custody plus is the type of short sentence that the courts 'have been waiting for',[105] there is the risk that it will be used even more frequently than short terms of imprisonment have come to be used in recent years. It could come to be regarded as a community sentence with teeth – a short spell behind bars, followed by intensive community programmes.[106] In an attempt to prevent this, the Sentencing Guidelines Council has emphasized the wording of s. 152(2) and the need to adopt a step-by-step approach in these cases, first ensuring that the custody threshold is passed and cannot be avoided, and then considering a suspended sentence and intermittent custody in turn, before resolving that custody plus may be imposed. This will be a stern test for the effectiveness of sentencing guidelines.

A third and related pitfall is that custody plus may lead to longer sentences for some offenders who currently receive only one or two months of imprisonment, particularly from a magistrates' court. The effective minimum will now be over six months (28 weeks). It is right to respond that the whole idea of the new sentence is different, with its emphasis on support and rehabilitation in the community.[107] But in terms of the totality of social control over these offenders, there is a lengthening. Moreover, there is a fourth and closely connected pitfall, even in cases where the decision to impose custody plus is within the spirit of the legislation. The basis for calculating the length and components of custody plus is not clear. It is not sufficient to say that courts should be guided by the same principles as they always have been, except that the minimum term of custody plus will, in effect, be over six months (28 weeks) and the maximum just below 12 months (51 weeks). This will not do, because the court will need to specify the length of each component. The primary task will be to set the term of custody at between two and 13 weeks; but immediately a court goes beyond the minimum of two weeks, the total length of custody plus begins to climb to seven months and longer, since there must be a minimum of 26 weeks on licence. The Sentencing Guidelines Council may be

105 Home Office (2002a), para. 5.23: 'there was widespread recognition of the need to make short sentences more effective in this respect'.

106 This possibility was raised by some sentencers interviewed by Hough et al. (2003), p. 39: 'it could substitute for community penalties rather than conventional custody, and serve to accelerate the increase in the prison population'.

107 Gullick (2004), for a thoughtful discussion.

expected to issue guidelines on this point and, once again, this will be a test of the practical effectiveness of guidelines. More generally, the danger of lengthier periods of compulsory intervention for these offenders is increased when one considers that the licence conditions take effect until the end of the nominal sentence, that these offenders include numbers of persistent offenders and that breach of licence will usually result in further custody. On the other hand, if the custodial part of a custody plus sentence is six weeks or longer, the offender will be eligible for early release on Home Detention Curfew – which has the potential to reduce the time actually served by up to one half.[108] This leads to a fifth possible pitfall – that some sentencers may take the view that custody plus fails to deliver the amount of custody they think appropriate in a given case, and that they may therefore impose a sentence of 12 months' imprisonment (i.e. just above the limit for custody plus) when in truth the case does not warrant a sentence of that length. It will be for the Sentencing Guidelines Council and subsequently the Court of Appeal to police this boundary, but how effectively this can be carried out remains to be seen. The worst outcome, combining the fourth and fifth pitfalls, will be for custody plus to be used for some cases that previously attracted only a community sentence, and for sentences of 12 months to be used for some cases that previously attracted only six or nine months' imprisonment. This would increase the use of imprisonment without justification.

9.5 Custodial sentences of twelve months and longer: release on licence

The discussion in Chapter 4 explored some of the parameters of proportionality in English sentencing. For the offences which are widely regarded as most serious, the courts have gradually produced a kind of framework or tariff which takes the sentence for murder as its starting point, and then works downwards towards robbery, attempted murder and rape. In Chapter 4 some questions were raised about the differentials between offences within this judicial structure. In part 2 of this chapter some international comparisons were discussed. Despite the difficulties of accuracy in those matters, it is widely accepted that English courts impose longer sentences than those of the courts in most other European countries (although shorter sentences than in the United States). However, in terms of the impact of those sentences, much depends on three factors – the release provisions, the application of Home Detention Curfew, and the effect of both these on sentencing practice.

9.5.1 Release provisions in the 2003 Act

Under the law as established by the Criminal Justice Act 1991 and the Crime (Sentences) Act 1997, release from sentences of less than four years was automatic after serving one-half, the third quarter being under supervision and the whole

108 Gullick (2004), pp. 654–5. HDC is examined below.

of the second half being on licence. For sentences of four years and over, prisoners were eligible for release after one-half but it was for the Parole Board to decide whether, and if so when, to release them between the half-way and two-thirds points. All long-term prisoners were released after two-thirds, with supervision until the three-quarters point and then a licence until the end of the sentence.

The effect of the Criminal Justice Act 2003 is to alter the release provisions in a significant way. All prisoners serving determinate sentences of 12 months or longer are automatically released after serving half the sentence. On release, however, all these prisoners will be subject to supervision on licence until the expiry of the full nominal sentence. The effect is to shorten the time served in prison by many of those sentenced to four years or longer, but at the same time to increase the amount of supervision of released prisoners significantly. Thus the length of compulsory intervention flowing from prison sentences is increased, but the length of time spent behind bars is reduced overall. Indeed, the reductions may be even greater than so far described, because Home Detention Curfew will now be available for prisoners serving four years or longer, as well as to those serving shorter terms. This may mean that a further period of up to four-and-a-half months (135 days) may be taken off some sentences.[109] For those who believe that imprisonment is over-used in this country to an extent that is unnecessary for public protection, the Act's provisions on early release will be most welcome. However, they do increase the burden on NOMS to provide sufficient and effective supervision. The changes can be defended in terms of public protection, because the supervisory element is much increased under the new arrangements; but the effectiveness of such supervision will have to be confirmed by experience.

One implication of the changes is that the Parole Board no longer has a function in relation to determinate sentences. Release is automatic, and it is for NOMS to take charge after that. Courts have the power to recommend certain licence conditions at the time of sentencing,[110] but the precise terms of the licence will be set by the Home Office on advice from the prison governor and from NOMS. Various resettlement programmes for released prisoners are in place or being developed, in order to address problems such as unemployment, lack of housing and addiction.[111] The work of the Parole Board will therefore be confined, as we saw in Chapter 6.8, to dealing with offenders serving 'dangerousness' sentences where release is determined by assessments of risk. Those offenders lie outside the category of determinate sentences now being discussed.

9.5.2 Home Detention Curfew

Home Detention Curfew (HDC) was introduced in 1999 as a means of releasing certain prisoners earlier than their normal release date, subject to curfew restrictions which are electronically monitored. Offenders thus released therefore have to be

---

109 See further Gullick (2004), pp. 660–1.   110 Criminal Justice Act 2003, s. 238.
111 Home Office (2002), paras. 6.19–6.25.

'tagged'. Under the pre-2003 Act regulations, certain prisoners serving sentences under 12 months (excluding sex offenders and some others) would presumptively be released on HDC unless an assessment in prison yielded 'exceptional and compelling reasons' to refuse it.[112] HDC was also available to prisoners serving sentences of 12 months and under four years, with certain exclusions of sex and violent offenders. There is a risk assessment process within the prison and, again, the decision to release is that of the prison governor. The maximum period of HDC was raised to 90 days in 2002 and then to its present 135 days in 2003. The regulations provide for recall to prison for non-compliance with the terms of the licence or, more broadly, if the offender is considered to represent a threat to public safety.

When announcing the extension of the HDC scheme in 2002, Lord Falconer stated:

> Home Detention Curfew has been very successful in providing prisoners with a smooth and more effective reintegration back into the community, enabling prisoners to be released from prison early while still subject to restrictions placed on their liberty. Increasing the curfew period will allow them to make the transition over a longer period and will help them resume employment or training at an earlier stage.[113]

It appears that some 30 per cent of those eligible for HDC in its first five years were released, that the rate of recall to prison was around 5 per cent, and that the subsequent reconviction rate of those released on HDC was little different from those released normally.[114] Details of the application of HDC to sentencing under the 2003 Act are not yet clear, but it will remain an administrative decision taken by the prison governor and will be available, for the first time, for those prisoners serving four years and longer. Its operation has prevented the prison population from rising even higher in the last few years, and it tends to demonstrate that considerations of public safety do not necessitate prison sentences of the lengths currently handed down.

9.5.3 The effect on sentencing practice

What will be the effect of the new provisions on early release and of HDC on the sentencing practices of the courts? The first step should be to apply s. 153(2), when calculating the length of a custodial sentence, and to impose 'the shortest term . . . commensurate with the seriousness of the offence'.[115] The word 'shortest' has not been used in this statutory context before, and should be taken as a clear indication that sentences in cases falling outside the dangerousness provisions of the 2003 Act should be brought down. The Court of Appeal has emphasized that the courts

---

112 For an analysis of the relevant regulations, see Livingstone, Owen and Macdonald (2003), pp. 287–94.
113 25 Nov. 2002, quoted by Lord Woolf CJ in *McInerney and Keating* [2003] 2 Cr App R (S) 240 at p. 249.
114 Nellis (2004), pp. 233–4.
115 Cf. the analysis of the last seven words in ch. 3.5 above.

should not take account of the possibility of release on HDC when calculating the length of a sentence.[116] However, there is the possibility that some sentencers might take the view that the new early release provisions reduce the custodial element of long sentences too greatly, and may try to counteract this by raising overall sentence levels. This would be to subvert the logic of the 2003 Act, and the Sentencing Guidelines Council has already attempted to prevent this. The Council points out that the supervisory element of all sentences of 12 months or more will be longer and more demanding and restrictive than hitherto. Its reasoning is that

> As well as restricting liberty to a greater extent, the new requirements will last until the very end of the sentence, rather than to the three-quarter point as at present, poten-tially making a custodial sentence significantly more demanding than under existing legislation. Breach of these requirements at any stage is likely to result in the offender being returned to custody and this risk continues, therefore, for longer under the new framework than under the existing legislation.[117]

The Council states that guidelines issued in the future will be lowered to take account of this, but it recognizes that all existing sentencing guidelines and informal tariffs will need to be lowered if the total penal bite of sentences is to be kept as it is, and not increased contrary to the legislative intention. It concedes that there are many factors to be considered in trying to 'achieve the best match' between old and new calculations, and its guideline is as follows:

> When imposing a fixed term custodial sentence of 12 months or more under the new provisions, courts should consider reducing the overall length of the sentence that would have been imposed under the current provisions by in the region of 15 per cent.[118]

This is an important injunction if Parliament's intention is to be carried through with fairness and due restraint. It means that all sentencing guidelines announced before April 2005, whether by the Court of Appeal or the Council, must now be interpreted subject to a deduction of some 15 per cent – a point that does not appear to have received specific endorsement or publicity among sentencers.

There are two obvious problems with the Council's guideline. One is that, if it is not carefully policed by the Court of Appeal, it will simply not happen – or, at least, not in all cases or to the required extent. The plasticity of English sentencing levels makes it difficult to ensure that changes of this kind are really occurring. In 1992 Lord Taylor as Lord Chief Justice issued a *Practice Statement* to try to prevent a similar malfunction resulting from the Criminal Justice Act 1991. Recognizing

---

116 *Al-Buhairi* [2004] 1 Cr App R (S) 496.
117 SGC, *New Sentences: Criminal Justice Act 2003* (2004), para. 2.1.5.
118 Ibid., para. 2.1.10. The Council, following the Panel, had originally proposed a reduction of 'up to one quarter' in its draft guideline. The Home Affairs Committee of the House of Commons did not comment on this, but the Home Secretary took the view that, while the reasoning was correct, the amount of the reduction should be less and should be consistent. Presumably in response to this, the Council replaced 25 per cent with 15, and 'up to' with 'in the region of '.

that the Act would effectively lengthen the time spent in prison as a proportion of a given sentence, he stated that courts should have regard to the longer periods served and to the risk of offenders 'serving substantially longer' if sentence lengths were not reduced.[119] The wording of the statement was much more tentative than that of the Council's guideline, and it is difficult to find any evidence that it had the effect of reducing nominal sentence lengths[120] – although that may be partly because sentence lengths began to go upwards during 1993 for unrelated reasons. That leads on to the second possible problem – that sections of the mass media may choose to portray this aspect of the 2003 Act, not as a means of increasing the length of control over offenders and increasing the chances of reducing reoffending and thus protecting the public, but rather as an underhand method of cutting the costs of the prison system. In relation to the increase of the maximum sentence for causing death by dangerous driving from 10 to 14 years, the effect of the early release provisions and of the Council's guideline may be to reduce the time spent by such offenders in custody rather than to increase it;[121] and there may be some who are more impressed by this fact than by the lengthening of the total period of control over such offenders.

9.6 Demographic features of the prison population

The composition of the prison population is almost entirely the result of decisions of the courts, either applying the law or using their discretion. While sentencers may state that they never send anyone to prison unless there is no alternative, and that prison is truly a last resort, it is instructive to consider the sorts of offender found in the prisons, and their proportions. This may say something about the functioning of the criminal justice system as a whole, and about sentencing decisions in particular. One enormous improvement in the last decade has been the steep decline in the number of fine defaulters sent to prison: from 1992 to 1995 some 20,000 or more offenders who defaulted on fine payments were committed to prison each year, whereas court decisions and a change of Home Office policy then led to a sharp decline and the greater use of other means of enforcement. In 2002 the number of fine defaulters received into prison was 1,192.[122] For other groups of offender, the position has been less positive – notably women, ethnic minorities and mentally disordered offenders. First, however, mention must be made of a class of prisoner that does not consist of convicted offenders – the remand population.

9.6.1 Remand prisoners awaiting trial

The average number of persons held in prison on remand has been around 11,000–12,000 since 1994: in 2002 the number was 12,790, an increase of some 14 per cent

---

119 *Practice Statement: Criminal Justice Act 1991* (1992) 95 Cr App R 456.
120 See also Hough et al. (2003), p. 19.
121 Cf. Gullick (2004), p. 660, written before the Council's guideline appeared.
122 Prison Statistics 2002, Table 1.13; see ch. 10.5 below.

over 2001, when the figure was 11,240. Although this now represents a lower proportion of the prison population than a decade ago, because of the steep rise in the numbers of sentenced prisoners, it remains a cause for concern. Putting the matter bluntly, those awaiting trial have not been convicted and should receive the benefit of the presumption of innocence; and yet they are not only deprived of their liberty but also, in many cases, subjected to the worst conditions in the English prison system (i.e. in local prisons). Although there are some new, purpose-built remand prisons, most of the overcrowding occurs in local prisons, as we saw in part 9.1.2 of this chapter. The position bears particularly harshly on those remandees who are acquitted at their trial or have their case discontinued – one-fifth of both male and female remand prisoners.[123] It also bears particularly harshly on women, for the reasons elaborated in part 9.6.2 below. Over a decade ago the Woolf Report placed strong emphasis on the special rights of remand prisoners and called for improved and separate facilities for them, describing the present situation as 'a travesty of justice'.[124] There has been some progress since then, but in essence the problem remains.

It has long been the case that persons who appear for sentence having been remanded in custody are much more likely to receive a custodial sentence. From one point of view this is unremarkable: the reasons why these people are remanded in custody may be very similar to the reasons for giving them custodial sentences. However, there is also the possibility that courts may occasionally react differently to offenders simply because they have been remanded in custody, or that remand in custody handicaps the presentation of mitigating factors. Flood-Page and Mackie showed that the proportionate use of custodial sentences for first offenders differed between 90 per cent (remanded in custody) and 36 per cent (on bail), and for those with previous convictions between 85 per cent (remanded in custody) and 44 per cent (on bail).[125] The authors rightly commented that 'factors which affect the sentencing decision overlap with those which influence remand decisions'; the question is whether that overlap is total, or whether some part of these wide divergences is attributable to other causes.

9.6.2 Women prisoners

Table 12 in part 9.2 of this chapter demonstrates the rapid increase in the female prison population, which almost trebled in the years from 1992 to 2002. Table 13 shows that it is the longer sentences that have increased most significantly, and Table 12 confirms that it is the numbers imprisoned for drug offences, robbery and burglary that account for most of the increase. Three strands of explanation are usually put forward – a rise in the number of women being prosecuted and convicted, a rise in the proportion of women being sentenced to custody, and an increase in the average length of custodial sentences.[126] The first factor appears not

123 Prison Statistics 2002, Table 4C, discussed in Ashworth and Redmayne (2005), ch. 8.
124 Woolf (1991), para. 10.55.   125 Flood-Page and Mackie (1998), p. 76.
126 Prison Reform Trust (2000), p. 2.

to be borne out, since the number of women found guilty or cautioned for indictable offences declined from some 101,000 in 1992 to fewer than 89,000 in 2002.[127] The last two factors apply to men also, as we saw in part 9.2 above, and yet the increase in women prisoners far outstrips the percentage increase in male prisoners in recent years. It could be argued that this is because the number of women prisoners was so low in the first place that expressing the increases in percentages may give a misleading impression; against that, however, there is surely no doubt that a major change has taken place.

The steep increase in women prisoners in the late 1990s led to various initiatives, including the creation in 2001 of a Women's Offending Reduction Programme designed to reduce women's offending by measures taken not only in the criminal justice system but also in the spheres of health, housing and employment.[128] It is not known what effect this programme has had, but certainly the figures for women's imprisonment appear not to have taken a downturn. Another initiative was the judgment of Lord Woolf CJ in *Mills* (2002),[129] referring to the overcrowding in women's prisons and to the need to consider the special position of women:

> Because of the smaller percentage of the prison population, the ability to imprison mothers close to their homes in the community is difficult. The difficulties in the prison population to which we have referred do not mean that if an offence is such that it is necessary to send an offender to prison, they should not be sent to prison for the appropriate time. But in a borderline case, in a case where the offence does not in particular involve violence but is one with financial consequences to a commercial concern, it is very important that those who have responsibilities for sentencing take regard to the prison population as well as the other matters. In a case of a person such as this appellant who is of previous good character, who has been performing useful acts in the community, where there is every reason to think that she will not re-offend, and where the offending behaviour is out of character with her normal behaviour, the courts should strive to avoid sending her to prison and instead use punishments in the community . . .

Well-intentioned as this passage was, its prospects as a sentencing initiative were never good, largely because each phrase restricts its application to fewer and fewer women offenders. Table 12 shows that the average number of women serving sentences for theft and related offences has not increased as greatly as for other types of offence. Probably most of the women in that category are persistent minor offenders,[130] sent to prison because they have long records and the courts, having tried other alternatives, use prison as 'a last resort'. Very few women 'economic' offenders sent to prison have the kind of background Lord Woolf described.

It is estimated that around half of all women received into prison have dependent children for whom they are the primary carer, and in Chapter 5.4.5 above the scope

127 Criminal Statistics (2002), Table 2.9.   128 Home Office (2001b).
129 [2002] 2 Cr App R (S) 229, above, n. 55 and accompanying text.
130 See the argument of Gelsthorpe and Morris (2002), emphasizing that 'women commit less serious crimes and pose fewer risks than men'.

for mitigation of sentence on this basis was discussed. In terms of the impact of the 2003 Act, it was noted in part 9.4.3 above that intermittent custody is said to be particularly appropriate for women offenders with responsibilities as carers. It is also possible that some women could benefit from the reinvigorated suspended sentence. However, as argued in parts 9.4.2 and 9.4.3 above, much turns on the courts' willingness to apply the spirit of the 2003 Act in this regard. If one rereads the passage from Lord Woolf's judgment in *Mills* just quoted, would it not now be easy for him to conclude by proposing a suspended sentence, or even intermittent custody, rather than a community sentence? This demonstrates the precarious prospects of the 2003 Act's measures, not least for women offenders. Moreover, for those women sent to prison for repeated minor property offences, the 2003 Act's provisions on persistent offenders appear more likely to toughen than to soften sentencing practice.[131] The Act does little to address the high proportion of women prisoners suffering from mental health problems, or the relatively high proportion of foreign nationals.

Finally, there is a strong argument that a sentence of imprisonment for a woman is correspondingly harsher than for a man. The argument would be that the existing prison estate for women means that, too frequently, they are held a considerable distance from their home and family, and that this constitutes an extra source of deprivation. Immediate steps should be taken to improve the situation. The Wedderburn Committee recommended, among other proposals, that the existing prison estate for women be replaced by 'suitable, geographically-dispersed custodial centres', that a Women's Justice Board (along the lines of the Youth Justice Board) be created and that in the community there should be a properly accessible network of Women's Supervision, Rehabilitation and Support Centres.[132] These changes have not occurred, and there remain major problems in respect of women's prisons and the offenders held in them. In 2003 the Chief Inspector of Prisons drew attention to the fact that 'one in four women in local prisons self-harm', and on the general issue of women prisoners concluded:

> The special needs of women, many of whom will not come from the region or area, need to be promoted vigorously in a system in which they will always be a small, and easily marginalized, minority. This Inspectorate will continue to do that; we will expect the Prison Service to do the same.[133]

The increasing numbers of women in the prisons makes it all the more urgent to deal with the well-known problems.

9.6.3 Ethnic minority prisoners

The sentencing of ethnic minority offenders was discussed in Chapter 7.2 above, and the points made there will not be repeated here. However, it must be recognized that the prison population contains a far higher proportion of people from ethnic

131 See above, ch. 6.3.   132 Prison Reform Trust (2000), ch. 6.
133 HMCI Prisons (2003), pp. 3–5.

minorities than does the general population of this country. While between 1 and 2 per cent of the general population is black, the proportion in male prisons is around 15 per cent and in female prisons around one-quarter.[134] The categories of 'South Asian' and 'Chinese and other' in the prisons stand at around 3 and 4 per cent respectively, about double their proportion in the general population. Whether these proportions are evidence of discriminatory practices in the criminal justice system was discussed in Chapter 7.

A somewhat related issue in the prisons is the number of foreign nationals held. In 2004 some 9,000 foreign national prisoners were among the prison population, representing some 12 per cent of male prisoners and 20 per cent of female prisoners. They present obvious problems of communication within the prisons, as well as suffering additional hardships concerned with communication with their families, some discriminatory treatment and a lack of preparation for release.[135] The Chief Inspector reports a lack of commitment to instituting foreign national policies in individual prisons, commenting that 'only 8 out of 38 prisons in full inspections had foreign national policies, and of these only two London prisons (Brixton and Wormwood Scrubs) could be described as making reasonable progress in implementing them'.[136] Difficulties of this kind make it particularly important to think further about the various regulations for the transfer of prisoners to their home country: repatriation is possible under the international Convention on the Transfer of Sentenced Prisoners 1983, incorporated into domestic law in the Repatriation of Prisoners Act 1984.[137]

9.6.4 Mentally disordered prisoners

Successive studies have found that a significant proportion of the prison population is suffering from mental disturbance, and that some prisoners – possibly as many as one-third – might be classified as mentally disordered. In a survey by Gunn, Maden and Swinton, some 37 per cent of the sentenced prisoners were diagnosed as mentally disordered, including 3 per cent whose conditions were severe enough to require hospital treatment.[138] A survey of the custodial remand population by Brooke, Taylor, Gunn and Maden put at 63 per cent the proportion suffering from mental disorder.[139] Whereas the proportion of the sentenced prison population suffering from a psychosis was put at 2 per cent, it rose to 5 per cent among remandees. A subsequent study by Singleton, Meltzer and Gatward found that as many as 78 per cent of male remand prisoners, 64 per cent of sentenced males and 50 per cent of sentenced females had some form of personality disorder, and also that 10 per cent of male prisoners and 20 per cent of female prisoners had been mental hospital patients at some time.[140]

---

134 Prison Statistics 2002, Table 6.3.   135 HMCI Prisons (2004), p. 20.
136 HMCI Prisons (2004), p. 20.   137 Livingstone, Owen and Macdonald (2003), pp. 302–9.
138 Gunn, Maden and Swinton (1991).   139 Brooke, Taylor, Gunn and Maden (1996).
140 Singleton, Meltzer and Gatward (1998).

Policy in this sphere has not been coherent. The Mental Health Act 1983 sought to restrict the use of hospital orders for offenders classified as mentally impaired or psychopathic, by requiring evidence that the condition is treatable. This has been effective in reducing the number of offenders admitted to mental hospital, but one consequence has been that mentally disordered offenders continue to be sentenced to custody, even though it is clear that prison is rarely a suitable place for mentally disordered people. The Richardson report quotes the Chief Inspector of Prisons' comment that the regime on the psychiatric ward at Wormwood Scrubs prison 'was barren and impoverished . . . [and] entirely unacceptable . . . The patients' rights to NHS equivalent health care were not being met.'[141] Although there have been some improvements since then, there have been unacceptable numbers of suicides and incidents of self-harm, many of which are associated with mental disturbance.

From the sentencer's point of view, there are two key steps when dealing with the mentally disordered. The first is to ensure that they are recognized as such, and this requires courts to take note of factors indicating the presence of some mental disturbance and to call for a medical report. Section 157 of the Criminal Justice Act 2003 imposes a duty to obtain and consider a medical report before passing any custodial sentence on a person who appears to be mentally disordered (although s. 157(2) qualifies that duty), and also requires the court to consider any other information bearing on the offender's mental condition and the likely effect of a custodial sentence on that condition and on any possible treatment for it.[142] This is a necessary provision, but a similar section has been in force for over a decade and its effects are difficult to discern.

Some sentencers argue that there is also a major problem at the next stage: that where an offender is said to be mentally disordered and to require treatment, doctors and hospitals are often unwilling to accept offenders as patients. This is what often leads a court to impose imprisonment. On the other hand, some years ago Lord Woolf's inquiry found at least one area of the country in which about half of the recommendations for hospital orders by psychiatrists were turned down by the courts,[143] perhaps because of concerns about release from mental hospitals. It remains the case that increased provision through the health and social services (including more secure and medium-secure hospital places) is likely to be the only practical way of dealing with the problem: without that, the courts and the criminal justice system are hampered, and more prison sentences are likely to result.

There are also provisions for the transfer of prisoners to mental hospital during their sentence. Although the use of transfers increased considerably during the 1990s, it has not removed the problem of mentally disordered offenders being kept

---

141 Richardson (1999), para. 16.1.
142 The section re-enacts s. 4 of the Criminal Justice Act 1991; see also s. 166(5) of the 2003 Act, preserving the courts' power to mitigate sentence in the case of mentally disordered offenders.
143 Woolf (1991), para. 10.120.

in unsuitable prison accommodation. This is one of many problems relating to mentally disordered offenders which will be revisited in Chapter 12.3.

9.7 Conclusions

This chapter has pointed out the strengths of the argument for restraint in the use of custody – arguments of principle, of effectiveness in preventing crime, and of economics. These arguments received some degree of acceptance at the beginning of the 1990s, at least in one part of the then government's twin-track approach to sentencing policy and among some members of the judiciary. But during the decade they lost virtually all political force, as the rhetoric of penal repression began to spiral upwards. The first five years of the new millennium have seen no change in the political rhetoric, although the government's policy does appear to be one of bifurcation and not unmitigated severity. Serious, 'dangerous' and persistent offenders are marked out for severe responses, whereas for other cases there is evidence of a commitment to reducing reoffending through rehabilitative programmes, manifest particularly in the emphasis on community sentences and the expansion of supervision under licence for both short-term and longer custodial sentences.

Overcrowding and poor regimes remain major practical concerns in relation to the prison system. Many inmates of the local prisons are suffering conditions that are likely to be found to violate Article 3 of the Convention. The CPT has given official warnings about this in its reports,[144] but overcrowding continues to be acute in certain prisons, and inmates are forced to endure unsatisfactory conditions in their cells for as many as 23 hours per day. The Scots courts have found certain prison conditions to be in violation of Article 3,[145] and it will not be long before this argument is tested in the English courts. The response that more prison places are 'on the way' fails to meet the human rights issue: the Convention rights of many individuals are being violated now, and one obvious remedial step should be taken – declaring that no prison shall admit prisoners above the number for which its certified normal accommodation provides.[146] The ramifications of this would cause difficulties for sentencing, although not necessarily difficulties for sentencers – the problem could be dealt with by means of executive release.

So far as sentencing is concerned, the impact of guidelines is a key issue. There have been so many other changes affecting sentencing in the years since 1999 that it is virtually impossible to identify any particular effect of guidelines without specially targeted research. Some of the sentencers interviewed by Hough, Jacobson and Millie suggested that

---

144 See part 9.2.2 above.
145 See the *Napier* decision, above n. 20 and accompanying text.
146 Cf. Woolf (1991), para. 1.190.

guideline judgments, in combination with the possibility of prosecutorial appeal, served to draw lenient judges' decisions up to the guideline level, whilst leaving those of tougher judges unchanged. And as with legislative change, one would expect guideline judgments for specific crime types to have a knock-on effect on other crimes, given the priority placed by sentencers on achieving parity and proportionality.[147]

Insofar as this implies that the tendency of guidelines has generally been to raise levels, it takes no account of the thrust of the Council's guidelines on general principles, on reduction for guilty plea and on new sentences under the 2003 Act. Much of the success of custody plus, suspended sentence and intermittent custody – which may be seen as a bold initiative to deal constructively with offenders who are on the custody threshold – is dependent, in the first place, on sentencers following the Sentencing Guidelines Council's guidance and adopting the spirit of the new legislation. Several possible malfunctions have been pointed out in this chapter, on the basis of experiences in the past, and avoidance of these will be no easy matter. Similarly, the provision for release of all prisoners serving determinate sentences of 12 months or longer after serving half of their sentence is to be applauded; but whether courts will follow the Council's instruction to reduce sentences by 15 per cent to take account of the longer period of supervision and licence remains to be seen, and there is a risk that those longer periods produce more breaches and reimprisonment. Even though the new legislation on persistent offenders and dangerous offenders is draconian, the government should receive some credit for taking some measures to reduce the use of custody and to reduce reoffending in other cases. It is now for the courts to attempt to apply these provisions faithfully.

147 Hough et al. (2003), p. 25.

CHAPTER 10

Non-custodial sentencing

In Chapter 9 the close connection between custodial and non-custodial sentencing was often evident, particularly when discussing the custody threshold. The present chapter aims to examine the principal non-custodial measures available to English courts, in the light of the Criminal Justice Act 2003.[1] In brief, four methods of disposal are unchanged (absolute discharges, conditional discharges and bind-overs, compensation orders and fines), but the 2003 Act has replaced the diverse forms of community order with a single, generic community sentence. It has also reshaped deferment of sentence. First, it is necessary to consider the route by which the English system arrived at its present position.

10.1 A brief history

Successive governments between the 1960s and the early 1990s stated a policy of reducing the use of custodial sentences, and regarded the provision of new forms of non-custodial sentence as a key element in this strategy.[2] Community service orders (and compensation orders) formed part of the 1972 Criminal Justice Act. New forms of probation order were introduced by a Schedule to the 1982 Act, the Act which also legislated for curfew orders on young offenders. The result was that courts in England and Wales had available a wider range of non-custodial measures than the courts of most European countries, most states in the United States and probably most countries in the world. What might be described as the policy of proliferation was not a conspicuous success. Simply widening the range of available non-custodial sentences did little to deflect courts from their use of custodial sentences. Changes in sentencing practice did take place, but these did not impinge significantly on the use of custody.

It was lack of progress in that direction, combined with concern among sentencers about laxity in the enforcement of non-custodial sentences, that led to changes in the 1991 Act. The notion of 'alternatives to custody' had not been found convincing or even comprehensible by many sentencers: there was, they would say, nothing

---

1 Non-custodial measures for young offenders are dealt with in ch. 12 below.
2 For an analysis of policy changes, see Bottoms (1987); Bottoms, Rex and Robinson (2004).

equivalent to prison, and certainly nothing in the available options. Major changes of direction were proposed in the 1990 White Paper: restraint in the use of custody for non-serious offences, a toughening of community sentences, more rigorous enforcement of community measures, and greater use of financial penalties. Perhaps the most important change was the abandonment of the 'alternatives to custody' rhetoric, and its replacement with the idea of punishment in the community:

> The Government believes a new approach is needed if the use of custody is to be reduced. Punishment in the community should be an effective way of dealing with many offenders, particularly those convicted of property crimes and less serious offences of violence, when financial penalties are insufficient. The punishment should be in the restrictions on liberty and in the enforcement of the orders. All community service orders place restrictions on an offender's liberty, and so may probation orders when, for example, they require an offender to attend a day centre for a lengthy period. The discipline exerted by these orders on offenders may extend over many months. These orders intrude on normal freedom, and the court should be satisfied that this is justified.[3]

Thus, responding to the views of sentencers, the then government announced more demanding, 'tougher' orders which restricted liberty, and a more regular system of enforcement. The Criminal Justice Act 1991 therefore separated out six sentences (i.e. probation, community service, combination orders, curfew orders, attendance centres and supervision) and termed them 'community sentences'. A seventh community sentence, the drug treatment and testing order, was added by s. 61 of the Crime and Disorder Act 1998. These were reinforced by the drawing up of National Standards, specifying the form that each community sentence should take, the contents of the order, the enforcement of the order and so forth.

Since the 1991 Act the proportionate use of community sentences has increased significantly for both male and female offenders, but these increases have not been accompanied by reductions in the use of custody, which has also risen steeply. The consequence, as is evident from Table 4 in Chapter 1, is that the community sentences rose from 18 per cent in 1992 to 25 per cent in 2002 for adult men at the same time as the proportionate use of custody rose from 18 per cent to 30 per cent for that age-group. For adult women the rise in community sentences was from 22 per cent to 33 per cent at the same time as custody for this group increased from 6 per cent to 17 per cent. Overall, therefore, the displacement has been, not from custody to community sentences, but rather from suspended sentences and fines to community sentences and custody. The aim of increasing courts' use of fines has not been realized, the abolition of the unit fine system by the Criminal Justice Act 1993 amounting to an abandonment of that policy. Thus, through their greater demands and tougher enforcement, community sentences have contributed to an increasingly punitive sentencing system.

3 Home Office (1990), para. 4.3.

Brief mention should be made of the Criminal Justice and Court Services Act 2000, which (among other changes) altered the names of several major community sentences. Immediately following the consolidation of sentencing law by the Powers of Criminal Courts (Sentencing) Act 2000, the government thought it desirable to rebrand certain community sentences. The probation order became the community rehabilitation order; the community service order became the community punishment order; and the combination order became the community punishment and rehabilitation order. Why this change was needed in 2000 remains difficult to fathom, not least because the new names were abandoned in the Criminal Justice Act 2003 in favour of a further set of names of (what are now) requirements forming part of a community sentence. This will be taken up again in part 10.6 below: its relevance here is to suggest that, at times, the development of community sentences has been more dogma than substance.

The Criminal Justice Act 2003 makes major changes to non-custodial sentencing, but most of those changes concern community sentences. The Halliday report concluded that discharges and fines are working well as part of the sentencing system, and proposed no significant changes.[4] It is with those measures that the discussion begins.

10.2 The absolute discharge

This is the least severe order which a court can make on conviction. It requires nothing from the offender, and imposes no restrictions on future conduct. The statutory provisions on discharges are consolidated in ss. 12–15 of the Powers of Criminal Courts (Sentencing) Act 2000. For many purposes an offence followed by an absolute discharge does not count as a conviction (s. 14 of the 2000 Act), but s. 134 of the Sexual Offences Act 2003 provides that a conviction followed by a discharge does count for the purpose of requiring sex offender notification.

Absolute discharges are relatively uncommon, being granted in around 1 per cent of cases. They are generally reserved for the most venial of offences, committed in circumstances of little moral blame. We saw earlier that one criterion for cautioning or discontinuing a case is that the court 'would be likely to impose a purely nominal penalty'.[5] If that test is conscientiously applied, most of the absolute discharge cases ought not to be prosecuted, and one might regard those that do end in an absolute discharge as 'failures' of the prosecution system. In his study, however, Martin Wasik argues that this might not always be so. He discusses three main reasons for granting an absolute discharge: where the offence is venial; where the offender had low culpability or high motivation, but the law does not provide a defence; and where the offender has suffered collateral losses or 'indirect' punishment as a result of the offence. Cases in the last category do not suggest any failure of prosecution

---

4 Halliday (2001), paras. 6.15–6.19.   5 Ch. 1.4 above.

policy: whether they should result in mitigation of sentence has been discussed elsewhere.[6]

10.3 Conditional discharges and bind-overs

The conditional discharge has a similar legal framework to the absolute discharge. The condition which forms part of the discharge is that the offender should commit no further offence during the specified period, which may be up to three years. If a further offence is committed during the specified period, the court may sentence the offender not only for that offence but also for the original offence which gave rise to the conditional discharge. The statutory provisions on discharges are consolidated in ss. 12–15 of the PCCS Act 2000. Section 134 of the Sexual Offences Act 2003 provides that a conviction followed by a conditional discharge does count for the purposes of sex offender notification and other orders under Part 2 of that Act.

The essence of the conditional discharge is therefore a threat or warning: the court is prepared to impose no sanction for the present offence, on condition that there is no reoffending within the specified period. This is different from the suspended sentence of imprisonment, which should only be imposed where the present offence is so serious as to justify custody, and under which the second court has a qualified duty to activate the suspended sentence, whereas the second court has a wide discretion on breach of a conditional discharge.[7] David Moxon's 1988 survey showed that in the Crown Court over half the conditional discharges were granted in theft cases, mostly involving little or no loss, often committed by people of fairly good character.[8] In their mid-1990s survey, Flood-Page and Mackie give no details on discharges granted by the Crown Court, but they report that in the magistrates' courts conditional discharges were given to 11 per cent of men and 21 per cent of women. Stress, mental health problems and being a first offender were associated with decisions to grant a conditional discharge, and their interviews with magistrates revealed that it was often regarded as a difficult choice between a fine (immediate bite, no lasting effect) and a conditional discharge (no immediate bite, but a 'sword of Damocles' for a year or more).[9]

The proportionate use of conditional discharges grew enormously in the 1980s but has steadied in more recent years. For males aged 21 or over, their use increased from 7 per cent in 1978 to 10 per cent in 1988 to 17 per cent in 1992, falling back to 14 per cent in 2002; for females aged 21 and over, the increase was from 19 per cent in 1978 to 27 per cent in 1988 and 36 per cent in 1992, falling back

---

6 Cf. Wasik (1985), pp. 229–33, with ch. 5.5.6 above.
7 The suspended sentence was discussed in ch. 9.4.2 above; cf. *Watts* (1984) 6 Cr App R (S) 61 for an example of the Court of Appeal replacing a suspended sentence with a conditional discharge.
8 Moxon (1988), pp. 47–8.
9 Flood-Page and Mackie (1998), pp. 53–4; it should be pointed out that many fines have more than an immediate bite, since many offenders pay by instalments over several months.

to 24 per cent by 2002.[10] The increases were unexpected because the police and the Crown Prosecution Service were receiving repeated guidance that it was not in the public interest to bring a prosecution where a nominal penalty was likely to result; if they had been predicting these cases accurately, one might have expected the discharge rate to decrease rather than increase. Similarly, the introduction of conditional cautions under the Criminal Justice Act 2003 might be expected to take away from the courts some cases that might otherwise result in a discharge,[11] but the effect on court disposals remains to be seen. Insofar as there is a policy on conditional discharges, it seems to be confused. The Halliday report referred favourably to conditional discharges, commenting that 'the evidence shows that they are an effective disposal, attracting better than predicted reconviction rates'.[12] However, in two types of case – conviction for breach of an anti-social behaviour order, and sentencing a juvenile within two years of receiving a final warning – Parliament has seen fit to prevent courts from imposing a conditional discharge.[13]

The power to 'bind an offender over' is a flexible creature of statute and common law, which may be applied to offenders, witnesses and indeed anyone involved in proceedings.[14] Some courts make considerable use of the 'bind-over' as a sentence, whereas others do not. In a survey for the Law Commission, almost three-quarters of bind-overs were for purposes other than sentencing[15] – a finding which raises important questions about the wide-ranging use of this power, especially where it operates as a *quid pro quo* in return for the dropping of a prosecution. As a sentence, the bind-over may amount more or less to a suspended fine. Under the Justices of the Peace Act 1361 an offender may be bound over in a certain sum to keep the peace for a specified period, on which there appears to be no limit. Breach leads to forfeiture of the sum. At common law an offender may be bound over in a certain sum to come up for judgment, apparently subject to almost any condition – in *Williams* (1982)[16] a condition of going to Jamaica and not returning for five years was not held unlawful. The common law power to bind a person over to be of good behaviour has been held to be too uncertain to be compatible with Article 10(2) of the Convention.[17] The Law Commission had warned of impending difficulties in 1994 and recommended the abolition of all forms of bind-over. However, many judges and magistrates continue to find the power 'flexible' and 'useful', and in 2003

---

10   See Tables 4 and 5 in ch. 1.3 above, and annual volumes of Criminal Statistics.
11   See ch. 1.4 above for brief discussion of conditional cautions.
12   Halliday (2001), para. 6.19, showing that the two-year reconviction rate was 2 per cent below expectation.
13   On ASBOs, Crime and Disorder Act 1998, s. 1(11), provides that 'it shall not be open to the court by or before which he is convicted' to impose a conditional discharge; s. 66(4) of the same statute prevents courts from imposing a conditional discharge on a juvenile who has received a final warning in the preceding two years unless the court finds 'exceptional circumstances'.
14   For review and reform proposals, see Law Commission (1994).
15   Law Commission (1994), para. 4.3.   16   (1982) 4 Cr App R (S) 239.
17   *Hashman and Harrup v. United Kingdom* (2000) 30 EHRR 24.

the Home Office issued a consultation document that proposed retention of some forms of bind-over with enhanced procedural protections.[18]

10.4 Compensation orders

Although the idea of making offenders pay compensation to their victims has a long history,[19] it is only in the last thirty years that it has become a regular and significant element in English sentencing. The Criminal Justice Act of 1972 introduced the compensation order for injury, loss or damage. In the Powers of Criminal Courts Act 1973 it took its place alongside other measures such as the confiscation order for property used in the commission of crime (s. 43) and also the restitution order (s. 28 of the Theft Act 1968). One of the objectives of the 1982 Criminal Justice Act was to increase the use of compensation orders by courts, and among the changes it introduced were the possibility of making a compensation order as the only order in a case, and the principle that the compensation order should have priority over a fine where an offender has limited means. The strongest measure is that introduced by s. 104 of the Criminal Justice Act 1988, which requires a court to consider making a compensation order in every case involving death, injury, loss or damage, and requires the court to give reasons if it makes no compensation order in such a case. The 1991 Act raised the maximum to £5,000 in magistrates' courts, and all the statutory powers and requirements are now consolidated in ss. 130–134 of the PCCS Act 2000.

Systems of criminal justice ought to be concerned to assist victims no less than to deal fairly with offenders. Crime is no less 'about' victims than it is 'about' offenders. Indeed, the explanatory memorandum of the Council of Europe's Convention on Compensation for the Victims of Violent Crimes includes the proposition that states have a duty to ensure that crime victims receive compensation, because the state is responsible for maintaining law and order, and crimes result from a failure in that duty.[20] There was, however, considerable reluctance to accept a state obligation in this country, although it was among the first to have a state scheme for criminal injuries compensation.[21] That has now developed into the Criminal Injuries Compensation Scheme, given a legislative framework by the Criminal Injuries Compensation Act 1995. The details of the scheme raise a number of important issues which cannot be pursued here,[22] but it is relevant to note that the minimum claim which the Criminal Injuries Compensation Authority will entertain is £1,000, and that the scheme is confined to crimes of 'violence'. This means that the victims of minor violence and the victims of all other forms of crime have to resort to civil proceedings or to hope for a compensation order in their favour from a criminal court.

18 Home Office (2003).
19 For debates in the nineteenth and early twentieth century, see Radzinowicz and Hood (1986), pp. 654–5.
20 Council of Europe (1984), Preamble.   21 Rock (1990), p. 273.
22 For full analysis see Miers (1997).

At a more pragmatic level, criminal justice systems rely heavily on victims for information about crimes and about offenders, and for evidence in court. It is only fair that, in return, the system should ensure that they receive the proper help and support. Apart from the Criminal Injuries Compensation Scheme, recognition of this is evident in government assistance for the spread of victim support schemes, to bring help, support and advice to the victims of burglary, rape and other crimes. Beyond that, there have been two Victim's Charters (in 1990 and 1996) setting out the services and information which victims can expect to receive, but these were unenforceable.[23] Now the Domestic Violence, Crime and Victims Act 2004 provides for the issue of a Code of Practice for Victims (s. 32), provides for victims to be informed of the impending release of 'their' offender and for them to make representations on the matter (ss. 35–44), creates the office of Commissioner for Victims and Witnesses (ss. 48–51) and provides for the appointment of a Victims' Advisory Panel (s. 55). These amount to the most visible attempt to recognize victims' rights in statutory form. Whether they will improve the lot of victims remains to be seen: they have little bearing on the question of compensation.

Returning to the compensation order made by a criminal court, this sits rather uncomfortably with other forms of sentence and order. It has a dual function: in many cases it operates simply as an ancillary order, to ensure some compensation to the victim in addition to the state punishment contained in the principal sentence; in other cases it becomes a central feature, as where it takes priority over a fine or accompanies a conditional discharge, and particularly where it is the sole order in the case. In the 'ancillary' cases it can be justified as a reparative element which accompanies the proportionate sentence. But some have found the task of justification harder when the compensation order is the principal or sole order in the case. How can this be regarded as sentencing when, in effect, the court is merely making a relatively 'rough and ready' award of damages to the victim? The offender would have been civilly liable to the victim in almost all cases and therefore, the argument goes, the court's order amounts to nothing in sentencing terms – no punishment, but rather a kind of civil award made by a criminal court.[24] One counter-argument to this is that, in practice, very few victims sue their offenders; therefore, in practice, the compensation order does transfer from the offender to the victim money which the offender would not otherwise have been made to pay. It may therefore be realistic to regard the compensation order as punitive in its effect on the offender, as well as reparative in relation to the victim. Another counter-argument would be that orders do not have to be punitive anyway: the compensation order should be applauded as a form of reparative justice, or at least as recognition that our system ought to be multi-functional rather than limited to punitive responses.

How ought compensation orders to be used by the courts? Section 130 of the PCCS Act 2000 requires a court to consider an order in every case involving death or injury, damage or loss. It is well established that an order can be made in a case

23 Fenwick (1997).   24 See *Barney* (1989) 11 Cr App R (S) 448.

where the offence causes distress and anxiety.[25] Courts are empowered to make a compensation order for 'such amount as the court considers appropriate', but appellate courts remain reluctant to uphold orders unless the amount of the loss is agreed or proved,[26] and unless the grounds for liability are clear and not complex.[27] It is the prosecution's duty to ensure that such evidence is available in court, and if there is no up-to-date evidence it would be wrong for the court to calculate the compensation on the basis of long-term effects which have not been proved.[28] The court should be satisfied that the offender caused the harm for which compensation is ordered,[29] although in public order cases where several offenders are convicted courts have not required proof that the particular offender actually inflicted the harm.[30]

Section 130 requires the court to have regard to the means of the offender when deciding whether to make a compensation order and when deciding on its amount. It will be apparent that the characterization of compensation orders as essentially civil measures breaks down at this point, because awards of damages are not reduced to take account of the means of defendants. The law on compensation orders is the same as applies to fines, and the justification for this must be that compensation orders which were too high to be paid would be prison sentences in disguise.[31] Compensation orders are enforced as if they were fines, and imprisonment is the ultimate sanction for non-payment. This blurring of the civil and the criminal continues when we consider what assets of a defendant may be used to pay a compensation order: a court may be justified in ordering the sale of a moveable asset such as a car to pay compensation, so long as it has reliable evidence of the car's value,[32] but it is usually regarded as wrong to order the sale of a family home in order to compensate the victim, unless the home was purchased substantially out of the proceeds of the offence.[33] No such indulgence would be granted by the civil courts, but the criminal courts prefer the interests of the offender's family over those of the victim, presumably on the grounds that to impose too severe a burden might encourage further crime or might lead to the offender being imprisoned for default. The payment of a compensation order out of income may be stretched over two or even three years, if the court thinks this appropriate.[34] Such long orders may fail to ensure that the victim receives compensation when needed, may prolong the memory of the offence, and may end in default. It is regrettable that governments have not acted on the proposal that the court should pay the full amount of the

25 *Bond* v. *Chief Constable of Kent* (1982) 4 Cr App R (S) 314, *Godfrey* (1994) 15 Cr App R (S) 536.
26 *Vivian* (1978) 68 Cr App R 53; however, if a certain minimum loss is beyond dispute and a greater loss is contested and difficult to assess, the court should make the compensation order for the minimum loss: *James* [2003] 2 Cr App R (S) 574.
27 *Horsham Justices, ex p. Richards* (1985) 7 Cr App R (S) 158; *White* [1996] 2 Cr App R (S) 58.
28 *Smith* [1998] 2 Cr App R (S) 400.   29 *Graves* (1993) 14 Cr App R (S) 790.
30 *Taylor* (1993) 14 Cr App R (S) 276.   31 *Panayioutou* (1989) 11 Cr App R (S) 535.
32 See e.g. *Martin* (1989) 11 Cr App R (S) 424, a case where the offender was also sentenced to custody.
33 Cf. *Holah* (1989) 11 Cr App R (S) 282, also a case where the offender was imprisoned, with *McGuire* (1992) 13 Cr App R (S) 332.
34 *Olliver and Olliver* (1989) 11 Cr App R (S) 10, discussed below, part 10.5.6.

compensation order to the victim immediately out of court funds, and should then recover it from the offender in the ordinary way.[35]

Soon after the introduction of compensation orders, the question of their relation to other sentences was raised. The words of Scarman LJ in *Inwood* (1974)[36] remain apposite:

> Compensation orders were not introduced into our law to enable the convicted to buy themselves out of the penalties for crime. Compensation orders were introduced into our law as a convenient and rapid means of avoiding the expense of resort to civil litigation when the criminal clearly has means which would enable the compensation to be paid.

It therefore follows that an offender's ability to pay compensation should not be allowed to deflect the court from imposing a custodial sentence or a community sentence, if that is what the offence justifies.[37] If this were not so, the law would permit wealthy offenders to receive reduced sentences, which would infringe the principle of equality before the law (see Chapter 7.1). It may be said that for less serious offences the law accords precedence to reparative over punitive elements, in that a compensation order has priority over a fine. But the priority is reversed for serious offences: thus, in *Jorge* (1999)[38] the Court of Appeal, reviewing the authorities, confirmed that it is generally wrong to impose a compensation order with a custodial sentence unless 'either the defendant has assets from which to pay it, especially no doubt the proceeds of his crime, or he is reasonably assured of income when he comes out from which it is reasonable to expect him to pay'.

How frequently do courts make compensation orders? The trend is for them to award compensation less and less frequently. Thus in the Crown Court some 21 per cent of offenders in 1989 and 1990 were ordered to pay compensation, but this had fallen to 7 per cent by 2002. One possible reason for this is that the rise in the use of custody has precluded the making of a compensation order in some cases. Thus, for example, in 2002 the Crown Court only made a compensation order in 17 per cent of cases of violence and 3 per cent of burglary cases.[39] There has also been a decline in the use of compensation orders by magistrates' courts for indictable offences, from 29 per cent in 1990 to 15 per cent in 2002. An order was made in some 33 per cent of cases of violence and 52 per cent of criminal damage cases in 2002, but that was for indictable offences, and since common assault and most offences of criminal damage are summary only, it is worth noting that the number of compensation orders made in non-motoring summary cases increased from some 35,000 to 59,000 between 1992 and 2002. If one adds indictable and summary offences, the use of compensation orders by magistrates' courts remained stable between 1992 and 2002. However, the study by Flood-Page and Mackie showed

---

35 See the prevarication in Home Office (1990), para. 4.25.   36 (1974) 60 Cr App R 70, at p. 73.
37 E.g. *Copley* (1979) 1 Cr App R (S) 55.   38 [1999] 2 Cr App R (S) 1.
39 *Criminal Statistics 2002*, Table 4.21.

that legal procedures were not being carried out in some cases: a magistrates' court is required to give reasons if it does not make a compensation order, but in over 70 per cent of cases this was not done; in some cases magistrates said that they did not award compensation because the victim did not request it, a clear breach of the statutory requirement to consider it in every case of harm.[40] However, the most common reason for not making a compensation order was that stolen goods were recovered, and in some cases the offender's income was thought too low to make an order. Some courts regarded it as pointless or counter-productive to make an order against an offender in the same household as the victim.

Although the theory behind compensation orders is right, there are two significant practical drawbacks from the victim's point of view. First, an order can only be made if the offender is detected, prosecuted, convicted and not penniless. Since fewer than one-quarter of all reported offences are 'cleared up', and since around two-thirds of defendants are unemployed, a victim's prospects of receiving compensation from this source are hardly bright. Second, the increased use of police cautioning has led to fewer cases being brought to court over the last twenty years. There are good reasons in favour of diversion, as we saw in Chapter 1.4, but the result of diversion was often to leave the victim without compensation. These two reasons, and the great increase in the use of custody, mean that fewer victims now receive compensation from their offenders than twenty years ago: in 1983 some 128,000 offenders were ordered to pay compensation to their victims, whereas in 1993 the figure was only 97,000, and in 2002 it stood at 103,000. The advent of the conditional caution may change this, since one of the conditions that may be imposed on cautioned offenders is that they pay specified compensation to the victim.[41] Surveys of victims have shown that they set particular store by receiving some money, even if not full compensation, from the offender rather than from any other source.[42]

10.5 Fines

10.5.1 Introduction

The fine is the standard penalty for summary offences, and may be imposed for almost all indictable offences. Maximum fines are ranged on five levels according to the seriousness of the offence. Magistrates' courts are in any event limited to a maximum of £5,000 in most cases, but the Crown Court has no overall limit. Over 90 per cent of all cases in magistrates' courts result in a fine. Looking at indictable offences tried in magistrates' courts or the Crown Court, around 60 per cent of adult male offenders were fined in the mid-1970s, but the figure had declined to 26 per cent by 2002, and to 20 per cent for adult women. Fines are the normal response to offences committed by companies, and the attendant difficulties are discussed in part 10.5.6 below.

40 Flood-Page and Mackie (1998), pp. 60–4.   41 See ch. 1.4 above.
42 Shapland, Willmore and Duff (1985).

The fine is often presented as the ideal penal measure. It is easily calibrated, so that courts can reflect differing degrees of gravity and culpability. It is non-intrusive, since it does not involve supervision or the loss of one's time. Indeed, it is straightforwardly punitive, 'uncontaminated by other values'.[43] It also seems to be relatively effective, since surveys show that it tends to be followed by fewer reconvictions than other sentences. The assertion of superior efficacy has been doubted, since Tony Bottoms rightly pointed out that courts tend to select for fines offenders with a certain stability in their lives (job, family) which would in any case indicate a lower risk of reoffending.[44] Justifiable as this is as a criticism of most studies of comparative effectiveness, it remains true that fines have emerged well from almost all of them. This is no reason to claim *superior* efficacy, but neither does it suggest that the decline in fining should be applauded. As a recent Home Office survey puts it, 'reconviction rates for fines compare favourably with community penalties. There is thus no evidence that the switch from fines to community penalties that has occurred over the last twenty years has achieved anything by way of crime reduction.'[45]

The 1990 White Paper promoted the twin aims of greater use of fines and greater justice in fining: 'Setting fairer fine levels should lead to the greater use of fines and less difficulty in enforcing them.'[46] However, as will be explained in part 10.5.3 below, the provisions of the Criminal Justice Act 1991 on unit fines were abandoned within a few months of their introduction, and the overall use of fines has continued to decline. In recent years there has been a revival of government interest in fines. The Courts Act 2003 makes provision for the Court Service to focus on the enforcement of fines, but the Criminal Justice Act 2003 does little to advance the Halliday report's support for the fine. Halliday argued that fines should be used 'at all levels of seriousness, both in isolation and in combination with [other] non-custodial penalties'.[47] He was aware that adding a financial penalty to a community sentence should not be allowed to take the 'punitive weight' of the sentence above the level proportionate to the seriousness of the crime, and he also argued that 'substantial fines in quite serious cases might be enough to meet the needs of punishment'.[48] However, little of this found its way into the White Paper of 2002. Instead it was Rod Morgan, then Chief Inspector of Probation, who demonstrated that low-risk offenders were increasingly being given community sentences instead of fines, taking those offenders more quickly up-tariff and also 'silting up' the probation service with offenders who did not really need their intervention.[49] The Carter Review took this argument forward and returned fines to the main agenda of sentencing reform. Carter argued that

---

43 Young (1989).   44 Bottoms (1973).
45 Moxon (1998), p. 98.   46 Home Office (1990), para. 5.2.
47 Halliday (2001), para. 6.15. Earlier (para. 6.5), he stated that 'the "serious enough" threshold [for imposing a community sentence] may have unintentionally created an impression that fines should be reserved for the least serious cases, which is not the case'.
48 Halliday (2001), para. 6.16.   49 Morgan (2003).

Fines should replace community sentences for low risk offenders. 30 per cent of community sentences are given to offenders at low risk of reoffending.[50]

Carter then went on to recommend the introduction of a day fine system – along similar lines to the system abandoned in 1993. In its reply, the government cited the fall in the use of fines as a principal reason for the 'increased severity in sentencing' and rising use of prison.[51] It accepted the recommendation that 'revitalized fines should replace a very substantial number of the community sentences that are currently given to low risk offenders', and promised to explore the feasibility of legislation to introduce day fines.[52] These are significant steps, but there remains the practical question of how to turn courts back towards fining and away from their reliance on community sentences and custody.

10.5.2 Fines and fairness

As we saw in Chapter 7.5, the fine may raise questions related to the principle of equality before the law and the principle of equal impact. Equality before the law is relevant in two ways. One is that courts should not fine a wealthy offender when the offence justifies a more severe measure which they would have imposed on a less wealthy offender. The striking decision in *Markwick*[53] was cited in support. The other aspect is that courts should not impose a more severe penalty on an offender who lacks the means to pay what is regarded as an adequate fine. In the past, the Court of Appeal struck down several suspended sentences on this ground:[54] the proper course, if a court declines to impose a fine, is to move down to a conditional discharge and not up to a more severe measure. There is no ready way of assessing how faithfully the principle of equality before the law is followed in practice.

The principle of equal impact points to another aspect of social justice in relation to fines. It has long been established that a court should have regard to the means of the offender when calculating the amount of a fine, but this principle had been somewhat blunted in practice in three ways – the old rule that fines should not be increased for the rich, the difficulties in obtaining accurate information about an offender's financial situation, and courts' reluctance to impose fines that appear derisory to them and to newspaper readers. The 1991 Act attempted to tackle these problems.

10.5.3 The rise and fall of unit fines

In an endeavour to achieve more and fairer fining, the 1991 Act introduced the unit fine. Day-fine systems operate in other European countries, such as Germany and Sweden, and it was decided to adapt them for use here. An experiment in the late 1980s showed that, after initial scepticism among local magistrates, the courts had

50 Carter (2003), p. 27.   51 Home Office (2004), para. 19.
52 Home Office (2004), paras. 34–35. See also Coulsfield (2004) for a similar proposal.
53 (1953) 37 Cr App R 125.
54 E.g. *McGowan* [1975] Crim LR 111; *Ball* (1981) 3 Cr App R (S) 283.

quickly become accustomed to calculating fines in units; that fine levels were more realistic; and that fine enforcement was improved, with less resort to the sanction of imprisonment for non-payment.[55]

The success of these schemes not only persuaded the then government to provide for their introduction into all magistrates' courts under the 1991 Act, but also led several benches to introduce them of their own accord, in advance of the legislation. In outline, the scheme introduced by the 1991 Act was that magistrates' courts, when dealing with an individual (not a company), should calculate the fine by deciding how many units, on a scale from 1 to 50, represented the relative seriousness of the offence. This would be the judicial or judgmental part of the decision. Then the court would turn to the more administrative task of deciding how much the offender could afford to pay. The Act, combined with rules made by the Lord Chancellor's Department, instructed courts to calculate each offender's weekly disposable income, to make some standard deductions to reflect ordinary living expenses, and then to move towards the decision of how much the offender should pay per unit. The minimum was set at £4 per unit, which was regarded as possible for an offender whose only income came from state benefits, and the maximum was £100 per unit.

The statutory unit fine system came into force on 1 October 1992, and was abolished in the summer of 1993 by the Criminal Justice Act 1993. What were the problems? First, the amount of unit fines under the statutory scheme was far higher than in the experimental schemes. It is said that this was at the insistence of the Treasury, but it resulted in a scheme with a quite different flavour: few of the experimental courts went above £25 per unit, whereas the statutory scheme went up to £100 per unit. Second, the scheme emphasized income to the exclusion of capital and other indicia of wealth – an approach aimed at simplicity, but productive of some injustice. Third, the statutory scheme became extremely complex, particularly in the regulations for calculating weekly disposable income. Since the scheme was never intended to be precise, but merely to mark a significant step towards equality of impact, it was unfortunate that it became so complex. Fourth, a vocal group of magistrates, particularly some stipendiary magistrates, felt that the scheme was misconceived because it was too rigid and overlooked the problems of determining the income of certain types of offender, such as prostitutes and foreign tourists.

However, it was a fifth difficulty that was probably the major factor in the decision to abolish unit fines. The system resulted in particularly high fines for offenders who might previously have received relatively low fines, particularly middle-class motoring offenders with moderately or well-paid jobs. This, of course, was one of its aims: the 1990 White Paper referred to the need to impose substantial fines on 'an increasing minority of offenders with greater resources'.[56] If courts had routinely announced fines in terms of the number of units imposed, rather than the total payment, this element in the new scheme might have been less open to

---

55 See Gibson (1990), and Moxon, Sutton and Hedderman (1990).
56 Home Office (1990), para. 5.5.

misinterpretation. As it was, the press, and particularly one newspaper group, began assiduously to collect examples of different levels of fines being imposed on people who had committed similar offences. One newspaper headline ran: 'Two cases, minutes apart, but with very different penalties. For a Mr Rothschild, a £2,000 fine; for a man named Bell, an £84 fine.'[57] No mention was made of the principle of equal impact that lay behind the new scheme. The journalists almost seemed to be assuming that the two men should have received the same fine, despite the vast difference in their incomes. The widely publicized case of a man who was fined £1,200 for dropping an empty crisp packet in the street increased the pressure on the government to 'do something about' the new scheme, even though it quickly became evident that the reason why the magistrates had fined this offender at £100 per unit was that he failed to disclose his income to the court.

In May 1993, at a time when the Magistrates' Association had put together some proposals for alterations to the scheme, the then Home Secretary, Kenneth Clarke, made the politically extravagant gesture of announcing the abolition of unit fines entirely. That decision was founded on two manifest confusions. One confusion was that between the principle of equal impact and the details of the actual scheme adopted. Politicians and the media would speak and write as if all offenders should receive similar fines, irrespective of differences in wealth. The principle 'that different financial penalties can provide the same punishment for offenders of different means'[58] seems to have been lost among the complaints about the practical details of the legislative scheme adopted. That was not the scheme that had been so successful in the experiments. The other confusion was that between the right amount of structure and the right amount of discretion. The unit fine system attempted to formalize and to structure the reasoning of magistrates when calculating fines. It probably formalized it to too great an extent. But if the balance between structure and discretion was wrong, it does not follow that the whole system should be abolished.

Whether the Carter review's proposals will provoke further legislation on day fines or will disappear discreetly from view is difficult to predict. There is relatively little in the Carter review on day fines:[59] not only is there no attempt to confront (even to mention) the controversial aspects of the 1991 unit fine system, but also there is a suggestion that the maximum weekly deduction from benefit should be increased from £2.70. It will take more than this to achieve Carter's avowed aim, 'fines rebuilt as a credible punishment'.

10.5.4 Fines in magistrates' courts: business as usual?

The legislation on fines as sentences has now been substantially re-enacted in the Criminal Justice Act 2003. Section 164(2) provides that the amount of the fine should reflect the seriousness of the offence. Section 164(3) provides that in fixing

---

57 *Daily Mail*, 28 Oct. 1992, p. 5.   58 Home Office (1990), para. 5.2.
59 Less than a page is devoted to the whole subject: Carter (2003), p. 27.

the amount of the fine a court should take account of the offender's financial circumstances. Section 164(4) adds that this applies whether it has the effect of increasing or reducing the amount of the fine. These provisions ought to be applied step-wise: first, the court should determine the level of fine that represents the seriousness of the offence; second it should make the appropriate adjustment to reflect the offender's means. Section 164(1) requires a court to inquire into the offender's financial circumstances before fixing the amount of a fine. Section 162 empowers a court to make a financial circumstances order, requiring the relevant person to provide the court with such financial details as it requests.

This legislative framework was first introduced in 1993 to replace unit fines. What were its effects? Figures from the Home Office data collection exercise show that the proportionate use of fines for indictable offences at magistrates' courts rose to 42 per cent in the final quarter of 1992, and then fell back to 35 per cent in the final quarter of 1993, following the abolition of unit fines. The decline in fining was most marked amongst those who were unemployed at the time of sentence (from 43 per cent down to 32 per cent), and by the end of 1993 average fines for the unemployed had risen from £66 to £78. Average fines for the employed, on the other hand, had declined from £233 to £158.[60] No such detailed figures have been produced since then, but they suggest the re-emergence of the very unfairness problems that had led to the introduction of unit fines.

Research by Charman, Gibson, Honess and Morgan (1996) found that in 1995 some 55 per cent of magistrates' courts substantially adopted the Magistrates' Association guidelines on calculating fines, a further 28 per cent had devised a significant modification of those guidelines for local use, and that 17 per cent were operating a unit fine approach, using the logic of the scheme to assist magistrates to calculate fines within the new legislative framework. Sentencing exercises carried out by magistrates from various courts showed that those from courts using unit fines reached the most concordant decisions, and 'graduated fines more radically in accordance with defendants' incomes' compared with other courts. Those other courts had some divergent approaches:

> For example, an unemployed defendant in receipt of income support was fined a total of £250 plus £20 costs for three offences of using a car with a defective tyre, handbrake and headlamp by one panel . . . For the same offences, two other panels from the same [court] fined two employed defendants – one with a medium and the other with a high net disposable income – totals of £80 plus £20 costs and £160 plus £20 costs respectively.[61]

These were 'only' sentencing exercises, one might say, but they do little to allay fears that disparities in fining occur to a considerable degree. Research by Robin

---

60 Home Office (1994).
61 Charman et al. (1996), p. 4; one problem with fining for some motoring offences, such as driving without insurance or without road tax, is that low fines make it profitable for those on low incomes not to pay car insurance or road tax. But that consideration does not apply to this example.

Moore at the turn of the century also reveals a failure of many benches to grasp the financial circumstances of some offenders.[62] There appear to be two major barriers to fairer fining – a reluctance to fine unemployed people amounts which look small through middle-class eyes, and a reluctance to impose on offenders with substantial incomes fines which look high in relation to the offence. As to the first barrier, Staughton LJ lamented:

> What troubles me about these cases is not the remedies which the magistrates had to choose from as means of enforcement, but the size of the fines which people on income support were expected to pay out of resources which are said to be only sufficient for the necessities of life.[63]

As to the second barrier, Flood-Page and Mackie concluded from their research, in which they questioned magistrates about their willingness to increase fines for the wealthy, that 'these contrasting opinions meant that wealthy offenders could receive very different fines at different courts as the size of the fine imposed depends largely on the views of the magistrates at that court'.[64] Translating the principle of equality of impact into practice seems difficult to achieve.

The 2004 version of the *Magistrates' Court Sentencing Guidelines* embodies a practical attempt to grapple with this difficult problem. For each offence for which a fine is the guideline sentence, the guidelines indicate fine A, B or C as the starting point. The commentary then urges the court to use its powers to obtain financial information, including not only income but also savings, disposable assets, level of outgoings and any unpaid fines. It then advises magistrates as follows:

> The suggested fines in these Guidelines are given as either A, B or C. These represent 50 per cent, 100 per cent and 150 per cent of the defendant's weekly take home pay/benefit. (Weekly take home pay or benefit means weekly income after all deductions made by an employer (take home pay) or the amount of weekly benefit.) These levels take into account ordinary living expenses. This guidance should not be used as a tariff and every offender's means must be individually considered.[65]

This is an attempt to combine structure with flexibility. Supporters of unit fines will still find it too woolly,[66] whereas it will be welcomed by those who think that courts should be left with maximum discretion. The problem with the latter group is that their approach is capable of leading to unfair fines because of their failure to recognize the two barriers outlined above.

10.5.5 Fines in the Crown Court

The unit fine scheme was confined to magistrates' courts, and the Crown Court continued with only one significant change – a statutory principle that fines should

---

62 Moore (2003).   63 *Stockport Justices, ex p. Conlon* [1997] 2 All ER 204 at p. 214.
64 Flood-Page and Mackie (1998), p. 53.   65 Magistrates' Association (2004), p. 85.
66 Cf. Moore (2003), who argues for a different structure based on payments for a set number of weeks.

be increased for the rich as well as reduced for the poor, now found in s. 164(4).[67] Section 163 empowers the Crown Court to impose a fine (not subject to any limit, other than the offender's means) 'instead of or in addition to' any other way of dealing with the offender. Questions remain about the extent to which the Crown Court adjusts fines according to the income of offenders, particularly poor offenders. Thus, Flood-Page and Mackie found that the average fine for an unemployed man was £340 (which would take 16 months to pay at £5 per week, then thought to be the maximum for those on state benefits), and that just under one-fifth of unemployed men who were fined had to pay over £500.[68] Section 152(2) of the 2003 Act requires courts to impose custody only where it is satisfied that 'neither a fine alone nor a community sentence can be justified for the offence', and that indicates a need for courts to consider imposing a substantial fine in cases approaching the custody threshold. The ensuing difficulty is that courts may fine those who can afford to pay large amounts and imprison those of lesser means.

A number of related issues of principle were raised in *Olliver and Olliver* (1989).[69] Two brothers were convicted of wounding and of assault occasioning actual bodily harm to a police officer. Such offences would often result in immediate custodial sentences, but the court imposed suspended sentences of two years and 18 months, combined with fines and compensation orders totalling over £5,000 for one of the brothers, and somewhat less for the other. The reason for taking this course was that the brothers ran a carpentry business on which the jobs of 23 others depended, and to imprison them would put the business and the jobs in jeopardy. The Court of Appeal dismissed an appeal against the fines, Lord Lane remarking that it is 'desirable if possible to keep people out of prison' and that 'if people can be dealt with properly by means of non-custodial sentences, and fines are possibly the best of all the non-custodial sentences, then that should be done'. This case was supremely difficult, involving as it did a conflict between the principle of equality before the law, the principle of restraint in the use of custody, and the avoidance of harmful consequences to innocent third parties. However, it is important that the last-mentioned point be emphasized. Surely it was the consequences to the 23 employees which turned the case:[70] restraint in the use of custody should not so easily outweigh the principle of equality before the law in general Crown Court sentencing.

10.5.6 Repayment periods

Courts should always be prepared to allow time to pay. Some offenders will be expected to pay the whole sum at once. Others may be allowed time to pay over a longer period, although subsequent adjustments are often regarded as an administrative decision and practices differ from court to court.[71] The normal maximum

---

67 In these cases there must still be some element of proportionality to the seriousness of the offence: *Jerome* [2001] 1 Cr App R (S) 316.
68 Flood-Page and Mackie (1998), p. 106.   69 (1989) 11 Cr App R (S) 10.
70 See the discussion in ch. 5.4.5 above.   71 Moore (2003).

repayment period was set at one year by judicial decisions in the 1980s,[72] but some commentators have assumed that the effect of *Olliver and Olliver* (1989)[73] is to overturn this. What the Lord Chief Justice said in that case was that there is nothing wrong in principle in the payment period being longer than one year, provided that it was not an undue burden or too severe a punishment. Two years would seldom be too long, and three years might be acceptable in an appropriate case. Care must surely be taken in ensuring that these longer periods are not used too readily, particularly since they apply to compensation orders as much as to fines. If the burdens are too great, the orders may be prison sentences in disguise.[74]

10.5.7 Fining companies

A company which is convicted of, or pleads guilty to, an offence may be sentenced in one of a number of ways – a compensation order, or an absolute or conditional discharge, would be possible. But fines are the most frequent penalty, and this immediately raises the issue of how such fines should be calculated. Magistrates' courts are subject to a maximum fine of £20,000 in most such cases, so many of the serious cases are committed to the Crown Court. In the leading cases on environmental offences, the Court of Appeal rightly emphasizes the importance of assessing the degree of the company's culpability, especially where the offence is one of strict liability. But, when summarizing the issues in *Anglian Water Services Ltd* (2004),[75] nothing was said about the relevance of the economic standing of the company to the size of the fine. This issue was discussed in the leading decision on fines for breaches of the health and safety legislation, *F. Howe & Son (Engineers) Ltd* (1999),[76] where the Court of Appeal took account of the fact that this was a small company with limited financial resources. The judgment sets out the main factors relevant in assessing culpability for health and safety breaches, and then adds that the state of the company's finances is a relevant factor. For larger companies, however, it seems that their financial standing is rarely discussed and the size of the fine is calculated by reference to fine levels in similar cases.[77]

In principle, the approach to fining companies should be the same as for individuals: s. 164(2) states that the fine should reflect the seriousness of the offence, s. 164(3) states that the court should take account of the financial circumstances of the offender ('whether an individual or other person'), and s. 164(4) states that this may have the effect of increasing or reducing the amount of the fine. Adjusting fines to the means of individuals is difficult enough: how can courts adjust fines to the ability of companies to pay? This question was broached by the Sentencing Advisory Panel in its first advice to the Court of Appeal, but it found the choice between

72 *Knight* (1980) 2 Cr App R (S) 82, *Nunn* (1983) 5 Cr App R (S) 203.
73 Above, n. 69 and accompanying text.
74 As recognized by Staughton LJ in the quotation above, text at n. 63.
75 [2004] 1 Cr App R (S) 374, summarizing the effect of *Milford Haven Port Authority* [2000] 2 Cr App R (S) 423 and *Yorkshire Water Services Ltd* [2002] 2 Cr App R (S) 37.
76 [1999] 2 Cr App R (S) 37.
77 E.g. *Avon Lippiatt Hobbs (Contractors) Ltd* [2003] 2 Cr App R (S) 427, reviewing the size of fines in earlier cases.

turnover, profitability and liquidity as measures of company wealth to be difficult to resolve.[78] Nonetheless, it remains important for the courts to take account of the means of companies, particularly when imposing a fine on a relatively small business. There is also the possibility of giving the company time to pay the fine.[79]

10.5.8 The enforcement of fines[80]

Practices differ considerably from one magistrates' court to another. There are various ways in which the rate of payment can be adjusted, sometimes by agreement with the court staff who deal with fine enforcement, sometimes as a result of a court appearance.[81] The speed at which offenders are brought back to court for default proceedings varies considerably, and the attitude of the courts at those proceedings varies also.[82] There has long been a range of enforcement measures, including reminder letters, money payment supervision orders, attachment of earnings orders, distress warrants, overnight detention in a police station and suspended committal to prison. The ultimate sanction is imprisonment for default, the maximum periods being regulated by statute.

In recent years there has been a concerted and successful effort to reduce the number of fine defaulters sent to prison. Over 22,000 fine defaulters were received into prison in 1993 and in 1994. More than three-quarters of these were unemployed, and were on state benefits, some two-thirds had been in prison before, and 80 per cent had more than one set of fines outstanding. The most frequent reason for default given by those interviewed in a small survey was that they could not afford to pay the fines; clearly it is important to distinguish between those who cannot pay and those who can but will not.[83] Another survey found that some magistrates were reluctant to consider some alternative enforcement measures, such as money payment supervision orders.[84] In the late 1990s courts were urged to make much greater use of alternative means of enforcement, both by guidance from the Lord Chancellor's Department and by the landmark decision in *Oldham JJ, ex p. Cawley*,[85] which requires courts to give active consideration to all alternatives before committing a young fine defaulter to prison and to state those reasons in open court. The provisions relating to the committal of adult fine defaulters to prison are less exacting, as the Divisional Court pointed out in *Stockport JJ, ex p. Conlon*,[86] but the court in that case none the less scrutinized the reasoning of the magistrates and remitted one case for reconsideration.

As a consequence of these developments, and a 'best practice' guide issued by the Lord Chancellor's Department, the number of fine defaulters received into prison dropped sharply – from its peak of 22,000 in 1994 to around 6,000 in 1997 and to

---

78 SAP, *Environmental Offences* (2000), paras. 22–25. This is the only advice from the SAP that has never been acted upon; on this particular issue, however, it invited the Home Secretary to give further examination to the problems.
79 *Rollco Screw and Rivet Co. Ltd* [1999] 2 Cr App R (S) 436.
80 For thorough recent reviews see Moore (2003), (2004), and Raine, Dunstan and Mackie (2004).
81 Charman et al. (1996), p. 3; Raine et al. (2004).
82 See Moore (2004).   83 Moxon and Whittaker (1996); Moore (2004).
84 Whittaker and Mackie (1997).   85 [1996] 1 All ER 464.   86 [1997] 2 All ER 204.

just over 1,000 in 2002.[87] A court may instead impose a community service order, a curfew with electronic tagging or disqualification from driving as a means of dealing with unpaid fines. Findings from two pilot areas showed that over three-quarters of the orders made were community service orders; that, although it remains possible for a fine defaulter to terminate the default order by paying off part or the whole of the fine, this rarely happened; and that both magistrates and fine defaulters seemed content with the new arrangements.[88] Fine default remains a problem, however, and this is largely because collection and enforcement policies have been so variable. In 2002 the national payment rate for financial penalties was 59 per cent, varying considerably from area to area, but the position seems to have improved since then. Further improvement may stem from the Courts Act 2003, which provides for the appointment of fines officers (s. 36) and strengthens the powers to require information and to enforce financial penalties against those who do not pay (ss. 95–97). But effective enforcement involves understanding the reasons why offenders default. In Moore's sample, over three-quarters of fine defaulters were unemployed, and there was little prospect of them paying the sums required.[89] Moore argues for a more sensitive approach that focuses on better decision-making by courts at the stage of imposing the fine, and then careful enquiries in cases of default, leading to properly targeted methods of ensuring payment.[90] Similarly, Raine, Dunstan and Mackie show that it is wrong to assume that non-payment is simply the fault of wilful or feckless offenders, and argue that it is preferable to consider a range of reasons for non-payment (including decisions of the court and its staff) which then require a range of appropriate responses.[91]

The significant move away from imprisonment for fine default is to be welcomed, particularly because the offences for which offenders are fined are usually well short of custody in their seriousness. But if the fine is to become more widely used again, care must be taken to ensure that initial decisions and subsequent enforcement are properly grounded. There should also be active consideration of whether custody should be regarded as a proper sanction for default: in principle it should not, and some European countries manage without it.[92]

10.6 The generic community sentence

10.6.1 Introduction

We now move away from discharges and fines and begin a lengthy consideration of community sentences. In the framework of the Criminal Justice Act 1991 this involved stepping from one level up to a higher level: a case was only considered serious enough for a community sentence if it was too serious to be dealt with by a fine or discharge. However, as we have seen, the Halliday report commended the

87 Prison Statistics 2002, Table 1.13.   88 Elliott, Airs and Webb (1999).
89 Moore (2003), p. 16.   90 Moore (2004).
91 Raine, Dunstan and Mackie (2004), at pp. 523–34.
92 Shaw (1989), and Council of Europe (1993).

use of substantial fines in serious cases – as an alternative or a supplement to a community sentence. Thus the 2003 Act retains the threshold test for a community sentence – the case must be serious enough to warrant such a sentence (s. 148(1)) – but does not exclude the use of fines for cases at that level. Thus the Sentencing Guidelines Council states that 'even where the threshold for a community sentence has been passed, a financial penalty or discharge may still be an appropriate penalty'.[93] Moreover, in cases where the court is considering a custodial sentence, it must only impose such a sentence if satisfied that 'neither a fine nor a community sentence can be justified for the offence'.[94]

Under the 1991 Act there was a choice of half a dozen or more forms of community sentence, many with familiar names (probation order, community service order), and each with its own statutory requirements. New orders had been added to the list (e.g. the drug treatment and testing order) but, as outlined in part 10.1 above, history shows that this policy of proliferation was not successful in its major objective – to reduce the use of imprisonment by expanding the use of community sentences.

The Halliday report found four major problems with the then approach to community sentences.[95] First, the law was unduly complex and therefore unclear to courts, offenders and the public. Different orders had different statutory restrictions, and so forth. Second, the positioning of community sentences was unclear: the idea of 'alternatives to imprisonment' had been abandoned, which suggested that community sentences were positioned just below custody in the hierarchy, but the requirements added to community sentences had become increasingly onerous and custody was frequently used in cases of breach. Third, there was confusion about the 'punitive weight' of the different forms of community sentence, making it difficult to achieve any kind of proportionality. And fourth, as just mentioned, the relationship between community sentences and fines was unduly rigid.

The Halliday report responded to these perceived problems by proposing a single, generic community sentence which would require the offender to be supervised and to fulfil one or more requirements as specified by the court, such requirements being proportionate in punitive weight to the seriousness of the offence(s). Halliday envisaged that the requirements would be made by the court after it had received a pre-sentence report which contained an assessment of the needs of, and risk presented by, the offender.[96] Although the purpose of the community sentence would be the reduction of reoffending, Halliday insisted on a proportionality constraint: once the sentencer has decided 'the amount of punishment that would be proportionate . . . the "punitive weight" should determine how much can and should be done to reduce the risks of reoffending and make reparation'.[97] The 2002 White Paper accepted the thrust of these proposals, and said very little about the details. Instead, it recalled that there was general public support for 'changing the existing arrangements for community sentences', and commented that 'they are still

93 SGC, *Overarching Principles: Seriousness* (2004), para. 1.36.
94 S. 152(2) of the 2003 Act, discussed in ch. 9.4.1 above.   95 Halliday (2001), paras. 6.2–6.5.
96 Halliday (2001), paras. 6.6–6.14.   97 Halliday (2001), para. 6.6.

not tough enough nor do they allow the sentence to be matched to the individual offender'.[98] This rhetoric was used to announce the introduction of 'a customized community sentence'.

The Criminal Justice Act 2003 simply terms this 'a community sentence'. There are five major issues to be discussed: the threshold tests for imposing a community sentence, the range of requirements, the choice of requirement(s), monitoring progress and dealing with breach. The Sentencing Guidelines Council has issued a relevant guideline – *New Sentences: Criminal Justice Act 2003* – and reference is made to that where appropriate.

10.6.2 The threshold tests for imposing a community sentence

There are two separate sets of circumstances in which a community sentence may lawfully be imposed. The first and more widely applicable threshold test is that created by s. 148(1):

> A court must not pass a community sentence on an offender unless it is of the opinion that the offence, or the combination of the offence and one or more offences associated with it, was serious enough to warrant such a sentence.[99]

The purpose of this provision is to ensure that community sentences are not used for minor cases, which should generally be dealt with by way of a discharge or fine. The key judgment here is one of relative seriousness, and it is very difficult to offer concrete guidance – this is one of those issues on which the spirit or disposition of the courts will always be more influential than any attempt at guidance. The Magistrates' Courts Sentencing Guidelines indicate a fine as the starting point for some offences and a community sentence as the starting point for others, but this amounts to general guidance and it covers whole offences (e.g. theft) without any differentiation. It will be important for the National Probation Service or NOMS to develop a means of indicating to the court that they do not regard a case as sufficiently serious for a community sentence. Such an intimation may be unwelcome to some courts, perhaps in the belief that assessments of seriousness are a judicial matter. The SGC's guidelines contain a gentle nudge in the direction of restraining the use of community sentences:

> Where an offender has a low risk of reoffending, particular care needs to be taken in the light of evidence that indicates that there are circumstances where inappropriate intervention can increase the risk of reoffending rather than decrease it. In addition, recent improvements in enforcement of financial penalties make them a more viable sentence in a wider range of cases.[100]

---

98 Home Office (2002), para. 5.20.
99 Broadly speaking, an offence is 'associated with' the current offence if it is one for which the court is passing sentence on the same occasion: *Baverstock* (1993) 14 Cr App R (S) 471, *Godfrey* (1993) 14 Cr App R (S) 804.
100 SGC, *New Sentences: Criminal Justice Act* (2004), para. 1.1.9.

This guidance is based on risk of reoffending, whereas the point at issue is the different one of avoiding a disproportionate response to a relatively minor offence. But its general thrust communicates to sentencers the need for restraint.

The second and less frequently used threshold is to be found in s. 151 of the 2003 Act.[101] This empowers a court to impose a community sentence on a person who has been fined on three or more occasions since the age of 16, whose current offence is not serious enough to warrant a community sentence (even taking account of previous convictions under s. 143(2)), and where the court concludes that it would be in the interests of justice to impose a community sentence. The SGC warns that in these cases 'great care will be needed in assessing whether a community sentence is appropriate since failure to comply could result in a custodial sentence'.[102] There may be some cases where an element of supervision will help some such offenders to overcome underlying problems, but the danger is that a number of minor offenders will be taken up-tariff and hence subjected to more severe sanctions than their minor crimes properly warrant.

10.6.3 The range of requirements

The 2003 Act provides 12 forms of requirement that a court may make as a community order (s. 177) that constitutes a community sentence for the purpose of the Act. These apply only to offenders aged 18 and over: a different list applies to younger offenders, and is discussed in chapter 12 below. The principles that should guide a court when determining which requirements to impose are discussed in part 10.6.4 below. Here, the focus is upon the meaning and legal framework for each of the 12 requirements.

1. Unpaid work requirement. Section 199 of the 2003 Act states that an offender may be required to perform between 40 and 300 hours of unpaid work, provided that the court is satisfied that the offender is a suitable person to perform such work. The work must be carried out within 12 months 'at such times as he may be instructed by the responsible officer' (s. 200(1)). This requirement is a new name for the measure introduced in 1972 as the community service order and renamed the community punishment order in 2000. When proposing these orders in 1970, the Advisory Council on the Penal System suggested that they would appeal to sentencers with various penal philosophies:

> To some, it would be simply a more constructive and cheaper alternative to short sentences of imprisonment; by others it would be seen as introducing into the penal system a new dimension with an emphasis on reparation to the community; others again would regard it as a means of giving effect to the old adage that the punishment should fit the crime; while still others would stress the value of bringing offenders into close touch with those members of the community who are most in need of help and support.[103]

101 It substantially re-enacts s. 59 of the PCCS Act 2000, and was discussed in ch. 6.5 above.
102 SGC (above, n. 100), para. 1.1.10.
103 Advisory Council on the Penal System (1970), para. 33.

Perhaps it was this range of reparative, retributive and rehabilitative functions which led to the swift adoption of community service orders into English sentencing practice. Since then they have become more onerous: the *2000 National Standards* state that work placements should 'occupy offenders fully and be physically, emotionally or mentally demanding',[104] and the 2003 Act raises the maximum from 240 to 300 hours. If the essence of the unpaid work requirement lies in its punitive function, in terms of the performance of hard work, the other functions may nevertheless be achieved as by-products. The element of reparation involved in unpaid work is symbolic, since it does not involve direct reparation to individual victims, although it may require repair work or construction work in the community which can be regarded as a rough equivalent to the harm done. The choice of work, however, is for the probation service and not the courts. The *National Standards* require that the probation officer should first issue the offender with a set of requirements. The probation service is responsible for maintaining a suitable range of work placements, usually run by voluntary agencies. Once the offender is assessed and is assigned to a particular work placement, the times of work should be agreed. The *National Standards* state that the first work placement should be arranged to take place within ten working days of the order being made, that offenders should be offered no fewer than five hours per week and that a weekly record should be given to the offender, detailing hours worked and giving comments on the satisfactoriness of the work. There are also standards relating to meal breaks, travelling time, bad weather and so on.[105]

The use of this type of community order has been relatively static over the last decade, declining from 9 per cent of adult male offenders in 1992 to 8 per cent in 2002, and increasing from 5 per cent of adult females in 1992 to 7 per cent in 2002. For what types of offender might unpaid work requirements be used? Evidence from Flood-Page and Mackie's survey in the mid-1990s suggests that magistrates made the choice between community service and probation on various grounds, often connected with their belief about the needs of the offender and the local organization of the two forms of sentence. Some said that unpaid work was more appropriate for unemployed offenders, since it might reintroduce them to a form of regular work, but the sentencing practices of magistrates in that study showed that a lower percentage of those on community service were unemployed compared with probation (65 per cent and 81 per cent respectively).[106] The same pattern was evident in the Crown Court cases (49 per cent and 83 per cent respectively). Fewer of those on community service had previous convictions (58 per cent, compared with 77 per cent for probation), and fewer stood convicted of more than one offence (31 per cent compared with 47 per cent for probation). As expected, fewer had problems of drug addiction, mental disorder or stress.[107] This may be taken to show that community service was not so high on the tariff as probation orders, but

---

104 National Standards (2000), D16.   105 National Standards (2000), D14.
106 Flood-Page and Mackie (1998), pp. 37–8.   107 Flood-Page and Mackie (1998), p. 102.

that is not a straightforward deduction. Offenders were often placed on probation because of their personal and social problems, and their previous convictions may be evidence of that rather than of serious offending, so the relationship between these two forms of community sentence probably has more to do with offender than with offence characteristics.

2. *Activity requirement.* Section 201 of the Act provides that an offender may be required to present himself and participate in specified activities for up to 60 days. This requirement may only be imposed if a probation officer has been consulted and if the court is satisfied that it is feasible to secure compliance with the requirement. The place where the offender must present himself should be a community rehabilitation centre or other approved premises. The activities may be reparative in purpose and involve 'contact between offenders and persons affected by their offences' (s. 201(2)). In effect, this is a rebranding of the former condition of attendance at a probation (day) centre, which could be added to a probation order. Now that supervision is an underlying element of all community orders, the activity requirement stands on its own. The *National Standards 2000* include detailed instructions for the organization of activities in what are now to be known as community rehabilitation centres. The activities may involve training in social skills, communication, being interviewed and so forth.

3. *Programme requirement.* Section 202 of the Act provides that an offender may be required to participate in an accredited programme for a specified number of days. This requirement may only be imposed if a probation officer has recommended the programme as suitable for the offender and if the court is satisfied that a programme is available at the place specified. The legislation does not lay down a maximum period for this requirement: no doubt the length of the particular programme will be a factor here, but the need to observe proportionality constraints means that the courts should not simply make a programme requirement of whatever length is requested, without reference to the seriousness of the offence. Progress is being made towards the accreditation of programmes by the Correctional Services Accreditation Panel. In the early years a variety of programmes was accredited – six sex offender treatment programmes; five general offender behaviour programmes, including Reasoning and Rehabilitation and Think First; and four others, dealing with such problems as anger management and drink-impaired drivers.[108] The aim of these programmes is to take advantage of 'What Works' findings and to apply and develop them for particular groups of offender.

4. *Prohibited activity requirement.* Section 203 of the Act empowers a court to make a requirement prohibiting the offender from participating in specified activities on specified days or for a certain period. There is a duty to consult a probation officer before making this requirement. The section mentions the possibility of requiring that the offender does not possess, use or carry a firearm; another possible

108 Rex, Lieb, Bottoms and Wilson (2003).

prohibition would be from driving a motor vehicle. No maximum duration for this requirement is stated.

5. *Curfew requirement.* Section 204 of the Act provides that a court may require an offender to remain, for periods specified in the relevant order (not less than 2 nor more than 12 hours per day), at a place so specified. The requirement may last for a maximum period of six months, and before making it the court must obtain and consider information about the place at which the offender is to remain under curfew. A court that decides on a curfew requirement must also impose an electronic monitoring requirement, unless an exception applies. One exception is where the consent of another person is needed and it is not forthcoming (s. 215(2)); another is where the court has not been notified that arrangements for electronic monitoring are available in the area (s. 218(4)); and a third is where 'in the particular circumstances of the case' the court considers it inappropriate to require electronic monitoring (s. 177(3)(b)). Beyond curfew cases, courts are empowered to add an electronic monitoring requirement to other requirements so long as all the necessary conditions are fulfilled (s. 177(4)).

Experiments with electronic monitoring began in 1990, the then government declaring that 'the criminal justice system should take advantage of modern technology when it is sensible and practical to do so'.[109] Some have argued that electronic monitoring is not acceptable because it breaches an offender's human rights: requiring an offender to wear an electronic anklet may be held incompatible with Article 3 of the Convention (no inhuman or degrading punishment) or with Article 8 (right to respect for private life), but there has not been a successful challenge on these grounds. Others have doubted whether it is practical to rely on the technology: however, after some early disappointments, equipment failures are now relatively rare, and successful completion rates of 82 per cent were comparable with other community orders.[110] Interviews of magistrates and probation officers suggest that tagging is inappropriate for those whose lifestyles are chaotic, who are substance misusers or who present risks to the family or the public. Tagging was thought particularly useful to disrupt 'pattern offending', such as shoplifting, night-time burglary or public order offences on Friday and Saturday nights.[111] Electronic monitoring is widely used for prisoners released early on home detention curfew.[112] Indeed, curfew orders may be seen as creating a 'virtual prison' for an offender, by placing strong restrictions on movement for certain periods.[113] But this raises the vexed issue of the relative position or 'penal bite' of a curfew with electronic monitoring: if it operates like a 'virtual prison', should it not be seen as one of the most onerous requirements for a community sentence? Or will it come to be seen as a normal requirement of most such sentences, perhaps even taking the place of supervision?[114]

---

109 Home Office (1990), para. 4.22.   110 Mortimer and May (1997).
111 Mortimer, Pereira and Walter (1999), p. 3.   112 See ch. 9.5.2 above.
113 See Roberts, J. (2004).   114 See further Nellis (2004), pp. 240–1.

6. *Exclusion requirement.* Section 205 of the Act empowers a court to prohibit an offender from entering a specified place for a specified period of up to two years. The order may limit the prohibition to certain hours, or to different places for different times. This power was first introduced in 2000, and it is similar in some ways to the anti-social behaviour order, which may also be used to prohibit a person from going to certain places (although supervision may be added in a community sentence but not in an ASBO, and ASBOs must be for a minimum of two years).[115]

7. *Residence requirement.* Section 206 of the Act provides that a court may make a requirement that the offender should reside, for a specified period, at a certain place. The court is required to consider the offender's home surroundings, and only to specify a hostel or other institution as the place of residence if so recommended by a probation officer. This requirement is a version of a long-standing condition that could be added to probation orders, usually requiring residence at an approved probation hostel. Much depends on the availability of hostel accommodation and the assessed suitability of the offender for a particular hostel. However, it will be noted that the residence requirement does not have to relate to a hostel: an offender may be required to reside at his home, or with a relative, for example. In appropriate cases a curfew order may be added, with or without electronic monitoring.

8. *Mental health treatment requirement.* Sections 207 and 208 of the Act provide that a court may require the offender to submit to treatment by or under the direction of a registered medical practitioner. This, too, is a long-standing requirement that was formerly added to a probation order in appropriate cases, and that may be used for offences that normally attract a substantial custodial sentence.[116] It will be discussed further in Chapter 12.3 below.

9. *Drug rehabilitation requirement.* Sections 209–211 provide that a court may require an offender to submit to drug treatment and testing for a period of at least six months. The court first has to be satisfied that the offender is dependent on, or has a propensity to misuse, drugs; that this may be susceptible to treatment; and that arrangements can be made for treatment, either as a resident or as a non-resident. This requirement may only be made if the offender consents. There are provisions for courts to review the offender's progress (s. 210) and to make changes to the requirement (s. 211), somewhat along the lines of 'drug courts' in the United States. This requirement replaces the DTTO (drug treatment and testing order), introduced in 2000 in order to provide a measure aimed directly at tackling the link between drugs and crime. As the name suggested, the two elements were that the offender should undergo a programme of treatment and that during that programme he should be subjected to periodic testing to see whether he was still taking drugs.

The DTTO had a broadly favourable reception in the courts: many sentencers have welcomed a measure that tackles addiction and welcomed the court's role

---

115 For further discussion, see ch. 6.5 above and ch. 13 below.
116 E.g. *Attorney General's Reference No. 37 of 2004 (Dawson)* [2005] 1 Cr App R (S) 295.

in monitoring progress, but one frequently heard complaint is that the resources were not available for a sufficient number of orders (and indeed some areas ran out of earmarked funds).[117] Enthusiasm for these orders is sometimes tempered by the frequency with which offenders lapse or fail to complete them, an expected outcome given the chaotic and troubled lives of most of the offenders involved.[118] The positioning of the DTTO in the sentencing hierarchy has also given rise to differences of opinion. There are certainly some cases in which a DTTO was thought appropriate for offences that would normally attract sentences of around three years,[119] although on other occasions the Court of Appeal has given priority to the seriousness of the offences over the prospect of preventing reoffending.[120] If the sentencing framework of the 2003 Act is applied, it seems unlikely that community sentences with drug rehabilitation requirements will be made for offences 'worth' three years' imprisonment.

10. Alcohol treatment requirement. Section 212 of the Act empowers a court to impose a requirement that the offender submits to treatment with a view to the reduction or elimination of the offender's dependency on alcohol. This requirement does not include submission to testing, but otherwise it has similar conditions to the drug rehabilitation requirement – the court must be satisfied that the offender is dependent on alcohol; that this may be susceptible to treatment; that arrangements can be made for treatment, either as a resident or as a non-resident; and that the offender consents. This requirement replaces the alcohol treatment condition that could be added to a probation order since 2000.

11. Supervision requirement. Section 213 of the Act introduces a supervision requirement, which may be made for the purpose of promoting the offender's reha-bilitation and which may last as long as the community order as a whole lasts. It seems that this will be regarded as the basic requirement of a community sentence, usually combined with one or more of the other requirements. It is, in effect, a replacement for the probation order, a long-standing feature of the English sen-tencing system. The welfarist approach that predominated in the 1960s and before has now given way, at least in rhetoric, to the idea of probation as an order of the court that is a 'tough and demanding' measure, which is 'credible' in the eyes of the courts and the public, and which is fair in the sense of imposing similar and proportionate restrictions on the offenders subject to it. The following extract from the 2000 *National Standards* sets the tone:

> C7 The purpose of a community sentence is to:
>
> provide a rigorous and effective punishment;
> reduce the likelihood of reoffending;
> rehabilitate the offender, where possible; and
> enable reparation to be made to the community.

---

117 See Hough et al. (2003), p. 49.
118 See generally Rumgay (2004), reporting (at p. 260) that breach proceedings were taken for 86 per cent of DTTOs in 2003.
119 E.g. *Kelly* [2003] 1 Cr App R (S) 472, *Belli* [2004] 1 Cr App R (S) 490.
120 E.g. *Attorney General's Reference No. 28 of 2001* [2001] EWCA Crim 1373.

C8 Supervision in the community . . . shall:

address and reduce offending behaviour;
challenge the offender to accept responsibility for the crimes committed and their consequences;
contribute to the protection of the public;
motivate and assist the offender towards a greater sense of personal responsibility and discipline . . .[121]

The language is far more controlling than would have been used ten or fifteen years previously, but this should be seen as emphasizing one long-recognized element of probation work rather than as a complete break with the past. There remains a commitment to rehabilitative techniques, and several of the aims set out above can be brought within Francis Allen's definition of rehabilitation – 'effect[ing] changes in the characters, attitudes and behaviour of convicted offenders'.[122]

What kinds of offender were made subject to probation orders? The proportionate use of probation orders has edged slowly upwards over the last decade, from 9 per cent of adult male indictable offenders in 1992 to 12 per cent in 2002, and from 16 per cent of adult female offenders in 1992 to 21 per cent in 2002. A study of the characteristics of offenders on probation shows that they are an unusual and troubled group. Only one-fifth are in regular work, some two-thirds have state benefits as their main source of income and are in debt, over two-thirds live in rented accommodation, over half reported health problems or disability, drug use was high but alcohol use low[123] – all these diverge considerably from rates in the general population. As noted when discussing unpaid work requirements in part 10.6.3.1 above, the recent tendency has been for those placed on supervision (previously probation) to be more likely to have previous convictions, suggesting that these are not low-risk offenders and (perhaps) that the penal bite of this requirement is relatively high.

12. Attendance centre requirement. Section 214 provides that a court may require an offender to attend at an attendance centre for between 12 and 36 hours, so long as local arrangements are available. Attendance centres were developed primarily for young offenders, and are discussed further in Chapter 12 below. Section 177(1) provides that this requirement cannot be made unless the offender is aged under 25 at the time.

10.6.4 The choice of requirement(s)

Assuming that the threshold test for a community sentence (considered in part 10.6.3.2 above) has been satisfied, the court's next step is to choose which requirement(s) are appropriate in the particular case. The relevant statutory provision is s. 148(2):

---

121 *National Standards* (2000), C2.   122 Allen (1981), p. 2.   123 Mair and May (1997), ch. 3.

Where a court passes a community sentence which consists of or includes a community order –

the particular requirement or requirements forming part of the community order must be such as, in the opinion of the court, is, or taken together are, the most suitable for the offender, and

the restrictions on liberty imposed by the order must be such as in the opinion of the court are commensurate with the seriousness of the offence, or the combination of the offence and one or more offences associated with it.

These provisions adapt those in s. 6 of the Criminal Justice Act 1991, and were built on suggestions made by Tony Bottoms (1989) and particularly by Martin Wasik and Andrew von Hirsch in 1988, demonstrating how the desert rationale might be applied to non-custodial sentencing. Those authors sketched a model based on the 'limited substitutability' of sanctions of roughly the same degree of severity,[124] and the statutory test goes some way in this direction – prescribing not only that the community orders must be commensurate with the seriousness of the offence, but also that the particular order(s) 'must be . . . the most suitable for the offender'. The statutory formula is therefore designed to ensure that measures to reduce reoffending are taken within the framework of a proportionate sentence.

A report from the Probation Service will in many cases be influential in the decision whether to make a community sentence rather than an alternative disposal. However, the guideline also states that, once a court has decided on a community sentence, it should ask for a pre-sentence report specific to the issues in the particular case.[125] There are three key issues to be addressed. First, as the Halliday report advocated,[126] as s. 148(2)(b) states and as the SGC's guideline emphasizes, the court must preserve proportionality between the restrictions on liberty entailed by the requirement(s) and the seriousness of the offence(s). The Halliday report rightly complained that this proportionality constraint in the 1991 Act had never worked properly, because no one had authoritatively established the punitive weight of the various forms of community sentence.[127] Halliday's recommendations on this have been put into effect by the SGC's guideline, which sets three ranges of sentence within community orders, graduated according to the degree of restriction they impose. Courts are required by the guideline to indicate, when they ask for a pre-sentence report on this point, 'which of the three sentencing ranges is relevant and the purpose(s) of sentencing that the package of requirements is required to fulfil'.[128] The second key issue, as the Halliday report advocated,[129] as s. 148(2)(a) states and as the SGC's guideline emphasizes, is that the court must determine

---

124 Wasik and von Hirsch (1988), p. 561.
125 S. 161 of the 2003 Act also empowers a court to make a pre-sentence drug testing order, for the purpose of ascertaining whether an offender has any specified Class A drug in his body.
126 Halliday (2001), paras. 6.6, 6.8.   127 Halliday (2001), para. 6.4.
128 SGC, *New Sentences: Criminal Justice Act 2003*, para. 1.1.16.
129 Halliday (2001), paras. 6.8 and 6.10.

the requirement(s) most suitable for this offender. The pre-sentence report will be crucial in advising courts of the programmes available to allow them to deal suitably with the particular offender. The third key issue concerns the court's obligation to indicate the purpose(s) that it wishes to achieve through the community sentence. This is a reference to the list of purposes in s. 142 of the 2003 Act, strongly criticized on other grounds in Chapter 3.3.1 above. The purposes that might be relevant to community sentences are punishment (by means of an unpaid work requirement, for example), the reform and rehabilitation of offenders (by means of a supervision requirement and, for example, an activity requirement or a drug treatment or alcohol treatment requirement), and the protection of the public (by means of a supervision order, a curfew order, and perhaps a prohibited activity requirement). Summarizing the guideline approach, the SGC states:

> The decision on the nature and severity of the requirements to be included in a community sentence should be guided by:
>
> the assessment of offence seriousness (low, medium or high);
> the purpose(s) of sentencing the court wishes to achieve;
> the risk of reoffending;
> the ability of the offender to comply; and
> the availability of requirements in the local area.
>
> The resulting restriction on liberty must be a proportionate response to the offence that was committed.[130]

The three sentence ranges set out in the SGC's guideline are Low, Medium and High.[131] The Low range may include 40–80 hours of unpaid work, a curfew requirement 'for a few weeks', a prohibited activity requirement (no maximum duration is mentioned), or an attendance centre requirement (for which the maximum is 36 hours). Community orders in this range are said to be suitable for offences below the community sentence threshold,[132] and for some thefts from shops and public order offences.[133] The Medium range may include a greater number of hours of unpaid work (e.g. 80–150), an activity requirement of 20–30 days, a curfew requirement lasting two–three months, or an exclusion requirement of around six months. The guideline indicates that community sentences in this band might be appropriate for handling stolen goods (less than £1,000 if for resale; more if for personal use), some burglaries of commercial premises, some cases of taking vehicles without the owner's consent, and some cases of obtaining property by deception.[134] The High range includes unpaid work of 150–300 hours, activity requirements up to the 60-day maximum, curfew orders lasting for four–six months and so forth. Such

---

130 SGC, above n. 128, para. 1.1.23.
131 The Sentencing Advisory Panel approached this issue, in its advice to the SGC, on the basis of the indications given in Halliday (2001), pp. 40–1.
132 I.e. offenders sentenced under s. 151 (see part 10.6.2 above), who have been fined three times but whose offence is not serious enough to meet the threshold for a community sentence.
133 SGC, above n. 128, para. 1.1.25.   134 Ibid., para. 1.1.28.

orders should be made in cases just below or around the custody threshold, where the court decides that a community sentence is appropriate, 'for example some cases displaying the features of a standard domestic burglary committed by a first-time offender'.[135] None of the bands mentions the supervision requirement, probably because it is assumed that this will form part of all community sentences.

It will be recalled that the Act contemplates the inclusion of more than one requirement in a community sentence, and indeed that the Act requires courts to consider whether to make an electronic monitoring requirement in various types of case (see part 10.6.3.5 above). Unfortunately the SGC's guideline appears to leave little room for combinations of requirements in its three bands, and this may perpetuate the lack of clarity of which Halliday complained. The new structure creates the danger that more requirements will be incorporated into a community sentence than would previously have occurred, without proper regard to proportionality and the increased possibility of breach. For example, if the court decides that a case falls within the medium band and the pre-sentence report recommends supervision for 12 months, an unpaid work requirement of 80 hours and a prohibited activity requirement lasting 12 months, does the guideline assist in determining whether this combination of requirements falls within the medium band? The guideline does state, specifically in relation to the medium band, that 'particular care needs to be taken with this band' to ensure proportionality,[136] but the guideline gives no authoritative lead on this point. It will therefore be left to the National Probation Service to work out some protocols on the combinations that may fall within each band.[137] Section 177(6) states that, wherever a community order is to include two or more requirements, the court must be satisfied that they are compatible with one another.

Once the court has reached the point of deciding on the requirement(s) satisfying the statutory conditions of suitability and proportionality in s. 148(2), it must then ensure that due credit has been given for any time spent in custody on remand. This would be a routine matter if a custodial sentence were imposed, and courts must take care not to overlook the same principle of fairness in cases where they decide on a community sentence. The guideline indicates how courts should approach this issue, particularly in cases around the custody threshold where there may be a choice between imposing a custodial sentence that (in fact) enables immediate release, and imposing a community sentence that is reduced in its onerousness to take account of the time spent on remand.[138]

---

135 Ibid., para. 1.1.31. Note that this refers only to first-time burglars, and makes no reference to the controversy over the recommended use of community sentences for first- and second-time burglars, in *McInerney and Keating* [2003] 2 Cr App R (S) 240 – see Chs. 2.2 and 4.4.10 above.
136 SGC, above n. 128, para. 1.1.30.
137 PSR request forms, using the three community sentence ranges of low, medium and high, are being piloted.
138 SGC, above n. 128, paras. 1.1.37–1.1.40.

The SGC's guideline is absolutely clear that the arrival of the generic community sentence should not be allowed to 'shorten the penal ladder'. In other words, where under previous law an offender might be given a curfew order on one occasion, a community service order on another occasion and a probation order on a third occasion, there is no obstacle to an offender being given two or three successive community sentences under the 2003 Act. Thus, the fact that there is only one form of community sentence in law

> does not mean that offenders who have completed a community sentence and have then reoffended should be regarded as ineligible for a second community sentence on the basis that this has been tried and failed. Further community sentences, perhaps with different requirements, may well be justified.[139]

In order to ensure that relevant information is properly transmitted, however, courts are urged to record their community sentences in terms of the purpose of the order and the range (low, medium or high) in which the sentence was placed.

10.6.5 Monitoring progress

Although the 2003 Act does not at this stage make detailed provision for courts to monitor and review the progress of offenders during their community sentences, s. 178 empowers the Home Secretary to make an order to that effect. In Chapter 9.4.2 it was noted that the idea of court review is now part of the new suspended sentence (to which one or more community requirements will usually be added), and some courts have in the past used their powers to review the progress of offenders on drug treatment and testing orders. However, 'the review process is by no means cheap, and it can create serious listing problems'.[140] If review proceedings for the new suspended sentence are thought worthwhile, the Home Secretary may exercise his power and extend them to community sentences.

10.6.6 Dealing with breach

Section 179 states that Schedule 8 to the 2003 Act governs the breach, revocation and amendment of community orders. The Schedule confers on the 'responsible officer' a discretion in relation to the first breach of a requirement without reasonable excuse, either to give a warning or to initiate breach proceedings; in relation to the second breach, however, the responsible officer must bring the offender back to court in breach proceedings. The court's powers on breach are tough, but the SGC's guideline is designed to ensure that 'the primary objective' of the court's response to breach proceedings is to ensure 'that the requirements of the sentence are finished'. Thus paragraphs 9 and 10 of Schedule 8 state that a court that finds a breach without reasonable excuse must either amend the terms of the community order 'so as to impose more onerous requirements' or revoke the order and deal with the offender

---

139 Ibid., para. 1.1.34.   140 Hough et al. (2003), p. 62; cf. also Rumgay (2004), p. 256.

as for the original offence. If the court finds that 'the offender has wilfully and persistently failed to comply with the requirements of the order', it must impose a prison sentence of up to 51 weeks.[141] However, the court must take account of the extent to which the offender has complied with the requirements of the order, and give any credit for 'part performance'; it should also take account of 'the reasons for the breach'.[142] In many cases, an appropriate response may be to lengthen the order or to include an extra requirement in it, but the Council's guideline warns that imposing a custodial sentence may be out of proportion to the original sentence, and that imposing extra requirements should not be allowed to make compliance with the terms of the order less likely. Indeed, on the use of custody for breach, the Council takes a strong line:

> Custody should be the last resort, reserved for those cases of deliberate and repeated breach where all reasonable efforts to ensure that the offender complies have failed.[143]

Nonetheless, the wording of Schedule 8 remains severe, and, as noted above, custody is permitted in all breach cases and is required where there is 'wilful and persistent' breach, even in cases where the original offence was non-imprisonable. This is another example of breach being punished more severely than the original offence, thereby regarding defiance of authority as a particularly serious wrong. As argued in Chapter 6.3.1 above, the reasons for breach may be much more complex and decisions on the appropriate response require flexibility.

10.7 Deferment of sentence

To the great surprise of many, the power to defer sentence – on the statute book since 1972 and hardly ever used – has been retained and slightly revived in the 2003 Act. Thus s. 278 of the Act introduces Schedule 23, which replaces ss. 1 and 2 of the Powers of Criminal Courts (Sentencing) Act 2000 with new substituted sections. Whereas the previous power could only be exercised if the condition specified either the making of reparation or 'any change in his circumstances', the new power enables a court to defer sentence for up to six months if 'the offender undertakes to comply with any requirements as to his conduct during the period of deferment that the court considers it appropriate to impose'. Courts can therefore impose conditions relating to attendance at a course of treatment, or relating to residence in a particular place, or whatever they think appropriate. A court is now empowered to deal with an offender before the end of the period of deferment (which is usually six months), and if the offender fails to comply with one or more of the requirements the court may pass sentence for the original offence – and also for any offence committed within the period of deferment. The new s. 1A empowers the court to

141 This power extends to cases where the original offence was non-imprisonable: Schedule 8, paras. 9(1)(c) and 10(1)(c).
142 SGC, above n. 128, para. 1.1.46.   143 Ibid., para. 1.1.47.

appoint a supervisor for the period of deferment, who will usually be a probation officer.

The idea of deferment is to allow the court to test the offender's resolve and intentions, and perhaps also to enable the offender to have a positive influence over the sentence ultimately imposed. The SGC's guideline provides that

> The use of deferred sentences should be predominantly for a small group of cases close to a significant threshold where, should the defendant be prepared to adapt his behaviour in a way clearly specified by the sentencer, the court may be prepared to impose a lesser sentence.[144]

It seems that most of these cases will be on the custody threshold, where a community sentence might be considered in favourable circumstances; but the Council also contemplates that there may be cases that pass the threshold for a community sentence but where a discharge or fine might be imposed if the conditions of the deferment are fulfilled. In the earlier leading case of *George*,[145] the Court of Appeal held that at the end of the deferment period the sentencer should 'determine if the defendant has substantially conformed or attempted to conform with the proper expectations of the deferring court . . . If he has, then the defendant may legitimately expect that an immediate custodial sentence will not be imposed'. It remains to be seen whether deferment will come to be regarded as a useful addition to the powers of the court at the sentencing stage.

10.8 Conclusions

Much of this chapter has been given over to the details of the new generic community sentence introduced by the 2003 Act, and to an assessment of its prospects for changing practice. In these conclusions, some of the main arguments for and against the new framework are brought together under four headings – the repositioning of thresholds, the operating realities of the community sentence, the drive towards effectiveness in reducing reoffending and the problem of malfunctions.

10.8.1 Repositioning the thresholds

There is broad agreement that what has happened in English sentencing in the last ten years or so is that the use of imprisonment has increased sharply, that many of those who would previously have received a community sentence or a suspended sentence are now sent to custody, and that many of those who would previously have been fined (and, latterly, some of those who would have received a conditional discharge) are being given community sentences. Thus, as the statistics confirm, the use of both custody and community sentences has increased. Some may argue that the increased use of community sentences shows a growing and welcome confidence among sentencers in what the National Probation Service can provide, but

---

144 Ibid., para. 1.2.7.   145 (1984) 6 Cr App R (S) 211.

Rod Morgan was right to reply that probation resources are scarce and that the service was being 'silted up' with low-risk offenders. Thus one fundamental error in recent penal policy was the peremptory abolition of unit fines in 1993. The scheme had several faults, but the proper approach would have been to remedy those faults. By giving way to a press campaign and to a small minority of magistrates, and preferring political kudos to sound policy, the Home Secretary of the time squandered the opportunity to make financial penalties fairer and returned the fine to its previous chaos. The obvious deleterious consequences – that fewer offenders would be fined, and that the poor would receive higher fines – have followed, as demonstrated in part 10.5 above. The only positive development on fines is the sharp decline in committals to prison for default, brought about partly by judgment of the Divisional Court and partly by sensible developments in government policy.

How can this trend be reversed? To bring offenders down-tariff is probably much more difficult than to take them up-tariff, and it means unravelling practices developed over a decade or so. The fine has to be made more attractive, and efforts to improve enforcement are already bearing fruit. The 2003 Act also makes it clear that the fine does not always stand beneath community sentences in order of 'penal bite', and that substantial fines may be used for offenders close to the custody threshold. That raises fairness problems, however, and the principle of equality before the law (Chapter 7, above) must be preserved. The Carter report has proposed a re-examination of the continental day-fine system, as has the Coulsfield report, and this must be done as a matter of urgency. Only if the fine is revived in a demonstrably fair way can it be hoped that the thresholds for community sentences and custody will be able to operate properly.

The revival of the fine must be accompanied by closer attention to the threshold of seriousness that must be met before a community sentence is passed (see part 10.6.2 above). This means that courts must reject the option of a community sentence in some less serious cases, and that the Probation Service should not be reticent about this lower boundary. As for the use of custody, everything depends here on a fresh approach to the custody threshold and to the range of new forms of sentence positioned just below and just above it – suspended sentences, intermittent custody and custody plus, discussed in Chapter 9.4 above. The judges and magistrates interviewed by Hough, Jacobson and Millie were clear that it was the power of certain mitigating factors, or of an expressed willingness to address the causes of offending behaviour, that might bring a custody case below the threshold.[146] However, they held to the notion of using custody only 'as a last resort', and this is an unsatisfactory principle insofar as it suggests that custody may be used when other forms of sentence have been tried and have failed, irrespective of the seriousness of the offence. The Council's guideline insists on this seriousness criterion, but in

146 Hough et al. (2003), pp. 36–41, discussed above.

practice much will turn on the extent to which sentencers follow the spirit of the new framework. The 1991 Act never really achieved sufficient judicial and magisterial support: will the 2003 Act?

10.8.2 The operating realities of community sentences

A key factor in the courts' response to the 2003 Act will be the approach of the National Probation Service. There is much that is imaginative and constructive in the requirements that may form part of a community sentence, and a great deal will depend on the leadership given by the National Offender Management Service. It will be for NOMS to secure adequate resources to ensure that facilities and services are available to the courts, and to develop policies to be followed in the preparation of pre-sentence reports. PSRs will be a crucial element in communication between the Probation Service and the courts, and will provide an opportunity for the Probation Service to ensure that the various programmes are directed at the most suitable types of offender. There are obvious dangers of imposing more onerous requirements than the offence justifies, and of imposing so many requirements that an offender is 'set up to fail', and the outcome of the piloting of PSR request forms (in which the court indicates whether a low, medium or high set of requirements is appropriate) is awaited.

The attempts to reduce reoffending embodied in some of the requirements may be constructive and imaginative, but there are also other issues arising from the set of 12 requirements. One is that the Probation Service has been encouraged to focus on risk and to conduct risk assessments of offenders. The danger here is that if the concept of risk is not interpreted carefully, it may lead to disproportionately onerous requirements on some offenders – most likely on offenders with several non-serious previous convictions or with a disadvantaged background or both.[147] Another issue is the possibility of a trend from supervision to surveillance. The 2003 Act appears to contemplate the frequent use of curfews with electronic monitoring in support of community sentences. If that does happen, then it should not be allowed to replace supervision as the underlying purpose of the community sentence. If the probation service is to focus on medium and high-risk offenders, some of whom might previously have been sentenced to custody, it must ensure that their problems are tackled constructively.

10.8.3 The drive towards effectiveness in reducing reoffending

This government committed itself at an early stage to taking evidence-based practice and developing the most effective ways of reducing reoffending. Catching the rising tide of enthusiasm embodied in the 'What Works' movement, it was determined in the late 1990s to press ahead with new programmes that promised significant reductions in offending behaviour. The Halliday report encouraged this approach,

147 See ch. 6.5 above.

with an optimistic claim about outcomes that Tony Bottoms has described as 'fairly reckless even at the time it was made'.[148] Unfortunately, it seems that the programmes were 'rolled out' on a large scale before rigorous evaluations had been completed. Now that some evaluations are beginning to become available, there is disappointment that the results do not appear to be encouraging. The fact is that, from the earliest Home Office review[149] through mid-term reviews[150] to the latest assessments of the evidence,[151] the reconviction rates of those who have completed these programmes are generally not superior to the rates of those who have experienced other measures. Most criminologists would not be surprised, since, even if reconvictions are an acceptable measure of success, the best that could be expected would be that some forms of intervention work more effectively with some forms of offender. James McGuire, perhaps the leader of the 'What Works' movement in this country, has insisted that overall reductions in reconviction rates can be produced, but that this can only occur if the various programmes and interventions are properly designed and delivered.[152] In practice there have often been problems of both design and delivery in this country, some resulting from underfunding and some from over-ambitious government targets. The search for effective forms of reducing reoffending should not be abandoned – indeed, the community sentence under the 2003 Act provides a good framework for it to be continued – but a greater sense of realism, planning and the investment of resources is necessary if the desired results are to be achieved.

10.8.4 101 malfunctions

It is obvious from remarks scattered through this chapter and Chapter 9 that, if the 2003 Act is to have a fair chance of achieving some of its objectives, the framework must be implemented as intended. The Sentencing Guidelines Council moved quickly in order to assist this, by promulgating definitive guidelines that were used in training sentencers prior to April 2005 and that bind all courts. But the fact remains that in the past even the plainest legislative intention has been thwarted by sentencers who have not applied the spirit of the law. The best-known 'malfunctions' are those affecting the suspended sentence in the years between 1967 and 1981, when courts misapplied the law by imposing suspended sentences on offenders to whom they would not have given immediate custody, and also gave them longer sentences because of the suspension.[153] In Chapter 9 we saw how fragile the custody threshold is, and how fine the line between a community sentence, a suspended sentence, intermittent custody and custody plus is. It is difficult to draw these lines even in theory. In practice, the disposition of the particular judge or magistrate will be a major factor. The Council's guideline sets out the process of reasoning to be adopted in these cases, but there are many possible malfunctions.

148 Bottoms (2004), p. 62.
149 Vennard and Hedderman (1998).   150 Rex (2001).
151 See Bottoms (2004), pp. 61–3; Raynor (2004); Roberts, C. (2004).
152 McGuire (2002).   153 See Bottoms (1981), and ch. 9.4.2 above.

Similarly, if fines are not used more widely, it is likely that community sentences will be overused. Even if the case is one for a community sentence, will the courts observe the seriousness bands? Will they avoid adding too many requirements to orders, and thus setting offenders up to fail? How will the courts deal with breaches? At several points, therefore, it is possible that the sentencing system will be subject to malfunctions. To avoid at least some will be a supreme test for the guideline system.

CHAPTER 11

Procedural issues and ancillary orders

The main aim of this chapter is to draw together most of the significant procedural steps in sentencing, but the second part of the chapter focuses on a major development in sentencing that will be further highlighted in Chapter 13 below – the expanding availability and use of preventive and other ancillary orders at the sentencing stage. As a prelude to that discussion the first part of the chapter summarizes the framework of sentencing. Afterwards, the third part sets out various requirements to give reasons. Following that, brief consideration is given to several issues arising in procedural context. Thus, before a court passes sentence in any case other than a minor summary one, there will usually be either a trial or, if the plea was guilty, a prosecution statement of facts. In some cases these provide the court with an insufficient basis on which to pass sentence: what is to be done? Again, what role do the advocates for prosecution and defence play in relation to sentencing, and what role should they play? When should pre-sentence reports be relied upon by sentencers? What place do victims have in the sentencing process, and what role should they have?

11.1 The sentencing framework of the 2003 Act

The framework of sentencing established by the Criminal Justice Act 2003 has been much discussed in Chapters 9 and 10 above, and the present summary eschews detailed statutory references in order to convey the essence of the decision-making scheme. The following sequence begins with the least onerous sentence and ends with the most onerous.

Is an absolute or conditional discharge sufficient?

Is the case suitable for a fine (which may be substantial enough to come close to the custody threshold)?

Is the case serious enough to warrant a community sentence?

Is the offence so serious that neither a fine alone nor a community sentence can be justified, and therefore a custodial sentence is unavoidable?

If the case passes the custody threshold, are there factors indicating that the sentence may either (i) be suspended or (ii) take the form of intermittent custody?

If neither of those alternatives is possible and an immediate custodial sentence is unavoidable, what is the shortest term commensurate with the seriousness of the offence (bearing in mind the effect of the early release provisions of the 2003 Act which indicate a reduction of some 15 per cent on previous levels)?

Is the case one to which a minimum sentence applies? Or

Is the case one to which the dangerousness provisions (life imprisonment, imprisonment for public protection or extended sentence) applies?

This is a simplified framework. It is phrased in terms of sentencing for a single offence, and we saw in Chapter 8 that sentencing for more than one offence brings various other complications. The framework leaves out of account the court's duty to consider making a compensation order (see Chapter 10.4 above), and also various duties relating to the ancillary orders set out in part 11.2 below. It also takes no account of the statutory requirements on aggravating and mitigating factors, examined in Chapters 5 and 6 above.

11.2 Ancillary orders

This part of the chapter sets out several of the many ancillary orders available to courts in criminal proceedings. In part 11.2.1 below there is discussion of three privatory orders, the purpose of which is to take from an offender something that he or she should not retain. In part 11.2.2 below the focus switches to preventive orders, the purpose of which is to prevent the offender from engaging in certain sorts of activity thought to represent a risk to others. Behind these two categories of ancillary orders lies a further distinction, between punishment and prevention. In the context of the European Convention on Human Rights, it is often important to determine whether a particular order amounts to a penalty (i.e. a punishment) or is merely preventive. If an order has a significant punitive element (even though it is also to some extent preventive), it must comply with certain standards. In particular, it must not operate retrospectively (Art. 7), its ambit must be clear (Art. 7), and it must only be imposed after all the safeguards appropriate to a criminal charge have been observed (Art. 6(3)). Thus in *Welch* v. *UK* (1995)[1] the European Court of Human Rights held that the confiscation procedures of the Drug Trafficking Act 1986 violated Article 7 of the Convention by imposing a retrospective penalty on the offender. Section 38(4) of the Act did expressly give retroactive effect to the powers of confiscation, provided the defendant had been *charged* after the Act came into force. The key question was therefore whether a confiscation order was a 'penalty'. In deciding that it was, the court noted that the measure had punitive as well as preventive and reparative aims; that the order was calculated by reference to 'proceeds' rather than profits; that the amount of the order could take account of culpability; and that the order was enforceable by a term of imprisonment in default. In *Ibbotson* v. *UK* (1997),[2] by

---

1 (1995) 20 EHRR 247.   2 (1999) 27 EHRR CD 332.

contrast, the European Commission on Human Rights held that the notification requirement under the Sex Offenders Act 1997 was not a 'penalty', since it was less severe than confiscation, there was no provision for imprisonment in default (a separate prosecution would have to be brought), and it was preventive 'in the sense that the knowledge that a person has been registered with the police may dissuade him from committing further offences'. This preventive/punitive distinction will be referred to as the various ancillary orders are discussed.

11.2.1 Privatory orders

Three forms of order that deprive the offender of some asset are set out here – restitution orders, deprivation orders and confiscation orders.

1. Restitution orders. Section 148 of the Powers of Criminal Courts (Sentencing) Act 2000 empowers a court to make an order, on conviction for a theft offence (or where one is taken into consideration on another charge), requiring the offender to restore to the victim the property stolen, or goods representing that property, or a sum equivalent to the value of the stolen property that was taken from the offender's possession on arrest. It will be seen that the conditions for making this order are precise, and it is relatively rare for courts to make restitution orders.

2. Forfeiture orders. Section 143 of the PCCS Act 2000 empowers a court to make an order depriving the offender of any property used (or intended for use) in committing or facilitating the commission of the offence, which was lawfully seized from the offender or under his control at the time of arrest or summons. Subsections (6) and (7) make it clear that a number of motoring offences fall within the rubric of 'facilitating the commission of the offence', and so a court may order that the offender be deprived of a car for the offence of driving whilst disqualified. However, as the Divisional Court held in *Highbury Corner Stipendiary Magistrate, ex p. DiMatteo* (1990),[3] the court must also request or receive information about the financial impact on the offender before making the order. The decision also emphasizes the importance of regarding the order as part of the total sentence on the offender, which ought not to be out of proportion with the seriousness of the offence(s). In *Ball* (2003)[4] the Court of Appeal quashed a deprivation order in respect of a Mercedes car with a personalized number plate, used in facilitating theft, on the grounds that the judge had failed to give counsel the opportunity to address the court in relation to a forfeiture order and its possible effects, and failed to follow the statutory requirement to make an estimate of the value of the property before deciding whether to make the order.

3. Confiscation orders. For several years there has been a mandatory procedure for the confiscation of the proceeds of drug trafficking, most recently under the Drug Trafficking Act 1994, and also a procedure for the confiscation of the proceeds of other forms of crime, under the Criminal Justice Act 1988. These two statutes remain in force in respect of events occurring before March 2003, whereas events

3 (1990) 12 Cr App R (S) 263.   4 [2003] 2 Cr App R (S) 92.

and offences occurring after that date are covered by the Proceeds of Crime Act 2002. This statute is an extensive and detailed piece of legislation, and it suffices here to mention the principal provisions of part 2 of the Act. Where an offender has been convicted in the Crown Court, the judge must initiate the confiscation procedure if there is an application from the prosecution or the judge believes that it is appropriate to do so (s. 6). The next step depends on whether the judge decides that the offender has a 'criminal lifestyle' or not. Section 75 sets out the elements of a 'criminal lifestyle', in terms of being convicted of one of a listed group of offences, or of 'conduct forming part of a course of criminal activity'. If the court decides that the offender has a 'criminal lifestyle', it must make certain assumptions about property possessed by the offender in the previous six years (s. 10). If the court decides that the offender does not have a 'criminal lifestyle', it must decide whether he has benefited from the particular criminal conduct in the case – not using the assumptions in s. 10, but possibly requiring the offender to furnish information on pain of adverse inferences (s. 18). Section 7 prescribes the way in which the court should arrive at the 'recoverable amount', and s. 9 prescribes what deductions and additions may be made. The court may then make an order, and must at the same time fix a term of imprisonment in default of payment.

The desirability of depriving criminals of the proceeds of their crime was discussed in Chapter 3.3.8 above and has received recognition from the Council of Europe, in its Convention of 1990 on Laundering, Search, Seizure and Confiscation of the Proceeds of Crime. One may take leave to doubt, however, whether the draconian powers and deprivation of normal rights now built into the Proceeds of Crime Act are justifiable or necessary. The courts are permitted to proceed on assumptions which sometimes have an extremely flimsy basis.

11.2.2 Preventive orders

The discussion now moves to several preventive orders, beginning with three forms of disqualification and then moving to various prohibitions and restrictions.

1. Disqualification from driving. Although sometimes regarded as an ancillary penalty, the court's power to disqualify road traffic offenders from driving may properly be treated – as it is by most recipients – as the primary penalty. The detailed rules may be found in the Road Traffic Act 1988. Disqualification from driving for at least 12 months is mandatory following the offences of driving with excess alcohol, failure to provide a sample for testing and causing death by reckless driving. Only in cases where 'special reasons' are found can the mandatory period of disqualification be avoided. Disqualification also ensues when an offender accumulates 12 penalty points as a result of two or more offences, and it is a discretionary penalty for various offences connected with motoring, such as taking a car without the owner's consent. There are also provisions in ss. 146–147 of the Powers of Criminal Courts (Sentencing) Act 2000 empowering courts to disqualify from driving any person who uses a vehicle for the purposes of crime, or any person convicted of an offence. It appears that, in general, the length of disqualification is influenced less by proportionality to the current offence than by the prevention of probable danger, to which the offender's driving record as a whole is relevant; but it is established that account should be taken, when setting a lengthy period of disqualification, of the effect on the offender's future prospects of employment and therefore of law-abidance.[5]

2. *Disqualification from acting as a company director.* The power to disqualify a person from acting as a director of a company was granted by the Company Directors Disqualification Act 1986. It is most frequently exercised in cases involving fraudulent trading or similar offences:[6] orders of over 10 years up to the maximum of 15 years should be reserved for very serious cases, with orders in the 6–10 year range more appropriate for offences committed over a shorter period of time and yielding less money.[7] It is unlikely that such emphasis should be placed on the offender's future prospects of employment, since the order – although fairly wide ranging – does not disqualify the person from being an employee.

3. *Disqualification from working with children.* Section 28 of the Criminal Justice and Court Services Act 2000 empowers a court to disqualify from working with children, indefinitely, an offender convicted of a sexual offence against a child.[8] A court has a duty to make an order where the offender is aged 18 or over and the court has imposed a custodial sentence of 12 months or more; it has the power to make an order where the offender is under 18 or the court has not imposed a 12-month sentence on conviction. The duty to make the order applies unless the court is satisfied that it is unlikely that the offender will commit any further offences against a child. Such an order is for an indefinite period, although there may be an application to discharge it. It appeared possible to construe the Act as requiring an order to be made when a trigger offence had been committed before the Act came into force, and so it was crucial to determine whether it was a 'penalty' (no retroactive effect permitted) or merely a preventive order (which could operate retrospectively). In determining this question in *Field and Young* (2003),[9] the Court of Appeal laid considerable weight on the fact that the order applies both where a person is convicted and where a person is found to be either unfit to plead or not guilty by reason of insanity, and concluded:

> It seems to us of considerable importance that a conviction is not a necessary condition for the making of such an order. When one considers the nature and purpose of such an order it points overwhelmingly to this being for preventative rather than punitive effect. Precisely the same order is made whether a person is convicted or not and the making of the order has no regard to the extent or seriousness of the offending but rather to whether a repetition of the conduct is likely.[10]

---

5 E.g. *Doick* [2004] 2 Cr App R (S) 203.   6 E.g. *Edwards* [1998] 2 Cr App R (S) 213.
7 *Millard* (1994) 15 Cr App R (S) 445 (eight years appropriate for fraudulent conduct lasting four years and yielding some £700,000).
8 For 2003 amendments, see Taylor, Wasik and Leng (2004), pp. 231–2.
9 [2003] 2 Cr App R (S) 175.   10 Ibid., at para. 58 per Kay LJ.

The Court therefore held that the order could operate retrospectively, since it is not a penalty and therefore not caught by Article 7. However, the reasoning is flawed. If the main arguments had been the preventive purpose and the fact that the effect of the prohibition was not unduly severe, that would arguably have been in line with earlier decisions. But the Court appeared to think that it would be difficult to regard the order as preventive if it could only be made after a conviction, and thus rested its conclusion on the provision for the making of an order after a finding of insanity or disability in relation to the trial. This is manifestly unsatisfactory: the whole point of that provision is to treat the severely mentally disordered (for these purposes) as if they had been convicted, rather than to suggest that these orders can be made generally on persons who have not been convicted. The Court of Appeal placed form above substance, and it seems highly unlikely that the Strasbourg Court would yield to a device which, if approved, could be deployed widely by draftsmen to transform truly punitive orders into preventive orders. The decision in *Welch*[11] demonstrates that such devices would be caught by the anti-subversion doctrine. Is it really suggested that, if the Drug Trafficking Act 1986 had provided for the making of confiscation orders not only on conviction but also after a finding of insanity or unfitness to plead, the Court in *Welch* would have reached a different conclusion and found the orders to be non-punitive?

4. *Sexual offences prevention orders.* Section 104 of the Sexual Offences Act 2003 empowers a court which has convicted an offender of a listed offence to make a sexual offences prevention order, if it is satisfied that this is necessary for the purpose of protecting one or more others from serious sexual harm. The terms of the order may prohibit an offender from doing 'anything described in the order' for a period of at least five years (s. 107). It is also possible for the court to make such an order outside criminal proceedings, on application by the police.[12] The contents of a SOPO are entirely negative or preventive, and may include a prohibition on making any contact or communication with a person under 16 and not residing in a private dwelling where there is a child under 16.[13]

5. *Risk of sexual harm orders.* Section 123 of the Sexual Offences Act 2003 empowers a magistrates' court to make a risk of sexual harm order on application from the police, in respect of a person who has on two or more occasions engaged in sexually explicit conduct or communication with children. The police may apply for this order in respect of someone who has a conviction or a person without any conviction: it appears that the police may apply to a court at the sentencing stage and invite it to make this order. The court must only make an order if satisfied that

11 Above, n. 1.
12 For commentary on this and the other preventive orders in sexual cases, see Shute (2004). That article also deals with the foreign travel order (s. 114 of the SOA 2003), which can only be made on application from the police and on evidence of conduct since a relevant conviction.
13 Cf. *B* v. *Chief Constable of Avon and Somerset* [2001] 1 WLR 340, where an unsuccessful challenge to the compatibility of SOPO's predecessor, the sex offender order, with the Convention was mounted.

it is necessary to protect one or more children from physical or psychological harm. Again, the essence of the order is a prohibition on 'doing anything described in the order' for at least two years. This is a particularly controversial power because it applies equally in respect of persons who have never been convicted, so long as the court receives evidence satisfying it as to the past conduct and future danger to children.[14]

6. *Travel restriction orders.* Section 33 of the Criminal Justice and Police Act 2001 requires courts to consider making a travel restriction order whenever they sentence an offender to four years or more for a drug trafficking offence. Guidance on the proper use of the power was given in *Mee* (2004),[15] where the Court of Appeal recognized that if the offence appeared to be opportunistic rather than part of a pattern, it might not be necessary to make an order. If a court apprehends a risk of further offences, it should make an order of a length appropriate to the degree of risk it finds, having invited submissions from counsel.

7. *Football spectator banning orders.* Section 14A of the Football Spectators Act 1989 (as amended by the Football (Disorder) Act 2000) provides that, on conviction of a relevant football-related offence, a court must make a banning order in respect of designated football matches if it is satisfied that this would help to prevent violence and disorder in connection with regulated football matches. If the court is not so satisfied, it must state this in open court and give its reasons. Banning orders may also be imposed by magistrates on application from the police. The duration of the order depends on the sentence imposed for the conviction: if immediate imprisonment is imposed, the order must be between 6 and 10 years, but in other cases it must be between three and five years.[16] A banning order is not a penalty but is merely a preventive order, although it has been held that the standard of proof should be equivalent to that in criminal proceedings.[17]

8. *Exclusion from licensed premises orders.* Under the Licensed Premises (Exclusion of Certain Persons) Act 1980 a court which is dealing with an offence committed on licensed premises which involved the use or threat of violence may make an exclusion order, excluding the offender from certain premises for a period of between three months and two years. The power should generally not be used for isolated incidents, but reserved for persistent nuisances.[18] However, in *Arrowsmith* (2003),[19] where an offender with previous convictions for violence was imprisoned for 12 months for assault occasioning actual bodily harm on another customer in a public house, the judge had made an order excluding the offender from all 165 licensed premises in the area of his residence for 18 months. The Court of Appeal held that this was not manifestly excessive, in view of the offender's history and the risk it suggested, but that procedurally all the premises had to be individually named.

---

14 See Shute (2004), p. 431.   15 [2004] 2 Cr App R (S) 434.
16 For an example of a three-year order, see *O'Keefe* [2004] 1 Cr App R (S) 404.
17 *Gough* v. *Chief Constable of Derbyshire* [2002] QB 459.
18 *Grady* (1990) 12 Cr App R (S) 152.   19 [2003] 2 Cr App R (S) 301.

9. *Anti-social behaviour orders*. Most of the prohibitions imposed under the orders listed above can also be brought about by the anti-social behaviour order, the broadest of the courts' powers to impose preventive restrictions. As outlined in Chapter 6.6 above, a court may make an ASBO either on application from the police, local council or others, or as an order following conviction. Most orders are now made on conviction. The court has to be satisfied that the offender has caused harassment, alarm or distress amounting to anti-social behaviour. It may then make an order, for a minimum period of two years, that prohibits the offender from doing anything described in the order. The number and breadth of the conditions may be considerable,[20] and the breach rate is around 42 per cent. On breach an offender commits an offence punishable with up to five years' imprisonment. This is a much higher penalty than is available for many criminal offences, and yet in *Hall* (2005)[21] the Court of Appeal accepted that the ASBO may be used to circumvent the (lower) maximum penalty for an offence. Parliament has provided a maximum of six months' imprisonment for driving whilst disqualified. The court in this case had made an ASBO prohibiting the offender indefinitely from driving a motor vehicle on any road in the United Kingdom without holding a valid driving licence and certificate of insurance. Breach of that condition would open up a maximum penalty of five years. This is yet another unsatisfactory feature of the ASBO.

10. *Preventive orders and sentencing for breach*. It is manifest from the foregoing paragraphs that the range of preventive orders is wide, and that they are capable of being very restrictive. They are entirely negative in content, and include no provision for support or for constructive activities. Yet the penalties for breach are high, many of them having a maximum sentence of five years for breach. As already stated, this maximum is often higher than would be available if a substantive offence were charged. The use of custody for breach is frequent: for ASBOs, the breach rate is 42 per cent, and of those some 55 per cent overall (and 45 per cent of juveniles) are sent into custody.[22] In sentencing for breach of any preventive order, the court should take account of the nature of the conduct amounting to a breach, and whether it was a single incident or persistent. Persistent serious breaches have been held to justify a sentence as high as three-and-a-half years,[23] whereas lesser breaches of a restraining order (now a sexual offences prevention order) have been sentenced in the 12–18 months range.[24] In *Clark* (2003)[25] it was held that the court should have regard to the maximum, so that a three-year sentence on a plea of guilty for a non-serious breach of a restraining order was too high (since it was equivalent

---

20 Cf. *C* v. *Sunderland Youth Court* [2004] 1 Cr App R (S) 443, where the Divisional Court granted judicial review of an order that prohibited the offender from 'exhibiting any behaviour towards any individual or group which would cause them harassment, alarm or distress', on the ground that this was too vague and uncertain. The magistrates had also failed to consider whether an area of application so wide as the whole of Sunderland was necessary.

21 [2005] Crim LR 152.   22 Home Office press release 042/2005.

23 *Braxton* [2005] 1 Cr App R (S) 167, discussed in ch. 6.6 above.

24 *Clark* [2003] 1 Cr App R (S) 6, *Wilcox* [2003] 1 Cr App R (S) 199.

25 [2003] 1 Cr App R (S) 6.

to about four years on a conviction). Nevertheless, there are many ASBO cases in which the courts use custody for breach and where the conduct was relatively minor. The effect is not only disproportionality of sentencing but also the taking of many non-serious offenders up the tariff at an early stage – an observation particularly relevant to young offenders. But the fault lies earlier in the process too, since the imposition of multiple conditions on young offenders[26] is inappropriate, and particularly inappropriate without an element of supervision. It is, in truth, setting a person up to fail.

11.3 The obligation to give reasons for sentence

It is a fundamental tenet of natural justice that decision-makers should give reasons for their decisions, and the argument is surely at its strongest where the decisions affect the liberty of the subject. The case for reasoned decisions in sentencing is therefore unanswerable in principle,[27] and is now reinforced by Article 6 of the Convention as a result of the Human Rights Act 1998. Offenders should be able to know the reasons for sentences imposed upon them. The public also has an interest in knowing. The duty to give reasons may conduce to decisions which are more considered and more consonant with legal principle. And the giving of reasons enables appellate courts better to assess the appropriateness of a sentence which has been challenged on appeal.

What counts as a reason for sentence? Clearly, a kind of moral expostulation about the offence, 'one of the worst of its kind', 'a dreadful and brutal attack', is hardly enough on its own. To amount to a 'reason', the sentencer's remarks must surely link the sentence to general levels of sentence for that kind of offence, and to other general principles. It has long been established that a court should make some effort to explain the length of custodial sentences. In the case of *Newman, Newman and Myers* (1979)[28] the judge had simply meted out sentences of three, four and five years' imprisonment without any comment or embellishment. Lord Widgery CJ held in the Court of Appeal that it is wrong, when sentences of that severity are passed, for a judge to give no clue as to how the sentences were arrived at. Similarly, in *Attorney General's Reference (No. 23 of 1992)* (1993)[29] Lord Taylor CJ chided a recorder for failing to give reasons:

> The learned recorder did not specify any reasons or explain the process by which she arrived at that sentence. It may be that if those who have to pass sentence do give some reasons for the sentence they pass, that brings them to consider the effect which the sentence they are minded to impose might have and the public perception of it.

This passage emphasizes the importance of explaining the process by which the court arrived at its sentence, and this means that the idea of giving reasons needs

---

26 The use of ASBOs for mentally disturbed people is also a matter of concern, not least because of the absence of support as part of the order.
27 Thomas (1963).   28 (1979) 1 Cr App R (S) 252.   29 (1993) 14 Cr App R (S) 759.

to be developed carefully. As the Council of Europe's 1992 recommendation on 'Consistency in Sentencing' proposed,

E.1 Courts should, in general, state concrete reasons for imposing sentences. In particular, specific reasons should be given when a custodial sentence is imposed. Where sentencing orientations or starting points exist, it is recommended that courts give reasons when the sentence is outside the indicated range of sentence.

E.2 What counts as a 'reason' is a motivation which relates the particular sentence to the normal range of sentences for the type of crime and to the declared rationales of sentencing.

Along these lines is the latest statutory provision on the duty to give reasons for, and explain the effect of, sentences. Section 174(1) of the Criminal Justice Act 2003 provides:

Subject to subsections (3) and (4), any court passing sentence on an offender –

(a) must state in open court, in ordinary language and in general terms, its reasons for deciding on the sentence passed, and
(b) must explain to the offender in ordinary language –
    (i)   the effect of the sentence,
    (ii) where the offender is required to comply with any order of the court forming part of the sentence, the effects of non-compliance with the order,
    (iii) any power of the court, on the application of the offender or any other person, to vary or review any order of the court forming part of the sentence,
    (iv) where the sentence consists of or includes a fine, the effects of failure to pay the fine.

Subsection (2) emphasizes that compliance with subsection 1(a) requires the court to explain why the appropriate threshold is passed, that is why the offence is serious enough to warrant a community sentence, or why the offence is considered too serious for a fine alone or community sentence. Subsection (2) also adds the requirement to give an explanation where the court reduces the sentence for a guilty plea, and where any aggravating or mitigating factors are of particular importance. Subsection 2(a) states that a court must

where guidelines indicate that a sentence of a particular kind, or within a particular range, would normally be appropriate for the offence and the sentence is of a different kind, or is outside that range, state the court's reasons for deciding on a sentence of a different kind or outside that range.

This reinforces the effect of the court's duty to have regard to definitive sentencing guidelines,[30] but this subsection applies to guidelines generally – presumably applying equally to those laid down by the Court of Appeal.[31] In addition to these statutory requirements, there is a Practice Direction requiring a court to give

---

30 S. 172 of the 2003 Act.   31 See the discussion in ch. 1.5.3 above.

a full explanation, when imposing a custodial sentence, of the applicable release provisions.[32]

Beyond all these duties of explanation, there is now the emergence of an obligation on judges to be more explicit about the calculations that lead them to a particular sentence – particularly in respect of custodial sentences, but not exclusively so. Thus the guideline judgment on sentencing in cases of racial aggravation states that courts 'should say, publicly, what the appropriate sentence would have been for the offence without the racial aggravation',[33] thus making it clear what was added to take account of the aggravating factor. Similarly, the Council's guideline on the guilty plea discount goes further than s. 174(2), mentioned above, by recommending that 'the court should usually state what the sentence would have been if there had been no reduction as a result of the guilty plea'.[34] This applies to all courts and to all forms of sentence. Whether obligations of this kind will become more detailed remains to be seen, but even these two obligations are significant steps in the direction of transparency in sentencing, with benefits both to the public and to counsel and appellate tribunals.

11.4 The factual basis for sentencing

Even after a full trial on a not guilty plea, the court may not have heard sufficient evidence on certain points to provide a proper factual basis on which to pass sentence. A carefully controlled trial will concentrate on the legal points at issue: if the offence is defined broadly by the law, some points relevant to sentence (e.g. provocation, knowledge of the class of drug possessed) might not be fully dealt with during the trial. Difficulties of this kind are much more likely to occur on a guilty plea, after which the prosecution may state the facts in one way and the defence may advance a different version. In a system of criminal law which includes many broadly defined offences, these difficulties are likely to be perpetuated. Yet the implications for offenders are considerable, sometimes amounting to the gulf between a custodial and a non-custodial sentence, or between a long or a shorter term of imprisonment. It is surely wrong that defendants should suffer a disadvantage simply because the legal system happens to assign certain issues to the sentencing stage rather than to the trial process. Issues which can affect sentence substantially and which are disputed should, as a matter of principle, be resolved only after a procedurally fair examination of the evidence which accords proper safeguards to the defendant. This proposition derives support from the general right to a fair trial in Article 6.1 of the European Convention on Human Rights, although the Strasbourg

---

32 *Practice Direction (Custodial Sentences: Explanations)* [1998] 1 WLR 278, subsequently consolidated in the Practice Directions, but now requiring amendment to take account of the changes in early release under the 2003 Act (see ch. 9.5 above).

33 *Kelly and Donnelly* [2001] 2 Cr App R (S) 341, at p. 347. The judgment presumably applies to religious aggravation, and also to aggravation related to disability or sexual orientation.

34 SGC, *Reduction in Sentence for a Guilty Plea* (2004), para. 3.1.

jurisprudence on this aspect of sentencing remains underdeveloped.[35] How do the rules and procedures evolved by the Court of Appeal measure up to principles of fairness?

11.4.1 Interpreting a jury verdict

The general principle is that the judge must base the sentence on a version of the facts which is consistent with the verdict. Occasionally, cases arise in which a crucial issue (e.g. whether the offender's acts were intentional or merely reckless; whether he was the perpetrator or a mere accomplice) is likely to be left unclear when the jury gives its verdict, because the definition of the crime charged does not draw the necessary distinction. Judges are usually discouraged from asking the jury for a special verdict in these circumstances, but they may do so. As the Court of Appeal explained in *Cawthorne* (1996),[36]

> Whether or not the judge asks the jury to indicate to him the basis of their verdict is entirely a matter for the judge's discretion. In many cases the judge will not wish to do so, and doing so will throw an unnecessary additional burden upon the jury. In a case such as the present . . . there are grave dangers in asking juries how they have reached a particular verdict. For example, they may not all have reached it by precisely the same route.

In that case it was unclear whether the manslaughter verdict was based on lack of intent, provocation or gross negligence. The judge's duty is to reach a conclusion on the basis of the facts proved during the trial. If the judge is left unsure, then the sentence should be based on the version of facts more favourable to the offender. In *McGlade* (1990)[37] D had been convicted of the buggery of a young woman on charges of rape and buggery. At this time (i.e. until 1994) the offence of buggery of a woman was committed whether or not she consented, and in this case it was unclear from the jury's verdict whether they concluded that she had or had not consented. The judge sentenced D to five years' imprisonment on the basis that she had not consented. The Court of Appeal held that this was proper: 'the learned judge, having heard all the evidence himself in the course of the trial, is free and, indeed, it is his duty to come to a conclusion, if he can, upon where the truth lies'. In this case the finding made the difference between five years' imprisonment and a short, even perhaps a non-custodial sentence. In principle, an issue not concluded by the verdict (and not relevant to the definition of the offence) should be explored after conviction and before sentence, in an adversarial proceeding. It appears from *Finch* (1993)[38] that a judge is not allowed to reject a version of facts accepted by the jury without holding a post-conviction hearing (see part 11.4.2 below for *Newton*

---

35 Cf. *De Salvador Torres* v. *Spain* (1997) 23 EHRR 601, where the Court found no violation but where the Commission discussed the application of the right to have adequate time and facilities for the preparation of a defence (Art 6.3(b)) in relation to statutory aggravating factors.
36 [1996] 2 Cr App R (S) 445, at p. 450.   37 (1990) 12 Cr App R (S) 105.
38 (1993) 14 Cr App R (S) 226.

hearings); but where the verdict is equivocal, as in *Cawthorne* and in *McGlade*, it seems that no *Newton* hearing is required. However, in those circumstances the judge must take care to give a reasonably full explanation of the conclusions reached on the evidence heard.[39] Where there has been a trial and the jury has convicted only on the lesser charge, it is clear that the judge should not pass sentence on a basis that presupposes the truth of the rejected evidence.[40]

11.4.2 Interpreting a guilty plea

Where an offender pleads guilty, the judge does not have the opportunity to hear the evidence. All that is provided are the case papers and the prosecution's statement of facts. That statement may disclose that the offence had particularly serious consequences, to the extent that a higher offence might have been charged, and the court is entitled to sentence on that basis unless there is a defence challenge.[41] On the other hand, the Court of Appeal has laid down that 'the prosecution should not lend itself to any agreement whereby a case is presented to a sentencing judge to be dealt with . . . on an unreal and untrue set of facts'.[42] In practice it is not uncommon for a defendant to submit a written basis of plea, when pleading guilty.[43] Assuming that the prosecution gave careful consideration to the statement of facts, the normal course will be for the court to pass sentence on that basis. However, as Lord Bingham CJ stated in *Tolera* (1999),[44]

> If the defendant wishes to ask the court to pass sentence on any other basis than that disclosed in the Crown case, it is necessary for the defendant to make that quite clear. If the Crown does not accept the defence account, and if the discrepancy between the two accounts is such as to have a potentially significant effect on the level of sentence, then consideration must be given to the holding of a *Newton* hearing to resolve the issue. The initiative rests with the defence . . .

This may occur, for example, where there is a disagreement about the extent of a defendant's involvement in a crime,[45] or where criminal liability is strict (i.e. no proof of culpability is required) and where the defence contend that the crime was committed inadvertently.[46] If the defence advance in mitigation a version of the facts which seems to lack foundation, it is the judge's duty to examine the allegedly mitigating material in order to form of a view about it: this has often occurred in drugs cases, where the offender alleges that all the drugs were for personal use only.[47]

---

39 *Byrne* [2003] 1 Cr App R (S) 338, where the jury's manslaughter verdict was equivocal between provocation and lack of intent.
40 *Gillespie* [1999] 2 Cr App R (S) 61.
41 *R v. Nottingham Crown Court, ex p. DPP* [1996] 1 Cr App R (S) 283 (plea of guilty to common assault, papers disclosed injuries serious enough to justify charge of assault occasioning actual bodily harm).
42 *Beswick* [1996] 1 Cr App R (S) 343 at p. 346.
43 For two recent examples see *Attorney General's Reference No. 70 of 2003* [2004] 2 Cr App R (S) 254 at p. 256, and *Attorney General's Reference No. 60 of 2003* [2004] 2 Cr App R (S) 376 at p. 378.
44 [1999] 1 Cr App R (S) 25 at p. 29.   45 *Anderson* [2003] 1 Cr App R (S) 421.
46 *Lester* (1975) 63 Cr App R 144.
47 See *Ribas* (1976) 63 Cr App R 147 and many subsequent decisions.

It appears that the judge may reject the defence version without hearing evidence if that version is 'manifestly false' and 'incredible', but the normal practice would be for the judge to call upon the defence to lead some evidence on the matter (if only the defendant's testimony) and this evidence should be tested in the normal way.[48]

The most significant procedural development in recent years has been the spread of so-called 'Newton hearings'. Again, the crime which produced the procedural problem in *Newton* (1982)[49] was buggery of a woman, in this case Newton's wife. Newton pleaded guilty, but he contended that his wife had consented, whereas the prosecution's version of the facts was that there were threats of violence and no consent. (The offence of buggery with consent in private was abolished in 1994.) In the Court of Appeal, Lord Lane CJ held that there are two alternative ways of resolving such a conflict. One is for the judge to hear no evidence but to invite submissions from counsel and then form a conclusion. If this approach is taken, and the submissions are substantially in conflict, the judge's duty is to accept the defence version. 'The second method which could be adopted by the judge in these circumstances is himself to hear the evidence on one side and another, and come to his own conclusion, acting so to speak as his own jury on the issue which is the root of the problem'. In the case of *Newton* the sentence of eight years' imprisonment was quashed because the judge had adopted the first approach, but without concluding in favour of the defence. It is the second approach which is now favoured in these cases, and a considerable jurisprudence has developed. Thus, where the defence contend that an attack was provoked and the prosecution maintain that there was no provocation, the judge ought to hold a *Newton* hearing before passing sentence.[50] Similarly, where the defence contend that the offender believed the drug was cannabis not cocaine, the judge should hold a *Newton* hearing – always subject to the judge's right to decide the issue if the defence version is considered incapable of belief.[51]

11.4.3 Towards procedural fairness

The advent of *Newton* hearings marked an important step forward in procedural fairness where facts are disputed after a guilty plea: bearing in mind the great effect on sentence which such issues may have, they ought properly to be resolved according to rules of evidence no less fair than those applicable at the trial.[52] However, as we saw in Chapter 5 above, aggravating and mitigating factors – some of them statutory – may also have a significant effect on the severity of the sentence. It is established that, if there is a dispute, the prosecution must establish aggravating factors to the criminal standard of proof, whereas the defence need only establish mitigating factors to the civil standard.[53] However, in the United States there has been constitutional debate about whether the defendant should have a right to trial

---

48 As set out in *Tolera* (above n. 44) and *Anderson* (above n. 45).
49 (1982) 4 Cr App R (S) 388.   50 *Costley* (1989) 11 Cr App R (S) 357.
51 *Broderick* (1993) 15 Cr App R (S) 476.   52 *McGrath and Casey* (1983) 5 Cr App R (S) 460.
53 *Kerrigan* (1993) 14 Cr App R (S) 179, *Guppy and Marsh* (1995) 16 Cr App R (S) 25.

by jury on such matters, rather than simply a bench trial or (in English terms) a *Newton* hearing. In *Apprendi* v. *New Jersey* (2000)[54] the Supreme Court held that

> Other than the fact of a prior conviction, any fact that increases the penalty for a crime beyond the prescribed statutory maximum must be submitted to a jury, and proved beyond a reasonable doubt.

That decision related to an offence with a maximum of 10 years, but which could have an enhanced maximum of 20 years if committed with a purpose to intimidate because of race, colour, gender, disability and so forth. It was held that the defendant had a right to jury trial on the issue of intimidation for discriminatory purposes. In *Blakely* v. *Washington* (2004)[55] this principle was extended by interpreting the 'maximum sentence' so as to include the maximum set by the applicable guideline. If this were to be applied to English law, that would mean that any judge who decided that the facts of the case took it outside the applicable range of sentences specified in a definitive guideline or guideline judgment – because the aggravating factors were so great, for example – should offer the defendant the opportunity of a jury trial on those issues, and not simply deal with it by means of a *Newton* hearing or other procedure. There is considerable substance in the argument, not least because of the substantial effect that certain factors may have on sentence (e.g. whether the offender knew that the victim was elderly or disabled), but the jurisprudence of the Convention would certainly not require jury trial. What it should require is the right to an adversarial hearing on the issue, and English law falls short of that insofar as it allows the court to dismiss without further enquiry any defence submissions it regards as 'incredible' or 'manifestly false'.

11.5 Police antecedents statements

In broad terms, a police antecedents statement will usually refer to the age, education, employment and domestic circumstances of the offender, and should contain details of previous convictions (if any). A further Practice Direction issued in 1997 and consolidated in the 2002 Practice Direction states that antecedents statements should be compiled by the police from the Police National Computer and provided to the CPS with the case file.[56] Antecedents statements should always include details on three matters – personal details, recorded convictions and recorded cautions – and in the Crown Court there should additionally be information on the circumstances of the last three similar convictions and, if the case involves breach of a community order, the circumstances of the offence for which that order was given. The Practice Direction also requires the police to check the details of convictions seven days before the court hearing, to ensure that any changes are drawn to the court's attention.

---

54 (2000) 120 S.Ct. 2348.   55 (2004) 124 S.Ct. 2531, discussed in ch. 2.2 above.
56 *Practice Direction (Criminal Proceedings: Consolidation)* [2002] 1 WLR 2870, para. 27.

11.6 The role of the prosecution

Where there is a guilty plea, the prosecution is expected to state the facts of the case. The process of constructing this statement depends on the police and on the Crown Prosecution Service. Sometimes the statement represents the outcome of a compromise in relation to plea; for example the prosecution may agree not to mention a certain factor in return for the defendant changing his plea from not guilty to guilty. In general, some defendants believe that the prosecution has given an unjustifiably serious impression of the facts of their case, whereas others acknowledge that certain inaccuracies in the statement militated in their favour.[57] We saw in part 4 above that if the defence wish to dispute the prosecution's version, there are various procedural methods at their disposal. It is equally true that the prosecution may, and indeed should, challenge any statement made by the defence in mitigation which it believes to be unjustifiable.

How far beyond presenting the facts of the case might the prosecution go? The English tradition, represented by the Bar's Code of Conduct, is that the prosecutor 'should not attempt by advocacy to influence the court in regard to sentence'. The defence may, more or less explicitly, refer to possible sentences in the plea in mitigation, but it is thought improper for the prosecution to do so. However, there have been significant changes and prosecuting advocates now have several duties in relation to sentence. In *Komsta and Murphy* (1990)[58] the Court of Appeal held that 'there is a positive obligation on counsel (not just counsel for defendants but counsel who represent the prosecution) to ensure that no order is made that the court has no power to make'. The Code for Crown Prosecutors (2004) now describes the prosecutor's principal duties as follows:

> Crown prosecutors should draw the court's attention to
> any aggravating and mitigating factors disclosed by the prosecution case;
> any victim personal statement;
> where appropriate, evidence of the impact of the offending on the community;
> any statutory provisions or sentencing guidelines which may assist;
> any relevant statutory provisions relating to ancillary orders (such as anti-social
> behaviour orders).[59]

This betokens a considerable change, and it was encouraged by Lord Bingham as Lord Chief Justice, when he urged judges to 'invite assistance from prosecuting counsel' and expressed the hope 'that judges will not be affronted if prosecuting counsel do offer to give guidance to the relevant provisions and appropriate authorities' in a case.[60] None of this detracts from the proposition that a prosecutor should not urge a particular sentence. It remains important that greater prosecutorial involvement be encased within a clear ethical framework: prosecutors should

57 Baldwin and McConville (1978), pp. 545–6.
58 (1990) 12 Cr App R (S) 63.   59 Crown Prosecution Service (2004), para. 11.1.
60 *Attorney General's Reference No. 7 of 1997 (Fearon)* [1998] 1 Cr App R (S) 268 at pp. 272–3.

act in the spirit of a Minister of Justice, not striving for severity but adopting a balanced view in the public interest.[61] This requires both familiarity and sympathy with the aims of sentencing policy.

11.7 Pre-sentence reports

In 1960 the Streatfeild Committee declared that 'our cardinal principle throughout is that sentences should be based on reliable, comprehensive information relevant to what the court is seeking to do'.[62] The next three decades saw great increases in the supply of social inquiry reports to courts. At their best, they would inform courts of the offender's background and situation and attitude to the offence; would inform courts of the available facilities which might be suitable for the offender, given his or her characteristics and needs; and might recommend one sentence in particular.

There was, however, frequent debate about the contents of social inquiry reports. In the 1970s, Thorpe found a tendency of probation officers to omit certain details when they might tell against the recommendation which the writer wished to make. Sentencers voiced various criticisms of reports – of the social work jargon in which they were sometimes written; of the gullibility of some probation officers in accepting the defendant's claims without checking them; and of the 'unrealistic' nature of some of the recommended sentences. Loraine Gelsthorpe and Peter Raynor reported on the variation in quality of reports and the need for tighter quality control procedures; but their research, which also contains interesting judicial reflections on reports, relates to a pilot study carried out in the months after the enactment of the 1991 Act.[63] Michael Cavadino reported on a 'before and after' study of reports immediately before the 1991 Act and in 1993, after the introduction of the Act. His research suggested a more positive attitude among report writers, and a strong change towards focusing on the seriousness of the offence and on the offending behaviour, although he also found that the quality of reports was variable.[64]

In some cases a court may adjourn the case before sentence to allow for the preparation of a pre-sentence report, for example where the defendant had pleaded guilty and no pre-sentence report had been prepared. The principle is that, if the court adjourns the case specifically in order to have the offender's suitability for a certain sentence assessed, and the report confirms suitability, it is then wrong for the court to impose a custodial sentence. In the leading case of *Gillam* (1980),[65] the case had been adjourned to assess suitability for community service, but the judge then imposed custody despite a favourable report. As Watkins LJ held,

> when a judge in these circumstances purposely postpones sentence so that an alternative to prison can be examined, and that alternative is found to be a satisfactory one in all respects, the court ought to adopt the alternative. A feeling of injustice is otherwise aroused.

---

61 See Blake and Ashworth (1998).   62 Streatfeild (1960), para. 336.
63 Gelsthorpe and Raynor (1995).   64 Cavadino (1997).   65 (1980) 2 Cr App R (S) 267.

The principle applies wherever a sentencer's remarks create a reasonable expectation of a non-custodial sentence, even if only over a lunchtime adjournment. If the court appears to go back on what it has stated, the ensuing sense of injustice will lead to the quashing of the subsequent custodial sentence.[66]

Section 156 of the Criminal Justice Act 2003 requires courts to obtain and consider a pre-sentence report (PSR) before imposing a community sentence, and before forming an opinion that the case passes the custody threshold, before deciding what is the shortest term commensurate with the seriousness of the offence, and before determining that an offender is 'dangerous' for the purposes of the dangerousness provisions. However, failure to obtain a report does not invalidate the sentence, and if the court is of the opinion that it is unnecessary to obtain a PSR in any of the stated circumstances, it need not do so.

The form and contents of pre-sentence reports are governed by the *National Standards for the Supervision of Offenders in the Community*. The relevant paragraphs from the 2000 version are set out below, but they are under revision and it is likely that the 2003 Act will usher in various changes – not least to take account of the new banding of community sentences, described in Chapter 10.6 above. At present, the standards for pre-sentence reports prescribe five main sections for each report: front sheet, offence analysis, offender analysis, risk to the public of reoffending, and conclusion.

- The front sheet should 'set out the basic factual information on the offender and the offence(s), and list the sources used to prepare the report, indicating clearly which information has been verified'.
- The offence analysis ought to include discussion of the context in which the offence occurred, the offender's 'culpability and the level of premeditation', the impact of the crime on the victim, the offender's awareness of the consequences of the crime, and any attempt to make reparation or to address offending behaviour since the offence.
- The offender assessment should focus on relevant personal or social details, ranging over such matters as 'domestic situation', social skills, schooling, employment, and so forth, and anything in the offender's background that might explain the motivation for the offence. In particular, report writers are urged to consider the impact of racism or of substance misuse on the offending. More broadly, the report should 'evaluate any patterns of offending, including reasons for offending, and assess the outcome of any earlier court interventions, including the offender's response to previous supervision'.
- The risk to the public of reoffending should be assessed on three fronts: first, 'the offender's likelihood of reoffending based on the current offence, attitude to it, and other relevant information'; second, 'the offender's risk of causing serious harm to the public'; and third, any risks of self-harm.
- The conclusion should evaluate the offender's motivation and ability to change. The shape of further conclusions depends on the proposal made, which should be 'a clear and realistic proposal for sentence designed to protect the public and reduce reoffending,

---

66 E.g. *Waterton* [2003] 1 Cr App R (S) 606.

including for custody where this is necessary'. If the offender is thought suitable for a community sentence, the report should explain what community sentence is appropriate and what form it might take. For serious sexual and violent offences the report should provide advice on the appropriateness of extended supervision. If custody is a possibility, the report should identify 'any anticipated effects on the offender's family circumstances, current employment or education'.

In order to assist with assessment the Home Office has developed or sponsored the development of various diagnostic tools relating to need and risk. Particularly significant is the risk assessment programme known as OASys, and a definitive evaluation of its predictive accuracy is awaited.[67]

However, the practice of passing sentence without a pre-sentence report ought to be reappraised. We have noted that the Criminal Justice Act 2003 allows this, as previous legislation did. It is also true that there are problems of delay in some areas, and even though 'stand down' reports are now prepared in many cases, they are but a pale reflection of the fuller report. What is more significant is that, on some occasions when courts pass sentence without obtaining a report, they do so on the spurious basis that they have learnt quite enough about the offender and his background from the trial. Moreover, one obvious danger – that more black offenders will be sent to custody, because more black offenders plead not guilty and are therefore unlikely to have pre-sentence reports prepared[68] – requires greater attention than it has received.

11.8 Defence speech in mitigation

In contrast to the prosecution statement of facts, the 'plea in mitigation' by the defence advocate has traditionally been allowed to range over the facts of the offence, the background and characteristics of the offender, and the suitability of possible sentences. According to Joanna Shapland's research in the 1970s, the factors most mentioned were, in order of frequency, (i) the reasons for the offence (e.g. provocation, sudden loss of temper, financial crisis); (ii) the relative seriousness of the offence; (iii) the offender's attitude to the offence (especially contrition, for which the plea of guilty was sometimes the only evidence); (iv) the offender's personal circumstances at the time of the court appearance (especially employment and family circumstances), probable future circumstances (e.g. continuing support from family), and the previous record (emphasizing, where possible, the absence of convictions or a gap since the last offence).[69] The best speeches in mitigation tended to be constructed in a way which appeared to show 'realism', by recognizing the gravity of the offence and any other factors against the offender. Shapland found that a common approach was for the advocate to acknowledge each aggravating

---

67 See Merrington (2004).
68 See Hood (1992), p. 156, showing a strong association between custody for blacks and the absence of a social inquiry report. See generally ch. 7.2 above.
69 Shapland (1981), ch. 3.

factor but to qualify it immediately by reference to a mitigating factor. As Shapland commented,

> this would seem to be one effective method of both being seen to be realistic and dealing with the [versions of the] offences given by the prosecution and the police, so turning them to the benefit of the offender.[70]

Such an approach would have been welcome to the judges interviewed in the Oxford pilot study, who stressed the importance of 'realism, in terms of pitching sentencing suggestions at an appropriate level; ready support for factual assertions, such as an employer's letter to confirm the availability of a job; and sound knowledge of the purpose and availability of the various sentences'. This kind of realism is related very much to the individual judge's view of the case, and requires counsel to modify the mitigating strategy according to indications from the judge.

How might defence speeches in mitigation measure up to the standard of providing reliable, comprehensive and relevant information, as the Streatfeild Committee expected of social inquiry reports? In one respect they would probably tend to be more comprehensive than social inquiry or pre-sentence reports: those reports tend not to recount factors going against the offender, whereas speeches in mitigation might do so. Judges seemed to value the speech in mitigation more highly because it tended to be more up to date, whereas social inquiry reports were often written some weeks before the hearing.[71] On the other hand, a speech in mitigation is less likely to be based on direct and probing interviews by a trained caseworker, although the defence advocate can incorporate comments from the pre-sentence report into the speech. In terms of reliability, both the probation officer and the defence advocate often have nothing more than the offender's word on which to base their submissions. Relevance is likely to be significantly higher for defence advocates, for three interrelated reasons. First, the concept of relevance is more or less defined by the judiciary and magistracy. Second, defence advocates are trained lawyers and should be more familiar with key offence-related issues than many probation officers. And third, the defence advocate has the great advantage of being in court and able to respond to any indications from the bench as to whether a certain line of argument is worth pursuing or not. In that way, the defence advocate may be able to change position in response to something as apparently slender as the eyebrow movements of the judge.[72]

The degree to which defence advocates make specific suggestions on sentence remains variable. Some judges discourage it, others appear willing to hear arguments in favour of a particular outcome. In *Ahmed* (1994)[73] an offender convicted of three cases of fraud involving the misrepresentation of his income in order to obtain further mortgage advances appealed against his sentence of 21 months. The Court of Appeal held that it was manifestly excessive, and that the judge could have been saved from this error if counsel had cited two recent Court of Appeal decisions on the

---

70 Shapland (1981), p. 82.   71 Oxford Pilot Study (1984), pp. 43–4.
72 Oxford Pilot Study (1984), p. 44.   73 (1994) 15 Cr App R (S) 286.

point. The Court added that 'we would urge members of the Bar when mitigating on sentence to draw the sentencing judge's attention to appropriate decisions of this court on sentencing'. This requires counsel to have a sound general understanding of sentencing principles, as well as to consult *Current Sentencing Practice* in relation to the particular offence – something which the judge might also have been expected to do. Where a guideline for the offence exists, counsel may be expected to frame the speech in mitigation in the terms of the guideline – in the expectation that the court will start from that point.[74] Most magistrates' courts make some use of the Magistrates' Courts Sentencing Guidelines, and the prudent advocate would make some reference to the factors which it mentions, even if it might not always be advisable to make direct reference to the guide.

A defence advocate is expected to give notice to the court of an intention to dispute the prosecution's version of the facts, on a guilty plea.[75] It is well established that the judge should give notice to defence counsel of an intention to impose certain types of sentence, in order to give counsel the opportunity to address the court on the issue – in particular severe sentences such as those imposed on 'dangerous' offenders under the 2003 Act, and also sentences that might be unexpected, such as disqualification from driving in a case where it is merely a discretionary penalty (e.g. for taking a car without consent).[76]

11.9 The role of the victim

What is, and what should be, the role of the victim in the sentencing process? Several other jurisdictions have created procedural rights for victims, and in this country the Domestic Violence, Crime and Victims Act 2004 has required the creation of The Victims' Code of Practice. This imposes obligations on several agencies within the criminal justice system, enforceable in the first place by complaint to the relevant agency and, in the absence of satisfaction, by way of complaint to the Parliamentary Commissioner for Administration (the Ombudsman). The 2004 Act also creates the office of Commissioner for Victims, to deal not with individual complaints but with issues surrounding the provision and co-ordination of victim policy.

The main thrust of The Victims' Code of Practice[77] is to set out the obligations of the various service providers to victims. The police are required, among other things, to inform the victim if a suspect has been arrested and then released on bail; if an offender has been given a caution, reprimand or warning; if no arrest has been made, to provide monthly updates on progress; if a date has been set for court proceedings; and if court proceedings have been concluded, to inform the victim

---

74 As s. 174 of the 2003 Act, discussed in part 11.3 above, implies that the court should.
75 *Gardener* (1994) 15 Cr App R (S) 667.   76 *Ireland* (1988) 10 Cr App R (S) 474.
77 Drafts of the code have been available since late 2003. In March 2005 the Home Office initiated a consultation on the Code (see www.homeoffice.gov.uk), and it is expected that a definitive version will be published later in 2005.

of the outcome. The police also have a duty to pass on details of relevant cases to the local Victim Support group within two days, unless the victim asks the police not to do so. And, when taking statements from victims, the police must inform them of their right to make a victim personal statement. The Crown Prosecution Service is required to tell the victim when charges have been dropped or altered, and to give an explanation for that outcome; to have in place a system for taking account of the contents of victim personal statements; and to ensure, so far as possible, that the prosecuting lawyer meets the victim before the start of any court hearing. Obligations are imposed on Victim Support to provide various contracted services, and also to provide the Witness Service at courts in accordance with the standards agreed. Court staff have various obligations to liaise with other agencies and to provide appropriate facilities, and so forth. The Code of Practice also imposes obligations on the Criminal Injuries Compensation Authority[78] and other agencies.

Although recent years have seen rather more promises than delivery in respect of victim services, especially in terms of keeping victims informed of events in 'their' case, the Code of Practice is to be welcomed as a major step in the formalization of victim services. However, whether victims should be granted procedural rights at the sentencing stage is a different question, and one can argue strongly in favour of improved services for victims whilst doubting the wisdom of victim participation in sentencing. Much depends, of course, on the rationale for sentencing and on its social and constitutional function. The issues are discussed briefly below in relation to two possible rights: a victim's right to convey to the court information about the offence and its impact, and a victim's right to voice an opinion on the sentence to be imposed.

11.9.1 Information from victims

It was noted above that the *2000 National Standards* stipulate that pre-sentence reports should 'assess the consequences of the offence, including what is known of the impact on the victim, either from the CPS papers or from a victim statement where available'.[79] Subsequently, and following pilot studies in certain areas, the government introduced the 'Victim Personal Statement' scheme in October 2001.[80] Whenever the police take a statement from a victim, they must also inform the victim of the right to make a victim personal statement. This provides victims with the opportunity to describe how the crime has affected them. Victims who make a VPS have the right to update it at any time before the trial. When a VPS is presented to a court, the proper approach is set out in a Practice Direction by the Lord Chief Justice:[81]

---

78 Discussed in ch. 10.4 above.   79 See this chapter, part 11.7 above.
80 Many other jurisdictions, particularly within the Commonwealth, have similar schemes. For that in Victoria, introduced after three official reports recommending against it, see Fox and Freiberg (1999), pp. 165–75.
81 Practice Direction (Victim Personal Statements) [2002] 1 Cr App R (S) 482.

(a) The Victim Personal Statement and any evidence in support should be considered and taken into account by the court prior to passing sentence.

(b) Evidence of the effects of an offence on the victim contained in the Victim Personal Statement or other statement must be in proper form, that is a S9 witness statement or an expert's report and served upon the defendant's solicitor or the defendant if he is not represented, prior to sentence. Except where inferences can properly be drawn from the nature of or circumstances surrounding the offence, a sentencer must not make assumptions unsupported by evidence about the effects of an offence on the victim.

(c) The court must pass what it judges to be the appropriate sentence having regard to the circumstances of the offence and of the offender taking into account, so far as the court considers it appropriate, the consequences to the victim . . .

The requirements in paragraph (b) are a response to the difficulties arising from unsubstantiated claims about the effects of crime: if the effect on the victim is relevant, and therefore is capable of amounting to an aggravating factor in sentencing, it is right that it should be proved in the normal way.[82] Similarly, just as it is unfair on victims that they should have their character or conduct attacked in the defence speech in mitigation,[83] without an opportunity to challenge what has been said, so it is unfair on an offender if unsubstantiated allegations are made by the victim without a proper opportunity to challenge them.

From the court's point of view, a victim statement may provide helpful information to 'complete the picture' of the offence, but this raises the deeper question of the relevance of this information. Insofar as it refers to the after-effects of an offence, should it be relevant at all? Why should the offender's sentence vary according to the chance circumstance of whether a particular victim suffers after-effects that are unusually great or unusually small? The general question of liability for unforeseen consequences was aired in Chapter 4 above.[84] Particularly controversial are cases such as *Hind* (1994),[85] where there was evidence that the victim of a rape, the offender's former lover, had not suffered much trauma as a result of the offence. The Court of Appeal held that this might be accepted as a factor reducing the seriousness of the offence. The guidelines on rape, it will be recalled, provide that particularly great trauma resulting from the offence is an aggravating factor.[86] Insofar as such effects are relevant to sentencing, it seems to follow that accurate and up-to-date information should be made available to the court through a VPS.

From the victim's point of view, is the VPS scheme a positive development? A study by Carolyn Hoyle and others of a pilot scheme in 1997–8 found that about 30 per cent of victims took advantage of the opportunity and that, if anything, the statements tended to understate rather than overstate the effects of the offence – largely

---

82 The early decision in *Hobstaff* (1993) 14 Cr App R (S) 605 made this point.
83 Para. 11(b) of the Code for Crown Prosecutors requires prosecutors to challenge such allegations.
84 See particularly ch. 4.4.4 above.
85 (1994) 15 Cr App R (S) 114; see also *Hutchinson*, ibid., 134.   86 Ch. 4.4.7 above.

because the statements were prepared so soon after the offence and not updated.[87] Whether victims feel that making a VPS has more advantages than disadvantages is unclear. Edna Erez is among those who claim that making such a statement can have a therapeutic effect for the victim: she points out that, in her surveys and others, victims who made a statement find that a positive experience.[88] However, much may depend on what the victim believes about the statement's reception: the English research concludes that 'most victims did not know the use to which their VS had been put, and few believed that it had much effect on charge or sentence even though this had been the hope of many'.[89] In other words, even if some victims do feel better for the experience, there is in other cases a danger of raising expectations that are then disappointed. One possible disadvantage of victim statements is that they may create or increase the fear of reprisals from the offender's family or associates. In the English survey a substantial minority of the 70 per cent of victims who declined to make a statement did so for fear of the offender's reaction if it became known to him.[90] Many of the criticisms of the VPS and similar schemes assume that the remaining aspects of the criminal justice system and social system will remain unchanged, however, and Andrew Sanders has made a powerful argument for a more inclusive approach to criminal justice that allows victims to inspect case files and reports and to engage in dialogue with decision-makers.[91]

11.9.2 Victim's opinion on sentence

Some of the jurisdictions which make formal provision for victim impact statements also allow the VPS to include an expression of opinion on the appropriate sentence. Some states in the United States go further and provide victims with a 'right of allocution', allowing a victim to make a statement in court in relation to the sentence.[92] From the victim's point of view, this may have even stronger advantages and disadvantages than merely making a factual statement. But what are the implications of such statements for the aims and purposes of sentencing? If the primary aim of sentencing is restorative,[93] then one possible route to the achievement of restorative justice might be to allow the individual victim to play a part in the determination of the sentence – provided that it must be a restorative sentence, not a purely punitive one, and provided that the individual victim does not decide what is necessary for the restoration of the community (an essential aspect of most modern restorative theories), since that ought to be the task of community representatives too. Thus, in the Family Group Conferences in New Zealand, convened to decide on the response to a young offender's crime, the conference includes not only the

---

87 Hoyle et al. (1998); also Sanders (2002), pp. 218–20.   88 Erez (1999), pp. 550–4.
89 Hoyle et al. (1998), p. 34.   90 Hoyle et al. (1998).
91 Sanders (2002); cf. Edwards (2004).   92 See Ashworth (1993) for some details.
93 See ch. 3.3.7 above.

offender and family and the victim and family, but also a police officer and (in some cases) a social worker.[94]

In the context of a sentencing system whose primary aim is not restorative, however, there must be grave doubts about allowing a victim to voice an opinion as to sentence. It is unfair and wrong that an offender's sentence should depend on whether the victim is vindictive or forgiving: in principle, the sentence should be determined according to the normal effects of a given type of crime, without regard to the disposition of the particular victim. If it is then said that allowing the victim to make a statement on sentence is not the same as allowing the victim to determine the sentence, one wonders about the point of the exercise. Victims' expectations might be unfairly raised and then dashed if a court declines to follow the suggestions made, and the whole process might appear to victims as a cruel pretence.

The English courts have now reached some such position, although not without some deviations. There are several cases in which victims and/or their families have written to the court to plead for mercy, to express forgiveness or otherwise to suggest that a lenient sentence is appropriate. In *Buchanan* (1980)[95] the Court of Appeal referred to a 'long and loving' letter from the victim, pleading for the offender's release so that she could live with him again, but the court held that he must receive the proper sentence for the offence. In *Darvill* (1987)[96] the Court of Appeal was equivocal, affirming that the offender must be sentenced for the offence he has committed but adding that 'forgiveness can in many cases have an effect, albeit an indirect effect, on the task of the sentencing judge. It may reduce the possibility of reoffending, it may reduce the danger of public outrage which sometimes arises when a defendant has been released into the community unexpectedly early . . . ' This theme was taken up in *Attorney General's Reference (No. 18 of 1993)* (1994),[97] where the offender struck a pregnant woman and a child with an iron bar. The sentencer was shown a letter from the then-pregnant victim and others from her family, stating that the offender had been forgiven and had been punished sufficiently by being remanded in custody pending trial. A probation order was made. The Court of Appeal, considering whether the sentence was unduly lenient, had received another letter from the victim. Referring to the 'very exceptional circumstances', the court did not alter the sentence, and clearly paid some attention to the forgiveness expressed by the victim and the family.

The leading decision is now *Nunn* (1996),[98] where a young man had caused the death by dangerous driving of a close friend. The mother and sister of the victim wrote to the court to say that, distressed as they were by their loss, the fact that the offender was in prison was also a continuing source of grief. The purport of their

94 See Morris, Maxwell and Robertson (1993), Morris and Maxwell (2000).
95 (1980) 2 Cr App R (S) 13.   96 (1987) 9 Cr App R (S) 225.
97 (1994) 15 Cr App R (S) 800.
98 [1996] 2 Cr App R (S) 136, endorsed by Lord Bingham CJ in *Roche* [1999] 2 Cr App R (S) 105 and incorporated into more general guidance in *Perks* [2001] 1 Cr App R (S) 66.

representations was that the sentence of four years should be reduced. Judge LJ said this:

> We mean no disrespect to the mother and sister of the deceased, but the opinions of the victim, or the surviving members of the family, about the appropriate level of sentence do not provide any sound basis for reassessing a sentence. If the victim feels utterly merciful towards the criminal, and some do, the crime has still been committed and must be punished as it deserves. If the victim is obsessed with vengeance, which can in reality only be assuaged by a very long sentence, as also happens, the punishment cannot be made longer by the court than would otherwise be appropriate. Otherwise cases with identical features would be dealt with in widely differing ways, leading to improper and unfair disparity . . .

In this case the court did reduce the sentence from four to three years, but it did so in response to the evidence that its length was adding to the grief of the victim's family, and not in response to their views on the appropriate sentence. Indeed, as Judge LJ pointed out, in this case the other two members of the deceased's family (his father and brother) did not share the views of the mother and sister.

In a system that treats proportionality to the seriousness of the offence as the primary determinant of sentence, this is clearly the right approach. The court's first duty is to impose the proper sentence for the case, by reference to the law and to sentences in similar cases. The Practice Direction[99] summarizes the effect of the above cases thus:

> The opinions of the victim or the victim's close relatives as to what the sentence should be are therefore not relevant, unlike the consequence of the offence on them. Victims should be advised of this. If, despite the advice, opinions as to sentence are included in the [victim personal] statement, the court should pay no attention to them.

The only exception for which there is authority is where some reduction in sentence is appropriate in order to mitigate the suffering of the victim's family. Thus in *Robinson* (2003),[100] the Court took note of the serious effects of the offender's imprisonment on the victim's family (who were close friends) and reduced a manslaughter sentence from four years to 18 months. Exceptional cases apart, the general approach in *Nunn* is consistent with that taken under the European Convention on Human Rights: in *McCourt* v. *UK* (1993)[101] a murdered woman's mother alleged a breach of Article 8 on the ground that she was denied the right to participate in the process of sentencing the convicted offender, to be informed of

---

99 See n. 81 above.
100 [2003] 2 Cr App R (S) 515; cf. *Attorney General's Reference No. 77 of 2002 (Scotney)* [2003] 1 Cr App R (S) 564, where the Court of Appeal, in a judgment delivered by Judge LJ (who also gave the leading judgment in Nunn), held that a community punishment order was not unduly lenient for causing death by careless driving while intoxicated in a case where the impact of the death on the offender and the victim's family (who were close) was so exceptional that a merciful course was justified.
101 (1993) 15 EHRR CD 110.

the date of his release and to express her views to those who decided on release. The European Commission on Human Rights noted that the Home Office does accept submissions from victims' families and places them before the Parole Board, and also has a practice of ensuring that victims' families are informed of any impending release of the offender. However, the Commission accepted that it would be inappropriate to recognize any role for the victim's family in setting the tariff period for the offender, since they would lack the requisite impartiality. The Commission concluded that the application disclosed no interference with the victim's family's right to respect for family life under Article 8.

CHAPTER 12

Special sentencing powers

This chapter deals with three sets of sentencing powers for particular groups of offender. It begins with the sentencing of young offenders under the age of 18, deals briefly with young adult offenders aged from 18 to 21, and then concludes with the various powers for dealing with mentally disordered offenders. In respect of each group, we will consider the justifications for separate sentencing powers, and the extent to which the rationale for special powers carries through into sentencing practice.

12.1 Young offenders

For almost the whole of the last century there were different sentencing procedures for younger offenders. Those aged under 17 (after the Criminal Justice Act 1991, under 18) were dealt with in different courts, formerly called juvenile courts and then renamed 'youth courts'. There is a considerable literature about the development of sentencing policy in respect of young offenders,[1] whereas the discussion here is necessarily briefer.

12.1.1 A short history of juvenile justice

Ever since 1933, the law has laid down that, in dealing with a juvenile offender, a court 'shall have regard to the welfare of the child or young person'.[2] This welfare ideology reached its apotheosis in the Children and Young Persons Act 1969, which sought to 'decriminalize' the juvenile court by regarding the commission of an offence as merely one way in which the court's powers to intervene for the welfare of the child could be activated. The legislation contemplated that children under 14 would be dealt with outside the criminal courts, and those aged 14–16 would only rarely be taken to court.[3] The 1969 Act failed, however, to resolve the long-standing tension between the welfare ideology and the tougher, punitive approach. In 1970

---

1 The leading legal text is Ball, McCormac and Stone (2001). For surveys see Newburn (2002), Ball (2004) and Bottoms and Dignan (2004).
2 Children and Young Persons Act 1933, s. 44(1).   3 Bottoms (1974).

there was a change of government, and some sections of the 1969 Act were never implemented. Much of its welfare ideology remained largely at the level of rhetoric: its foundations had lain in the belief that juvenile courts should work through and with the family, and should be seen chiefly as welfare-providing agencies. But some magistrates were unhappy with the greater power and discretion it bestowed upon social workers, and campaigned vigorously against the changes. The 1970s saw an expansion in the cautioning rather than prosecution of juveniles, but it also saw an unprecedented increase in the imposition of custodial sentences on young offenders. The struggle between welfare and punishment, between local authority social work departments and the magistracy, was joined in 1980 by the government, which issued a White Paper proclaiming a tougher approach. Tougher regimes were introduced into some detention centres, on an 'experimental basis', and the Criminal Justice Act 1982 restored to the magistracy some of the powers taken away by the 1969 Act.

Perhaps the most significant provision in the 1982 Act was the introduction of restrictions on custodial sentences for young offenders, introduced by way of backbench amendment rather than government policy. This, together with the expansion of cautioning for young offenders, meant that the 1980s turned out to be a decade of decreasing severity in the approach to young offenders.[4] The cautioning rate rose steeply, prompted by a Home Office circular of 1985. The number of recorded juvenile offenders began to fall significantly, and not merely because there were fewer young people in the population. Thus, between 1979 and 1989 the number of juveniles in the population fell by 25 per cent, whereas the number of recorded juvenile offenders declined by 40 per cent. A government-funded initiative to expand schemes of 'intermediate treatment' gathered momentum, and seems to have been reasonably successful in dealing with young offenders who might formerly have been sent into custody. And the number of juveniles sentenced to custody, which had risen steeply in the 1970s, fell spectacularly in the 1980s, from a peak of 7,900 in 1981 to merely 1,600 in 1991. These trends suggested a considerable momentum towards diversion from the courts and diversion from custody, but in the early 1990s the tide began to turn.

The Criminal Justice Act 1991 replaced the juvenile court with the youth court, and expanded its jurisdiction to cover all defendants aged under 18. New forms of community sentence were made available for young offenders, and, in line with those for adults, they were somewhat tougher. But the real changes of direction came around 1993 and 1994. The then Home Secretary announced that the high use of cautioning should be restrained, especially in respect of fairly serious offences and repeat offenders.[5] This seemed to go against the United Nations Convention on the Rights of the Child, but that fact was suppressed amid the growing media ferment about 'law and order', particularly in respect of young offenders. The mood continued after the election of 1997. The new government proposed wide-ranging

4 See further Harris and Webb (1987).   5 Home Office circular 18/1994.

and significant reforms of the youth justice system. In the preface to the White Paper *No More Excuses*, the then Home Secretary, Jack Straw, explained the government's approach in these terms:

> For too long we have assumed that young offenders will grow out of their offending if left to themselves. The research evidence shows this does not happen. An excuse culture has developed within the youth justice system. It excuses itself for its inefficiency, and too often excuses the young offenders before it, implying that they cannot help their behaviour because of their social circumstances. Rarely are they confronted with their behaviour and helped to take more personal responsibility for their actions . . . This White Paper seeks to draw a line under the past and sets out a new approach to tackling youth crime.[6]

Although parts of this are contestable – what 'the research evidence' shows about policies of minimum formal intervention, how often the courts have 'excused' young offenders – its drift is clear, and the change of language from government pronouncements in earlier decades is clear. The White Paper was followed by two sets of statutory changes, in the Crime and Disorder Act 1998 and the Youth Justice and Criminal Evidence Act 1999, some of the powers (but not others) being consolidated in the PCCS Act 2000, and their broad structure must now be analysed.

12.1.2 The structure of the youth justice system

The principal agency is the Youth Justice Board, created by s. 41 of the 1998 Act, with the tasks of monitoring the operation of the youth justice system, advising the Home Secretary on how the aims of the system might be pursued most effectively, for example promoting good practice and commissioning research. In practice the Board has achieved some success in steering youth justice policy in respect of matters such as reducing the use of custody, expanding forms of community sentence and creating initiatives in respect of (for example) ethnic minority young people and those placed on anti-social behaviour orders.[7] Beneath the Board, each local authority must establish a youth offending team (s. 39 of the 1998 Act). These teams (or YOTs, as they are known) draw from at least five local agencies: probation, social work, police, health and education. Their main tasks are to co-ordinate youth justice services, to carry out functions assigned to them under local youth justice plans and to arrange youth offender panels (YOPs) for individual offenders referred to them under the 1999 Act (see below). The third and fourth agencies to be mentioned are the police, who retain the decision to prosecute (under the usual arrangements with the Crown Prosecution Service), and the youth courts themselves.

Turning to the aims of the new youth justice system, the official rationale is to be found in s. 37 of the 1998 Act:

---

6 Home Office (1997), Preface.
7 For its annual reports, see www.youth-justice-board.gov.uk.

(1) It shall be the principal aim of the youth justice system to prevent offending by children and young persons.

(2) In addition to any other duty to which they are subject, it shall be the duty of all persons and bodies carrying out functions in relation to the youth justice system to have regard to that aim.

The system relies quite heavily on the idea of expert diagnosis (by a youth offender panel) of a young offender's predicament, for which an assessment tool known as Asset has been developed.[8] The assessment should lead the YOP to propose a contract, making certain requirements of the offender, of which 'the aim (or principal aim) is the prevention of reoffending by the offender'.[9] There is a potential problem here with the multiplicity of aims: although the five new 'purposes of sentencing' set out by the Criminal Justice Act 2003 do not apply in respect of young offenders under 18,[10] the youth justice legislation alludes to two aims of punishment, prevention and restorative justice. These potential conflicts are not merely academic or theoretical, nor do they suggest that all elements of the new scheme are open to attack. Many will agree with the emphasis on bringing offenders (of all ages) to recognize what they have done by 'confronting' them with their crime and its consequences, even if they do not agree with the implication in some government statements that all young offenders must take (full?) responsibility for their crimes. But the difficulty is that the scheme also draws elements of reparation and even restorative justice into the response to young offenders, as we shall see below, and there are questions about their role in an essentially punitive framework.

Before considering the youth court stage, however, it is important to emphasize the place of diversion in youth justice. Sections 65 and 66 of the Crime and Disorder Act 1998 created a system of reprimands and warnings. Section 65(1) is addressed to 'a constable [who] has evidence that a child or young person has committed an offence', and therefore replaces all the informal warnings and more formal cautions given by the police to persons under 18. However, the system is strongly prescriptive. No young offender should receive more than one reprimand and one warning; and, if the offence is too serious for a mere reprimand, the police must proceed straight to a warning. In cases where a warning is given, the constable must refer the offender to a YOT, and the YOT must assess the offender and, 'unless they think it inappropriate to do so, shall arrange for him to participate in a rehabilitation programme'.[11] Although the Youth Justice Board set a target of 80 per cent of final warnings to have an intervention programme by the end of 2004, the Audit Commission has warned against imposing too many requirements at an early stage, so as to avoid a rapid escalation towards custody.[12]

---

8 See Baker (2004).   9 S. 8(1) of the 1999 Act.   10 Criminal Justice Act 2003, s. 142(2)(a).
11 S. 66(2)(b) of the 1998 Act. See more fully Ball, McCormac and Stone (2001), ch. 4.
12 See Mair (2004), p. 153, for further argument.

Table 14. *Cautioning rate for young offenders, given*
as a percentage of offenders found guilty or cautioned

	Boys			Girls		
	10–11	12–14	15–17	10–11	12–14	15–17
1992	96	86	59	99	96	81
1997	93	74	49	98	89	68
2002	83	63	41	94	84	62

Source: Criminal Statistics 2002, Table 2.3.

Although the rate of diversion (formerly by cautions, now by reprimands and warnings) remains high for young offenders, it has continued to decline in the last few years, as Table 14 shows. While the Youth Justice Board writes of reprimands and warnings as 'light-touch, minimal interventions',[13] critics have pointed out that the implications of diversion for young offenders are more onerous than for older offenders, who may receive a simple caution.[14] The introduction of conditional cautions will alter the balance somewhat, but not entirely. There is some evidence that reconviction rates are some 7 to 10 per cent lower than the predicted rate, but those estimates require confirmation.[15]

There is evidence to suggest that there may be some unfair treatment at the diversion stage in respect of racial origin. Feilzer and Hood found that 'the odds of a case involving a mixed-parentage youth being prosecuted was 2.7 times that of a white youth with similar case characteristics', whereas the odds for a black youth were only slightly higher than for a white youth.[16]

If a young defendant is taken to court, the youth court is required (subject to an exception mentioned below) to make a referral order wherever a young offender who has not previously been convicted by a court pleads guilty to an offence.[17] The order may be for a period, to be specified, between 3 and 12 months. The referral is to the local YOT, which is then bound to establish a youth offender panel for the offender, with a view to drawing up a programme of behaviour to which the offender is invited to agree. This procedure must involve the offender's parent or guardian, but may not involve a legal representative. The programme may involve the payment of financial compensation to the victim, attendance at mediation sessions with the victim, the performance of unpaid work in the community, participation in certain activities and so forth. If the offender agrees, this becomes a 'youth offender contract', with provisions for a return to court in the event of breach. If the offender does not agree, the case is returned to the youth court and it is supposed to proceed to deal with the offender as normal. This whole procedure is framed in contractual terms,

13 Youth Justice Board (2004), p. 3.   14 Ball (2004), p. 37.
15 Audit Commission (2004); but cf. the questions raised by Bottoms (2004), pp. 72–3.
16 Feilzer and Hood (2003), p. ix.   17 S. 16 of the PCCS Act 2000.

but it is suffused with coercion, and that which is being coerced derives from large elements of expert diagnosis and discretion.[18] However, the study of referral orders by Newburn, Crawford and others showed that the new system was welcomed by all groups of participants:

> Within a relatively short period of time the panels have established themselves as constructive, deliberative and participatory forums in which to address young people's offending behaviour. The informal setting of youth offender panels would appear to allow young people, their parents/carers, victims (where they attend), community panel members and YOT advisers opportunities to discuss the nature and consequences of a young person's offending, as well as how to respond to this in ways which seek to repair the harm done and to address the causes of the young person's offending behaviour. This view is echoed by all participants in panels . . .[19]

The same study reported that apology and reparation were recurrent features of the contracts resulting from the panel meetings. However, the involvement of victims was lower than expected, with only 13 per cent of panel meetings attended by a victim and some 28 per cent overall in which a victim had some input (e.g. by written statement).[20] One substantial criticism of the referral order system was that its mandatory nature meant that many relatively minor cases were receiving undue attention. National figures for 2002, the year in which referral orders were made available to all courts, show that of some 19,000 referral orders made, the largest group was for summary non-motoring offences (5,800), followed by theft and handling (4,200), followed by summary motoring offences (3,000).[21] The law was amended by Order in 2003 by giving the youth court a discretion not to make a referral order in minor cases.

Apart from referral orders, the youth court's powers remain broadly unchanged, save for the introduction of some new powers and requirements by the Criminal Justice Act 2003.

12.1.3 The youth court and non-custodial sentences

The framework of sentencing is somewhat similar to that for adults, in the sense that the power to make an absolute discharge, conditional discharge, bind-over, compensation order and fine remain available in most cases.[22] If a financial penalty is imposed, the parents may be ordered to pay if the offender is aged 16 or 17, and they must be ordered to pay if the offender is aged under 16. The parents have a right to be heard before being ordered to pay, and it is their means that should be taken into account. Although fining is not a common response to juvenile offending, reconviction figures suggest that it is relatively effective, as is the conditional discharge.[23]

---

18 See Ball (2000).   19 Newburn, Crawford et al. (2002), p. 62.
20 Newburn, Crawford et al. (2002), ch. 8.   21 Criminal Statistics 2002, Table 4F.
22 For further discussion of these measures see ch. 10 above.
23 Mair (2004), p. 151, with qualifications.

Indeed, when dealing with offenders under 16, the youth court's powers and duties extend to the parents of the offender. Thus, a youth court is required to order parents to attend court if their child is being prosecuted, unless it would be unreasonable to require this. There is also a presumption that a court should bind over the parents of a child aged under 16 to exercise proper care and control over the child: if it declines to do so, it should state its reasons. There is a further power to bind over the parents of a child who is placed on a community sentence, requiring them to ensure that the child completes it. The general theme of encouraging greater parental responsibility is undoubtedly right, insofar as family units are critical to much social behaviour. But a more constructive approach than court orders, threats and coercion would be to provide greater support for parents through local authority social workers and parental support groups. Thus the Children Act 1989 provides for local authorities to provide support and assistance to parents based on assessment of the needs of the child, without resort to care proceedings and without any attribution of blame. However, parents may have other duties imposed on them, such as that of attending all meetings of a young offender panel relating to their child, where a referral order has been made. Indeed, ss. 8–10 of the Crime and Disorder Act 1998 also empower a court to make a parenting order, requiring a parent to attend guidance sessions and so on as specified. The questions of the appropriate degree of coercion on parents of offending children remains controversial.[24]

Where a youth court is contemplating making a community order, it must comply with all the statutory requirements applicable to such orders (see Chapter 10.6 above). However, the 2003 Act is not yet in force for offenders aged 16 and 17, so the old community sentences apply. Where a youth court is dealing with an offender aged 10–15, it is empowered to make a youth community order, and that may take one of five forms:

a curfew order,
an exclusion order,
an attendance centre order,
a supervision order, or
an action plan order.

The appropriate statutory provisions for these five orders are to be found in the Powers of Criminal Courts (Sentencing) Act 2000, and not in the Criminal Justice Act 2003. Nothing more needs to be said here about curfew orders and exclusion orders. *Attendance centres* operate for three hours on a Saturday afternoon, and involve the offenders in physical training and constructive work, among other things. The maximum number of hours that can be ordered is 24 for offenders under 16 (36 for those aged 16 and under 25). *Supervision orders* involve supervision of the offender by a local authority social worker. They may include additional requirements, similar to those included in activity requirements, programme requirements

24 See Zedner (1998), pp. 176–81.

and other requirements for adults. The *action plan order* involves supervision for three months, during which the offender may be ordered to do one or more of a whole range of things found in other orders (e.g. participate in specified activities, attend an attendance centre, report at certain times and places, make non-financial reparation to the victim or the community).

A major objective of the Youth Justice Board has been to tackle persistent young offenders, and one prominent initiative has been the development of the Intensive Supervision and Surveillance Programme (ISSP) aimed at this group. As the name suggests, this programme attempted to combine the supervision of this difficult and often troubled group of offenders with surveillance of them. The Audit Commission commended ISSPs as 'a more constructive and cheaper option for persistent young offenders than a spell in custody'.[25] An evaluation of the ISSP by an Oxford University team showed that there was some reduction in reoffending in the short term, which may or may not have been attributable to ISSP, but a proper follow-up study is awaited. The research also showed that ISSP was largely successful in ensuring that underlying needs, such as education, were tackled. However, the study showed some variation in the delivery of ISSP, with standards not uniformly high.[26] These findings are sufficient to justify further development of ISSP, but they counsel caution in making claims about its effectiveness.

The youth court may also make certain ancillary orders, of which the *anti-social behaviour order* is the most prominent. We have seen that ASBOs may be made in civil proceedings or, alternatively, after sentence; we have also noted that around half of all ASBOs are made against persons under 18 – even though the government stated during the parliamentary debates that ASBOs were not intended for the young. Accepting the reality that young people are going to become subject to ASBOs in considerable numbers, the Youth Justice Board has pressed for greater involvement of Youth Offending Teams with these young people.[27] This is now facilitated by s. 292 of the Criminal Justice Act 2003, which inserts into the legislative framework for ASBOs a new power to make an 'individual support order', assigning the young person to a 'responsible officer' and requiring the young person to comply with directions for a period of up to six months. This promises to furnish some support to young people on ASBOs, although the maximum of six months is well below the minimum period of two years for the ASBO.

As we saw in Table 6 in Chapter 1, the proportionate use of community sentences has increased considerably between 1992 and 2002, from 39 to 64 per cent of boys aged 10–17 and from 27 to 71 per cent of girls. Discharges are now little used, and instead the youth court is more frequently imposing a community sentence – sometimes, it may be argued, on offenders whose crimes are not serious enough to warrant this degree of intervention. There appears to be much local variation in youth justice: the study of some 17,000 cases by Feilzer and Hood found considerable evidence of 'justice by geography' in the disposal of cases by youth courts. Looking

---

25 Audit Commission (2004).   26 Moore et al. (2004).   27 Youth Justice Board (2004), p. 7.

at ethnic origin in relation to community sentences, they found that Asian youths and mixed-parentage youths were more likely to receive one of the more restrictive community penalties than could be explained by their case characteristics.[28]

12.1.4 Custodial sentences

In Chapter 9 above we noted the sharp increase in the use of custody in English sentencing. However, the sentencing of young offenders is an exception to this, at least in respect of boys. Thus as Table 6 in Chapter 1 demonstrates, the proportionate use of custody for boys aged 10–17 increased from 10 per cent in 1992 to 14 per cent in 1997 and then fell back to 13 per cent in 2002. For girls, however, the trajectory has been upwards – from 2 per cent in 1992 to 5 per cent in 1997 and to 7 per cent in 2002. These are increases, but not of the same magnitude as for adult offenders. The Youth Justice Board has endeavoured to generate a movement of young offenders away from custodial sentences to community sentences, and 2003 saw a downturn in the numbers of sentenced young offenders in custody, from 9,079 in November 2002 to 8,330 in November 2003.[29] The Audit Commission's report in 2004 advocates a reduction of the use of custodial sentences in favour of the more demanding community orders, by means of greater emphasis on and information about 'the costs and the effectiveness of custody and community alternatives'.[30]

The custodial sentence for offenders aged 10–17 is the detention and training order (DTO), the statutory provisions on which are to be found in the Powers of Criminal Courts (Sentencing) Act 2000. Section 100 provides that no such order may be made unless the provisions on the custody threshold are satisfied.[31] If the court is satisfied that the case passes the custody threshold, it may only impose a DTO on an offender aged under 15 if it is of the opinion that he is a 'persistent offender', which is not defined.[32] Also, a court may only impose a DTO on an offender aged 10 or 11 if of the opinion 'that only a custodial sentence would be adequate to protect the public from further offending by him'. Section 101 provides that a DTO may only be for one of the specified lengths – 4, 6, 8, 10, 12, 18 or 24 months. Not surprisingly, this restriction has been criticized for playing havoc with courts' attempts to reflect differences in culpability between offenders, and mitigating factors such as a plea of guilty. Under a DTO the young offender serves half the sentence in a young offender institution and is then released under supervision for the remainder of the sentence. To some extent, therefore, the order already incorporates some of the elements to be introduced as 'custody plus' for older offenders under the Criminal Justice Act 2003.[33] The new measures for adults, including custody plus, suspended sentences and intermittent custody, are not available for offenders under 18.

---

28 Feilzer and Hood (2004), p. xi.   29 Lewis (2004), pp. 49–50.
30 Audit Commission (2004).   31 See ch. 9.4.1 above.
32 It appears that a young offender with no previous convictions who is convicted of multiple offences on his first court appearance may be classed as a 'persistent offender': *AS* [2001] 1 Cr App R (S) 62.
33 See ch. 9.4.4 above.

Section 91 of the Powers of Criminal Courts (Sentencing) Act 2000 provides for the long-term detention of young offenders for serious offences. The power may only be exercised where the offender is convicted of an offence with a maximum penalty of 14 years, or of a few listed offences. Guidelines on the proper use of the s. 91 power were laid down in *Mills* (1998).[34] Whereas previously it had been held that the power should only be used in cases of exceptional gravity, this guidance makes it clear that s. 91 simply authorizes the use of that part of the tariff which lies above the range of ordinary sentences of detention. Thus, if a court concludes that a particular case warrants a sentence longer than two years, it may use the s. 91 power so long as the offence falls within the purview of that power. In *Mills* Lord Bingham CJ emphasized that no young offender should be given a custodial sentence unless absolutely necessary, and then for no longer than is necessary. And, of course, the length of sentence should be calculated in a way that makes allowance for the offender's youth and for any plea of guilty. Severe sentences are imposed on very young offenders from time to time, such as the three-year sentence of long-term detention imposed on a boy of 11 for causing grievous bodily harm to a younger boy when he was 10.[35]

However, the power under s. 91 is now joined by the much more severe power under part 12 of the Criminal Justice Act 2003 dealing with 'dangerous offenders'. Part 12 of the new Act was discussed in some detail in Chapter 6.9 above, and it therefore suffices here to repeat that there are three new forms of sentence. Detention for life must be imposed in certain cases, where the offence is one to which s. 91 of the 2000 Act applies (above) and where the court considers that the seriousness of the offence justifies detention for life (s. 226). Detention for public protection must be imposed in a case where the court believes that there is a serious risk to the public from which an extended sentence would not provide adequate protection (s. 226(3)). And an extended sentence must be imposed if a young offender stands convicted of a specified offence and the court believes that there is a significant risk of serious harm otherwise (s. 228). These are very severe sentences for young offenders, and it is to be hoped that the courts will use them restrictively.

12.2 Young adult offenders

Offenders aged 18, 19 and 20 are tried and sentenced in adult courts, but there is some difference in the orders available to the court. There is a lengthy tradition of separate custodial institutions for offenders aged under 21 – borstals, detention centres, youth custody centres and now young offender institutions. The reasoning is partly to prevent the 'contamination' of young offenders by older and more experienced criminals, and partly to enable more constructive regimes with a greater emphasis on education and on industrial training. The Younger report justified special attention to this group thus:

---

34 [1998] 1 Cr App R (S) 128.　35 *Jamie Craig W.* [2003] 1 Cr App R (S) 502.

This is a highly delinquent group making a major demand on the penal system. While offenders in the group often have records of serious delinquency behind them, many are not yet set in their ways. They may be failures of the school system or immature in other respects, and the few years after leaving school may offer a last chance of helping them to make good the ground they have lost. A special concentration of public effort upon this group of young adults, who are in danger of going on to long and costly criminal careers, is a sensible investment by society at a time when resources, both human and material, are too scarce to allow a similar degree of attention to be paid to all age groups.[36]

There is now reason to doubt that the 'special concentration' for which the Younger report argued is thought appropriate. The different category of 'young adult offenders' is fast disappearing and, although young offenders can still expect some mitigation for their age, they are for most purposes aggregated with adult offenders.

12.2.1 Cautioning young adults

The high rate of cautioning for juveniles has never been matched by a similar rate for young adults. Initiatives were begun in the late 1980s to increase the cautioning rate for young adults, with considerable success. For young adult males the cautioning rate reached 29 per cent in 1992, rose to 35 per cent in 1997, and then returned to 29 per cent in 2002; for young adult females there has been a steady decline, from a high of 50 per cent in 1992, through 48 per cent in 1997, and down to 41 per cent in 2002 – a rate still considerably higher than that for young men, however. The overall figures are higher than for adults aged 21 and over, which stood at 19 per cent for men in 2002 and 32 per cent for women. Research by Roger Evans showed that, as with many other decisions in criminal justice, much depends on the ground-level views of those who decide whether or not to caution: in one of the two police divisions he studied, there was a distinct uneasiness about a higher use of cautions for young adults,[37] and there is still considerable variation across the country. Some of the reluctance may stem from the fact that 18 is now the peak age of offending for males, but it can be pointed out that the peak age was previously 16 and the expansion of juvenile cautioning took place nevertheless. It remains to be seen how the advent of conditional cautioning under the 2003 Act will affect this age-group, in terms of reducing the number of simple cautions and/or reducing the numbers prosecuted.

12.2.2 Sentencing young adults

The sentencing framework for young adults is largely that for adults, with a few exceptions. It was noted in Chapter 10.6.3 that one form of requirement in a community sentence, the attendance centre order, is available only up to the age of 25. So far as custodial sentences are concerned, since 1982 custody for young adults has

36 Advisory Council on the Penal System (1974), para. 9.   37 Evans (1993).

not been imprisonment but detention in a young offender institution, preserving the segregation that has long been a feature of the system. However, s. 61 the Criminal Justice and Court Services Act 2000 will reverse this policy when it is brought into force, which has not yet happened. Custodial sentences on offenders aged 18 and over will take the form of imprisonment. This will mean that the new raft of sentences introduced by the Criminal Justice Act 2003 and discussed in Chapter 9.4 above will become available for this age-group – custodyc plus, intermittent custody and (reverting to the position before 1982) the suspended sentence.

As Table 5 in Chapter 1 shows, the use of custody for this age group has risen considerably in the last decade – from 15 per cent in 1992 to 26 per cent in 2002 for young men, and from 3 to 14 per cent for young women. At the same time the proportionate use of community sentences has remained unchanged for young men (30 per cent in 1992, 31 per cent in 2002) and has risen steadily for young women, from 26 to 38 per cent. Fines have declined for both men and women, but there has been a marked decrease in conditional discharges for young women, which seems to link with the increase in community sentences and custody.

12.3 Mentally disordered offenders[38]

It is generally accepted that people who commit offences while mentally disordered, or who are mentally disordered at the time of trial, should not be dealt with in the same way as other offenders. The criminal law provides a procedural bar to trial, unfitness to plead, and also a defence of insanity, and if either is upheld the court has a discretion in the order it may make: Criminal Procedure (Insanity and Unfitness to Plead) Act 1991. The test of unfitness to stand trial relates to the defendant's ability to follow the proceedings and to instruct counsel: more than 30 defendants a year are found unfit to plead.[39] The test for the defence of insanity is still restrictive and, despite the flexibility of powers on a verdict of insanity, its use since the 1991 Act remains low.[40] Most of those who are mentally disordered tend not to plead insanity, but instead acquiesce in conviction and seek a medical disposal at the sentencing stage. This means that sentencers have to deal with far more people in this category than they would need to if there were proper adherence to the principle that persons whose responsibility was significantly affected at the time of the offence should not be subjected to criminal conviction.

At the sentencing stage there is a long tradition of regarding (some) mentally disordered offenders as either deserving of mitigation, or requiring treatment instead of punishment. This approach can be rationalized on the basis that such offenders may not have sound powers of reasoning or control, and may therefore not understand the significance of punishment or may not deserve it. Sentencing has a communicative element, which cannot be realized where it is the offender's

---

38 For fuller discussion, see Peay (2002).   39 Mackay and Kearns (1999).
40 Mackay and Kearns (1999), reporting an average of nine insanity pleas per year.

understanding that is impaired.[41] However, not all mentally disordered people lack understanding: some suffer affective disorders, which reduce their ability to control their behaviour and thus supply a different ground for doubting that punishment is deserved.

Insofar as the orientation of sentencing for mentally disordered offenders has been towards treatment and rehabilitation, this raises its own difficulties. If there is no proportionality requirement, the compulsory treatment may endure far longer than any compulsory powers taken against a non-disordered offender. Moreover, treatment may bestow far more discretion on the psychiatrist or hospital than would be acceptable in most sentences. This makes it important to ensure that there is a proportionality constraint upon the duration of compulsory powers in the name of criminal justice, and also to ensure that the rights of mentally disordered offenders are respected and not subjugated to assumptions about dangerousness. The recent trend to phrase a more repressive policy towards mentally disordered offenders in terms of risk and public protection fails, as we shall see, to place a proper interpretation on the empirical foundations and normative implications of assessments of dangerousness.

12.3.1 Diversion of mentally disordered offenders

The police have long had the power to remove to a place of safety any person who appears to be suffering from mental disorder and to be in need of care and control. The power, now in s. 136 of the Mental Health Act 1983, is used in over 1,000 cases each year, more in some areas than others. If a mentally disordered person is arrested in the normal way, the disorder may be regarded as a reason for cautioning the offender or as a reason for discontinuing a prosecution, under the Code for Crown Prosecutors. Home Office circular 60/1990, *Provision for Mentally Disordered Offenders*, encourages the diversion of mentally disordered offenders away from the criminal justice system where possible. There are many diversion schemes across the country, either at police stations or at courts, which draw upon mental health professionals in order to assess and, where appropriate, divert mentally disordered people from the formal criminal process.[42] The difficulties of achieving this in practice remain, however. Geoffrey Pearson and Elizabeth Burney, in their study of one such scheme, demonstrated that other problems bulk large in many of these cases – notably accommodation needs, the overlap between mental health problems and substance abuse, and the over-representation of black people with psychotic illness – and that their solution requires considerable inter-agency co-operation and financial resources.[43] Moreover, the schemes do not cover all areas, and there is no requirement on courts to consider the effect of a custodial remand on a defendant's mental health.[44]

---

41 Duff (1986).   42 Laing (1999).
43 Burney and Pearson (1995).   44 See Cavadino (1999).

12.3.2 Special orders for the mentally disordered

Absolute or conditional discharges may be appropriate in some cases where the offender is suffering from mental disorder. Beyond that, the courts have various orders available for the mentally disordered. If the offence is of sufficient seriousness, the court may consider a community sentence with a mental health treatment requirement, a guardianship order or a hospital order. All these orders depend on the presence of mental disorder, which includes mental illness, severe mental impairment, mental impairment or psychopathic disorder. Section 1 of the Mental Health Act includes definitions of all except mental illness.[45]

The powers in the Mental Health Act 1983 were intended to enhance the possibility of treatment, but it is important to signal at the outset a major difference between medical and penal disposals. The prisons cannot refuse to accept persons sentenced to imprisonment, but psychiatrists and the hospitals can and do refuse to accept people on whom the criminal courts might wish to make a particular order. The availability of a place remains a precondition of all the orders discussed below.

Section 35 of the 1983 Act permits remand to hospital for the preparation of a report for the court, but many psychiatric reports for the courts are still prepared when the defendant is in prison, which may be a manifestly unsuitable environment. Since few of these defendants present a danger to the public, it seems unnecessary to remand them to prison, but at present it is doubtful whether the mental hospitals could cope with the large numbers of people on whom the courts want reports. Although there are court-based assessment schemes in some areas, enabling a psychiatric assessment to be carried out promptly without the need for a remand, the power under s. 35 is relatively little used.[46]

Section 36 provides for remand to hospital for treatment, and s. 38 creates the interim hospital order. Again, these have not been greatly used, and this may stem partly from the difficulties over hospital beds and admission policies, discussed below. An example of the operation of these powers is provided by *Attorney General's Reference (No. 34 of 1992)* (1993).[47] The offender pleaded guilty to wounding with intent and was remanded to prison for psychiatric reports. Four months later, on considering the reports, the court made an interim hospital order and the offender was admitted to Broadmoor Hospital under s. 38: the purpose was to see whether he was susceptible to treatment that would justify the making of a hospital order. Five months later, the psychiatrist reported to the court that, although treatment was exceedingly difficult, it would be appropriate to make a full hospital order with restrictions. However, the defendant then changed his plea and, by the time the case ultimately came to court for sentence a further 12 months later, two psychiatrists reported that the defendant's condition was not susceptible to treatment.

Turning to special sentences for the mentally disordered, a court may make a community sentence with a mental health treatment requirement under

45 See Ashworth and Gostin (1984).   46 Peay (2002), p. 759.   47 (1993) 15 Cr App R (S) 167.

ss. 207–208 of the Criminal Justice Act 2003. This replaces what used to be known as the psychiatric probation order, and it is subject to all the conditions that must be fulfilled if a community sentence is to be imposed.[48] Before making this particular requirement the court must receive a report from a duly qualified medical practitioner, and must satisfy itself that the offender's mental condition requires and may be susceptible to treatment, and that it is not such as to warrant the making of a hospital order or guardianship order. The treatment prescribed may be as a resident at a specified hospital or as an outpatient, or by or under the direction of a specified doctor or chartered psychologist, and the offender must consent to it. The requirement was formerly subject to a maximum of one year, but that limit has now been removed and it is for the court to specify the duration of the requirement. This form of sentence was for many years the most frequently used of the special orders, averaging around 1,000 cases per year. However, the figures for the early part of this century show a decline, and in 2002 there were just 521 such orders made – 30 for treatment as a resident in a mental hospital, 319 for treatment as a non-resident (out-patient) at a hospital, and 172 for treatment under the direction of a duly qualified medical practitioner.[49] This order may occasionally be made in a case that might otherwise justify a substantial custodial sentence, as where an offender suffering from a depressive illness was sentenced for attempting to rob a post office using a sawn-off air pistol.[50]

Guardianship orders are rarely used: they place an offender under the guardianship of a local authority or a person approved by such an authority, and might be suitable for mentally impaired people who would benefit from occupational training and other guidance. Much more frequently used are hospital orders, made in around 700 cases per year in the mid-1990s, and most recently made in 626 cases in 2000 and in 614 cases in 2001.[51] In order to make a hospital order under s. 37 of the Mental Health Act 1983, the court must have evidence from two qualified practitioners, of whom one is approved under s. 13 of the 1983 Act, to the effect that the offender is suffering from a mental disorder which makes detention for medical treatment appropriate.[52] An order cannot be made unless a hospital has signified its willingness to admit the offender for treatment. There are two main reasons why hospital orders cannot be made on more mentally disordered offenders: first, the 1983 Act includes a treatability condition, so that in cases where the offender is suffering from mental impairment or psychopathy, the court must be satisfied that treatment is 'likely to alleviate or prevent a deterioration of the condition', which is unlikely in cases of psychopathic disorder; second, local mental hospitals tend

---

48 See ch. 10.6 above.   49 Probation Statistics 2002, Table 3.10.
50 *Attorney General's Reference No. 37 of 2004 (Dawson)* [2005] 1 Cr App R (S) 295: the Court refused the reference and thus the community sentence stood.
51 Home Office Statistical Bulletin 13/2002, Table 18.
52 In *Nafei* [2005] Crim LR 409 the Court of Appeal reiterated that s. 37 confers a power. In a case where psychiatrists recommended a hospital order for a man who was not suffering from mental disorder at the time of the offence but was at the time of sentence, the Court upheld a sentence of 12 years' imprisonment for drug importation.

to pursue fairly restrictive criteria for admission, and offender-patients are sometimes refused admission on the basis that they are likely to disrupt the regime. In the debates on the legislation that became the 1983 Act the government resisted an amendment that would have required hospitals to accept offender-patients sent by the courts: s. 39 of the Act requires regional hospital authorities to respond to requests from courts for information on hospital accommodation in their area, but this is merely a prompting device. The effect of a s. 37 hospital order is that the patient may be detained for six months initially, and this is renewable for a further six months and then for one year at a time. If the offender-patient is not discharged by the hospital, the case will be reviewed periodically by a Mental Health Review Tribunal.

For some mentally disordered offenders, a hospital order is not considered sufficient, because local hospitals can provide little security and the offender is regarded as a danger to others. In this sphere there is often a casual mixture of fact and fiction. It is sometimes assumed that mentally disordered offenders pose greater dangers than others because of their disorder, whereas in fact the offence categories of the mentally disordered are similar to those of other offenders (in fact mentally disordered offenders are slightly more likely to have committed property offences), and they are no more likely to be reconvicted than other offenders.[53] A number of much publicized cases of ex-patients killing on release have led to the institution of mandatory inquiries after homicide by released patients; but, as Jill Peay argues,

> it is particularly galling to those involved in treating mentally disordered offenders that such concerns persist despite repeated demonstrations that 'reoffending rates are in fact no higher than for any other class of offender' and the knowledge that when psychiatric patients kill, they are more likely to kill themselves than others.[54]

This is not to deny that there are mentally disordered offenders who appear dangerous. But it is necessary to warn against the too-ready progression from mental disorder, to unpredictability, to danger and to long-term detention (whether for 'treatment' or not). This brings us to the strongest of measures available for mentally disordered offenders: the Crown Court has the power to add to a hospital order a restriction order, under s. 41 of the 1983 Act. A restriction order may be for a determinate number of years, but in most cases is without limit of time. Before adding a restriction order, the court must have heard oral evidence from at least one of the medical practitioners, and it must be satisfied that a restriction order is necessary for the protection of the public from serious harm – a formula subsequently used in the dangerousness provisions of the Criminal Justice Act 2003.[55] In *Kearney* (2003)[56] the Court of Appeal quashed a restriction order in a case where the judge had not addressed himself to the phrase 'necessary for the protection of the

53 Peay (2002), p. 774.   54 Peay (1997), p. 662.
55 See ch. 6.9 above.   56 [2003] 2 Cr App R (S) 85.

public from serious harm', and where the facts and the psychiatrists' reports were equivocal on this. Some general considerations for the making of restriction orders were set out by Mustill LJ in *Birch* (1989).[57] Where the potential harm from further offences is serious, a low risk of repetition might be sufficient; but a high probability of the recurrence of relatively minor offences should not suffice. Moreover, it is only where there is a firm prognosis that a restriction order for a fixed period should be made: the norm is for the s. 41 restrictions to be without limit of time. In recent years the courts have tended to make around 200 restriction orders per year (the figure for 2001 was 239). Research by Street into the imposition of restriction orders found that some 94 per cent of them were without limit of time; that 77 per cent were diagnosed as suffering from mental illness, and 13 per cent as psychopathic; that some 69 per cent had been psychiatric in-patients before; and that 20 per cent were black (compared with 1.6 per cent of the general population).[58]

Fewer than half of all offenders who are subject to restriction orders are held in high-security hospitals: in 2001 some 1,144 were held in the high-security hospitals and a further 1,858 in other hospitals, chiefly medium-secure units.[59] The high-security hospitals have limited space, and hold a considerable number of patients who no longer require high security but for whom there are not suitable places elsewhere. The development of medium-secure units to cater for mentally disordered patients who require medium security has been slow: it appears that there are now over 1,500 medium-secure beds, but pressure on them is great – not only from the courts, but also from patients transferred from prison and patients awaiting transfer from high-security hospitals.

There have been many occasions over the years when judges have lamented the unavailability of a place in a special hospital; if such a place is not forthcoming a judge will often feel that security concerns require the imposition of a prison sentence, despite the unsuitability of prison for many mentally disordered offenders. As a general principle it is wrong for a judge to impose a sentence of life imprisonment if there is unanimous medical opinion in favour of a s. 41 order and a bed is available in a special hospital.[60] The Court of Appeal deviated from this principle in the 'unusual and exceptional' case of *Fleming* (1993),[61] upholding life imprisonment where the offender had previously been released from hospital following a restriction order but killed two people three years later. However, the Court of Appeal has now disapproved that decision in *Mitchell*, pointing out that the decision to release a person serving a discretionary life sentence is in the hands of the Parole Board, not the Home Secretary, and that the Board's composition is similar to that of a Mental Health Review Tribunal. The decision in *Fleming*, held Otton LJ, 'is better disregarded'.[62]

---

57 (1989) 11 Cr App R (S) 202.   58 Street (1998), s. 1.
59 Home Office Statistical Bulletin 13/2002.   60 *Howell* (1985) 7 Cr App R (S) 360.
61 (1993) 14 Cr App R (S) 151.   62 *Mitchell* [1997] 1 Cr App R (S) 90 at p. 93.

Once admitted under s. 41, the offender will be detained until either the Home Secretary or a Mental Health Review Tribunal decides that the criteria for release are satisfied, i.e. that the offender-patient's confinement is no longer necessary for the protection of the public. Street found that, of those released, some 62 per cent were discharged by the Tribunal and the remainder by the Home Secretary. On average they had spent around nine years in hospital before discharge.[63]

Brief mention should also be made of the 'hospital and limitation direction' introduced by s. 45 of the Crime (Sentences) Act 1997. It applies only to offenders suffering from a psychopathic disorder, and provides for courts to sentence them to imprisonment while directing that they be admitted to hospital for treatment. The order has been little used,[64] and there is a strong argument that it was ill-conceived.[65]

12.3.3 Prisons and the mentally disordered

The previous paragraphs disclose at least some explanations of the process by which mentally disordered offenders come to be sent to prison. First, if the treatability requirement in s. 37 of the Mental Health Act is not fulfilled, a hospital order becomes impossible and the court might feel that prison is the only alternative. This is often the outcome for offenders diagnosed as suffering from psychopathic disorder, as it is rare for such a person to be regarded as treatable. Second, even where the treatability requirement is fulfilled, no hospital place may be available. Thus, every year, numerous offenders suffering from mental disorder are given custodial sentences. As we saw in Chapter 9.7, studies suggest that around one-third of all convicted prisoners and almost two-thirds of remand prisoners have some form of mental disorder: even though a substantial proportion of those mentally disordered prisoners have disorders related to substance abuse, the magnitude of the problem is considerable.[66] A third and related point is that there are simply not enough available beds for all the mentally disordered offenders who are in prison. With only around 3,500 beds in the high-security hospitals and medium-secure units, and relatively few available for offender-patients in local mental hospitals, the numbers in prison could not be accommodated. This shows that the matter is largely one of allocation of resources: the community care policy must be enhanced, but there will still be cases where the practical choice lies between hospital and prison. Since it is widely accepted that prison is unsuitable for people suffering from mental disturbance, it is unjust to send them there. It remains a fact, however, that mentally disordered offenders are being sent to prison and will continue to be sent there. And, although the Chief Inspector of Prisons has recently reported 'a considerable improvement' in prison healthcare as a whole, she adds that 'healthcare staff struggle with the scale of the task. Mental health in-reach teams in some prisons can do little but skim the surface of the severity and breadth of mental illness contained in prisons.'[67]

---

63 Street (1998), s. 2.
64 Home Office Statistical Bulletin 13/2002 records three cases in 2000 and in 2001.
65 Eastman and Peay (1998).   66 See ch. 9.6.4 above.   67 HMCI Prisons (2004), p. 7.

Concerns about the inadequacy of prison medical care for the mentally disordered were recorded by the Joint Committee, referring to 'an over-reliance on medication and no therapy available'.[68]

A possibility in some cases is to have a prisoner transferred to mental hospital, under Mental Health Act powers that treat him or her as a restricted patient. Although the number of transfers remains fairly low compared with the number of mentally disordered offenders in prison, it has increased significantly in the last decade. The figure for 2000 was 662, and for 2001 it was 624. Some two-thirds of transfers each year are of remand prisoners, and in their study of this group Mackay and Machin found that transfers were both humane and in some cases useful in testing the treatability of mental conditions.[69] They also found that some 19 per cent of those transferred were black.[70] These transfers mark an overdue recognition of the inappropriateness of prison for the mentally disordered, but in turn they create further pressure on beds in medium-secure units and high-security hospitals – as noted recently by the Joint Committee.[71]

In cases where custody is being contemplated, s. 157 of the Criminal Justice Act 2003 imposes a duty to obtain and consider a medical report before passing any custodial sentence on a person who appears to be mentally disordered (although s. 157(2) qualifies that duty), and also requires the court to consider any other information bearing on the offender's mental condition and the likely effect of a custodial sentence on that condition and on any possible treatment for it.[72] This is a necessary provision, but a similar section has been in force for over a decade and its effects are difficult to discern. However, there are provisions to ensure that the possibility of making a hospital order or a guardianship order is preserved in spite of certain mandatory provisions: in the case of an offence for which sentence would fall to be imposed under s. 51A of the Firearms Act 1968 (mandatory minimum of five years for possessing firearm), or under ss. 110 or 111 of the Powers of Criminal Courts (Sentencing) Act 2000 (minimum sentences for third class A drug dealing or third domestic burglary), or under ss. 225–228 of the Criminal Justice Act 2003 (new dangerousness provisions), 'nothing in these provisions shall prevent a court from making an order ... for the admission of the offender to a hospital'.[73] These are important provisions, particularly in respect of the dangerousness provisions, the severity of which was discussed in Chapter 6.8 above. However, given the number of mentally disordered offenders who are sent to prison, it remains possible that this statutory provision will have little effect in practice, and that the severity of the dangerousness provisions will bite here too.

---

68 Joint Committee on the draft Mental Health Bill (2005), para. 256.
69 Mackay and Machin (2000).   70 Cf. the similar finding of Street, n. 58 above.
71 Joint Committee on the draft Mental Health Bill (2005), para. 256.
72 The section re-enacts s. 4 of the Criminal Justice Act 1991; see also s. 166(5) of the 2003 Act, preserving the courts' power to mitigate sentence in the case of mentally disordered offenders.
73 Criminal Justice Act 2003, Schedule 32, para. 38.

12.3.4 Conclusions

The proper approach to the sentencing of mentally disordered offenders remains a matter of controversy. There has tended to be a major division of policy between mentally disordered and other offenders: for the former, a treatment approach is essential, but increasingly an approach based on risk and public protection is providing the framework for the sentence, even if treatment is provided within it. A better approach is to recognize that both the treatment approach and the risk-based approach lend the awesome authority of the criminal justice system to wide therapeutic discretion, and that respect for the rights of the mentally disordered means that they should not be compulsorily detained under 'criminal' powers beyond the point at which a non-disordered offender would be released from prison.[74] It is therefore important that proportionality of sentence should be reasserted as a constraint on sentencing the mentally disordered, no less than in respect of sentencing generally.

The controversy over the proper response to mentally disordered offenders is evident from various sets of proposals issued in recent years. The Richardson report, reviewing the Mental Health Act 1983, is chiefly concerned with the civil powers over mentally disordered people, and it is firmly based on the principle of non-discrimination or equal treatment (that 'wherever possible the principles governing mental health care should be the same as those which govern physical health') and on a number of other principles such as patient autonomy, the principle of the least restrictive alternative, and the principle of reciprocity (that 'where society imposes an obligation of compliance on a patient, there should be a corresponding public duty to provide adequate services').[75] The Richardson committee was unable to devote sufficient time to a thorough examination of the proper response to mentally disordered offenders, but noted the complexity of the issues and called for a thorough and independent inquiry. The committee did make a number of recommendations, however, in line with the principles adopted for the civil powers. Treatment ought to be given priority over punishment, as the 1983 Act requires; a 'health order' (replacing the hospital order) should be available to criminal courts; there should be wider use of interim orders, and also of community orders for treatment; a restriction order should remain, but the powers to grant leave and to authorize transfer between hospitals should not lie solely with the Home Office but should also be given to tribunals; prisoners should have a right to a mental health assessment, and there should be no compulsory treatment in prisons – only in hospitals.[76]

The government, however, has been moving in a different direction. Shortly after the publication of the Richardson report, it issued a Consultation Document, *Managing Dangerous People with Severe Personality Disorder* (1999), suggesting that there are around 2,000 people in England and Wales who fall into this category

---

74 See Gostin (1977), p. 96.   75 Richardson (1999), pp. 21–3.
76 Richardson (1999), chs. 15 and 16.

and for whom special measures should be taken, in order to ensure public safety. The proposals were widely opposed by psychiatrists and lawyers, but they have nevertheless been put before Parliament on two or three occasions. On each occasion they have met a cool response and outright opposition, and have not been pressed. The essence is that courts should be able to make a Dangerous People with Severe Personality Disorder (DSPD) order against any person who is assessed 'as suffering from a severe personality disorder' and 'as presenting a danger to the public as a result of the disorder', even though that person has not committed an offence and even though the condition is not thought to be treatable. Detention would be in a separate system of facilities, and not either the regular prisons or hospitals. In their heavy reliance on prediction and indeterminate detention, these proposals are extraordinary in a government that has proclaimed that it is 'bringing human rights home'. While the document assures readers that the proposals are compatible with the European Convention, very few human rights lawyers would take that view. Moreover, a sound evidential basis for the risk assessment and any treatment of DPSD people is lacking: the government says that it must press ahead none the less, but the tendency to over-predict dangerousness is so well known[77] that there is inadequate empirical foundation for any curtailment of individuals' rights, even if on a policy level that were thought justifiable.

In autumn 2004 the government published a draft Mental Health Bill, after consultations with various groups in the years since the Richardson report. It is principally concerned with civil orders, but the bill contains several clauses relating to mentally disordered offenders. Clauses 87–92 deal with remand to hospital for a mental health report; clauses 93–96 with remands for medical treatment; clauses 114–124 with the mental health order (replacing the hospital order), with provisions for care plans; clauses 125–129 with restriction orders; and clauses 130–132 with hospital directions for prison sentences. In all these clauses there are changes to the existing framework, most notably in the shift towards risk as the criterion for the framework in which treatment is to be provided. Thus, before making a mental health (hospital) order, the court is required to take account of risk factors; but on the other hand there is no requirement that the court be satisfied that detention is necessary in order to provide the needed treatment.[78] The Joint Committee has made several criticisms of the bill as a whole and of the proposals for mentally disordered offenders in particular, and it remains to be seen whether and to what extent the government alters the bill. The thrust of the bill is strongly in the direction of risk and public protection, with less emphasis on diversion and treatment, but at least in its present form the bill contains no provisions for the detention of so-called 'dangerous people with severe personality disorder'.

77 See ch. 6.8 above.   78 Joint Committee on the draft Mental Health Bill (2005), para. 271.

CHAPTER 13

Conclusions

The purpose of this chapter is to draw together various themes emerging from the topics examined in the 12 substantive chapters, and to offer some concluding reflections. The chapter begins by returning to a fundamental issue, that of the role sentencing should be expected to fulfil in criminal justice. It then looks at the more positive aspects of the new sentencing framework introduced by the Criminal Justice Act 2003, and at their prospects in practice. This links to the third issue – the new sentencing guideline mechanism and its ability to ensure that the new sentencing framework is translated faithfully into practice. The fourth part of the chapter looks at less constructive aspects of the new sentencing framework, notably its reliance on the rhetoric of protection, its use of the concept of risk and the proliferation of preventive orders in sentencing. The fifth part reassesses the place of proportionality in the new system and the impact of the framework on issues of social justice. The chapter concludes with some reflections on political courage and the need for leadership on criminal justice policy in general and sentencing policy in particular.

13.1 The responsibility of sentencing

There is no doubt that the task of sentencing imposes a great burden on magistrates and judges, and that many of them say that it is the hardest and most disturbing of judicial tasks. In view of the momentous consequences it may have for offenders, in terms of deprivations or restrictions on liberty, that is as it should be. In the present context, however, a more significant question is what sentencers and sentencing should be held responsible *for*. Discussions of criminal justice sometimes appear to assume that sentencers are responsible for crime rates in society, or for the subsequent conduct of offenders, and these are the issues that need to be confronted.

As argued in Chapter 1.4 and in various other places, the very concept of 'the crime rate' is a difficult one. Recorded crime has been measured for years, but it is well known that it does not measure the total number of crimes committed. The British Crime Survey comes closer to this (although it leaves out crimes against and by companies, crimes without direct victims, and some other offences), and it is the most complete measurement available. It has shown a downward trend in overall crime rates in recent years, but there are few policy-makers, politicians or members of the public who appear to accept this, let alone to use it as a basis for policy. A decline in the crime rate may be influenced by other factors, such as a decline in the number of young people in society (stemming from a decline in the birth rate at some time past) and that is true of the last few years. Other social factors, such as the ready availability of a new and stealable expensive consumer product (notably mobile phones in recent years) may have an influence on the crime rate, as may crime prevention measures that reduce the susceptibility to theft of major items (such as manufacturers' improvements in the security systems of cars). The willingness of victims to report certain crimes (serious sexual offences, 'domestic' violence) may increase, as a result of initiatives within criminal justice.

This list of possible influences on the crime rate could be expanded, but the fundamental point remains the same and was made in Chapter 1.4 above. Such a low proportion of crimes are reported to the police and recorded by the police, and such a low proportion of those are detected (fewer than a quarter), that the criminal justice system makes a formal response to only around 3 per cent of offences committed in any one year. Of those about a third (or 1 per cent) receive a caution, reprimand or warning. This means that the courts sentence only around 2 per cent of offenders. The idea that sentencing policy in respect of this 2 per cent – which is admittedly higher in some categories such as serious violence (10 per cent) but not so as to weaken the argument here – can have a significant effect on the overall crime rate is difficult to sustain. There is a whole range of broader social trends and changes that have an impact on offending rates: one of them, mentioned at various stages in this book and highlighted in the report *Rethinking Crime and Punishment*,[1] is the link between drug-taking and crime. Thus the simple notion that increasing sentences will have a kind of hydraulic effect in reducing criminality is unsustainable. As we saw in Chapter 3.3 above, the evidence on deterrence and incapacitation does not bear this out.[2] Some judges seem either to be unaware of this or to doubt it, since general deterrent rhetoric remains common when justifying sentences.[3] Some politicians, especially ministers, must be well aware of the evidence, since there is ample support for it in Home Office-conducted or -commissioned research. But by setting over-ambitious targets for sentencing and by subscribing to a notion of 'public confidence' that too readily dissolves into beliefs about sentence severity (and may be influenced by media representations anyway), the government goes against the evidence that it possesses.[4]

On this first issue, then, the conclusion is that too much should not be expected of sentencing. It should aim to be fair and proportionate, and any exceptions to this aim call for strong and evidence-based justification. Sentencing is a form of

1 Rethinking Crime and Punishment (2004), ch. 7. See also Coulsfield (2004), ch. 6.
2 See further the brief but penetrating analysis by Bottoms (2004), pp. 60–72.
3 See ch. 4.4 above; Tonry (2004), pp. 110–12; and *Attuh-Benson* [2005] Crim LR 243.
4 For the fragile relationships between public opinion and public assessments of the sentencing system, see Hough and Roberts (1998) and Hough et al. (2003).

public censure, and the sentences imposed should convey the relative degree of censure for the particular offence(s). Sentencing is but a small part of criminal justice policy, and it is wrong to treat it as a primary form of crime prevention: there are several other kinds of initiative that have a greater crime-preventive potential than modifications of sentencing levels, although it is of course necessary to have in existence a sentencing system that operates so as to exert an overall or underlying preventive effect.

13.2 The new penal ladder

The concept of a penal ladder has two applications in sentencing. Its fundamental meaning is to describe the hierarchy of sentencing options, from the least restrictive (or that with the lowest punitive weight) to the most restrictive or onerous sanction. It is also used, however, to describe how some sentencers apply those options in the 'typical' case of an offender who commits a further offence following an earlier conviction and sentence, the tendency being to select a sentence on a higher 'rung' of the penal ladder on the premise that the previous sentence (on a lower rung) did not 'work'. More will be said about the approach to sentencing persistent offenders in parts 13.4 and 13.5 below, and the primary concern here is with the hierarchy of sentences and how they are intended to operate in the new sentencing framework.

In Chapters 9 and 10 above there was much discussion of the custody threshold, and how the various new forms of sentence might fit together. But possibly a more important starting point is the fine. In Chapter 7.5 and in Chapter 10.5 above we noted that the use of the fine has declined spectacularly in the last thirty years, and indeed that the changes in sentencing in the last decade have been affected by courts' apparent lack of confidence in the use of the fine. The aim of increasing the use of community sentences has been achieved, but this has not been successful in the sense that it has not diminished the use of custody – it appears that the increase in community sentences has been at the expense of fines and discharges, with the result that there has been a general raising of the severity of penal interventions. If this movement is to be reversed – and the government accepts that it should be reversed – then the fine must be regenerated and revitalized as a penal measure. This book has argued strongly in favour of the day fine system in successive editions, and in the last few years there has been greater interest in revisiting a system of this kind. It has grave dangers, of course, because when a version of day fines was tried in the early 1990s some sections of the media misrepresented it. The result of the ensuing furore was its abolition, and the result of its abolition was that poorer people were again fined more. That leads to problems of collection and problems of default. Considerable effort has been put into improving the collection of fines in recent years, and there is acceptance that part of the problem is the imposition of unduly onerous fines in the first place. So, bearing in mind these pitfalls, it is now imperative that the government both introduces a form of day fine system without delay and ensures that it is properly explained to everyone – to the extent that when certain sections of the press attack it for 'inconsistency' (i.e. for fining rich people more than poor people, which is the whole purpose of the system), ministers are prepared to defend it in public, to explain the principle of equal impact, and to weather any negative publicity.

If the fine becomes accepted as a viable option in some cases of moderate seriousness, this may begin the process of 'unsilting' the resources of the National Probation Service by relieving it of the need to provide community sentences for offenders who are not really serious enough to warrant them. The next step is to ensure that community sentences are given to offenders of moderate seriousness, and that the community sentence is not regarded as a single 'rung' on the penal ladder. The danger, in other words, is that courts may take the view that if a community sentence has been tried and failed, another community sentence should not be imposed for a further offence of moderate seriousness. We saw in Chapter 10.6 that attempts have been made in the definitive guidelines to ensure that this view is not taken, and that the range of requirements that may be made as part of a community sentence is used constructively and not just once for each offender.[5] There are other dangers, too, such as the imposition of too many requirements in an individual case to the extent that an offender – particularly one with a disorganized lifestyle or other personal problems – is 'set up to fail'. The role of NOMS and the National Probation Service, in preparing sensitive pre-sentence reports and in ensuring that there is a sufficient range of relevant programmes available in each area, is no less crucial than that of the courts in ensuring that the guidelines are properly followed, that the statutory threshold for a community sentence is treated as meaningful (which appears not to have been the case in recent years), and that breaches are dealt with in context and proportionately. NOMS and the National Probation Service must also continue to strive to improve the effectiveness of the programmes they offer, without succumbing to the temptation to make excessive claims about their results.

The next statutory threshold is also critical to the application of the new sentencing framework. Again, there is little evidence that in recent years courts have taken a proper view (or indeed any view) of the requirement to impose custody only if the offence is too serious for a fine or a community sentence. It would not be appropriate here simply to repeat the warnings collected in Chapter 10.7.4 above under the provocative heading, '101 malfunctions'. But we must recall that the new framework – with custody plus, suspended sentences and intermittent custody all clustered around the custody threshold – will require careful handling in both the magistrates' courts and the Crown Court. The guidelines set out the principles, but at the point of application there will be a considerable degree of judgment to be exercised on whether the custody threshold has been passed and whether there are sufficient reasons to take the case back down to a community sentence or a suspended sentence or (in a small number of cases) to intermittent custody. The success of these sentences will depend considerably on how NOMS and the National

5 See SGC, *New Sentences: Criminal Justice Act 2003* (2004), discussed in ch. 10.6 above.

Probation Service carry out their 'parts of the bargain', as it were, in terms of providing relevant and persuasive pre-sentence reports, in sustaining a sufficient range of programmes in each area, and in ensuring that any requirements imposed are duly supervised. But it will be court decisions that make or break the bold initiatives taken by the government in creating this part of the new framework.

13.3 Delivering change: the guideline system

Previous editions of this book have argued strongly in favour of the creation of a system of sentencing guidelines, tailored to English requirements, for several reasons – particularly for improving consistency in the delivery of sentencing policy and broadening the range of professionals having an input into sentencing guidance. As we saw in Chapters 1 and 2, the Sentencing Advisory Panel began work in 1999 and it proposed guidelines to the Court of Appeal for five years until 2004. The Panel's method of working involves wide consultation among interested organizations, considers the opinions of members of the public (there are three lay persons on the Panel too) and takes several months to come to fruition. The process then changed, as a result of the Criminal Justice Act 2003, with the introduction of the Sentencing Guidelines Council. The Council now issues its definitive guidelines. It is a cumbersome system, and all the arguments about consulting Parliament, and not leaving a purely judicial body to issue the guidelines, could equally have been met by adapting the Sentencing Advisory Panel rather than creating an extra tier. However, that is the mechanism we now have: will it work?

Michael Tonry has argued that the new system is flawed because it ignores the lessons of other guideline systems that have been operating for up to 25 years.[6] In particular, a body with a judicial majority and a judicial chair is said to be too conservative to make the kind of changes that are needed if the idea of guidelines is to be taken seriously – for example, reassessing relativities between offences, reviewing the evidence on the effectiveness of prisons and non-custodial options and then acting on the results. One reply is that the English system required a tailor-made solution and was and is not ready for the kind of radical change advocated by Tonry. The system has long had guidelines, in the form of Court of Appeal judgments, and the new system can be seen as a further evolutionary step rather than a revolution. Judges and magistrates will resist the changes if they do not consider that they have some 'ownership' of them. The kinds of deviant behaviour seen among some US judges, sometimes (as in the case of the federal system) resulting in greater compulsion and rigidity in the guidelines, could become much more common in this country if there was substantial alienation from the approaches adopted in the guidelines. It remains an open question whether the government was right in the model it chose. The early days of the Sentencing Guidelines Council have been directed by a sympathetic and knowledgeable Lord Chief Justice, although not

6 Among several writings, see most recently Tonry (2004), ch. 5.

without some misgivings among other senior judges. When Lord Woolf retires, the orientation of the whole exercise could change.

Are the published guidelines well conceived and well drafted? Those questions are for others to answer. A particular style was adopted by the Panel, and the Council appears to wish to simplify the format so that the essence of the guidelines can be conveyed more simply and succinctly. If there is to be progress towards the goal of comprehensive guidelines – albeit that that will take many years, in view of the consultation process and the part-time nature of the two bodies – then a simpler format for guidelines is surely a proper objective. Are the guidelines self-consistent? Efforts have been made to ensure that there is no incompatibility of approach or outcome among the 15 sets of guidelines and the other drafts that are in the public domain, but the stage has now been reached at which some hard thinking needs to be done about relativities between offences and their sentence ranges. In many US guideline jurisdictions this was one of the first tasks – to rank the major offences. The English system has proceeded piecemeal up to this stage, although with occasional discussions of wider relativities, but an effort to devise a coherent framework (even if it may need to be adapted) must now be made.

What impact do the guidelines have on sentencing practice? Anecdotal evidence has been mentioned, but the fact is that there is no research evidence on this point. If relevant evidence were available, it would tell us whether sentences for rape, handling stolen goods, domestic burglary or causing death by dangerous driving had been affected by the sentence levels proposed by the Panel and laid down by the Court of Appeal. But a far more difficult test is the one set by the guideline on the new sentences introduced by the Criminal Justice Act 2003.[7] Thus the government has abandoned the policy of proliferating the number of community sentences, and the new Act incorporates a single community sentence with a range of possible requirements, but this renders critical the various thresholds provided by the law. As is apparent from part 13.2 of this chapter, how sentencers approach community sentences and the suspended sentence (and, where available, intermittent custody) will be absolutely crucial in determining the impact of the new Act. The guideline captures the spirit of the legislation and tries to convey it, in practical detail, to sentencers. The horses have been taken to the water: will they drink?

13.4 Risk, public protection and trifurcation

English sentencing has sometimes been depicted as a bifurcated system, in which a policy of lowering the penal response towards non-serious offenders has been combined with a much more severe policy in respect of those committing serious crimes. The 'lower track' of sentencing is one that tries to avoid custody, or at least to keep it short in those cases where it is thought 'unavoidable'. The 'upper track' of sentencing is characterized by long sentencers for armed robbers, drug

---

7 SGC, *New Sentences: Criminal Justice Act 2003* (2004).

smugglers and serious sexual and violent offenders. In this context, the operative conception of proportionality becomes an elongated or stretched scale that accentuates the extremes of the spectrum of penalties, rather than spacing offences out 'evenly'. Changes of emphasis in recent years, and particularly some provisions in the Criminal Justice Act 2003, suggest that there is a third 'track' emerging in English sentencing, and that a word such as 'trifurcation' might better convey contemporary sentencing policies.

This third track is one that places the emphasis on the risk that an offender is believed to present rather than upon the offence(s) already committed. Public protection is seen as an important rationale for sentencing, and so the assessment of risk becomes a key factor. This element is evident in the burgeoning range of preventive orders discussed in Chapter 11.2 above: these orders are not regarded as punitive, but are rather seen as protective and justified by the need to prevent a person from doing harmful acts in the future. Whatever the justification for such measures in principle – and several counter-arguments were put in Chapter 6.6 and Chapter 11.2 above – there are acute difficulties raised by practice. One is that the conditions imposed, particularly in anti-social behaviour orders, may be numerous and very restrictive, often aimed at a young offender or someone with a disorganized lifestyle. The order is entirely negative, although there is now some provision for the supervision of juveniles. The second practical difficulty is that sentencing for breach of such orders has tended to be severe, particularly in respect of breach of an ASBO, which constitutes a separate offence with a maximum penalty of five years' imprisonment.

The preventive orders, and sentencing for their breach, constitute one new strand of a risk-based penal strategy. Persons (usually, but not always, offenders) are identified as posing a risk to others, on the basis of behaviour that may or may not amount to a criminal offence and may only have been proved in civil proceedings.[8] Two more strands of this strategy are the new approach to persistent offenders and the new provisions on 'dangerous offenders'. The approach to persistent offenders, discussed in Chapter 6.3 above, urges courts to treat each recent and relevant previous conviction as an aggravating factor when sentencing for the current offence. This has the potential to increase sentences for persistent offenders well beyond the level appropriate to the seriousness of the current or indeed the previous offences, and thus to lead to swingeing sentences for persistent minor offenders – notably property offenders such as shop thieves, handbag thieves and pickpockets. It is questionable whether these offences are so serious in the scale of things as to warrant sentences of three, four or five years' imprisonment, which were handed down in some such cases even before the new law came into force. As for the new provisions on 'dangerous offenders', these are likely to lead to a sharp rise in the number of offenders sentenced to life imprisonment or to imprisonment for public protection.

---

8 The admissibility of evidence would be governed by the civil law, but the standard of proof is equivalent to that in criminal proceedings, i.e. beyond reasonable doubt.

Provisions on dangerous offenders form a part of many sentencing systems across the world, despite the well-documented problems of identifying the dangerous and the poor prediction rates revealed by almost all studies.[9] What is particularly objectionable about those in the 2003 Act is that they have an enormously wide range of application and could lead to long indeterminate sentences for two offences of only moderate seriousness committed some years apart. Moreover, the so-called 'test' of dangerousness in s. 229 of the new Act is broad, unspecific and skewed by a presumption of dangerousness that may arise from one previous conviction for a qualifying offence.

Even if some justifications for longer, incapacitative sentences for a group of 'dangerous' offenders can be found,[10] this new law is condemned by its 'overbreadth'. The preventive orders such as ASBOs and the new law on previous convictions are vitiated by the shared presumption that a person who breaches an order or commits another offence (as the case may be) ought to receive a more severe sanction for going against the authority of the state in that way. There is ample evidence that people breach preventive orders or commit further offences for a variety of reasons, some of which reflect the situation they are in, defects in their personality or a response to unusual pressures. This is not to say that all such persons should be excused or their wrongdoings mitigated, but rather that the approach of these two laws presumes that courts should not look first into the reasons for what has happened. When the Council of Europe recommended that previous convictions should not mechnically be treated as making an offence more serious,[11] they were pointing to this multiplicity of reasons. These English laws are wrong to presume otherwise, and to take the notion of defiance of authority as a strong reason for severity.

13.5 Proportionality and social justice

A further objection to these three elements of the risk-based penal strategy is that they, like most other severe elements in the criminal justice system, are likely to impinge disproportionately on offenders from disadvantaged backgrounds. In all the debate about sentencing and criminal justice policy in the last few years, the impacts on members of ethnic minorities, on the unemployed and on the mentally disordered have received little examination, and although the treatment of women offenders has received discussion, there has been little by way of concrete changes of approach. Some general points were made on race, poverty and gender in Chapter 7 above and on mental disorder in Chapter 9.6 and 12.3 above, but one salient feature is the extent to which these and other disadvantaged categories overlap. The criminal justice system, and particularly the prison system, contains a disproportionate number of people with not just one but more than one of these characteristics.

---

9 See generally ch. 6.8 above.   10 See further von Hirsch and Ashworth (2005), ch. 5.
11 See ch. 6.3 above.

Thus black people may be over-represented among the mentally disordered; a high proportion of mentally disordered offenders are unemployed and without settled accommodation; many women offenders are also very poor and/or have a drug problem; and so forth. These facts, as well known to the government as to criminologists, have been marginalized in policy-making and debate, probably because they do not have the vote-winning potential of the new dangerousness sentences or the approach to persistent offenders.

If the Sentencing Guidelines Council follows its declared line on the centrality of the proportionality principle in sentencing,[12] then we should see new guidelines that may – at least for offenders not caught by the previous convictions premium or the dangerousness provisions – see the emergence of some more definite sentence levels that focus on the offence itself and restrict the possibility of discrimination. Whether English guidelines will be so fine-grained as to exert such control over sentencers must be doubted, however. Moreover, there is a whole range of questions about the application of the proportionality principle in English sentencing. The question of the relativities between offences ('ordinal proportionality') has been raised in part 13.3 above, and the current structure calls for a root-and-branch reconsideration. But in Chapter 5 above we identified another issue on proportionality. For some offences the presence or absence of an aggravating factor appears to have a greater effect on sentence than the basic offence itself. Thus where an offence is committed against an older person or indeed any vulnerable victim, the extent to which that aggravates the sentence may be 100 per cent or more of the basic offence. The same may prove to be true of previous convictions, as we saw in Chapter 6.3. On the other hand, where an offender pleads guilty and satisfies the sentencer that he or she is genuinely remorseful, the reduction in sentence may reach 40 per cent or more. Enhancements or reductions of sentence of this magnitude are questionable in the light of the proportionality principle, and it is important that they be re-examined.

13.6 Political courage and criminal justice

It was argued in parts 13.2 and 13.3 of this chapter that recent legislation has introduced some potentially worthwhile reforms into English sentencing, although some manifestly unsatisfactory features of the new system have been pointed out in parts 13.4 and 13.5. The paradox is that it is those features here described as unsatisfactory that the government has promoted most vociferously, and those features here described as in principle worthwhile that have received far less coverage in public speeches. The government remains nervous about criminal justice policy and unwilling to give the leadership necessary to explain to the public exactly what it is doing. It seems that every reform package must contain elements of greater severity, and they then become the focus of public discussion.

---

12 SGC, *Overarching Principles: Seriousness* (2004).

This is wrong for two main reasons. It is wrong because the Home Office knows that imprisonment is no more effective that other forms of sanction in preventing reoffending, and indeed that the hydraulic hypothesis (an increase in sentence lengths brings a decrease in offending rates) is simply not sustainable. The Halliday report set out the research findings very clearly, even though it rather overestimated the ability of rehabilitative programmes to reduce reoffending, but the government has not taken heed. Despite its rhetoric about evidence-led policies, its approach to sentencing has been to promote what it conceives to be a populist agenda in defiance of the research findings. The government is also wrong in the second place because it knows from its own and other research that the public tends to be ill-informed about crime and sentencing in general, and that when members of the public are asked to focus on the facts of particular cases they are not necessarily more punitive than the courts – indeed, they are more interested in exploring rehabilitative and restorative responses. Nonetheless, the Home Office has taken few measures to deal with this phenomenon of ignorance and latent support, and seems more concerned about the popular press and its probable reactions. The upshot is that the constructive side of its agenda (outlined in part 13.2 above), which is an immense undertaking involving large numbers of criminal justice professionals and large numbers of offenders, is not explained to the public as the centrepiece of its sentencing policy.

The government should take advantage of falling crime rates to reorganize its criminal justice policy, to reassert a sharpened proportionality principle, and to push forward its more constructive agenda while allowing the policies outlined in part 13.4 above to wither on the vine. Unless it has the courage to take these steps, we are likely to witness a spiralling prison population with relatively non-serious offenders being swept into custody in their thousands, many of them falling within the disadvantaged groups mentioned in part 13.5 above. A change of priorities is much overdue.

References

Advisory Council on the Penal System (1970), *Non-custodial and Semi-custodial Penalties*, London: HMSO.

Advisory Council on the Penal System (1974), *The Young Adult Offender*, London: HMSO.

Advisory Council on the Penal System (1977), *The Length of Prison Sentences*, London: HMSO.

Advisory Council on the Penal System (1978), *Sentences of Imprisonment: A Review of Maximum Penalties*, London: HMSO.

Allen, F. (1981), *The Decline of the Rehabilitative Ideal*, New Haven: Yale University Press.

Andenaes, J. (1974), *Punishment and Deterrence*, Ann Arbor: University of Michigan Press.

Archbold (2005), *Archbold's Criminal Pleading, Evidence and Practice*, London: Sweet & Maxwell.

Ashworth, A. (1975) 'Sentencing in Provocation Cases', *Criminal Law Review*, 553.

Ashworth, A. (1983), *Sentencing and Penal Policy*, London: Weidenfeld & Nicolson.

Ashworth, A. (1993), 'Victim Impact Statements and Sentencing', *Criminal Law Review*, 498.

Ashworth, A. (2002a), 'Robbery Reassessed', *Criminal Law Review*, 851.

Ashworth, A. (2002b), 'Rights, Responsibilities and Restorative Justice', *British Journal of Criminology*, 42: 578.

Ashworth, A. (2003a), *Principles of Criminal Law*, 4th edn, Oxford: Oxford University Press.

Ashworth, A. (2003b), 'Sentencing and Sensitivity', in L. Zedner and A. Ashworth (eds.), *The Criminological Foundations of Penal Policy: Essays in Honour of Roger Hood*, Oxford: Oxford University Press.

Ashworth, A. (2004a), 'Social Control and Anti-social Behaviour: The Subversion of Human Rights?' *Law Quarterly Review*, 120: 263.

Ashworth, A. (2004b), 'Criminal Justice Reform: Principles, Human Rights and Public Protection', *Criminal Law Review*, 516.

Ashworth, A., and Gostin, L. (1984), 'Mentally Disordered Offenders and the Sentencing Process', *Criminal Law Review*, 195.

Ashworth, A. and Player, E. (1998), 'Sentencing, Equal Treatment and the Impact of Sanctions', in A. Ashworth and M. Wasik (eds.), *Fundamentals of Sentencing Theory*, Oxford: Oxford University Press.

Ashworth, A. and Redmayne, M. (2005), *The Criminal Process*, 3rd edn, Oxford: Oxford University Press.

Ashworth, A. and von Hirsch, A. (1997), 'Recognising Elephants: The Problem of the Custody Threshold', *Criminal Law Review*, 187.

Audit Commission (2004), *Youth Justice 2004*, London: Audit Commission.

Auld, Lord Justice (2001), *Review of the Criminal Courts of England and Wales*, London: The Stationery Office.

Bagaric, M. (2001), *Punishment and Sentencing: A Rational Approach*, London: Cavendish.

Baker, E. (1998), 'Taking European Criminal Law Seriously', *Criminal Law Review*, 361.

Baker, K. (2004), 'Is Asset Really an Asset?' in R. Burnett and C. Roberts (eds.), *What Works in Probation and Youth Justice*, Cullompton: Willan.

Baldock, J. C. (1980), 'Why the Prison Population has Grown Larger and Younger', *Howard Journal of Criminal Justice*, 19: 142.

Baldwin, J. and McConville, M. (1978), 'Sentencing Problems Raised by Guilty Pleas', *Modern Law Review*, 41: 544.

Ball, C. (2000), 'A Significant Move towards Restorative Justice, or a Recipe for Unintended Consequences?' *Criminal Law Review*, 211.

Ball, C. (2004), 'Youth Justice? Half a Century of Responses to Youth Offending', *Criminal Law Review*, 167.

Ball, C., McCormac, K. and Stone, N. (2001), *Young Offenders: Law, Policy and Practice*, 2nd edn, London: Sweet & Maxwell.

Banks, R. (2003), *Banks on Sentencing*, London: Butterworths.

Barker, K. and Sturges, J. (1986), *Decision Making in Magistrates' Courts*, London: Fourmat.

Bennett, T. and Wright, R. (1984), *Burglars on Burglary*, London: Gower.

Bentham, J. (1789), *The Principles of Morals and Legislation*, London.

Bingham, T. (1996), 'The Courts and the Constitution', *King's College Law Journal*, 7: 12.

Blackstone (2005), *Blackstone's Criminal Practice*, Oxford: Oxford University Press.

Blake, M. and Ashworth, A. (1998), 'Some Ethical Issues in Defending and Prosecuting Criminal Cases', *Criminal Law Review*, 16.

Blumstein, A. et al. (1986), *Criminal Careers and Career Criminals*, Washington: National Institute of Justice.

Bottomley, A. K. and Coleman, C. (1981), *Understanding Crime Rates*, London: Saxon House.

Bottoms, A. E. (1973), 'The Efficacy of the Fine: The Case for Agnosticism', *Criminal Law Review*, 543.

Bottoms, A. E. (1974), 'On the Decriminalisation of the Juvenile Court', in R. Hood (ed.), *Crime, Criminology and Public Policy*, London: Heinemann.

Bottoms, A. E. (1981), 'The Suspended Sentence in England', *British Journal of Criminology*, 21: 1.

Bottoms, A. E. (1987), 'Limiting Prison Use: Experience in England and Wales', *Howard Journal of Criminal Justice*, 26: 177.

Bottoms, A. E. (1990), 'Crime Prevention Facing the 1990s', *Policing and Society*, 1: 3.

Bottoms, A. E. (1995), 'The Philosophy and Politics of Punishment and Sentencing', in C. Clarkson and R. Morgan (eds.), *The Politics of Sentencing Reform*, Oxford: Oxford University Press.

Bottoms, A. E. (1998), 'Five Puzzles in von Hirsch's Theory of Punishment', in A. Ashworth and M. Wasik (eds.), *Fundamentals of Sentencing Theory*, Oxford: Oxford University Press.

Bottoms, A. E. (2004), 'Empirical Research Relevant to Sentencing Frameworks', in A. Bottoms, S. Rex and G. Robinson (eds.), *Alternatives to Prison: Options for an Insecure Society*, Cullompton: Willan.

Bottoms, A. E. and Brownsword, R. (1982), 'The Dangerousness Debate after the Floud Report', *British Journal of Criminology*, 22: 229.

Bottoms, A. E. and Dignan, J. (2004), 'Youth Justice in Great Britain', *Crime and Justice: A Review of Research*, 31: 21.

Bottoms, A. E., Rex, S. and Robinson, G. (2004), 'How Did We Get Here?' in A. Bottoms, S. Rex and G. Robinson (eds.), *Alternatives to Prison: Options for an Insecure Society*, Cullompton: Willan.

Bottoms, A. E., Shapland, J., et al. (2004), 'Towards Desistance: Theoretical Underpinnings for an Empirical Study', *Howard Journal of Criminal Justice*, 43: 368.

Bottoms, A. E. and Wilson, A. (2004), 'Attitudes to Crime in Two High-Crime Communities', in A. Bottoms, S. Rex and G. Robinson (eds.), *Alternatives to Prison: Options for an Insecure Society*, Cullompton: Willan.

Bowling, B. and Phillips, C. (2002), *Racism, Crime and Justice*, Harlow: Longman.

Braithwaite, J. and Pettit, P. (1990), *Not Just Deserts*, Oxford: Oxford University Press.

Bridge, Lord Justice (1978), *Report of the Working Party on Judicial Studies and Information*, London: HMSO.

Brody, S. R. (1976), *The Effectiveness of Sentencing*, Home Office Research Study 35, London: HMSO.

Brody, S. R. and Tarling, R. (1981), *Taking Offenders out of Circulation*, Home Office Research Study 64, London: HMSO.

Brooke, D., Taylor, P., Gunn, J. and Maden, A. (1996), 'Point Prevalence of Mental Disorder in Unconvicted Male Prisoners', *British Medical Journal*, 313: 1524.

Brown, M. (1998), 'Serious Violence and Dilemmas of Sentencing', *Criminal Law Review*, 710.

Brown, M. and Pratt, J. (eds.), (2000), *Dangerous Offenders: Punishment and Social Order*, London: Routledge.

Burnett, R. (1994), *Recidivism and Imprisonment*, Home Office Research Bulletin 36: 19.

Burnett, R. and Maruna, S. (2004), 'So Prison Works, Does it?' *Howard Journal of Criminal Justice*, 43: 390.

Burney, E. (2002), 'Talking Tough, Acting Coy: What happened to the Anti-social Behaviour Order?' *Howard Journal of Criminal Justice*, 41: 469.

Burney, E. and Pearson, G. (1995), 'Mentally Disordered Offenders: Finding a Focus for Diversion', *Howard Journal of Criminal Justice*, 34: 291.

Campbell, S. (2002), *A Review of Anti-Social Behaviour Orders*, Home Office Research Study 236, London: Home Office.

Canadian Sentencing Commission (1987), *Sentencing Reform: A Canadian Approach*, Ottawa: Ministry of Supply and Services.

Carter, P. (2003), *Managing Offenders, Reducing Crime*, London: Strategy Unit.

Cavadino, M. (1997), 'Pre-Sentence Reports: The Effects of Legislation and National Standards', *British Journal of Criminology*, 37: 529.

Cavadino, M. (1999), 'Diverting Mentally Disordered Offenders from Custody', in D. Webb and R. Harris (eds.), *Managing People Nobody Owns*, London: Routledge.

Cavadino, M. and Dignan, J. (2002), *The Penal System: An Introduction*, 3rd edn, London: Sage.

Charman, E., Gibson, B., Honess, T. and Morgan. R. (1996), *Fine Impositions and Enforcement Following the Criminal Justice Act 1993*, Home Office Research Findings 36, London: Home Office.

Christie, N. (1977), 'Conflicts as Property', *British Journal of Criminology*, 17: 1.

Clarke, A., Moran-Ellis, J. and Sleny, J. (2002), *Attitudes to Date Rape and Relationship Rape*, Guildford: Department of Sociology, University of Surrey.

Cook, D. (1989), *Rich Law, Poor Law*, Milton Keynes: Open University Press.

Cook, D. and Hudson, B. (eds.) (1993), *Racism and Criminology*, London: Sage.

Cooke, R. K. (1987), 'The Practical Problems of the Sentencer', in D. Pennington and S. Lloyd-Bostock (eds.), *The Psychology of Sentencing*, Oxford: Centre for Socio-Legal Studies.

Corbett, C. (1987), 'Magistrates' and Court Clerks' Sentencing Behaviour: An Experimental Study', in D. Pennington and S. Lloyd-Bostock (eds.), *The Psychology of Sentencing*, Oxford: Centre for Socio-Legal Studies.

Cornish, D. B. and Clarke, R. (1986), *The Reasoning Criminal: Rational Choice Perspectives on Offending*, New York: Springer-Verlag.

Coulsfield, Lord (2004), *Crime, Courts and Confidence: Report of an Independent Inquiry into Alternatives to Prison*, London: Esmee Fairbairn Foundation.

Council of Europe (1976), *Alternative Measures to Imprisonment*, Recommendation R (76) 10, Strasbourg: Council of Europe.

Council of Europe (1984), *Convention on Compensation for the Victims of Violent Crime*, Strasbourg: Council of Europe.

Council of Europe (1992), *European Rules on Community Sanctions and Measures*, Recommendation No. R (92) 16, Strasbourg: Council of Europe.

Council of Europe (1993), *Consistency in Sentencing*, Recommendation R (92) 17, Strasbourg: Council of Europe.

Cox, E. (1984 [1877]), *The Principles of Punishment*, London: Garland.

CPT (European Committee for the Prevention of Torture, Inhuman and Degrading Treatment) (1992), *Report on the European Committee on the Prevention of Torture and Inhuman or Degrading Treatment, Visit to the United Kingdom*, Strasbourg: Council of Europe.

CPT (2001), *European Committee for the Prevention of Torture and Inhuman or Degrading Punishment, Report of Inspection of English Prisons*, Strasbourg: Council of Europe.

Criminal Statistics, England and Wales 2002, Cm 6054, London: The Stationery Office.

Crow, I. and Simon, F. (1989), *Unemployment and Sentencing*, London: NACRO.

Crown Prosecution Service (2003), *Annual Report 2002–2003*, London: Crown Prosecution Service.

Cullen, E., and Newell, T. (1999), *Murderers and Life Imprisonment*, Winchester: Waterside Press.

Daly, K. (2002), 'Mind the Gap: Restorative Justice in Theory and Practice', in A. von Hirsch, J. Roberts et al. (eds.), *Restorative Justice and Criminal Justice*, Oxford: Hart.

Darbyshire, P. (1984), *The Justices' Clerk*, Chichester: Barry Rose.

Darbyshire, P. (1997a), 'An Essay on the Importance and Neglect of the Magistracy', *Criminal Law Review*, 627.

Darbyshire, P. (1997b), 'For the New Lord Chancellor – Some Causes for Concern about Magistrates', *Criminal Law Review*, 861.

Darbyshire, P. (2000), 'The Mischief of Plea Bargaining and Sentence Rewards', *Criminal Law Review*, 894.

Davies, M. and Tyrer, J. (2003), '"Filling in the Gaps" – A Study of Judicial Culture', *Criminal Law Review*, 243.

Diamond, S. S. (1981), 'Exploring Sources of Sentencing Disparity', in B. Sales (ed.), *The Trial Process*, New York: Plenum.

Dodd, T., Nicholas, S., Povey, D. and Walker, A. (2004), *Crime in England and Wales 2003/2004*, Statistical Bulletin 10/04, London: Home Office.

Doob, A. and Webster, C. (2003), 'Sentence Severity and Crime: Accepting the Null Hypothesis', *Crime and Justice: A Review of Research*, 30: 143.

Dove-Wilson (1932), *Report of the Departmental Committee on Persistent Offenders*, London: HMSO.

Dowds, L., and Hedderman, C. (1997), 'The Sentencing of Men and Women', in C. Hedderman and L. Gelsthorpe (eds.), *Understanding the Sentencing of Women*, Home Office Research Study 170, London: Home Office.

Downes, D. (1988), *Contrasts in Tolerance*, Oxford: Oxford University Press.

Duff, R. A. (1986), *Trials and Punishments*, Cambridge: Cambridge University Press.

Duff, R. A. (2001), *Punishment, Communication and Community*, New York: Oxford University Press.

Eastman, N. and Peay, J. (1998), 'Sentencing Psychopaths', *Criminal Law Review*, 93.

Eaton, M. (1986), *Justice for Women?* Milton Keynes: Open University Press.

Edwards, I. (2004), 'An Ambiguous Participant: The Victim and the Criminal Justice System', *British Journal of Criminology*, 44: 967.

Edwards, S. (1993), 'Perspectives on Race and Gender', in E. Stockdale and S. Casale (eds.), *Criminal Justice under Stress*, London: Blackstone.

Ekblom, P. (1998), 'Situational Crime Prevention: Effectiveness of Local Initiatives', in C. Nuttall (ed.), *Reducing Offending: An Assessment of Research Evidence on Ways of Dealing with Offending Behaviour*, Home Office Research Study 187, London: Home Office.

Elliott, R., Airs, J. and Webb, S. (1999), *Community Penalties for Fine Default and Persistent Petty Offending*, Home Office Research Findings 98, London: Home Office.

Emmerson, B. and Ashworth, A. (2005), *Human Rights and Criminal Justice*, 2nd edn, forthcoming, London: Sweet & Maxwell.

Erez, E. (1999), 'Who's Afraid of the Big, Bad Victim?' *Criminal Law Review*, 545.

Evans, R. (1993), 'Evaluating Young Adult Cautioning Schemes', *Criminal Law Review*, 490.

Fairhead, S. (1981), *Persistent Petty Offenders*, Home Office Research Study 66, London: HMSO.

Farrington, D. (1997), 'Human Development and Criminal Careers', in M. Maguire, R. Morgan and R. Reiner (eds.), *Oxford Handbook of Criminology*, 2nd edn, Oxford: Oxford University Press.

Farrington, D. (2002), 'Developmental Criminology and Risk-Focused Prevention', in M. Maguire, R. Morgan and R. Reiner (eds.), *Oxford Handbook of Criminology*, 3rd edn, Oxford: Oxford University Press.

Farrington, D. and Langan, P. (1992), 'Changes in Crime and Punishment in England and America in the 1980s', *Justice Quarterly*, 9: 5.

Farrington, D. and Morris, A. (1983), 'Sex. Sentencing and Reconvictions', *British Journal of Criminology*, 23: 229.

Feilzer, M. and Hood, R. (2003), *Minority Ethnic Young People in the Youth Justice System*, London: Youth Justice Board.

Fenwick, H. (1997), 'Procedural "Rights" of Victims of Crime', *Modern Law Review*, 60: 317.

Field, S. (1990), *Trends in Crime and their Interpretation*, Home Office Research Study 119, London: HMSO.

Fitzgerald, M. (1993), *Ethnic Minorities and the Criminal Justice System*, Royal Commission on Criminal Justice Research Study 21, London: HMSO.

Fitzmaurice, C. and Pease, K. (1986), *The Psychology of Judicial Sentencing*, Manchester: Manchester University Press.

Fletcher, G. P. (1978), *Rethinking Criminal Law*, Boston: Little, Brown.

Flood-Page, C. and Mackie, A. (1998), *Sentencing Practice: An Examination of Decisions in Magistrates' Courts and the Crown Court in the mid-1990s*, Home Office Research Study 180, London: Home Office.

Floud, J. and Young, W. (1981), *Dangerousness and Criminal Justice*, London: Heinemann.

Folkard, S. (1976), *IMPACT volume II*, Home Office Research Study 36, London: HMSO.

Fox, D. and Freiberg, A. (1999), *Sentencing: State and Federal Law in Victoria*, 2nd edn, Melbourne: Oxford University Press.

Galligan, D. (1987), 'Regulating Pre-trial Decisions', in I. Dennis (ed.), *Criminal Law and Criminal Justice*, London: Sweet & Maxwell.

Gardner, J. (1998), 'Crime: In Proportion and in Perspective', in A. Ashworth and M. Wasik (eds.), *Fundamentals of Sentencing Theory*, Oxford: Oxford University Press.

Gardner, J. and Shute, S. (2000), 'The Wrongness of Rape', in J. Horder (ed.), *Oxford Essays in Jurisprudence: Fourth Series*, Oxford: Oxford University Press.

Garland, D. (1990), *Punishment and Modern Society*, Oxford: Oxford University Press.

Garland, D. (2000), *The Culture of Control*, Oxford: Oxford University Press.

Gelsthorpe, L. and Loucks, N. (1997), 'Magistrates' Explanations of Sentencing Decisions', in C. Hedderman and L. Gelsthorpe (eds.), *Understanding the Sentencing of Women*, Home Office Research Study 170, London: Home Office.

Gelsthorpe, L. and Morris, A. (2002), 'Women's Imprisonment in England and Wales', *Criminal Justice*, 2: 277.

Gelsthorpe, L. and Raynor, P. (1995), 'Quality and Effectiveness in Probation Officers' Reports', *British Journal of Criminology*, 35: 188.

Gibson, B. (1990), *Unit Fines*, Winchester: Waterside Press.

Glidewell, Lord Justice (1992), 'The Judicial Studies Board', in M. Wasik and C. Munro (eds.), *Sentencing, Judicial Discretion and Judicial Training*, London: Sweet & Maxwell.

Goldsmith, P. (2004), 'The Charter of Rights: A Brake not an Accelerator', *European Human Rights Law Review*, 473.

Gostin, L. (1977), *A Human Condition*, vol. II, London: MIND.

Graham, D. (1998), 'What Works in Preventing Criminality', in C. Nuttall (ed.), *Reducing Offending: An Assessment of Research Evidence on Ways of Dealing with Offending Behaviour*, Home Office Research Study 187, London: Home Office.

Greene, J. (1998), 'The Unit Fine: Monetary Sanctions Apportioned to Income', in A. von Hirsch and A. Ashworth (eds.), *Principled Sentencing*, Oxford: Hart Publishing.

Greenwood, P. (1982), *Selective Incapacitation*, Santa Barbara: RAND.

Guldenmund, B., Harding, C. and Sherlock, J. (1995), 'Sentencing and EU Law', in C. Harding et al., *Criminal Justice in Europe: a Comparative Study*, Oxford: Oxford University Press.

Gullick, M. (2004), 'Sentencing and Early Release of Fixed-Term Prisoners', *Criminal Law Review*, 653.

Gunn, J., Maden, A. and Swinton, M. (1991), 'Treatment Needs of Prisoners with Psychiatric Diagnoses', *British Medical Journal*, 303: 338.

Hadden, T. (1968), 'Offences of Violence: The Law and the Facts', *Criminal Law Review*, 521.

Halliday (2001), *Making Punishments Work: Report of a Review of the Sentencing Framework for England and Wales*, London: Home Office.

Hammond, W. H. and Chayen, E. (1963), *Persistent Offenders*, London: HMSO.

Harding, R. (1990), 'Rational-Choice Gun Use in Armed Robbery', *Criminal Law Forum*, 1: 427.

Harris, J. and Grace, S. (1999), *A Question of Evidence? Investigating and Prosecuting Rape in the 1990s*, Home Office Research Study 196, London: Home Office.

Harris, R. and Webb, D. (1987), *Welfare, Power and Juvenile Justice*, London: Tavistock.

Hart, H. L. A. (1968), *Punishment and Responsibility*, Oxford: Oxford University Press.

Hawkins, K. (2003), *Law as Last Resort*, Oxford: Oxford University Press.

Hedderman, C. (1990), *The Effect of Defendants' Demeanour on Sentencing in Magistrates' Courts*, Home Office Research Bulletin 29, London: Home Office.

Hedderman, C. and Gelsthorpe, L. (1997), *Understanding the Sentencing of Women*, Home Office Research Study 170, London: Home Office.

Hedderman, C., and Hough, M. (1994), *Does the Criminal Justice System Treat Men and Women Differently?* Home Office Research Findings 10, London: Home Office.

Hedderman, C. and Moxon, D. (1992), *Magistrates' Courts or Crown Courts? Mode of Trial Decisions and Sentencing*, Home Office Research Study 125, London: HMSO.

Hedderman, C. and Sugg, D. (1997), 'The Influence of Cognitive Approaches', in J. Vennard (ed.), *Changing Offenders' Attitudes and Behaviour: What Works?* Home Office Research Study 171, London: Home Office.

Heidensohn, F. (2002), 'Gender and Crime', in M. Maguire, R. Morgan and R. Reiner (eds.), *Oxford Handbook of Criminology*, 3rd edn, Oxford: Oxford University Press.

Henham, R. (1991), *Sentencing Principles and Magistrates' Sentencing Behaviour*, Aldershot: Avebury.

Henham, R. (2001), *Sentence Discounts and the Criminal Process*, Aldershot: Ashgate.

HMCI Prisons (1997), *Annual Report of Her Majesty's Chief Inspector of Prisons for 1996–97*, London: HMSO.

HMCI Prisons (2003), *Her Majesty's Chief Inspector of Prisons, Report 2002–03*, London: The Stationery Office.

HMCI Prisons (2004), *Her Majesty's Chief Inspector of Prisons, Report 2003–04*, London: The Stationery Office.

Hogarth, J. (1971), *Sentencing as a Human Process*, Toronto: University of Toronto Press.

Home Office (1965), *The Adult Offender*, London: HMSO.

Home Office (1977), *Prisons and the Prisoners*, London: HMSO.

Home Office (1986), *Criminal Justice: Plans for Legislation*, London: HMSO.

Home Office (1990), *Crime, Justice and Protecting the Public*, London: HMSO.

Home Office (1996), *Protecting the Public: The Government's Strategy on Crime*, Cm 3190, London: HMSO.

Home Office (1997), *No More Excuses: a New Approach to Tackling Youth Crime in England and Wales*, Cm 3089, London: The Stationery Office.

Home Office (1999), *Digest 4: Information on the Criminal Justice System in England and Wales*, London: Home Office.

Home Office (2001), *Criminal Justice: The Way Ahead*, London: The Stationery Office.

Home Office (2002), *Justice for All*, Cm 5563, London: The Stationery Office.

Home Office (2003), *Respect and Responsibility: Taking a Stand against Anti-social Behaviour*, Cm 5778, London: The Stationery Office.

Home Office (2004), *Reducing Crime, Changing Lives*, London: Home Office.

Home Office Special Data Collection Exercise (1994), *Monitoring of the Criminal Justice Acts 1991 and 1993*, Statistical Bulletin 20/94, London: Home Office.

Hood, R. (1962), *Sentencing in Magistrates' Courts*, London: Tavistock.

Hood, R. (1972), *Sentencing the Motoring Offender*, London: Heinemann.

Hood, R. (1987), 'Some Reflections on the Role of Criminology in Public Policy', *Criminal Law Review*, 527.

Hood, R. (1992), *Race and Sentencing*, Oxford: Oxford University Press.

Hood, R. (2002), *The Death Penalty: A World Wide Perspective*, 3rd edn, Oxford: Oxford University Press.

Hood, R. and Shute, S. (1996), 'Protecting the Public: Automatic Life Sentences, Parole and High Risk Offenders', *Criminal Law Review*, 788.

Hood, R., Shute, S., Feilzer, M. and Wilcox, A. (2002), 'Sex Offenders Emerging from Long-Term Imprisonment', *British Journal of Criminology*, 42: 371.

Hood, R., Shute, S. and Seemungal, F. (2003), *Ethnic Minorities in the Criminal Courts: Perceptions of Fairness*, Oxford: Centre for Criminology.

Hood, R. and Sparks, R. (1970), *Key Issues in Criminology*, London: Hutchinson.

Hope, T. (1998), 'Community Crime Prevention', in C. Nuttall (ed.), *Reducing Offending: An Assessment of Research Evidence on Ways of Dealing with Offending Behaviour*, Home Office Research Study 187, London: Home Office.

Horder, J. (1989), 'Sex, Violence and Sentencing in Domestic Provocation Cases', *Criminal Law Review*, 546.

Hough, M., Jacobson, J. and Millie, A. (2003), *The Decision to Imprison: Sentencing and the Prison Population*, London: Prison Reform Trust.

Hough, M. and Roberts, J. (1998), *Attitudes to Punishment: Findings from the British Crime Survey*, Home Office Research Study 179, London: Home Office.

House of Commons Expenditure Committee (1978), *The Reduction of Pressure on the Prison System*, London: HMSO.

House of Commons (2004), *Draft Sentencing Guidelines 1 and 2*, Home Affairs Committee, Fifth Report of Session 2003–04, HC 1207, London: The Stationery Office.

House of Lords (2003), *Criminal Justice Bill*, Select Committee on the Constitution, London: The Stationery Office.

Hoyle, C. et al. (1998), *Evaluation of the One-Stop Shop and Victim Statement Pilots*, London: Home Office.

Hoyle, C. and Young, R. (2003), 'New, Improved, Police-Led Restorative Justice?' in A. von Hirsch, J. Roberts et al. (eds.), *Restorative Justice and Criminal Justice*, Oxford: Hart.

Hudson, B. (1995), 'Beyond Proportionate Punishment: Difficult Cases', *Crime, Law and Social Change*, 22: 59.

Hudson, B. (1998), 'Doing Justice to Difference', in A. Ashworth and M. Wasik (eds.), *Fundamentals of Sentencing Theory*, Oxford: Oxford University Press.

Hudson, B. (2003), *Justice in the Risk Society*, London: Sage.

Hutton, N. (1999), 'Sentencing in Scotland', in P. Duff and N. Hutton (eds.), *Criminal Justice in Scotland*, Aldershot: Ashgate.

Jareborg, N. (1988), *Essays in Criminal Law*, Uppsala: Iustus Forlag.

Jareborg, N. (1995), 'The Swedish Sentencing Reform', in C. Clarkson and R. Morgan (eds.), *The Politics of Sentencing Reform*, Oxford: Oxford University Press.

Jareborg, N. (1998), 'Why Bulk Discounts in Multiple Sentencing?' in A. Ashworth and M. Wasik (eds.), *Fundamentals of Sentencing Theory*, Oxford: Oxford University Press.

Jefferson, T. and Walker, M. A. (1992), 'Ethnic Minorities in the Criminal Justice System', *Criminal Law Review*, 83.

Jennings, W. I. (1959), *The Law and the Constitution*, London: University of London Press.

Johnstone, G. (2002), *Restorative Justice*, Cullompton: Willan.

Johnstone, G. (2003), *A Reader on Restorative Justice*, Cullompton: Willan.

Joint Inspection Report (2002), *Streets Ahead – A Joint Inspection of the Street Crime Initiative*, London: Home Office.

Joint Inspection Report (2004), *Joint Inspection Report into Persistent and Prolific Offenders*, London: Home Office.

Jones, P. (2002), 'The Halliday Report and Persistent Offenders', in S. Rex and M. Tonry (eds.), *Reform and Punishment: The Future of Sentencing*, Cullompton: Willan.

Jordan, P. (1998), 'Effective Policing Strategies for Reducing Crime', in C. Nuttall (ed.), *Reducing Offending: An Assessment of Research Evidence on Ways of Dealing with Offending Behaviour*, Home Office Research Study 187, London: Home Office.

Judicial Studies Board (1988), *Triennial Report 1984–87*, London: HMSO.

Judicial Studies Board (2004), *Annual Report of the Judicial Studies Board 2003–04*, London: The Stationery Office.

Kenny, A. (1978), *Freewill and Responsibility*, Oxford: Oxford University Press.

Kleinig, J. (1998), 'The Hardness of Hard Treatment', in A. Ashworth and M. Wasik (eds.), *Fundamentals of Sentencing Theory*, Oxford: Oxford University Press.

Kurki, L. (2001), 'Restorative and Community Justice in the United States', *Crime and Justice: A Review of Research*, 26: 355.

Lacey, N. (1988), *State Punishment*, London: Routledge & Kegan Paul.

Lacey, N. (1998), *Unspeakable Subjects*, Oxford: Hart.

Laing, J. (1999), 'Diversion of Mentally Disordered Offenders: Victim and Offender Perspectives', *Criminal Law Review*, 805.

Landau, D. and Nathan, G. (1983), 'Selecting Delinquents for Cautioning', *British Journal of Criminology*, 23: 28.

Lappi-Seppala, T. (2001), 'Sentencing and Punishment in Finland', in M. Tonry and R. Frase (eds.), *Sentencing and Sanctions in Western Countries*, New York: Oxford University Press.

Law Commission (1994), *Binding Over*, Law Com No. 222, London: HMSO.

Lawson, A. and Mukherjee, A. (2004), 'Slopping out in Scotland: The Limits of Degradation and Respect', *European Human Rights Law Review*, 645.

Lea, J. and Young, J. (1993), *What Is To Be Done about Law and Order?* Harmondsworth: Penguin.

Lemon, N. (1974), 'Training, Personality and Attitudes as Determinants of Magistrates' Sentencing', *British Journal of Criminology*, 14: 34.

Levi, M. (2002), 'The Organization of Serious Crimes', in M. Maguire, R. Morgan and R. Reiner (eds.), *Oxford Handbook of Criminology*, 3rd edn, Oxford: Oxford University Press.

Lewis, C. (2004), 'Trends in Crime, Victimisation and Punishment', in A. Bottoms, S. Rex and G. Robinson (eds.), *Alternatives to Prison: Options for an Insecure Society*, Cullompton: Willan.

Livingstone, S., Owen, T. and Macdonald, A. (2003), *Prison Law*, London: Sweet & Maxwell.

Lloyd, C., Mair, G. and Hough, M. (1994), *Explaining Reconviction Rates*, Home Office Research Study 135, London: HMSO.

Lord Chancellor's Department (2002), 'Home Secretary and Lord Chancellor: Clear Message on Sentencing', press notice 194/02, 14 June.

Lovegrove, A. (1997), *The Framework of Judicial Sentencing*, Cambridge: Cambridge University Press.

Lovegrove, A. (2004), *Sentencing the Multiple Offender: Judicial Practice and Legal Principle,* Canberra: Australian Institute of Criminology.

McBarnet, D. (1981), *Conviction: Law and State,* Oxford: Martin Robertson.

McConville, M. and Bridges, L. (1993), 'Convicting the Innocent', *New Law Journal,* 160.

MacCormick, N. and Garland, D. (1998), 'Sovereign States and Vengeful Victims', in A. Ashworth and M. Wasik (eds.), *Fundamentals of Sentencing Theory,* Oxford: Oxford University Press.

McGuire, J. (ed.) (1995), *What Works?* London: Sage.

McGuire, J. (ed.) (2002), *Offender Rehabilitation and Treatment,* Chichester: Wiley.

Mackay, R. and Kearns, G. (1999), 'More Fact(s) about the Insanity Defence', *Criminal Law Review,* 714.

Mackay, R. and Machin, D. (2000), 'The Operation of Section 48 of the Mental Health Act 1983', *British Journal of Criminology,* 40: 727.

Magistrates' Association (2004), *Magistrates' Courts' Sentencing Guidelines,* London: The Magistrates' Association.

Maguire, M. (1982), *Burglary in a Dwelling,* London: Heinemann.

Maguire, M. (2004), 'The Crime Reduction Programme in England and Wales: Reflections on the Vision and the Reality', *Criminal Justice,* 4: 213.

Mair, G. (2004), 'Diversionary and Non-supervisory Approaches to Dealing with Offenders', in A. Bottoms, S. Rex and G. Robinson (eds.), *Alternatives to Prison: Options for an Insecure Society,* Cullompton: Willan.

Mair, G. and May, C. (1997), *Offenders on Probation,* Home Office Research Study 167, London: Home Office.

Martinson, R. (1979), 'New Findings, New Views: A Note of Caution Regarding Sentencing Reform', *Hofstra Law Review,* 7: 242.

Martinson, R. et al. (1974), 'What Works? Questions and Answers about Prison Reform', *The Public Interest,* 22.

Maruna, S. (2001), *Making Good: How Ex-convicts Reform and Rebuild their Lives,* Washington: American Psychological Association.

Maruna, S. and Immarigeon, R. (eds.) (2004), *After Crime and Punishment: Pathways to Offender Reintegration,* Cullompton: Willan.

Mathiesen, T. (1990), *Prison on Trial,* London: Sage.

Merrington, S. (2004), 'Assessments Tools in Probation', in R. Burnett and C. Roberts (eds.), *What Works in Probation and Youth Justice,* Cullompton: Willan.

Miers, D. (1997), *State Compensation for Criminal Injuries,* London: Blackstone.

Mitchell, B. (1998), 'Public Perceptions of Homicide and Criminal Justice', *British Journal of Criminology,* 38: 453.

Monahan, J. (2004), 'The Future of Violence Risk Management', in M. Tonry (ed.), *The Future of Imprisonment,* New York: Oxford University Press.

Moore, M. (1988), 'The Moral Worth of Retribution', in F. Schoemann (ed.), *Responsibility, Character and the Emotions,* Cambridge: Cambridge University Press.

Moore, R. (2003), 'The Use of Financial Penalties and the Amounts Imposed: The Need for a New Approach', *Criminal Law Review*, 13.

Moore, R. (2004), 'The Methods for Enforcing Financial Penalties: The Need for a Multi-dimensional Approach', *Criminal Law Review*, 728.

Moore, R. et al. (2004), *ISSP: The Final Report*, London: Youth Justice Board.

Morgan, R. (2002), 'Imprisonment', in M. Maguire, R. Morgan and R. Reiner (eds.), *Oxford Handbook of Criminology*, 3rd edn, Oxford: Oxford University Press.

Morgan, R. (2003), 'Thinking about the Demand for Probation Services', *Probation Journal*, 50: 7.

Morris, A. (1988), 'Sex and Sentencing', *Criminal Law Review*, 163.

Morris, A. (2002), 'Critiquing the Critics', *British Journal of Criminology*, 42: 596.

Morris, A. and Gelsthorpe, L. (2000), 'Something Old, Something Borrowed, Something Blue but Something New?' *Criminal Law Review*, 18.

Morris, A. and Maxwell, G. (2000), 'Restorative Conferencing', in G. Bazemore and M. Schiff (eds.), *Restorative and Community Justice*, Cincinnati: Anderson Publishing.

Morris, A., Maxwell, G. M. and Robertson, J. P. (1993), 'Giving Victims a Voice: The New Zealand Experience', *Howard Journal of Criminal Justice*, 32: 304.

Morris, N. (1974), *The Future of Imprisonment*, Chicago: University of Chicago Press.

Morris, N. and Tonry, M. (1990), *Between Prison and Probation*, New York: Oxford University Press.

Mortimer, E. and May, C. (1997), *Electronic Monitoring in Practice*, Home Office Research Study 177, London: Home Office.

Mortimer, E., Pereira, E. and Walter, I. (1999), *Making the Tag Fit*, Home Office Research Findings 105, London: Home Office.

Moxon, D. (1988), *Sentencing Practice in the Crown Court*, Home Office Research Study 103, London: HMSO.

Moxon, D. (1998), 'The Role of Sentencing Policy', in C. Nuttall (ed.), *Reducing Offending: An Assessment of Research Evidence on Ways of Dealing with Offending Behaviour*, Home Office Research Study 187, London: Home Office.

Moxon, D., Sutton, M. and Hedderman, C. (1990), *Unit Fines: Experiments in Four Courts*, Research and Planning Unit Paper 59, London: Home Office.

Moxon, D. and Whittaker, C. (1996), *Imprisonment for Fine Default*, Home Office Research Findings 35, London: Home Office.

Munro, C. (1992), 'Judicial Independence and Judicial Functions', in M. Wasik and C. Munro (eds.), *Sentencing, Judicial Discretion and Judicial Training*, London: Sweet & Maxwell.

Myhill, A. and Allen, J. (2002), *Rape and Sexual Assault of Women*, Home Office Research Study 237, London: Home Office.

Nagin, D. (1998), 'Criminal Deterrence Research at the Outset of the 21st Century', *Crime and Justice: A Review of Research*, 23: 51.

Narayan, U. (1993), 'Appropriate Responses and Preventive Benefits: Justifying Censure and Hard Treatment in Legal Punishment', *Oxford Journal of Legal Studies*, 13: 166.

National Standards (2000), *National Standards for the Supervision of Offenders in the Community*, London: Home Office.

Nellis, D. (2004), 'Electronic Monitoring and the Community Supervision of Offenders', in A. Bottoms, S. Rex and G. Robinson (eds.), *Alternatives to Prison: Options for an Insecure Society*, Cullompton: Willan.

Newburn, T. (2002), 'Young People, Crime and Youth Justice', in M. Maguire, R. Morgan and R. Reiner (eds.), *Oxford Handbook of Criminology*, 3rd edn, Oxford: Oxford University Press.

Newburn, T., Crawford, A. et al. (2002), *The Introduction of Referral Orders into the Youth Justice System*, Home Office Research Study 242, London: Home Office.

Nicholson, C. G. B. (2001), *The Law and Practice of Sentencing in Scotland*, 3rd edn, Edinburgh: W. Green.

NOMS (2004), 'Reducing Reoffending: National Action Plan', at www.noms. homeoffice.gov.uk.

Nuttall, C. and Pease, K. (1994), 'Changes in the Use of Imprisonment in England and Wales', *Criminal Law Review*, 316.

Oxford Pilot Study (1984), *Sentencing in the Crown Court: Report of an Exploratory Study*, by A. Ashworth, E. Genders, G. Mansfield, J. Peay and E. Player, Oxford: University of Oxford Centre for Criminology.

Padfield, N. (2003), *Text and Materials on the Criminal Justice Process*, 3rd edn, London: Butterworths.

Parker, H., Sumner, M. and Jarvis, G. (1989), *Unmasking the Magistrates*, Milton Keynes: Open University Press.

Pease, K. (1988), *The Seriousness of Offences: Findings from the 1988 British Crime Survey*, London: Home Office.

Pease, K. (1994), 'Cross-National Imprisonment Rates: Limitations of Method and Possible Conclusions', *British Journal of Criminology*, 34: 116.

Pease, K. (1998), 'Changing the Context of Crime Prevention', in C. Nuttall (ed.), *Reducing Offending: An Assessment of Research Evidence on Ways of Dealing with Offending Behaviour*, Home Office Research Study 187, London: Home Office.

Pease, K. et al. (1974), 'The Development of a Scale of Offence Seriousness', *International Journal of Criminology and Penology*, 182.

Peay, J. (1997), 'Mentally Disordered Offenders', in M. Maguire, R. Morgan and R. Reiner (eds.), *Oxford Handbook of Criminology*, 2nd edn, Oxford: Oxford University Press.

Peay, J. (2002), 'Mentally Disordered Offenders, Mental Health and Crime', in M. Maguire, R. Morgan and R. Reiner (eds.), *Oxford Handbook of Criminology*, 3rd edn, Oxford: Oxford University Press.

Philpotts, G. and Lancucki, L. (1979), *Previous Convictions, Sentence and Reconviction*, Home Office Research Study 53, London: HMSO.

Prison Reform Trust (2000), *Justice for Women: The Need for Reform*, London: Prison Reform Trust.

Prison Service (2004), *Report of the Prison Service 2003–04*, London: The Stationery Office.

Pyle, D. (1995), *Cutting the Costs of Crime*, London: Institute of Economic Affairs.

Radzinowicz, L. and Hood, R. (1979), 'Judicial Discretion and Sentencing Standards', *University of Pennsylvania Law Review*, 1288.

Radzinowicz, L. and Hood, R. (1980), 'Incapacitating the Habitual Criminal: The English Experience', *Michigan Law Review*, 1305.

Radzinowicz, L. and Hood, R. (1986), *The Emergence of Penal Policy in Victorian and Edwardian England*, London: Stevens.

Raine, J., Dunstan, E. and Mackie, A. (2004), 'Financial Penalties: Who Pays, Who Doesn't, and Why Not?' *Howard Journal of Criminal Justice*, 43: 518.

Ramsay, P. (2004), 'What is Anti-social Behaviour?' *Criminal Law Review*, 926.

Ranyard, R., Hebenton, B. and Pease, K. (1994), 'An Analysis of a Guideline Case as Applied to Rape', *Howard Journal of Criminal Justice*, 33: 203.

Raynor, P. (2004), 'Rehabilitative and Reintegrative Approaches', in A. Bottoms, S. Rex and G. Robinson (eds.), *Alternatives to Prison: Options for an Insecure Society*, Cullompton: Willan.

Raz, J. (1979), *The Authority of Law*, Oxford: Oxford University Press.

Rethinking Crime and Punishment (2004), *Rethinking Crime and Punishment: The Report*, London: Esmee Fairbairn Foundation.

Rex, S. (1998), 'Applying Desert Principles to Community Sentences', *Criminal Law Review*, 381.

Rex, S. (2001), 'Beyond Cognitive-Behaviouralism? Reflections on the effectiveness Literature', in A. E. Bottoms, L. Gelsthorpe and S. Rex (eds.), *Community Penalties: Change and Challenges*, Cullompton: Willan.

Rex, S., Lieb, R., Bottoms, A. and Wilson, L. (2003), *Accrediting Offender Programmes*, Home Office Research Study 273, London: Home Office.

Richardson, G. (1999), *Review of the Mental Health Act 1983: Report of the Expert Committee*, London: Department of Health.

Riley, D. (1985), 'Drinking Drivers: The Limits to Deterrence', *Howard Journal of Criminal Justice*, 24: 241.

Riley, D. (1991), *Drink Driving: The Effects of Enforcement*, Home Office Research Study 121, London: HMSO.

Riley, D. and Vennard, J. (1988), *Triable-Either-Way Cases: Crown Court or Magistrates' Court*, Home Office Research Study 98, London: HMSO.

Roberts, C. (2004), 'Offending Behaviour Programmes: Emerging Evidence and Implications for Practice', in R. Burnett and C. Roberts (eds.), *What Works in Probation and Youth Justice*, Cullompton: Willan.

Roberts, J. (1997), 'Paying for the Past: The Role of Criminal Record', *Crime and Justice: An Annual Review*, 22.

Roberts, J. (2003), 'Evaluating the Pluses and Minuses of Custody', *Howard Journal of Criminal Justice*, 42: 229.

Roberts, J. (2004), *The Virtual Prison*, Cambridge: Cambridge University Press.

Roberts, J. and Stalans, L. J. (1997), *Public Opinion, Crime and Criminal Justice*, Boulder: Westview.

Robinson, P. and Darley, J. (1995), *Justice, Liability and Blame*, Boulder: Westview.

Rock, P. (1990), *Helping Victims of Crime*, Oxford: Oxford University Press.

Roording, J. (1996), 'The Punishment of Tax Fraud', *Criminal Law Review*, 240.

Royal Commission on Criminal Justice (1993), *Report*, London: HMSO.

Rumgay, J. (2004), 'Dealing with Substance-Misusing Offenders in the Community', in A. Bottoms, S. Rex and G. Robinson (eds.), *Alternatives to Prison: Options for an Insecure Society*, Cullompton: Willan.

Sanders, A. (2002), 'Victim Participation in an Exclusionary Criminal Justice System', in C. Hoyle and R. Young (eds.), *New Visions of Crime Victims*, Oxford: Hart.

Sanders, A. and Young, R. (2000), *Criminal Justice*, 2nd edn, London: Butterworths.

Sebba, L. (1980), 'Is Mens Rea a Component of Perceived Offense Seriousness?' *Journal of Criminal Law and Criminology*, 71: 124.

Sellin, T. and Wolfgang, M. (1978), *The Measurement of Delinquency*, New York: Wiley.

Shapland, J. (1981), *Between Conviction and Sentence*, London: Routledge and Kegan Paul.

Shapland, J., Willmore, J. and Duff, P. (1985), *Victims in the Criminal Justice System*, London: Heinemann.

Shaw, S. (1989), 'Monetary Penalties and Imprisonment', in P. Carlen and D. Cook (eds.), *Paying for Crime*, Milton Keynes: Open University Press.

Sherman, L. et al. (1997), *Preventing Crime: What Works, What Doesn't, What's Promising*, Washington: US Congress.

Shetreet, S. and Deschenes, J. (eds.) (1985), *Judicial Independence: The Contemporary Debate*, Dordrecht: Kluwer.

Shute, S. (1999), 'Who Passes Unduly Lenient Sentences?' *Criminal Law Review*, 603.

Shute, S. (2004), 'New Civil Preventative Orders', *Criminal Law Review*, 417.

Singer, R. (1979), *Just Deserts: Sentencing based on Equality and Desert*, New York: Ballinger.

Singleton, N., Meltzer, H. and Gatward, R. (1998), *Psychiatric Morbidity among Prisoners in England and Wales*, London: The Stationery Office.

Smith, A. T. H. (1983), 'The Prerogative of Mercy', *Public Law*, 203.

Social Exclusion Unit (2002), *Crime and Social Exclusion*, London: Office of the Deputy Prime Minister.

South African Law Commission (2000), *Report on a New Sentencing Framework*, Pretoria: South African Law Commission.

Sparks, R., Genn, H. and Dodd, D. (1977), *Surveying Victims*, Chichester: Wiley.

Sprack, J. (2004), *A Practical Approach to Criminal Procedure*, 10th edn, Oxford: Oxford University Press.

Stephen, J. F. (1885), 'Sentencing', *The Nineteenth Century*, 17: 795.

Stevens, R. (1993), *The Independence of the Judiciary: The View from the Lord Chancellor's Office*, Oxford: Clarendon Press.

Streatfeild, Mr Justice (1960), *Report of the Interdepartmental Committee on the Business of the Criminal Courts*, London: HMSO.

Street, R. (1998), *The Restricted Hospital Order*, Home Office Research Study 186, London: Home Office.

Suhling, S. (2003), 'Factors Contributing to the Rising Imprisonment Figures in Germany', *Howard Journal of Criminal Justice*, 42: 55.

Tarling, R. (1979), *Sentencing Practice in Magistrates' Courts*, Home Office Research Study 56, London: HMSO.

Tata, C. (1997), 'Conceptions and Representations of the Sentencing Decision Process', *Journal of Law and Society*, 24: 395.

Taylor, Lord (1993), 'Judges and Sentencing', *Journal of the Law Society of Scotland* 129.

Taylor, Lord (1996), 'Continuity and Change in the Criminal Law', *King's College Law Journal* 7: 1.

Taylor, R., Wasik, M. and Leng, R. (2004), *Blackstone's Guide to the Criminal Justice Act 2003*, Oxford: Oxford University Press.

Thomas, D. A. (1963), 'Sentencing – The Case for Reasoned Decisions', *Criminal Law Review*, 243.

Thomas, D. A. (1974), 'The Control of Discretion in the Administration of Criminal Justice', in R. Hood (ed.), *Crime, Criminology and Public Policy*, London: Heinemann.

Thomas, D. A. (1978), *The Penal Equation*, Cambridge: Institute of Criminology.

Thomas, D. A. (1979), *Principles of Sentencing*, London: Heinemann.

Thomas, D. A. (1997), 'Sentencing Legislation – The Case for Consolidation', *Criminal Law Review*, 406.

Tonry, M. (1994), 'Proportionality, Parsimony and Interchangeability of Punishments', in A. Duff et al., *Penal Theory and Practice*, Manchester: Manchester University Press.

Tonry, M. (1995), *Malign Neglect: Race, Crime and Punishment in America*, New York: Oxford University Press.

Tonry, M. (1996), *Sentencing Matters*, New York: Oxford University Press.

Tonry, M. (2004), *Punishment and Politics*, Cullompton: Willan.

United Nations (1990), *The United Nations and Crime Prevention and Criminal Justice*, New York: United Nations.

Van Zyl Smit, D. (2002), *Taking Life Imprisonment Seriously*, The Hague: Kluwer.

Van Zyl Smit, D. and Ashworth, A. (2004), 'Disproportionate Sentences as Human Rights Violations', *Modern Law Review*, 67: 541.

Van Zyl Smit, D. and Dünkel, F. (2001), *Imprisonment Today and Tomorrow*, 2nd edn, The Hague: Kluwer.

Vennard, J. and Hedderman, C. (1998), 'Effective Interventions with Offenders', in C. Nuttall (ed.), *Reducing Offending*, Home Office Research Study 187, London: Home Office.

Von Hirsch, A. (1986), *Past or Future Crimes*, Manchester: Manchester University Press.

Von Hirsch, A. (1993), *Censure and Sanctions*, Oxford: Oxford University Press.

Von Hirsch, A. and Ashworth, A. (eds.) (1998), *Principled Sentencing*, 2nd edn, Oxford: Hart.

Von Hirsch, A. and Ashworth, A. (2005), *Proportionate Sentencing*, Oxford: Oxford University Press.

Von Hirsch, A., Bottoms, A. E., Burney, E. and Wikstrom, P.-O. (1999), *Criminal Deterrence: An Analysis of Recent Research*, Oxford: Hart.

Von Hirsch, A. and Jareborg, N. (1988), 'Provocation and Culpability', in F. Schoemann (ed.), *Responsibility, Character and the Emotions*, Cambridge: Cambridge University Press.

Von Hirsch, A. and Jareborg, N. (1989), 'Sweden's Sentencing Statute Enacted', *Criminal Law Review*, 275.

Von Hirsch, A. and Jareborg, N. (1991), 'Gauging Criminal Harm: A Living Standard Analysis', *Oxford Journal of Legal Studies*, 11: 1.

Von Hirsch, A. and Roberts, J. (2004), 'Legislating Sentencing Principles', *Criminal Law Review*, 639.

Walker, N. (1982), 'Unscientific, Unwise, Unprofitable or Unjust?' *British Journal of Criminology*, 22: 276.

Walker, N. (1991), *Why Punish?* Oxford: Oxford University Press.

Walmsley, R. (1986), *Personal Violence*, Home Office Research Study 89, London: HMSO.

Walmsley, R. (2003), *World Prison Population List* (4th edn), Home Office Research Findings 188, London: Home Office.

Wasik, M. (1982), 'Partial Excuses in the Criminal Law', *Modern Law Review*, 45: 515.

Wasik, M. (1983), 'Excuses at the Sentencing Stage', *Criminal Law Review*, 450.

Wasik, M. (1985), 'The Grant of an Absolute Discharge', *Oxford Journal of Legal Studies*, 5: 211.

Wasik, M. (1987), 'Guidance, Guidelines and Criminal Record', in M. Wasik and K. Pease (eds.), *Sentencing Reform*, Manchester: Manchester University Press.

Wasik, M. (2000), 'Sentencing in Homicide', in A. Ashworth and B. Mitchell (eds.), *Rethinking English Homicide Law*, Oxford: Oxford University Press.

Wasik, M. (2003), *Emmins on Sentencing*, 4th edn, London: Blackstone.

Wasik, M., and von Hirsch, A. (1988), 'Non-custodial Penalties and the Principles of Desert', *Criminal Law Review*, 555.

Wasik, M. and von Hirsch, A. (1997), 'Civil Disqualifications attending Conviction', *Cambridge Law Journal*, 599.

Wells, M. (1992), *Sentencing for Multiple Offences in Western Australia*, Perth: University of Western Australia Crime Research Centre.

West, D. J. (1963), *The Habitual Prisoner*, London: Heinemann.

West, D. J. (1973), *Who Becomes Delinquent?* London: Heinemann.

Whittaker, C. and Mackie, A. (1997), *Enforcing Financial Penalties*, Home Office Research Study 165, London: Home Office.

Wilczynski, A. (1997), 'Mad or Bad? Child-Killers, Gender and the Courts', *British Journal of Criminology*, 37: 419.

Wilkinson, J. (2005), 'Evaluating Evidence for the Effectiveness of the Reasoning and Rehabilitation Programme', *Howard Journal of Criminal Justice*, 44: 70.

Willcock, H. D. and Stokes, J. (1963), *Deterrents and Incentives to Crime among Youths Aged 15–21 Years*, London: HMSO.

Wilson, J. Q. and Herrnstein, R. (1985), *Crime and Human Nature*, New York: Simon and Shuster.

Windlesham, Lord (1996), *Responses to Crime: Vol. III*, Oxford: Oxford University Press.

Wintemute, R. (2004), 'Filling the Article 14 Gap', *European Human Rights Law Review*, 484.

Wood, D. (1988), 'Dangerous Offenders and the Morality of Protective Sentencing', *Criminal Law Review*, 424.

Woolf, Lord Justice (1991), *Prison Disturbances, April 1990: Report of an Inquiry*, London: HMSO.

Young, P. (1989), *Punishment, Money and the Legal Order*, Edinburgh: Edinburgh University Press.

Youth Justice Board (2004), *Annual Review 2003/04*, London: Youth Justice Board.

Zander, M. and Henderson, P. (1993), *Crown Court Study*, Royal Commission on Criminal Justice Research Study 19, London: HMSO.

Zedner, L. (1994), 'Reparation and Retribution: Are They Reconcilable?' *Modern Law Review*, 57: 228.

Zedner, L. (1998), 'Sentencing Young Offenders', in A. Ashworth and M. Wasik (eds.), *Fundamentals of Sentencing Theory*, Oxford: Oxford University Press.

Zedner, L. (2002), 'Dangers of Dystopias in Criminal Theory', *Oxford Journal of Legal Studies*, 22: 341.

Zedner, L. (2003), 'The Concept of Security: An Agenda for Comparative Analysis', *Legal Studies*, 23: 153.

Zeisel, H. and Diamond, S. (1977), 'The Search for Sentencing Equity', *American Bar Foundation Research Journal*, 881.

Zimring, F. and Hawkins, G. (1995), *Incapacitation: Penal Confinement and the Restraint of Crime*, New York: Oxford University Press.

Zimring, F., Hawkins, G. and Kamin, J. (2001), *Punishment and Democracy: Three Strikes and You're Out in California*, New York: Oxford University Press.

Index